Web Accessibility

Web Standards and Regulatory Compliance

Jim Thatcher
Michael R. Burks
Christian Heilmann
Shawn Lawton Henry
Andrew Kirkpatrick
Patrick H. Lauke
Bruce Lawson
Bob Regan
Richard Rutter
Mark Urban
Cynthia D. Waddell

friendsof ED

DESIGNER TO DESIGNER™

an Apress® company

Web Accessibility: Web Standards and Regulatory Compliance

Credits

Lead Editor Chris Mills	**Copy Editor** Marilyn Smith
Development Editor Adam Thomas	**Assistant Production Director** Kari Brooks-Copony
Technical Reviewers Bruce Lawson, Gez Lemon	**Production Editor** Laura Esterman
Editorial Consultant Bruce Lawson	**Compositor** Dina Quan
Editorial Board Steve Anglin, Ewan Buckingham, Gary Cornell, Jason Gilmore, Jonathan Gennick, Jonathan Hassell, James Huddleston, Chris Mills, Matthew Moodie, Dominic Shakeshaft, Jim Sumser, Keir Thomas, Matt Wade	**Artist** April Milne **Proofreader** Elizabeth Berry **Indexer** Michael Brinkman
Project Manager Beth Christmas	**Interior and Cover Designer** Kurt Krames
Copy Edit Manager Nicole LeClerc	**Manufacturing Director** Tom Debolski

To Jon B., who kept me going without even knowing it.
—Shawn Lawton Henry

To my wife, Nongyow, and our kids, Marina and James,
without whom life would be monochrome.
—Bruce Lawson

CONTENTS AT A GLANCE

CONTENTS

Chapter 3: Implementing Accessibility in the Enterprise 69

PART 2: IMPLEMENTING ACCESSIBLE WEBSITES 84

Chapter 4: Overview of Accessible Technologies 85

Chapter 9: CSS for Accessible Web Pages 247

Chapter 14: Introduction to WCAG 2.0 459

Chapter 15: Retrofitting Case Study: Redesign of
a University Website 475

PART 3: ACCESSIBILITY LAW AND POLICY 510

Chapter 16: U.S. Web Accessibility Law in Depth 511

The Challenge of Accessibility

When Tim Berners-Lee created the Web, he had some very specific goals in mind. Certainly, creating a technology that allowed the sharing of information was a main part of that goal, but an interesting piece of Berners-Lee's vision has always had to do with the human side of the Web. After all, it's not machines that use the Web, but people.

Accessibility has become a hot topic in web design, despite the fact that it has always been a part of the original vision. In a broad sense, accessibility simply means ensuring that a given page on the Web is able to be accessed. Accessibility is not about disability; rather, it's about people getting to the shared information that the vision of the Web has made manifest.

There has also been a lot said about how accessibility relates to web standards and vice versa. Realistically, accessibility relies on aspects of related web standards, but has in fact become a science, art, and practice of its own. It's a deep specialty, and one that is highly problematic, as what might make a page accessible to one person could conceivably render it inaccessible to another.

What's more, myths about accessibility and what it really means to the web designer and developer abound. To some, accessibility means merely the addition of alternative text for images. That's what folks were taught to do years ago, and that's as far as many go. To others, accessibility is considered an afterthought—something that's added to a site after it has been built. To a certain less than honorable group, web accessibility has become an opportunity for selling unnecessary or inappropriate services to unsuspecting clients, who think they're really doing the right thing and have no way as consumers to verify that what they're asking for is what they're getting.

There is good news though, and much of it has to do with a rising awareness in the industry not just of what accessibility really is, but why it's so important to the entire creation and long-term vision of well-constructed websites. This awareness is coming about through advocacy groups such as the Web Standards Project's Accessibility Task Force (ATF), World Wide Web Consortium (W3C), and independent web designers and developers who keep blogs and contribute to forums such as Accessify. And, personal politics aside, it's a fact that many organizations and companies have no choice but to comply with accessibility guidelines because they are being required to do so by legislative actions around the globe.

Hope and help are most certainly at hand here, in a book dedicated to blasting through myths and providing a deep understanding along with real-world practicalities to help the working web professional grasp the complexities of accessibility. By combining the skills and vision of some of the world's foremost accessibility specialists, web designers and developers now have a handbook to help them not only create accessible websites from the get-go, but retrofit sites as well. There's plenty of information about the laws governing accessible site design around the world, as well as how to properly test sites for accessibility, which is no easy task.

If you, like me, are concerned that the sites you work on provide the best possible experience for site visitors, and are concerned with retrofitting sites and managing the accessible site for the long haul, I am confident that *Web Accessibility: Web Standards and Regulatory Compliance* will become a constant help and much used resource that no web professional should be without.

Molly E. Holzschlag
Tucson, Arizona
May 2006

ABOUT THE AUTHORS

 **Jim Thatcher** received his PhD from the University of Michigan in 1963, one of the first PhDs in Computer Science. Together with his thesis advisor, Dr. Jesse Wright, Jim then joined the Mathematical Sciences Department, IBM Research, in Yorktown Heights, New York. His research was in the area of mathematical computer science, automata theory, and data abstraction. Jim began moving away from the abstract and toward the practical when he and Dr. Wright, who is blind, began working on access to the PC for people who are blind. That project led to one of the first screen readers for DOS which, in 1986, became IBM Screen Reader (and the term later became generic). After that, Jim led the development of IBM Screen Reader/2 for OS/2, which was the first screen reader for the graphical user interface on the PC (1991).

In 1996, Jim left his research post to join the IBM Accessibility Center in Austin, Texas. There, he led the effort to establish the IBM accessibility guidelines specifically for use by IBM's development community.

Jim served as Vice-Chair of the Electronic and Information Technology Access Advisory Committee (EITAAC), which was impaneled by the Access Board to propose standards for Section 508. He chaired the subcommittee on Software Standards. He wrote the course on Web Accessibility for Section 508 for the Information Technology Technical Assistance and Training Center (ITTATC), which was funded by the General Services Administration and the Department of Education to support Section 508.

Jim has received numerous awards for technical work over his 37-year career with IBM. He received a Distinguished Service award from The National Federation of the Blind in 1994 and the Vice President's Hammer Award for his work with the Department of Education on the development of Software Accessibility Standards in 1999.

Jim is coauthor of *Constructing Accessible Web Sites* (along with Paul Bohman, Michael Burks, Shawn Lawton Henry, Bob Regan, Sarah Swierenga, Mark D. Urban, and Cynthia Waddell), published by glasshaus in 2002, and published again by Apress in 2003.

Michael R. Burks currently serves as Section 508 Analyst working on the accessibility of electronic and information technology. He is also the Webmaster and Public Information Officer of the International Center for Disability Resources on the Internet (www.icdri.org), a nonprofit organization dedicated to presenting disability resources and information to those who are dealing with disability issues.

Michael works with the Internet Society (www.isoc.org) on disability issues, and has made presentations and taught tutorials on web accessibility and disability issues around the world.

Christian Heilmann grew up in Germany and, after a year working with people with disabilities for the Red Cross, spent a year as a radio producer. From 1997 onwards, he worked for several agencies in Munich as a web developer. In 2000, he moved to the U.S. to work for Etoys and, after the dot-com crash, he moved to the UK, where he led the web development department at Agilisys. In April 2006, he joined Yahoo! UK as a web developer.

Christian publishes an almost daily blog at www.wait-till-i. com and runs an article repository at www.icant.co.uk. He is a member of the Web Standards Project's DOM Scripting Task Force.

Shawn Lawton Henry leads the World Wide Web Consortium's (W3C) worldwide education and outreach activities promoting web accessibility for people with disabilities. She develops online resources to help web developers understand and implement web accessibility guidelines, and provides presentations and training on accessible web design and development with the Web Accessibility Initiative (WAI). Shawn has presented and published papers on accessibility and usability for Human Factors and Ergonomics Society (HFES), Computer-Human Interaction (CHI), Usability Professionals' Association (UPA), Web Design World, and many other conferences around the world (http://uiaccess.com/pres.html). Her publications also include the "Everyone Interfaces" chapter in *User Interfaces for All* (Lawrence Erlbaum Associates, 2000), *Accessibility in the User-Centered Design Process* (Georgia Tech Research Corporation, 2004), and other online resources (www.uiaccess.com/pubs.html).

Prior to joining W3C WAI, Shawn consulted with international standards bodies, research centers, government agencies, nonprofit organizations, education providers, and Fortune 500 companies to develop and implement strategies to optimize design for usability and accessibility (www.uiaccess.com/experience.html). She developed UIAccess.com to share information on universal user interface design and "usable accessibility." Although Shawn holds a research appointment at the Massachusetts Institute of Technology (MIT)

Computer Science and Artificial Intelligence Laboratory (CSAIL) and has a Massachusetts phone number, she actually lives in Madison, Wisconsin. When not typing on her small laptop, she can often be found paddling her long sea kayak.

Andrew Kirkpatrick serves as the cross-product Accessibility Engineer for Adobe Systems. Prior to joining Adobe, Andrew was Principal Accessibility Engineer at Macromedia, and Director of Technology at the National Center for Accessible Media (NCAM) at WGBH in Boston, with a focus on accessibility consulting for corporate clients including America Online, Yahoo!, BT, Apple, and Macromedia. In addition to activities with corporate clients at NCAM, Andrew managed projects focused on web and interactive media accessibility, and was the product manager for MAGpie (NCAM's software for creating captions and audio descriptions) and developer of STEP (NCAM's Simple Tool for [Accessibility] Error Prioritization).

Andrew is also Principal for Kirkpatrick Consulting, a web accessibility consultancy. Andrew lives in Massachusetts with his wonderful wife and three of the cutest kids ever.

Patrick H. Lauke currently works as Web Editor for the University of Salford (www.salford.ac.uk), where he heads a small, central web team, which provides development, training, and advice to departmental web authors across the institution. In 2003, he implemented one of the first web standards-based, XHTML/CSS-driven UK university sites.

Patrick has been engaged in the discourse on accessibility since early 2001, regularly contributing to a variety of web development and accessibility-related mailing lists and forums, taking an active role in the running of Accessify.com (www.accessify.com), moderating the Accessify forum (www.accessifyforum.com), and joining the Web Standards Project Accessibility Task Force (WaSP ATF) (www. webstandards.org) in June 2005. In his spare time, Patrick pursues his passion for photography and runs a small web/design consultancy (www.splintered.co.uk).

With two years of Computer Sciences at the Swiss Federal Institute of Technology (ETH) in Zurich, followed by a switch to a Bachelor's degree in Graphic Design and a Masters in Creative Technology at the University of Salford, Patrick's background spans both technical and creative disciplines, which he feels are essential for a holistic approach to web design and development.

An outspoken accessibility and standards advocate (although he has been called an "evangelist," with only slight negative connotations, by some of his colleagues), Patrick favors a pragmatic hands-on approach to web accessibility over purely theoretical, high-level discussions.

"I'm an idealist by nature, but a pragmatist by trade. I'd never class myself as an expert, and I certainly don't have all the answers. . . I'm just an opinionated guy eager to find real-world solutions where the rubber meets the road."

Bruce Lawson dreamed up *Constructing Accessible Web Sites*, the forerunner of this book. Previously, he worked as an actor and theater director, and a programmer with AT&T, before becoming a singer, guitarist, and tarot card reader in Istanbul, a volunteer pharmacist in Calcutta, a movie extra in Bombay, and a kindergarten teacher and tutor to the princess's daughter in Thailand.

Now, Bruce is a member of the Web Standards Project's Accessibility Task Force, and was one of the reviewers of the British Standards Institution's Publicly Available Specification (PAS) 78 - "Guide to Good Practice in Commissioning Accessible Websites." His interest in web standards is both philosophical (a good artisan uses the right tools, in the right way) and practical (I can get smaller pages, which Google likes). His interest in accessibility is thinly disguised self-interest, having been diagnosed with multiple sclerosis in 1999.

He blogs at www.brucelawson.co.uk, and lives in the UK, but wishes he lived somewhere warm.

Bob Regan is a solutions architect for vertical markets at Adobe Systems, Inc. In that role, he serves as the technical lead for the education, government, financial services, manufacturing, telecommunications, and life science markets. It is his responsibility to connect with the specific needs, challenges, and successes of customers working to create digital content and applications. He works with each team to help them collect customer experiences and communicate them into the product organization, and assemble solutions based on these requirements.

Bob's first role in the software world as an accessibility advocate continues to play an important part of his day-to-day life. Now with Adobe, he is part of a much larger team looking at accessibility issues from product design to engineering, from content authoring through to the end user. Ensuring that the Web is a great experience to us all remains a great passion of his.

Richard Rutter has been developing commercial websites for ten years. In 2000, he joined Citria as a user interface lead, where he introduced web standards to a staff of 150 in three offices across Europe. Richard was the producer on large e-commerce projects for clients including Barclaycard, on a finance portal that was the first commercial site to be built using CSS throughout and to meet Royal National Institute of the Blind (RNIB) accessibility requirements.

After two years at Citria, Richard joined Multimap. He was responsible for rebuilding Multimap's hugely successful website using web standards and for making the site accessible to a far wider audience. While at Multimap, Richard acted as accessibility consultant to a number of high-profile clients, including Ford Europe, Yell, and BT.

Richard is now cofounder and Production Director of Clearleft, a web consultancy specializing in accessible websites. Richard is also coauthor of the book *Blog Design Solutions*, in which he explains how to push the envelope of what can be achieved with weblog software and design. A more personal side of Richard can be found at Clagnut.com, a popular weblog where he writes about accessibility and web standards issues, as well as his passion for music and mountain biking.

The Honorable **Mark Urban** is Chairman of the North Carolina Governor's Advocacy Council for Persons with Disabilities. He is a member and past Chair of the Board of Directors for the International Center for Disability Resources on the Internet (www.icdri.org), and a member and past Vice Chairman of the International Committee for Information Technology Standards, V2 (IT Access Interfaces). He was chief executive of a municipality during the implementation of the Americans with Disabilities Act, and a reservist in the United States Navy. He is an experienced technical architect and IT policy developer. Mark currently does project management and consulting on accessibility and related IT and disability matters with federal, state, and local agencies and the businesses that supply them.

Mark lives in Raleigh, North Carolina, with his supportive friends and family, two cats, and two "attack Chihuahuas." To them and their support of his endeavors, he sincerely dedicates this book.

Cynthia D. Waddell is the Executive Director of the International Center for Disability Resources on the Internet (ICDRI). She provides leadership and project oversight in carrying out ICDRI's mission to increase opportunities for people with disabilities by identifying barriers to participation and promoting best practices and universal design of technology for the global community.

In the world of accessibility, Cynthia Waddell is a nationally and internationally recognized expert in the field of electronic and information technology, as well as employment and construction. Named in the "Top 25 Women on the Web" by Webgrrls International in 1998, she received the first *U.S. Government Technology Magazine* award in 2003 for Leadership in Accessibility Technology and For Pioneering Advocacy and Education.

The free Cynthia Says web accessibility tool and portal was named after her and endorsed by the American Council of the Blind. The Cynthia Says portal (www.cynthiasays.com) is a joint Education and Outreach project of ICDRI, The Internet Society Disability and Special Needs Chapter, and HiSoftware.

Seeking a solution for access to information on the Web for the community of people with disabilities, Cynthia Waddell authored the first accessible web design standard in the U.S. that was recognized as a best practice by the federal government and contributed to the eventual passage of legislation, including the Electronic and Information Technology Accessibility Standards (Section 508). Her seminal paper, "The Growing Digital Divide in

Access for People with Disabilities: Overcoming Barriers to Participation," was commissioned by the Clinton Administration and has been translated and cited by foreign governments, businesses, universities, disability organizations, and entities around the world.

Cynthia Waddell combines her expertise in disability legislation, public policy, and technology to provide education and professional consulting services for government, higher education, and businesses. She serves as the accessibility quality assurance lead for award-winning government portals and provides Section 508 VPAT assistance for technology vendors. Active in a number of organizations, she is the North America Chair of the International Commission on Technology and Accessibility (ICTA), a Standing Commission of Rehabilitation International, and Vice-Chair of The Internet Society Disability and Special Needs Chapter.

Cynthia Waddell's work includes consultancies for the United Nations as an expert in accessible information and communication technologies (ICT) and for the body developing an international treaty on the rights of persons with disabilities. This is similar to her participation on the Portuguese International Accessibility Board that led to Portugal's adoption of the Portuguese Accessibility Guidelines for websites in 1999.

In 2003, Cynthia Waddell served as the accessible technology expert for the Bush Administration UK-U.S. seminar exchange on employment and technology; following her work for several years in the "Boosting the UK Digital Economy—A Virtual Think Tank." In addition, she was the sole U.S. speaker at the 2001 "Design for All European Day of Disabled People" at the invitation of the European Commission and the European Disability Forum.

Cynthia Waddell has keynoted at many government, university, and industry forums in the U.S. and abroad. For example, in 2005 she presented at the UN World Summit on the Information Society at the invitation of Pacific Rim consortium. In 2004, she spoke at the U.S. National Summit for Disability and Distance Education in Washington D.C. She also spoke in Tokyo, Japan at an ICT symposium and at a meeting of Diet members in conjunction with the launch of the first accessible web requirements in the Japanese Industrial Standards. She also spoke at the "Accessibility for All" conference in Nice, France for the European Union (EU) Standardization bodies, an event that was part of the EU "Design for All" initiative for access to products, services, and the environment.

Cynthia Waddell is a Lecturer in Law at her alma mater and holds a Juris Doctor from Santa Clara University School of Law. She was designated a Public Interest Disability Rights Scholar and a Dan Bradley Fellow for the Employment Law Center in San Francisco, California. In addition, she was a Rotary International Foundation Fellow at Exeter University, England, as well as an USC-Cambridge University Scholar at Cambridge University, England. She received her B.A., *cum laude*, from the University of Southern California.

ABOUT THE TECHNICAL REVIEWERS

Gez Lemon works as an accessibility consultant for The Paciello Group. A keen accessibility advocate, Gez participates in the Web Content Accessibility Guidelines Working Group and is a member of the Web Standards Project's Accessibility Task Force. In his spare time, Gez talks about accessibility issues on his blog, Juicy Studio (`http://juicystudio.com`).

Bruce Lawson was both an author and technical reviewer of *Web Accessibility: Web Standards and Regulatory Compliance*. For more information about Bruce, please see his biography in the "About the Authors" section.

ACKNOWLEDGMENTS

Infinite thanks to my husband, Karl, my amazingly intuitive voice-recognition software.

Shawn Lawton Henry

Thanks to Zeldman and Shawn Lawton Henry, whose conversations in 2001 planted the seed of the idea for the first edition of this book, and Lou Barr (www.frogboxdesign.co.uk/) who believed in that idea. Big respect to my fellow WaSP Task Force members, and Julie Howell, Rachel Andrew, Bob Regan, Isofarro, and Joe Clark, whose research and advocacy have taken accessibility into the mainstream.

Bruce Lawson

I'd like to thank my friends and colleagues at Clearleft (www.clearleft.com), Jeremy Keith and Andy Budd, for their support and advice in writing my chapter. Thanks must also go to my technical reviewers, Gez Lemon and Bruce Lawson, for their invaluable insight, suggestions, and of course, corrections; and to Marilyn Smith for sterling work in organizing my thoughts. Last but not least, thank you Wendy for putting up with me.

Richard Rutter

INTRODUCTION

It's easy for a non-disabled person to browse the Web. Point your mouse, see the screen, ignore (or read) the ads and the navigation on a page, and concentrate on the central area of a web page that contains the content. Skim through the headings, search for an interesting picture, and then settle your eye down to read the actual information.

Fine and dandy, if you aren't old and don't have arthritis, Parkinson's disease, or multiple sclerosis, and therefore have the motor control necessary to point your mouse. It's a piece of cake to listen to that news report if you aren't deaf, and easy as pie to find the main content if your vision is good enough to read—or if you are sighted at all. No problem ignoring all those flashing ads, if you don't have an attention deficit disorder, and no danger of a seizure, if you don't have photosensitive epilepsy.

But what about those people with disabilities? How can they ever hope to use the Web, which was designed for people who can see and use a mouse? The answer is in this book.

First, the Web was *explicitly* designed to be usable without a mouse, and without eyes if necessary. A good deal of what drives the Web and makes it so popular is animation, color, and images. But behind the scenes, underneath the hood of any website (choose your metaphor), lurks the computer code that powers it all. Because the Web was designed to be available to people with disabilities, carefully crafting that code (the "markup") can make your site much more accessible to people with disabilities.

Without damaging the attractiveness of your site to your non-disabled visitors, you can allow users with disabilities to reach, perceive, operate, and understand your content. Therefore, more people will have the opportunity to experience your brand, buy your products, or participate in whatever activity you hope to stimulate with your web presence.

> *It's a huge and utterly untruthful myth that accessible websites must be boring, text-heavy, and ugly. Many are, but that's a failure of imagination on the authors' part. The good news is that, in the vast majority of cases, a skilled developer can make websites accessible without any changes to the look of your website.*

Many disabled people use extra gadgets to help them use the Web, known as *assistive technologies*. Some blind people use the Web with a program called a *screen reader*, which has a speech synthesizer that reads aloud the web page. Some deaf/blind people have a refreshable Braille display, which allows users to feel a set of pins that the computer moves up and down to form Braille characters.

Some people have voice recognition software to understand spoken commands, and others with motor problems don't use a mouse, so they navigate with the keyboard. Paraplegics may sip and blow into a straw to control the computer. People with low vision can use a screen magnifier. (Chances are, if you have a Windows operating system, there's a magnifier built into your system already; check out Start ➤ All Programs ➤ Accessories ➤ Accessibility.)

Many, many other people who don't necessarily define themselves as having a disability (such as older people) just soldier on without any assistance, peering at low-contrast, unscalable, 10-point type or trying to click tiny radio buttons on order forms.

To allow these gadgets (or strategies, in the case of increasing the font size) to hook into your site, it must be coded (marked up) the right way. This is nearly always about the code that underpins your site. The majority of the work is transparent to the surfer who doesn't require assistive technologies, yet vital to those who do.

To help include everyone in the Web, the Web's governing body, the World Wide Web Consortium (W3C), formed a group called the Web Accessibility Initiative (WAI), whose mission was to develop "strategies, guidelines, and resources to help make the Web accessible to people with disabilities." It issued the Web Content Accessibility Guidelines (WCAG) version 1.0 in May 1999 (see www.w3.org/TR/WAI-WEBCONTENT/) to help make content both "understandable and navigable." These are generally considered by web developers, lobbying groups, and many legislatures to be the "touchstone" by which one should code, or judge, the accessibility of a website. WCAG 1.0 gives 14 guidelines, plus checkpoints explaining how the guidelines may be implemented. Each checkpoint has a priority, ranging from Priority 1 to 3. Not conforming to Priority 1 guidelines means some of your content is impossible to access for some groups; conforming to Priority 1 but not Priority 2 can mean it's very difficult for some groups, and so on.

Grotesquely oversimplifying, putting the WAI guidelines into practice on your pages means making sure that important pictures have text equivalents (hidden or otherwise) that can be accessed by blind people, audio is subtitled/transcribed for those who are hard-of-hearing, links and form controls can be easily accessed by those with motor problems, and the site is well structured for use by those with learning difficulties or problems with the language. A handful of the techniques suggested in WCAG 1.0 no longer apply, given that many were written to overcome deficiencies in 1999 browsers, and arguably some of its edicts are ambiguous, contradictory, or even impossible to measure objectively, but most of them have stood the test of time well and continue to be useful today. It's certainly possible to argue with the guidelines, but generally, they still remain the yardstick for all new techniques that come along. They are also unusual in the panoply of W3C documentation—in that it's possible to read them *and understand them*. A new version (imaginatively called WCAG 2.0) is in Working Draft form and may appear sometime in 2006. Don't worry that this book will be redundant; the new rules restate (and clarify) the old ones, but the techniques for making your site accessible remain equally applicable.

The WCAG guidelines help authors make sites accessible for consumption by disabled people. There are also the lesser-known Authoring Tool Accessibility Guidelines (ATAG, www.w3.org/TR/WAI-AUTOOLS/), which define how to make web authoring tools (such as Dreamweaver, Adobe Acrobat, content management systems, and blogging tools) usable by people with disabilities, and also ensure the output is accessible to end users. As fewer people make websites than surf them, this is WCAG's snot-nosed younger brother.

Then there are the even more obscure User Agent Accessibility Guidelines (UAAG, www.w3.org/TR/WAI-USERAGENT/), which you need to read only if you're developing a browser or media player, or you have a worrying fascination with the arcane.

Accessibility can also be used to refer to the coding of web pages needed to comply with legislation. The U.S., for example, has Section 508 of the Rehabilitation Act that requires federal agencies to make their electronic and information technology accessible to people with disabilities, and which gives a recipe of technical requirements. Other countries, such as the UK, have nontechnical laws that outlaw discrimination against disabled people and so are of obvious significance to the web professional or site owner, but don't describe the technical hoops that they should jump through in order to comply. It is generally considered that complying with these human rights-based laws requires at least WCAG Priority 2 compliance (that is, all Priority 1 and 2 checkpoints and some Priority 3).

Why Should You Care?

I'm not going to try to convince you of the need for accessibility. I'm assuming that you're interested because you're reading this. But if you need evidence, or need to convince others, here are some objective facts:

- It's very likely, if your company operates in the developed world, that there is a legal obligation not to discriminate against people with disabilities if you provide some kind of goods or services on your site.

- It makes financial sense, as people with disabilities account for up to 15 percent of the population. And if you're not pitching your wares to that 15 percent, you can be pretty sure that one of your competitors will be. (Neither should you assume that your business isn't of interest to disabled people; a client of mine sold skateboards online, and he was threatened with court action by a blind man who couldn't complete his order for a board for his son's birthday present.)

- It has been shown that your average "mostly text with a few images" website will reduce in size by approximately 50 percent if recoded using the techniques outlined in this book. That's a 50 percent savings in bandwidth costs for you, and the reduction of page size means a zippier load time for your customers. "It's a win-win situation," the marketing director might say.

- Google loves accessible websites; they are much easier for Google's indexing robot (Googlebot) to follow. This means your Google rank goes up, so your site is easier to find. (Check out www.google.co.uk/intl/en/webmasters/guidelines.html if you think I'm fibbing!)

- An April 2004 report by the UK Disability Rights Commission suggests that accessible coding makes sites more usable for non-disabled people. Of course, if your organization never gets a shopping cart abandoned before checkout, and you never have to pay staff to answer e-mail from people unable to find something on your website, you don't need to worry about increasing usability. Ahem . . .

- At a recent conference to launch the UK PAS 78 (see Appendix C), there was a very illuminating presentation by David Rhys Wilton, Internet Marketing Manager at Legal and General, a large UK financial services company. Mr. Wilton explained that Legal and General were concerned about their exposure to litigation under disability discrimination laws, and rewrote their consumer sites to be more accessible. As a side-effect, they noted the following benefits:

  - A 30 percent increase in natural search-engine traffic
  - A "significant improvement" in Google rankings "for all target keywords"
  - A 75 percent reduction in time for pages to load
  - Browser-compatibility (not a single complaint since)
  - Accessible to mobile devices
  - Time to manage content "reduced from average of five days to 0.5 days per job"
  - Savings of £200,000 annually on site maintenance
  - A 95 percent increase in visitors getting a life insurance quote
  - A 90 percent increase in life insurance sales online
  - A 100 percent return on investment in less than 12 months

Many would also add "Including people with disabilities is the ethical thing to do" to this list. I'm not going to, as I promised you objective facts.

What Accessibility Isn't

Let's get this horrible statement out of the way right now. Ready? Here we go: *You will never be perfectly accessible to everybody.* There is not a simple binary opposition between accessible and inaccessible. There are more than five billion people on the planet, and they're all individuals. (Lone voice in background: "I'm not.")

All you can do is make the best accommodation for the people who come your way. An extreme example: What's good for a person with Down Syndrome may very well be the opposite of what benefits someone with an attention deficit disorder. A bread-and-butter example: What's good for a blind person might enrage your company's brand manager, who will just *die* unless every word of the website is in that gorgeous typeface that was commissioned for the logo.

"Hang on!" I hear you saying, "That stupid brand manager isn't disabled—why bring him into it?" Because, I respond (neatly segueing into my next point), *accessibility is emphatically not about bringing every web page down to the lowest common denominator*. It is *not* about abandoning branding, beauty, creativity, passion, or soul. Quite the contrary, it is about preserving all of those, while simultaneously maximizing the number of people invited in to experience them. Also, although there could never be a solution to suit all disability groups, creating content that can easily be repurposed goes quite some way to achieving that goal.

Have I cheered you up again? Okay, so here's some more bad news.

Because there's no simple polar opposition between accessible and inaccessible, it's very, very difficult to *test* for accessibility. Unlike the validity of the markup that makes your web page, which is a language for machines so it can be tested by machines, websites are for people and can't be stuffed through a validator for a definitive thumbs up or thumbs down.

Yes, there are products out there, some free and some pricey, that claim to test accessibility, but they're only labor-saving devices. (See Chapter 13 of this book for a detailed discussion of automated checkers.) They can do the heavy lifting and check the obvious stuff. And while this automation is welcome in a site of more than a dozen pages, never *ever* assume that because some package has found no errors, your site is therefore accessible, or I'll huff and I'll puff and I'll blow your monitor in (unless you have an iMac G5; in which case, I'll just take it home with me).

Why Another Accessibility Book?

This book is a totally revamped, rewritten, shiny new version of *Constructing Accessible Web Sites*, originally published back in 2002 by a sister brand of friends of ED.

"Ah, Bruce," you may be complaining, "I've already got that book. I've just wasted my money buying this one." Fear not. A lot has changed in the past few years.

The CSS and XHTML Combo Is the New Black *and* the New Rock 'n' Roll

A whole raft of better tools has come on the scene since 2002. Internet Explorer 6 is no longer the most advanced browser out there; in fact, it's looking shakier than Methuselah's grandfather with a hangover, and is imminently going to be replaced with Internet Explorer 7. In the meantime, Firefox, Safari, and Opera have blazed a trail in modern browsers, encouraging web professionals everywhere to use modern web standards to produce some staggeringly attractive designs.

There has been a mutual advancement between accessibility and web standards: Web professionals have been encouraged to use Cascading Style Sheets (CSS) and Extended Hypertext Markup Language (XHTML) on the grounds that the combination "increases accessibility." That has made a whole lot of designers—who were initially excited by the typographic possibilities of CSS—think about accessibility. It's also shown accessibility boors that accessibility can be good looking, too; see, for example, the work of Andy Clarke (http://stuffandnonsense.co.uk/) or many of the CSS Zen Garden entries curated by Dave Shea (www.csszengarden.com/). "Synergy," our marketing director might say.

The Web Has Grown Up

Web designers are no longer exclusively ex-print designers. At the beginning of the Web, almost anyone who worked making sites with a credible claim to have an eye for design had previously worked in print. These are the fantastic pioneers who built the modern Web by making it more interesting than a bunch of hyperlinked physics papers, but whose expertise was almost entirely based on making things visually gorgeous, with pixel-perfect layouts that preserved the design's integrity. For the majority of these pioneers, the idea of designing beauty while keeping in mind the people with no visual faculties at all was simply too much for their paradigms to cope with.

We now have a generation of designers who've grown up with the Web, and the world of accessibility gets a boost because of that (although the world of computer book prefaces has suffered a blow at my gratuitous use of the word *paradigm*).

We've Learned New Techniques

Through trial and error, community websites, and the occasional ill-tempered argument, the accessibility community has learned a great deal, too. We've learned that screen readers no longer simply read the screen; instead, they read the source—so the text is read out in source-order rather than in the order that the CSS positions it. (Don't worry if you didn't understand that last sentence; you will soon.)

We've learned that not everyone with a disability is blind, and that not everyone with a visual impairment uses a screen reader.

We've also learned that while a website can be technically accessible (so, theoretically, a user with unlimited time and patience could get to the content), it's not always *easily* accessible. A good example would be a portal page with dozens of links before each page's main content. With no way for screen reader users or keyboard navigators to "jump over" the links, they're forced to listen to them or tab through them again and again and again as they move though your site.

Maybe most important, we've learned that online accessibility validators (which compare code against the rules for that language) cannot replace knowledge, testing, and understanding.

Accessibility: The Three-Legged Stool

It's a truism that retrofitting a completed project for "accessibility" is much more expensive than designing for it, and that it leads to a lower level of accessibility than if it were a design goal from the very beginning. The reason is that full accessibility is a combination of the WAI guidelines, web standards, and semantic coding. Think of these as the three legs of a stool; if one is shorter or weaker than the others, at some point, you're going to fall over and land painfully on your backside.

This is a fairly technical section, so if you're a site owner/technology officer, you might want to skip it, while making it mandatory reading for your developers. (You may want to make them memorize it and recite it at your holiday party—in which case, please video it and send me a copy.)

Web Standards

A couple of the WCAG 1.0 Priority 2 checkpoints are maddeningly vague. The following two checkpoints are taken to require web standards:

3.2 Create documents that validate to published formal grammars

3.3 Use style sheets to control layout and presentation

Web standards are a big subject and deserve a whole book in their own right (and friends of ED publishes a splendid introductory guide/cookbook by Dan Cederholm called *Web Standards Solutions*; see www.friendsofed.com/books/1590593812/).

Putting it simply, by *web standards*, I mean using a markup language (HTML or XHTML—totally up to you) to describe the structure of the web page. Every single page of every single website across the world uses one of these languages, but most don't follow the rules properly. The markup languages have rules published by the W3C, and you'll get the most benefit if you follow those rules.

Unlike testing for accessibility, it's easy to test whether your (X)HTML conforms to the specification, as there are free online validators that pass or fail the code (see http://validator.w3.org). However, once you've made sure your code validates to the rules, you'll get extra accessibility, cleaner code, and depending on how well you've separated your content and presentation, easier maintenance.

Yes, I know that sounds like gobbledygook, but it simply means that *you should use the markup language to describe what something is* (is it a paragraph? a list? a heading?) *and not what it looks like*. Describing what it looks like in the markup mixes up presentation with content, and can therefore feed a lot of useless stuff to a device like a screen reader. By definition, a screen reader doesn't care what something looks like; it only cares if the current bit of the web page is a header, a link, or a quote, and will probably indicate that to its user. Mixing structure and presentation also makes maintenance a nightmare, as it's far more difficult to make site-wide changes without editing every page.

So instead of markup that looks like this:

```
<h1>
 <font color="#CC0000" size="+4" face="Times New Roman",➡
                   Times, serif">
 The launch</font>
</h1>
<p><img src="chiefExec.jpg" alt="The chief executive" width="150"➡
 height="75" hspace="5" vspace="5" border="1" />
<font color="#FF00FF" size="2" face="Verdana, Arial, Helvetica, ➡
sans-serif ">
Chief Exec, Brendan Gerrard and Technology Officer, Lisa Perry ➡
 at the launch of new document, "Pushing the Envelope: ➡
A Synergistic Paradigm to leverage the New Millenium's Challenges "➡
.</font></p>
<h2>
<font color="#CC0000" size="+4" face="Times New Roman", Times, serif">
The lunch</font></h2>
<p><font color="#FF00FF" size="2" face="Verdana, Arial, Helvetica,➡
 sans-serif ">
The lunch was a scrumptious smorgasbord of roast paradigm, eaten➡
Out of the Box, with a refreshing glass of Blue Sky Thinking.
</font></p>
```

You can strip out the styling and have simply:

```
<h1>The launch</h1>
<p><img src="chiefExec.jpg" alt="The chief executive" />Chief ➡
 Exec, Brendan Gerrard and Technology Officer, Lisa Perry at the ➡
launch of new document, "Pushing the Envelope: A Synergistic ➡
Paradigm to leverage the New Millenium's Challenges".</p>
<h2>The lunch</h2>
<p>The lunch was a scrumptious smorgasbord of roast paradigm, eaten ➡
Out of the Box, with a refreshing glass of Blue Sky Thinking.</p>
```

The place to describe the look of your content is in a style sheet (aka Cascading Style Sheets aka CSS), which tells the browser where on the page your headings, images, copyright section, and so on should go, plus what colors to use, which fonts to use, and all other styling considerations.

This is now standard practice among web developers, as it means that changing all fonts, colors, and so on throughout an entire site can be done by editing one style sheet, and not having to update the information on *every* page.

The single CSS file for the whole site for the preceding example might be:

```
h1 {font: xx-large "Times New Roman", Times, serif; color: #c00;}
p {font: small Verdana, Arial, Helvetica, sans-serif; color: #f0f;}
img {margin: 5px; height: 75px;width: 150px; border: 1px; }
```

Semantic Code

Semantic code is alluded to in three WCAG 1.0 checkpoints:

3.5 Use header elements to convey document structure and use them according to specification

3.6 Mark up lists and list items properly

3.7 Mark up quotations. Do not use quotation markup for formatting effects such as indentation

It's really the practice of using the best HTML element for the job. So, don't use `<blockquote>` just because you want some indented text, merely because many browsers just happen to indent text inside a `<blockquote>` tag. Use it only if your content actually is a quote. If it isn't, enclose it in another element that more accurately describes what it is and use CSS to format it with an indent.

Similarly, if you have a navigation menu, don't mark it up as being a paragraph or a table. A menu is really a list of links, so mark it up as an unordered list. You can style it, remove the bullets, or even set it as a horizontal navigation bar later using (can you guess?) CSS.

This will make your code cleaner, more maintainable, and more useful for search bots like Googlebot to work out which content is important. There's also an accessibility benefit, especially for the blind, as the most popular screen readers (such as JAWS for Windows by Freedom Scientific and Window-Eyes by GW Micro) allow users to jump between certain types of content. In JAWS, for example, the H key jumps from header to header, and the 2 key jumps to the next second-level header. It's a way of allowing a blind user to "scan" a document in a manner similar to how a sighted user would read a newspaper: jumping from headline to headline, rather than listening to every word of every story in order. Imagine how tedious you would find it to listen to ten pages of sports news before you got to the horoscopes that you wanted.

> *Not all screen readers can take full advantage of web standards yet. This is because, historically, most websites have been so badly marked up that the screen reader developers spent most of their time developing the products to make a silk purse out of the bad code of the sow's ear. But screen readers do like well-marked-up code, and the influential lobby group, the Web Standards Project, set up the Accessibility Task Force to lobby assistive technology vendors to support even more web standards. It's a long-term job, but it's the way the wind is blowing, so you can be certain that you will be enhancing your accessibility by adopting a design methodology of semantic markup that separates content and presentation.*

Remember my analogy of a stool? It's all too possible to write code that validates but isn't semantic. Here is an example:

```
<p class="header"> This is big and bold and should be a h1 tag</p>
<span class="paragraph">No earthly reason why this isn't a paragraph,➡
but I've marked it up as a span.</span>
```

It's perfectly possible to write code that separates content and presentation, but doesn't validate (usually due to a typo or small error). It's incredibly common to see a page that is semantic and valid but inaccessible (perhaps the main point of the page is a graph that is just a picture, but with no alternative text description that the visually impaired can understand).

Current Hot Potatoes

I wouldn't want you to think that making your sites accessible is just a matter of following a recipe; to make nourishing accessibility pudding, add one part CSS, one part valid code, a pinch of semantic markup, and a cupful of WCAG guidelines. It would be nice if I could guarantee that slavishly following such a recipe would make everything lovely, but there are two reasons why I can't. The first is that annoying fact that people are people, and insist on having different needs and abilities. The second reason is that, when discussing a discipline that's as new as web standards/accessibility, there are the expected disagreements between practitioners. In fact, when three accessibility practitioners are gathered together, there will be four or more different opinions.

I don't want this to discourage you from learning about accessibility. The most important accessibility techniques are uncontroversial and will help the huge majority of those people who are currently ill-served or locked out of the Web. However, there are several different authors following me, and they will occasionally disagree with each other. We think that glossing over these differences of opinion would do you, the book, and the discipline of accessibility a disservice, but you *might* want to skip these and return to them after you've read the rest of the book.

Accessibility Isn't the Same As Device-Independence

Some highly erudite and respected accessibility practitioners will claim a site isn't accessible if it can't be viewed and understood with images and CSS off, and over a dial-up modem. They feel that *accessibility* means that anyone with an Internet-enabled device—however slow or old—should be able to access the content.

The W3C, however, explicitly says that its guidelines are purely aimed at making sites available for people with disabilities, but "following them will also make Web content more available to all users, whatever user agent they are using or . . . constraints they may be operating under." That is, the "all users" part is a happy *by-product* of accessibility for people with disabilities.

It's a debate that hangs on your understanding of the word *accessible* and how prepared you are to sacrifice imagery and design to accommodate those who choose to use very old or very slow technology. This book generally defines accessibility as dealing with disabilities, and not user choice, although making pages accessible goes a long way toward making them universal, just as the W3C says.

It Takes Two to Tango

A close relative of the accessibility vs. device-independence debate is the question of to what extent you can expect users to own the right tools to help them access the Web. If, for example, someone has an ancient version of a screen reader that can't use a well-established accessibility technique that I've sweated to implement, is that my fault?

The British Standards Institution's recently released PAS 78 "Guide to Good Practice in Commissioning Accessible Websites" says:

> 8.3.3.2 If a website conforms to WCAG, assistive technologies should work with the site. Although it is not the responsibility of the website commissioners to change their code to make an assistive technology work correctly they may wish to provide work arounds if they exist.

(Read more about PAS 78 in Appendix C.)

On this subject, we agree. The authors of this book believe that it takes two to tango—a user must be equipped to use the page that you spent so long making accessible. That means visitors must come with a reasonably modern browser, a reasonably recent version of any assistive technology (such as a screen reader or Braille display), and a reasonable knowledge of how to use their setup.

But note that even if a user does have the most up-to-date tools available, if one of the items brought to the party is a screen reader, it will most likely be deficient. Most screen readers can't process important bits of HTML. For example, the <ins> and <del> tags that indicate inserted and deleted text are ignored by some screen readers—making legal documents at best incomprehensible and at worst misleading or incorrect. JavaScript support is patchy, undocumented, and thus unpredictable. New techniques, like Ajax (a kind of fancy JavaScript-driven way to make websites feel more slick and responsive that you may have seen if you've used Google Maps or Google's Gmail), are very difficult to make accessible.

However, there's one reason for optimism with the screen reader inadequacies. There are numerous screen readers competing aggressively with each other. The vendors sell their products for hundreds of dollars, and lock the customers in by their screen readers being incredibly difficult to learn and difficult to replace, due to the costs.

So when Flash was first made accessible by its manufacturers, the Window-Eyes screen reader from GW Micro could read it from day one. Another screen reader, JAWS (from Freedom Scientific), raced to catch up because so many websites were Flash-based, so

Flash support was a selling point. As all software manufacturers know, to fall behind is to die slowly. The same has happened with support for JavaScript, PDF, and the Firefox browser.

It seems that when a technique or technology becomes popular, the screen readers will vie for each other to support it. Whether that means that it is legitimate to use a technology like Ajax and wait for the assistive technologies to catch up is not something I can decide for you.

"Until User Agents . . ."

Some of the WAI checkpoints are obsolete or badly worded—so do we have to follow them? For example, checkpoint 10.1 commands, "Until user agents allow users to turn off spawned windows, do not cause pop-ups or other windows to appear." Now, some browsers do allow me to turn off spawned windows, but others don't. Do I need to follow this checkpoint or not?

This book generally assumes that if the majority browser (currently Internet Explorer 6 for Windows) is one of the user agents that doesn't do what the checkpoint is primarily concerned with, then it may *not* be safely disregarded.

Fortunately, WCAG 2.0 is desperately trying to avoid using terms like "until user agents." See Chapter 14 for more information about WCAG 2.0.

Cognitive Disabilities

Cognitive disabilities are a tricky and emotive area. It's relatively straightforward to ensure your animations won't trigger photosensitive epilepsy, or to design a typography that is accessible to people with dyslexia. But will the plain, nondistracting design hold the attention of those with an attention deficit disorder?

To what extent can you make your pages accessible to those with cognitive disabilities? Can someone with Alzheimer's disease navigate your site? Is there a technique to make your site appealing to autistic people? There's an entire book to be written about cognitive accessibility; this book isn't that book.

What This Book Will Do

We'll show you how to make your websites as accessible as possible, to the broadest range of people as possible, in a way that should—at a minimum—make sure you're in compliance with the law.

We'll do that in the most modern way possible, using semantic markup, CSS for presentation, and valid code—except for those rare occasions in which accessibility is better served by invalid code. We'll show you how to make sure that the behavior layer of your page is accessible, too, using the emerging techniques of "unobtrusive" JavaScript.

We'll be pragmatic, too. Many of us, whether by choice or requirement, need to use Adobe PDF or Adobe Flash. There are techniques to enhance the accessibility of those technologies, and we'll show you those and examine the advantages as well as the pitfalls in the chapters dedicated to accessible PDF, Flash, and JavaScript.

Finally, I promised pragmatism, so we'll cut back on the philosophy.

Conventions Used in This Book

To keep this book as clear and easy to follow as possible, the following text conventions are used throughout (you've already seen many of these in this introduction):

- Code is presented in `fixed-width font`.
- New or changed code is normally presented in **`bold fixed-width font`**.
- Pseudo-code and variable input are written in *`italic fixed-width font`*.
- Menu commands are written in the form Menu ➤ Submenu ➤ Submenu.
- Notes and additional information are in the following style:

> *Ahem, don't say I didn't warn you.*

- Sometimes code won't fit on a single line in a book. Where this happens, we use an arrow, like this:

```
This is a very, very long section of code that should be ➡
written all on the same line without a break.
```

So Let's Start!

Are you still here? Good. Then let's get started. Quick! Turn the page . . .

Bruce Lawson

PART 1 UNDERSTANDING THE IMPACT OF WEB ACCESSIBILITY

1 UNDERSTANDING WEB ACCESSIBILITY

by Shawn Lawton Henry

The Web is providing unprecedented access to information and interaction for people with disabilities. It provides opportunities to participate in society in ways otherwise not available. With accessible websites, people with disabilities can do ordinary things: children can learn, teenagers can flirt, adults can make a living, seniors can read about their grand-children, and so on. With the Web, people with disabilities can do more things themselves, without having to rely on others. People who are blind can read the newspaper (through screen readers that read aloud text from the computer), and so can people with cognitive disabilities who have trouble processing written information. People who are deaf can get up-to-the-minute news that was previously available only to those who could hear radio or TV, and so can people who are blind and deaf (through dynamic Braille displays). People with quadriplegia who cannot move their arms or legs can shop online to get groceries, gadgets, and gifts delivered. People who cannot speak can participate in online discussions, such as through blog comments.

However, this possibility is not a reality throughout the Web. The problem is that most websites have accessibility barriers that make it difficult or impossible for many people with disabilities to use them. And most web software tools are not sufficiently accessible to people with disabilities, making it difficult or impossible for them to contribute to the Web. This is a very big deal. Many millions of people have disabilities that affect their use of the Web.

Web accessibility is about removing those barriers so that people with disabilities can use and contribute to the Web. This chapter helps you get started improving your website to remove accessibility barriers and avoid adding new barriers.

What Is Web Accessibility?

Web accessibility basically means that people with disabilities can use the Web. More specifically, web accessibility means that people with disabilities can perceive, understand, navigate, and interact with the Web.

Web accessibility encompasses all disabilities that affect access to the Web, including visual, auditory, physical, speech, cognitive, and neurological disabilities. Here are just a few examples of disabilities that affect web use and some real people with those disabilities:

- Some people cannot use their arms or hands to type or move a mouse. Carl had polio and cannot move his arms. He uses a mouth stick, which is just a wooden dowel with an eraser on the end. Sarah has cerebral palsy and has limited control of her arms and mouth. She uses a head pointer, as illustrated in Figure 1-1.

- Some people with tremors and older people with diminishing fine motor control can use a keyboard, but not a mouse. Richard has multiple sclerosis and can move his arms but not with enough precision to control a mouse.

Figure 1-1. Web accessibility tutorial participant using computer with head pointer

- Some people cannot see at all and use a screen reader that reads aloud the information in the web page. Neal was born blind. John started losing his sight from retinitis pigmentosa when he was a young adult. Screen readers are also used by people like Tracy, who can see just fine but have trouble processing written language.

- Some people have blurry vision and cannot read text unless it is very large. Shawn has a neurological condition that makes it hard to focus on small text, so she increases the size of text and images in her browser. Richard also has blurry vision. It is common for people to have multiple disabilities.

While access to people with disabilities is the primary focus of web accessibility, it also benefits people *without* disabilities. For example, a key principle of web accessibility is designing websites that are flexible to meet different user needs. This flexibility also increases general usability and lets people without disabilities use websites according to their preferences, such as using whichever browser they want and using keyboard shortcuts. Web accessibility also provides financial and technical benefits to organizations, as described in the "Additional Benefits from a Business Perspective" section later in this chapter.

There are many more examples throughout this chapter of how web accessibility benefits people with and without disabilities.

An Example of Web Accessibility: Alt-Text

Alternative text equivalents, called *alt-text*, are a clear example of web accessibility. Web pages often include images, but some people cannot see images. People who cannot see images can get the information contained in the images when web developers include alternative text equivalents for images. An alternative text equivalent provides the same functional information in text as the image provides visually. The markup for image alt-text looks like this:

```
<img src="thunder.gif" alt="storms" />
```

(By the way, alt is an *attribute*, not a tag.)

Alt-text is provided as follows:

- Read by screen readers and voicing browsers
- Displayed in text browsers
- Displayed in graphical browsers when images are not downloaded

Alt-text is rendered differently by different browsers and configurations, as shown in Figures 1-2, 1-3, and 1-4. Figure 1-2 shows a page in Microsoft Internet Explorer with images loaded and the mouse hovering over an image, which displays the alt-text (rain) in a pop-up.

Day	Mon	Tues	Wed	Thur	Fri
Outlook					
High (°C)	25°	20°	15°	10° rain 5°	
Low (°C)	15°	10°	5°	0°	-5°

Figure 1-2. Common browser showing the alt-text "rain"

Figure 1-3 shows the same page in Opera with images turned off in the browser settings. For images with alt-text provided, the alt-text is displayed. Where alt-text is missing (the middle image), IMAGE is displayed.

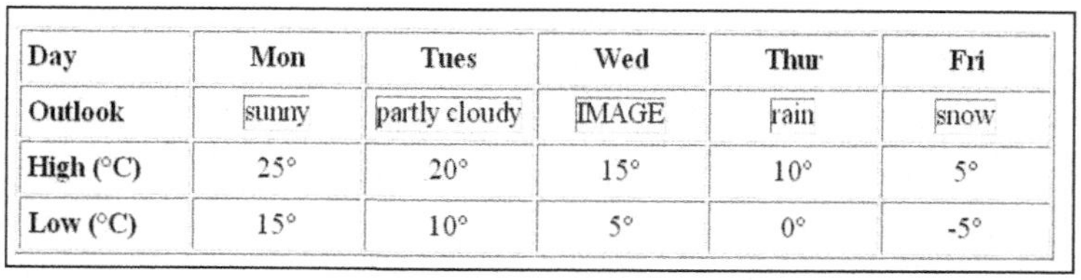

Day	Mon	Tues	Wed	Thur	Fri
Outlook	sunny	partly cloudy	IMAGE	rain	snow
High (°C)	25°	20°	15°	10°	5°
Low (°C)	15°	10°	5°	0°	-5°

Figure 1-3. Images turned off and alt-text showing

Figure 1-4 shows the display of IBM Home Page Reader set to read images without alt-text. Home Page Reader is a voicing browser that reads aloud web pages, as a screen reader does. The text in the bottom pane indicates what a person using this browser hears. At the time of the screen capture, it was reading across the Outlook row. Notice that for the image with missing alt-text, it reads the filename. (Browsers and assistive technologies handle missing alt-text differently, and some have multiple settings so the user can choose.)

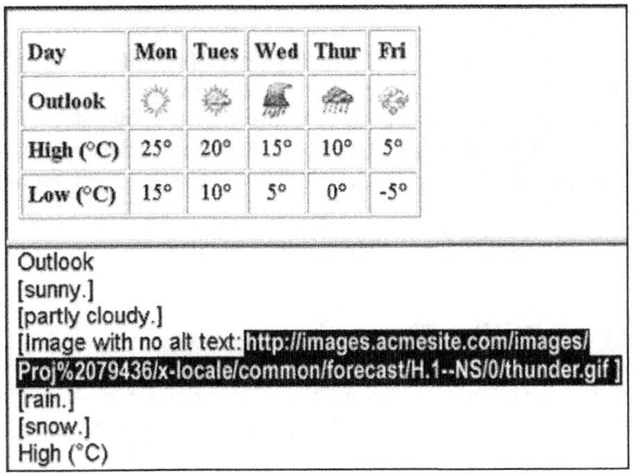

Day	Mon	Tues	Wed	Thur	Fri
Outlook					
High (°C)	25°	20°	15°	10°	5°
Low (°C)	15°	10°	5°	0°	-5°

Outlook
[sunny.]
[partly cloudy.]
[Image with no alt text: http://images.acmesite.com/images/
Proj%2079436/x-locale/common/forecast/H.1--NS/0/thunder.gif]
[rain.]
[snow.]
High (°C)

Figure 1-4. The image filename is read where alt-text is missing.

These examples are missing alt-text for only one image. Imagine if all the images were missing alt-text (which is, unfortunately, quite common). In that case, a person who cannot see images wouldn't have any idea when it was forecast to be sunny or storming. However, if all the images had alt-text, a person who cannot see would get the same information as someone who can see.

> With equivalent alt-text, the page is equally useful with or without images.

Many websites today use images for navigation, where missing alt-text makes the site totally unusable.

Note that providing alt-text improves accessibility without changing the visual appearance of the website. Indeed, most accessibility improvements are "under the hood" and don't change the user experience for users without disabilities.

The World Wide Web Consortium (W3C) Web Accessibility Initiative (WAI) is developing a demo site that shows an inaccessible site and then the same site with the accessibility barriers fixed, where the visual design (on a common browser configuration) is the same. To find the latest version, search for "before after demo" on the W3C WAI site (for example, www.google.com/search?q=site:www.w3.org/WAI+before+after+demo).

Alt-text is also an example of an accessibility technique that has benefits beyond accessibility for people with disabilities. The following are some ways that alt-text is useful to people without disabilities and to organizations:

- Alt-text is useful for people using a mobile phone, PDA, or other handheld device that doesn't display images.

- Alt-text is useful for people who turn off image downloading because they have a slow Internet connection.

- Alt-text can increase usability. Most visual browsers display the alt-text for an image as the image is downloading. For long downloads, this helps with both user perception and interaction. Users are likely to be less bothered by a slow image download when they are getting information about the image from the alt-text. When the image is a link, users can click the alt-text without waiting for the image to download.

- Alt-text helps with search engine optimization.

Other Web Accessibility Examples

The alt-text example focuses on people who are blind. It's important to also address other disabilities. Here are some other web accessibility issues, along with some additional benefits:

- **Captions for audio:** Captions are text describing sound in video or audio, such as people speaking and other important sounds. Captions are vital for people who are deaf. Captions are also beneficial for people in a noisy environment who cannot hear audio, as well as for people in a very quiet environment where it is not appropriate to play audio. Search engines don't index the content of audio files; however, when you provide the captions as a text transcript, the information is available to search engines. Also, users can more easily find information in a text transcript, rather than trying to locate it in an audio file; for example, a reporter looking for a quote from a speech can search through a transcript.

- **Device independence:** Websites should be designed so that they don't require a specific type of device, such as a mouse. This also helps "power users" who are faster with keyboard shortcuts, people needing to limit mouse use due to repetitive stress injuries (RSI), and people using mobile phones and other devices without a mouse.

- **Clear and consistent design and navigation:** People with some kinds of cognitive disabilities have difficulty processing visual information. They may not be able to use a site if the navigation is not clearly distinguished and consistent throughout the site. Clear and consistent design and navigation also benefit people who magnify web pages significantly and people with "tunnel vision" who see only a small part of the web page at a time. When the navigation is clearly distinguished, as in Figure 1-5, it is much easier to tell if you are in a navigation area or a content area. Clear and consistent design and navigation also help people without disabilities using mobile phones and other PDAs that have small displays (a "situational limitation"). Additionally, clear and consistent design and navigation increase usability for all users.

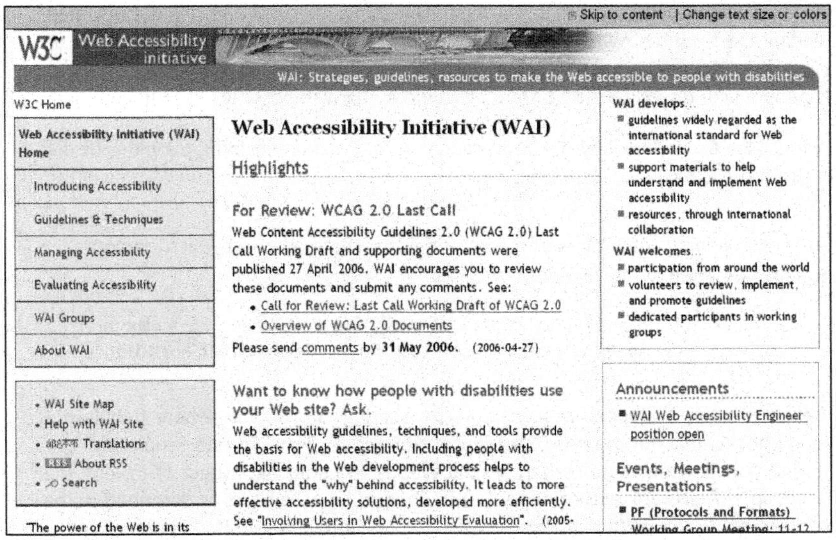

Figure 1-5. Website with navigation clearly distinguished in the blue box

The preceding examples apply to websites. Examples of browser accessibility issues include providing keyboard access and the following options:

- Resizing text, images, and areas on web pages
- Turning off background images
- Changing text and background colors

Examples of authoring tool accessibility issues are in the "Interdependent Components of Web Accessibility" section later in this chapter. Now let's look at why accessibility is so important.

Web Accessibility Is Essential for Equal Opportunity

Use of the Web is spreading rapidly into most areas of society and daily life. In many countries, the Web is increasingly used for government information and services, education and training, commerce, news, workplace interaction, civic participation, health care, recreation, entertainment, and more. In some cases, the Web is replacing traditional resources. Therefore, it is essential that the Web be accessible in order to provide equal access and equal opportunity to people with disabilities.

The Web is an opportunity for unprecedented access to information for people with disabilities. Many accessibility barriers to print, audio, and visual media can be much more easily overcome through web technologies. For example, when the primary way to get certain information was go to a library and read it on paper, there were significant barriers for many people with disabilities, such as getting to the library, physically getting the resource, and reading the resource. When that same information is also available on the Web in an accessible format, it is significantly easier for many people to get. In some cases, the Web allows people with disabilities to do things that were nearly impossible without it.

The Web is also an opportunity for unprecedented *interaction,* enabling people with disabilities to more actively participate in society.

> The dream behind the Web is of a common information space in which we communicate by sharing information.
>
> Tim Berners-Lee, inventor of the World Wide Web, "The World Wide Web: A very short personal history" (www.w3.org/People/Berners-Lee/ShortHistory)

The Web was initially designed as a medium for sharing information, where people not only read information, but they also contribute information. Ensuring that people with disabilities are able to contribute content to the Web is an important aspect of making the Web accessible. Therefore, authoring tools also need to be accessible, as described in the "Interdependent Components of Web Accessibility" section later in this chapter.

> *Making the Web accessible can dramatically improve people's lives and benefit society as a whole.*

Understanding that web accessibility is a social issue can help position it within an organization, particularly an organization committed to corporate social responsibility (CSR). Providing an accessible website is one way an organization can demonstrate its commitment to providing equal opportunities. (And just as an accessible website demonstrates CSR, an inaccessible website demonstrates lack of CSR.) More on how web accessibility relates to CSR and to the digital divide is available in "Social Factors in Developing a Web Accessibility Business Case for Your Organization" (www.w3.org/WAI/bcase/soc).

Benefits for People Without Disabilities

Organizations interested in CSR and the digital divide may want to know how accessibility also improves access for the following groups:

- Older people
- People with low literacy and people not fluent in the language
- People with low-bandwidth connections to the Internet and those using older technologies
- New and infrequent web users

The following sections describe the benefits for each of these groups.

Older People

The statistics and trends point to an increasing number of people with functional limitations in the future. As we age, most people experience a decrease in vision, hearing, physical abilities, and cognitive abilities. Figure 1-6 shows the increase in disability as we age, while Figure 1-7 depicts an example increase in the aging population. (Figures 1-6 and 1-7 are used with permission of the Trace R&D Center. For data sources, see http://trace.wisc.edu/docs/function-aging/.)

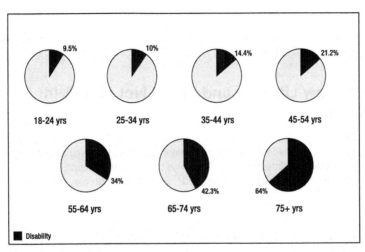

Figure 1-6. Disability by age groups

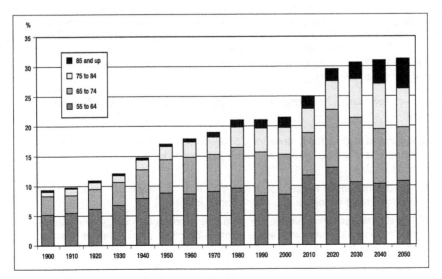

Figure 1-7. Example of increase in aging population

As shown in the graph in Figure 1-7, the portion of the population considered "senior" is dramatically increasing. This has created greater interest in technologies that reduce the impact of various impairments. Older users are an important market for many organizations online.

While older people often experience changes in vision, hearing, dexterity, and memory as they age, they might not consider themselves to have disabilities. Yet the accessibility provisions that make the Web accessible to people with disabilities also benefit older people with diminishing abilities. For example, many people with age-related visual deterioration benefit from sufficient contrast between foreground and background colors. Some older people cannot use the mouse because of diminishing fine motor control and eye-hand coordination. For more information, see "Web Accessibility and Older People" (www.uiaccess.com/andaging.html).

People with Low Literacy and Those Not Fluent in the Language

Accessible websites can benefit people with low literacy levels and people who are not fluent in the language of the website. Specifically, many of the aspects of web accessibility for people with cognitive disabilities help people who do not know the language well. In addition, accessible sites can be read by screen readers, so people who can understand the spoken language but not read can listen to sites.

People with Low-Bandwidth Connections and Older Technologies

Some aspects of web accessibility benefit people with low-bandwidth connections. Low bandwidth can be due to connection technology (for example, mobile phone or personal data assistant), location (for example, rural), or financial situation (a high-speed connection is unaffordable). Some older technologies load pages very slowly and don't support features used on newer sites. These issues are common in some developing countries and areas of developed countries.

People with low-bandwidth connections and older technologies can benefit from the following:

- Redundant coding for information conveyed with color, and sufficient contrast between text and background colors, for people who have devices with black-and-white displays

- Text descriptions of images, for people who turn off images to speed download and for devices or software that don't display images

- Text alternatives for multimedia, for people whose older technology cannot access new multimedia formats and people whose connections are too slow to download multimedia files

- Style sheets used effectively to separate content from presentation, which can decrease file size and file download requirements, and thus increase download speed

- Sites that are organized so they can be read without style sheets, because some older technologies cannot handle style sheets (accessible pages can use style sheets and still be usable, although not great looking, when style sheets are not supported)

- Sites that are usable when scripts, applets, or other programmatic objects are turned off or not supported

New Web Users

Some people have little opportunity to use the Web because of socioeconomic issues. New and infrequent web users benefit from aspects of accessibility such as the following:

- Clear and consistent design, navigation, and links
- Redundant text links for server-side image maps
- Information about new, spawned browser windows

For more examples see the "Web Accessibility Benefits People With and Without Disabilities" section of "Social Factors in Developing a Web Accessibility Business Case for Your Organization" (www.w3.org/WAI/bcase/soc).

Interdependent Components of Web Accessibility

Much of the focus of web accessibility has been on the responsibilities of web content developers. This view misses the crucial interdependence of other components of web development and interaction, including browsers, assistive technologies, and authoring tools.

If you understand the interdependencies between the components, you can better perform the following:

- Evaluate the source of accessibility barriers in your site. For example, if during testing you identify problems with a data table, it could be for one of the following reasons:

  - The developer did not mark up/code the data table properly (most likely).

  - The tester does not know how to use the assistive technology's table-reading feature (not uncommon if the tester is a novice assistive technology user).

  - The tester's assistive technology doesn't facilitate reading data tables effectively (rare these days).

- Fix accessibility barriers in your site and develop effective solutions.
- Encourage accessibility improvements in the other components that would make the whole system work better and easier (see the "Call to Action" section later in this chapter).

It is essential that all of the components of web development and interaction work together in order for the Web to be accessible to people with disabilities. When the components don't fulfill their responsibilities, the result is more work for others and a less accessible web. For example, inconsistencies between browsers have by one estimate added "at least 25% to the cost of developing all sites" because of the extra effort required of content developers (Web Standards Project, "WaSP: Fighting for Standards," http://webstandards.org/about/mission/).

Improvements in browsers, authoring tools, and other components could significantly reduce the amount of effort spent on accessibility overall and substantially improve web accessibility. For example, if the few hundred authoring tools provided ample accessibility support, it would save many millions of content developers an untold amount of effort on accessibility and result in much more accessible sites. (Authoring tools cannot automatically take care of all accessibility issues. There will always be things that developers need to do for accessibility. However, there are many ways that tools can facilitate accessibility and make it much easier.)

Description of Components

One way to look at the components is grouped by technical and human. The following can be considered the technical components:

- **Web content:** Generally refers to the information in a web page or web application, including text, images, forms, sounds, and such, as well as the markup and code that defines the structure, presentation, and interaction.
- **Technical specifications:** Refers to Extensible Hypertext Markup Language (XHTML), Cascading Style Sheets (CSS), and such. They are also called *web technologies* and *markup languages*.
- **Authoring tools:** Refers to any software or service that developers use to produce, create, or modify web content, including these:
  - Web page editors (such as Dreamweaver, FrontPage, and so on)
  - Word processors and desktop publishing software that save files in web formats
  - Tools that transform documents into web formats, such as filters to transform desktop publishing formats to HTML

■ Multimedia tools

■ Content management systems (CMSs), tools that automatically generate websites dynamically from a database, on-the-fly conversion tools, and website publishing tools

■ Websites that let users add content, such as blogs, wikis, and sites like Flickr and MySpace

■ **Evaluation tools:** Software programs or online services that help determine if a web page meets accessibility guidelines or standards. See the "Myth: Evaluation Tools Can Determine Accessibility and Conformance" section later in this chapter for more about evaluation tools.

■ **User agents:** Web browsers, media players, assistive technologies, and other software that people use to access and interact with web content.

■ **Assistive technologies:** Software and hardware that people with disabilities use to improve interaction with the Web. Examples include screen readers that read aloud web pages for people who cannot see or read text, and voice-input software and switches for people who cannot use a keyboard or mouse. An official definition is: any item, piece of equipment, product, system or software, whether acquired commercially off the shelf, modified, or customized, that is used to increase, maintain, or improve functional capabilities of individuals with disabilities.

The human components of web accessibility are as follows:

■ **Tool developers:** The people and organizations who develop user agents, assistive technologies, authoring tools, and evaluation tools.

■ **Users:** People using the Web, sometimes called website visitors.

■ **Content developers:** The people and organizations who design, code, write, edit, update, and otherwise create web content. This includes web programmers, graphic designers, technical writers, project managers, blog commenters, wiki contributors, secretaries who edit their organization's website, and others.

Figure 1-8 illustrates the relationship between the basic components of web accessibility. Content developers usually use authoring tools and evaluation tools to create web content according to technical specifications. Users use web browsers and sometimes assistive technologies to get and interact with the content. Tool developers provide features and functionality in their authoring tools, evaluation tools, and user agents based on user needs (well, really, market demands).

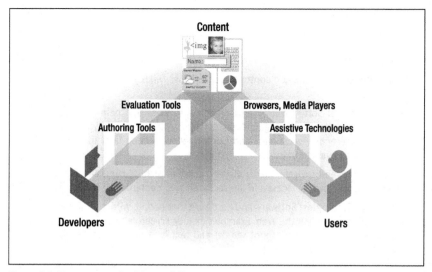

Figure 1-8. Components of web accessibility

*Figures 1-8, 1-10, 1-11, and 1-12 are based on art by Michael Duffy,
DUFFCO. See* www.w3.org/WAI/intro/components *©W3C.*

Let's look at providing and using alt-text for images as an example of how the components
must work together in order for the Web to be accessible. Figure 1-9 illustrates the
responsibilities of the components.

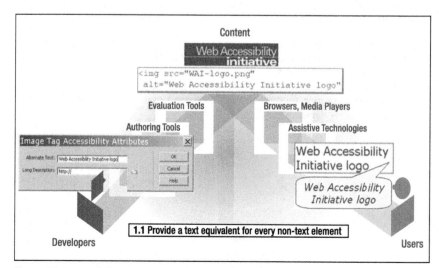

Figure 1-9. Responsibilities of components for alt-text

The technical components have the following responsibilities for alt-text:

- **Technical specifications:** Provide a standard for marking up alt-text. For example, in HTML 4.01 the img element used to put images into content has an alt attribute for a text alternative for the image. The World Wide Web Consortium (W3C) HTML 4.01 Specification (www.w3.org/TR/html4/struct/objects.html#adef-alt) describes alt as follows:

    For user agents that cannot display images, forms, or applets, this attribute specifies alternate text. The language of the alternate text is specified by the lang attribute.

    Specifying alternate text assists users without graphic display terminals, users whose browsers don't support forms, visually impaired users, those who use speech synthesizers, those who have configured their graphical user agents not to display images, etc.

    The alt attribute must be specified for the IMG and AREA elements.

- **Authoring tools:** Enable, facilitate, and promote providing alt-text. The interface to insert an image and provide alt-text should also be accessible to content developers with disabilities.
- **Evaluation tools:** Check that alt-text exists and help determine if it is appropriate.
- **User agents:** Provide human and machine interfaces to the alt-text.
- **Assistive technologies:** Provide human interfaces to the alt-text in different modalities, such as in synthetic speech.

The Web Accessibility Initiative (WAI) guidelines, which are described in the "Bringing Together the Components" section later in this chapter, define how to implement alt-text for accessibility in the different technical components.

The human components have the following responsibilities for alt-text:

- **Content developers:** Provide the appropriate alt-text, often using authoring tools and evaluation tools.
- **Users:** Need to know how to get the alt-text from their user agent and assistive technologies.
- **Tool developers:** Provide the functionality of authoring, evaluating, and rendering alt-text in the tools.

Accessibility in the Implementation Cycle

The interdependencies between components have historically led to a "chicken-and-egg" problem of who goes first in implementing an accessibility feature. Figure 1-10 illustrates this implementation cycle without a clear beginning.

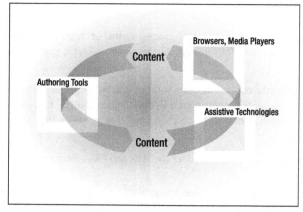

Figure 1-10. Cycle of accessibility implementation

If an accessibility feature is not implemented in one component, there is little motivation for the other components to implement it when it does not result in an accessible user experience. For example, content developers are unlikely to implement an accessibility feature that most browsers or assistive technologies do not implement consistently or that is difficult to do with their authoring tool. Similarly, browser developers have little motivation to support accessibility features that are not implemented in most content. And authoring tools have little motivation to add accessibility support when content developers (their customers) are not demanding it. The result is that some accessibility features are not implemented at all, and others take a long time to be implemented in all components effectively.

When accessibility features are effectively implemented in one component, the other components are more likely to implement them. The "Call to Action" section later in this chapter discusses ways to encourage implementation of accessibility features throughout the components.

Technical specifications must also be designed with accessibility in mind; otherwise, the technology might not support necessary accessibility features. Indeed, many web technologies were developed without accessibility support. Due largely to customer demand, technologies such as Portable Document Format (PDF) and Flash are improving their accessibility support.

Many web technology organizations now have explicit focus on accessibility. The W3C's Protocols and Formats Working Group (PFWG, www.w3.org/WAI/PF/) coordinates across W3C Working Groups to improve the level of accessibility support in W3C technical specifications. The PFWG works to ensure the following:

- Web content and applications implemented using the specified technologies can be adapted for people with disabilities.

- Web technologies interoperate well with assistive technologies.

- Accessibility features are integrated into and a natural part of technical specifications and do not require a high level of additional effort by content developers.

Compensating for Weak Accessibility Support

If one technical component has poor accessibility support, sometimes other components can compensate through work-arounds that require extra effort both initially to create and in the long-term to maintain. Figure 1-11 illustrates the compensation for lack of accessibility support in tools.

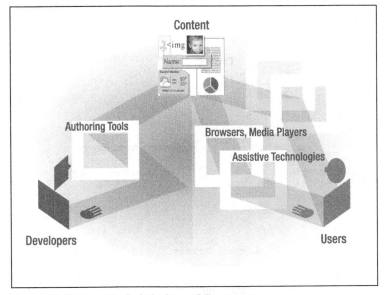

Figure 1-11. Compensating for lack of accessibility support

When authoring tools and user agents do not support an accessibility feature, sometimes the content developer can do more work to compensate with work-arounds. For example, if the authoring tool does not produce accessible markup, the content developer can write the markup "by hand." If a user agent does not provide the ability to navigate through the structure of the content, the content developer can provide additional navigation within the web content.

In some cases, users can compensate for lack of accessibility in browsers or content by using different combinations of user agents or assistive technologies, even for the same web page. Unfortunately, for many accessibility issues, there is no work-around for the user, and the content is inaccessible.

Bringing Together the Components

The W3C WAI (www.w3.org/WAI) helps coordinate international web accessibility efforts to bring together the technical and human component considerations. Figure 1-12 illustrates how WAI's work fits into the components of web accessibility. WAI works with the following:

- W3C Working Groups to produce technical specifications that support accessibility

- User agent, authoring tool, and evaluation tool developers to create the Authoring Tool Accessibility Guidelines (ATAG) documents (www.w3.org/WAI/intro/atag) and User Agent Accessibility Guidelines (UAAG) documents (www.w3.org/WAI/intro/uaag)

- Content developers and tool developers to create the Web Content Accessibility Guidelines (WCAG) documents (www.w3.org/WAI/intro/wcag)

- Users to understand issues and advocate for aspects of accessibility in each of the other components

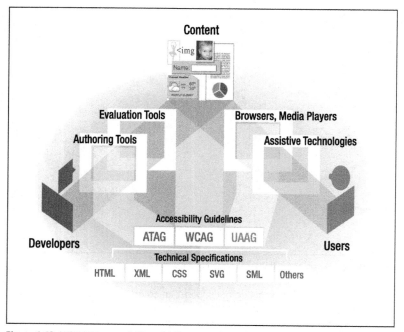

Figure 1-12. W3C WAI accessibility guidelines covering web accessibility components

This coordinated effort developing accessibility guidelines provides the framework for how the components can work well together. It defines what each component needs to do for accessibility. This also helps reduce the chicken-and-egg problem by clarifying what each component should expect from the others.

Authoring Tool Accessibility Guidelines (ATAG)

The ATAG documents explain how to make authoring tools accessible to people with disabilities and define how authoring tools should help web developers produce web content that conforms to WCAG. Through prompts, alerts, templates, and other features, authoring tools can enable, encourage, and assist content developers to create accessible web content. As described earlier, people with disabilities must also be able to contribute content. Therefore, the authoring tools themselves must be accessible.

While ATAG is primarily written for authoring tool developers, ATAG and supporting documents are also intended to meet the needs of many different audiences, including policy makers, managers, and others. For example, the following may use ATAG:

- People who want to choose authoring tools that are more accessible can use ATAG to evaluate authoring tools (see "Selecting and Using Authoring Tools for Web Accessibility," www.w3.org/WAI/impl/software).
- People who want to encourage their existing authoring tool developer to improve accessibility in future versions can refer the authoring tool vendor to ATAG.

ATAG 1.0 (www.w3.org/TR/ATAG10) was published as a W3C Recommendation in February 2000. ATAG 2.0 (www.w3.org/TR/ATAG20/) is currently under development to clarify minor issues with ATAG 1.0 and to update references to other guidelines.

> *A W3C Recommendation is a specification or set of guidelines that, after extensive consensus-building, has received the endorsement of W3C Members and the Director. W3C recommends the wide deployment of its Recommendations. Note that W3C Recommendations are similar to the standards published by other organizations. See* www.w3.org/2005/10/Process-20051014/tr.html#RecsW3C *for more details on the W3C Technical Report Development Process.*

Web Content Accessibility Guidelines (WCAG)

The WCAG documents explain how to make web content accessible to people with disabilities. WCAG is written for content developers as well as for the following:

- Authoring tool developers to create tools that generate accessible content
- User agent developers to create tools that render accessible content
- Evaluation tool developers to create tools that identify accessibility issues in content

WCAG 1.0 (www.w3.org/TR/WCAG10/) was published as a W3C Recommendation in May 1999. The WCAG 2.0 (www.w3.org/TR/WCAG20/) documents are being developed to apply to more advanced web technologies, be easier to use and understand, and be more precisely testable.

For more up-to-date information on WCAG, see "Web Content Accessibility Guidelines (WCAG) Overview" (www.w3.org/WAI/intro/wcag) and "Overview of WCAG 2.0 Documents" (www.w3.org/WAI/intro/wcag20).

User Agent Accessibility Guidelines (UAAG)

The UAAG documents explain how to make user agents (web browsers, media players, and assistive technologies) accessible to people with disabilities, and particularly to increase accessibility to web content. For example, UAAG defines that users should have control over how browsers display content, and browsers should use standard programming interfaces to enable interaction with assistive technologies.

UAAG is primarily for user agent developers. UAAG and supporting documents are also intended to meet the needs of many different audiences, including policy makers, managers, and others. For example, the following may use UAAG:

- People who want to choose user agents that are more accessible can use UAAG to evaluate user agents.
- People who want to encourage their existing user agent developer to improve accessibility in future versions can refer the user agent vendor to UAAG.

UAAG 1.0 (www.w3.org/TR/UAAG10/) was published as a W3C Recommendation in December 2002.

Approaches to Web Accessibility

The importance of accessibility to people with disabilities and the benefits to others are rarely reflected in how organizations and individuals approach accessibility. Many web projects look at accessibility guidelines and evaluation reports well into the development cycle. There are guidelines that should be at the center of your accessibility efforts—just not the only focus. This section suggests a different approach.

Start Now

Accessibility is often left for the end of web projects. At the end, it costs more and is burdensome and frustrating. For example, if you wait until the end, you could find that your authoring tool or CMS complicates accessibility, whereas a different one with good accessibility support would have made designing an accessible site much easier. Or you could find that one simple thing you did wrong has been propagated throughout the entire website. If you had done it right from the start, it would have taken almost no effort; to go back and fix it will take significant effort.

Incorporating accessibility from the beginning of a website development or redesign process is significantly easier, more effective, and less expensive than waiting until the end of a project. When accessibility is incorporated from the beginning, it is often a small percentage of the overall website cost. (If you already have a website and are going back to address accessibility, most of the following advice still applies, and the "Accessibility Barriers on Existing Sites" section later in this chapter provides additional guidance.)

Start by Understanding the Issues

When people do finally get to accessibility in their project, most approach it as a checklist to tick off. They dive into standards. They run an evaluation tool. Then they are totally overwhelmed. To use a few expressions, they started by "drinking from a fire hose" and became "deer in the headlights."

This approach also has problems (besides turning you into a soaking wet deer about to be hit by a truck). If your project uses only accessibility standards, it will take longer, be more frustrating, and produce less effective results.

Here is an example: A developer (who doesn't know what it's like to use a screen reader) comes to the guideline "Provide text alternatives for all non-text content." To meet this guideline, the developer provides the alt-text: "This image is a line art drawing of a dark green magnifying glass. If you click on it, it will take you to the Search page for this Acme Company website." He writes similarly verbose alt-text for hundreds of different images on his website. He has just wasted a whole lot of time and effort on a totally ineffective solution. For the image that takes you to the search page, the alt-text "Search" is all that was needed. His overly descriptive text throughout the site will be extremely frustrating for people who need the alt-text, because they will have to wade through all the extraneous information.

I have a collection of real-life examples of accessibility efforts gone wrong. A couple are amusing, like the following markup for decorative images: `<img src="blue-space.gif" alt=" ">`. But most are sad, such as the developer who had coded by hand for every cell in several large data tables:

```
<td row="1" col="1">…
<td row="1" col="2">…
. . .
<td row="57" col="15">. . .
```

It's regretful when developers spend a lot of time but their efforts are ineffective, just because they didn't have some basic understanding of accessibility and how people with disabilities use the Web.

There is a better approach that can save you from wasting effort developing ineffective solutions.

> *Before jumping into guidelines, before studying evaluation tool results, first understand the issues. Learn the basics of how people with disabilities use the Web.*

You can find many free resources to help understand accessibility issues. For example, "How People with Disabilities Use the Web" (www.w3.org/WAI/EO/Drafts/PWD-Use-Web/) describes in detail how different disabilities affect web use and includes scenarios of people with disabilities using the Web, and "Introduction to the Screen Reader" (www.doit.wisc.edu/accessibility/video/intro.asp) is a short video. Organizations that can afford it might want to engage a web accessibility consultant or employee who has firsthand experience with how people with different disabilities interact with the Web.

Involve People with Disabilities in Your Project

After some background reading, the best way to understand accessibility issues is to actually work with some people with disabilities to learn how they interact with the Web and with assistive technologies. This will give you firsthand experience with accessibility barriers and solutions.

Including people with disabilities in your project may seem like a daunting proposition. Stick with me for a bit; there's a lot of guidance in this section and references to more. While it might be out of the question for some small projects, if you can do it, it will be well worth the effort.

From a little effort to include people with disabilities in your web development, you will get a lot of benefit, including the following:

- **Motivation:** When web developers, managers, and other project stakeholders see people with disabilities use their website, most are highly motivated by a new understanding of accessibility issues.

- **Efficiency:** Including users with disabilities *early* in a project helps web developers be more efficient in addressing accessibility, thus maximizing the results from investment in accessibility. You can more quickly develop accessibility solutions, and spend less time guessing and having to go back and fix things.

- **Effectiveness:** The better you understand the issues, the better you can implement more effective accessibility solutions (for example, using "search" for alt-text instead of "this image is a line art drawing of a dark green magnifying glass . . .").

Recruiting People with Disabilities

Start by finding a few people with disabilities. "Recruiting Participants with Disabilities" (www.uiaccess.com/accessucd/ut_plan.html#recruiting) lists places to contact when looking for people with disabilities. Find people close to your "target users." For example, if your site is about applying for college loans, it would be better to get an 18-year-old rather than an 80-year-old.

Find people who are fairly experienced using the Web. Later in testing you might want to include some novices, but for now, you want people who can teach you well. The "Users' Experience Interacting with the Web" section of "Involving Users in Web Accessibility Evaluation" (www.w3.org/WAI/eval/users) includes a bit about considerations for people's experience with their assistive technology (which applies when including users at the beginning of projects, as well as for evaluation later).

Include more than one person, with different disabilities. People with disabilities are as diverse as any other people. They have diverse experiences, expectations, and preferences. They use diverse interaction techniques, adaptive strategies, and assistive technology configurations. People have different disabilities: visual, auditory, physical, speech, cognitive, and neurological—and many have multiple disabilities.

Even within one category, there is considerable variation; for example, "visual disability" includes people who have been totally blind since birth, people who have distortion in their central vision from age-related degeneration, people who temporarily have blurry vision from an injury or disease, and more. A common mistake is assuming that people who are blind represent all people with visual disabilities.

Figures 1-13, 1-14, and 1-15 demonstrate very different needs of people whose conditions are both in the broad category of "low vision." Figure 1-13 is a web page in a common configuration with default settings. Figure 1-14, is a sample setup of a person with blurry vision (poor visual acuity), who needs to increase font and image size to be able to read the page. She also maximizes her browser window and wants the web page to use the full width so that the text line length isn't too short, as it is in Figure 1-14. Figure 1-15 is a sample setup of a person with tunnel vision and good eyesight (sharp visual acuity). He makes fonts and images small so that he can see more at a time. It's easier for him to read when the line lengths are shorter, so he wants to be able to decrease the window width and have the text reflow (rather than requiring horizontal scrolling, as shown in Figure 1-15).

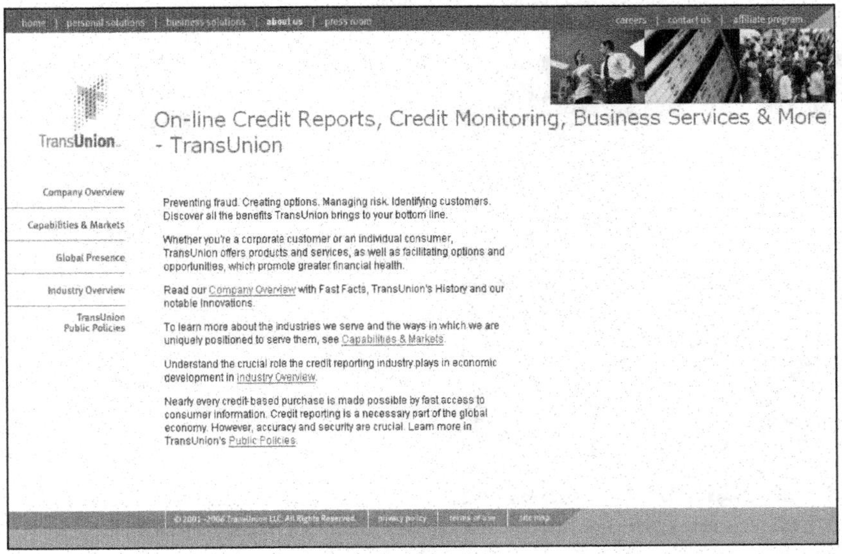

Figure 1-13. Site in common configuration

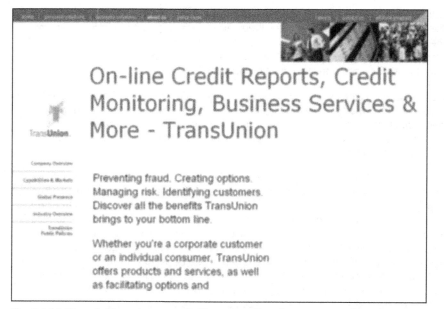

Figure 1-14. Site scaled larger by a user with blurry vision. Note that some text scales and some doesn't. Also, the main text area does not scale wider, causing very short line lengths.

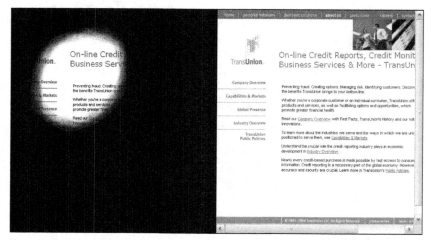

Figure 1-15. Site scaled smaller by a user with tunnel vision. On the left is what the user sees. The right shows how the whole page looks; note the horizontal scrollbar.

Because of this diversity in user needs, ideally you would include several users with different disabilities and user characteristics. In reality, the number of users will be limited by time and money constraints. That's okay, because you have a resource to cover the diversity (WCAG, as explained in the "Understand the Vital Role of Guidelines" section later in this chapter). For some guidance on choosing which disabilities to include in your recruiting, see "Determining Participant Characteristics" (www.uiaccess.com/accessucd/ut_plan.html#characteristics). While it's written for usability testing, some of the information applies to including users early in a project.

In deciding the number of people with disabilities to include, consider that users with disabilities also address general usability issues. For example, if you do usability testing with people with disabilities, you will find both accessibility issues and general usability issues that impact all users (including users without disabilities). Knowing that people with disabilities also address general usability can help get more time and money budgeted to include people with disabilities throughout your project.

When recruiting people with disabilities and planning to work with them, remember that if a person uses specific assistive technology, you'll need to arrange for it during your work together. If she has a laptop that she can bring to your site, that's probably best. If not, you could get the assistive technology for your site. However, many assistive technologies are very expensive and demo versions are limited. Also, people may have their own system customized, and that might be difficult to reproduce with your configuration. This is less likely to be a problem with an advanced user. In some cases, it might be best to go to the user's work or home, rather than having the user come to you. A downside to this is that fewer people from your project team get hands-on interaction.

Learning from People with Disabilities

Once you're sitting down with the user, make sure that he had a chance to get the computer and assistive technology set up how he likes. Then start out having him show you some websites that work well for him. It's important to do this first, so you get an idea how things can work well, and he can confirm that the setup is as he expects. Ask a lot of questions to learn how things work. Then you can have him show you things that don't work. Keep in mind that any problems are probably because of the site markup or design; however, if your user is a novice, there is a chance he doesn't know how to get his assistive technology to work with the site. If you already have a website that you are modifying, have him go over your website, particularly the areas that you are redoing. If you already have an idea of how you might redesign your site, ask him to use sites that have similar design, such as sites with the same type of navigation interaction.

Tell your users ahead of time what you'll want them to do. Ask them to prepare to show you good sites and bad sites. Tell them which sites you want them to show you, and what things to concentrate on, such as navigation, data tables, or forms. The better prepared they are, the more comfortable everyone will be and the more you'll get out of it.

To maximize the benefit of this time with users, include several people from your web project: developers who will be doing the coding, managers who approve the budget, and so on. Consider videotaping it to share with those who couldn't participate. Of course, make sure you find users who are comfortable with this. Some people will appreciate a large audience learning about accessibility; others would be uncomfortable with several people watching them.

In addition to involving users early in a project to help you understand accessibility issues, include them throughout the project as you develop accessibility fixes for existing sites or prototypes for new projects. When you have a draft (of a form, or navigation scheme, page layout template, or anything in between) that you are considering, have your users with disabilities test it. That way, you can make any necessary fixes before you propagate it throughout your site.

A word of caution: Avoid assuming that feedback from one person with a disability applies to all people with disabilities. A person with a disability doesn't necessarily know how other people with the same disability interact with the Web, nor know enough about other disabilities to provide valid guidance on other accessibility issues.

More information on including people with disabilities is included throughout "Usability Testing for Accessibility" (www.uiaccess.com/accessucd/ut.html). This is written for formal usability testing, so some of it won't apply to informal interaction early in project development. Much of it does apply, such as ensuring the facility is accessible, setting up the room, and interacting with people with disabilities. Don't worry about getting everything just right. As long as you are respectful, most people with disabilities will appreciate your efforts and not be bothered by any blunders.

To learn more about how to effectively involve users, turn to the usability field and the user-centered design (UCD) process, which we'll look at next.

Understand the Relationship Between Accessibility and Usability

UCD is a user interface design process that focuses on usability goals, user characteristics, environment, tasks, and workflow in the design of an interface, such as a website. UCD follows a series of well-defined methods and techniques for analysis, design, and evaluation. The UCD process is an iterative process, where design and evaluation steps are built in from the first stage of the project and throughout implementation. Accessible design techniques fit well into UCD processes. With a few additions and adaptations, design teams can use UCD practices to focus design on accessibility.

While there is a lot of overlap between accessible design, UCD, and usability, the relationship between accessibility and usability is not clear-cut.

First, let's start with a definition of *usability*. The International Organization for Standardization (ISO) defines usability as the "extent to which a product can be used by specified users to achieve specified goals effectively, efficiently and with satisfaction in a specified context of use" (in ISO 9241-11: Ergonomic Requirements for Office Work with Visual Display Terminals, Part 11: Guidance on Usability). Using this definition, accessibility focuses on the following:

- Including people with disabilities as "specified users"
- A wide range of situations, including assistive technologies, as the "specified context of use"

Put more simply, usability means designing your website to be effective, efficient, and satisfying. Accessibility makes sure it is effective, efficient, and satisfying for more people, especially people with disabilities, in more situations—including with assistive technologies.

Looking at definitions is easy. In practice, the relationship between accessibility and usability is more complex. For some people, it's a hotly debated topic. For most people, it's not an issue at all: When designing websites, it is rarely useful to differentiate between usability and accessibility.

However, there are times when the distinction between accessibility and usability is important, such as when looking at discrimination against people with disabilities and when defining specific accessibility standards. Yet the distinction is a common debate when defining accessibility standards such as WCAG. It is not clear what should be included in accessibility standards and what is purely usability and should not be included in accessibility standards.

One way to start looking at the distinction between the two is to categorize interface problems:

- Usability problems impact all users equally, regardless of ability; that is, a person with a disability is not disadvantaged to a greater extent by usability issues than a person without a disability.
- Accessibility problems decrease access to a website by people with disabilities. When a person with a disability is at a disadvantage relative to a person without a disability, it is an accessibility issue.

The distinction between usability and accessibility is especially difficult to define when considering cognitive and language disabilities. Many of the accessibility guidelines to improve accessibility for people with cognitive disabilities are the same as general usability guidelines. The distinction is further blurred by the fact that features for people with disabilities benefit people without disabilities because of situational limitations (that is, limitations from circumstance, environment, or device—such as using the Web on a mobile phone in bright sunlight with one hand because you're holding a sleeping baby with the other), and accessibility increases general usability.

Another point to cloud the distinction is "usable accessibility"—how usable are accessibility solutions. For example, if a site uses images for navigation and there's no alt-text, the site is clearly not accessible. If the site has frustratingly verbose alt-text (such as "This image is a line art drawing of a dark green magnifying glass. If you click on it . . ."), one might say that the site is technically accessible because there is alt-text; however, the alt-text is so bad that the usability of the site is awful for anyone who relies on the alt-text (which won't happen when you understand accessibility issues and include people with disabilities in your project).

There can be problems when people don't understand the issues around the distinction between usability and accessibility. For example, if a study reported that sites were not accessible but the problems were general usability issues (that impact all users, not just users with disabilities), the study could report incorrect conclusions about accessibility guidelines. Academic discussions of accessibility and usability can actually harm the cause of accessibility if they are not presented carefully for people who don't understand the complexity of the issue.

The bottom line on the issue of the relationship between accessibility and usability can be summarized as follows:

- Clearly, there is significant overlap between the two.
- The nuances of how they relate is of no consequence for most web development, which should have as its goal both accessibility and usability for all.
- In some specialized situations, such as legal policies, the distinction is important.
- It's a tricky issue; be careful what you do with it.

Using both UCD and WCAG as the basis for addressing accessibility ensures that the broad range of issues is covered well, at both the technical level and the user interaction level. You should be able to get most of what you need from WCAG. Involving users and using the UCD approach makes it easier and better.

For more on this topic, see "The Relationship Between Accessibility and Usability" (www.uiaccess.com/andusability.html) and "Accessibility in the User-Centered Design Process" (www.uiaccess.com/accessucd/).

Understand the Vital Role of Guidelines

Now to a topic that is clearer: the role of guidelines in web development projects. I've talked a lot about including people with disabilities in your web development project. While there are many benefits, that alone will not lead you to develop an accessible site, because even large projects cannot include the diversity of disabilities, adaptive strategies, and assistive technologies that would be necessary to sufficiently cover all the issues. WCAG covers the diversity. It was developed with input from people with many different backgrounds, experiences, and perspectives from around the world.

WCAG is comprehensive, covering the wide range of accessibility issues and addressing all disabilities in all situations, as much as possible.

There are other web accessibility guidelines and standards; probably the most well known is Section 508 in the U.S. But note that the web provisions in Section 508 cover only a small subset of WCAG, and a site that meets Section 508 Standards will not be fully accessible to some people with disabilities.

WCAG 1.0 was published in 1999 and is still the stable reference version. WCAG 2.0 is in development and nearing completion. In April 2006, WAI published fairly complete Working Drafts of WCAG 2.0 (www.w3.org/TR/WCAG20/) and very robust supporting documents "Understanding WCAG 2.0" (www.w3.org/TR/UNDERSTANDING-WCAG20/), "Techniques for WCAG 2.0" (www.w3.org/TR/WCAG20-TECHS/), and Overview of WCAG 2.0 Documents (www.w3.org/WAI/intro/wcag20). The April 2006 versions are sufficiently complete to start using as reference material for web development. Although some details may change between now and finalization of the documents, the main points are stable, and WCAG 2.0 is much more robust and flexible than WCAG 1.0.

While I suggest starting with users rather than guidelines, I also suggest that WCAG be central in web development projects. In most cases, the WCAG documents will be the primary reference for accessibility information. A common pattern would be as follows:

- First read about how people with disabilities use the Web. Learn from some real users the basic issues around accessibility barriers and solutions, and generally how common assistive technologies work.

- Mostly use WCAG and supporting documents throughout development to make sure you are covering all issues and for implementation techniques.

- Work with your users as you develop accessibility solutions to check that the solutions are effective.

WCAG should be the guiding force in accessibility efforts, yet be careful to keep it in perspective. The goal of accessibility is not to check off a guidelines list; the goal is to make your site accessible. Using WCAG helps ensure that all issues are addressed, and involving people with disabilities helps address them efficiently and effectively.

Accessibility Barriers on Existing Sites

It's all well and good to say that the best time to start accessibility is at the beginning of a project. However, most websites are already out there. Most were developed without considering accessibility and have accessibility barriers that make it difficult or impossible for some people with disabilities to use the site. Some sites have several significant barriers; others have only a few minor barriers. Sites developed to meet web standards such as XHTML and CSS usually have fewer barriers.

This section provides specific guidance for fixing accessibility barriers in existing websites; in other words, *repairing* accessibility problems, or *retrofitting* a site to improve accessibility. The previous sections also apply to retrofitting.

Fixing accessibility barriers on an existing website can be simple or complex, depending on many factors, such as the type of content, the size and complexity of the site, and the development tools and environment. Sometimes, complex sites are easier to fix than simple sites because they use templates and CMS.

The key word for retrofitting is *prioritize* (to avoid the whole wet-deer-in-headlights thing).

In order to define a prioritized retrofitting plan, it is usually best to first identify all of the accessibility barriers on your site. However, if you have a few serious accessibility barriers that are fairly easy to repair, it may be best to fix those immediately before going further. For example, if your primary site navigation is images without alt-text and you can fix it once in a template that takes care of the whole site, do that first.

Focusing Evaluation

Evaluating before retrofitting has specific goals: to define the accessibility barriers on your site and gather information to help plan an efficient retrofitting project. Rather than thoroughly evaluating every page on your site, you can focus on representative areas in order to get more valuable information with less effort. For example, elements that are the same across pages, such as navigation bars and footers, need to be evaluated only once and can then be skipped on pages where they are repeated. Make sure that your evaluation covers each feature and functionality (for example, data tables, forms, and scripts) from each developer or development group.

Evaluation can focus on specific points to help guide your retrofitting plan, such as determining if a particular accessibility barrier is widespread or isolated. For example, if only a few of your data tables are missing necessary markup, your retrofitting plan would include adding table markup to quality assurance (QA) processes. However, if none of the tables are properly marked up, you would add data table markup to your education plan. If tables from one development group are done properly, but those from another development group are not, this further clarifies where education is needed.

Prioritizing Evaluation and Repairs by Area

One aspect of prioritizing retrofitting is determining which areas of your website to work on first. It is usually best to first evaluate and repair the areas that have the greatest impact on users' experience with your website. Depending on how your site is developed, you may be able to repair many barriers through the following:

- Templates that impact many pages
- Style sheets that impact many pages
- Elements that impact many pages, such as navigation bars and scripts

Certain pages have higher priority, such as these:

- The homepage, which is often the first entry point to the site
- The main pages and functionality based on the purpose of the site (such as ordering products for an office supply site), including the following:
  - The path to get there from the common entry points (usually the homepage, but can be other pages as well)
  - The path to complete transactions (such as entering shipping address, payment details, and so on)
- Frequently used (high-traffic) pages and functionality, including the path to get there and complete transactions

Prioritizing by area helps scope what to do first. Prioritizing by barriers, described next, helps determine what to do first from a different perspective.

Prioritizing Repairs by Barrier

Accessibility barriers are often identified by WCAG 1.0 checkpoints. Each checkpoint has a priority (Priority 1, Priority 2, or Priority 3) that helps determine the impact of a particular accessibility barrier. An approach to retrofitting is to fix all of the Priority 1 barriers first, and then fix lower-priority barriers later. However, this approach has several disadvantages: You must go back over templates, style sheets, and pages multiple times; you will miss easy-to-do, lower-priority items; and you can get hung up on a few hard problems, instead of getting a lot of easy things done quickly.

A more effective approach in most cases is to do all of the high impact *and* easy repairs while you are working on a page, template, style sheet, and so on. Then address harder problems later. This approach has several advantages: It usually takes less time overall, and you get many fixes done quickly. This helps make your website more accessible sooner and demonstrates your commitment to improving the accessibility of your website as soon as is feasible.

Consider two parameters for prioritizing the order in which to address accessibility barriers: impact and effort. For each accessibility barrier, determine the following:

- **Impact on people with disabilities:** The actual impact on users of a specific barrier depends on the context of your site. For example, poor color contrast in the main content has high impact on some people with disabilities, whereas in generic footers, it may have low impact. Evaluating with users with disabilities, as described earlier in this chapter, helps determine the impact of accessibility barriers in your website.

- **Effort required for repair:** The time, cost, and skills to repair a barrier vary greatly based on parameters such as the type of repair and your development environment. For example, repairing barriers in navigation could require a simple change to the template that is automatically propagated throughout the website, or it could require changing every page manually. Repairing missing alt-text equivalents requires knowing the content and understanding how the text is used; whereas changing a site to effectively use style sheets requires CSS skills.

Imagine that you plot the repairs on a graph with impact on people with disabilities on one axis and effort required for repair on the other, as in Figure 1-16. Your retrofitting project should cover all those repairs that have high impact, and all the repairs that are easy. Repairs that are lower impact and harder to do can be left for later (often in conjunction with a redesign project).

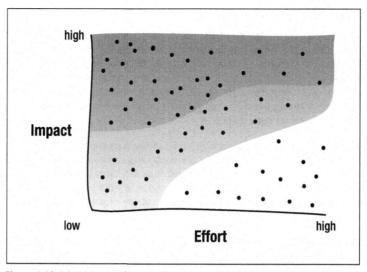

Figure 1-16. Prioritizing repairs by barrier: graph of impact and effort

Focusing evaluation to answer the specific questions for retrofitting, prioritizing by area, and prioritizing repairs by barriers helps you to define an effective retrofitting plan.

Harmful Myths About Web Accessibility

There are many myths about web accessibility. A few have some basis, but are focused on one side of the issue and are mitigated when you look at the whole picture. Several are downright wrong. Many of the myths hurt the cause of accessibility overall. I hope that you'll take a little time to understand the truths and help clarify the myths for others.

Long ago (in web time), it was nearly impossible to make visually appealing, complex, dynamic websites that were also accessible. Web technologies didn't adequately support accessibility, and they were not robust enough to provide elegant ways to produce complex visual designs. Web browsers also had little accessibility functionality. Common assistive technologies were not able to handle complex web page designs; for example, screen readers read across the screen, so multicolumn newspaper-style layouts were not usable. Back then, web developers wanting to make accessible sites were faced with the choice of either significant constraints on their design or providing a separate text-only version.

Now technologies let you develop visually appealing, complex, dynamic websites that are also accessible. Web technologies (such as XHTML and CSS), browsers, and assistive technologies have evolved. Style sheets offer more presentation functionality. Browsers provide text resizing. Assistive technologies can handle complex tables.

There is no longer a need to make text-only versions for accessibility, and there hasn't been for quite some time.

This history is part of the reason behind the first two myths I'll cover here: that text-only versions are an acceptable accessibility solution and that accessibility makes sites dull and boring.

Myth: Text-Only Versions Are an Acceptable Solution

Text-only versions refer to pages vwithout images or graphics, and often with single-column layout, little or no color, and simplified navigation interaction. Figure 1-17 shows a main site page (National Institute of Neurological Disorders and Stroke, NINDS, www.ninds.nih.gov/disorders/repetitive_motion/repetitive_motion.htm), and Figure 1-18 is the text-only version of the same page.

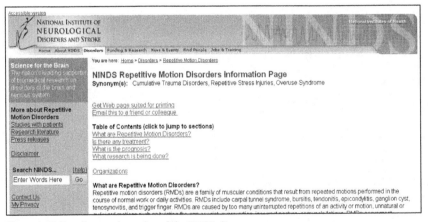

Figure 1-17. Page from main version of the NINDS site

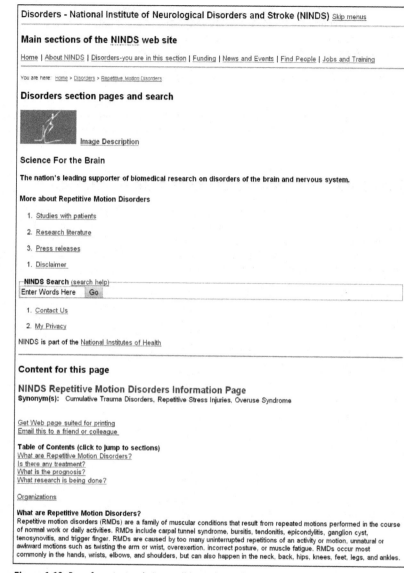

Figure 1-18. Page from text-only "accessible version" of the NINDS site

Text-only versions should have disappeared long ago, but unfortunately, they are still around. Text-only versions are not adequate accessibility solutions for several reasons.

Most text-only versions are not accessible for some people with disabilities. In Figure 1-17, the navigation in the main site is easy to distinguish because of the design and colors. The navigation is difficult to distinguish in the text-only version in Figure 1-18. People with some types of cognitive disabilities would not be able to use this text-only version because they couldn't differentiate the navigation from the content.

Separate versions are rarely fully equivalent and often outdated. When there are two versions of a website, invariably, the text-only version doesn't get updated as frequently as the main version. Even when organizations and individuals have the best intentions of keeping two versions in sync, the realities of deadlines and limited resources interfere. Some tools generate both a main version and a text-only version from a single source of content, supposedly eliminating the problem of separate versions not being in sync. Other tools facilitate creating a text-only version of an existing site. Despite claims that these tools provide totally equivalent versions, I have yet to see it. In one such implementation that I reviewed, the text-only version was fairly close in content with the main site; however, the text-only version was missing promotional material. Therefore, users of the text-only version missed out on special offers available through the website. This was not only not equivalent, but in this case, it also was discriminatory.

The main version often lacks even the most basic accessibility. When organizations develop text-only versions, they usually spend little effort to make the main site accessible. Many people with disabilities can use websites with only minor adjustments. For example, take the case of a person who has low vision where she can read text that is just a little larger than what most sites use by default. She doesn't need screen magnification software (which is costly), and instead just increases the text size through browser settings. Providing basic accessibility in the main site allows her and others like her to use it, rather than forcing them to use text-only versions that are usually much more difficult for sighted people to use, as demonstrated in Figure 1-18. Also, people who regularly use the main site may sometimes have accessibility issues from temporary disability or situation limitation (for example, they break their arm, break their glasses, or break their mouse). If the main site is inaccessible, they would be forced to use the text-only version that looks and acts very differently from the one they are used to using.

Clearly, text-only versions are not an acceptable substitute for making the main version of your site accessible. There are rarely good reasons to provide a text-only version. That's not to say that you should never provide a text-only version. If the main site is fully accessible and the text-only version is fully equivalent, then it's acceptable. It would be wise to clarify that, lest people see the text-only version and assume that you're using it as a cop-out for making the main site accessible.

Myth: Accessibility Makes Sites Dull and Boring

The myth that accessible sites have to be dull and boring, visually and technologically, is another one that comes from the olden days. If you still think that, you are not up with the times . . . except that, in theory, this myth is no longer true; however, in practice, there sadly is some truth to it. This section looks at the causes of this myth, as a starting point for correcting it.

In the past, most sites that focused on web accessibility were dull and boring. But this was not because of the limitations of accessibility. It was primarily because the organizations providing these sites did not have the resources (skills or money) to spend on good design. They focused the limited resources on their main goal, such as providing information and services to people with a particular disability or developing guidelines for web accessibility. When people went looking for examples of accessible sites, all that they found were dull and boring. Unfortunately, the W3C WAI site (www.w3.org/WAI/) was one of those. One of the premier web accessibility sites in the world was perpetuating this myth. We have fixed that. In 2005, WAI redesigned its website. Figure 1-19 shows the WAI homepage before redesign, and Figure 1-20 shows it after redesign.

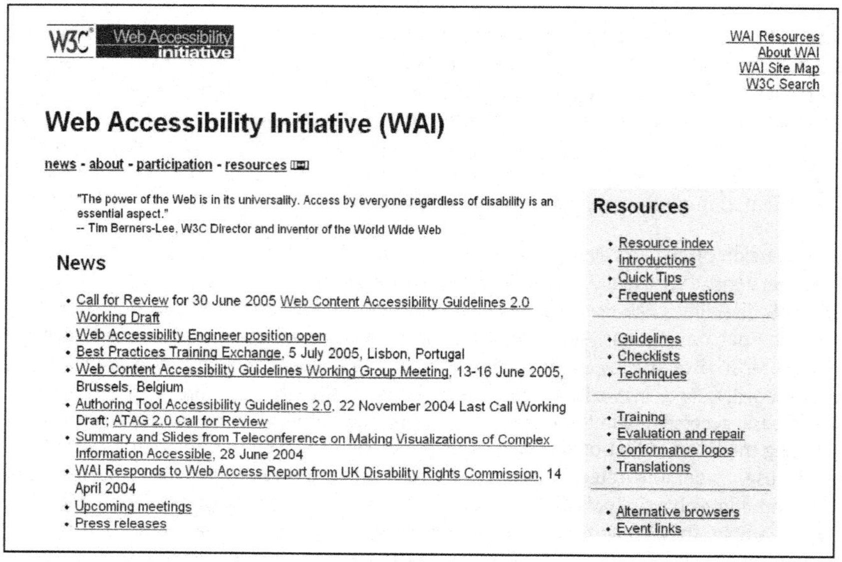

Figure 1-19. WAI homepage before 2005 redesign

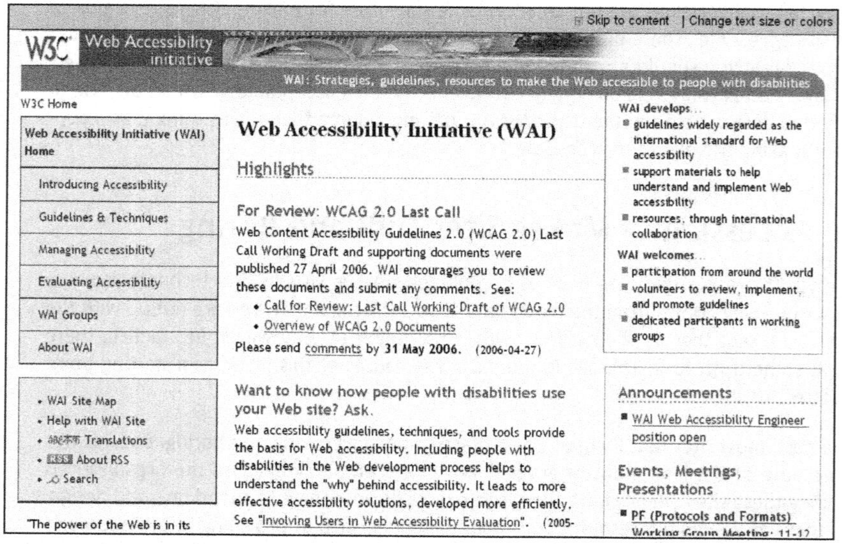

Figure 1-20. WAI homepage after 2005 redesign

As the lead on the redesign project, I will say that, unfortunately, it is not a shining example of visual design (we still have limited resources); however, it is no longer dull and boring. (And the information architecture, usability, and other aspects are top-notch.) Many other sites that focus on accessibility have also given their site a "face lift" recently and are now much more visually appealing.

Another problem that contributed to the dull-and-boring myth is that web developers misinterpreted accessibility requirements and guidelines as more restrictive than they actually are. People have misinterpreted that WCAG 1.0 says that you cannot use JavaScript and cannot open new browser windows. In fact, the guidelines say that web pages need to be accessible without scripts:

> 6.3 Ensure that pages are usable when scripts, applets, or other programmatic objects are turned off or not supported. If this is not possible, provide equivalent information on an alternative accessible page.

However, this doesn't prevent you from using scripts. It just means that you also need an alternative method to get the job done without scripts. For example, if you use client-side scripting for error checking, you should have backup server-side error checking for when scripting is not available. If you use scripting for things such as interactive navigation, you should make sure that users can get the navigation without scripting.

WCAG 1.0 Checkpoint 10.1 addresses opening new windows:

> 10.1 Until user agents allow users to turn off spawned windows, don't cause pop-ups or other windows to appear and don't change the current window without informing the user.

The checkpoint doesn't say don't do it; the checkpoint says inform users if you're doing it. WCAG Checkpoint 10.1 is another good example of why not to start your accessibility work with guidelines or standards, and instead to start with understanding the issues. If you first learn about how people with disabilities use the Web, you'll see the problems that new windows and changes in windows can cause when users don't know about them. Also note this is a big problem for users without disabilities who are new to the Web, as described in "On Spawned Windows" (www.uiaccess.com/spawned.html). We hope that with continuing education and with the rollout of WCAG 2.0, such harmful misinterpretations will dissolve.

Yet another major contributor to the dull-and-boring problem is that some "flashy" web technologies were developed without accessibility support. Web developers couldn't use these new, trendy technologies and make accessible sites without a lot of extra work to develop alternative versions. To fix this problem, we need to do the following:

- Understand that it's vital that web technologies support accessibility (as explained in the "Interdependent Components of Web Accessibility" section earlier in this chapter).
- Use technologies that support accessibility.
- Encourage those developing technologies to support accessibility.

All W3C technologies are now developed with accessibility support. Other technologies, such as Flash and PDF, have made significant progress toward accessibility support.

Perhaps the strongest reason for the dull-and-boring problem is more cultural. Websites and web designers are not judged on or rewarded for accessibility. From internal managers to external customers, people mostly have based their opinions of a site on the visual design, with no consideration for accessibility (or usability). Most web design competitions have not included accessibility as criteria. For example, in February 2006, I skimmed through the South by Southwest web awards finalists' sites, and the accessibility was abysmal. Most depressing were the accessibility problems in the CSS category that "show-cases sites . . . with standards compliant and accessible code."

As a web culture, we need to shift the definition of "cool site" to include accessible. Managers need to include it in the criteria on which their web developers are judged, as do web design contests. As consumers, we can use accessibility as criteria for supporting sites, as discussed in the "Call to Action" section later in this chapter.

Developing and promoting more sites that are accessible and visually exciting will help dissolve the myth that accessibility makes sites dull and boring.

Myth: Accessibility Is Expensive and Hard

Certainly, web accessibility is not cheap and easy. However, it's not as expensive and hard as it often seems at first. When an organization gets started with web accessibility, much of the cost is up-front knowledge and skill acquisition. Accept this as an initial investment, and plan to help it pay off later.

> *The additional benefits of web accessibility can result in overall cost savings in the long term, and high return on investment from increased site use. Specific examples of financial and technical benefits are discussed in the "Additional Benefits from a Business Perspective" section later in this chapter.*

If you are coming up against the expensive-and-hard myth in a particular case, figure out what's behind it. There could be a misunderstanding. For example, one reason people think web accessibility is expensive and hard is that they try to use screen readers. Screen readers *are* expensive and hard to learn to use. You can save some time, money, and hassle by doing the following:

- Using a voicing browser for initial testing. Currently, the main one is Home Page Reader from IBM, which is much cheaper and easier to use than most screen readers. It is usually sufficient for first-line testing. For example, see "Testing Web accessibility with Home Page Reader" (www-306.ibm.com/able/guidelines/web/webhprtest.html).

- Have regular screen reader users do testing for you. See "Involving Users in Web Accessibility Evaluation" (www.w3.org/WAI/eval/users) and "Usability Testing for Accessibility" (www.uiaccess.com/accessucd/ut.html).

A few aspects of accessibility, such as captions for multimedia, are costly, no matter how efficient your approach. But you can significantly decrease the cost of most aspects of web accessibility by following the suggestions earlier in this chapter:

- Start accessibility at the very beginning of a web development project.
- Start by understanding the issues, including the different components of web accessibility, then using "Understanding WCAG 2.0" (www.w3.org/TR/UNDERSTANDING-WCAG20/) to cover all the issues.
- Involve people with disabilities throughout.
- Prioritize by area and by barrier.

Finally, given that web accessibility is essential for equal opportunity for people with disabilities (and is required by law in some cases), not doing accessibility is expensive and hard in different ways.

Myth: Accessibility Is the Sole Responsibility of Web Developers

Web content developers will always have some responsibility for making their websites accessible. However, content developers currently have more work to do for accessibility than they should.

The "Interdependent Components of Web Accessibility" section earlier in this chapter describes multiple responsibilities for web accessibility. If the other components did a better job at accessibility, content developers would have an easier time of it. For example, authoring tools could make accessibility easier to implement, and if browsers had better and more consistent standards support (especially for CSS), content developers wouldn't waste so much time on browser-compatibility issues. The "Call to Action" section later in this chapter provides guidance on encouraging all components to do their part in web accessibility.

Myth: Accessibility Is for People Who Are Blind

A poorly developed website can have accessibility barriers for people with different disabilities, including visual, auditory, physical, speech, cognitive, and neurological. The examples of accessibility issues with different types of disabilities throughout this chapter illustrate different accessibility barriers.

Much of the work that you do in your accessibility efforts will be related to providing accessibility to people who are blind. Also, several "big names" have focused their accessibility studies and publications on people who are blind. Because of this focus on blindness, you might need to make a conscious effort to keep in mind accessibility issues of people with other disabilities.

One way to keep other disability issues in mind is using personas for people with different disabilities. For help developing personas, see "Accessibility in the Analysis Phase: Personas" (www.uiaccess.com/accessucd/analysis.html) and "How People with Disabilities Use the Web" (www.w3.org/WAI/EO/Drafts/PWD-Use-Web/).

Myth: Evaluation Tools Can Determine Accessibility and Conformance to Standards

Web accessibility evaluation tools are software programs and online services that help determine if a website meets accessibility guidelines or standards. Evaluation tools are very helpful and can reduce the time and effort required to evaluate a website. However, no tool can determine that a site is accessible and meets accessibility guidelines. Knowledgeable human evaluation is required to determine if a site is accessible.

The most well-known accessibility evaluation is Bobby, which was developed by CAST, the Center for Applied Special Technology. (Old-timers might enjoy http://web.archive.org/web/20020805071053/bobby.cast.org/html/en/index.jsp). Watchfire purchased it in 2002 and integrated it into WebXACT.

There are different types of evaluation tools, as described in "Selecting Web Accessibility Evaluation Tools" (www.w3.org/WAI/eval/selectingtools). For a comprehensive list of web accessibility evaluation tools, see "Web Accessibility Evaluation Tools: Overview" (www.w3.org/WAI/ER/tools/Overview), which is a searchable and sortable database of more than 100 tools.

Some tools check a website against a set of standards, such as WCAG 1.0 checkpoints. For some checkpoints, tools can determine automatically if the web page meets the checkpoint. For other checkpoints, tools cannot tell if the page meets the checkpoint, because the issue is not something that a computer can determine. Those checkpoints must be evaluated manually. Many tools provide help with those manual checks; however, human judgment is still required.

Webster's definition of "tool" as an "instrument used by a craftsman or laborer at his work" is useful in understanding the role of web accessibility evaluation tools. Rather than thinking of tools as a substitute for human evaluation, think of tools as an aid to human evaluation.

Consider spell checkers as an analogy for evaluation tools. Spell checkers identify possible spelling errors by evaluating against a set of known words. A human must then determine whether or not the word is indeed misspelled; correctly spelled proper names, technical terms, and such might not be in the spell checker's word list. The human must know the language, and if the document is about a subject with uncommon words (for example, with medical terms), the human evaluator must have some knowledge of the subject.

Similarly, web accessibility evaluation tools identify possible accessibility errors by evaluating web pages against a set of accessibility standards. A human must then determine whether the identified issue indeed doesn't meet standards and is an accessibility barrier. The human must have knowledge of accessibility issues and solutions. "Using Combined Expertise to Evaluate Web Accessibility" (www.w3.org/WAI/eval/reviewteams) lists recommended knowledge for evaluating web accessibility: an understanding of web technologies, evaluation tools, barriers that people with disabilities experience, assistive technologies and approaches that people with disabilities use, and accessibility guidelines and techniques.

To carry the analogy further, spell checkers help fix spelling errors by providing a list of similar words. A knowledgeable human is required to pick the correct spelling or provide the correct spelling if it is not listed. Some evaluation tools help fix accessibility problems, and a knowledgeable human is required to implement the fix properly. A spell checker can have false positives and false negatives. For example, if I type "good text tool," when I meant to type "good test tool," the spell checker will not identify it as an error. Similarly, there are many errors that evaluation tools will not identify. For example, a tool that checks HTML and not CSS would miss absolute font sizes in CSS.

Checking alt-text for images is a good example of using web accessibility evaluation tools to increase efficiency and of the requirement for human judgment. To meet web accessibility standards and guidelines, images must have equivalent alt-text. Evaluation tools help in checking alt-text. Many tools list all images that are missing alt-text. Some tools flag suspicious alt-text. However, no tool can determine if the alt-text is equivalent as required for accessibility. Judging if the alt-text is equivalent requires human evaluation. Some tools help a human evaluator judge if alt-text is equivalent. For example, the WAVE tool (www.wave.webaim.org/) displays the alt-text adjacent to the image so that you can see the image and the alt-text together in the context of the page. Some tools help fix missing or poor alt-text by providing a dialog box to enter the alt-text and then inserting the alt-text in the markup.

Alt-text is also a good example of the benefits of involving users in evaluation. Evaluation tools focus on assessing conformance to accessibility standards. With this focus on the technical aspects of accessibility, the human interaction aspect can be lost. Include people with disabilities in usability evaluation techniques to assess "usable accessibility" and make sure that your implementations of accessibility solutions are done well and are usable by people with disabilities. Usable accessibility is a term introduced in: "Another -ability: Accessibility Primer for Usability Specialists" (www.uiaccess.com/upa2002a.html).

There are many benefits to including participants with disabilities in traditional usability testing. However, large-scale formal usability testing is not necessary to evaluate usable accessibility. Short, informal evaluation can gather valuable feedback from people with disabilities without the rigor of formal usability testing.

The "Involve People with Disabilities in Your Project" section earlier in this chapter provides some guidance on including users with disabilities in web development and evaluation. Additional guidance on including people with disabilities ("users") in accessibility evaluation throughout web development is available in "Involving Users in Web Accessibility Evaluation" (www.w3.org/WAI/eval/users) and "Usability Testing for Accessibility" (www.uiaccess.com/accessucd/ut.html). The latter is written for formal usability testing, yet much of the information also applies to including people with disabilities in informal evaluation focusing on accessibility issues.

Effective and efficient evaluation combines the following:

- Screening techniques (including using assistive technologies, as described in "Screening Techniques for Accessibility" (www.uiaccess.com/accessucd/screening.html) and "Preliminary Review of Web Sites for Accessibility" (www.w3.org/WAI/eval/preliminary)
- Accessibility expert review
- Evaluation with people with disabilities
- Evaluation tools

Myth: Guidelines Are Not Sufficient for Accessibility

A myth I've been hearing more often lately is that accessibility guidelines aren't sufficient to ensure that a website is accessible. I'm in the process of addressing this myth; see "Myth: Guidelines Aren't Sufficient for Accessibility" (www.uiaccess.com/myth-guidelines.html).

Additional Benefits from a Business Perspective

The reason to make the Web accessible is equal access for people with disabilities, period. It is also useful to know the many additional benefits of web accessibility. It is often easier for organizations to allocate more resources to accessibility when they learn that it can increase their potential market, decrease maintenance efforts, and result in many other benefits.

> *While the primary focus of web accessibility is on access by people with disabilities, for a broader business perspective, you can say that accessibility is about designing your website so that more people can use it effectively in more situations.*

Technical Benefits

Implementing web accessibility solutions in a website often results in improved technical performance. The importance of various technical benefits of web accessibility is different for specific organizations and situations. For example, reducing server load might be most important to an organization with a large, mission-critical, high-traffic site; whereas another organization that focuses on cutting-edge technology might be more interested in interoperability and being prepared for advanced web technologies. And these same technical benefits might not be very important for organizations with small, simple sites.

Accessibility is an aspect of high-quality websites. Some developers and organizations pride themselves on producing high-quality websites that meet technical standards. WCAG and other WAI guidelines are widely recognized international standards. Several resources online address the benefits of and business case for web standards in general; use a search engine with the search text "benefits web standards" for more information.

Reduced Site Development and Maintenance Time

Accessibility can reduce site development and maintenance time. Incorporating accessibility usually increases site development time initially. However, in the long term, web accessibility can reduce the time an organization spends on site development and maintenance.

Defining presentation through a style sheet and using proper markup (for example, in XHTML) for structure reduces time and effort needed to change presentation across a site. Presentation includes design and style, such as font size, font face, background color, and page layout. If the presentation is defined in an external style sheet, it can be changed throughout the site by making the modification to that one style sheet. However, if the presentation is improperly defined throughout the HTML, the presentation markup will need to be changed in every instance on every web page.

Using standard markup and style sheets to style and format text, instead of using bitmap images of text, reduces updating and, for sites in multiple languages, reduces translation time and skills. Site designers often use bitmap images for stylized text. In such cases, to change or translate text content or style, each image must be manipulated. If the text is not in an image, and the style is provided in a style sheet, then the text can be changed or translated without touching the image, and the style can be changed in the style sheet.

Reduced Server Load

Web accessibility techniques often reduce the server load, thus reducing the need for additional servers and increasing the download speed. Defining presentation in style sheets rather than in the markup of each page and using text rather than bitmap images of text reduces the size of each page served.

Improved Interoperability

Accessibility can help enable content on different configurations. Many organizations are increasingly interested in web interoperability and device independence—that is, developing websites that work with multiple technologies, devices, and so on. Web accessibility can enable web content to be rendered (displayed) and interacted with on various configurations, including different browsers, operating systems, and devices.

W3C technologies—such as Extensible Hypertext Markup Language (XHTML), Extensible Markup Language (XML), Resource Description Framework (RDF), Synchronized Multimedia Integration Language (SMIL), Cascading Style Sheets (CSS), Extensible Stylesheet Language (XSL), XSL Transformations (XSLT), and Portable Network Graphics (PNG)—were designed to support accessibility. Using current versions of W3C technologies should provide the best rendering across different configurations. Designing for device independence benefits some people with disabilities as well as people without disabilities using input devices other than keyboards, such as with phones and other handheld devices. Using markup for structure and style sheets for presentation allows users and user agents to request content in a way that suits their capabilities.

Preparation for Advanced Technologies

Web accessibility can help organizations take advantage of advanced web technologies and be prepared for future web technologies. Using metadata and representing it using RDF, as described in the "What is RDF?" section of "Frequently Asked Questions about RDF" (www.w3.org/RDF/FAQ.html#What), allows content reuse. Defining presentation in a style sheet, using proper markup structure, and using the latest standards simplify forward migration and backward-compatibility.

Financial Benefits

An organization's efforts to make its website accessible often have a financial impact, and can result in positive return on investment and cost efficiencies. Benefits to organizations that provide accessible websites include financial benefits from increased website use and direct cost savings.

Search Engine Optimization

Making your site accessible can significantly improve search engine optimization (SEO). For some organizations, SEO is a big deal. In such cases, this additional benefit of accessibility is a good selling point if you need to make a business case for spending effort on accessibility.

Several accessibility techniques are exactly the same as SEO techniques—that is, employing accessibility techniques will most surely improve your web pages' ranking. Take, for example, Google's Webmaster Guidelines (from www.google.com/webmasters/guidelines.html):

Following these guidelines will help Google find, index, and rank your site.

- Make sure that your TITLE and ALT tags [sic] are descriptive and accurate.
- Try to use text instead of images to display important names, content, or links. The Google crawler doesn't recognize text contained in images.
- Check for . . . correct HTML.
- Make a site with clear . . . text links.
- Keep the links on a given page to a reasonable number (fewer than 100).
- Offer a site map to your users.
- Use a text browser such as Lynx to examine your site, because most search engine spiders see your site much as Lynx would. If fancy features such as JavaScript, cookies, session IDs, frames, DHTML, or Flash keep you from seeing all of your site in a text browser, then search engine spiders may have trouble crawling your site.

All of these are accessibility guidelines and best practices. And there are other examples of accessibility techniques that improve SEO, such as text equivalents for multimedia. Just as search engines need alt-text for images, they need alternatives for multimedia. Providing a transcript with visual descriptions meets an accessibility requirement and makes the material available for search engines.

Headings are another overlap between optimizing for search engines and accessibility techniques. People with some types of cognitive disabilities greatly benefit from information grouped with clear headings. People who use screen readers benefit from the headings being properly marked up with heading tags (h1, h2, and so on). People who can see are able to visually skim through the headings on a page to get an overview of the content of the page. People who are blind and use a screen reader are not able to do this. Instead, they access the page one word at a time. When headings are properly marked up, screen reader users can also skim through the headings using a screen reader feature. If headings aren't marked up, users who are blind cannot use this feature.

To find several very good articles on the SEO benefits of accessibility, search the Web for "accessibility search engine."

Increased Website Use

A major benefit of web accessibility is the potential for direct and indirect financial gains from increased website use. Web accessibility can make it easier for people to find a website, access it, and use it successfully, thus resulting in more users and increased use.

Many organizations benefit financially when more people successfully use their website. For example, commercial companies can get more sales, educational institutions can get more students, and nonprofit organizations can get more funding by demonstrating successful outreach and dissemination. Increasingly, websites are used to cut costs by decreasing customer support services and letting customers complete transactions online, rather than requiring personnel and paper interactions. The many examples of cost savings from online transactions include citizens renewing licenses, investors trading stock, and students registering for classes online. Thus, more users using the site more often can result in financial gains and cost savings.

Accessible sites can be used by more people (as described earlier in the "Benefits for People Without Disabilities" section), thus increasing the market segments and number of people who can successfully use the site. An important potential market for many organizations is older people. In many countries, older people are the fastest growing group of new web users.

When web use is a significant part of a job, web pages and applications that are accessible to more people can help with employee recruiting and employee retention. Employees, customers, and other users who become temporarily or permanently disabled or impaired due to accident, illness, or aging are more likely to be able to continue using a website if it is accessible.

Accessible sites are generally more usable to everyone, including people with disabilities and people without disabilities. Increased usability means website users achieve their goals effectively, efficiently, and satisfactorily. When users have a positive experience with a website, they are more likely to use the site more thoroughly, return to the site more often, and tell others about the site (called *viral marketing*). Some accessibility guidelines can indirectly increase usability; for example, by making web pages load faster.

Some accessibility guidelines directly increase usability for all users, such as the following:

- Clear and consistent design, navigation, and links
- Blocks of information divided into groups
- Clear and simple language as appropriate
- Supplemental images and illustrations
- Good color contrast

An organization's efforts in web accessibility are a public relations opportunity to increase its positive image, which can increase website use. As mentioned earlier in the chapter, web accessibility is a social issue and an aspect of CSR. CSR has been shown to improve financial performance, enhance brand image and reputation, increase sales and customer loyalty, increase ability to attract and retain employees, and provide access to capital and funding. To find CSR information such as statistics that show how it impacts customers, search the Web for "corporate social responsibility" and "corporate citizenship."

Direct Cost Savings

In addition to the benefits from increased website use, many organizations realize direct cost savings from efforts to improve web accessibility. Many of the aspects of web accessibility that are discussed earlier in the section about the technical benefits can provide direct cost savings:

- Decreases personnel costs for maintaining the site when accessibility reduces site maintenance over the long term
- Decreases the amount of server capacity needed and saves on additional server costs when accessibility reduces server loading
- Decreases the need for creating multiple versions of a site for different devices when accessibility enables content to work on different devices
- Decreases the cost of upgrading to new technologies when accessibility helps take advantage of advanced web technologies and being prepared for future web technologies

Potential direct cost savings also result from decreasing the potential for high legal expenses, decreasing the cost of alternative format materials, and decreasing the cost of translating. Ensuring that websites are accessible reduces the risk of high legal costs associated with defending against legal action for not complying with web accessibility requirements.

For organizations that provide printed materials in alternate formats (large print, embossed Braille, and computer disk), an accessible website can reduce the demand for alternate formats when people choose to use the Web, thus saving some production and distribution costs. The cost of translating a website to other languages can be decreased by following accessibility guidelines for the following:

- Clear and simple language as appropriate
- Clear and consistent design, navigation, and links
- Separating content from presentation
- Text and markup rather than bitmap images of text to convey information

The Business Case for Web Accessibility

For more details on the technical and financial benefits of web accessibility, see "Developing a Web Accessibility Business Case for Your Organization" (www.w3.org/WAI/bcase/Overview). It is designed to help develop a customized business case for web accessibility for a specific organization, and presents many different aspects of web accessibility, along with guidance on incorporating these aspects into a specific organization's business case.

Call to Action

Incorporating accessibility is *an act of enlightened self-interest*, both for organizations and individuals. If individuals and organizations are aware of the benefits of accessibility (they are "enlightened"), they will address accessibility issues in order to benefit themselves as well as others. Most people will experience temporary or permanent disability in their lifetime, and will benefit from technology that is accessible. While some people are born with a disability, others acquire disabilities from accident, illness, disease, or aging. The point is that even if you don't have a disability now, you very well could acquire one at any time.

For many people, understanding that accessibility is the right thing to do is motivation enough. Most who know people with disabilities or have included people with disabilities in their development process, and have witnessed firsthand the failures of inaccessible sites and the successes of accessible sites, are passionate about accessibility. If you understand the social inequality that results from an inaccessible web, and the power of an accessible web for people with disabilities, you will want to do your part for web accessibility.

> *Perhaps the most influential thing that you can do is foster a positive attitude about accessibility.*

A few years ago, I consulted with a company that approached accessibility as a frustrating, burdensome legal requirement. The developers were only trying to tick off a checklist with as little effort as possible, and with that approach, they wasted a lot of effort trying to get around accessibility and developing ineffective solutions that had to be redone. It was no fun for anyone. Another company I consulted with at the time had a totally different approach to accessibility. The management saw accessibility as a market differentiator that would put the company above its competition. The developers took on challenging issues like engineers with a puzzle. They almost welcomed finding difficult accessibility problems because they loved coming up with innovative solutions. They also had a couple of people with disabilities come into the office periodically to help them understand the issues and test potential solutions. It was an exciting project for everyone involved.

These examples illustrate the importance of attitude. Embrace accessibility as a rewarding challenge.

If you've already had some success with web accessibility, you can help foster a positive attitude throughout the web development community by sharing success stories. This will also help others who are trying to get support for accessibility in their projects. We need more data or even empirical evidence of how improving accessibility of a website (Internet or intranet) resulted in improved SEO, increased business, decreased maintenance, and other benefits. Write a conference paper or a web article, or post to a web accessibility list (such as the WAI Interest Group at www.w3.org/WAI/IG/#mailinglist and WebAIM at www.webaim.org/discussion/) telling of the additional benefits that your organization realized. (You can also get some marketing value out of this for your own organization.)

Another way to mutually benefit yourself, your organization, and web accessibility in general is to encourage accessibility improvements in the different components (browsers, authoring tools, and so on). Earlier in this chapter, I talked about the chicken-and-egg issue of which component implements an accessibility feature first. Encourage each to go first in order to prompt others. When accessibility features are effectively implemented in one component, the other components are more likely to implement them:

- When web browsers, media players, assistive technologies, and other user agents support an accessibility feature, users are more likely to demand it and developers are more likely to implement it in their websites.

- When developers want to implement an accessibility feature, they are more likely to demand that their authoring tool make it easy.

- When authoring tools make a feature easy to implement, developers are more likely to do it.

- When an accessibility feature is implemented in most websites, developers and users are more likely to demand that browsers and other user agents support it.

As the customers for authoring tools, web developers have particular clout to encourage authoring tool developers to make their tools accessible. Send e-mail saying that accessibility support and conformance to ATAG will be criteria in your future authoring tool purchasing. Provide feedback on specific accessibility improvements you would like implemented in their future releases.

You don't have to be directly involved in web development to help make the Web more accessible. Anyone can contribute by communicating to others the importance and benefits of web accessibility. Encourage sites to be accessible. Send e-mail messages (and letters and phone calls) to sales, marketing, customer service, and web development departments, asking them to improve the accessibility of their website. Point them to resources to learn more about accessibility. Explain how the accessibility barriers on their site affect people with disabilities.

Please use a positive, encouraging approach, rather than an attacking, threatening, or otherwise negative approach. While you may feel negative, that approach is not the best way to get accessibility. I've seen organizations make some accessibility improvements in their sites and get harshly criticized because they didn't do it well enough. One manager said with exasperation, "Why even try? We get attacked when we're doing the best we can." When you approach organizations, I think it's best to assume that they don't understand accessibility, rather than as if they are purposely excluding people with disabilities. What's usually needed is education and encouragement, not criticism. Certainly, there is a time for different approaches, but they should be a last resort after you've tried more cooperative approaches.

Reward accessible sites by giving them your business and telling others about them. Send an e-mail message saying that you appreciate that they've made their site accessible. This will help them know the benefits of their accessibility efforts, and can help them budget for additional accessibility enhancements in the future.

Be an accessibility evangelist.

Summary

This chapter addressed key issues in understanding web accessibility, including its essential role in equal opportunity for people with disabilities, additional benefits to others and to organizations, interdependent components, approaching web accessibility by including people with disabilities throughout development, and myths surrounding web accessibility. For updates to this chapter, see www.uiaccess.com/understanding.html.

Some of the information in this chapter was developed through the W3C WAI (www.w3.org/WAI/), and the Education and Outreach Working Group (www.w3.org/WAI/EO/) in the following documents. Check the latest online version of these resources for additional and updated information.

- "Introduction to Web Accessibility," S.L. Henry, ed. www.w3.org/WAI/intro/accessibility
- "Essential Components of Web Accessibility," S.L. Henry, ed. www.w3.org/WAI/intro/components
- "How People with Disabilities Use the Web [Draft]," J. Brewer, ed. www.w3.org/WAI/EO/Drafts/PWD-Use-Web
- "Developing a Web Accessibility Business Case for Your Organization," S.L. Henry, ed. www.w3.org/WAI/bcase

- "Improving the Accessibility of Your Web Site," S.L. Henry, ed. www.w3.org/WAI/impl/improving ("Prioritizing the Repairs" section at www.w3.org/WAI/impl/improving#prior)
- Web Content Accessibility Guidelines (WCAG) documents
  - "Web Content Accessibility Guidelines (WCAG) Overview," S.L. Henry, ed. www.w3.org/WAI/intro/wcag
  - "Web Content Accessibility Guidelines 1.0," W. Chisholm, G. Vanderheiden, I. Jacobs, eds. www.w3.org/TR/WCAG10
  - "Overview of WCAG 2.0 Documents," S.L. Henry, ed. www.w3.org/WAI/intro/wcag20.php
  - "Web Content Accessibility Guidelines 2.0," B. Caldwell, W. Chisholm, J. Slatin, G. Vanderheiden, eds. www.w3.org/TR/WCAG20
  - "Understanding WCAG 2.0," B. Caldwell, W. Chisholm, J. Slatin, G. Vanderheiden, eds. www.w3.org/TR/UNDERSTANDING-WCAG20
  - "About Baselines and WCAG 2.0," D. MacDonald, J. Slatin, G. Vanderheiden, eds. www.w3.org/WAI/WCAG20/baseline/Overview
- Authoring Tool Accessibility Guidelines (ATAG) documents
  - "Authoring Tool Accessibility Guidelines (ATAG) Overview," S.L. Henry, ed. www.w3.org/WAI/intro/atag
  - "Authoring Tool Accessibility Guidelines 1.0," J. Treviranus, C. McCathieNevile, I. Jacobs, J. Richards, eds. www.w3.org/TR/ATAG10
  - "Authoring Tool Accessibility Guidelines 2.0," J. Treviranus, J. Richards, M. Matt, eds. www.w3.org/TR/ATAG20
  - "Selecting and Using Authoring Tools for Web Accessibility," J. Brewer, ed. www.w3.org/WAI/impl/software
- User Agent Accessibility Guidelines (UAAG) documents
  - "User Agent Accessibility Guidelines (UAAG) Overview," S.L. Henry, ed. www.w3.org/WAI/intro/uaag
  - "User Agent Accessibility Guidelines 1.0," I. Jacobs, J. Gunderson, E. Hansen, eds. www.w3.org/TR/UAAG10
- Web accessibility evaluation documents
  - "Evaluating Web Sites for Accessibility: Overview," S. Abou-Zahra, ed. www.w3.org/WAI/eval/Overview
  - "Preliminary Review of Web Sites for Accessibility," S. Abou-Zahra, ed. www.w3.org/WAI/eval/preliminary
  - "Involving Users in Web Accessibility Evaluation," S.L. Henry, ed. www.w3.org/WAI/eval/users

- "Using Combined Expertise to Evaluate Web Accessibility," J. Brewer, ed. www.w3.org/WAI/eval/reviewteams
- "Selecting Web Accessibility Evaluation Tools," S. Abou-Zahra, ed. www.w3.org/WAI/eval/selectingtools
- "Web Accessibility Evaluation Tools," S. Abou-Zahra, ed. www.w3.org/WAI/ER/tools/Overview
- "Basic Glossary for WAI Documents," H. Snetselaar, S.L. Henry, eds. www.w3.org/WAI/glossary/basic

References from other than W3C include the following:

- *Accessibility in the User-Centered Design Process*, S.L. Henry and M. Grossnickle, Georgia Tech Research Corporation, Inc, 2004, www.uiaccess.com/accessucd
- *Interdependent Components of Web Accessibility*, W. Chisholm and S.L. Henry, Proceedings of the 2005 International Cross-Disciplinary Workshop on Web Accessibility (W4A), 2005, ISBN:1-59593-219-4
- "Introduction to the Screen Reader" video, University of Wisconsin-Madison, www.doit.wisc.edu/accessibility/video/intro.asp
- *Another -ability: Accessibility Primer for Usability Specialists*, S.L. Henry, Proceedings of UPA 2002 (Usability Professionals' Association annual conference), www.uiaccess.com/upa2002a.html
- "The Relationship Between Accessibility and Usability," S.L. Henry, www.uiaccess.com/andusability.html
- "Myth: Guidelines aren't sufficient for accessibility," S.L. Henry, www.uiaccess.com/mythguidelines.html
- "On Spawned Windows," S.L. Henry, www.uiaccess.com/spawned.html
- "Web Accessibility Evaluation Tools Need People," S.L. Henry, www.uiaccess.com/evaltools.html
- "Web Accessibility and Older People," S.L. Henry www.uiaccess.com/andaging.html

There are now many good resources on accessibility—too many to list here. And if I listed some, it would be bad not to list others. So I've (mostly) listed only those from WAI or that I wrote elsewhere. Of course, the remainder of this book covers details on many of the issues introduced in this chapter.

2 OVERVIEW OF LAW AND GUIDELINES

by Cynthia D. Waddell

Throughout history, disability law and public policy have reflected the norms of the many governments of the world and the varying socioeconomic environments. But one common thread in many societies has been the tendency to isolate and segregate persons with disabilities because of ignorance, neglect, superstition, or fear. Within this social environment, disability policy has evolved from the early social welfare approach, under the medical model of institutional care, to rehabilitation and education.

Because of the growing body of laws and public policies requiring the accessible design of products and websites, it's important for both policymakers and designers of this technology to be able to recognize the barriers that restrict access, and how to comply with these laws and policies. Just as security, cybercrime, privacy, and copyright are important issues for technologists, so too is accessible web design.

This chapter will introduce you to the emergence of global legal and policy issues for accessible web design standards. Since many jurisdictions now require adherence to standards of accessibility in web design, it is important for web designers to understand which technical standards to apply. This chapter includes the following:

- A general introduction to the legal and public policy issues
- A discussion of two disability rights complaints based on inaccessible web design
- An introduction to the industry standards recommended by the World Wide Web Consortium (W3C), as well as the U.S. legislation establishing Electronic and Information Technology Accessibility Standards

Evolution of Public Policy

Since World War II, a new concept of integration has emerged along with a growing awareness of the capabilities of persons with disabilities. For example, the 1960s saw the United Nations reevaluating its policy and establishing both the foundation for the human rights of people with disabilities and the goal for their full participation in society.

Raising the alarm, the United Nations noted that more than half a billion persons were disabled worldwide and that approximately 80 percent of this population lived in developing countries. Declaring a "silent crisis," the United Nations said that the public policy issue "affects not only disabled persons themselves and their families, but also the economic and social development of entire societies, where a significant reservoir of human potential often goes untapped" (see *United Nations Commitment to Advancement of the Status of Persons with Disabilities*, www.un.org/esa/socdev/enable/disun.htm).

The 1980s brought the formulation of the current World Programme of Action (WPA) concerning Disabled Persons, adopted by the General Assembly in December 1982 (*General Assembly resolution 37/52*). The theme of the WPA is the equalization of opportunities for persons with disabilities and the need to approach disability from a human rights perspective:

One of the most important concerns is **accessibility: to new technologies, in particular information and communications technologies, as well as to the physical environment**. The notion of "mainstreaming" will also be given prominence, that is, including a **disability dimension in policy recommendations** covering a wide spectrum of social and economic concerns.

United Nations Commitment to Advancement of the Status of Persons with Disabilities,
www.un.org/esa/socdev/enable/disun.htm (emphasis added).

As a result, Rule 5 of the *Standard Rules on the Equalization of Opportunities for People with Disabilities* (*General Assembly resolution 48/96* of 20 December 1993, annex) addresses "Accessibility" and measures to provide access to the physical environment, as well as access to information and communication (see www.un.org/esa/socdev/enable/dissre04.htm).

Other examples of public policy initiatives include the European Union activities discussed in Chapter 17, as well as various initiatives addressing the global digital divide—for example, see www.bridges.org.

What Is the Problem?

We have reached a significant crossroads, where our global policies, technologies, and purchasing choices will determine whether or not every person will benefit from, and directly participate in, the digital economy. The explosive growth of electronic commerce continues to erect new barriers to participation for people with disabilities, as well as for anyone without the latest technology.

We are now seeing a significant shift from using the Web to post essentially static information to using it for dynamic applications. The impact is systemic and reaches all sectors of our economy. Whether or not the web application is for e-government (communications, services, and Internet voting), e-commerce (shopping, kiosks, personal digital assistants, and product design), e-banking (online banking), or e-education (long-distance learning and research), a shift in methodology is in progress, affecting the delivery of communications and services. For a detailed discussion of this issue and the new barriers being created, see *The Growing Digital Divide in Access for People with Disabilities: Overcoming Barriers to Participation* commissioned by the U.S. Department of Commerce, National Science Foundation, and authored by Cynthia D. Waddell (www.icdri.org/CynthiaW/the_digital_divide.htm).

Information technology has evolved from command-line text interfaces, through graphical user interfaces, and today to other modalities such as speech input and output. Accessible web design seeks to integrate the four user interface modalities (visual, auditory, tactual, and kinesthetic) previously reserved for assistive computer technologies so that the widest possible audience can benefit regardless of disability, age, or limitations of the end user's technology. As the Internet evolves and technology advances, it is important for information technology managers and public policy technologists to understand accessible web design so that they can recognize public policy issues as they arise.

One particular example of a public policy problem is the language used to establish contract formation on the Web in the U.S. Electronic Signatures in Global and National Commerce Act passed in 2000. The language of this digital signature act not only creates problems for enabling accessible contract formation on the Web, but it also has an adverse impact on the use of alternative Internet access devices such as cell phones and personal digital assistants (PDAs). See The Internet Society Press Release, *Landmark U.S. Digital Signature Legislation Falls Short with Regard to Persons with Disabilities* (www.isoc.org/isoc/media/releases/000703pr.shtml) and related June 2000 commentary, *Questions about Electronic Signature Bill: Will Everyone Be Able to Participate?* (www.icdri.org/CynthiaW/questions_about_electronic_signa.htm).

Nevertheless, the growing recognition that disability rights laws demand equal access to information and online services and programs has contributed to the development of accessible web design standards. In fact, the development of these standards, user agent accessibility guidelines, and web authoring tool accessibility guidelines is an acknowledgement of the practical and public policy needs for functionality and interoperability for the Web. This book is timely in that it provides the premier tools necessary for constructing accessible websites for a sustainable digital economy.

Complaints Filed Due to Inaccessible Web Design

At least two types of complaints can be filed against entities for creating and maintaining inaccessible websites. We will take a look at two examples and examine the facts of these cases. This will help you to better understand the legal liability and disability rights issues that can arise from failure to design an accessible website. These cases illustrate some of the public policy reasons for the importance of accessible design. Decisions made at the design phase for a website can have a profound impact on its navigation and usability, as well as legal liability for certain jurisdictions.

First, we will go back in Internet pioneering time to 1995 and the Wild, Wild Web—where there were no laws and every frontier website was on its own. At the time, an Americans with Disabilities Act (ADA) administrative complaint was filed against the City of San José. It was the resolution of that complaint that led to the first accessible web design standard for local government in the U.S. Next, we will fast-forward to 1999–2000 and examine the facts of the first fully adjudicated case in the world on the issue of constructing accessible websites. This case is the 1999 Australian complaint filed against the Sydney, Australia Organising Committee for the Olympic Games.

ADA Complaint Against the City of San José, California

In 1995, I served as the ADA Compliance Officer for the City of San José, California, and was responsible for citywide compliance with State and Federal disability access laws. In that capacity, I was also designated to receive, investigate, and resolve ADA administrative complaints filed against the City. These complaints would be filed by, or on behalf of, people with disabilities who alleged discrimination on the basis of disability in their access to City programs, services, and facilities. San José was the third largest city in California and the eleventh largest in the nation.

At that time, my office received an ADA complaint against the City of San José for operating an inaccessible website. A City Commissioner, who was blind, complained that she was unable to access City Council documents as part of her City Council advisory role because the documents were posted in an inaccessible format, Portable Document Format (PDF). This was a case where the posting of inaccessible City Council documents violated the "effective communication" requirement of the ADA. Because the ADA is a civil right, it did not matter if the webmaster did not know that the format was inaccessible. The mere fact that the Commissioner was discriminated against was enough.

Even four years later in 1999, the U.S. Department of Education reported on the accessibility challenges of posting documents in Adobe Acrobat's PDF format (for more, go to www.usdoj.gov/crt/508/report/web.htm#N_20_):

> The Portable Document Format (PDF) has provided one of the most controversial accessibility problems of the decade. . . . Unfortunately, documents displayed by the Adobe suite of products are totally unusable by those using screen reader technology to retrieve information from a computer display.

This accessibility problem remains a difficulty even today, as discussed in more detail in Chapter 16 of this book.

At the time the web access complaint was filed, my office was familiar with screen reader access, since we had initiated the practice of e-mailing Commission agendas and supporting documentation to the Chair of the San José Disability Advisory Commission, who also was blind. Not only did this practice eliminate the staff time, cost, and delivery delay for creating an accessible audiotaped document, but also the electronic version provided word searchability not available to the Commissioner with the audiotape format.

As I researched the web access complaint, I found that I, too, was a stakeholder in the accessible web effort, since I needed captioning to understand webcasts and streaming audio. As a person with a lifetime significant hearing loss, who had taken years and years of speech and lip-reading lessons, I found it simply impossible to lip-read audio on the Web!

In my capacity as a city manager, it was imperative that a policy be developed to manage the ADA violation on a proactive, rather than reactive basis. My legal analysis found that websites constituted a program or service of the City and were thus subject to the ADA. Already, a growing number of administrative complaints were being filed against U.S. entities operating inaccessible websites. Not until the following year was my legal analysis confirmed by a policy ruling from the U.S. Department of Justice (see Chapter 16 for further information).

By June 1996, I had written the *City of San José Web Page Disability Access Design Standard*. This standard was developed in response to the monitoring of ADA Internet complaints and the need to incorporate City ADA implementation policies. Seven minimum requirements were identified for web accessibility, and it was understood that these standards would evolve as new technologies and information systems emerged to solve the problem:

1. Provide an Access Instruction page for visitors (explaining the accessibility features of the website and providing an e-mail hyperlink for visitors to communicate problems with web page accessibility).

2. Provide support for text browsers and descriptive hyperlinks (links such as this and click here do not alone convey the nature of the target link).

3. Attach alt-text to graphic images so that screen readers can identify the content.

4. For each photograph contributing meaningful content to the page, provide a D hyperlink to a page providing descriptive text of the image.

5. Provide text transcriptions or descriptions for all audio and video clips.

6. Provide alternative mechanisms for online forms since forms are not supported by all browsers (such as e-mail or voice/TTY phone numbers).

7. Avoid access barriers such as the posting of documents in PDF, nonlinear format, Frame format, or requiring visitors to download software for access to content. If posting in PDF, then accessible HTML or ASCII must also be posted by the webmaster converting the document.

In 1996, the City of San José Web Page Disability Access Design Standard was the first governmental policy to be implemented in the U.S. and was adopted by jurisdictions both in the U.S. and abroad. Designated as a "best practice" by the federal government, the standard was featured in former President Clinton's January 1997 inauguration as a virtual technology bridge to the Presidential Technology Tent on the mall. That same year, the League of California Cities named the City of San José as the winner of the prestigious Helen Putnam Award for Excellence for implementing the standards at the San José Public Library website.

Maguire v. Sydney Organising Committee for the Olympic Games

In 1999, Mr. Maguire, a blind citizen of Australia, tried to request an Olympic Games ticket book in Braille format. He was told that blind people could have access to it if it was available on the Internet. Mr. Maguire, a user of refreshable Braille technology, explained that he could access information only if it was presented in accordance with international accessibility guidelines. He also stated that since the Sydney Organising Committee for the Olympic Games (SOCOG) website did not comply with those guidelines, a lot of information was not accessible to him. The SOCOG response was that he should seek assistance from a sighted person.

On June 7, 1999, Mr. Maguire filed a complaint with the Australian Disability Discrimination Act (DDA) enforcement agency—the Human Rights and Equal Opportunity Commission (HREOC). His complaint alleged that he was unlawfully discriminated against by SOCOG in three respects:

- Failure to provide Braille copies of the information required to place orders for Olympic Games tickets
- Failure to provide Braille copies of the Olympic Games souvenir program
- Failure to provide a website that was accessible to the complainant

The ticket book and souvenir program allegations were dealt with separately and are not the subject of this discussion.

Ultimately, in August 2000, the SOCOG was found to have discriminated against the complainant in breach of Section 24 of the DDA in that the website did not include alt-text on all images and image map links, the Index to Sports could not be accessed from the Schedule page, and the Results Tables were inaccessible. The SOCOG was ordered to make the website accessible by the start of the Sydney Olympics, but because they were found only partly compliant in November 2000, damages were awarded in the amount of $20,000. (For more on the decision, see www.hreoc.gov.au/disability_rights/decisions/comdec/Maguire%20v%20SOCOG3.htm.)

By unlawfully breaching Section 24 of the DDA, the SOCOG decision confirmed the view that the DDA applied to the online provision of goods, services, or facilities to the public in Australia, whether or not for payment. According to the August 28, 2000, press release of the Internet Industry Association: www.independentliving.org/docs5/sydney-olympics-blind-accessibility-decision-press-release.html:

> Disability access is therefore a serious consideration for any Australian business wanting to establish a presence on the Net. Sites which targeted customers overseas might also be liable under equivalent legislation in the US, Canada, the UK, and elsewhere.

Expert witnesses for accessible web design on Maguire's behalf were Mr. Worthington and Ms. Treviranus. Mr. Worthington was the first Webmaster for the Australian Department of Defence. He is also one of the architects of the Commonwealth Government's Internet and web strategy. Ms. Treviranus is from the University of Toronto, where she is the manager of the Adaptive Technology Resource Center at the University. She also chairs the W3C Authoring Tool Guidelines Group.

I'll highlight a few points from the case, although I recommend that you review the entire decision of <u>Maguire v. Sydney Organising Committee for the Olympic Games</u> at www.hreoc.gov.au/disability_rights/decisions/comdec/2000/DD000120.htm.

Direct Discrimination

First, it is important to note that the HREOC held that Mr. Maguire was subject to direct discrimination and rejected the argument that he was not treated less favorably in respect to the website than a person who was not blind (see page 9 of the decision):

The respondent in constructing its web site (and its Ticket Book) was intending to offer a service to the public. In the case of the web site that service consisted in the provision of a large body of information. By the form and content of its web site the respondent sought to make the information available. Because of the manner in which that information was made available, a sighted person could access it. Because of the manner in which that information was made available it could not be accessed by a blind person because of his or her disability.

Unjustifiable Hardship vs. Remediation

Second, although the respondent argued that remediation of the website constituted unjustifiable hardship, this defense was rejected. The decision noted that the respondent argued that the W3C Web Content Accessibility Guidelines 1.0 had been released by the W3C on May 5, 1999, just the previous month, and that they "appeared subsequent to the planning and 'substantial implementation' of its site."

However, the HREOC noted that the website had been in the process of continual development until the day of the decision in August 2000. For an example of the accessibility difficulties at the website, see Mr. Worthington's demonstration and link to expert testimony at www.tomw.net.au/2000/sports.html.

Additional facts presented by both sides on the issue of unjustifiable hardship versus remediation demonstrate a significant variance in website analysis. The respondent made a number of arguments for unjustifiable hardship, including the following:

- That there were 1,295 sports web templates
- That the Table of Results was made up of data sources from a number of different databases for each of the 37 sporting disciplines and that the tables contained wrapped text within cells
- That making the website accessible would require the development of a new or separate site
- That extensive changes to infrastructure were required as well as specialized skills, both of which were limited and expensive
- That it would require one person to work 8 hours a day for 368 days
- That $2.2 million of additional infrastructure would be required to separately host the additional designs necessary for an accessible Table of Results

In contrast, Mr. Maguire offered a number of arguments for website remediation, including:

- That the number of templates was significantly less than 1,295, and that the reformatting of the templates would take considerably less than the 2 hours for each alleged by the respondent—in fact, 10 minutes each
- That wrapping in each cell could be addressed by simply including an invisible end-of-cell character for the screen reader to signal the end of the text in each cell

- That the cost of making the site accessible was a modest amount

- That no new infrastructure would be required because it was in place

- That a team of one experienced developer with a group of five to ten assistants could provide an accessible site at W3C Level A compliance within 4 weeks

Effect of Addressing Access Early in Web Design

Lastly of interest was the comment by HREOC that, according to Ms. Treviranus, if accessible web design had been addressed early in the web development process, the cost would have been less than one percent of the total effort (see page 12 of the decision).

Development of Accessible Web Design Guidelines and Laws

Across the globe, there are now public policies and laws protecting the rights of people with disabilities to access the content of the Web. Web developers need to understand the types of accessible design guidelines and standards that govern their work. In general, you will find that there are statutes and regulations, treaties and public policies, industry codes, technical recommendations, and good practice guides.

Let's start with statutes and regulations.

Statutes and Regulations

A *statute* is an act of legislation declaring, commanding, or prohibiting something—such as a website design element. In other words, a statute is a law created by legislature as opposed to law generated by case law or judicial opinion. The corresponding regulations are the rules issued by governmental agencies to carry out the intent of the statute.

In the U.S., specifications for accessible design have been mandated through legislation. Congress enacted the *Workforce Investment Act* in 1998, which strengthened *Section 508 of the Rehabilitation Act*. Also known as the *Rehabilitation Act Amendments of 1998*, the legislation authorized the U.S. Access Board to enter into rule-making and the publication of the *Electronic and Information Technology Accessibility Standards* on December 21, 2000. (See *36 CFR 1194, Electronic and Information Technology Accessibility Standards, Final Rule*; for English, Spanish, and Japanese translations, see www.access-board.gov/508.htm.)

These standards became effective on June 21, 2001, and are broad in scope, covering technical standards in the following areas:

- Software applications and operating systems

- Web-based intranet and Internet information and applications

61

- Telecommunications products
- Video and multimedia products
- Self-contained, closed products
- Desktop and portable computers

The *Electronic and Information Technology Accessibility Standards* also include a section on "Functional Performance Criteria," as well as a section on "Information, Documentation, and Support." Technologists responsible for help desk assistance should particularly note the rules under the latter section.

Web developers and managers creating or maintaining websites for U.S. entities subject to Section 508 must implement these standards in order to participate in the U.S. market. Careful attention must be paid to the following Section 508 standards: "Software Applications and Operating Systems" (1194.21), "Web-Based Intranet and Internet Information and Applications" (1194.22), and "Information, Documentation, and Support" (1194.41).

When we look at U.S. web accessibility law in depth in Chapter 16, you will find that not understanding the legal technical requirements can lead to serious consequences. Not only will your expertise and credibility as a web designer be questioned, but when your client becomes a target for litigation, the client will seek you out to recover any damages incurred. One reason for this is that U.S. contracts for web design services typically include an indemnification clause seeking recovery of damages.

In Chapter 17, we will look at statutes, laws, and policies that govern accessible web design for countries outside the U.S. As you will see, every web design project you take on requires you to look at all relevant legal and technical requirements for accessible design. Any liability the web developer may be subject to is dependent upon the laws of the country and the nature of the contract you have entered into for the provision of web design services. The Maguire v. Sydney Organising Committee for the Olympic Games case is an example of liability that occurred outside the U.S. It is important to be informed as global web accessibility laws evolve.

Australia has a web design law. But what if you are developing a website for an entity in a country that does not have accessible web design laws? And what do you do if your country has a public policy or has signed on to a treaty requiring web accessibility but provides no guidance on implementation? The good news is that the remaining sources—industry codes, technical recommendations, and good practice guides—are your friends.

Industry Codes, Recommendations, and Good Practice

A treaty or public policy is only as good as its implementation requirements. For example, at this time, a new international treaty or convention is under development to protect the rights of people with disabilities around the world. Accessible information and communication technologies (ICT) is a core component of this United Nations effort, and it has been a privilege to serve as one of its Accessibility Subject Matter Experts. Hopefully, the final treaty language will point to specific technical requirements for implementation so that it will be clear how web developers in the affected countries can conform to the treaty requirements. When the treaty is finalized, affected countries with accessible web design laws or policies will need to harmonize with the treaty requirements, and countries without accessible web design laws will need to enact legislation for conformance.

Even if the treaty does not address accessible web design, there is technical guidance that may be helpful for you. For example, one industry code includes the Australian Bankers' Association (ABA) and its *Industry Standards for Accessibility of Electronic Banking* (www.bankers.asn.au/Default.aspx?FolderID=105).

Examples of good practice guides include the European *Guidelines for the Design of Accessible Information and Communication Technology Systems* (www.tiresias.org/guidelines/index.htm), as well as those practices referenced throughout this book.

And an important technical recommendation includes the specifications developed by the *World Wide Web Consortium (W3C) Web Accessibility Initiative (WAI)* discussed next. The *World Wide Web Consortium Web Content Accessibility Guidelines 1.0 (WCAG)* is a stable international specification developed through a voluntary industry consensus. Released in May 1999, it has since been adopted by many countries. In Chapter 16, you will see many instances where the W3C WCAG has been given the force of law in litigation settlement agreements in the U.S. In Chapter 17, you will see the important role the W3C WAI has played in the standards of 25 countries worldwide.

Because the U.S. Section 508 is based on the W3C WCAG 1.0, let's first discuss the W3C WAI. We will then conclude with an introductory discussion of Section 508. For an in-depth discussion, see Chapter 16.

W3C Web Accessibility Initiative (WAI)

In April 1997, the W3C announced the launch of the WAI to "promote and achieve Web functionality for people with disabilities" (see the press release at www.w3.org/Press/WAI-Launch.html). The project began with a WAI workshop on April 6, 1997, which I attended by invitation. I provided assistive technology for presenters with hearing loss, as well as copies of the first accessible web design standard written for the City of San José, California, in 1996.

The W3C WAI envisioned the establishment of an International Program Office (IPO), and in October 1997, one was launched. In the press release about the launch, Tim Berners-Lee, W3C Director, commented that

> The power of the Web is in its universality. Access by everyone regardless of disability is an essential aspect. The IPO will ensure the Web can be accessed through different combinations of senses and physical capabilities just as other W3C activities ensure its operation across different hardware and software platforms, media, cultures, and countries.

This press release also announced the appointment of Judy Brewer as Director of the IPO and noted that the IPO was sponsored by a partnership of government, industry, research, and disability organizations (see the press release at www.w3.org/Press/IPO-announce).

Currently, the WAI (www.w3.org/WAI/), in coordination with organizations around the world, pursues accessibility of the Web through five primary areas of work:

- Ensuring that core technologies of the Web support accessibility
- Developing guidelines for web content, user agents, and authoring tools
- Facilitating development of evaluation and repair tools for accessibility
- Conducting education and outreach
- Coordinating with research and development that can affect future accessibility of the Web

WAI sponsors and funders include the following:

- Assistive Devices Industry Office, Industry Canada, Government of Canada (www.at-links.gc.ca/as/)
- Fundación ONCE (www.fundaciononce.es/WFO/Castellano/default.htm)
- Hewlett-Packard Development Company (www.hp.com/)
- IBM Corporation (www.ibm.com/us/)
- Information Society Technologies Programme (http://europa.eu.int/information_society/text_en.htm)
- Microsoft Corporation (www.microsoft.com/)
- National Institute on Disability and Rehabilitation Research, grant H133A000500, U.S. Department of Education (www.ed.gov/about/offices/list/osers/nidrr/index.html)
- SAP (www.sap.com/index.epx)
- Verizon Foundation (www22.verizon.com/)
- Wells Fargo (www.wellsfargo.com/)

The W3C WAI technical activity has produced many significant work products, including the following:

- Web Content Accessibility Guidelines 1.0 – W3C Recommendation, May 5, 1999 (www.w3.org/TR/WCAG10/), WCAG-accessible web design standards

- Authoring Tool Accessibility Guidelines 1.0 – W3C Recommendation, February 3, 2000 (www.w3.org/TR/ATAG10/), web content authoring tool guidelines that facilitate accessible web design, including making the tool interfaces accessible

- User Agent Accessibility Guidelines 1.0 – W3C Candidate Recommendation, September 12, 2001 (www.w3.org/TR/UAAG10/), web user agent guidelines for any software that retrieves and renders web content for users, such as browsers, media players, plug-ins, and other programs, including assistive technologies

WCAG Priorities

The WCAG has three priorities, and each checkpoint has a priority level assigned by the Working Group based on the checkpoint's impact on accessibility, as follows:

- **Priority 1:** A web content developer *must* satisfy this checkpoint. Otherwise, one or more groups will find it impossible to access information in the document. Satisfying this checkpoint is a basic requirement for some groups to be able to use web documents.

- **Priority 2:** A web content developer *should* satisfy this checkpoint. Otherwise, one or more groups will find it difficult to access information in the document. Satisfying this checkpoint will remove significant barriers to accessing web documents.

- **Priority 3:** A web content developer *may* address this checkpoint. Otherwise, one or more groups will find it somewhat difficult to access information in the document. Satisfying this checkpoint will improve access to web documents.

Some checkpoints specify a priority level that may change under certain (indicated) conditions. The complete list of WCAG checkpoints and their priority level can be found at www.w3.org/TR/1999/WAI-WEBCONTENT-19990505/full-checklist.html.

Today, governments around the world have adopted or are in the process of implementing W3C WCAG 1.0 or some form of a technical design standard. As of the writing of this chapter, the W3C WAI has issued a call for comments on a working draft for WCAG 2.0, as well as a draft document titled *Understanding WCAG 2.0*. As explained in the W3C call for comments, the working draft is a significant reorganization and includes individual success criteria and support documents. Once comments are received by December 21, 2005, an evaluation will be made as to how close they are to publishing a Last Call Working Draft. Once the Last Call is entered, it will take several months to progress through the W3C Recommendation Track. Until WCAG 2.0 becomes a W3C Recommendation, WCAG 1.0 will continue to be the current and stable document to use. For more information about accessible web activity outside the U.S., see Chapter 17.

Section 508: U.S. Web Accessibility Standards

Rather than adopt W3C WCAG, the U.S. has taken a different track by legislating *Electronic and Information Technology Accessibility Standards* (also known as *Section 508*). Although a majority of the Web Section 508 rules are based on Priority Level 1 of the W3C WCAG 1.0, additional rules are particular to U.S. law. In fact, web developers and decision makers need to understand when to follow the technical specifications for W3C WCAG and when to follow Section 508.

On August 7, 1998, the U.S. Congress enacted Public Law 105-220—the Rehabilitation Act Amendments of 1998. This law significantly expanded and strengthened the technology access requirements of Section 508 of the Rehabilitation Act of 1973 (Section 508).

Today, U.S. Federal agencies and entities subject to Section 508 must make their electronic and information technology accessible to people with disabilities. As you saw in the earlier discussion on website disability discrimination complaints, inaccessible technology interferes with an individual's ability to obtain and use information quickly and easily. Section 508 was enacted to eliminate barriers in information technology, to make available new opportunities for people with disabilities, and to encourage development of technologies that will help achieve these goals. As a result, accessible web design falls within the scope of Section 508.

The law applies to all covered entities whenever they develop, procure, maintain, or use electronic and information technology. The scope of electronic and information technology is expansively defined. It includes computers (such as hardware and software, and accessible data such as web pages), facsimile machines, copiers, information transaction machines or kiosks, telephones, and other equipment used for transmitting, receiving, using, or storing information.

Section 508 requires Federal agencies to give disabled employees and members of the public access to information that is comparable to the access available to others. Federal agencies do not need to comply with the technology access standards if doing so would impose an undue burden. This is consistent with language expressed in the ADA and other U.S. disability rights legislation, where the term *undue burden* is defined as "significant difficulty or expense." However, agencies shall continue to have long-standing obligations under Sections 501 and 504 of the Rehabilitation Act to provide reasonable accommodation to qualified individuals with disabilities upon request.

For the first time in U.S. history, Section 508 seeks to create a marketplace incentive for accessible technologies and utilizes the power of the Federal government purse to require accessible web design. A ripple effect is currently underway throughout U.S. state and local governments—Section 508 now informs state and local governments on how to meet their ADA obligations to provide accessible websites for their citizens. Already we see states adopting Section 508 policies and legislation as part of their institutional electronic and information technology standards. Chapter 16 covers Section 508 in depth.

Summary

In this chapter, you were introduced to the emergence of global law and policy guidelines pertaining to accessible web design. You learned that we have reached a significant cross-road, where our global policies, technologies, and purchasing choices determine whether or not every person can participate on the Web. You discovered the following:

- The United Nations World Programme of Action seeks the equalization of opportunities for persons with disabilities and that access to information and communication is a human right.

- The global emergence of accessible web design laws and policies is a product of disability rights laws demanding equal access to information and online services and programs.

- There are two types of specifications for accessible web design: *W3C WCAG 1.0*, an international voluntary standard, and a statute such as *Section 508*, a U.S. legislative mandate for *Electronic and Information Technology Accessibility Standards*.

- It is imperative for web developers and decision makers to understand what accessible web design guideline or standard they should apply for their client.

- Depending on the laws of the jurisdiction, complaints can be filed by people with disabilities against institutions that develop, procure, maintain, or use an inaccessible website.

As for the future of the Web, today's outreach and education on this important issue provide the foundation for tomorrow's accessible design of new technologies. By designing accessibly, everyone will benefit from this effort.

3 IMPLEMENTING ACCESSIBILITY IN THE ENTERPRISE

by Mark Urban and Michael R. Burks

In order for an enterprise to successfully implement an accessibility solution, the enterprise needs to be some sort of organization that will handle and support accessibility issues and enforcement. We'll refer to this as an *accessibility organization*. The details of how this accessibility organization works will differ depending on the type of organization. Certainly, there will be differences in the way it is implemented in nonprofit organizations, governmental entities, for-profit businesses, and educational institutions. However, there will also be important similarities.

This chapter will describe the basics of implementing web accessibility in an enterprise. We will look at the development of a model accessibility organization that could be set up within any large enterprise. While this chapter is geared towards web accessibility, this process could also be used to implement other accessibility solutions, such as enterprise-wide standards for assistive and adaptive technology or employment practices related to disabilities.

Why Set Up an Accessibility Organization?

In many organizations that consider accessibility, the common approach is to create a project that will add accessibility to existing services, or offer accessibility on an ad hoc or as-needed basis—addressing accessibility only when persons with disabilities raise issues. There are at least two dangers in this approach:

- Adding accessibility to existing products and services is expensive, requiring accessibility personnel to understand the product or service and to develop a specific accessibility interface, often reinventing or reengineering the product or service in the process.

- The law, policy, and technical aspects of accessibility are often focused into a small team, which can disappear (due to attrition, illness, or competition), leaving no resource base for the organizations.

The U. S. federal government also realized that an ad hoc approach would not be effective in resolving some of the issues on an enterprise basis. The U.S. Department of Justice, in a report to the federal agencies (www.usdoj.gov/crt/508/report/intro.htm), stressed the need for a broad-based architectural approach:

> Data provided by the agencies suggest that the majority of agencies that continue to handle IT accessibility issues exclusively on an "ad hoc" or "as needed" basis, instead of integrating accessibility into the development and procurement of their mainstream IT products (sic). Many IT officials hold the mistaken belief that persons with disabilities can always be accommodated upon request by using widely available assistive technology devices (e.g., screen readers, screen enlargers, volume control apparatuses, pointing devices that serve as alternatives to a computer

mouse, voice recognition software, etc.) in conjunction with mainstream technology applications. Indeed, the goal of section 508 is to ensure that the agency will always be able to provide reasonable accommodations. Without adequate planning, however, the possibility of providing an accommodation to person with a disability may be foreclosed. . . . Use of an "ad hoc" or "as needed" approach to IT accessibility will result in barriers for persons with disabilities. A much better approach is to integrate accessibility reviews into the earliest stages of design, development, and procurement of IT. Once an accessible IT architecture is established, then and only then can persons with disabilities be successfully accommodated on an "as needed" basis.

The point is that if you take the ad hoc approach, your web-based architecture may require so much retrofitting that it will be unusable to a large degree. Designing from the beginning and using good planning can avoid this trap. It can also save an enormous amount of money. Retrofitting anything is expensive, and it should be avoided whenever possible.

Setting up an accessibility organization for the enterprise will help to avoid the dangers of taking an ad hoc approach.

Makeup of the Accessibility Organization

A model accessibility organization (AO) within a larger enterprise must have certain qualities. One of the most important is the ability to cut across lines within an organization to maximize knowledge and awareness of accessibility itself. Its ultimate goal should be to build a group of qualified people within the company who can manage and oversee accessibility projects, rather than overseeing them itself. To that end, the AO should be a resource within the enterprise, not a controlling organization. Its management should be carefully structured, and its members should have a mix of characteristics directly related to their role in implementing accessible web technology.

The AO should consist of members of stakeholder departments and internal experts in the field of web accessibility. Very few of the members of the AO should be full-time workers in the AO. Most should work in the group only part-time, having their primary responsibilities in their departments. The reason for this is that (for the most part) members of actual design, development, sales, strategy, and management will have a greater day-to-day feel for the status of accessibility within an organization. Also, such a team spreads accessibility awareness and concerns throughout an organization, creating a culture of understanding regarding accessibility concerns that no amount of drum-beating by "purist" accessibility staff can create. Most should be drawn from the departments that will be affected by the implementation of accessibility in web technology.

Figure 3-1 illustrates how an AO might be structured.

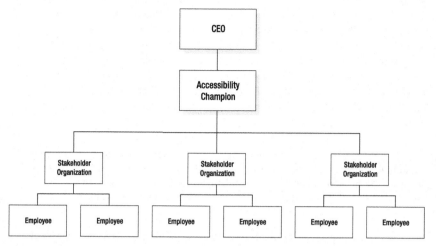

Figure 3-1. Model accessibility organization structure

Accessibility Organization Authority

One of the most important factors in implementing accessibility is seeing to it that the organization charged with this implementation has the *authority* to implement change, as well as the responsibility to do so. This organization must be able to set standards, make decisions on the tools needed, and lay out the processes to be followed. Without such authority, the implementation of accessible web technology will be difficult, if not impossible.

In addition, the AO must also have authority to do the following:

- Bring various groups together to discuss accessibility and discover, define, and articulate issues related to accessibility of concern to both the whole enterprise and to its individual parts.

- Use both the "carrot" and the "stick." It must be able to reward innovation and discourage nonproductive actions to ensure proper implementation of accessibility within the entire organization.

- Arbitrate disputes and settle misunderstandings about accessibility within and between departments. On occasion, it will need to make decisions on issues that cannot be decided any other way.

The AO must have authority from the highest levels of an enterprise. It must be able to assist or consult on all related projects. The upper management of your enterprise will need to make a commitment to implementing web accessibility. It must make this commitment publicly and provide financial backing for the AO. It is preferable for this empowerment and commitment to come from the head of your organization, such as the chancellor of a university or the CEO of a corporation.

Good examples of the types of organizations that have made such a commitment can be seen in the three letters sent to President Clinton by technology executives and research university presidents. These letters committed the organizations to various aspects of accessibility, but the principle is the same. Visit www.icdri.org/DD/digital_divide_summary_page.htm to see these letters.

After the head of your organization has committed to making your web technology accessible, a web accessibility "champion" should be chosen, or should volunteer. This should be a member of upper management who is familiar with web accessibility issues, and has enough authority and prestige to ensure that everything that needs to be done is done.

A bottom-up approach is fine for implementation and understanding of accessibility; however, for this to succeed and to be implemented in an efficient and effective manner, at least one member of upper management must be able to "push" solutions when needed. This person must have a good grounding in this area and believe in what he is doing.

It is likely that if there are no consequences for noncompliance within organizational policy, low levels of compliance will follow. The AO must be authorized to punish noncompliance. Conversely, it is just as important to reward meaningfully the efforts of those who do make the effort to implement web accessibility. The AO must be empowered to use both types of consequences as tools to implement web accessibility throughout the enterprise efficiently.

Accessibility Organization Scope, Goals, and Functions

Defining the scope of the AO is critical to its success. Its scope must be narrow and well defined to keep the organization small and compact. This will also help to keep the workload of its members from becoming too large to handle. A clear and focused scope will also keep the organization from becoming bogged down in a morass of side issues not directly related to accessibility. The departments using the AO should be prepared to handle these issues.

The goals and mission of the AO should be clear and simple, helping members to understand clearly what is expected of them. This will keep the group on target for achieving its goals. For the initial implementation of accessibility, clear timelines must be set with checkpoints for the organization's goals.

An AO should be responsible for the following:

- Raising accessibility awareness
- Encouraging feedback to share problems and solutions
- Implementing quality assurance procedures

- Providing web accessibility support
- Handling legal matters related to accessibility
- Developing internal accessibility standards
- Representing the organization in public affairs related to accessibility

The following sections describe these functions in more detail.

Accessibility Awareness

The AO must make education and raising accessibility awareness top priorities. On its own, this awareness can solve many of the accessibility issues in your organization and go a long way toward making your enterprise's websites accessible to people with disabilities.

Awareness is very low among those who have not had any reason to implement accessibility in web-based technology. Many people do not even know there is an issue. The very act of educating those who will be responsible for making the web technology accessible will alleviate many problems. If properly trained, many people who work with web-based technologies not only start to work to the required accessibility standards, but also go on to help develop new and innovative accessibility techniques.

Two ways to raise accessibility awareness are through training and by providing an electronic knowledge base.

Training

Training should be closely focused to give personnel not only a good grounding in the technical aspects of web accessibility, but also a clear understanding of the laws involved and how they can be applied to their work. Depending on their level, personnel will need different depths of accessibility awareness. Higher-level managers should need to know only enough to understand the issues. This should be the first level of training, which everyone involved will need. As you move deeper and deeper into the various departmental roles, training will need to be provided in greater detail on a need-to-know basis.

Training should be done both with live instructors and with online training. Instructors can give the initial coursework, answer questions, and get personnel started with accessibility training. The remainder of the training can be done using online distance-learning techniques. Externally developed online coursework can be considered both for basic and advanced courses. A number of online courses in web accessibility are available, such as those offered by WebAIM (www.webaim.org/).

Using these resources can save your enterprise considerable time and money, while giving staff a good grounding in accessible web design. This can be supplemented by supplying personnel with a good textbook (such as this book!), which can also serve as a reference manual.

If the distance-learning site is set up properly, it can also be used for reference and reviews. It should not be the only option for this type of information, but it should be set up with the idea that those who are implementing web accessibility in your organization will use it as a reference.

Knowledge Base

The AO should set up a knowledge base—an accessible collection of practices (internal and external) that can be queried. This electronic knowledge base should serve as the central hub for people looking for solutions. Employees should be encouraged to use the solutions stored in this repository and also to contribute new ones. Those who develop new and usable solutions to accessibility issues should be rewarded, which will encourage others to do the same.

The knowledge base should be easy to get to by everyone who needs it, including internal *and* external support personnel (if you have any). If the knowledge base isn't easily accessible, the simple fact is that it will be unused. It is therefore very important to ensure that the knowledge base is designed and deployed well, via a company intranet, for example.

A mechanism should be set up so people can easily enter information that would be appropriate to the knowledge base and increase the information it holds for dissemination to the organization. This information should be easy to submit *and* extract, and checked and formatted to ensure its validity before being posted. This method should be known throughout the enterprise, and people should be constantly reminded of its existence. Reminders of how to use the knowledge base can be placed in company newsletters, e-mail messages, and internal articles on a regular basis.

Feedback

One of the functions of the AO should be to encourage the sharing of solutions within the enterprise. It should also encourage the sharing of common issues and problems. The feedback mechanisms should allow the expression of problems that are perceived in the implementation of the standards set up by the AO. This will allow problems to be aired, investigated, and resolved quickly. It is very important to answer the feedback in a timely and accurate manner, so people know that you are indeed supporting them and that they can count on getting help.

A feedback process must be developed so that the AO can work to improve its methods. Changes may be made both in procedures for implementing accessibility into new areas in the enterprise and in existing processes already in use. It should be easy for internal and external "users" to submit feedback. A "user" of the AO (that is, someone who can benefit from it) can be any person who needs access to the services you provide: another division or group within your organization, a student, another organization, or a consumer. Customers should be given every opportunity to provide feedback on accessibility on a continuing basis, without complaints being the only measure. This is important, because in electronic services, customers rarely complain about a cumbersome or inaccessible interface—they just leave.

Focus groups can help your organization to understand the needs of users and usability studies during the development of your web pages and websites can increase your customer satisfaction ratings. These should be small groups of individuals from within and outside your organization, with an interest in using your services. They should talk about what they would like to see provided by your services, and test your sites to see what problems they can uncover. Obviously, users with disabilities will be best to test the accessibility of your sites. Testing with real users is vital. Merely relying on the available accessibility guidelines is never enough. Focus groups and usability studies can help you achieve good, usable pages that meet the needs of your customers. In the long run, this will be cheaper and more cost-effective for both the enterprise and the customer than the cost of lengthy remediation. Usability is critical. No matter how many accessibility features a page has, if it is not usable, it is not accessible. You can find Information on how to develop focus groups and usability studies through many online resources. One of the best places to start is Jakob Nielson's site, www.useit.com/. Chapter 1 of this book includes suggestions for how to include users with disabilities in projects.

Quality Assurance

While feedback is one method of ensuring that accessibility initiatives constantly improve, the AO also needs to implement more formal procedures for monitoring and assessing the quality of web accessibility initiatives in the enterprise. Milestones, monitoring, and periodic reviews should be part of a quality assurance program.

Milestones

The AO and its member organizations should set department-specific milestones that quantify accessibility. Those people responsible for implementing and managing the work necessary to reach each milestone should be involved in setting what should be accomplished by when. This will give you the best chance of success. The following are some examples of milestones:

- Hiring of an accessibility subject matter expert (SME)
- 100 percent of accessibility-centric staff trained
- Deployment of testing methodology and tools
- Creation of a style guide or template that enforces/assists in accessibility
- Strategic partnership with a disability expert, organization, or contractor

An SME should audit quality and expenditure when each milestone is reached. This information should be recorded and made available for future reference in the knowledge base. These reports should also be integrated with larger periodic reviews to make sure that a good overall picture of the progress of the enterprise is produced on top of the snapshot at each milestone.

Technological Monitoring

There must be a consistent way to determine if the company-wide standards are being followed. These can be in the form of checklists, accessibility analyses, repair tools, or a combination of these things. Depending on the size of the enterprise, the number of web pages, and the type of web pages, there will have to be a suite of methods to determine if standards are being met. Whatever they are, the methods should be consistent across the enterprise. This will ensure that there is at least a level of consistency for both the compliance and the understanding of what the compliance is supposed to be.

Periodic Objective Reviews

SMEs or experts in accessibility should conduct regular reviews of enterprise web accessibility. These should be done within a framework of clearly delineated sets of checklists, standards, and milestones that have been set up by the AO for the entire enterprise.

This review should be able to clearly show where the enterprise is in achieving this goal. The information can be placed in the AO knowledge base so the entire enterprise will have access to it. Your enterprise may want to consider using an outside service for this assessment. This reduces the chance of the assessment being influenced by internal politics and pressures.

Support

Having support personnel devoted to web accessibility is not recommended, unless your organization is huge. Much of this support probably can be done by electronic means. A well-laid-out set of web pages addressing the major concerns of the organization can greatly assist your organization's support needs for accessible web design. As noted earlier, a good feedback mechanism can help keep the electronic support up-to-date, and it can help highlight new problems your organization is facing.

To enable the talents of persons with disabilities to be utilized most effectively in an organization, a clear infrastructure for support and integration of assistive technology is essential. Ideally, the following questions should be asked:

- **Do you have standard configuration and support for assistive systems?** Standard configurations and software support help you define service options with the specific vendors you need. Specifying operating systems for computers and browsers for use with internal documents can go a long way in reducing cost for supporting internal web accessibility. Web documents and sites intended for people outside the company are another matter. They should be coded to be used by the largest audience possible—not only those with disabilities, but also those with diverse browsers and devices utilizing web standards.

- **Will you have outsourced or internal assistive technology support?** It is best to have both: internal support for applications, and external support for hardware, purchased software, and integration issues. You know your applications best, so you should support them. The vendors should support the hardware and the software, except where they are integrated into your operations. Where the two meet—when the software and hardware your organization uses interfaces with your localized web-based applications and development—your personnel should supply support. For generalized support of the hardware and software used in the web-based applications in your enterprise, you should rely on vendor support. The vendors know the product the best, and you have probably already paid for the support anyway.

- **Is procurement of web-based technology coordinated with the AO?** Accessible technology systems are often destabilized by changes in "standard" PC components, such as CPUs, video cards, sound cards, and monitors. Procurement officials within an organization have members on the AO to prevent inaccessible systems from being introduced into the enterprise.

Support for systems and applications for persons with disabilities should be formalized. Often, the problems experienced by users of adaptive systems can be resolved once, and the solutions applied throughout the enterprise. A model assistive technology support structure could follow this pattern:

1. A call goes into internal support.
2. Support checks for standard browser and assistive technology issues.
3. Support checks with the knowledge base for known problems and resolutions.
4. If necessary, the problem is escalated to outside vendor support.
5. Solutions are entered into the knowledge base.

Legal Matters

The AO should ideally have at least one legal expert on staff, and the heart of the legal contribution should be a section of the knowledge base devoted to the laws, regulations, and policies that apply to web accessibility in the enterprise (Section 508, for example). These should be explained clearly, with examples illustrating the relationship to the enterprise's web activities.

The main job of the legal person on staff should be to deal with exceptions, and to make sure the knowledge base is usable and understandable to both attorneys and personnel whose main expertise is not in the area of law and policy.

It is critical that the AO and the legal department maintain strict control over the dissemination of governmental communications that could affect the future of the entire enterprise. All such communications should be routed through the AO. This is critical to both the health of the AO and the enterprise in general. The legal department representative should be an integral part of the AO.

Standards

Standards are the framework upon which an organization will be able to base its solutions to accessibility issues. Most organizations will deal with two types of standards: external and internal.

External standards have a national or international scope. Standards bodies have representatives from many areas of expertise. These bodies meet, discuss, and decide on standards for web accessibility, developing rules that are designed to promote web accessibility. The standards include the three sets of World Wide Web (W3C) guidelines (as explained in Chapter 1 and discussed throughout this book) and Section 508 of the Rehabilitation Act (also discussed throughout this book; Appendix B contains the section of it most relevant to web developers).

Internal standards should be through a manual, or style guide, and software. The manual addresses the consistency of style on websites. It should have accessibility built into the guidelines, as well as the standards that authors use to produce accessible websites. The software will be used by the enterprise to produce websites. This can consist of several types of software and will ensure consistency of results across the enterprise. These software packages should meet the needs of developers and be able to produce accessible websites. This approach should also reduce training costs, as a limited number of software packages will need to be supported.

Internal standards must be developed carefully with the input of the people who will actually be doing the work. This is critical to the success of the program. The people in the field who are building the websites and using the software on a daily basis are the ones who should have the main input into what tools will be chosen.

3

> *A good example of integrating accessibility standards is the North Carolina State University (U.S.) implementation. This enterprise architecture incorporates WCAG 1.0 requirements, along with telecommunications, software, and biometric accessibility requirements. See* http://ncsu.edu/it/access/webreg.html *for more information.*

A standard that is not applied is no standard at all. Your internal standards must not only be applied on a consistent basis, but they also must be applicable to the situations that exist within the organization. If the standards are not realistically chosen, they will not be applied. If they are not applicable to the web technology that your organization is using, they cannot be applied.

The style guide should be developed using the experience of your developers and institute accessibility standards. It should reflect best practices that have been developed both internally and externally, and should be tailored to fit the specific situations that your developers are likely to encounter. This ensures that document developers feel they are being listened to, that their expertise is being respected, and that the best tools are chosen to accomplish the tasks at hand. The people who are going to use the style guide should have a sense of "ownership" of it. This will ensure that it gets used and that new knowledge, acquired by experience, will be integrated into the document.

The best way for developers to address accessibility while dealing with your customer needs is for it to be incorporated in the design phase of planning. A style guide can contain the rules for accessibility, as well as all the other rules for how you will produce websites (such as spelling, colors used, copyright and trademark issues, scripting page layout, navigation issues, and so on), both internally and externally. Accessibility should be dealt with both specifically in a separate section and elsewhere in the style guide where appropriate. For example, alternative text for images should be discussed in the section on image use and presentation, as well as in the section on accessibility (see Chapter 6 for more information about alternative text requirements). Having such a style guide will make web developers' jobs a good deal easier, allowing them to concentrate on building the website's infrastructure and content.

Another important consideration for internal standards is that project personnel should be informed of the functional requirements of accessibility, not their implementation. Don't tell people how to do things; tell them what needs to be done. Personnel must be educated to the fact that most standards do not give specifics of how to achieve a desired functionality. In general, the standards should specify what must be done and not go into great detail of how it must be done. This allows developers to exercise creativity in implementing the desired functionality in any particular situation. Where possible, the AO should not only encourage creative solutions to problems, but also collect these solutions and make them available to all through the knowledge base.

Public Representation

The AO should represent the parent organization in public affairs related to accessibility. Since the AO will be the single most concentrated area of accessibility expertise in the enterprise, its members should be the ones facing the public and representing the enterprise to the accessibility community. This will present a unified front to the public and prevent misunderstandings about your organization's web accessibility policies in the wider arena.

The AO can also represent the entire enterprise in standards groups, such as the Web Standards Group Accessibility Task Force (WaSP ATF). This will serve the needs of everyone. Even if there are members of the organization who are on standards bodies and are not formally members of the AO, they should be listed as associated with the AO and should coordinate their activities with it to keep everyone informed and to be sure a united front is presented. The best way to ensure that people are committed to this goal is to make sure that the AO helps to finance these activities.

Standards committees can be difficult to work with, and it takes a certain type of person to be effective within them. This person must be able to work within the standards process, and to collect and integrate all of the concerns of the member organizations. She must then be sure that these concerns are addressed by the standards committee, as well as fairly representing your organization's interests and accessibility issues.

Implementation Approach

It is not realistic to suppose that you can simply convert every single web page overnight and make it accessible. Had they been designed that way from the beginning, then it would not be much of an issue. However, if that were the case, you would probably not be reading this chapter!

A phased approach is the most workable and realistic approach. The following are suggested steps for implementing such a phased approach in your organization:

1. Decide upon a standard for web accessibility.
2. Announce the standard to the entire organization.
3. Announce support and training for the standard.
4. Set a date beyond which all new web-based technology must be accessible according to the standard you have chosen.
5. Have each organizational member of the AO analyze his web-based systems to determine which technology will be changing first, since this will need to be accessible.

6. Determine if any critical web-based technology must be made accessible.

7. Determine if any critical web-based technology cannot be made accessible.

8. Have each member department in the AO present a plan phasing in accessible web technology.

9. Begin implementation of accessible technology, including retrofitting inaccessible websites, as discussed in Chapter 15. The phased-in approach will help ensure that members of the AO are ready by launch date.

10. Make sure all support systems are in place, including technical support and training.

11. Monitor the progress and supply help where needed.

Before you take any implementation steps, you need to make an initial assessment. If you do not know where you are, then you will never figure out how to get where you want to be! The initial assessment gives you a starting point. You will then be able to gauge how long it will take to achieve the goals you have set and how many resources are required.

Initial Assessment (Where Are You?)

The most effective way to begin accessibility integration is to make an objective analysis of the current situation in your organization. An honest and thorough assessment, along with a detailed, time-limited plan for remediation, can help an organization meet its accessibility needs in a cohesive, cost-effective way, as well as limiting liability during the remediation process. Although some organizations may have the resources to do accessibility analysis internally, one of the most effective methods is to have an independent assessment. This rules out the possibility of political forces (internal and external) or subjective attachments and conceptions skewing the assessment.

An assessment should involve answers to the following questions:

- Do senior policy makers understand what accessibility is and what its implementation means?

- Which departments and personnel within your organization are responsible for legal compliance?

- Do your IT managers (department heads, IT service and planning directors, webmasters, and so on) understand electronic and information technology accessibility issues?

- Have you adopted an architecture and web design standards (external and internal, as described in the "Standards" section earlier in this chapter) for accessibility? Did you include all organizational stakeholders in their development?

- Do you have training and technical support available for those who do not understand the practical implementation of those standards?

- Are the standards applied throughout your organization?

- Do you have a phased, cost-effective approach to limit undue burden?

- Do your e-commerce/e-government sites have a consistent, accessible interface?

- Do your customers have alternatives to e-commerce/e-government services?
- How will you evaluate your progress towards accessibility (checklists, checkpoints, timelines, assessment tools, and so on)?
- Are your web-based documents and databases (public and internal) accessible?

When conducting a review of your existing web technologies, you should ensure that you include the following:

- Web portals
- Web pages
- Internal documents
- Kiosks
- Telecommunications web-based devices, such as cell phones
- All other web-based documents and services

All devices and services that use web-based technology must be accessible to people with disabilities, including your employees and any others who may use your devices and services. These must be tested with a wide range of access devices where appropriate.

Implementation Plan

When looking at the costs associated with retrofitting existing inaccessible technology, it becomes apparent that the implementation plan should stress implementing accessibility as part of new development, procurement, and use of electronic and information technology. This "forward accessibility" focus will maximize the resources within the enterprise by making accessibility simply part of the natural development of the organization. This plan will need to deal with both retrofitting old web material and seeing that standards are developed to make sure that all new web-based projects are implemented in an accessible manner.

Once this plan is in place, you can then start to monitor against it using the feedback and quality assurance procedures that are included in the functions of the AO.

Handover to AO

Accessibility, if being handled by a special team as a project, should be handed off to the AO upon completion of the initial integration. The AO should meet no less than quarterly to ensure enterprise-wide accessibility maintains momentum. Between the meetings, information should be gathered so that progress reports and agenda items can be brought to the AO for action.

If properly handled, and the initial integration completed, the requirements for keeping web-based products and services accessible should be no more onerous than making sure any other required design features are included in the next site redesign. It is a simple matter of raising awareness and keeping a good set of requirements available to designers, developers, and those who must implement the technology.

Summary

When considering web accessibility in any organization, it is essential to do so by coordinating all its resources. Without this holistic view, accessibility can be both expensive and difficult. Additionally, there is a danger of creating pockets of inaccessible web-based technologies within the enterprise. By having management and field personnel participation in accessibility integration, an understanding of the needs of people with disabilities can be disseminated throughout the enterprise, creating an environment that allows the largest number of people to be as productive as their talents permit. By having the personnel who are actually developing and implementing solutions as ongoing participants in the implementation process, you will get commitment from the people who know the most about the web-based technology being used by your enterprise.

The following steps can be used to create an accessibility organization successfully:

1. Get commitment from the top manager.
2. Get an accessibility champion to head the organization with authority to implement accessible web design.
3. Clearly lay out the purpose of your organization and its goals and scope.
4. Recruit its membership from the people doing the work and the people managing them.
5. Develop your accessibility plan.
6. Set your specific goals and timeline.
7. Begin your implementation.
8. Monitor your progress.
9. Make needed corrections.
10. Provide feedback mechanisms.
11. Create a central resource for ongoing use.
12. Meet with field personnel on a regular basis to monitor progress, introduce new technologies, collect internal methodologies, and reward progress.

Keep in mind that the U.S. and other countries have developed standards for accessible web technologies. As described in Chapters 2, 16, and 17, there may be laws that apply to your enterprise. Even in instances where these laws do not directly apply, the regulations and standards that are being set up are bound to have a great influence in many places. Therefore, it is a good idea to keep informed of what these regulations and standards are, and how they are being applied in the technical venue.

PART 2 **IMPLEMENTING ACCESSIBLE**
        WEBSITES

4 OVERVIEW OF ACCESSIBLE TECHNOLOGIES

by Andrew Kirkpatrick

Web technologies aren't accessible by chance. When a new technology is developed, inattention to accessibility translates most often to inaccessible technology. The fact that the Web and the technologies used to interact with it are ever-changing means that it demands constant monitoring in order to ensure that the needs of users with disabilities are not ignored. More often than not, even with constant monitoring, access to new technologies lags well behind their large-scale adoption—a fact that is not lost on users with disabilities.

The excitement felt and expressed by many developers about a new strategy or technology is infectious. Articles and blog entries are churned out by the hundreds, and product strategies shift to take advantage of the interest. Eventually, somewhere, a few people ask, "Is this accessible?" From there (and assuming the answer is, in large part, no), the process is neither rapid nor linear.

Concerned developers need to learn about the strengths and limitations of a technology in order to maximize accessibility. Assistive technologies need to create new ways to interpret information from and interact with this technology. Users need to acquire and learn how to use new and improved versions of assistive technologies. These events occur iteratively, improving access incrementally, but with plenty of frustration for users and developers along the way.

As a result of this indirect route toward providing access, whether a technology is regarded as accessible is often subjective. The World Wide Web Consortium's (W3C's) Synchronized Multimedia Integration Language (SMIL) is usually regarded as an accessible technology, but no assistive technologies are able to interact with buttons in a media presentation. SMIL does provide the best way to add closed captions and audio descriptions to media for Real Media players, and few developers use SMIL for anything more than linear media layout and display, so screen reader and even keyboard access is not frequently an issue. Flash, on the other hand, usually includes interactive elements and nonlinear or interrupted-linear media. Authoring accessible Flash requires some knowledge on the part of the developer, so it is not unusual to encounter Flash content that has been authored inaccessibly. As a result, Flash, while enjoying greater accessibility support in screen readers than SMIL and having similar capabilities for captions and audio descriptions, is often regarded as an inaccessible format. We'll look into both SMIL and Flash in this chapter.

Excluding users is never the intended goal when choosing any technology for a project, but you will almost always bar access for some. There are always users who don't own the latest version of a screen reader, who don't use a browser that supports JavaScript, who use Windows 3.1, or who access the Web using their mobile phone. The best you can do is choose the most accessible technology that is appropriate for your content and business needs. When using a newer or less accessible technology, you can make good efforts to ensure that your website or application degrades gracefully and retains comparable functionality for users who don't have the targeted configuration of hardware and software.

In this chapter, I will discuss many different technologies and highlight accessibility benefits and shortcomings for each. I'll put my stake in the ground and indicate whether or not the technology is accessible. If the technology is not accessible, it doesn't necessarily mean that you shouldn't use it, but that you should provide alternative ways to access the content. My opinion—built with knowledge of the state of assistive technologies, browsers, players, and development strategies that exist in 2006—is certainly subject to change, and I am hopeful that it will do so.

HTML and XHTML

Web developers use HTML and XHTML (for convenience, this pair is hereafter referred to as *HTML*) to create the majority of web documents. Purists view HTML (www.w3.org/MarkUp/) as the vehicle for web content and structure, with the presentation and behavior aspects to be handled separately, typically with Cascading Style Sheets (CSS) and a scripting language such as JavaScript.

Depending on the version of HTML being used, style elements built into the HTML recommendations can be utilized to control the visual presentation within the HTML document itself, but these are gradually being phased out. In XHTML 2.0 (www.w3.org/TR/xhtml2/), all presentation elements and attributes will be removed, and authors will be required to handle presentation aspects via a style sheet. The practice of using external style sheets, to be required in XHTML 2.0 (not a W3C recommendation as of writing), represents good practice for web development today, and efforts to separate content and presentation should be made for any redesign or new site construction.

HTML enjoys substantial support for accessibility in a wide range of user agents (for our purposes, this refers to browsers and assistive technologies such as screen readers). The *X* in XHTML stands for extensible, and if the existing recommendation doesn't meet specific needs, it can be extended (using XHTML 1.1 as the base from which to extend). One example of this is the W3C's XHTML + MathML + SVG Profile (www.w3.org/TR/XHTMLplusMathMLplusSVG/). It is important to note that extending the recommendation is only a small part of the challenge. Getting user agent support to deliver accessible information for documents with extended namespaces is the web accessibility equivalent of trailblazing, and no assumptions should be made regarding the accessibility of the resulting content.

Accessibility became a part of HTML with the release of HTML 3.2 in 1997. Since then, additional elements and attributes have been added to support accessibility, such as the summary attribute for tables and the label element to explicitly associate form elements with identifying information. You'll find in-depth advice on how to implement these accessibility features in Chapters 6, 7, and 8.

Screen reader support for HTML has improved incrementally over time. Support for HTML headings was added to JAWS in version 4.01 (February 2002), Window-Eyes in version 4.5 (September 2003), and Home Page Reader 3.02 (spring 2001). Adoption of new versions of screen readers is never quick. As a result, developers interested in accessibility for a broad audience have only begun to feel comfortable using HTML headings to provide blind users the ability to skip around a page easily. Screen reader support for HTML's accessibility features is very solid, with most tools supporting most elements and attributes. However, this statement changes when scripting and CSS are added to HTML. More information is available in Chapter 5, which discusses screen readers and other assistive technologies in depth.

Keyboard users are also able to have positive experiences with HTML. Not all browsers have the same level of support for non-mouse interaction, but the most commonly used browsers (Microsoft's Internet Explorer, Mozilla's Firefox, Apple's Safari, and Opera) allow users to press a key to move the focus through hyperlinks and form controls. Support for heading navigation is not as good. At this time, only Opera natively supports navigation through HTML headings. The result of this is that keyboard users who benefit from skip navigation links to jump past navigation features of web pages are not able to enjoy the same experience that screen reader users have when a developer provides a rich heading structure but no skip navigation link.

Browser support for users with color-related impairments or who need fonts resized is strong for HTML, as shown in the example in Figure 4-1. But difficulties crop up when using CSS or inline styles to specify font sizes or colors. You'll find solutions to these issues in Chapter 6.

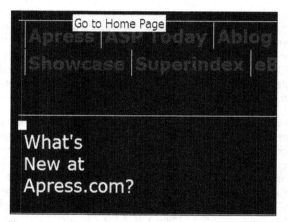

Figure 4-1. HTML fonts and colors can respond well to system settings.

Cascading Style Sheets (CSS)

CSS is wonderful for accessibility—more for how it makes developers think than for what it enables for users. Developers love CSS because it separates the structure and content of a site from the presentation. CSS makes major and minor updates to the presentation layer much easier by allowing edits in a single CSS file to affect the appearance of all pages that use it. As a result of this separation, the semantic structure of the HTML is right out in the open for the developer to see, and many developers like clean, logical code.

Whether it is due to an interest in conveying semantics, a need to save a few characters because `<h2>` is shorter than `<p class="maintopic">`, or some other reason, whenever developers pay closer attention to the HTML, the result is often more accessible code. It's true that a developer can create a website that is as accessible using "old school" web design techniques, but sites where the developer completely separates the presentation elements into CSS usually work better for more users.

CSS is regarded as supporting accessibility, but another way of looking at it is that CSS is transparent to accessibility. (See www.w3.org/TR/CSS-access for a W3C discussion of CSS accessibility features.) Users who need larger fonts or increased line spacing can use the browser font size controls or author a replacement style sheet to apply these changes. Users with screen readers can read the semantic information and content within a web page. Users needing keyboard access have uninterrupted access to the default tab order. Still, there are instances where CSS needs to be authored in particular ways to avoid specific issues, and this topic is addressed in Chapter 9.

Screen reader support for CSS is very solid, but one area merits specific mention here. Use of two CSS properties to hide content can create different results in screen readers. visibility:hidden and display:none are the CSS property/value combinations that developers use most often to make items like drop-down menus and occasionally content appear only when needed. There is a difference between these two properties. visibility:hidden should hide the content, reserve the space on the screen, and be voiced by assistive technologies. display:none should hide the content in every way, reserve no space on the screen, and not be voiced by assistive technologies. How screen readers actually deal with these CSS properties depends (at least in JAWS) on how the CSS is associated with the page. The results for the same properties differ in some cases when the CSS is linked versus when @import is used. I maintain a test page for this issue at http://webaccessibility.info/lab/displaytest.html. The results are surprising, and it's good to be aware of them.

CSS is also used in technologies other than HTML. For example, Flash makes use of CSS, and authors can utilize that support to author more accessible Flash content. Other technologies, including SVG and a timed-text format for displaying caption data (currently being developed by the W3C), also use CSS.

JavaScript

For many web developers, JavaScript meant image rollovers and occasional client-side form calculations or data validation. Users with browsers that lacked JavaScript support usually didn't miss much when rollovers didn't work, and developers worth their salt always implemented server-side form validation as well to ensure data quality. When developers discovered document.write and figured out how to generate web page markup dynamically, problems became more common, as some content simply didn't exist without a JavaScript-enabled browser.

In the past year, JavaScript has been used to create content and interface elements more than ever. Interactive web applications that exchange data with the server using the XMLHttpRequest object (popularized with the acronym AJAX, which stands for Asynchronous JavaScript and XML) are discussed regularly and promoted widely. Examples of such applications are Google's Gmail and Kiko's calendar application (www.kiko.com), shown in Figure 4-2. Many AJAX applications are models of inaccessibility for many users. However, it is not as simple as "JavaScript is inaccessible."

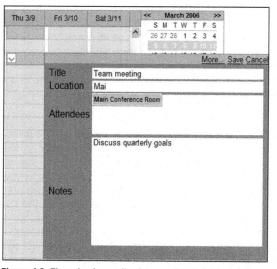

Figure 4-2. The calendar application uses JavaScript to create interface elements dynamically.

The traditional advice for developers using JavaScript was to use the <noscript> element to deliver replacement content. More often than not, the message non-JavaScript users received read like this: "Your browser is too old and doesn't support scripting. Please come back after you update your browser!"

Screen reader users had difficulties also. Older versions of screen readers usually built an off-screen model of the page being viewed and didn't change the structure or content of that page model. The user happily navigated the model, unaware (or at least not notified) of changes to the page. Content generated within a <noscript> element isn't much help, at least in JAWS. As of version 7.0, JAWS doesn't read <noscript> content in the standard reading mode, whether or not scripting is disabled.

Screen readers have improved support for JavaScript in recent versions. There are more and more events that will trigger updates to the page models and data structures on which screen readers rely. As a result, more and more JavaScript-created content is accessible to screen readers, at least in theory. The big problems revolve around notification of page changes and the lack of role and state information for scripted interface elements. A user may or may not be aware that something on the page has changed. If the screen reader user knows that a change has taken place, the user has a new problem: locating the change. Ideally, the change is very close to the point on the page where the user's focus is located, but this doesn't always happen, nor is it necessarily sufficient for comprehension. Interface elements are often created, but HTML doesn't have any way to identify a set of four pairs of nested <div> elements as an accordion or nested navigation menu, so the unsighted user is at a considerably greater disadvantage.

There is ongoing work in the W3C's Protocols and Formats Working Group developing a roadmap (www.w3.org/WAI/PF/roadmap/) to address accessibility issues in web content, including the lack of roles and states (see www.w3.org/WAI/PF/adaptable and www.w3.org/WAI/PF/GUI/). Firefox 1.5 has an interesting implementation of this group's work that is worth a closer look (see www.mozilla.org/access/dhtml/).

Keyboard users are the other group who are often excluded in complex JavaScript. Interface elements are often created using simple HTML elements that are modified by the script, but sometimes the modifications add behaviors to the elements using mouse-driven events. The onclick event responds to keyboard input as well as mouse clicks, as long as the user can reach the element with this event using the keyboard. If the keyboard user can't move the focus to the element that uses onclick (for example, by using the Tab key), it is effectively mouse-only.

Keyboard support is more readily achievable than screen reader support, but without attention from developers, keyboard users will be left behind. Chapter 10 tackles accessible JavaScript in far more detail, with suggestions and techniques to help you address the issues you are likely to encounter.

Flash

Adobe Flash offers a growing list of features that support users with disabilities (see www.macromedia.com/resources/accessibility/flash8/). This is quite an accomplishment, considering how it once shared the dubious distinction with PDF as the "web format most likely to be a target for accessibility advocates' criticism." Support for assistive technologies was built into version 6 of the Flash Player, and improvements to this support have followed with every new release. In addition to these, Flash has always been a format that users with learning disabilities (such as dyslexia or other forms of cognitive impairments) found helpful. The interactive, multisensory experiences that developers often create in Flash can provide built-in concept reinforcement to the textual information provided, as is demonstrated at www.clubndss.org/StartWebFun.html, a site designed to teach kids with Down Syndrome how to surf the Web safely.

A new type of Flash called Flex provides a rich set of components (a text area component, an accordion component, a calendar component, and others) and a simple XML authoring file format called MXML. Authors can write MXML by hand or by using an authoring tool such as Adobe's Flex Builder to create rich internet applications that have built-in keyboard support and that provide information to screen readers via Microsoft's Active Accessibility API. Support for the Flex components among screen readers is growing. It is already possible to use JAWS to interact with a Flex application such as the Flex BlogReader sample application. For more information about Flex and sample applications, see www.macromedia.com/macromedia/accessibility/features/flex.

Flash provides support for keyboard access, captioning, font resizing, and color contrast. The ongoing challenge for Flash is to make it easier for developers to implement these features. Keyboard support became easier in Flash Player 8 when a change was made to allow partial tab orders to be provided. Previously, developers needed to assign a tab index value for every object, or else the default tab order would be used. Captioning is possible in multiple ways; Figure 4-3 shows one example. Many developers have crafted straightforward solutions for parsing and displaying XML caption data, and HiSoftware has created a captioning component that makes adding captions easier. The Flash Player's support for CSS and filters in Flash 8 make it easier for developers to support font and color contrast changes, but these changes exist separately from browser and operating system settings at present.

Figure 4-3. Captioning is available in AOL's Flash-based Princess Natasha series.

Flash accessibility support is not complete yet (the same can be said for any format/player combination), but improvements that move it in the right direction are included with every release of the player. Chapter 11 covers Flash in depth.

Portable Document Format (PDF)

Adobe PDF is the de facto standard for offering documents digitally. Adobe's work on PDF accessibility since version 5 has yielded great results, with support in a variety of assistive technologies and on multiple platforms (see www.adobe.com/enterprise/accessibility/ pdfs/acrobat7_accessibility_aag.pdf). PDF has addressed issues for many different types of users. It includes support for screen readers, magnifiers, keyboard users, users who need enlarged fonts and different document colors, and more. Even users who lack assistive technology or who have difficulty reading benefit since Adobe implemented a Read Out Loud feature.

The most significant obstacle in PDF accessibility is in authoring. Since Adobe published the details for the PDF format, the number of tools that can create PDFs has increased dramatically. However, few non-Adobe tools author accessible PDFs, and Adobe's on-the-fly accessibility "tagging" that is available in Adobe Reader is not infallible. Authors need to spend additional time making their PDF documents accessible, and unfortunately, few don't know how or want to try.

Chapter 12 covers the accessibility features, limitations, and accessibility authoring and remediation process for PDF documents.

Synchronized Multimedia Integration Language (SMIL)

SMIL is used to define the layout of multimedia presentations. In this case, *layout* includes both the position of elements in coordinate space (x, y, and z position) as well as defining when different elements occur in the overall timeline. SMIL is supported by several media players, but the most popular is the RealPlayer. QuickTime Player (4.1 and newer) also supports a subset of SMIL.

SMIL is not specifically for accessibility, but it is needed for accessibility purposes. By using SMIL, authors can create complex presentations, including audio, video, text, animations, and other media elements that are supported by the player that is interpreting SMIL. Using SMIL, an author can add caption tracks, audio descriptions, and alternative audio sources easily (see www.w3.org/TR/SMIL-access). SMIL allows authors to provide multiple versions of parts of a media presentation for different languages. The author can also add markup for bandwidth negotiation so that users with different connection speeds can receive content tuned for their environment. These features are well supported in RealPlayer and QuickTime.

Here's a basic SMIL file that defines the presentation of a 320 × 240 video with captions and an audio description that starts ten seconds into the video:

```
<!DOCTYPE smil PUBLIC "-//W3C//DTD SMIL 2.0//EN"➡
"http://www.w3.org/TR/REC-smil/SMIL20.dtd">
<smil xmlns="http://www.w3.org/2001/SMIL20/Language">
<head>
  <layout>
    <root-layout backgroundColor="black" height="315" width="330"/>
      <region id="video" backgroundColor="black" top="5" left="5" ➡
      height="240" width="320"/>
      <region id="captions" backgroundColor="black" top="250"➡
      height="60" left="5" width="320"/>
  </layout>
</head>
<body>
  <par>
    <video src="video.rm" region="video" title="myVideo Title"➡
    alt="Demonstration of RAM chip installation"/>
    <textstream src="captions.rt" region="captions"➡
    systemCaptions="on" title="captions"/>
    <audio src="ad.mp3" begin="10s" systemAudioDesc="on"/>
  </par>
</body>
</smil>
```

The root-layout defines the overall size, and the region elements define the position of media elements within the root-layout. In this case, the root-layout is defined by the combined sizes of the video and caption regions, plus a 5-pixel border between these elements and around the outer edge of the presentation.

The <par> (parallel) element indicates that the three elements nested within (in this example) should maintain synchronization with each other. The opposite of <par> is <seq> (sequence), which indicates that items should be played serially.

In the example, notice the presence of alt and title attributes. If a screen reader provided access to this information in an SMIL player, these attributes would be very useful in providing access to additional information for the screen reader user; however, at present, no such support exists. In this case, and in the case of many SMIL presentations, real access to the content is provided through audio descriptions. If a SMIL presentation includes text or HTML that users need to read to understand the content, this text will not be accessible to screen reader users and should be provided in an alternate manner.

Also in the SMIL code example are SMIL test attributes for captions and audio descriptions. For captions, systemCaptions acts as an indication to the player that the textstream element should play only when the user has selected to view captions. The systemAudioDesc attribute operates in the same way for audio descriptions. RealPlayer provides a Preferences panel for accessibility settings, shown in Figure 4-4, which it uses to compare to the SMIL test attributes to determine what should display. QuickTime does not make use of the test attributes.

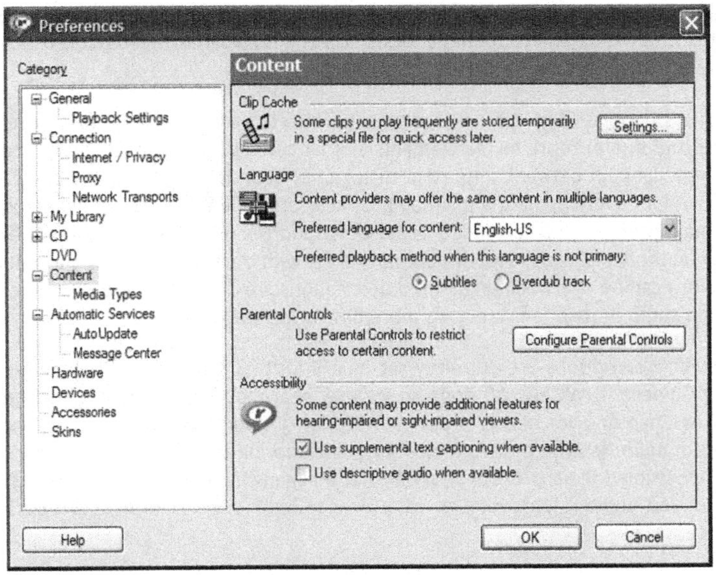

Figure 4-4. Accessiblity settings in the Preferences panel for RealPlayer 10

Providing multiple languages is similar. The systemLanguage test attribute is used by the player to identify what language choice the user should have to view specific content. Here is a variation on the previous code:

```
<body>
  <par>
    <video src="video.rm" region="video" title="myVideo Title"
    alt="Demonstration of RAM chip installation"/>
    <switch>
      <textstream src="captions_fr.rt" region="captions"
        systemLanguage="fr" systemCaptions="on"/>
      <textstream src="captions_es.rt" region="captions"
        systemLanguage="es"systemCaptions="on"/>
      <textstream src="captions_en.rt" region="captions"
        systemCaptions="on"/>
    </switch>
    <audio src="ad.mp3" begin="10s" systemAudioDesc="on"/>
  </par>
</body>
```

In addition to the systemLanguage attribute, a switch element is also used. The switch element indicates an ordered set of options. In this case, the first choice in the switch is French captions, which display only when captions are on and the language is set to French; the next choice is Spanish captions, which display only when captions are on and the language is set to Spanish; and the final choice is English captions, which display when captions are enabled but there is no language restriction set. The third choice will play only if neither the first or second option plays, and by not setting the systemLanguage attribute, it acts as the default caption file for all non-English languages except French and Spanish.

RealPlayer also supports SMIL 2.0's excl element. This element provides a way to temporarily interrupt one or more media elements so that audio descriptions that take more time than is available in between important dialogue or sounds in a movie can be heard completely without overlapping the main audio. These are called *extended audio descriptions*. The main problem with extended audio descriptions is that they make the movie longer. If the authors of the descriptions are not thrifty with their use of words, the resulting descriptions can be overwhelming. Audio descriptions are difficult to author correctly, and extended audio descriptions are even more difficult to write.

Extended audio descriptions are currently set as a Priority 3 item in the Web Content Accessibility Guidelines (WCAG) 2.0 draft, so we may hear more descriptions of this type someday. (See Chapter 2 for details about WCAG priority levels.) You won't get any help with extended audio descriptions from any current authoring tools for, but the National Center for Accessible Media (NCAM) at WGBH has a page with SMIL templates, including one for extended audio descriptions, at http://ncam.wgbh.org/richmedia/tutorials/smiltemplates.html.

QuickTime, Windows Media, and RealPlayer

The QuickTime, Windows Media, and RealPlayer players are most often used for playing simple movie files, but each has capabilities beyond that basic feature. These media players can display textual information, as well as include interactive sprites, images, text, secondary audio, and more. When it comes to accessibility however, these tool's main strengths are in the area of captions and audio descriptions.

QuickTime supports QTtext, its own proprietary caption data format. Developers can easily add captions to a QuickTime movie using QuickTime Pro's Add Track feature or by using SMIL (see http://developer.apple.com/documentation/QuickTime/IQ_InteractiveMovies/), described in the previous section. Real uses its own proprietary caption data format, called RealText, and it is associated with the primary media file using SMIL (see http://service.real.com/help/library/guides/ProductionGuide/prodguide/realpgd.htm). Windows Media also has its own proprietary caption data format, called Synchronized Accessible Media Interchange (SAMI). The hardest part of the captioning process is getting the caption data file with all the necessary caption data and timing. Fortunately, a large number of caption vendors are able to do the captioning work and create these file types for you. If you prefer to handle the captioning in-house, tools like MAGpie (http://ncam.wgbh.org/webaccess/magpie/) and Hi-Caption (www.hisoftware.com/hmcc/) can help you do the work yourself. See http://ncam.wgbh.org/richmedia/tutorials/captioning.html for more information about adding captions to rich media.

Adding audio descriptions is easy in QuickTime, using either QuickTime Pro or SMIL. RealPlayer can also include audio descriptions, again using SMIL to associate them with the main movie. Windows Media is unable to play audio descriptions separately from the movie. To include audio descriptions for Windows Media, it is necessary to encode the additional audio as part of the audio track for the main media. For audio descriptions, MAGpie will author an SMIL file or just help record the files and locate the correct timing for the supplementary audio track. The challenge is in the authoring of the information voiced in the descriptions themselves. See http://ncam.wgbh.org/richmedia/tutorials/audiodesc.html for more information about adding audio descriptions to rich media.

These media players have poor or no support for most other disabled user profiles. Text in the QuickTime Player doesn't resize or respond to operating system contrast settings, and interactive controls that can be added are not accessible to keyboard or screen reader users. There is promise now that Apple is offering its own screen reader, VoiceOver, but a cross-platform accessible QuickTime Player seems unlikely in the near term.

Each player has some measure of keyboard support for access to the player controls. In all cases, the support is far better in the stand-alone player than the version that displays within a web page. Offering users the ability to view media in the stand-alone player will help keyboard and screen reader users control your media offerings.

Scalable Vector Graphics (SVG)

Scalable Vector Graphics (SVG) is a W3C recommendation (www.w3.org/TR/SVG) that defines an XML-based format for creating graphics and graphical interfaces. SVG has received increased attention recently, in large part due to Mozilla Firefox 1.5 shipping with built-in SVG rendering. In general, SVG has not caught on for the desktop in the same way that another vector-based tool (Flash) has. SVG faces many of the same accessibility concerns that Flash did prior to Flash 6, most of which are currently unresolved. (See www.w3.org/TR/SVG-access/ for SVG accessibility features.)

Being vector-based, SVG has incredible potential for users who need magnification. Text and graphics that are part of an SVG file can increase in size considerably (Adobe SVG viewer claims 1,600 percent magnification; see www.adobe.com/svg/viewer/install/main.html), but unfortunately, the user doesn't get particularly usable control over the magnification. A talented SVG developer can design an interface to facilitate magnification by the user, but this is not often done. Firefox 1.5's implementation of SVG (www.mozilla.org/projects/svg/) solves this problem in part by making text within an SVG document increase in size along with text in the HTML page. Unfortunately, this can wreak havoc on the layout of the SVG content, and often decouples text from related graphical elements that do not resize and creates overlapping text elements. Figure 4-5 shows an example of this problem.

Figure 4-5. Increasing the font size in SVG documents in Firefox is possible, but can have undesirable results.

The SVG recommendation does offer ways to include alternative information within an SVG file. Each element in SVG can have a title and description element, so a developer can provide information to be used by assistive technologies to display for users. Unfortunately, no mainstream SVG viewer makes this information available to assistive technologies, so there is no screen reader support for SVG. The IVEO Viewer (www.viewplus.com/products/touch-audio-learning/IVEO/) is one commercially available tool that makes use of accessibility data in SVG files. This tool works in conjunction with a touch-sensitive pad. Users can print out SVG graphics with a tactile printer and calibrate the tactile print-out with the touchpad, so that the computer can announce the title and description for the SVG element that is touched on the printout overlaying the touchpad. This tool also works using a mouse and can display the entire SVG document tree, so it is a potentially useful tool for SVG accessibility testing.

SVG developers can include interactive buttons within an SVG file. Unfortunately, no SVG viewers support keyboard access to these elements.

The other area in which SVG might be expected to offer benefits to users with disabilities is in color contrast. Unfortunately, like the support for magnification, a developer might implement a solution in a particular graphic or interface, but there is no current support in existing players to modify document colors or follow the settings of the operating system.

For more on SVG implementations, see www.svgi.org/directory.html?type=1.

Java

Java applets are another way that developers can provide applications via the Web. With the Swing components, Sun created a set of commonly used components that application developers would need and built in support for its Accessibility application program interface (API). This makes authoring accessible Java applications and applets possible.

Assistive technologies can gather accessibility information from Java applets as long as the Java Access Bridge is running. The Java Access Bridge is able to gather information from the Accessibility API and make it available for accessibility tools not running inside Java.

Java's Swing components also allow developers to attend to keyboard support for non-mouse users. Although keyboard shortcuts can be easily assigned and the tab order controlled, as with any application, developers should pay close attention during development and testing to ensure that all functionality is keyboard accessible.

In general, Sun has paid attention to accessibility, and Java is worth a closer look. For the most complete and up-to-date information, visit Sun's accessibility resources on the Web:

- Developing Accessible JFC Applications: www.sun.com/access/developers/developing-accessible-apps/
- Java Look and Feel Guidelines: http://java.sun.com/products/jlf/ed2/book/
- Java Access Bridge for Windows: http://java.sun.com/products/accessbridge/

XML and XSL

People often ask whether Extensible Markup Language (XML) or Extensible Stylesheet Language (XSL) is accessible. Any XML document is accessible for what it is, which is a text file. When a user agent interprets a text file that claims to be a particular type of XML, at that time, the user agent's logic can look for and display data structures that are important for accessibility (for example, the alt attribute on an image in XHTML). If the XML is not understood by any user agents as a file type that can be interpreted and rendered, it is impossible to say whether it is accessible. XML is accessible like a database is accessible or like a binary file is accessible. It's only when you try to turn it into something that problems, and benefits, appear.

If you have an XML document that contains address data, the information in that file is as accessible to a blind user as it is to a sighted user in the text form of the XML. In the case of most users, it is better to see the data in a different format, perhaps HTML. The XML with the address data needs to be a specific type of XML file—one that allows a browser to make certain assumptions about the content. (Browser: "OK, I know or assume that this is XHTML. Hey, an XML element called img. I'll look for a source file, display that on the page, and keep the value of that alt attribute here in this DOM location for easy access.")

So how do you get the XML to turn into XHTML? XSL is one way (see www.w3.org/Style/XSL/). Using XSL transformations, you can define a document that contains some or all of the data from the original file. That new document could be made so that it validates as XHTML, or it could be made so that it lacks every possible accessibility feature. Both are possible—it all depends on the experience and knowledge of the person writing the XSL transformations. It's the same when you use structured data to create web documents with Perl, Java, or any other scripting language. If you know what you need to make the document look like in order for it to be accessible, you can do it with any of these, as long as the necessary information exists in the data file.

If you are designing an XML data structure for an online application, you need to make sure that all of the information that is needed for accessibility in the final documents exists in the database. Usually, this means that when you have an XML file that includes a URL or filename for an image that will be displayed by the final document, you need to make sure that the XML data structure has a place for an equivalent of that image. Not having that image doesn't make the XML data file less accessible, but it clearly could make the final document less accessible. See www.w3.org/TR/xag for W3C's XML Accessibility Guidelines.

Summary

A broad range of technology choices is available today for developing websites and applications, and each technology has its own strengths and weaknesses. The information presented in this chapter is a starting point, not the final analysis. Formats and user agents are guaranteed to change, so it is incumbent on those involved in drafting specifications for and developing web content to make efforts to regularly update their knowledge on the accessibility of these technologies. I am hopeful that this overview helps in this pursuit. The chapters ahead cover many of the technologies discussed in brief here and will provide essential information on how to implement accessibility successfully.

5 ASSISTIVE TECHNOLOGY: SCREEN READERS AND BROWSERS

by Jim Thatcher

Assistive technologies are an indispensable assessment tool for the web developer. It is not possible to determine a website's compliance with most of the requirements of accessible web design using a conventional browser alone.

Many requirements are *indirect*, in that they require information to be available to users *through* their assistive technology. This information may not be exposed by conventional browsers. An example of this is the requirement for markup in data tables to indicate which cells are heading cells (Section 508 provisions §1194.22(g, h) and WCAG 1.0 Checkpoints 5.1 and 5.2). Sometimes, this markup is reflected in the visual presentation. For example, if the <th> tag is used to define the heading cells, then the text contained in those cells will be bold and centered *by default*. If, instead, the headers attribute is used to indicate heading cells, then there may be no visual manifestation. Another example is that text equivalents for nontext elements may or may not be available for normal visual examination. Also, some guidelines are quite subjective, such as the WCAG 1.0 Checkpoint 14.1 to use the clearest and simplest language appropriate for a site's content. The decision about whether a site complies with this checkpoint can be reached only after careful assessment.

Screen readers are the primary assistive technology through which website content is funneled. People who are blind use them to have the information that is displayed on the computer screen spoken to them with synthesized speech.

This chapter will provide a brief overview of the assistive technologies used in later chapters for exemplifying and examining accessible web techniques, and will also illustrate how to assess a website's accessibility with a standard browser.

Screen Readers

Screen reader products in the DOS days literally read the 80×25 display buffer to speak the screen. The ASCII codes stored in the display buffer were sent directly to a hardware device to produce synthesized speech. With the advent of the graphical user interface (GUI), screen readers had to become a lot smarter. Now they can capture text as it is written to the display through display driver software. These sophisticated technologies create what is called an *off-screen model* (OSM), which is, in effect, a database of all the text displayed on the graphical screen. When a screen reader user requests information, it is read from this database, the OSM, rather than from the screen itself.

Even speech synthesis has changed. The first developments in speech synthesis were hardware synthesizers that cost around $1,000. Now speech synthesizer software is included in screen readers and talking browsers, and has even been built into some operating systems.

How Screen Readers Work with Web Pages

With the advent of the Web, the way in which screen readers work has changed yet again. Now screen readers look at the document object model (DOM) of the page to know what the browser would display. For the Web, as well as for some other applications, screen readers are not reading the screen any more; instead, the screen reader is using the DOM to provide a speech rendering of data that is a web page.

A screen reader must present the two-dimensional graphical web page to a user who is blind as a one-dimensional stream of characters, which is usually fed to a speech synthesizer. There is an alternative to speech for people who know Braille called *refreshable Braille* displays. These units can cost as much as $30,000 and typically have 20, 40, or 80 individual eight-dot Braille cells, where the individual dots are raised and lowered with tiny solenoids. Figure 5-1 shows four Braille cells from the Robotron Group (www. sensorytools.com).

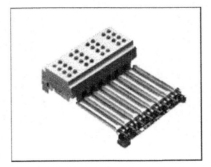

Figure 5-1. Four eight-dot Braille cells

It is very important to recognize that this screen-reading process is converting a two-dimensional page to a one-dimensional text string, whether spoken or displayed in Braille. This is aptly called *linearizing* the page. If you are familiar with HTML, the simplest way of picturing linearization is by imagining an HTML document stripped of all its tags, leaving just the text together with the textual values of some attributes like alt and title. The resulting text file is the linearized version of the page. Different parts of that text document will be presented to a screen reader user through synthesized speech or Braille.

Another way to picture the linearization process is to read the page from left to right and from top to bottom. Tables are read left to right and top to bottom before continuing, and each cell is read completely before continuing to the next cell. Of course, there is more to this linear view than just characters. It must also include form elements and links in order to capture the function of the page.

It seems that those users who are blind rarely listen to a page in full. Often, they navigate to the content and controls of the page. Tab and Shift+Tab move forward and backward through the active elements of the page—that is, through the links and form controls. Screen readers have key commands to read by characters, by words, by lines, and by sentences, as well as HTML features like headings, paragraphs, tables, and lists.

Screen readers do much more than read web pages. They can be used with any software running on the computer; therefore, they must be keyboard-compatible with all of that software. This makes screen reader-specific key combinations complicated and even arcane. For example, to move around the cells of a table with JAWS for Windows, you need to use Ctrl+Alt+arrow; to go into table mode with Window-Eyes, you need to use Ctrl++ (plus), and then use Ins+arrow to move around the table.

It is in this linearized world that some of the accessibility requirements begin to make better sense. Clearly, the images that are on the visual page need to be replaced with the text equivalents, the alt-text; otherwise, the information or function they contain will be lost.

Additional help is essential. If the user is reading in the middle of a data table, the screen reader technology needs a way of informing the user of the headers for the current data cell that is being read. Try to imagine—in this linearized text world—making an online order. Having selected the product you want to purchase, you reach the checkout page, only to find several fields where you are required to enter your details, but no clue as to which data goes where. This is the kind of information that must be included in web page markup to make it accessible to a person who is blind.

> *You can find an excellent short video demonstration of how screen readers work on the DoIT website, www.doit.wisc.edu/ (University of Wisconsin-Madison, Division of Information Technology), "Introduction to the Screen Reader" with Neal Ewers of the Trace Research Center www.doit.wisc.edu/accessibility/video/intro.asp.*

Specific Screen Readers

In later chapters, three screen readers will be used to illustrate techniques for addressing web accessibility requirements: Hal, JAWS for Windows, and Window-Eyes. These screen readers are probably used by more than 95 percent of users of the Web who are blind.

Hal is a screen reader developed in the UK by Dolphin Oceanic, Ltd. (Dolphin Computer Access, www.dolphincomputeraccess.com/). The price for Hal is either $795 or $1,095, depending on whether you choose Hal Standard or Hal Professional. The tests in later chapters use Version 6.5 of Hal Professional. The demonstration version of Hal is fully functional but will time out after 30 minutes. You can run it again after you restart Windows.

JAWS for Windows is the most popular screen reader. JAWS, an acronym for Jobs Access With Speech, is developed by Freedom Scientific (www.freedomscientific.com/). The cost of JAWS is either $895 or $1,095, depending on whether you want the Standard or Professional edition. You can download a demo version, which will operate for 40 minutes before it times out. You can do that again, after the system is rebooted. The tests in the later chapters were run with JAWS Professional Versions 6.2 and 7.0.

Window-Eyes, developed by GW Micro (www.gwmicro.com/), costs $795. A timed demonstration is available from GW Micro. The demo version is fully functional and will time out after 30 minutes. You may reboot your machine for another 30-minute crack at Window-Eyes. The tests in later chapters use Window-Eyes Versions 5.0 and 5.5.

In the past, one commercial screen reader for the Apple Macintosh was available. outSPOKEN, by the Alva Access Group, was the first screen reader to provide access to a GUI (in 1988). Unfortunately, outSPOKEN did not keep up with Windows screen readers, especially in the way web information is handled. Now, outSPOKEN is no longer available. Apple has developed its own screen reader for Mac OS X, called VoiceOver (www.apple.com/accessibility/voiceover/). Jay Leaventhal of The American Federation for the Blind (www.afb.org) wrote a review of VoiceOver for AccessWorld (www.afb.org/aw), titled "Not What the Doctor Ordered: A Review of Apple's VoiceOver Screen Reader."

The picture for UNIX is also cloudy. There are no commercial screen readers for X-Windows, the windowing system for UNIX, although there are shareware attempts at accessing X-Windows for people who are blind. In particular, the open source software GNOME (a UNIX and Linux desktop suite and development platform) project has a screen reader project called Gnopernicus (www.baum.ro/gnopernicus.html). There is at least one sophisticated access system (http://emacspeak.sourceforge.net/) for text-based UNIX, Emacspeak, but that environment is usually accessed with terminal software under Windows, using Windows screen readers.

The bottom line is that when we talk about access to the Web for people who are blind, we are talking about the Windows platform. Examples and samples in subsequent chapters are all taken from Windows, using Microsoft Internet Explorer, Netscape Navigator, or Mozilla Firefox. Among those browsers, Internet Explorer is most effective with screen readers because of the way it exposes the DOM and provides information through Microsoft Active Accessibility (MSAA) (www.microsoft.com/enable). The latest version of JAWS and Window-Eyes are providing access to Firefox (Version 1.5.0.2). Representatives of Freedom Scientific (JAWS) say that their support is not yet as good as it is for Internet Explorer 6, and they don't offer customer support for Firefox yet. Although GW Micro (Window-Eyes) has not made such a statement, I found table reading to fail with both screen readers. There are also problems with maintaining point of regard. When you are reading in one page, go to another, and return to where you started, the screen reader should pick up where you were. That doesn't work with either screen reader with Firefox.

In later chapters, I will describe techniques for using screen readers in special circumstances, especially for forms, tables, and skipping blocks of links. The following sections cover the basics of using the screen readers used in the tests and examples for this book.

With the screen readers (and also IBM Home Page Reader, the talking browser) described in the following sections, the active elements of a page, including links and form controls, can be navigated with the Tab key (Shift+Tab goes backwards). The order in which these links and form elements appear in the tab sequence is the same as the linearized page unless the attribute tabindex is used in the HTML source of the document. Then those active elements with valid tabindex attributes appear first and according to the number assigned as the value of the tabindex. The active elements without the tabindex attribute are placed at the end of the sequence. The tabindex feature is supported by JAWS and Home Page Reader and with MSAA Mode off by Window-Eyes; it is not supported by Hal.

5

Using Hal

When Hal is started, its settings dialog box is displayed, as shown in Figure 5-2.

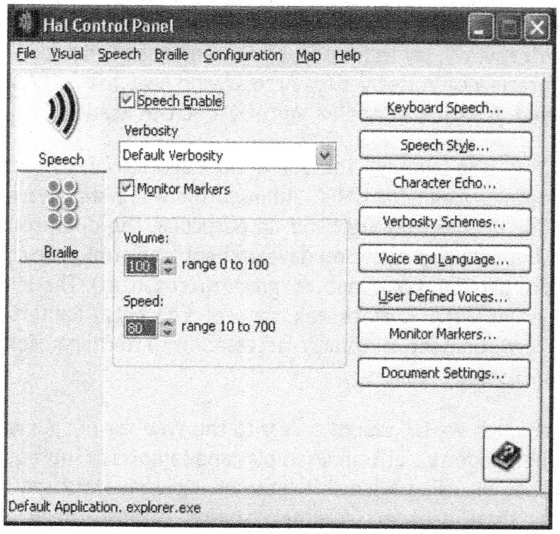

Figure 5-2. Hal Control Panel

All the screen readers have some kind of specialized web mode for reading web pages, because there is usually no focus point on the page, like a text cursor, selector, or focus rectangle. For Hal, the web mode is called Virtual Focus because the screen reader must create its own focus point. Virtual Focus mode can be toggled with the minus key on the number pad.

When a web page is loaded in Internet Explorer, Hal announces "Hypertext, Virtual Focus," followed by the page title, and then the number of links, frames, and headings. Hal uses the left Ctrl key to stop speech, rather than the right Ctrl key, which is my habit for the other screen readers and Home Page Reader.

The up and down arrow keys move through a web page line at a time. Hal doesn't have the convenient letter keys shared by other assistive technologies for moving around structures on the page. Some of Hal's advanced navigation keys are listed in Table 5-1.

Table 5-1. Advanced Navigation Keys in Hal

Key	Function
Left Shift+left Ctrl+Home	First edit field
Left Ctrl+Page Up/Page Down	Previous/Next control
Left Shift+left Ctrl+Page Up/Page Down	Previous/Next frame
Left Shift+left Ctrl+left arrow/right arrow	Previous/Next text
Left Shift+left Ctrl+up arrow/down arrow	Previous/Next link

Hal also has a useful "more information" key, left Shift+0 (zero on the number pad) which, for example, speaks the href when virtual focus is on a link.

Using JAWS for Windows

In JAWS for Windows, the web mode is known as Virtual PC Cursor (VPC) mode. The screen reader automatically switches to VPC mode when Internet Explorer is the foreground process. VPC mode can be turned on and off manually using Insert+Z, which is a useful command to know when things aren't working quite right and you need to toggle between modes.

When JAWS loads a page, it announces the title, the number of links, and begins reading from the top. The Ctrl key stops speech. The down and up arrow keys give you the next and previous line. Insert+down arrow reads the rest of the page (Say All).

You can move among active elements (links and controls) with Tab and Shift+Tab. Move from heading to heading with H (use Shift+H to move backward through the headings).

To find and read form controls, use Ctrl+Insert+Home to go to the first input element on the page, and then use F to move through the controls (to go backwards, use Shift+F). You need to press Enter to go into forms mode to actually enter text in an input field, and then you can use the plus key on the number pad to exit forms mode and return to VPC mode. This is actually a problem area in assessing the accessibility of forms. When you are in forms mode, the arrow keys don't speak the previous and next line; instead, they are used to move through the input form, so it may be difficult to find (listen to) surrounding information about the control without leaving forms mode. This is one of the reasons that precise labeling of form controls is so important (see Chapter 8).

It is possible to obtain a copy of what JAWS *will* read—that is, the JAWS view of the page. After the page loads, stop the speaking speech with Ctrl. Then use Ctrl+A to select all (the whole page) and use Ctrl+C to copy all the text to the clipboard. Now you can paste (Ctrl+V) into a word processor or text editor. Some of the metatext used by JAWS, like link, is not included in that JAWS view.

Rather than tabbing to each link, you can open the JAWS Links List with Ins+F7, as shown in Figure 5-3.

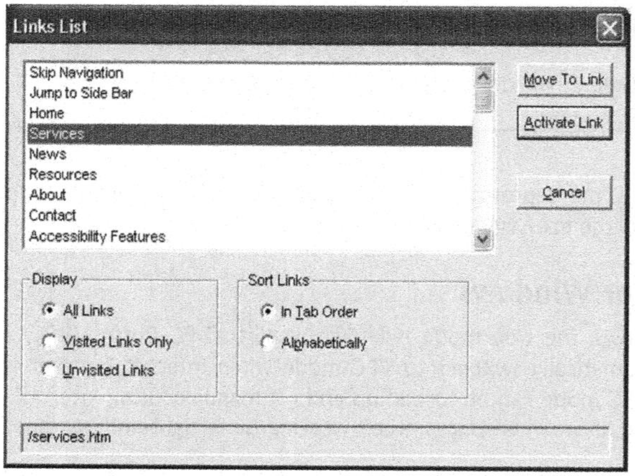

Figure 5-3. JAWS links list

Other lists are available with Ins+F5 (Form Fields), Ins+F6 (Headings), and Ins+F9 (Frames).

Using Window-Eyes

For Window-Eyes, the special web mode is called MSAA Application mode or Browse mode. It is toggled with Ctrl+Shift+A.

Like JAWS, Window-Eyes switches to web mode automatically when Internet Explorer is the foreground process. As the page is loaded, Window-Eyes announces the page title, then "Loading Page, Looking for Visible Line, Visible Line found, Load done." Then it begins speaking with an announcement of the number of links, tables, and headings, followed by the text of the page.

The Esc or Ctrl key stops speech, and the up and down arrow keys speak the previous and next line. Ctrl+Home takes you to the beginning of the document, and Ctrl+End takes you to the end. The Ctrl+Shift+R combination causes Window-Eyes to read from the current point to the end (Say All).

Move among active elements (links and controls) with Tab and Shift+Tab, or move from link to link with L (use Shift+L to go backwards through the links). Move from heading to heading with H (Shift+H to go backwards through the headings).

To find the form controls on a page, use the C key (Shift+C to go backwards). When you are reading a web page with Browse mode (MSAA Application mode), there are many keys that facilitate reading and navigation (like C and Shift+C). When you want to use an input control, say to put text in an edit field, you want those keys to go into the edit field, not to move to the next control. So, it is necessary to leave Browse mode. To do this, press Enter when the focus is on a form control, and then you can type in the input field. Use the Tab key to navigate the form controls. You can return to Browse mode with Ctrl+Shift+A.

To get the Window-Eyes view of the web page, use Ctrl+A to select all, Ctrl+C to copy to the clipboard, and Ctrl+V to paste the text into a text editor or word processor. This is an excellent way for a sighted developer or tester to study the web content for accessibility, especially because the screen reader is unfamiliar and the synthesized speech may be difficult to understand.

Use Ins+Tab when viewing any page with Window-Eyes to bring up a dialog box containing a list of all the links on the web page, as shown in Figure 5-4. By selecting different radio buttons in the Information Selection section of that dialog box (like Headings, Alt+H) you can list and then move to or activate (if appropriate) each item.

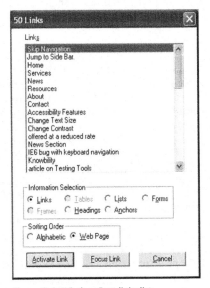

Figure 5-4. Window-Eyes links list

You can activate any link by moving to it and pressing Enter because Activate Link is the default push button. Alternatively, you can move to the link in the web page with the Focus Link push button. The same dialog box that brings up the list of links also provides the option to see lists of tables or frames.

Talking and Text-Only Browsers

Screen readers are inherently difficult to use because they must be able to read any application, which means that they must be compatible with any application. Since applications have built-in commands, you often need to use complex keyboard commands that don't clash with any other application commands, such as Ctrl+Alt+down arrow, which are difficult to remember and may be difficult to execute. If you don't have to use a screen reader and if you don't use it every day, chances are that you will have a hard time working with one.

Another way of checking for accessibility with assistive technology and understanding how your web page sounds to someone who is blind is to use talking browsers, which are designed specifically to speak web pages. One of the first such browsers was pwWebSpeak by Productivity Works, but that was discontinued in January 2001. Currently, the most commonly used talking browser is IBM Home Page Reader.

Another helpful type of browser is one that is text-only. Because a text-only browser does not support graphics or technologies such as JavaScript and Cascading Style Sheets (CSS), it offers a way to evaluate whether your page is usable with these technologies turned off.

A Talking Browser

Home Page Reader from IBM (www.ibm.com/able/hpr.html) has a retail cost of $149 through one of IBM's authorized dealers; I found HPR for as low as $90 on the Web. IBM used to offer a 30-day trial, but now the demo version is not restricted in time but instead restricted in the sites you can browse. The allowed sites are www.ibm.com, www.adobe.com, www.macromedia.com, and www.w3.org.

Home Page Reader is available in six languages: Brazilian Portuguese, French, German, Italian, Spanish, and English. It is also available in Japanese as a separate product. In addition to having the product in a specific language, Home Page Reader will begin reading a page in the language specified with the lang or xml:lang attribute of the <html> tag if that is present. If there is no language specified in the <html> tag, Home Page Reader will speak using its default language, such as French for a French product. However, in this case, Home Page Reader will also apply its heuristic algorithm to see if it can detect the language of the page (assuming Automatic Language Detection is enabled) and if successful, speak in that language. You can specify changes of languages in a web page using the lang attribute, on a span element, for example. Upon encountering the lang attribute, Home Page Reader will change the speaking language if the designated language is available. Home Page Reader does not try to detect changes in language in a page, except those specified with the lang attribute.

Home Page Reader was originally designed by a blind IBM researcher, Chieko Asakawa, and was first produced in Japanese in 1997. Asakawa was motivated to develop Home Page Reader because Japanese screen readers did not accommodate the Web at all.

Using Home Page Reader is a much easier way for sighted developers to understand the view of the Web experienced by a user who is blind. This is because it is a normal Windows application for speaking the Web with conventional menus and much simpler keyboard commands.

As shown in Figure 5-5, Home Page Reader has four main panes: a graphical browser on the top right, a text pane on the bottom right, a history view to the left, and an information view at the bottom of the window. The important panes for this discussion are the graphical view and the text view. The other two can be closed through the View menu.

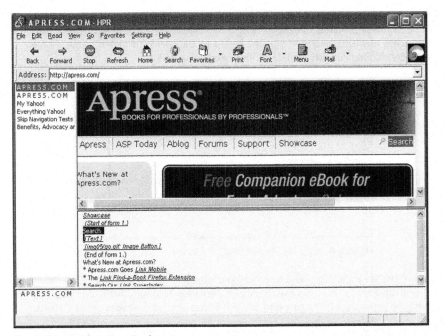

Figure 5-5. IBM Home Page Reader

When Home Page Reader opens a web page, it begins speaking, and the text that is being spoken is displayed in the text view. About eight or ten lines are displayed, and as speaking proceeds, the text pane is refreshed. The current word is highlighted in both the text and graphics views. In Figure 5-5, "Search" is being spoken.

If you would like to see all the text of the page as the Home Page Reader view of the page, put the focus on the text view with the mouse or with F6, use Ctrl+A (for select all) and then Ctrl+C to copy the resulting text to the clipboard. Then use Ctrl+V to paste the text view in your favorite word processor or text editor. This is a useful tool for studying the accessibility of your page, as it is with the screen readers.

When using Home Page Reader, the spacebar begins reading from the current point. As mentioned earlier, people rarely listen to the whole page, but instead choose to navigate around the content. Home Page Reader's philosophy for navigation is to always use the arrow keys: left arrow for previous, right arrow for next, and down arrow for current. By choosing a reading mode (from the Read menu), you can specify the size of the "chunk" you move to with the navigation keys. The options available are character, word, line, paragraph (item), link, control, heading, and table. There is a special reading mode for reading tables, and in this case, all four arrow keys navigate the cells of the table. Home Page Reader defaults to item reading mode, which is similar to line-at-a-time with screen readers.

In addition to using the arrow keys in various reading modes, Home Page Reader also implements the single-letter navigation keys: O for controls, H for headings, T for tables, Tab for active elements, and Shift plus the key to go backwards for any of those. Home Page Reader also has link lists (Ctrl+L), as illustrated in Figure 5-6.

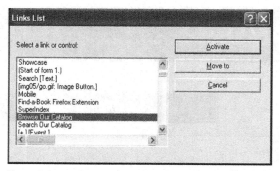

Figure 5-6. Home Page Reader Links List dialog box

These link lists are especially useful when you know the link text. In addition to navigating with the arrow keys, letter keys move to the next item beginning with that letter. They also illustrate the importance of making sure link text makes sense when taken out of context.

There is no question that Home Page Reader is the easiest assistive technology for sighted people to learn to use. If you want to test your forms or tables for accessibility, try them with Home Page Reader.

A Text Browser

If you have never seen Lynx, you are in for a surprise. Lynx is a text browser that is available on UNIX, DOS, and Windows (through DOS emulation). Because it doesn't support graphics, dynamic HTML, or CSS, it is incredibly fast. When you enter a URL for opening a page with Lynx, the page is displayed almost immediately.

Like Home Page Reader and the screen readers, Lynx (http://lynx.browser.org) uses a linearized view of the page. If you don't want to try Lynx, you can visit www.delorie.com/web/lynxview.html and submit a URL in order to see what your page looks like as if it were viewed with Lynx—that is, when it is linearized.

Figure 5-7 shows the Lynx screen for www.jimthatcher.com.

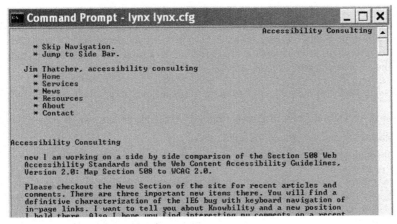

Figure 5-7. Lynx with www.jimthatcher.com open

The user interface for Lynx is first and foremost command keys, including G (Go) for entering a URL to open, O (Options) for setting user preferences, and H (Help) for an extensive help document. You navigate by using the up and down arrow keys to move through the links on the page. After passing the bottom of the current screen, the next screen of information is presented, or you can use the spacebar to go to the next page.

Lynx makes extensive use of colors to present HTML structures like links, headings, titles, and lists. Those colors can be set in an .lss file. The colors do not carry over well to the black-and-white rendition shown in Figure 5-7. That figure is using the default color settings, including black for normal text, purple (with *) for list items, blue for links, and red for the current link (Home) The down arrow key moves through the links, Services, News, Resources, and so on. To follow a link, use the right arrow. To return to the previous page, use the left arrow. Page Up takes you to the previous screen if you have moved past the first screen display. These are default settings, which can be changed using the Options (O) command.

Any time you need to input text, such as when you need to enter a URL as a result of the Go command, a command line opens at the bottom of the window. Text can be entered in that command line.

Lynx does not support graphics, plug-ins, JavaScript, Java, or CSS. Thus, it is an excellent test vehicle to evaluate whether or not your page is usable and readable with these technologies turned off.

Screen Magnification

Screen magnification software uses standard display monitors. It increases the size of everything in the display, including text and images in a web page. Screen magnification software provides various degrees of magnification, typically between 1.5x and 32x. Because of the physical limitations of the monitor, the greater the magnification, the smaller the amount of content that is shown.

The following are the primary issues when using screen magnification software:

- Small display area preventing users from getting the big picture view of a page
- Missing the context around the visible area
- Difficulty in finding page elements, such as navigation or form elements

Screen magnifiers provide multiple settings for magnification. Some also provide a split screen that shows both the magnified page and a nonmagnified page, as shown in Figure 5-8 with 3x magnification using the Windows XP Magnifier.

Figure 5-8. Magnifiication in Windows XP

Windows XP comes with a simple magnifier (Start ➤ All Programs ➤ Accessories ➤ Accessibility ➤ Magnifier). With its default setting, the magnified part of the screen is a banner across the top (see Figure 5-8). Displayed in that banner (in the default setting) is a section of the screen centered on the mouse pointer.

Commercial magnification programs include ZoomText from AI Squared and Magic from Freedom Scientific. The commercial magnifiers offer amazing features. Figure 5-9 is an example comparing ZoomText magnification with its xFont technology (on the top) versus that of Windows Magnifier (both at 5x). The simple magnification enlarges each pixel, and the result becomes very difficult to read at higher magnification (except for letters that have no round parts). With ZoomText, the result is clean and crisp at all magnifications. Also, ZoomText offers screen reading—the menus and dialog boxes talk as focus changes, just as with a screen reader. A trial version of ZoomText can be downloaded from the AI Squared website at www.aisquared.com.

Figure 5-9. Comparison of ZoomText and Magnifier

Consistent layout is a very important design consideration for users who depend on screen magnifiers. Placing the navigation links in the same position on every page, for example, will make it considerably easier for users who can see only a small portion of the screen at one time to find their way around your site.

Some users view the magnified and nonmagnified page simultaneously. This lets them see the general layout of the page in the nonmagnified section and the details in the magnified section. Some users will view a page at less magnification first to get the big picture, and then increase the magnification to read the text.

> *Another assistive technology used by people with reduced vision is large display hardware, such as large monitors and Fresnel lenses. Users can also project the screen display onto a large desk area or a wall. Such solutions may not be feasible depending on the environment. For example, you probably would not want your coworkers to be able to see your display from across the room!*

Browser Checks of Website Accessibility

Visual web browsers can be used to assess the accessibility of a website in several ways:

- Certain sites provide an online analysis of active pages.
- Browser settings can be modified to simulate the way in which a user with disabilities experiences a page.
- A new player in this arena, the browser toolbar, allows you to evaluate accessibility of individual pages as you view them.

Websites That Analyze a Page

You can visit some websites that will help you analyze a live web page. Two of these are the Lynx Viewer and the WAVE.

Due to security concerns and abuse of the Lynx Viewer service, Delorie Software (www.delorie.com/web/lynxview.html) now requires actions on the part of site owners to permit the Lynx Viewer to work. In effect, a file, delorie.htm, must be present in any directory that the Lynx Viewer is asked to access. I have done this on my site (www.jimthatcher.com), so you can check Lynx View there.

The WAVE was conceived and developed by the late Dr. Leonard Kasday at Temple University, Institute on Disabilities. It is being further refined and is now hosted by WebAIM, www.wave.webaim.org/. There are several ways to use the WAVE. The simplest is to just enter the URL of the page, as shown in Figure 5-10.

Figure 5-10. Access to the WAVE

The WAVE tool inserts icons in the page to indicate errors, warnings, and successes relating to accessibility. Figure 5-11 shows the WAVE annotation using the default setting of all annotations.

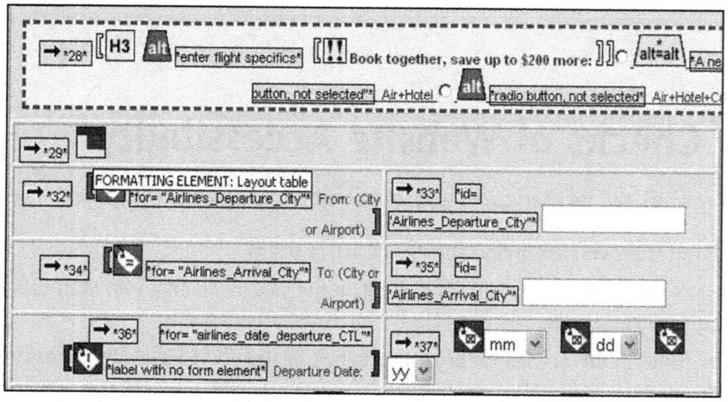

Figure 5-11. WAVE annotation of a part of Priceline.com

118

As shown in Figure 5-11, the WAVE analyzes the page and provides a lot of accessibility information through annotation. There are a total of 75 possible icons, which makes the display daunting at first. But you can quickly recognize a few common icons, and you can check the meaning of unusual ones by moving the mouse over the icon to see its alt-text, as illustrated with the Layout Table icon in Figure 5-11. Table 5-2 describes the function of the icons in Figure 5-11.

Table 5-2. A Small Sample of the Icons Used by the WAVE

Icon	Function
	The reading order in the linearized page is displayed by the arrow icon, followed by a numeral. The numerals indicate the order in which the page will be read by a screen reader.
	The alt-text icon (green for an "accessibility feature") shows the alt-text right next to it.
	This interesting warning icon alerts the user to the fact that there is possible redundant information, typically where two images have the same alt-text.
	This accessibility feature icon indicates a form control label that seems to be correct.
	This accessibility error icon indicates a form control that seems to be improperly labeled. (Because of the use of title attributes on this page, these are not errors.)

Browser Settings for Testing a Page

One method of assessing how a screen reader will handle a page is by browsing it with images turned off. In Internet Explorer, choose Tools ➤ Internet Options, and then click the Advanced tab. In the resulting list, check Always expand alt text for images at the top of the list. Then move down two pages in the list, under Multimedia, and uncheck the item Show Pictures. (To return the system to normal, use the Restore Defaults button at the bottom of the Advanced tab.) With these settings, images will not be displayed and alternative text will appear instead. Figure 5-12 illustrates how these settings work with www.borders.com.

The small rectangles, each with an icon or part of an icon (the icon just indicates a missing image), are placeholders where images would be. Of thirteen image placeholders in Figure 5-12, three show that alt-text is present: Search, Borders.com, and Browse. All the other images lack text equivalents.

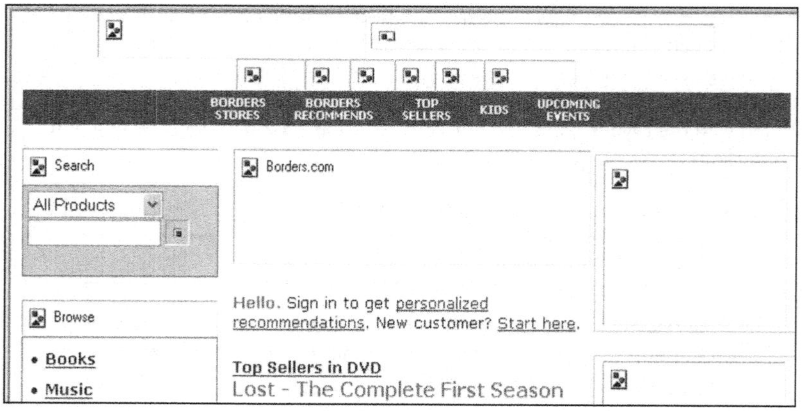

Figure 5-12. Viewing Borders.com with images off in Internet Explorer 6

When you want to turn off images in Netscape (7.2), select Edit ➤ Preferences. In the Preferences dialog box, select (double-click) the Privacy & Security category, and in the resulting submenu, select Images. In the Images dialog box, select the Do not load any images radio button. Now Netscape will not load any images. But there is a fundamental difference from the treatment with Internet Explorer. Images that have alternative text do not have rectangles around them, so if your page is done well (more in the next chapter), the Netscape view is even appealing, and the pages load very quickly. Figure 5-13 shows the top half of the www.priceline.com homepage viewed in Netscape 7.2 with images off.

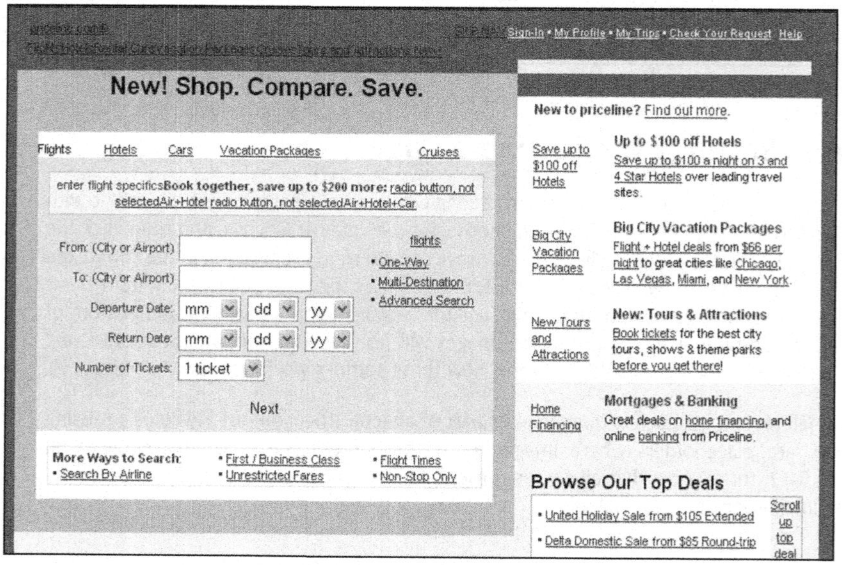

Figure 5-13. Viewing Priceline.com with images off in Netscape 7.2

With Opera (8.51), you also can view the page without images by selecting View ➤ Images ➤ No Images. The effect is similar to Netscape; however, Opera displays a fine-lined box, so you can tell which text comes from the images.

With Firefox (1.5.0.1), select Tools ➤ Options ➤ Content and uncheck the Load Images check box. Similar to the treatment by Netscape, Firefox replaces each image with its alt-text if it is available. When the alt-text is not available, Firefox places a border around the place where the image would be.

Toolbars and Favelets

The newest tools for checking accessibility are favelets and favelet toolbars that display in-line information about a page. This is a lot like what the WAVE does, except it overcomes the problem of information overload that is found in the WAVE by targeting the markup of specific elements or issues. We will look at three of these tools: the Accessibility QA Favelet from WGBH (http://ncam.wgbh.org), the Web Accessibility Toolbar from Vision Australia (www.visionaustralia.org.au/), and the Section 508 Toolbar for Firefox from RampWEB (www.rampweb.com).

Each of these tools is a collection of what are called *favelets* or *bookmarklets*. These consist of code, usually JavaScript, which can analyze the current page open in the browser, temporarily change it, and report accessibility information, such as the alternative text or headings on the page. That code is saved as a favorite in Internet Explorer or bookmark in Netscape, which is the reason for the terminology (favelet or bookmarklet).

The NCAM Accessibility QA Favelet

The NCAM Accessibility QA Favelet is a single favelet available from the National Center for Accessible Media (NCAM, http://ncam.wgbh.org/webaccess/favelet/), authored by Andrew Kirkpatrick and Rich Caloggero. The NCAM favelet provides a number of functions. This favelet creates a form at the top of the current page with a drop-down menu of options and an Analyze submit button, as shown in the example in Figure 5-14.

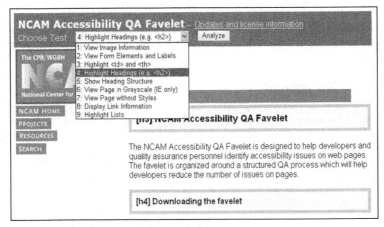

Figure 5-14. The NCAM Accessibility QA Favelet

I have applied the NCAM QA Favelet once, selecting Highlight Headings in the drop-down menu, and then clicking the Analyze button. As a result of that analysis, two headings are highlighted on the page (one h3 and one h4). After applying that transformation, I then opened the menu again for the purpose of the screenshot. Highlighting of lists, headings, and table markup is done in-page. The other options list information in a new window.

The Web Accessibility Toolbar

The Web Accessibility Toolbar (www.visionaustralia.org.au/info.aspx?page=619) was written by Steven Faulkner of Accessible Information Solutions (www.visionaustralia.org.au/). Whereas the NCAM favelet adds a menu to the page, the Web Accessibility Toolbar is a collection of menus, as shown in Figure 5-15. These provide three kinds of functions: information resources, other tools like the WAVE and W3C validation, and in-page markup or lists like those available with the NCAM Accessibility QA Favelet.

Figure 5-15. The Web Accessibility Toolbar

Figure 5-15 shows the Images menu with Show Images highlighted. I had already performed the Show Images operation on the Vision Australia page. The only foreground image visible in the figure is highlighted, and its alt text is displayed just above the image.

The Web Accessibility Toolbar is a rich collection of tools for people who want to conveniently explore the effects of accessibility or to carry out serious human reviews of pages for accessibility.

The Section 508 Toolbar

RampWEB (www.rampweb.com) offers a toolbar for both Internet Explorer and Firefox with functions similar to those of the Web Accessibility Toolbar, called The Section 508 Toolbar (www.rampweb.com/Accessibility_Resources/Section508/).

The basic human review functions of the Section 508 Toolbar mark up the page with icons, similar to those used by the WAVE. Figure 5-16 shows the 508 Accessibility Toolbar for Firefox. After I activated Display Tab Order and Display Headings, these functions were applied, so that each heading is highlighted and each tab stop is indicated with an icon and a number.

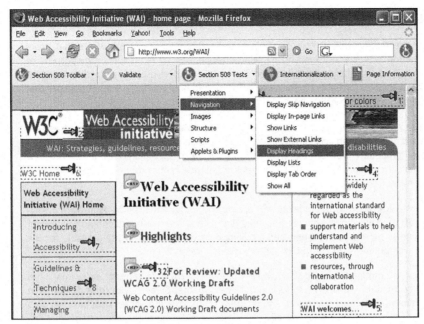

Figure 5-16. The Section 508 Toolbar from RampWEB

The following two icons appear in Figure 5-16:

  Indicates the tab order

Specifies the presence of an HTML heading, in this case <h1>

In addition to Display Headings and Display Tab Order, you can use the 508 Accessibility Toolbar to test forms, mark up lists, test images, and find online accessibility resources for web accessibility.

As I suggested at the beginning of this section, the favelets and toolbars that have become available recently are the best thing that has happened for experimenting with web accessibility and for human review of web page accessibility. Many other favelets and toolbars are available, including the Web Developer Extension toolbar (http://chrispederick.com/work/webdeveloper/) for Firefox, which stands out with more than 150 distinct functions. For accessibility with Firefox, however, the Section 508 Toolbar from RampWEB is superior.

Summary

The indirect requirements for accessible web development are mostly those that make information available to users who are blind through their screen readers. One purpose of this chapter was to help you understand how screen readers use a linearized text view of a page to speak information to their users. This should help you understand the issues that will be discussed at length in later chapters.

The chapter also discussed several ways in which a web developer or designer can use the standard browser as an accessibility checker. These ideas suggest "sniff tests" for the developer or procedures to be integrated into a quality assurance plan. Plus, it covered new accessibility checking favelets and toolbars that provide remarkably simple techniques to assist in the evaluation of web page accessibility.

The best verification of the indirect web accessibility requirements will result from involving professionals with disabilities who fully understand the assistive technology. Short of that, one or more screen readers and a talking browser should be made available for the web development team and the quality assurance process.

With even a moderately sized site, it is very difficult to check to see that every image has alt-text (Chapter 6) or that every form has a label (Chapter 8), even with tools described in this chapter. A number of software tools, both client side and server side, can test web content for the presence of accessibility features. We will explore the question of what can and cannot be tested by such tools and investigate five commercial testing tools in Chapter 13.

6 ACCESSIBLE CONTENT

by Jim Thatcher

The subject of accessibility on the Web can be divided into three main categories: accessible web content, accessible navigation, and accessible interaction. This chapter addresses the first of these: creating accessible content, including the text, images, and audio files that might be available on a web page. Accessible navigation is covered in Chapter 7, and accessible interaction is the subject of Chapter 8. In addition to these basic treatments of accessibility for the Web, see also the coverage of advanced topics, especially Cascading Style Sheets (CSS) in Chapter 9 and JavaScript in Chapter 10.

Content is accessible only if it can be "viewed" or accessed by people with disabilities. Besides getting the information from the page, people with disabilities must be able to use all the functions available to nondisabled users: links, buttons, form controls, and so on. Accessible content must be compatible with assistive technologies, particularly screen readers. There must be alternatives to pure visual content for people who can't see and alternatives to pure auditory content for people who can't hear.

To explain issues and solutions for accessibility, I will refer to four assistive technologies discussed in Chapter 5: one talking browser and three screen readers. The screen readers are Hal Version 6.5 (www.dolphincomputeraccess.com/); JAWS for Windows Version 7.0, by Freedom Scientific (www.freedomscientific.com); and Window-Eyes Version 5.5, by GW Micro (www.gwmicro.com/). The talking browser is IBM Home Page Reader Version 3.04 (www.ibm.com/able/hpr.html). All are intended to be used by people with very limited or no useful vision. As explained in Chapter 5, demonstration versions of these products are available from their respective websites.

Guidelines for Accessible Web Development

The two important sets of guidelines for accessible web development are the Web Content Accessibility Guidelines (WCAG) and the Section 508 Standards. In order to share in the wisdom of the corresponding community of experts and to give context to the discussion, each of the topics in this chapter will include a review of what the guidelines have to say on the subject. Here, I will provide an overview of these guidelines.

WCAG 1.0

WCAG 1.0, from the Web Accessibility Initiative (WAI, www.w3.org/WAI) of the World Web Consortium (W3C, www.w3.org) became an official Recommendation of the W3C on May 5, 1999. The WCAG consists of 14 guidelines, or principles of accessible design (www.w3.org/TR/WCAG10). Each guideline includes a set of checkpoints that explain how the guideline applies to web development. The checkpoints (www.w3.org/TR/WCAG10/full-checklist.html) are prioritized according to the following criteria:

> [Priority 1] A web content developer **must** satisfy this checkpoint. Otherwise, one or more groups will find it impossible to access information in the document. Satisfying this checkpoint is a basic requirement for some groups to be able to use web documents.

[Priority 2] A web content developer **should** satisfy this checkpoint. Otherwise, one or more groups will find it difficult to access information in the document. Satisfying this checkpoint will remove significant barriers to accessing web documents.

[Priority 3] A web content developer **may** address this checkpoint. Otherwise, one or more groups will find it somewhat difficult to access information in the document. Satisfying this checkpoint will improve access to web documents.

There are 65 checkpoints in all; 16 of them are Priority 1, 30 are Priority 2, and 19 are Priority 3.

WCAG 2.0

The 1999 WCAG is being revised by the WAI at the time of this writing. The WCAG revision process has taken about five years and entered "Last Call" on April 27, 2006. Last Call comments were allowed through late June. After processing Last Call comments, and assuming none are showstoppers, the WCAG Working Group will solicit and then verify WCAG 2.0 compliant websites. This testing phase will last about four months.

There are two dramatic differences between the first edition of these guidelines, WCAG 1.0, and the second edition, WCAG 2.0 (www.w3.org/TR/WCAG20). Like WCAG 1.0, the second edition is organized around guidelines. WCAG 2.0 includes 13 guidelines, and each contains a list of items similar to the checkpoints of WCAG 1.0 that are called *success criteria*. These are testable statements of what needs to be done to satisfy each guideline. These success criteria are technology-independent and thus very general. The generality is the first dramatic difference between WCAG 2.0 and WCAG 1.0 and it leads to wording like this:

> SC 2.4.4 Each link is programmatically associated with text from which its purpose can be determined.

Instead of this:

> 13.1 Clearly identify the target of each link. [Priority 2]

With more general constructs, the applicability is also generalized. Success Criterion 2.4.4 (as of Last Call) about link text also applies to server-side image maps requiring text links for each image map hotspot.

After you have become accustomed to the style and the vocabulary of the WCAG 2.0 document, the technology-neutral approach begins to make sense.

The second major difference between WCAG 1.0 and WCAG 2.0 is that the success criteria under each guideline are not prioritized by their importance or priority, as they were in

6

WCAG 1.0. Instead, they are ranked by the extent to which the web design and development process must be modified in order to meet the success criteria. The ranking is by levels, as follows (as defined at the time of this writing):

- Level 1 success criteria:

  1. Achieve a minimum level of accessibility.

  2. Can reasonably be applied to all web resources.

- Level 2 success criteria:

  1. Achieve an enhanced level of accessibility.

  2. Can reasonably be applied to all web resources.

- Level 3 success criteria:

  1. Achieve additional accessibility enhancements.

  2. Cannot necessarily be applied to all web resources.

Whereas Level A conformance with WCAG 1.0 required complying with all Priority 1 checkpoints, Level A conformance with WCAG 2.0 requires compliance with all Level 1 success criteria.

Read more about this very important set of guidelines in Chapter 14.

Section 508 Standards

The U.S. Access Board (www.access-board.gov) has issued access standards (www.access-board.gov/508.htm) for federal electronic and information technology as required under Section 508 of the Rehabilitation Act: *The Electronic and Information Technology Accessibility Standards, 36 CFR Part 1194, Web-based Intranet and Internet Information and Applications* (1194.22). The Access Board has also published an online guide (www.access-board.gov/sec508/guide) for all the standards. This guide site is the easiest route to view the 16 provisions of the Section 508 Standards for the Web.

The force of the Section 508 Standards is that electronic and information technology purchased by the U.S. federal government must comply with these provisions. Because of that force of law, these provisions are seen as playing an important role in defining accessibility, especially in the U.S. There are additional applications of the Section 508 Standards. Several states, including my home state of Texas, use the Section 508 Standards as at least a reference for state accessibility requirements.

Many of the Section 508 provisions correspond to Priority 1 WCAG checkpoints with minor changes for regulatory wording. Some of the Priority 1 checkpoints were deemed by the Access Board to be too restrictive on web development or too difficult to judge for compliance. In addition, the Section 508 Standards add provisions that combine WCAG 1.0 checkpoints of lower priorities, like the Section 508 provision for accessible forms.

The Association of Assistive Technology Act Projects (ATAP, www.ataporg.org/) sponsored a detailed side-by-side comparison (www.jimthatcher.com/sidebyside.htm) of the Section 508 provisions and the Priority 1 WCAG 1.0 checkpoints. In the same spirit, I have compiled a mapping from the Section 508 Standards to the WCAG 2.0 success criteria, which you can find at www.jimthatcher.com/508wcag2.htm.

This chapter will address the individual WCAG guidelines and Section 508 web accessibility provisions, and show how each one can be met.

Using Text Equivalents for Images

The one accessibility issue that is probably more important than all others is providing text information for web content that is nontextual. Nontext items include images, image maps, image buttons, audio files, and multimedia files that provide both audio and video.

The reason text is so important is that people with sensory disabilities have ways of accessing text even if they are unable to access the nontext content. If there is a textual equivalent for an image, users who are blind will be able to listen to that text with their screen reader or talking browser. Most images on web pages are simple, and so their text equivalents are simple, too. Even when the images carry more information—as with charts or graphs—there are techniques for conveying that information textually.

A person with impaired hearing may find it difficult or impossible to get information from an audio file. The text equivalent of an audio file is a word-for-word transcript. The transcript can be read by itself or viewed while listening to the audio. In this way, the person who is hearing impaired can get the equivalent information. (See the "Using Text Equivalents for Audio" section later in this chapter.)

It would be convenient if there were a mechanism for creating some sort of word-for-word transcript of an image, but, of course, there is no such thing. Therefore, the process of providing adequate and useful alternative text for images—text that does not overburden the user—requires judgment and style.

Guidelines and Standards for Text Equivalents

One measure of the perceived importance of the text equivalents can be gleaned from the fact that the requirement for text equivalents is the first item in most guideline lists.

WCAG 1.0

The first checkpoint in the WAI WCAG deals with providing text equivalents for nontext elements.

> 1.1 Provide a text equivalent for every non-text element (for example, via "alt", "longdesc", or in element content). This includes: images, graphical representations of text (including symbols), image map regions, animations (for example, animated GIFs), applets and programmatic objects, ascii art, frames, scripts, images used as list bullets, spacers, graphical buttons, sounds (played with or without user interaction), stand-alone audio files, audio tracks of video, and video.

This checkpoint from the Guidelines Working Group of the WAI lists more types of nontext elements than we will be considering in this chapter. Applets, programming objects, and scripts can often be very textual. The issues with these kinds of content are much more serious than suggested by including them among the candidates for alternative text. Applets and programmatic objects, frames, scripts, and multimedia will be covered elsewhere in this book.

There are also duplications in the WCAG list of nontext elements. Images, graphical representations of text, animations, images used as list bullets, and spacers are all instances of uses of the img element. The classification of nontext elements I'll use in this chapter is discussed in the upcoming "Classification of Images" section.

Section 508

The first provision of the Section 508 Standards for web content accessibility is very similar to the WCAG, but without the "This includes" remarks.

§1194.22(a) A text equivalent for every non-text element shall be provided (e.g., via "alt", "longdesc", or in element content).

The guide for this provision (www.access-board.gov/sec508/guide/1194.22.htm#(a)) includes mention of most of the examples included in WCAG Checkpoint 1.1. The Access Board guide also mentions "check boxes" in the discussion of nontext elements, which, I think, is an error.

WCAG 2.0

The WCAG 2.0 success criteria for text equivalents (version as of Last Call) help us understand how to write alt-text. Here is the main guideline and corresponding success criterion (SC):

Guideline 1.1 Provide text alternatives for all non-text content.

SC 1.1.1 For all non-text content, one of the following is true:

- If non-text content presents information or responds to user input, text alternatives serve the same purpose and present the same information as the non-text content. If text alternatives cannot serve the same purpose, then text alternatives at least identify the purpose of the non-text content.

- If non-text content is multimedia; live audio-only or live video-only content; a test or exercise that must use a particular sense; or is primarily intended to create a specific sensory experience; then text alternatives at least identify the non-text content with a descriptive text label. (For multimedia, see also, Guideline 1.2 Provide synchronized alternatives for multimedia.)

- If the purpose of non-text content is to confirm that content is being operated by a person rather than a computer, different forms are provided to accommodate multiple disabilities.

- If non-text content is pure decoration, or used only for visual formatting, or if it is not presented to users, it is implemented such that it can be ignored by assistive technology.

Note that the success criteria are numbered with the guideline and an index. So, SC 1.1.1 is the first success criterion for Guideline 1.1.

It is refreshing that these success criteria do a very good job in elaborating on and explaining how Section 508 §1194.22(a) and WCAG 1.0 Checkpoint 1.1 should be handled. SC 1.1.1 covers information-bearing images, for which the alt-text should convey the same information as the image. Here is a sample from www.borders.com.

But image buttons, image links, and image map hotspots are also covered by SC 1.1.1. If the image has text like About us or Go, then the alt-text should be the same. If the image is a question mark that opens a help screen, then the alt-text should be "help" (the purpose of the image link). WCAG 2.0 recognizes that there will be places where it does not make sense to try to provide a text equivalent, and SC 1.1.1 says to identify the purpose of that nontext content. The last clause of SC 1.1.1 covers formatting or spacer images, where alt="" is appropriate for XHTML.

Classification of Images

Most of the pictures we see on web pages are images, including animated GIFs. There are also images we do not see, so-called *spacer* images, which may be used for formatting purposes when tables are used for layout.

Text equivalents for images are provided through the alt attribute, which is a required attribute on the <img> tag. For example, consider the following image link:

Here is the code for this link:

```
<a href=". . .><img src= "go.gif" width="21" height="21" alt= "go" />
</a>
```

Every img element must have alternative text specified in the alt attribute. That text is referred to as *alt-text*. As specified in SC1.1.1, alt-text should convey the information in the image or the purpose (function) of the image.

Let's look at the different types of images.

Image Links

An image link is an image inside an anchor tag, <a>, like the following simple example of a logo at the top of a commercial page (www.corda.com).

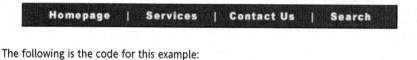

Here is the code for this image link:

```
<a href="http://www.corda.com/" >
  <img src="images/logobutton2.gif" alt="Home"  ... />
</a>
```

In an earlier version of the page, the Corda logo had alt="Corda Logo", which I accepted without comment, but that alt-text is not really correct. The alt-text should specify the *function* of the link, and "Corda logo" is not the function of the link. It could be alt="Home page" or possibly alt="Corda home page". But "page" is redundant (we don't say "contact us page"), as is "Corda", because what other homepage would it be? And we just heard "Corda" from the page title. The bottom line is that alt="Home" is the correct choice for the alt-text.

Image Map Hotspots

A client-side image map is an image (img element) with the usemap attribute whose value is the name of a map element. Here is an example of a client-side image map with four hotspots:

The following is the code for this example:

```
<img src="banner.gif" width="500" alt="navigation banner"
    usemap="#banner" />
<map name="banner" id="banner">
  <area href="home.htm" alt="homepage"
        shape="rect" coords="0,0 110,24" />
  <area href="services.htm" alt="services"
        shape="rect" coords="111,0 215,24" />
  <area href="comntact.htm" alt="contact us"
        shape="rect" coords="216,0 326,24" />
  <area href="search.htm" alt="search"
        shape="rect" coords="327,0 435,24" />
</map>
```

Image Buttons

An image button is an input element with type="image". The following shows a typical image button.

The source for the image is specified with the src attribute of the input element:

```
<input type="image" src= "llogon.gif" alt="log on" />
```

Decorative and Formatting Images

Some images are primarily for visual appeal, serving as decoration, or sometimes they carry absolutely no information, as is the case with spacer images used for formatting. For this type of image, alt="" is appropriate:

```
<img src="images/1-pix.gif" width="1" height="1" alt="" />
```

Charts and Graphs

Some images carry a lot of information—more than can reasonably be placed in alt-text—and they require special accommodation. Here is an example:

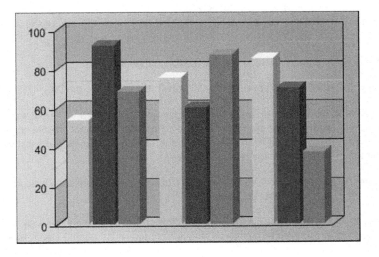

The following is the code used for the sample chart image:

```
<img src="images/bargraph.gif" width="400" height="250"
        alt="bar graph of results for three groups"
        longdesc="bargraph.htm" />
```

6

Accessible Image Links

Images that play some active role in the navigation of the site must have meaningful and simple alt-text. Without that text, users with disabilities will not be able to navigate or otherwise interact with your site. Since a user who is blind will be listening to the links, it is very important to make those alternative text strings simple and short while still clear.

Typical of this kind of image are the ones that look like buttons for navigation. Here is an example:

This image typifies groups of images that look like the horizontal tabs on file folders. Here is what the code for this image *should* look like:

```
<img src="video-tab.gif" width="39" ...alt="Electronics" />
```

I say "should" because this simple image actually does not have any alternative text at all on the site where it was found. Since there is no alt-text on the image on the subject site, a screen reader must try to hunt for some information about the image elsewhere in order to try to convey the target of the link.

When there is no alt-text, different assistive technologies look in different places: sometimes the href attribute of the anchor tag (<a>), and sometimes the src or the name attribute.

Here is the href attribute (in elided form) for the link in this case:

```
href="exec/obidos/tg/browse/-/172282/ref=tab_gw_e_4/104-9411283-476802"
```

Because values of href attributes are often very long and complicated (as in this case), with many initial segments that are redundant and do not carry information, IBM Home Page Reader tries to pick a part of the href that is shorter and will hopefully carry some information to the user. Here is the result in this case:

- **Home Page Reader:** "ref equal tab underscore g w underscore e underscore 4 divided by 104 minus 9411283 minus 476802"

I have spelled out the way Home Page Reader reads this href to underscore how ugly it is. The numbers are also spoken as numbers: "nine million, four hundred and eleven thousand, two hundred and eighty three." This is not only meaningless, it is painful. The visually impaired Home Page Reader user will not be able to participate in this navigation.

Hal users are better off because they only have to listen to the numbers!

- **Hal:** "104 minus 9411283 minus 476802 not visited link press insert to click"

Things are different for the Window-Eyes user, but they are not better. They get to hear the whole `href`, without punctuation and reading only digits instead of spelled-out numbers.

- **Window-Eyes:** "link exec obidos tg browse 172282 ref = tab g w e 4 104 9411283 476802"

JAWS for Windows takes a different approach, which, in this case, is more helpful. It tries to read a part of the `src` attribute of the image. Here is the `src` attribute (slightly elided):

```
src="http://.../G/01/nav/personalized/tabs/electronics-off-sliced.gif"
```

The part that JAWS reads contains valuable information but it is cluttered with meaningless stuff; however, the keyword, *electronics*, is present!

- **JAWS:** "Link graphic tabs slash electronics dash off dash sliced"

The fact that there is anything good about what JAWS speaks is the result of fortune rather than foresight, and it is still far from ideal! Accessibility should never rely on the use of comprehensible filenames in your web page (not that they are a bad idea, but clear and simple alt-text is the real answer). Because this page does not have alt-text where it needs it, the link becomes completely incomprehensible for the Home Page Reader, Hal, and Window-Eyes users, and even JAWS users are left guessing.

After pulling this terribly inaccessible example into pieces, let's look at a simple example of a nicely accessible image link. This is a common button-like navigation link (on www.evite.com), which is basically a picture of text tailored and refined by graphic designers and then sealed in pixels.

All of the images of text raise a serious problem. If an Internet Explorer user wants to adjust text size for more comfortable viewing (View ➤ Text size ➤ Largest), it will have no effect on these images. Opera's text enlargement (View ➤ Zoom ➤ 200%) does work with images. When you use images of text, be sure to use large fonts and adequate contrast. By the way, the sample image link here fails all the measures of contrast; see the "Color Contrast" section later in this chapter.

This image link is correctly coded with the alt-text, `"Planning Ideas"`, which matches the text in the image and the function of the image link.

```
<a href="/app/home/viewPlanningHome.do">
    <img id="plan" src="/images/nav/orng.gif" ...alt="Planning Ideas" />
</a>
```

6

Each assistive technology handles this link in pretty much the same way—in the way that the web author intended and the way that the user can understand. Here are the results:

- **Hal:** "Planning Ideas, not visited link, press insert to click"
- **Home Page Reader:** "[Planning Ideas]"
- **Window-Eyes:** "Link Planning Ideas"
- **JAWS:** "Link Graphic Planning Ideas"

The fact that an item is a link is indicated with Home Page Reader speaking in a female voice (with default settings). In the text view, Home Page Reader displays alt-text in square brackets. Hal, Window-Eyes, and JAWS all speak some variation of the word "link" together with the alt-text, Planning Ideas.

This is why alt-text for images is so very important: because the necessary information is quickly and clearly conveyed to the user. It is also important for website owners, because without it, visitors who use screen readers or talking browsers will not be able to use or even understand their site.

The Role of Positional Information or Context

Often, context provides information that is not available to a screen reader user listening to links. (This topic is also addressed in the discussion of link text in Chapter 7 and the discussion of forms in Chapter 8.)

Consider the following part of a checkout procedure at Amazon.com.

You could save $30 today with the Amazon.com Visa® Card :

Your current subtotal:	$61.13
Amazon Visa discount:	- $30.00
Your new subtotal:	$31.13

Find out how

The natural alt-text for the image link is alt="find out how" (the fact that Amazon has no alt-text on this image is not the point). If that were the case, when blind users listened to links, all they would hear is "Find out how." How to do what? This is a case where the alt-text on the image can easily and conveniently solve this context problem: alt="Find out how to save $30 with the Amazon Visa Card".

Accessible Image Map Hotspots

The importance of text equivalents for image map hotspots is just as great as that for image links. The difference is the form that these client-side image maps take.

An Accessible Client-Side Image Map

Let's begin with an accessible client-side image map instead of an inaccessible one—it's more fun that way. The following is an image from the University of Arizona Web Resources Page (as it was in 2001).

This image is specified in the HTML code as an img element with the usemap attribute, as follows:

```
<img src=" . . ." alt="Web Resources at The University of Arizona" ...
        usemap="#banner" />
```

Notice that the image does have an alt attribute, but the image itself is not the important accessibility issue. In the University of Arizona website case, the image has alt-text that corresponds to the text on the image, which is good, in principle. But that text is repeated as image map hotspots. I tend towards the idea of using alt="" on the image itself, since it is not active and conveys no information beyond the hotspots.

Then the <map> tag with name="banner" specifies areas of the image that will be hotspots. In this example, all the areas are simple rectangles (shape="rect"):

```
<map name="banner" id="banner">
  <area shape="rect" alt="UA Web Resources Homepage"
        coords="10,05 90,75" href=" ..." />
  <area shape="rect" alt="UA Homepage" coords="95,05 360,35"
        href=" ..." />
  <area shape="rect" alt="Search" coords="260,52 305,70"
        href=" ..." />
  <area shape="rect" alt="Comments & questions" coords="311,52 37,70"
        href=" ..." />
  <area shape="rect" alt="Web Resources Homepage"
        coords="385,52 502,70" href=" ..." />
  <area shape="rect" alt="UA Homepage" coords="515,52 572,70"
        href=" ..." />
</map>
```

> *A* map *element can be placed anywhere on the page. Its position is irrelevant to the position of the image, but the hotspot links will appear in the reading order where the* area *elements appear.*

6

The six hotspot rectangles specified by the area elements in the map surround the text headings in the image. Each rectangle is given by x/y pixel coordinates, where (0,0) is the top left and, in this case, (588, 81) is the bottom right.

If you had visited the University of Arizona site (the image map is no longer there) or if you visit any site with image maps using a traditional browser like Internet Explorer or Netscape, you may be able to see the href of the different areas in the browser status window as you move the mouse around the image. The tooltip also changes to the alt-text of the area element. In parts of the image that are not designated as hotspots, the status window goes blank and the tooltip changes to the alt-text of the image. (As discussed in Chapter 7, much more complicated client-side maps are possible, such as a map of the U.S.)

Assistive technology can cope with a correctly implemented image map just as well as it does with normal links (text or image). Home Page Reader does an even better job because only the number of links in the map is announced initially, so as not to burden the listener when the screen reader is just reading the page. If you want to hear the actual hotspots, you just stop and step through them with the arrow keys. This is the way they sound:

- **Home Page Reader:**
  - "(Start of map with 6 items.)"
  - "[UA Web Resources Homepage]"
  - "[UA Homepage]"
  - "[Search]"
  - "[Comments & Questions]"
  - "[Web Resources Homepage]"
  - "[UA Homepage]"
  - "(End of Map.)"

> *For sighted people using Home Page Reader as an analytical tool to check their websites for accessibility, it is convenient to see all the text, including the links within image maps. You can do this by moving the focus to the text area and pressing Ctrl+A to highlight the entire text view. Home Page Reader will then load all of the text and highlight it. If you want to make a copy, you can press Ctrl+C to copy the entire text view to the clipboard, and then press Ctrl+V to paste it into another application. That is what I did here in order to display the links corresponding to the areas of the sample image map shown here.*

Using Home Page Reader, the value of the alt attribute is always displayed within square brackets, [ ]. So-called *metatext*, which is text that is generated by Home Page Reader and does not appear on the page, is enclosed in parentheses, as in "(End of Map.)".

Window-Eyes, Hal, and JAWS all treat image map links with alt-text just like any other kind of link. This makes sense because, in function, image map links are no different from any other kind of link, and so they should not be treated differently when spoken.

Style of Alternative Text

The choice of specific alternative text is a matter of style and judgment. For the six areas of the client-side image map shown in the previous section, I would use alt-text that is the same as that on the image, except where it makes sense to make it *shorter*. Here is a comparison of the alt-text that the developers at the University of Arizona used and what I would recommend instead:

Text in Image	Actual Alt-Text	Suggested Alt-Text
Web Resources	UA Web Resources Homepage	Web resources
The University of Arizona	UA Homepage	U of A
Search	Search	Search
Comments	Comments & questions	Comments
Web Resources Home	Web Resources Home	Web Resources
UA Home	UA Home	U of A

The reason I prefer shorter alt-text is that people using a screen reader must sit and listen to all this. When sighted people look at the text on an image, they have the ability to filter out the "visual noise" and focus on the main concept. It is true that this is still possible when you have to listen to the content, but it is more difficult.

I tend to avoid "homepage" when identifying links. If the link says "The University or Arizona" or "IBM," I know it is going to the respective homepage, so "homepage" is redundant.

Bearing in mind the importance of conciseness when considering alt-text, it is not surprising that my preference is "U of A" over "University of Arizona." But why, you may ask, "U of A" over "UA"? That comes from my experience with screen readers occasionally *pronouncing* abbreviations like UA (or IBM for that matter) instead of spelling them out. If "UA" is pronounced, it truly fails in conveying the desired information. In this case, it turns out that all of the assistive technologies discussed here spelled out "UA" rather than pronouncing it, probably because it is capitalized. However, since there are other voice-assistive technologies available, it is best to adopt a safe approach.

Sometimes web designers prefer to see longer mouse-over tooltip text than the alt-text so that the mouse user gets more information than that on the image. To do this, you keep the alt-text the same as the image text and put the longer text in the title attribute of the anchor element. With Internet Explorer, this trick works for links, but it does not work for the area elements. Only Internet Explorer displays the alt-text as a tooltip. Firefox and Opera display the title attribute; Opera adds the prefix Title:.

An Inaccessible Client-Side Image Map

As an example of an inaccessible image map, consider this Yahoo! banner image from late 2001.

> You may be interested in how to find such older pages. Try the Wayback Machine (www.archive.org), where you can get archived copies of most sites. Unfortunately, the site seems to have stopped saving pages in mid 2005, but there is still an incredible amount of history available—approximately 40 billion pages!

This banner image looks like it contains text—Finance, Messenger, Check Email, What's New, Personalize, and Help—but it doesn't. The text under each button-looking image is made to look like link text, but it is really part of the image. For mouse users, the text works like a link because the banner is an image map. Had the Yahoo! developers decided to add alt-text to the area elements as follows, the image map would work just like a list of text links for a blind user as well (in fact, that is exactly what they did in mid 2002).

```
<map name=m>
    <area coords="0,0,52,52" href=r/a1 alt="Finance" />
    <area coords="53,0,121,52" href=r/p1 alt="Messenger" />
    <area coords="122,0,191,52" href=r/m1 alt="Check Email" />
    <area coords="441,0,510,52" href=r/wn alt="What's New" />
    <area coords="511,0,579,52" href=r/i1 alt="Personalize" />
    <area coords="580,0,637,52" href=r/hw alt="Help" />
</map>
```

The Yahoo! page was designed with efficiency in mind. The web designers tried to minimize the download time by reducing the number of characters on the page; however, the additional text that makes the navigation banner solidly accessible amounts to only 186 bytes—less than 0.6 percent of the size of the page—and increases the download time by only about 0.05 seconds, even on a slow modem.

Without the alt-text, all the assistive technologies were stuck with the meaningless href information like r/11, r/p1, and so on. To make matters worse in this case, Hal adds the full URL http://www.yahoo.com in front of the href. But that has all passed; Yahoo! did it right eventually, and currently the site doesn't even use an image map for the banner.

Accessible Image Buttons

Image buttons are `input` elements with `type="image"`. The idea is to create something more interesting and eye-catching than the standard push buttons. Here are examples of a search button from IBM and a simple text-based submit button.

The code for image button is as follows:

```
<input type="image" src="isearch.gif" ,,,  alt="Search" />
```

Obviously, the key again is `alt="Search"`. When screen readers encounter an image button, they treat it much like a push button (command button) and use the alt-text instead of the value. Here is the code for the submit button.

```
<input type="submit" name="Search" value="Search" />
```

Hal, JAWS, and Window-Eyes don't distinguish between the two buttons (which is appropriate). Home Page Reader says "search image button" and "search submit button," respectively.

It is interesting to notice the difference in the ordering of the information presented. Window-Eyes says "button search," while Hal, JAWS, and Home Page Reader all, in effect, say "search button." A strategy for communicating with speech synthesis is to rank the importance of the specific information and speak the most important first. To me, in this case, the most important information is the label, Search. The fact that it is a button is secondary.

> *As one tabs through active elements with a talking browser or a screen reader, the new item cancels the speaking of the previous one. As soon as you hear enough information to know you are not interested, you can press Tab again, and the speech of that item is stopped and the next one started. In this case, if you hear "button" first, you have to wait to hear "search" (Window-Eyes) before you can move along. On the other hand, if you hear "search" first and are not interested in searching, you can move on right away. This observation can be applied to multiple-word alt-text, encouraging the placement of the "most important" words first.*

6

Here is another image button, this time without alternative text.

Here is the code for the button with some minor changes:

```
<input type="image" value="Go" src=" ...images/go-button.gif" />
```

In the case of Window-Eyes and Home Page Reader, the careful listener might be able to guess the purpose of the image button because the source filename is go-button.gif. Hal uses the entire source URL, including the main domain, which makes picking out the name difficult. Surprisingly, JAWS finds the value attribute and speaks "Go button." The value attribute provides the text equivalent for submit buttons, so it is natural that JAWS would look there.

Using alt="Go" would make life so much easier with all the screen readers. The simple change of adding alt="Go" makes such a total difference—the difference between gibberish and smooth sailing.

Because many, if not most, active images on the Web today do *not* have a text equivalent, users of screen readers must try to find other ways to interpret those images, and these rarely produce comprehensible results. It is a discouraging and frustrating experience, and it certainly does not make sense for business.

A few screen reader users do find ingenious ways of coping with sites that lack the most basic accessibility considerations. However, they make up only a small percentage of blind users; most struggle through like the rest of us. If web designers make their sites accessible, all those potential customers can have an experience that is comfortable and supportive, rather than frustrating and annoying.

Treatment of Formatting and Decorative Images

In the preceding sections, I have raised issues of judgment and style on the nature of the alternative text used for active images. Some of these are minor issues; for example, whether to use two or three words. However, everyone agrees that for active images, you always use words. When it comes to images used for decoration, there are some more substantial differences of opinion.

So, let's begin with one area where there is no disagreement: images used purely for formatting.

Spacer Images

Spacer images are the small "clear GIFs," with filenames like clear.gif, c.gif, or spacer.gif. They are typically placed in otherwise empty table cells so that those cells do not appear empty to the browser. They ensure consistent formatting of layout tables in different browsers.

These spacer images should always have null alt-text. This means using alt="" (two quotes and no space). Although everyone agrees that formatting images should be treated this way, some still continue to write alt=" " (quote, space, quote).

What is wrong with quote, space, quote? First, to a mathematician and logician, null alt-text means null alt-text—that is, *none*. Quote, space, quote is something; it is one space. Quote, quote is nothing. Second, and confirming the first point, if you use alt=" " (quote, space, quote) for your image, Internet Explorer will display the tooltip, [ ]. If you write alt="", Internet Explorer will not display anything.

An example of good practice with handling formatting images can be found on the Department of Defense (DOD) homepage (www.defenselink.mil/), which has *70* instances of spacer.gif in various places for formatting purposes. The code looks like this:

```
<img src="/home/images/spacer.gif" alt="" width="10" height="18" />
```

Figure 6-1 shows part of the DOD home page with 25 of the formatting images highlighted in medium gray rectangles (red in the original).

Figure 6-1. The Department of Defense homepage with formatting images (indicated here with rectangles)

You can check out formatting images using the WAVE tool discussed in Chapter 5. Submit the URL to www.wave.webaim.org/. The WAVE inserts the following graphic everywhere it finds an image with null alt-text:

Other Formatting Images

Other images are used only for visual effect and should also be assigned empty alt-text. Figure 6-2 shows part of an IBM page (from 2001), which has a number of these formatting images.

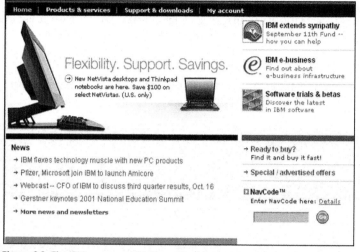

Figure 6-2. The IBM.com page with formatting images

In Figure 6-2, the small, black right-facing arrows down the left side, in the News section, indicate list items, as they do on the right side. When special images are used instead of the bullets in bulleted lists, as you see on this page, it is the author's decision whether to use alt="" or, say, alt="bullet" or alt="item". Certainly, you do *not* want to lengthen the alt-text with words like alt="small right arrow" or alt="right facing arrow", because the information content of the graphic is at most "bullet" or "item," and it is just plain burdensome to have to listen to such descriptions over and over. The IBM site uses alt="" for all the graphical bullets, which is the way I would do it as well.

There are more images on the IBM page in Figure 6-2 that should (and do) have alt="", including the faint lines between items on the right (dotted_rule_197pc.gif) and the arrow graphic:

To repeat, I would use empty alt-text for these graphic arrows indicating list items because nothing is gained by hearing "Bullet ready to buy?," "Bullet special / advertising offers," and so on. But there *is* something to be gained by marking up these bulleted lists *as* HTML unordered lists. Those HTML lists can be styled with your favorite bullet symbol, and the issue of alt-text doesn't even come up. In this way, users of assistive technology will hear lists announced in a way that is familiar to them, and they will navigate the lists in a familiar way as well.

Images That Repeat Textual Information

Another issue that the IBM site shown in Figure 6-2 demonstrates well is images that repeat textual information. Notice that near the top of the right side of Figure 6-2 are three items, each of which has an image followed by text: IBM extends sympathy, IBM e-business, and Software trials & betas. Here is what Home Page Reader speaks for these three highlights:

- **Home Page Reader:**
  - "link: [IBM extends sympathy.]"
  - "link: IBM extends sympathy"
  - "link: September 11th Fund - - Find out how you can help"
  - "link: [IBM e-business.]"
  - "link: IBM e-business"
  - "link: Find out about e-business infrastructure"
  - "link: [Software trials & betas.]"
  - "link: Software trials and betas"
  - "link: Discover the latest in IBM software"

Notice the repetition of the link text. First, the image has alt-text (within the square brackets), IBM extends sympathy. Then there is the text, identical to the alt-text of the image, which is also a link. Next, there is the descriptive text, saying more about the link. All three links have the same target, so effectively, there are three links in a row with the same target, and two with repeated text. How did this come about? An abbreviated fragment of the code will help to explain.

```
<tr><td . . .>
<a href=X. . .>
         <img src=". . .UnitedWay.gif" alt="IBM extends sympathy " />
</a></td>
<td. . .><a href= "X...">IBM extends sympathy </a> <br />
         <a href= "X..."> September 11th Fund - -<br />
                   Find out how you can help</a>
</td>
...</tr>
```

The best thing to do in a case like this is to combine the image with the text, all within one anchor tag, and then give the image alt="". This is the *only* situation where an active image could have null alt-text—when there is text there anyway. Essentially the code should look like this:

```
<a href= "X...">
    <img src="... UnitedWay" alt="" ... /> <br />
    IBM extends sympathy
</a>
```

This idea works for the second two links in each group. They can and should be combined, but it won't work to combine the image with the text, because as you can see from the original code shown earlier, the image and the text are in different table cells and the anchor element is not allowed to span table cells (or contain table data tags, <td>).

There are two possible solutions to this problem. You could change the layout so that the image and the text are in the same table cell. In this way, the anchor tag can include both pieces of text and the image. Since there is some text in the anchor, using alt="" on the image is fine. Alternatively, don't include the image in the anchor, make it inactive, and simply use alt="" on the image.

> One practice that is remarkably common and should always be avoided is putting alt="" on an image that is a link. Never use null alt-text on an image that is a link, unless text explaining the target of the link is contained in the same anchor.

Decorative Images

One last category of images that may have null alt-text is the decorative image that is just "eye-candy." Figure 6-3 shows part of a Corda Technologies web page (www.corda.com) with an example of such an image.

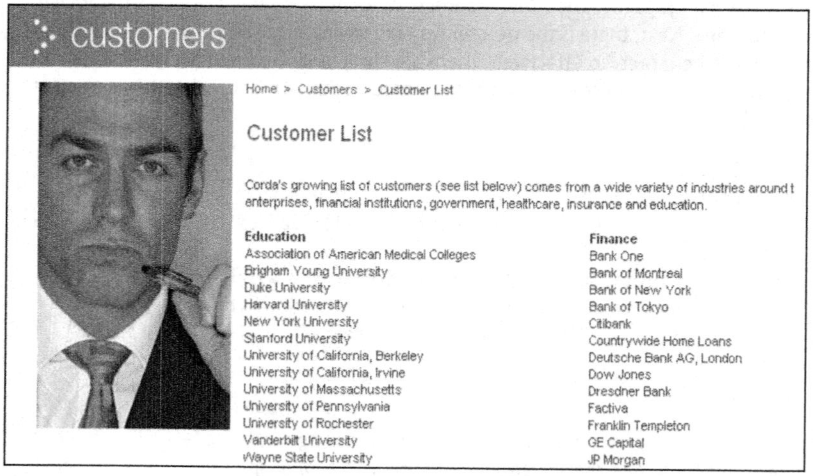

Figure 6-3. A page with an image that does not carry information

I think the picture of a man holding a pen is supposed to symbolize a thoughtful and careful customer. So you might use alt="thoughtful and careful customer" for that image. So then, if you listened to the page, you would hear "Customers thoughtful and careful customer home > customers customer list." That does not make sense, and it is long-winded besides.

For any such image, there are probably just as many accessibility experts who would want to use non-null alt-text as those who would say to use alt="". But I come down strongly on the side that such eye-candy images convey no information whatsoever, so alt="" precisely describes the information conveyed!

Treatment of Images That Carry a Lot of Information

It is easy (at least it should be easy) to decide on alt-text for image links and image map hotspots because the information of the image is the function of the link—that is, where the link will go, like alt="home", alt="products", or alt="services". It is also easy when images convey no information; just put alt=""! But sometimes, there is more information in the image than the concise alt attribute should hold.

It is a pretty standard recommendation that alt-text should have fewer than 150 characters—a number that first appeared because JAWS cut off alt-text at 150 characters. I think alt-text of 150 characters is too long.

Images that typically require more than alt-text are graphs, PowerPoint slides as images, or charts like the pie chart shown in Figure 6-4.

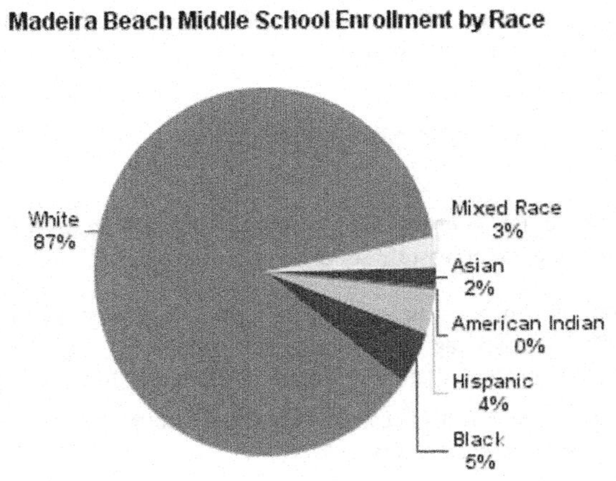

Madeira Beach Middle School Enrollment by Race

Figure 6-4. A pie chart showing middle school enrollment by race

What is the information in the pie chart in Figure 6-4? You could write out that information as follows:

"The enrollment by race at Madeira Middle School is 87% White, 5% Black, 4% Hispanic, 3% Mixed Race, 2% Asian, and 0% American Indian."

That is 132 characters, so some might allow that as alt-text, but I wouldn't, because it is too long. The information given in a sentence could just as well be given in a data table, like this:

Madeira Beach Middle School Enrollment by Race

Race	Percent
White	87%
Black	5%
Hispanic	4%
Mixed Race	3%
Asian	2%
American Indian	0%

Some hold the idea that a pie chart like the one in Figure 6-4 is conveying more information than that relayed by the corresponding data table. The message in the pie chart is something like this:

"The enrollment by race at Madeira Middle School is mostly White with other races less than 13% combined."

So that's the idea about the "information in the image." But how do we convey that information in XHTML? There are at least three ways:

- The description can be included in a file, which is referenced in the `longdesc` attribute of the `<img>` tag, like `longdesc="longdescriptions.html#piechart1"`. The information presented this way will be available only to screen reader users.
- The long description HTML file can be referenced through a link in the body of the page so that everyone can access it.
- The long description may literally be part of the body, as done on the Yahoo! News Photos page, shown in Figure 6-5. For example, you might have a sentence introducing the pie chart: The pie chart shows the enrollment by race at Madeira Middle School to be mostly White with other races all less than 13% combined.

> In the past, before the `longdesc` attribute was supported, I suggested using the d link as another way to handle long descriptions. The d link, placed next to the image, opened the long description file: `<a href="longdescription.htm#piechart1">d</a>`. The d link idea uses inadequate link text and repetitive link text, and the `longdesc` attribute is now supported. So, do not use the d link!

Figure 6-5. Yahoo news photos when enlarged have long descriptions included.

After you have decided on a way to convey the information of your complex image, don't forget to include alt-text for the image itself. Every image must have it. In the example in Figure 6-4, the alt-text might be as follows:

    alt="Pie chart of middle school enrollment by race"

The image in Figure 6-5 has alt="photo", which at first seems okay, but I would prefer alt="", because the information is conveyed by the text adjacent to the picture.

Summary for Text Equivalents for Images

Here is a summary of the main considerations for text equivalents for images:

- Every active image (image link, image map area, and image button) must have clear and succinct alt-text that conveys the function of the active element.
- Every inactive image must have a valid alt attribute conveying the information in the image.
- All images that are not active and do not convey information or are redundant should have alt=""; that is, null alt-text.
- If images contain information beyond what can be conveyed in a short alt attribute, use the long description attribute (longdesc) on the img element or in-line descriptions of the image that convey the same information the image conveys.

In an earlier publication, I randomly picked 10 of *PC Magazine*'s top 100 sites and analyzed them for missing alt-text. I listed the results of this unscientific survey as the number of images, image map hotspots, and image buttons that lacked alt-text. I thought that it would be interesting to see how these pages have changed. Table 6-1 shows the percentage of images (all types) that have alt-text for 2001 and 2006.

Table 6-1. Percentage of Images with Alt-Text

Site	2001	2006
About (www.about.com/)	8%	39%
Andale (www.andale.com/)	0%	58%
Bizrate (www.bizrate.com/)	89%	22%
Expert City (www.expertcity.com/)	15%	11%
Lonely Planet (www.lonelyplanet.com/)	74%	50%
Britannica (www.britannica.com/)	19%	79%
HotBot (www.hotbot.lycos.com/)	94%	100%
Schwab (www.schwab.com/)	77%	28%
Backflip (www.blackflip.com/)	94%	92%
MyPalm (www.palm.com/)	96%	88%

The unfortunate news from this (unscientific) study is that some sites improved, some completely changed (like HotBot), and others got worse, but there does not seem to be much of a trend. In 2001, the average for the 10 sites was 47 percent of their images included alt-text. In 2006, that was up to 57 percent. Remember that the alt attribute is a *required* attribute. Yet in 2006, only a little over half of the images on these sites had alt-text.

Using Text Equivalents for Audio

More and more audio is becoming part of the user experience on the Web. Most common types of streaming audio (RealPlayer, QuickTime, and Windows Media) provide access to news and events, while WAV files add sound to the user experience. If audio is decoration (sounds that the web author feels add to the experience of the site and do not carry information), then there is no need to add text equivalents for those sounds. Text equivalents are needed when audio includes spoken words—when the audio is in fact the message. To be accessible to people who are deaf or hearing-impaired, speeches or news reports need to have associated text transcripts.

Guidelines and Standards for Audio

As well as applying to the needs of users who are visually impaired, the Section 508 provision §1194.22(a) also applies to audio files:

§1194.22(a) A text equivalent for every non-text element shall be provided (for example, via "alt", "longdesc", or in element content).

WCAG Checkpoint 1.1 specifically applies to audio:

1.1 Provide a text equivalent for every non-text element (for example, via "alt", "longdesc", or in element content). This includes: . . . sounds (played with or without user interaction), stand-alone audio files, audio tracks of video, and video.

WCAG 2.0 does not change the picture as far as the transcripts are concerned, relying on the requirement that text equivalents be provided for nontext content.

Transcripts

Compared with the subtleties of text equivalents for images and the judgment required to decide on how much text will be adequate, it is refreshing to talk about text equivalents for audio, which are defined simply as *transcripts*. If you have audio information on your site, provide a link to a transcript of that audio.

There are few examples of websites that include transcripts with their audio content. One site is National Public Radio (NPR, www.npr.org/news/specials/mideast/transcripts). In the example in Figure 6-6, transcripts of programs on Mideast news are offered.

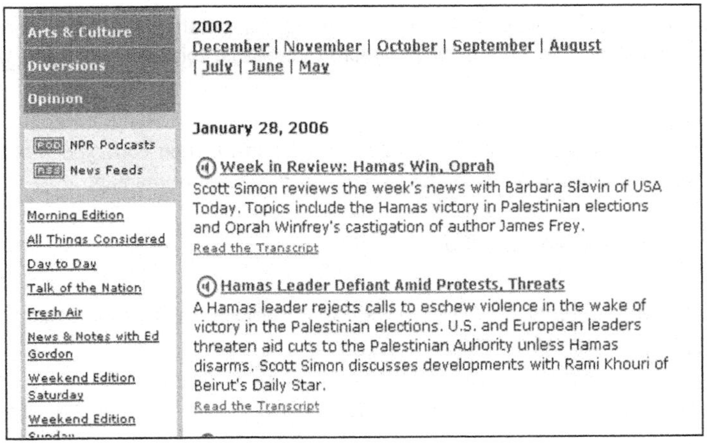

Figure 6-6. NPR offers transcripts of some of its stories.

Unfortunately, the transcripts of many of the NPR programs are only available for purchase, starting at $3.95 per broadcast (www.npr.org/transcripts/).

Using Color

Color may enhance the experience of visitors coming to a website. It can be eye-catching, add emphasis, or just add to the visual pleasure of the site. However, under some conditions, the use of color will make your website inaccessible to people who are not able to distinguish colors. Another issue regarding color is that of providing sufficient contrast for people with different types of color deficits or for people who are using monochrome displays.

Color to Convey Information

It is estimated that 1 in 20 visitors to a website will have some form of color vision deficiency and may find the website either difficult or impossible to use if color by itself is used to convey information. People who are color-blind (achromatopsia) will have difficulty finding the required fields if they are coded in red, as is often the case. If a library site indicates currently available books using only green text, color-blind visitors to the site will not know which books are available.

Isn't this an issue for users of the Web who are blind? It shouldn't be a problem, because screen readers can provide information about colors to their users; however, that color information is not provided by default, so screen reader users may also be left out when information is conveyed using color by itself.

It is good to use color to convey information. The key is not to use color *alone*.

All three of our sources of guidance have a top-level requirement that information not be conveyed by color alone. The Section 508 provisions require that color not be the sole way information is conveyed:

§1194.22(c) Web pages shall be designed so that all information conveyed with color is also available without color, for example from context or markup.

This is almost exactly the same wording as WCAG Priority 1 Checkpoint 2.1:

2.1 Ensure that all information conveyed with color is also available without color, for example from context or markup.

WCAG 2.0 addresses this color issue with the following level 1 success criterion (as of Last Call):

SC 1.3.2 Any information that is conveyed by color is also visually evident without color.

There are many ways that information, such as required fields in forms, can be conveyed with color and additional text or markup. Figure 6-7 shows a sample form where the required fields are visually highlighted with red, but prefaced with an asterisk as well.

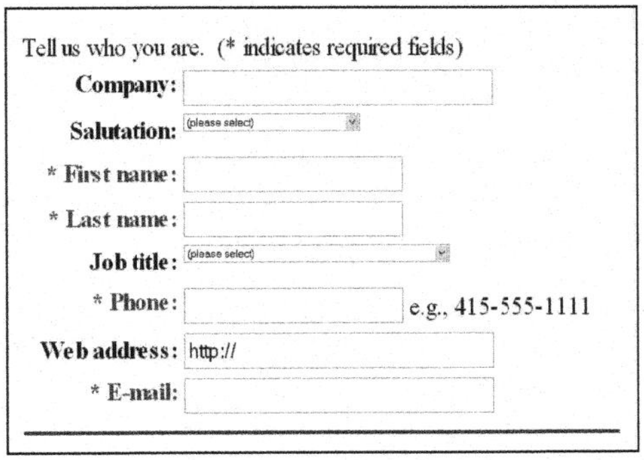

Figure 6-7. A form with required fields indicated by an asterisk

In the example in Figure 6-7, the asterisk precedes the label. This is by far the best method because this adaptation helps screen reader users, too. With the asterisk placed before the prompt, it will be the first thing these users hear, serving effectively as a notice to the user that the field is required.

In the default situation with Internet Explorer, links are blue and underlined, and visited links are magenta and underlined. This is a clear case of using color and also conveying the information in another way, in case the color is not perceived. The underlining does that. Independent of color, screen readers will know that text is a link and announce that property to blind users. But today, links are rarely presented in the default blue underline because it seems so old-fashioned. Styling often makes it difficult to detect links for those who have impaired vision or are color-blind. Designers frequently rely on color change or adding underlines with a mouse-over event handler; however, these methods do not benefit those who must use the keyboard for navigation.

Be sure your links are easy to detect. Use onFocus and onBlur event handlers in addition to onMouseOver when you are highlighting links—or better, use CSS to specify the visual behavior for the :hover and :focus pseudo classes.

Color Contrast

In addition to the concern about using color alone to convey information, web designers need to be aware of the combinations of foreground and background colors used on their web page, especially in images. If the foreground and background are too close to the same hue, they may not provide sufficient contrast for some visitors.

The reason images are especially important is that users with color deficits may choose to use their own contrast setting in the browser or their own style sheet to provide high contrast and possibly enlarged text. Such adaptations generally apply to the text on the page, not to the images.

Section 508 does not have a provision regarding contrast on web pages, but WCAG 1.0 specifies adequate contrast as a Priority 2 checkpoint, Priority 3 for text:

> 2.2 Ensure that foreground and background color combinations provide sufficient contrast when viewed by someone having color deficits or when viewed on a black and white screen. [Priority 2 for images, Priority 3 for text]

You can find an excellent discussion of issues of contrast for people with vision loss at the Lighthouse site, www.lighthouse.org/color_contrast.htm. Images in the article do a good job of illustrating effective and ineffective contrast.

With WCAG 2.0 (as of Last Call), the requirement for contrast is specific and measurable, it is one of the welcome benefits of the WCAG working group. Note that there is no Level 1 requirement relating to color contrast.

> 1.4.1 Text or diagrams, and their background, must have a luminosity contrast ratio of at least 5:1. [Level 2]

> 1.4.3 Text or diagrams, and their background, must have a luminosity contrast ratio of at least 10:1. [Level 3]

The luminosity contrast ratio is defined as follows (from WCAG 2.0):

> (L1 + 0.05) / (L2 + 0.05), where L1 is the luminosity of the lighter of the text or background colors, and L2 is the luminosity of the darker of the text or background colors.

Note 1: The luminosity of a color is defined as $0.2126 * ((R / FS) \wedge 2.2) + 0.7152 * ((G / FS) \wedge 2.2) + 0.0722 * ((B / FS) \wedge 2.2)$.

- R, G, and B are the red, green, and blue RGB values of the color;
- FS is the maximum possible full scale RGB value for R, G, and B (255 for eight bit color channels); and
- the "^" character is the exponentiation operator.

Note 2: Luminosity values can range from 0 (black) to 1 (white), and luminosity contrast ratios can range from 1 to 21.

The WCAG 2.0 luminosity formula is a bit daunting, but there are tools to help you evaluate the contrast ratio. One of these is the Web Accessibility Toolbar (www.visionaustralia.org.au/info.aspx?page=619), introduced in Chapter 5, which offers a contrast analyzer tool that will grab the color numbers from a page. It is really quite neat.

Figure 6-8 shows an example of the analysis of colors on Amazon.com. After clicking the eye-dropper button in the center of the Colour Contrast Analyser window, a zoom window about two inches square appears. As you position the mouse over a color (either foreground or background), its hex value appears in the main window, along with a sample of the color. You can do the same with the eye dropper in the lower-center area of the window.

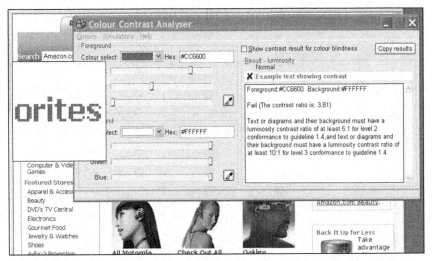

Figure 6-8. Checking out the luminosity contrast ratio

This Colour Contrast Analyser tool provides a calculation of the luminosity contrast ratio on the right side of the window, along with a reminder of the Level 1 and Level 2 success criteria cutoffs. You can also set the tool so that it calculates the color brightness/difference formulas (Options ➤ Algorithm ➤ Colour Brightness/Difference). By the way, the tool is available independent of the Accessibility Toolbar, also from Vision Australia (www. visionaustralia.org.au/info.aspx?page=628).

The test illustrated in Figure 6-8 was a surprise to me. This is an example of "heading text" on Amazon.com that should be marked up as an HTML heading (see Chapter 7). The color is a kind of burnt orange. It seems to me to have enough contrast, but the luminosity contrast ratio is only 3.81, which doesn't even meet the Level 2 success criterion cutoff of 5.

Gez Lemon has an excellent discussion of the luminosity contrast algorithm and other measures of contrast (http://juicystudio.com/article/luminositycontrastratioalgorithm. php). Linked to this article are color samples that meet Level 2 and 3 success criteria (http://juicystudio.com/services/coloursaferatio.php), as well as color brightness and difference requirements. Figure 6-9 is a composite drawn from the table for color combinations with a white background, including the sample from Amazon.com in Figure 6-8. The web-safe color comparisons are listed with fixed background and variable foreground. The table shows a sample of each color combination and icons indicating whether the combination passes the contrast tests. It is remarkable how few combinations pass one or more of the WCAG thresholds.

Luminosity Ratios with background: #fff				
Foreground Colour	Sample	Luminosity Contrast Ratio	Difference in Brightness	Difference in Colour
#000	Sample	❸ 21.00	✅ 255	✅ 765
#003	Sample	❸ 20.16	✅ 249	✅ 714
#006	Sample	❸ 17.61	✅ 243	✅ 663
#c0f	Sample	❌ 4.16	✅ 164	❌ 306
#c30	Sample	❷ 5.23	✅ 164	✅ 510
#c33	Sample	❷ 5.17	✅ 158	❌ 459
#c36	Sample	❌ 4.99	✅ 152	❌ 408
#c39	Sample	❌ 4.68	✅ 146	❌ 357
#c3c	Sample	❌ 4.28	✅ 140	❌ 306
#c3f	Sample	❌ 3.85	✅ 134	❌ 255
#c60	Sample	❌ 3.81	✅ 134	❌ 459
#c63	Sample	❌ 3.78	✅ 128	❌ 408
#c66	Sample	❌ 3.68	❌ 122	❌ 357

Figure 6-9. Part of the color samples table from Juicy Studio

Creating Accessible Tables

HTML tables are widely used on the Web. Most of those tables are not used to display data but are used for formatting purposes instead. With regard to accessibility, tables used for data are the primary concern. But before getting to data tables, let's briefly investigate how tables are used to format web pages and the consequences for people using screen readers.

Layout Tables

In the past, very few websites did *not* use tables for formatting pages. Today, that is changing. CSS offers a robust and effective alternative to using table cells to position content on the page (see Chapter 9). However, browser-dependency issues for CSS can make the conversion difficult. Yahoo!, for example, used tables for layout as late as March 2005 (the last page in the Wayback Machine, www.archive.org). Today, Yahoo! does not use tables for basic page layout, but there are still nine layout tables scattered around the homepage.

How Tables Linearize

Let's begin with a very basic table to see how it is spoken with a screen reader or other assistive technology. Figure 6-10 shows a simple table with two columns and two rows. The arrows indicate the order in which the table contents are read by a screen reader.

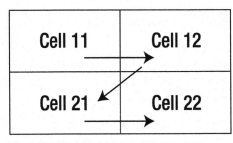

Figure 6-10. A simple two-by-two table, with arrows indicating the reading order

Here is the HTML code for the table in Figure 6-10:

```
<table border="1">
  <tbody>
    <tr>
      <td>Cell 1 1</td>
      <td>Cell 1 2</td>
    </tr>
    <tr>
      <td>Cell 2 1</td>
      <td>Cell 2 2</td>
    </tr>
  </tbody>
</table>
```

Home Page Reader and the screen readers all start with the first row, completely read each cell there, and then proceed to the second row, repeating that process, as follows.

- **Home Page Reader:**
  - "Cell 1 1"
  - "Cell 1 2"
  - "Cell 2 1"
  - "Cell 2 2"

This method of reading the contents of a table is called *linearization*. The way the reading (linearizing) is done is to start in the first row, first column ("Cell 1 1"), read the entire contents of that cell, including any nested tables, and then proceed to the next column, going across the first row. When row 1 is complete, proceed to row 2, and so on, as is illustrated by the arrows in Figure 6-10.

Even if there is a lot of information in any cell, all of it is read before proceeding to the next cell. This is a very important aspect of the linearization of tables, and it is different from the way screen readers worked just a few years ago. Today, they take advantage of the HTML structure of the document. They used to read the screen, so they would, in effect, speak the first line from each cell, then the second line from each cell, and so on. Often, this made no sense whatsoever.

6

When the linearization process comes to a cell that includes a nested table, that table must be completely linearized before continuing on to the next cell.

Another characterization of this linear reading order is source code order. If you look at an HTML file and strip out all the tags, leaving only text (and alt-text of the images), the resulting file is the linearized version of the page. You can check that out with the code for the simple table in Figure 6-10.

Spanning Cells in Layout Tables

Figure 6-11 shows a typical layout table and illustrates the way tables are used for laying out content on the page.

Sample Layout Table		
Navigation link 1 Navigation link 2 Navigation link 3 Navigation link 4	Banner ad	Right Navigation 1 Right Navigation 2 Right Navigation 3
	Main content area with lots of text and content filling the center part of the window	

Figure 6-11. A prototype layout table

What is especially important here is that some of the cells "span" rows or columns. In the HTML code for this table, you can see that the very first cell has colspan="3". That means that the first cell goes across (spans) the entire table. Here is the HTML code for the table in Figure 6-11:

```
<table border="1">
    <tr>
        <td colspan="3">Sample Layout Table</td>
    </tr>
    <tr>
        <td rowspan="2">
            Navigation link 1<br />
            Navigation link 2<br />
            Navigation link 3<br />
            Navigation link 4
        </td>
        <td>Banner ad</td>
        <td rowspan="2" >
            Right Navigation 1<br />
            Right Navigation 2<br />
            Right Navigation 3
        </td>
    </tr>
    <tr>
        <td>Main content area with lots of text and<br />
            content filling the center part <br />
            of the  window
        </td>
    </tr>
</table>
```

So, this is really a table with three rows and three columns, as shown in Figure 6-12.

Title (colspan #1)	Title (colspan #2)	Title (colspan #3)
Left Navigation (rowspan #1)	Banner	Right Navigation (rowspan #1)
Left Navigation (rowspan #2)	Content	Right Navigation (rowspan #2)

Figure 6-12. How spanning cells yield the layout of the table in Figure 6-11

The three cells across the top are merged into one with `colspan="3"` to give the title bar area across the top of the page. The lower two cells in the first and third columns are combined in a single cell with the attribute `rowspan="2"`. The left navigation panel includes the bottom two cells combined into one, and similarly, the right navigation panel is formed by combining the last two cells of the last column.

The spanning of columns and rows affects the way tables are linearized or spoken. The basic rule is that everything in a cell (independent of its spanning properties) is read when the cell is *first* encountered.

In the layout table in Figure 6-11, the complete title panel is read first. Then moving to the second row, the *entire* left navigation panel is read, followed by the "Banner" and all of the right navigation. In the middle row, only the cell called "content" remains to be read, and this is read last.

The formatting illustrated here raises a serious issue for access to a site. The main message of a page may be very hard to find. If you are listening to the page, chances are you want to hear that "main content." With layout like this, it takes a long time before you get to hear the information you were seeking. We will return to this example in Chapter 7 when we talk about accessible navigation.

Guidelines and Standards for Layout Tables

The WAI addresses table linearization in two Priority 2 checkpoints of WCAG 1.0. The first checkpoint cautions against the use of tables for layout, unless they linearize well:

> 5.3 Do not use tables for layout unless the table makes sense when linearized. Otherwise, if the table does not make sense, provide an alternative equivalent (which may be a linearized version). [Priority 2]

WCAG 2.0 (as of Last Call) offers Success Criterion 1.3.3, which addresses the concerns of Checkpoint 5.3.

> SC 1.3.3 When the sequence of the content affects its meaning, that sequence can be programmatically determined.

6

To give an example, my personal Yahoo! page used to have the stock prices for a set of stock symbols in a table with just two cells. All the symbols were in the first cell, and all the prices were in the second cell. Visually, the important sequence was stock symbol, stock price, repeated, but there is no way to determine that sequence from the code—the linearized version of the table made no sense at all.

The second Priority 2 checkpoint about layout tables from the WAI recommends the avoidance of structural markup inside a layout table:

> 5.4 If a table is used for layout, do not use any structural markup for the purpose of visual formatting. [Priority 2]

In general, it is important to use markup for its intended purpose, not to artificially create visual effects. For example, it is a bad idea to use the blockquote element in order to create indenting. When using tables for site layout, don't use the th element to have text centered and bold. If you do, then the assistive technology will think the table is a data table and try to deal with it accordingly.

The WCAG also has a further Priority 3 checkpoint related to how screen readers speak text on the web page:

> 10.3 Until user agents (including assistive technologies) render side-by-side text correctly, provide a linear text alternative (on the current page or some other) for all tables that lay out text in parallel, word-wrapped columns. [Priority 3]

User agents, including assistive technologies, actually do render side-by-side text correctly, so in my opinion, this checkpoint is moot.

Section 508 has no provision that specifically addresses layout tables because, apparently, these issues are interpreted as less pressing.

Tools for Checking Linearization

It is next to impossible to look at the source of a large commercial web page and determine what it will look like when it is linearized. The linearization algorithm is somewhat hard to apply, even when you know the structure of your page. Fortunately, some readily available tools let developers look at their linearized page.

Lynx (http://lynx.browser.org/) is a text-only browser that is popular in the UNIX world and is available for Windows. It is shareware, so you can download Lynx and try it yourself to get a first-hand feeling of linearized view of pages.

Additionally, various "Lynx viewers" emulate Lynx and display what Lynx would display. You can find one such viewer at www.regionet.ch/cgi-bin/lynxview/lynxview.html. I ran the sample layout table in Figure 6-11 through this Lynx viewer. Figure 6-13 shows the result.

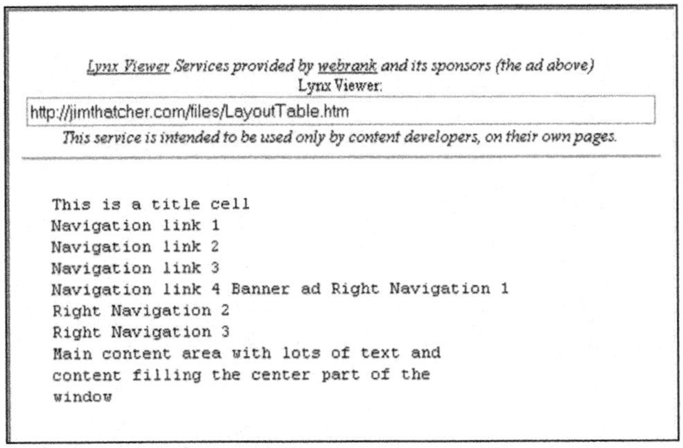

```
        Lynx Viewer Services provided by webrank and its sponsors (the ad above)
                                 Lynx Viewer:
  http://jimthatcher.com/files/LayoutTable.htm
        This service is intended to be used only by content developers, on their own pages.


  This is a title cell
  Navigation link 1
  Navigation link 2
  Navigation link 3
  Navigation link 4 Banner ad Right Navigation 1
  Right Navigation 2
  Right Navigation 3
  Main content area with lots of text and
  content filling the center part of the
  window
```

Figure 6-13. A Lynx view of the prototype layout table shown in Figure 6-11

Data Tables

So what are data tables? How are they distinguished from layout tables? Data tables present things like financial results, rainfall totals by city and month, or bus schedules. What do these have in common? It is that the meaning of data in most cells of the table depends on heading information, which is usually in the first row and the first column of the table. You cannot know what the data means unless you are aware of the contents of the corresponding headings.

For layout tables, information in various cells stands on its own. There are no headings—just table cells containing text and images. In contrast, headings are crucially important for understanding (or reading) data tables. That is the problem! Your tables must be designed and marked up in such a way as to ensure that assistive technology will know where the headings are and be able to announce them.

As an example, consider the data table shown in Figure 6-14. This table lists rainfall in Florida cities by month.

Month	Year	Pensacola	Milton	Crestview	Niceville	DeFuniak Springs	Chipley	Panama City	Wewa-hitchka	Apalach-icola
Jan	1971-00	5.41	6.24	6.51	5.79	5.40	6.09	5.85	5.70	4.94
Feb	1971-00	4.78	5.04	4.55	5.34	5.52	4.90	4.77	4.59	3.76
Mar	1971-00	6.39	7.39	6.92	6.45	6.23	6.13	6.20	6.07	4.90
Apr	1971-00	3.91	4.40	4.31	4.21	3.93	3.80	3.92	3.38	2.96
May	1971-00	4.38	4.78	4.93	4.20	4.98	4.37	3.81	3.56	2.65
Jun	1971-00	6.37	7.06	7.41	6.00	6.66	5.19	6.13	6.50	4.19
Jul	1971-00	7.99	8.23	7.17	9.32	7.89	6.73	8.81	9.00	7.32
Aug	1971-00	6.60	6.86	6.41	6.77	6.76	5.41	7.45	8.24	7.25
Sep	1971-00	5.83	6.23	4.26	6.95	6.33	4.88	6.38	5.68	6.73
Oct	1971-00	3.96	3.74	2.97	4.60	3.28	2.93	3.73	3.19	4.41
Nov	1971-00	4.46	5.39	4.34	4.67	4.87	4.07	4.57	3.44	3.44
Dec	1971-00	3.92	4.44	3.87	4.67	4.46	3.89	4.14	3.87	3.54
Total	1971-00	64.00	69.80	63.65	68.97	66.31	58.39	65.76	63.22	56.09

Figure 6-14. A data table showing rainfall totals in Florida

Notice that the meaning of each number depends on the corresponding heading information: the city from the first row and the month from the first column. This is especially obvious when the same number, say 5.41, appears more than once (for January in Pensacola and for Chipley in August). Additionally, given a row heading, say June (row 7) and column heading, say Niceville (column 6), you can look at the cell at (7, 6) (row 7, column 6) and find the average rainfall of 6.00 inches in Niceville in June.

If you can see the table, then you can look at the March row and see 6.45 for the rainfall in Niceville in March, or 4.67 in December. You can scan for row and column heading information to get the meaning of the data in the table.

If you are listening to the table, you must do it a cell at a time. When you are sitting on any cell, 5.41, for example, you need to know what the row and column headings are—Jan, Pensacola or Aug, Chipley, for example.

What screen readers try to do is to announce the row and column headers *as they change*. So as you move across the September row, you should hear something like "Year, 1971-00, Pensacola, 5.83, Milton, 6.23, Crestview, 4.6," and so on. Similarly, moving down the Pensacola column, you should hear something like "Jan, 5.41, Feb, 4.78, Mar, 6.39," and so on. The purpose of the guidelines for data tables is to ensure that this will be the behavior of assistive technology when reading such a table. Let's look at those guidelines.

Guidelines and Standards for Data Tables

The guidelines distinguish between what I call *simple* tables and all the others. A data table is simple if it satisfies two conditions:

- The column header for any given data cell is in the same column as the cell and all column headings are in the same row.

- The row header for any given data cell is in the same row as the cell and all the row headings are in the same column.

The Section 508 provisions require that row and column headers be identified with markup:

§1194.22(g) Row and column headers shall be identified for data tables.

This provision is essentially the same as Checkpoint 5.1 from the WCAG:

5.1 For data tables, identify row and column headers. [Priority 1]

These guidelines are designed so that the assistive technology can provide information about tabular structure to people who use screen readers or talking browsers.

The following guideline is for tables that are complex (not simple); that is, those that have "two or more logical levels of row or column headers."

5.2 For data tables that have two or more logical levels of row or column headers, use markup to associate data cells and header cells. [Priority 1]

The Section 508 provision again uses essentially the same language:

§1194.22(g) Markup shall be used to associate data cells and header cells for data tables that have two or more logical levels of row or column headers.

I will distinguish between two kinds of complex tables: those that are *layered*, where the headings are always in the same row and column as the data, and those that are *irregular*, where there are headings for data cells that are not in the row or column of the data. You will see examples in the following sections.

The treatment of the requirements on accessible data tables by WCAG 2.0 (as of Last Call) is very different. It is abstract, and it covers the two preceding cases.

SC1.3.1 Information and relationships conveyed through presentation can be programmatically determined and notification of changes to these is available to user agents, including assistive technologies.

This is saying that whatever the structure of the data table (simple, layered, or irregular), assistive technology must be able to figure out which cells are heading cells.

Simple Data Tables

Simple tables like the one in Figure 6-14 will speak properly with a screen reader if you follow the first Section 508 provision, §1194.22(g) (the same as WCAG Checkpoint 5.1), and identify the row and column headers of the table. The way you do that is to use the th (table header) element instead of the td (table data) element for all header cells. In addition, it is recommended that you use the scope attribute on the th; scope="row" if it is a

6

row header cell, and scope="col" if the cell is a column header. The following is part of the rainfall table in Figure 6-14 with correct table markup satisfying Section 508 §1194.22(g) and WCAG Checkpoint 5.1.

```
<table>
  <tr>
    <th scope="col" >Month</th>
    <th scope="col" >Year </th>
    <th scope="col" >Pensacola </th>
    <th scope="col" >Milton </th>
    <th scope="col" >Crestview </th>
    <th scope="col" >Niceville </th>
    <th scope="col" >DeFuniak Springs</th>
    <th scope="col" >Chipley </th>
  </tr><tr align="center" >
    <th scope="row">Jan </th>
    <td>1971-00 </td>
    <td>5.41</td>
    <td>6.24</td>
    <td>6.51</td>
    <td>5.79</td>
    <td>5.40</td>
    <td>6.09</td>
  </tr><tr>
    <th scope="row">Feb</th>
    <td>1971-00</td>
    <td>4.78</td>
    <td>5.04</td>
    <td>4.55</td>
    <td>5.34</td>
    <td>5.52</td>
    <td>4.90</td>
  </tr> . . .
```

Those th elements are identifying the row and column headers as required by the first of the two table provisions of the Section 508 Standards for web accessibility and the WCAG 1.0 checkpoints. With the table coded like this, it also meets WCAG 2.0 Success Criterion 1.3.1 because it is possible to programmatically recognize the cells that are marked as headers.

Layered Data Tables

The second table provision in the Section 508 Standards and of the WCAG talks about "tables that have two or more logical levels of row or column headers." What does that mean? Well, I think the intent is that if the previous technique does *not* work, then you need more complicated markup.

Figure 6-15 shows a table (from `http://frec.cropsci.uiuc.edu/1992/report2/table2.htm`) filled with absolutely fascinating information! This table has two (logical) levels of column headers. For its meaning, each number in the data part of the table depends on two column heading cells and one row heading cell.

Planting Date	Moldboard		No-Till	
	0P/0K	25P/25K	0P/0K	25P/25K
April 23-26	152	168	154	153
May 2-3	158	161	153	159
May 11-14	156	171	143	154
May 23-24	147	156	122	142

Figure 6-15. A data table with two logical levels of column headers

Tables like this are called *layered*. They have the property that, for any data cell, heading cells are always in the same row and column as the data, but there is more than one heading cell in the data cell's row or column. This characterization needs to take spanning into account. Data in a spanned cell is viewed as existing in all the cells it spans. For example, in the table in Figure 6-15, Moldboard occurs in row 1, columns 2 and 3, while No-Till appears in row 1, columns 4 and 5.

The accepted technique for specifying which heading cells apply to which data cells is called headers/id markup. The technique is error-prone when done manually, but the basic idea is straightforward. Each heading cell is given an id, and each data cell has a string of ids that are its headers. The string is specified as the value of the headers attribute of the data cell—the string of ids is *space-delimited*.

In the table in Figure 6-15, let's use ids that tell us which cell we are referencing. Let hxy be the id of the heading cell in row x and column y. So h25 contains 25P/25K (as does h23) and h61 contains May 23-24. Now the markup for the data cell in row 6, column 3 (156) is headers="h61 h12 h23".

Here is the code (with headers/id markup) for part of the table in Figure 6-15.

```
<table>
  <tr >
     <td></td>
     <th id="h12" colspan="2">Moldboard</th>
     <th id="h14" colspan="2">No-Till</th>
  </tr><tr align="center">
     <th id="h21">Planting Date</th>
     <th id="h22">0P/0K</th>
     <th id="h23">25P/25K</th>
     <th id="h24">0P/0K</th>
     <th id="h25">25P/25K</th>
```

```
    </tr><tr align="center">
      <td id="h31" headers="h21">April 23-26</th>
      <td headers="h31 h12 h22">152</td>
      <td headers="h31 h12 h23">168</td>
      <td headers="h31 h14 h24">154</td>
      <td headers="h31 h14 h25">153</td>
    </tr><tr align="center">
      <td id=h41 headers="h21">May 2-3</th>
      <td headers="h41 h12 h22">158</td>
      <td headers="h41 h12 h23">161</td>
      <td headers="h41 h14 h24">153</td>
      <td headers="h41 h14 h25">159</td>
    </tr>
    ...
```

The bottom line in this kind of markup is that you should avoid tables that require headers/id markup. The process is confusing at best, and the chance of error is very high.

Irregular Data Tables

It certainly can be argued that the fertilizer table (Figure 6-15) has two or more logical levels of row headers, and thus it brings headers/id markup into play. But I want to distinguish this kind of table from one where header information is not in the same row or column as the data. An example that is often used is the expense report table (www.w3.org/TR/WCAG10-HTML-TECHS/#identifying-table-rows-columns), as shown in Figure 6-16.

Travel Expense Report

	Meals	Hotels	Transport	subtotals
San Jose				
25-Aug-97	37.74	112.00	45.00	
26-Aug-97	27.28	112.00	45.00	
subtotals	65.02	224.00	90.00	379.02
Seattle				
27-Aug-97	96.25	109.00	36.00	
28-Aug-97	35.00	109.00	36.00	
subtotals	131.25	218.00	72.00	421.25
Totals	196.27	442.00	162.00	**800.27**

Figure 6-16. The "classic" complex table from the W3C

Notice how most numeric values in the table depend on a row header (date) and a column header (type of expense), *plus* the information as to the city where the expense occurred, and this information is not in the same row and the same column as the data. The first expense entry, 37.74, in row 3, column 2, has the heading **San Jose** in row 2, column 1, in addition to the date (25-Aug-97) and the expense type (Meals).

This is an example of an *irregular* table, in which heading information for a data cell occurs in cells that are not in the row or column of the data. Irregular tables *require* headers/id markup to make them accessible. Here is the markup for the table in Figure 6-16.

```
<table border="1"
            summary="expenses by date and city">
<caption>Travel Expense Report</caption>
<tr>
  <td></td>
  <th id="c2">Meals</th>
  <th id="c3">Hotels</th>
  <th id="c4">Transport</th>
  <td id="c5">subtotals</td></tr>
<tr>
  <th id="r2">San Jose</th>
  <td></td><td></td><td></td><td></td> </tr>
<tr> <td id="r3" >25-Aug-97</td>
  <td headers="c2 r2 r3">37.74</td>
  <td headers="c3 r2 r3">112.00</td>
  <td headers="c4 r2 r3">45.00</td>
  <td></td></tr>
<tr>
   <td id="r4">26-Aug-97
  <td headers="c2 r2 r4">27.28</td>
  <td headers="c3 r2 r4">112.00</td>
  <td headers="c4 r2 r4">45.00</td>
  ...
<tr><th id="r10">Totals</th>
  <td headers="c2 r10">196.27</td>
  <td headers="c3 r10">442.00</td>
  <td headers="c4 r10">162.00</td>
  <td headers="c5 r10">800.27</td></tr>
</table>
```

The specific cell with value 37.74 is highlighted in the preceding code. The cell has a headers attribute consisting of a list of three ids: c2 r2 r3. c2 is the id for the cell containing Meals. Cell r2 contains San Jose, and cell r3 contains 25-Aug-97.

Coding these headers/id combinations is very time-consuming and very error-prone. Every attempt should be made to simplify the table or break up the table, to avoid the need for headers/id markup.

There are very few good reasons to use irregular tables. The expense account example in Figure 6-16 could be converted to a layered table by having the location cells span all of the columns. What is so good about a layered table? When marked up with just th (and scope attributes when the applicability to a row or to a column is otherwise ambiguous), screen readers could, in principle, reliably speak the headings for all cells without needing to revert to complex and error-prone headers/id markup. In particular, a layered table marked up this way would meet WCAG 2.0 Success Criterion 1.3.1, because there is a simple algorithm to determine all the relevant heading cells for any data cell.

The Caption Element and Summary Attribute

The expense table in Figure 6-16 has the `caption` element—Travel Expense Report—which appears as a title (or caption) for the table. This could be just placed on the page and formatted to appear as a caption (bold and centered), but when you use the `caption` element, you are programmatically connecting the table and its caption, and that is a good thing to do, although use of the `caption` element is not a Section 508 requirement.

The purpose of the `summary` attribute on the `table` element is to give a blind user the kind of table structure overview that a sighted user gains by scanning the table. Michael Moore, of Knowbility (www.knowbility.org) gives a great example (www.knowbility.org/whatNot/tableExamples.html). The wrong `summary` for a table listing three courses is as follows:

```
summary="schedule of classes for May 23, 2005. There are three classes:
Web Development from 8 am to 9:20 am in Meyer 2.100 with Zeldman.
Creative writing from 11 am to 12:20 pm in Orwell 3.206 with Melville
and Advanced Calculus in Pascal 1.503 with Kepler"
```

And here is a corrected `summary`:

```
summary="schedule by course time, location and instructor"
```

The first `summary` is giving details that will be found by reading (listening to) the table, but the overall structure is what is needed in the `summary` attribute, and that is what the second example illustrates.

Like the `caption` element, the `summary` attribute is not a requirement of Section 508.

When you are listening to a page, the content is linearized and when tables are linearized, information is lost unless steps are taken to recover it. The intent of the guidelines is to allow a screen reader to recover the lost information and present it to the user. In particular, a screen reader or talking browser needs to know which cells contain header information for any given data cell.

Assistive Technology and Tables

The screen readers and IBM Home Page Reader handle tables quite differently. The way you initiate table reading is different, and the results are different. Because of those differences and subtleties, it is a good idea to check your accessible table with the assistive technology.

Home Page Reader and Tables

Home Page Reader has a setting (Settings ➤ Miscellaneous) to read row and column headers. That setting has two check boxes, and both should be checked (they are not checked by default). Pressing T or Shift+T moves to the next or previous table, respectively. Once on a table, press Alt+T to enter table reading mode. In table reading mode, the four arrow keys (up, down, left, and right) move around the cells of the table.

As you move left and right, changing the column, the new column header will be spoken, followed by the data in the cell. When you move up and down, the new row header will be spoken, followed by the data in the cell.

In the example shown earlier in Figure 6-15, as you move from column 2 to column 3, the spanning header, Moldboard doesn't change, and I would hope that Home Page Reader would not speak it, but it does. In fact, that spanning heading is also spoken by Home Page Reader when you move up and down a row, which is not good.

At any time, you should be able to hear all the headers for a current cell using the "Where-Am-I" key, which for Home Page Reader is Alt+F1; however, the information delivered to the user includes only row numbers and column numbers; it does not announce heading information.

Home Page Reader is very strict about accessible table markup. If you have some accessible table markup, Home Page Reader assumes you know what you are doing and that all of the headers will be appropriately marked up. So, for example, if you place ids on header cells and only one data cell has a headers attribute, then the header information on that *one* cell will be the only header information that is spoken. In the process of testing the sample table in Figure 6-15, I removed all the headers attributes, but left the ids. The only heading information that Home Page Reader spoke was the "Planting" cell, which has a <th> tag with scope="col".

JAWS and Tables

JAWS does not have a table reading mode, as such. As with Home Page Reader, the T key moves you to the next table and Shift+T moves to the previous table. When you are in a table, you can press Ctrl+Alt+arrow keys to move around the table. So, Ctrl+Alt+right arrow moves right one cell, Ctrl+Alt+down arrow moves down one table cell, and so on.

The speaking of the header information in the sample table in Figure 6-15 is the same as Home Page Reader, with two exceptions. JAWS seems to ignore the scope attribute and speaks "Planting" as a row header as well as a column header, which the scope attribute "requires". Also, JAWS does not read the spanning headings (like Moldboard) when moving up and down (thank goodness).

JAWS does have a useful "Where-Am-I" key combination. Use Ctrl+Alt+num pad 5 to hear the row and column and all heading information (as well as contents) for the current cell.

Window-Eyes and Tables

Like Home Page Reader, Window-Eyes has a setting that determines the way table headers are spoken. Use Global ➤ Verbosity ➤ MSAA ➤ Tables. In that dialog box, I think it is best to check the Default header to column or row radio button. This will speak column headings when the column changes and row headings when the row changes. I found the Window-Eyes description of how it handles table reading to be somewhat obscure. Here is that explanation:

Window-Eyes uses three methods to examine table headers: header attributes, <th> tags, and first row/first column (the method used is determined by the verbosity options listed below). You can override the header announcement method by enabling the Header Attrib Override verbosity option. If this option is enabled, and header attributes exist for the current cell, Window-Eyes will read only the header attributes for table headers for that cell. If this option is enabled, and header attributes do not exist, Window-Eyes will revert to the selected table header method for reading table headers. If this option is disabled, Window-Eyes will use the selected table header method for reading table headers. If the table header method "Default Header To Off" is enabled, this option becomes irrelevant. These radio buttons control how Window-Eyes will handle table headers on startup. The table headers hot key will not effect [sic] this radio button group (although changing this option will immediately affect the hot key). If Window-Eyes is restarted, the table header rotor will return to the default option (specified with these radio buttons).

At any rate, you can try it for yourself by using Ctrl+Shift+H (the default table headers hotkey) to cycle through the various options for headers announcement, try the table, and decide which you like best.

Window-Eyes, like Home Page Reader and JAWS, enables the T and Shift+T keys to move from table to table.

Window-Eyes also has a table reading mode that you enter by pressing Ctrl+num pad + (plus) and leave by pressing Ctrl+num pad – (minus). When in table reading mode, pressing Ins+arrow keys moves around the table cells.

Default Behavior

What happens if there is no accessible table markup (th, scope, headers/id)? JAWS, Window-Eyes, and Home Page Reader will read headings from row 1 and column 1 by default when there is no specific heading markup on the table. It is therefore reasonable to conclude that placing table headers in the first row and the first column amounts to *identifying row and column headers* as required by all the guidelines. To be certain, it is better to programmatically identify the headers of each data table using th for header cells, td for data cells, and the scope attribute on th or td elements when the scope of the cell is ambiguous.

However, here is a warning (again). If you use some accessible markup, you must do a complete job because Home Page Reader, once it detects accessible markup, will speak only the headings information that you specify.

It is not completely true with any assistive technology today, but I wish they always read (or had an option to always read) *only* the heading information that changes as the user moves through the table, one cell at a time. In addition, there should be a general "Where-Am-I" function, which in the case of table cells would announce all heading information for the current cell. For example, as you move across the fourth row in the expense table shown earlier in Figure 6-16, you would hear only the column headings because the date and city headings don't change. Of course, users would have heard that additional heading information the first time they landed on the row.

Summary for Accessible Tables

In terms of money and workload, implementing accessible tables can be an expensive proposition, but that expense can be totally avoided with careful design of data tables. In a table with 10 rows and 10 columns, an irregular table requires that all 100 cells be specially coded. When the table is simple but the header positions are not in the first row or first column, about 20 cells must be specially coded. When the headers are in the first row and first column, you don't need any specially coded cells.

Here is a summary of the main considerations for accessible tables:

- Identify row and column headers by placing them in the first row and first column.
- Use the table header element, th, for all header cells that do not contain data. Use td together with scope or headers attributes for cells containing data together with heading information. You must use the scope on any heading cell if the purpose of the cell is ambiguous. For example, a th in the top-left corner could be either a row or column header, and the scope attribute is needed to resolve the ambiguity.
- Use ids on the header cells the headers attribute on the data cells to explicitly associate header information with data cells. This is essential if the table is irregular, meaning there are data cells whose header information is not in the same row and the same column as that cell.
- Do not use any of the accessible data table markup (th, scope, headers, or summary) on a table used for layout. In particular, avoid gratuitous announcements resulting from summary="This table used for layout".

Flicker Issues

Rapid visual changes, flashes, or blinking objects on a web page can cause photosensitive epileptic seizures in susceptible individuals. This is particularly true when the flashing has a high intensity and is in the frequency range between 2 Hz and 55 Hz. All of the accessibility guidelines contain some advice on avoiding flicker.

Guidelines and Standards for Flicker

The first and most specific requirement is from the Access Board, in Section 508 provision §1194.22(j):

§1194.22(j) Pages shall be designed to avoid causing the screen to flicker with a frequency greater than 2 Hz and lower than 55 Hz.

The specific frequency range is a region of concern due to the possibilities of inducing seizure upon visitors with photosensitive epilepsy. The wording of this provision was intended to be consistent with that of WCAG 1.0, but phrased in regulatory language and testable.

The WCAG cautions web developers to avoid flicker as long as users have no control over it:

> 7.1 Until user agents allow users to control flickering, avoid causing the screen to flicker. [Priority 1]

The major browsers permit users to stop animation in GIFs by pressing the Esc key. Opera more effectively allows users to turn off animation by using a dialog box option. Choose File ➤ Preferences, select the Multimedia section, and uncheck the check box labeled Enable Animation (GIF images). But other sources of flickering or blinking content cannot be so easily controlled.

A second checkpoint from WCAG 1.0 is Priority 2 and refers to blinking, rather than flicker.

> 7.2 Until user agents allow users to control blinking, avoid causing content to blink (i.e., change presentation at a regular rate, such as turning on and off). [Priority 2]

It may be helpful to have an idea of what the frequencies of concern are like. The flashing rate of my text cursor is just shy of 1 Hz. To put this in context, the caret blink rate (or cursor blink rate) in Windows (set in the Keyboard settings from the Control Panel) varies from 0.4 Hz at the slowest setting to 3.1 Hz at the fastest; the middle setting is about 0.8 Hz.

The WCAG 2.0 guideline (as of Last Call) is more specific and less restrictive in the treatment of the problems raised with photosensitivity:

> Guideline 2.3 Allow users to avoid content that could cause seizures due to photo-sensitivity.

> SC 2.3.1 Content does not violate the general flash threshold or the red flash threshold. [Level 1]

> SC 2.3.3 Web units do not contain any components that flash more than three times in any one second period. [Level 3]

The important difference here is that the technical concepts of "general flash threshold" and "red flash threshold" have replaced the Section 508 reference to the frequency range of 2 Hz through 55 Hz. And these new concepts specify not only frequencies, but also the concept of "flash" and the area of the screen to be involved.

Here is the definition of the general flash threshold:

- A sequence of flashes or rapidly changing image sequences where both the following occur:

  1. the combined area of flashes occurring concurrently (but not necessarily contiguously) occupies more than one quarter of any 335 × 268 pixel rectangle anywhere on the displayed screen area when the content is viewed at 1024 by 768 pixels and

  2. there are more than three flashes within any one-second period.

     Note 1: For the general flash threshold, a flash is defined as a pair of opposing changes in brightness of 10% or more of full scale white brightness, where brightness is calculated as .2126*R + .7152*G + .0722B using linearized R, G, and B values. Linearized-X = (X/FS)^2.2 where FS is full scale (usually 255 today). An "opposing change" is an increase followed by a decrease, or a decrease followed by an increase.

     Note 2: Based on Wisconsin Computer Equivalence Algorithm for Flash Pattern Analysis (FPA).

6

This characterization of the problematic condition includes the area of flashing (which has not been mentioned in guidelines before) and frequencies greater than 3 Hz.

The Blink and Marquee Elements

There are other ways that web pages can be caused to have flicker. One way is by using the blink element, which is not officially part of HTML 3.2 or 4.0:

```
<blink>This is Blinking text</blink>
```

Here is how it is described on Webmonkey, "Authoring HTML Basics" (http://hotwired. lycos.com/webmonkey/teachingtool/blink.html):

> Blink may well be the most irritating tag available, and not just because it's only supported by Netscape (that is, it doesn't work on IE).

The frequency of the Netscape implementation of the blink element is around 0.8 Hz, so it is not in the dangerous range specified by the Access Board. However, it cannot be controlled by the Esc key. Opera does not support it.

Whereas Internet Explorer does not implement the blink element and Netscape does, the situation is unfortunately reversed for the marquee element. Here's the description of the marquee element on the Advanced HTML site (www.advancedhtml.co.uk/advancedhtml.htm#Marquees):

> A pretty useless tag and like the dreaded <BLINK> tag it could get very annoying if overused (or even used at all). You can use it to scroll messages across the screen.

In my opinion, the `marquee` tag is even worse than `blink`, both in annoyance value and in potential for causing accessibility issues. Admittedly, a simple application of the `marquee` is not too offensive:

```
<marquee>This text will scroll right to left quite slowly.</marquee>
```

However, attributes of the `marquee` element can be modified so that the text is jumping and moving well above the 2-Hz limit, and the Esc key will not stop the movement.

In summary, don't use the `blink` or `marquee` elements—because they are not valid HTML and because their effects cannot be controlled in the browsers that support them. Keep flashing frequencies of animated GIFs well below the 2-Hz limit, or much better, avoid animated GIFs altogether.

Bear in mind also that things that jump, flicker, and move about are a nightmare for people who use screen magnification or a magnifying glass and so can see only part of the screen at any one time. Such moving content can also be confusing for people with cognitive disabilities.

Summary

Let's distill the message of this chapter into a checklist of specific techniques for creating accessible content relating to text equivalents, use of color, accessible tables, and flicker rate.

1. Every image must have a valid `alt` attribute. The `alt` attribute should convey the information or purpose of the image.

2. When an image stands by itself as a link (inside an anchor) it must have a nonempty `alt` attribute that clearly specifies the purpose of the link or function of the image.

3. All images that are not active and that do not convey information should have `alt=""`, null alt-text (that is, `alt=` quote quote with no spaces between).

4. Avoid duplicate adjacent links. If both an image and text are links with the same `href`, enclose them both in the same anchor tag, and then place `alt=""` on the image. Inside a `button` element put non-null alt-text on any image to the extent that the information conveyed by the image is not redundant.

5. Each `input` of type image must have alt-text specifying the function of the button.

6. On every area of an image `map`, include alt-text that clearly identifies the purpose of the corresponding hotspot.

7. Use the long description attribute (`longdesc`) to provide text equivalents for images like charts or graphs that carry more important information than can be conveyed with their short `alt` attribute, or include the long description as part of the page.

8. Include a readily available text transcript for each informational audio file.

9. Whenever color carries information, make sure that other parts of the page convey the same information, for example, additional characters, images (with alt-text), or font changes.

10. Identify the row and column headers of every data table by *at least one* of the following methods:

    a. Place column headings in the first row and place row headings in the first column.

    b. Use the th element on heading cells that contain no data, and the td element together with the scope attribute when the cell contains data together and acts as a heading.

    c. Use the scope attribute on all heading cells in which the scope is ambiguous.

    d. Assign an id to each heading cell and string of ids as the headers attribute for each data cell to say which are heading cells for that data cell.

11. To obtain the widest possible coverage of assistive technology along with actual programmatic identification of headers, use positioning of the headings (10a) together with the scope attribute on heading cells (10b).

12. Any of the alternatives, 10a through 10d, can be used alone or combined with others to make simple data tables accessible. *Simple* tables are ones in which the row headings for every data cell are in the same row as the cell, and the column headings are in the same column as the cell.

13. For *irregular* tables, in which headings for some data cells are not in the same row and/or column as the cell, you must use the headers attribute approach (10d).

14. The frequency of flicker (image appearing and disappearing) in animated GIFs or other objects must be less than 2 Hz or greater than 55 Hz. But it is best to avoid moving content all together.

6

177

7 ACCESSIBLE NAVIGATION

by Jim Thatcher

The previous chapter focused on creating accessible content—content that is compatible with assistive technologies and that provides alternatives to nontext elements such as images and audio. We discussed how web pages can be constructed more effectively and designed to be easily accessible by people with disabilities.

In this chapter, we will discuss the accessibility issues of getting around a given page, within the website and to other websites. The distinction between navigation and content is somewhat unrealistic. Several of the issues discussed in Chapter 6 certainly influence navigation. For example, if you don't provide text equivalents for images that are links, then people using screen readers or text browsers won't be able understand the links on the page as they navigate through them. Similarly, if you have not included alt-text for image map hotspots (<area> tags), then large portions of the page will make no sense at all to people using assistive technologies. Unrealistic though the distinction may be, this chapter will cover the navigation topics of reading order, headings navigation, skipping over navigation links, accessible frames, accessible image maps, layout effects on navigation, and accessible links. First, let's take a look at some of the obstacles that people with disabilities face when they try to navigate through a web page.

Navigation Considerations

Usually, when web designers or developers think about "navigation," it is navigation within the website—getting from section to section to accomplish some task like searching for an item, finding it, and going through the process of checking out and purchasing it. These web professionals are probably not thinking about navigating *within a single page* because that is not what a sighted user does.

Let's look at a sample page, the homepage of the U.S. Department of Agriculture (USDA, www.usda.gov), shown in Figure 7-1.

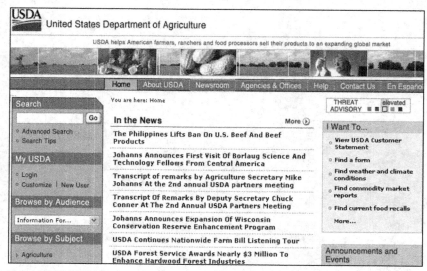

Figure 7-1. The USDA homepage

The headlines for news items on the USDA homepage are listed in the center of the page, about an inch and a half down from the top. Since I can see the screen, those headlines are very easy for me to spot and read. But if I wanted to read those same news headlines with a screen reader, it would take a while. There are about 106 words before the section heading, In the News, and it takes around 51 seconds to listen to those words with the JAWS for Windows screen reader (at its default speech rate).

The difference between what a mouse user is able to do to focus on the news items and what a keyboard user must go through is really quite astounding. If you can see the screen and want to read the details of the first news item, you simply click the corresponding link, such as The Philippines Lifts Ban On U.S. Beef And Beef Products. It is so easy and takes less than a second. It is what most web designers and developers do and expect others to do. But if you can't use the mouse, you must use the keyboard (or another more cumbersome input device) to move the input focus from wherever it is on the page (if you can find it) to the link that you want to follow (of course, you may not be able to know what link you want to follow), and then press Enter. The USDA homepage has about 28 links before the first news item. If you are starting from the top, that is the number of times you must hit the Tab key to get there.

Many users can see the screen, but are not able to use a mouse. If you are one of those users, as you tab through the links towards your desired target, you must follow the focus rectangle in order to know where you are. That is often very difficult and even impossible. In Figure 7-1, input focus is on Newsroom (in the center of the horizontal navigation bar at the top of the page), but that certainly isn't obvious. If you are using a screen reader, at least you have the advantage of being able to hear each link as you go along.

Keyboard navigation of the web page is very important for many users, whether or not they use a screen reader. As a web author or web designer, you can do some simple things to make that process of page navigation much easier for your site visitors, especially those with disabilities. And there are important things that must be done if your page is going to comply with the U.S. Access Board Section 508 Standards for web accessibility or the Web Content Accessibility Guidelines (WCAG) from the Web Accessibility Initiative (WAI) of the World Wide Web Consortium (W3C).

Reading Order

Whether you use tables or standards-compliant Cascading Style Sheets Version 2 (CSS 2) positioning (see Chapter 9) to lay out your page, a screen reader will find (speak) the page in the order of the HTML source code. The speaking order may have very little to do with the way you see the page, in the sense that blocks of text could appear in quite different positions than those apparent from looking at the page.

If the page uses tables for layout, you can have a general idea about the order in which items will be visited or spoken just by knowing where the table cells are. *Linearization*, as described in the discussion of layout tables in Chapter 6, is what happens when source code order is applied to a layout table. A table is spoken by starting with the first cell and speaking everything in that cell, including any nested tables. Then you go to the next cell in the first row, speak that, and continue until you finish the first row. Then on to the second row, and so on, continuing in this way through the whole table.

Table reading order becomes confusing or surprising when spanned rows come into play. In the table shown in Figure 7-2, the first row consists of a single cell spanning three columns and that is spoken first ("Sample Layout Table"); it is first in the source code order. The first cell of the second row spans two rows, but the content of that cell comes next in the source code, and so is spoken next ("Navigation link 1 Navigation link 2 Navigation link 3 Navigation link 4"). Then the second cell of the second row ("Banner ad") is spoken. Next, the screen reader speaks the third cell of the second row, which spans two rows ("Right Navigation 1 Right Navigation 2 Right Navigation 3"). The last part of this hypothetical layout table might be a main content area of a page. It is the second cell of the third row and last in the source code order ("Main content area with lots of text and content filling the center part of the window").

Sample Layout Table		
Navigation link 1 Navigation link 2 Navigation link 3 Navigation link 4	Banner ad	Right Navigation 1 Right Navigation 2 Right Navigation 3
	Main content area with lots of text and content filling the center part of the window	

Figure 7-2. A hypothetical layout table

The only thing complicated about this idea of source code order is that you cannot know what source code order is by looking at the page. You need to look at the source code, which can be awkward at best! There are tools that can help. Figure 7-3 shows the CNN homepage (www.cnn.com) modified using the Web Accessibility Toolbar (www.visionaustralia.org.au/info.aspx?page=619; see Chapter 5). Use the Structure ➤ Table Cell Order menu item to indicate the reading order of table cells.

Figure 7-3. CNN homepage showing the reading order of table cells

If the site uses CSS positioning to present the page, there is no way you can be sure of the order in which blocks of content will be spoken—that is, which blocks come before others in the source code order. Again, there are tools to help with this. The WAVE tool (http://dev.wave.webaim.org; see Chapter 5) can be used to indicate the order in which a section of a page will be spoken.

Figure 7-4 shows my homepage (www.jimthatcher.com) modified by the WAVE to highlight the "chunks" on the page (divs) and their position in the source code order.

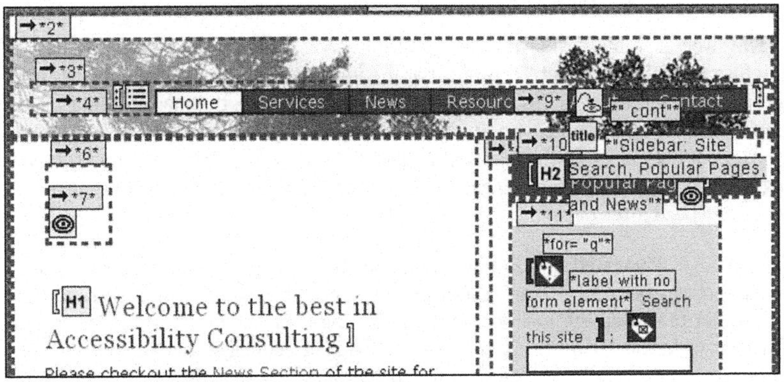

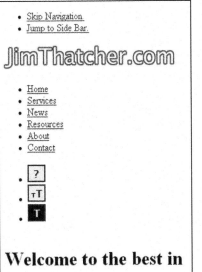

Figure 7-4. Using the WAVE to highlight reading order

For CSS-based pages, I think it is much simpler to just view the page with CSS turned off. This is most conveniently handled with the Web Accessibility Toolbar. Use the CSS ➤ CSS On/Off menu item. With Firefox and the Web Developer Extension toolbar, use the CSS ➤ Disable Styles ➤ All Styles menu item. Figure 7-5 shows part of my homepage, this time with CSS turned off. This is precisely the order in which the page will be spoken or visited with a screen reader.

Figure 7-5.
View reading order with CSS disabled

7

Heading Navigation

Now you know that text will be spoken and links visited in the order of the text in the source code. How can a user get around a web page conveniently with just the keyboard, without using the mouse? "Get around" means being able to read different areas and being able to follow links scattered through the page.

As you saw in the example of a layout table in Figure 7-2, it is possible that *everything* is spoken before the "main content." It is not that the information with that layout does not make sense, because it does. In this very simple mockup of a page, the main content takes up a quarter of the page. People who are listening to the page may need to wait through three-quarters of the words when what they really want is that main content. The problem of having to navigate through the navigation links in order to find the main content reoccurs, page after page after page.

In the late 1990s, I advocated a "skip navigation" link at the top of every page (discussed in the next section) because screen reader users were being overwhelmed with all the information that preceded the main content on the page. As vice-chair of the Electronic and Information Access Advisory Committee (EITAAC), empanelled by the U.S. Access Board to propose accessibility standards, I urged the adoption of a provision addressing this issue, and here is the result:

> §1194.22(o) A method shall be provided that permits users to skip repetitive navigation links.

Even though it is far from perfect, it was very important that this provision became part of the Section 508 Standards for web accessibility. It raised awareness of the problems with keyboard navigation and now serves to encourage (or require) headings navigation.

It was disappointing that WCAG 1.0 hardly addressed this fundamental problem of keyboard page navigation at all. Two Priority 3 checkpoints in WCAG 1.0 are related to the issue of keyboard navigation:

> 13.5 Provide navigation bars to highlight and give access to the navigation mechanism. (Priority 3)

> 13.6 Group related links, identify the group (for user agents), and, until user agents do so, provide a way to bypass the group. (Priority 3)

But these checkpoints really do not address the problem. The Last Call current draft of WCAG 2.0 brings this issue to the forefront through Guideline 2.4 and its Level 1 success criterion:

> Guideline 2.4 Provide mechanisms to help users find content, orient themselves within it, and navigate through it.

> 2.4.1 A mechanism is available to bypass blocks of content that are repeated on multiple Web units. [Level 1]

HTML has heading tags, <h1> through <h6>. Viewed as navigational features, when you use these heading tags, their presence can be programmatically determined. If you have "section headings" just styled with bold or certain background colors, their status as section headings or navigational features cannot be determined. Refer back to the USDA web page shown in Figure 7-1. I think it is obvious that Search, My USDA, In the News, and I Want To are section "headings," but they are not marked up that way. In fact, all of these section headings are images. They have appropriate alt-text, and those images could easily be wrapped in heading tags to provide significantly improved navigation.

The reason this is all so important is that recent versions of screen readers allow a user to navigate the headings on a page by simply pressing the H key (Shift+H to go to the previous heading). If a page is well structured and the headings are marked up as HTML heading elements (h1 through h6), then a screen reader user can easily get a useful survey of the page content and useful access to that content by just navigating through (listening to) the headings on the page with the H key.

To satisfy Section 508 provision §1194.22(o), if the main content begins with a heading (which certainly should be the case), it is an easy matter to skip over repetitive navigation links to get to the main content.

Figure 7-6 shows the Green Methods homepage (www.greenmethods.com). This is an interesting site with several accessibility features, including headings markup. I have used the Web Accessibility Toolbar (discussed in Chapter 5) to mark up those places where heading tags are used. Note that all the section headings are, in fact, HTML headings as they should be, and a keyboard user can, with eight keystrokes, get a quick and comprehensive outline of the structure on the page, and begin to read the section of interest.

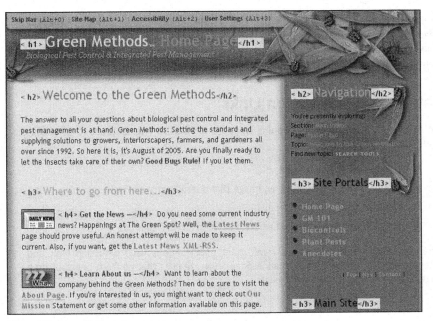

Figure 7-6. Green Methods homepage

You might be concerned as to whether or not the U.S. federal government accepts headings markup *instead* of skip links for Section 508 compliance. The U.S. Access Board developed the Section 508 standards and provides guidance, technical assistance, and resources on accessible design. The Section 508 page of the Access Board site (`www.access-board. gov/508.htm`) has no skip links and uses headings navigation instead. That should put that concern to rest.

You should use headings markup to address keyboard navigation of your page, in particular to be able to skip over repetitive navigation links and to get to the main content. Additionally, if you think about the sections of each page, and label those sections with headings, your whole site will be clearer and easier for *everyone* to use.

> *What about keyboard users who are not using an expensive screen reader? The Opera Browser (`http://opera.com/`) provides headings navigation from the keyboard. Use the S key to move forward from heading to heading; use the W key to move through headings in reverse direction. Remember that with Opera, links are accessed with the A key instead of Tab, and the Q key goes through links in reverse direction, like Shift+Tab. At the time of this writing, only the first beta of Microsoft Internet Explorer 7 has been released to a small set of MSDN subscribers. I hope that headings keyboard navigation will be implemented in that version.*

Skip Navigation Links

As discussed in the previous section, the correct way to deal with page navigation is to use headings. This section reviews techniques used to provide the ability to skip navigation links (you may still want to use that approach, in addition to headings). Then we will look at how skipping text blocks works with assistive technologies.

Creating Skip Navigation Links

Let's survey the techniques for skipping links. We will look at four methods for providing skip navigation links:

- Placing a link in normal text
- Creating a link as alt-text on an image that doesn't carry information
- Using a text link styled to be invisible
- Using CSS to expose the text of the link when it receives focus

After reviewing these techniques, I will point out a serious issue with skip links and Internet Explorer 6 that applies to all in-page links—all links that go from one spot on a page to another spot on the same page.

Placing a Link in Normal Text

The simplest technique is to just place a text link at the top of the page. I believe that one of the first skip navigation links was that used by the American Council of the Blind (ACB, www.acb.org). The ACB site has a link at the top of the page in a small font with link text, Skip Navigation Links, as shown in Figure 7-7.

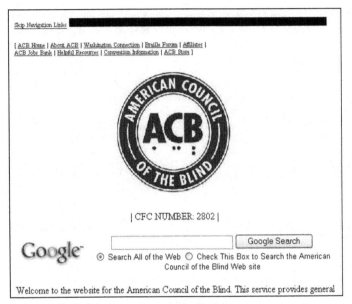

Figure 7-7. The ACB homepage has a visible skip link.

When a visitor using a screen reader opens the ACB homepage, the first announcement is "Link skip navigation links." If users want to listen to the navigation links, they can just ignore this skip link, just as they can ignore any other link. On a first visit to the page, the user might indeed want to listen to those navigation links, but the presence of the skip link empowers the screen reader user with the choice.

The code for the skip link at the top of the ACB homepage looks like this:

```
<a href="#nonav"><font size="-2">Skip Navigation Links</font></a>
```

The ACB web developers placed the defining anchor with name="nonav" on the ACB logo image:

```
<a name="nonav">
    <img src="acob5.gif" alt="American Council of the Blind"...>
</a>
```

That means when the skip link is followed, the alt-text for the logo, "American Council of the Blind," is the next item to be announced.

The definition of the local anchor does *not* need to have content. The code <a
name="nonav" id="nonav"></a> is valid and could have been placed just before the
Welcome to the website for the American Council of the Blind text on the page (see the following discussion of in-page links). This is a very important part of the skip navigation idea.
The target anchor does *not* need to enclose any content. As such, it can easily be placed in
a template to be used for all pages based on the template.

The ACB site seems to take the words *skip navigation links* literally. Their skip link just
skips over the two lines of text links at the top of the page and does not skip over the logo
or the search fields. I would code the target of the skip just before the main content,
starting with Welcome farther down the page.

A contemporary CSS-based page is the Guild of Accessible Web Designers (GAWDS) homepage (www.gawds.org). Part of that page is shown in Figure 7-8.

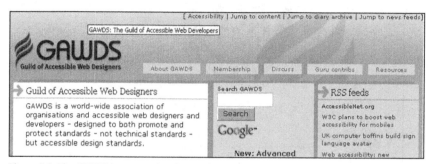

Figure 7-8. The GAWDS homepage has three visble skip links.

Notice that there are three navigation links at the top of the page, offering jumps to the
content, diary archive, and news feeds. This page includes 15 headings (one h1, three h2,
and eleven h3), so heading navigation is well supported. The three navigation links provide
access to key areas of the page in addition to heading navigation.

People with disabilities are best served when the skip navigation links are on-screen and
normal text. Users who can see the screen but do not use a mouse will not be surprised
when links appear or disappear. For example, on the GAWDS page, users can set about a
task to read about RSS feeds by first tabbing to the Jump to news feeds link, activating that
link, and then reading in the resulting section. When the links are hidden, as discussed
next, their existence is a surprise and, on an unfamiliar site, a plan of action is hard to
establish.

Creating a Link As Alt-Text on an Invisible Image

The CNN site (www.cnn.com), shown in Figure 7-9, has had a skip navigation link for a
number of years. The CNN page has a top area, including a logo and a search field, and
then a long list of navigation links down the left and right sides of the page. The left navigation is site navigation. The MORE NEWS navigation on the right changes from day to day
and is local to the area of the site (U.S. in Figure 7-9). If you tried to use the Tab key to get
to the main story (the main content)—in this case, 9/11 recordings, documents released—
without using the skip link, you would tab about 28 times through the left navigation links.

The surprising aspect of this site is that it has *exactly one* HTML heading: an h2 on the title of the main story. There are about ten other places on the CNN page that could use HTML headings; MORE NEWS is one that is visible in Figure 7-9.

Figure 7-9. CNN.com has an invisible skip link.

An invisible GIF on the top-right of the CNN page is the skip navigation link. If you turn off images (for example, for Internet Explorer, under Windows, choose Internet Options ➤ Advanced, check the Always expand ALT text for images option, and uncheck the Show pictures option), the link will appear far off to the right. Instead of turning off images, you can view the source code (View ➤ Source Code in Internet Explorer), and here is what you will find, first for the image link, then the local anchor:

```
<a href="#ContentArea">
    <img src="http://i.cnn.net/cnn/images/1.gif"
            alt="Click here to skip to main content"
            width="10" height="1" >
</a>

<a name="ContentArea"></a>
```

This local anchor, ContentArea, is just before the U.S. headline in red (which is actually an image with alt="U.S. News"). The anchor is in the template and above the content that changes hourly.

Let's summarize this method. At the top of the page, you place a link on an invisible image with alt-text such as "skip navigation" or "skip to main content" and with an href that points to a local anchor with empty content just above the main content. But do not say "Click here to . . .", as on the CNN site; instead, just express the function of the link, "Skip to main content" (see the "Accessible Links" section later in this chapter for more on link text). This is a very practical method of providing a skip navigation link, satisfying the Section 508 provision without changing the visual appearance of the page or site.

The same technique is used on many sites, including IBM (www.ibm.com). Unlike CNN, which used one heading, IBM (at the time of this writing) uses no headings markup, and the only assistance for page navigation is that provided by one skip link.

This technique is designed so that the visual appearance of the page isn't changed at all. But what about keyboard users who are not using a screen reader? The accommodation of an invisible skip navigation link almost entirely leaves them out. I say "almost" because a keyboard user could, if desperate for keyboard access, watch the status area of the browser and notice the href of the skip navigation link appear, as shown in the example from Netscape 7.2 in Figure 7-10.

Figure 7-10. The href of the focused link shows in the status bar.

Using a Text Link Styled to Be Invisible

Figure 7-11 shows the top of the FirstGov portal site (www.firstgov.gov) for the U.S. federal government.

Figure 7-11. The FirstGov.gov banner

In October 2001, the banner was similar to what it is today. There were five links at the top of the page using very small text, which was the same color (white) as the background, styled like this:

```
<a href="#content">
  <font color="#ffffff" size="-6">Skip to content</font>
</a> 
...
```

The skip links served as a kind of hidden table of contents, with a link to each of the main content areas of the page. They were Skip to content, Skip to Government search, Skip to Departments and Agencies, Skip to Reference, and Skip to Customer Survey. That table of contents was hidden from all users except those with a screen reader or those viewing the page with all styling turned off. Figure 7-12 shows the current page (as of this writing) with styling turned off using the Web Accessibility Toolbar (see Chapter 5).

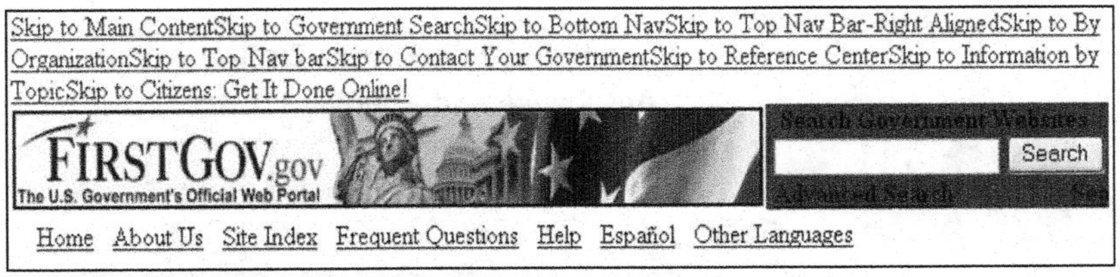

Figure 7-12. Turn off CSS to expose the skip links on FirstGov.gov.

Now there are twice as many skip links as before, *ten* of them at the top of the page preceding the banner, the search field, and the main navigation links: Skip to Main Content, Skip to Government Search, Skip to Bottom Nav, Skip to Top Nav Bar-Right Aligned, Skip to By Organization, Skip to Top Nav bar, Skip to Contact Your Government, Skip to Reference Center, Skip to Information by Topic, and Skip to Citizens: Get It Done Online!. The first skip link, Skip to Main Content, is a skip skip links link! These links are styled like this:

```
<a class="invisiblelink" href="#content">
<span class="invisiblelink">Skip to Main Content</span></a>
<a name="content"></a>
```

The style sheet includes invisiblelink styling:

```
.invisiblelink {
    font:bold 1pt Arial, Helvetica, sans-serif;
     text-transform:none; color:#ffffff; text-decoration:none}
```

These ten links are available (essentially) only to a screen reader user. How does this accommodation compare to using heading navigation (if headings had been coded on the page, which they were not)? There is no comparison. First, the many links added to the top of the page become a burden for a blind user with a screen reader. Second, if headings were used, then simple navigation keys can be interspaced with further line-by-line browsing, then continuing with previous or current heading. With the skip link table of contents, the user wanting to browse like that would need to go back to the top and step through the links again in order to skip to a different place.

Exposing the Link When It Receives Focus

A fairly new accommodation combines the idea of not cluttering the page with skip links and, at the same time, having links available to keyboard users who are not using screen readers. Figure 7-13 shows an example of a site that uses this approach. The figure shows the top part of the homepage of the Information Technology Technical Assistance and Training Center (ITTATC), which is funded to support Section 508.

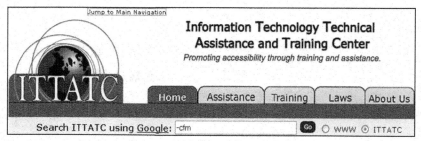

Figure 7-13. The skip link on ITTATC.org appears when it receives focus.

Three links at the top of the page are styled with a white font on a white background, until the link receives focus. Then the link becomes visible. In Figure 7-13, Jump to Main Navigation has input focus and is visible. The ITTATC skip link looks like this:

```
<a href="#Content" class="InvisiLink" title="">Jump to Page Content</a>
```

From the ITTATC style sheet, named ultimate.css, here is the style associated with the class InvisiLink:

```
A.InvisiLink {text-decoration: underline;  color : #ffffff;
    font-family : Verdana, Arial,
      Helvetica, sans-serif, "MS sans serif";  }
```

For both pseudo class selectors :active and :hover, the style is slightly different.

```
A.InvisiLink:active  {text-decoration: underline; color: #000000;
    font-family : Verdana, Arial,
      Helvetica, sans-serif, "MS sans serif"; }
```

The only change for the :active and :hover pseudo classes is to specify font color black (#000000), so that when you tab to the link or move your mouse over the link, it becomes visible.

A second example of this kind of accommodation is from my own site, www.jimthatcher.com, as shown in Figure 7-14.

Figure 7-14. The skip navigation link becomes visible on JimThatcher.com.

Here, the skip link becomes visible when it receives focus, but is styled off-screen so it does not occupy screen space. The skip link looks like this:

```
<li class="skip"><a href="#cont" id="skpnav">Skip Navigation.</a></li>
```

In the next section, I will talk about the target of this skip link, which is a bit of a surprise.

Let's look at the styling of the class skip:

```
.skip a {padding: 0 0.5em; display: inline; z-index: 2;
  text-decoration:none; position: absolute; width: 14em; left: -200em}
.skip a:focus, .skip a:active {position: absolute; left: 0.5em;
  border: solid #333 2px; color: #fff; background: #555}
```

With this styling, the inactive, unfocused skip link lies off-screen (left: -200 em) and is also available to a screen reader user. When the link receives focus using the Tab key, it is repositioned to be on-screen and is made visible.

The In-Page Link Problem with Internet Explorer 6

The target of the skip link on my website *used to* look like this:

```
<table><tr><td><a name="cont" id="cont"></a></td></tr></table>
```

Why a table? The answer is that there is a bug in Internet Explorer 6 that causes in-page links to not work from the keyboard. But when the target of any in-page link is placed at the top of a table cell, it will work correctly from the keyboard with Internet Explorer 6. What does *work correctly* mean? This description seems to be daunting for many web developers so focused on and dependent on the mouse. Here is how to test any in-page link:

1. Hide the mouse so you don't mess up this experiment.

2. Use the Tab key to move to the in-page link that is to be tested.

3. Press Enter. That will (probably) reposition the visual focus on the page so that the target of the in-page link is at the top of the visual window (if there is enough of a page to refocus).

4. Now, and this is the key, press Tab again. This time, the Tab key should move to the first link *below* the target of the in-page link. Often, this is not what happens; instead, this Tab key press puts focus on the first link of the page, or generally some other unwanted place.

If you follow these steps with Netscape 7.2, Mozilla Firefox 1.04, or Opera 7.54 (substitute the A key for the Tab key in Opera), everything will work as you would hope and expect. This is not so with Internet Explorer 6.

For table-based sites like CNN and IBM (as of this writing), the skip links usually work because it is natural that the target is at the top of a table cell (td). For more contemporary sites like that of the WAI, for example, the in-page links do not work. Try the WAI homepage at www.w3.org/WAI/. Tab to the Skip to Content link and press Enter, and the visual focus moves, but when you press Tab again, the input focus is back at the top of the

7

page. It should work, but it doesn't, at least as of this writing. This is true of many sites, and not just for skip links. For example, I have a short "table of contents" at the top of my comparison of Section 508 and WCAG (www.jimthatcher.com/sidebyside.htm). Though they are fixed now, up until recently, if you activated one of those from the keyboard, then tabbed again, you would be back at the top of the page.

What is the solution (read "work-around") for this problem? Through discussions on various mailing lists over several months in the spring and summer of 2005, the nature of the Internet Explorer 6 bug became clearer. In May 2005, Becky Gibson (of IBM) and Mike Scott (of MSF&W) independently recognized that when targets of in-page links were contained in elements "with width defined" (whatever that means), they generally worked from the keyboard. It was Terrence Wood who put it together with the hasLayout property.

When a link is activated, Internet Explorer 6 places input focus on one of the following:

- The target if the target is active (a link or an object with tabindex specified)
- On the first ancestor object of the target, which is a div or span with the property hasLayout equal to true
- A td or body object

The fact that table cells are in this list explains why in-page links usually work in table-based pages. The presence of a body element explains why the input focus after an in-page link often goes to the first link on the page.

A Google search for "hasLayout property" will yield a Microsoft MSDN page at the top of the list that describes this property and methods for setting it to true; setting width and height is one such method. That same Google search will turn up a number or articles about in-page links and the Internet Explorer 6 bug.

With that said, here is the work-around that I use to ensure that my in-page links work from the keyboard with Internet Explorer 6. This is the coding for a typical target:

```
<span style="position:absolute;">
<a name="content" id="content"> </a>
</span>
```

The anchor element (a) is not empty, but contains a nonbreaking space, which is invisible because it is given position:absolute. Without that content of the anchor tag, it turns out that visual focus doesn't work correctly. I hope that the next version of Internet Explorer will have this fixed, but Internet Explorer 6 will be around for a while, and this work-around is not too offensive.

Skipping Text Blocks with Assistive Technologies

Unfortunately, many important websites do not provide any of the simple accommodations discussed in the previous sections to permit people who cannot or do not use the mouse to quickly get to the main content of the page and around the major sections of the page. As is typically the case, the assistive technology developers recognize this problem and make valiant efforts to solve it for users of screen readers and talking browsers.

Navigation with screen readers has become quite sophisticated with keys to move through (forwards and backwards) headings, tables, links, lists, form elements, frames, and "chunks."

In this section, we'll look at the commands to jump over blocks of links in Window-Eyes 5.0, IBM Home Page Reader 3.04 (two updates since 3.00), and JAWS for Windows 6.2.

Skipping Links with Window-Eyes

Window-Eyes was the first screen reader to build in significant mechanisms for skipping over blocks of links, and now has about 20 different commands that have that effect. You can jump to more specific points in the document, such as to the next form control (C), the next link (L), next list (S), or next table (T).

You can also jump to the next block of normal inactive text (X). This next text jump can be configured as to how much text will be considered a block of normal text, so that a word or two, or a heading can be ignored. Settings for the number of characters and number of lines for the X jump are in the Window-Eyes Verbosity Settings (Ins+V). Choose MSAA ➤ Miscellaneous ➤ Next Text Minimum Line Length and Next Text Consecutive Lines. Both of these values default to 1, meaning that, in the default environment, any single nonactive word will be considered to be a block. The reason this jump might be important is the possibility of letting the screen reader jump over those "repetitive navigation links" all on its own, with no help from the web page designer.

With the default settings, from the top of the CNN homepage (Figure 7-9), you need to use about six next text jumps (X) to arrive at the main content targeted by CNN's skip link. If you change the Next Text Minimum Line Length to 25 text characters and the Next Text Consecutive Lines to 2 text lines, three next text jumps work (in a 2001 version of CNN.com, it took only one next text jump, but now there seems to be an iframe on CNN.com that is complicating the process). But the main story begins with a heading (h2), and it is the only heading, so a simple H key press takes you to the main story.

The difference between a single H key press to move among headings (for Home Page Reader and JAWS as well) and activating the skip link (with Enter) is a difference between day and night. With the H key, Window-Eyes responds by announcing the level of the heading (2) and the heading text. When you press Enter on the skip link, Window-Eyes announces that it is reloading the page and presents the table of statistics for the page (links, frames, Flash objects, and so on), and finally, the text at the target of the link if the jump worked (and sometimes it doesn't work). I don't know why Window-Eyes reloads the page when an in-page link is activated, but it does. And the fact that it does is reason enough that a skip link is a poor accommodation compared with proper headings markup. With the H key, you hear the headline in 2 seconds; it takes about 25 seconds to get through the page reloading message and get to the news.

Skipping Links with Home Page Reader

IBM Home Page Reader includes a command (Ctrl+down arrow) to jump to the next block of text or links, similar to Window-Eyes. So if you are positioned on link text, then this jump takes you to the next nonlink text. If you are positioned on nonlink text, this jump takes you to the next link.

The idea of the next block jump (Ctrl+down arrow) is to skip over the groups of links. But the problem is that very often, there are short stretches of nonlink text scattered among the links, so it still may take a long time to reach the main content. To add to this problem, Home Page Reader inserts metatext, such as "Internal frame 2: Untitled," in its text view, which is then counted as nonlink text. Similarly, "Start of form 1" and "End of form 1" are both stops for this jump command. Home Page Reader uses six jumps to get to the headline on the homepage of CNN.com (Figure 7-9).

Skipping Links with JAWS

JAWS provides single-character commands for skipping to most object types, including controls (C), buttons (B), edit fields (E), frames (M), headings (H), same element (D), different element (D), and many more. For headings, you can even jump by level using keys 1 through 6.

JAWS Version 6 introduced the new concept of *place markers*. You can insert a place marker at any position of and page (Ctrl+Shift+K), then return to it with K (Shift+K goes to the previous marker). I experimented by adding place markers at the beginning of the main content of CNN.com (Figure 7-9) and at MORE NEWS. A week later, much to my surprise, the main content place markers still worked, but the MORE NEWS place marker was off by a line. I am not sure how this is implemented. But it is a cool idea enhanced by the possibility of community-based place-marking, since place markers can be shared among JAWS users.

Accessible Frames

Although few websites use frames these days, when coded correctly, websites with frames can (in principle) achieve access improvements.

The U.S. Access Board advises that frames be identifiable with titles in this Section 508 provision:

> §1194.22(i) Frames shall be titled with text that facilitates frame identification and navigation.

The wording of WCAG 1.0, Checkpoint 12.1 on frames is nearly the same:

> 12.1 Title each frame to facilitate frame identification and navigation.

So where are these "titles" that the guidelines require? The problem with all of these guidelines is that the word *title* in them is ambiguous.

Guideline 4.1 of the Last Call draft of WCAG 2.0 is the key to accessible frames:

> Guideline 4.1 Support compatibility with current and future user agents (including assistive technologies).

The corresponding Level 1 success criterion is the following:

> 4.1.2 For all user interface components, the name and role can be programmatically determined, values that can be set by the user can be programmatically set, and notification of changes to these items is available to user agents, including assistive technologies. [Level 1]

Success Criterion 4.1.2 requires that it is possible to determine the role of a frame, and the simplest way to do that is by providing meaningful title attributes on those frames.

Let's see how frames work, to help make the issues raised by the guidelines clearer.

How Frames Work

A frame page is actually a collection of pages displayed in separate windows (or frames) within the main window. The main page of a frame site is called the *frameset page*, and it specifies the layout of the various pages (frames). What is appealing about this design is that the different functions of various parts of the page are separated into different files, which can contribute to helpful navigation for all users.

Figure 7-15 shows an example of a frame site that duplicates the structure of the table shown earlier in Figure 7-2. This frame page consists of five frames; a title frame, two navigation frames, a banner, and the main content, corresponding to the cells of the table in Figure 7-2.

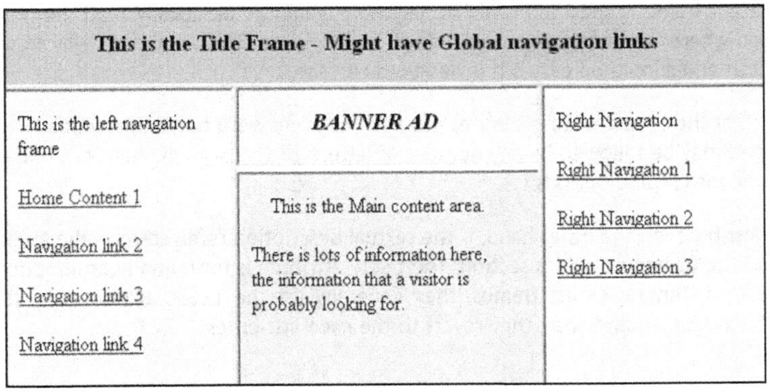

Figure 7-15. A frame example

Here is the code for the frame structure in Figure 7-15:

```
<frameset rows="40,*" >
   <frame src="Title.htm" … id="toptitle"
               name="TopTitle"  title="Top Title">
   <frameset cols="150,*,150">
      <frame src="Left.htm" … id=leftnavigation"
               name="LeftNavigation" title="Left Navigation">
```

```
<frameset rows="40,*"  border="2">
 <frame src="Banner.htm" … id="bannerad"
              name="BannerAd"   title="Banner Ad">
      <frame src="Content1.htm" … id="maincontent"
                  name="MainContent" title="Main Content">
</frameset>
<frame src="Right.htm" … id="rightnavigation"
              name="RightNavigation" title="Right Navigation">
</frameset>
</frameset>
```

Notice that each <frame> is provided with a title attribute together with both an id and a name attribute. The name and id attributes are how code in the HTML page refers to a frame (the id attribute replaces the name attribute for XHTML, so for a while both should be used). Often, the name attribute is totally obscure, like name="frame0978", and that is okay, because only programmers are supposed to see this. Links should specify a target frame in which the new page will open. When a link in the navigation frame opens up a page in the main content window, the navigation link should specify MainContent as its target attribute:

```
<a href="Content2.htm" target="MainContent">Navigation link 2</a>
```

The beauty of this for all audiences is that, when this link is activated, *only* the new main content page is opened or refreshed; the other frames, perhaps with a table of contents or large banner images, all stay as they were. If you want to read the main content of this sample frame site, just open the main content frame. If you want to check out the navigation links, read the navigation frame. And when you decide to follow a navigation link, since the target frame is specified, assistive technology can automatically read the main content page where the page you requested will be displayed. This scenario is why frame navigation can and should be easy if it is designed correctly.

Remember that the name and id attributes must be only one word beginning with a letter (A–Z; a–z) and may be followed by any number of letters, digits (0–9), hyphens (-), underscores (_), colons (:), and periods (.).

The title attribute, on the other hand, is the textual description referred to in the guidelines cited at the beginning of this section. The title attribute is for human consumption. When assistive technologies list frames, they generally list the title attributes of the frames when available; otherwise, they revert to the name attributes.

How Assistive Technologies Support Frames

When the Lynx text browser opens a frame site, it presents the user with a list of links to the various frame pages. Although assistive technologies use title attributes, Lynx identifies the frames by the name attribute if one exists; otherwise, each frame is identified with a number.

Figure 7-16 shows the list of frames as Lynx sees the example in Figure 7-15. The current link is MainContent. If the Lynx user follows that link (using the right arrow key), the main content page is opened, as shown in Figure 7-17.

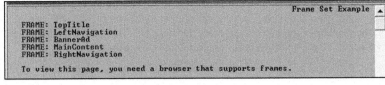

Figure 7-16. The Lynx view of a frame page

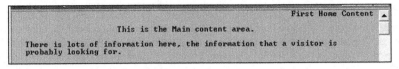

Figure 7-17. A single frame page displayed by Lynx

With a meaningful name attribute on every frame, the Lynx user can easily identify which frame to open. This Lynx view of the frame world captures the idea of frame browsing as a list of named HTML pages and their contents.

The situation is similar in the case of JAWS for Windows. However, when JAWS opens a frame page, it begins reading frame content one frame at a time in the order seen in the Lynx view shown in Figure 7-16, and which is explicit in the <frameset> page. As a new frame is encountered, JAWS announces "Frame," along with the value of the title attribute (or the name attribute if the title attribute is not available) of the frame. The JAWS user can also request a list of frames using the Ins+F9 command, and the list looks like Figure 7-18.

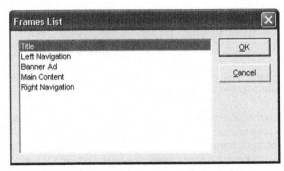

Figure 7-18. The JAWS list of frames

Window-Eyes and Home Page Reader do the same thing. If no title attribute is available, these technologies will revert to the name attribute of the frame. With no title or name attribute, Home Page Reader will try to use the <title> element on the actual frame page instead. But very often, frame pages do not have <title> elements because the developers of those pages don't see those titles in the title bar; they see only the title of the <frameset> page.

When Home Page Reader encounters the sample frame site in Figure 7-15, it opens the first frame, announces the `<title>` element of the `<frameset>` page ("Frame Set Example"), the number of the frame to be read, "Frame 1 of 5," the `<title>` attribute of the `<frame>` page ("Title"), and then finally reads the frame page itself.

Frames and Focus

Figure 7-19 shows a test frame site hosted on the Freedom Scientific website (www. freedomscientific.com/HTML_challenge/files/frames_demo2.html). The site actually has three frames; the top frame containing an image has been cropped from the view to save space. The two frames shown in the figure are a table of contents frame on the left and a content frame on the right. So, when you want to read one of the sections, say The HTML Frames Challenge, you find that link in the table of contents frame and activate it. Then the section will open on the right in the content frame, ready to be studied and navigated. Well, for some it is ready—if you can see and don't rely on the keyboard for navigation, it is ready.

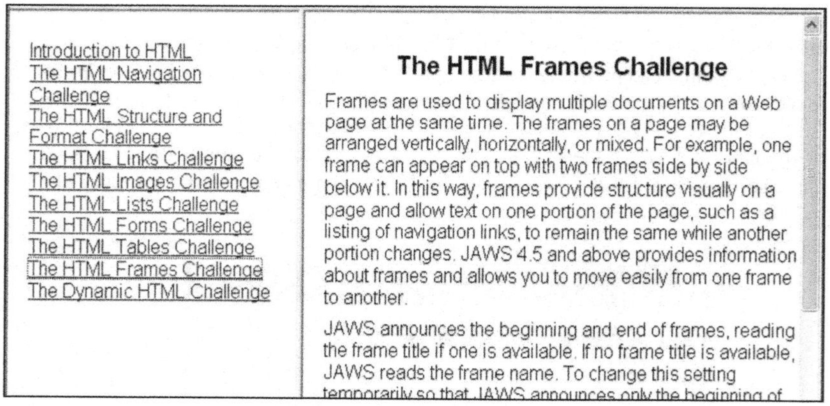

Figure 7-19. Sample frame page showing table of contents

Before capturing the screen in Figure 7-19, I had just used the Tab key to navigate down the table of contents page and pressed Enter on The HTML Frames Challenge. This opened the material in the content frame on the right. But notice in the figure that Internet Explorer has left focus on the link just activated. The focus rectangle is just barely visible. So, the next tab will not move around the content page as it should; it will still be locked in the table of contents frame. The same thing happens in the Firefox 1.04, Netscape 7.2, and Opera 8.02 browsers.

Basically, this browser focus problem negates the value of frames that I talked about earlier for people who rely on the keyboard. Two of the assistive technologies compensate for this and correctly take care of focus. Both JAWS and Home Page Reader start reading "The HTML Frame Challenge" (and put input focus there, too) after the table of contents link is activated. Unfortunately, Window-Eyes and Hal both continue reading in the table of contents where Internet Explorer has left the input focus.

Summary for Frames

There are fundamental usability problems with frames because they break the unified model of the Web—pages are not represented by unique URLs. Bookmarking, printing, and sharing of URLs don't work as they should. However, in some cases, a web application requires frames. When you must use frames, adding `title` attributes to the frameset components is a very small task compared to the development of a framed site. Therefore, you should have no difficulty following these guidelines:

- Use a meaningful `title` attribute for each `<frame>` element that clearly describes the purpose of the frame, such as Main Content, Site Navigation, or Table of Contents.

- Every page should have a meaningful `<title>` element. Make sure this is true for all frame pages as well.

Accessible Image Maps

There are two kinds of image maps: client-side and server-side. Client-side image maps are by far the most common type of image map to be found on the Web today. In fact, server-side image maps should be avoided.

Client-Side Image Maps

I talked about client-side image maps in the previous chapter, where I emphasized the requirement of text equivalents for all image map hotspots. These text equivalents are absolutely essential for accessibility.

The image map is called *client-side* because the browser (the client) must figure out how to handle the result of a click on the image. Any time there is a click on the page, the client (browser) figures out whether or not the coordinates of that click fell inside one of the regions specified as an `<area>` of the client-side map. If the click is inside one of those regions, then the browser opens the corresponding URL—that is, the value of the `href` for that `<area>`.

Figure 7-20 shows a client-side image map from an earlier version of the U.S. Senate website (`www.senate.gov/`). The alt-text on the image that creates the map is `alt="Quick List"`.

Figure 7-20. Client-side image map

Here is the code that designates the image in Figure 7-20 as a client-side image map:

```
<img src="sidebar.gif" alt="Quick List" ... usemap="#subnav">
```

Client-side maps need to have a usemap attribute, *not* an ismap attribute. In this case, the usemap attribute points to a map called subnav, which defines the areas of the image map that are hotspots. In the example, there are four areas:

```
<map name="subnav">
    <area shape="rect" coords="4,33,76,72" href=" ... "
        alt="Committee Hearing Schedule">
    <area shape="rect" coords="5,78,88,117" href=" ... "
        alt="Yesterday's Senate Floor Activity">
    <area shape="rect" coords="5,121,75,140" href=" ... "
        alt="Senate Art">
    <area shape="rect" coords="5,143,59,172" href=" ... "
        alt="Senate History">
</map>
```

The four image map areas have alt-text that is exactly the same as the text in the image; this is perfect. The way that this client-side image map works is that each <area> specifies a region of the image in which a click will open a certain URL, namely the href of the <area>.

The shape and coord (coordinates) attributes define the region of each <area>. There are three possible shapes: rect for rectangle, circle, and poly for polygon. The coordinates are pixel coordinates measured from the top left of the image. For a rectangle, the developer must specify the top-left and bottom-right corners. A circle is given by the center point and radius. A polygon is specified by a series of points corresponding to the corners of the polygon.

Server-Side Image Maps

Figure 7-21 shows another image map, from www.metrokc.gov/services.htm. It is fundamentally different from the previous example in Figure 7-20.

Figure 7-21. Server-side image map for King County

Figure 7-21 is a server-side image map, with the following elided code.

```
<a href= "wwwnav.map">
    <img src=" ... navbar.gif" border="0" ismap="ismap"
        alt="King County Navigation Bar (text navigation at bottom)" >
</a>
```

Since this is a server-side map, there is no usemap attribute. Instead, the image itself is enclosed in an anchor tag (<a>) and the img element has the Boolean ismap attribute. That attribute tells the browser to send the coordinates of the user mouse click directly to an associated map file on the server that is referenced by the href attribute of the anchor element. For any person who cannot use the mouse, this is a fundamentally *inaccessible* form of navigation because it requires positioning the mouse on some part of a picture indicating a desired action (pressing Enter on a server-side image map sends click coordinates 0,0 to the server).

The U.S. Access Board recognized the problem with server-side maps and recommends having redundant text links if you do use a server-side map, in this Section 508 provision:

§1194.22(e) Redundant text links shall be provided for each active region of a server-side image map.

WCAG 1.0 has the same requirement at Priority 1:

1.2 Provide redundant text links for each active region of a server-side image map.

Indeed, the King County site in Figure 7-21 has redundant text links at the bottom of the homepage, and the alt-text for the server-side map tells the user to find *text navigation at bottom*.

I can't see any reason why the King County site would use a server-side map for its main navigation. The equivalent text links at the bottom of the page make it accessible and compliant. The King County site, however, does not satisfy the second provision of the Section 508 rule on web accessibility:

§1194.22(f) Client-side image maps shall be provided instead of server-side image maps except where the regions cannot be defined with an available geometric shape.

The Section 508 provision is again almost identical to Checkpoint 9.1 of the WCAG:

9.1 Provide client-side image maps instead of server-side image maps except where the regions cannot be defined with an available geometric shape.

In the Last Call draft of WCAG 2.0, three success criteria relate to server-side maps under Guidelines 2.1, 2.4, and 4.2, respectively:

Guideline 2.1 Make all functionality operable via a keyboard interface.

SC 2.1.1 All functionality of the content is operable in a non time-dependent manner through a keyboard interface, except where the task requires analog, time-dependent input. (Level 1)

7

Guideline 2.4 Provide mechanisms to help users find content, orient themselves within it, and navigate through it

SC 2.4.4 Each link is programmatically associated with text from which its purpose can be determined. (Level 2)

Guideline 4.2 Ensure that content is accessible or provide an accessible alternative

SC 4.2.1 At least one version of the content meets all level 1 success criteria, but alternate version(s) that do not meet all level 1 success criteria may be available from the same URI. (Level 1)

There is nothing about the regions in the King County image map that would make them difficult to define with available geometric shapes; simple rectangles would work well. In fact, the main navigation map on the homepage has now been changed to a client-side image map, as shown in shown in Figure 7-22.

Figure 7-22. King County client-side image map

Complex Client-Side Image Maps

As mentioned earlier, client-side maps provide three shapes to describe regions: rectangles (shape="rect"), circles (shape="circle"), and polygons (shape="poly"). Effectively, any shape can be described with a polygon or collection of polygons.

Figure 7-23 shows a good example of a client-side image map with rather complex hotspots, which are regions defined by polygons. It is Microsoft's Local District Information map at www.microsoft.com/usa/map.asp.

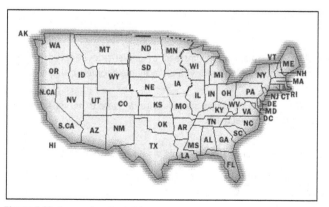

Figure 7-23. A complex client-side map

Using the Tab key, I moved the focus indicator in Internet Explorer to the upper Midwest area in the map in Figure 7-23 so that the focus polygon is visible. The source code for that area in the map uses a polygon determined by about 45 points:

```
<area shape=poly
    coords="173,7,181,9,180,10,227,9,232,10,233,12,238,11,244,12,
        250,13,257,14,263,15,267,17,259,27,251,27,245,36,249,41,246,48,
        254,53,256,57,257,61,258,66,262,68,263,73,264,75,263,77,
        262,78,260,78,259,80,258,82,257,84,256,86,254,87,243,87,243,88,
        229,88,229,92,207,92,206,90,186,90,184,85,173,82,170,45,
        172,30,172,7,174,8"
    href=" ... "
    alt="Twin Cities: ND, MN, SD, NE, IA">
```

In principle, any region of a finite image can be defined by one of the available geometric patterns of a client-side map. In the worst case, individual areas could consist of individual pixels. But, as the map in Figure 7-23 illustrates, complex regions also can be defined using polygons. It is therefore my conclusion that there is no case where a server-side map is permitted under the Section 508 provision §1194.22(f) or WCAG Checkpoint 9.1.

Even though it is hard to imagine, there may be cases where a designer wants every pixel to be a hotspot with different actions. You might argue that there are too many regions in this case. But that is a different issue than the one raised by provision §1194.22(f) and Checkpoint 9.1. A client-side image map still could be used.

Summary for Image Maps

The following points apply to accessible image maps:

- If you want to use an image map, make it a client-side image map.
- Include meaningful alt-text for every <area> of the <map> and also don't forget alt-text on the image that creates the map.
- If you must use a server-side map, also include equivalent text links on the page for all hotspots of your server-side map (and please write to me explaining why you need to use a server-side map, because I would like to know).

Layout and Navigation

Most of us will navigate *within* a page intuitively. If you can see the page, you can visually move to the main content of the page and read the story, or indeed look across the top global navigation buttons to find the Search form or Contact Us link that you need. You look down the right column to find the other top stories or shopping specials. The process of finding those items is as much navigation as the process of moving from page to page. While reading the main content, a sighted user may have to page down or use the mouse to move down with the vertical scroll bar. Clearly, layout is affecting the process of navigating the content of the page. This process is much more complicated and difficult if you cannot use the mouse or you are partially sighted or blind.

As you've seen, using HTML headings for the sections of your page can make a huge difference in user navigation. A skip navigation link can facilitate movement to the main story. The hidden table of contents at the top of the site (as in the FirstGov site at www.firstgov.gov, shown earlier in Figure 7-11) is another approach.

You have also seen how layout tables can make it very time-consuming to find the main content in a page, as in the example shown earlier in Figure 7-2. However, some simple tricks with layout tables actually make it easier to find the main content with a screen reader or talking browser.

It is not clear why at least one column of navigation links is routinely placed on the left side of web pages. On my site in 2004, I used to use a tabular structure like that shown in Figure 7-24, which places the navigation column on the right and the main content on the left.

This is a title cell	
Main content area with lots of text and content filling the left-hand part of the window	Right Navigation 1 Right Navigation 2 Right Navigation 3

Figure 7-24. Simple table layout with navigation on the right

With this layout, the main content follows the "title" in a text or linearized view of the page. There is no need to provide a skip navigation link in order to comply with the Section 508 provision §1194.22(o). However, in this situation, I did add a skip navigation link attached to an invisible GIF at the top of the page. This certainly is not required for compliance with the Section 508 Standards or WCAG 1.0.

When all the layout of a page is controlled with CSS positioning, the web developer is in control of the reading order of the sections (divs) of the page, because the source code order does not determine the visual presentation order. When you are using CSS, make sure that your reading order makes sense and mark up the sections of the page with HTML headings.

Accessible Links

The link text you use can have a major impact on your web page accessibility. But before we look at link text, let's review how link navigation works.

Link Navigation

Some users of the Web are so mouse-dependent that they may not be aware of the fact that you can tab through all the active elements of a web page. As you do that, usually a dotted enclosing polygon, called a *focus rectangle*, moves along with the focus, highlighting the current link text inside. This was illustrated in the image map from Microsoft

(Figure 7-23) and the frame page from Freedom Scientific (Figure 7-19). Figure 7-25 shows another example, which is a piece of the right navigation panel of my current site as seen in Firefox 1.04.

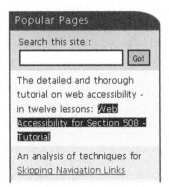

Figure 7-25. Link with focus

The link text that currently has focus is marked with a dotted rectangle, but the foreground and background colors are also changed by the CSS style on the site. The text enclosed inside this focus rectangle is called the *link text*, which is the content of the anchor element (a):

```
<a href="webcourse1.htm">
    Web Accessibility for Section 508 - Tutorial
</a>
```

As you navigate around the links of a page with the Tab key (and Shift+Tab to go backwards; A and Q in Opera), you can use the Enter key at any time to activate a link. This action corresponds to clicking the link.

When you are listening to a page, the link text will be identified in one of a number of ways, but generally screen readers precede the text of a link by saying "link" or "visited link." Home Page Reader has several options for indicating links. With the default settings, Home Page Reader changes to a higher-pitched, so-called "female" voice on a link. Alternatively, you can set Home Page Reader to produce a sound alerting the user as the link is spoken, or you can set it to speak some metatext (such as "link") before, or even after, the link.

Link Text

The actual link text is important. What does it say? Is the link text clearly explaining what the link is pointing to? WCAG Checkpoint 13.1 captures an important requirement:

13.1 Clearly identify the target of each link. [Priority 2]

Under Guideline 2.4, the Last Call draft of WCAG 2.0 has one Level 2 success criterion and one Level 3 success criterion that relate to link text:

> 2.4.4 Each link is programmatically associated with text from which its purpose can be determined. (Level 2)
>
> 2.4.8 The purpose of each link can be programmatically determined from the link. (Level 3)

You must be able to understand where a link will take you, even if you read the link text out of the context of the page. As you tab from link to link, the focus rectangle highlights the link text. Whether you are using magnification, focusing on the focus rectangle, or listening to the page, it is the link text that is important. At Level 3, WCAG 2.0 requires only that the purpose of the link can be programmatically determined from the link. The requirement at Level 2 is that purpose of the link be available to assistive technology in some way. I think the wording of this success criterion must change; "programmatically associated" is not defined.

The page excerpt shown in Figure 7-26 has a service to sell, but the targets of the links are not clearly identified.

Starting at $44.90 per month	$34.95 per month	$24.95 per month	$9.95 per month
Learn more.	Try it free or learn more.	Try it free or learn more.	Try it free or learn more.

Figure 7-26. Examples of bad link text

With link text such as Learn more and Try it free, a disabled user is left asking, "Learn more about what?" and "Try what free?" The link text needs to be much more meaningful, such as Learn more about our content management system and Try our testing tool for free.

The worst offender is Click here. All of the assistive technologies discussed in this chapter can help users by generating a list of links. With JAWS, Ins+F7 brings up the list. With Home Page Reader, Ctrl+L generates a list. The Window-Eyes command is Ins+Tab. Figure 7-27 shows the Window-Eyes link list for a site that just does not understand the importance of identifying the target of links.

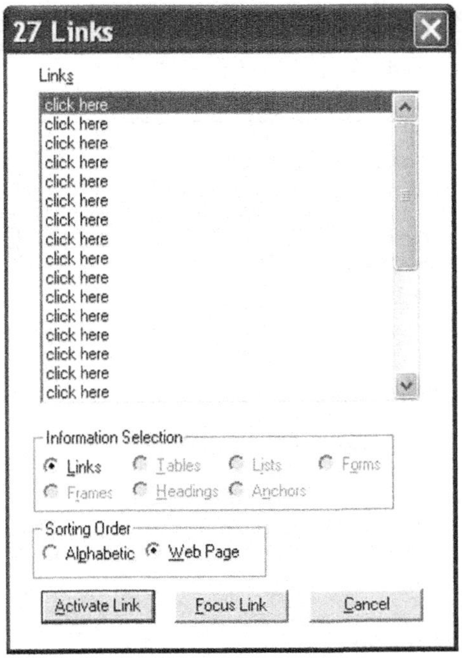

Figure 7-27. Window-Eyes link list for a site where all links are "click here"

There are other, less crucial but still important, aspects of accessible link text. As I just mentioned, links are read as "links" by screen readers and talking browsers, so there is no need to include link to in the link text, as is commonly done in alt-text for image links. Don't include verbs like open our contact form here; instead, just say contact us. The latter would be typical of visual text, while the longer version might appear as alt-text on a contact us image. You already saw an example of annoying link text in the CNN.com skip link (described in the "Creating a Link As Alt-Text on an Invisible Image" section), with Click here to skip to main content. It should be just main content. Unfortunately, there is historical precedent for using skip to main content and skip navigation, but both are poor choices because of the presence of the verb and, in the second case, because the destination cannot even be determined.

Every image that is a link must have nonempty and meaningful alt-text because when you tab to a link, there must be something there. When the link text is the alt-text of an image, it should convey the target of the link. Remember from the previous chapter that an image inside an anchor tag *may* have null alt-text if text describing the nature of the link is also included within the *same* anchor.

Finally, there are times when fully spelling out the target of a link really becomes overbearing and annoying for both the visual and auditory experience of a page. Figure 7-28 shows a section of a page on Priceline.com.

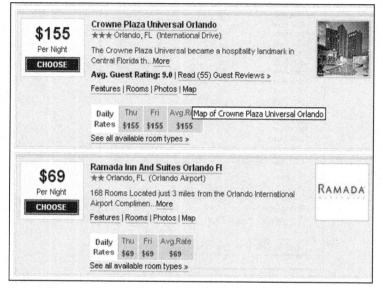

Figure 7-28. Generic link text augmented with title attribute

Each of the generic links, including More, Choose, Features, Rooms, and Photos, is relevant to the specific hotel property. Those generic links are repeated for each hotel. Some interpret WCAG Checkpoint 13.1 to require that each generic link must include the specific hotel, such as Features of the Crowne Plaza Universal Orlando. That is the wrong thing to do for all users because the visual design would become highly cluttered, as would the audible presentation. The examples in Figure 7-28 do comply with Success Criterion 2.4.4 because there is text available with which to understand the purpose of the link. In cases like these, you should add a `title` attribute to the anchor element that specifies the details and thus comply with WCAG Checkpoint 13.1 and WCAG 2.0 Success Criterion 2.4.8. That is what Priceline.com does, as suggested by the tooltip in Figure 7-28.

I am often asked, "What good does that `title` attribute do?" Can screen readers access that information? The answer is, "not very easily." For example, JAWS has three options for speaking a link: the link text, the title text, or the longer of the two. The default, thank goodness, is link text. I hope one day that screen readers will add an option to speak additional information about this object, which could announce the `title` attributes on links and other elements, long descriptions of images, and additional information about form controls (see Chapter 8), as just three examples.

Summary

In this chapter, we looked at several ways of providing navigation that is accessible to users who depend on screen readers or cannot use the mouse. The most important thing you can do to provide accessible navigation of your page is to mark up the sections of your page with HTML headings, including one at the beginning of the "main content." You also saw how a link to the main content at the top of the page can be a useful facility for users who are visually impaired. You then looked at how frames can be fairly accessible if meaningful title attributes are placed on the frame elements and title elements are included on the frame pages themselves.

Next, you saw how client-side image maps can provide an accessible form of site navigation, as long as you provide alt-text on each area of the map that clearly describes the target of the corresponding hotspot. Server-side image maps are fundamentally inaccessible, so redundant text links for all hotspots of the map should be provided whenever server-side maps are used. It is best not to use server-side maps at all.

Good page layout is another important factor that can increase a website's accessibility, especially for pages with CSS layout.

Finally, you looked at accessible links. All link text, whether it is visible on your page or the alt-text on image links, must clearly tell the user the purpose of the link. Phrases like Click Here or Learn More are of little use to someone using an assistive technology. Not only that, but there is no need to preface link text with link to; instead, simply specify the target.

7

8 ACCESSIBLE DATA INPUT

by Jim Thatcher

Increasingly, businesses and government agencies are adopting a web presence for sales and services to their customers and clients. In the U.S., these businesses are required by the Americans with Disabilities Act (ADA) to make their physical bricks-and-mortar facilities accessible to people with disabilities. Many believe that the ADA also applies to the virtual world of the Internet as a "place of public accommodation," and thus web services and sales must also be accessible.

The local bank has a website where you can check your balances, make transactions, and fill out a loan application. Similarly, if you own a mutual fund, you can probably open an online account where you can check the status of your funds and transfer assets from one fund to another. However, the chances are that these shopping and financial sites are *not* tuned to the simple requirements of web accessibility. While these sites stress the importance of being able to interact with the web page to enter data and submit information, their developers and designers may not have considered how customers with disabilities will deal with that interaction.

All of the issues about accessible content come into play when we think about how people with disabilities interact with a web page to input information—whether to fill out a survey, to purchase a software product, or to request information. Is there convenient access to the form elements with the keyboard? Are there images that convey information about the form, and do those images have clear text equivalents? Are image buttons in use and do those images include alt-text? Is color being used to convey information? Is there a redundant method conveying the same information?

When you can look at the screen, you can make associations easily; for example, you can quickly focus on the main content of a page. In a similar way, when you input data (name, address, phone number, and so on) into an online form, it is usually quite easy to understand what information goes where, what is required, and how to submit the results. If you have trepidation about passing personal data across the Internet, then consider how your concern would be heightened if you weren't absolutely certain of which information goes where. If you cannot see the screen and rely on a screen reader, the task can be daunting at best. This is the principal issue to be discussed in this chapter.

Guidelines for Data-Input Forms

The Section 508 Standards for web accessibility are very clear on the point that data input should be accessible:

> §1194.22(n) When electronic forms are designed to be completed online, the form shall allow people using assistive technology to access the information, field elements, and functionality required for completion and submission of the form, including all directions and cues.

A fundamental difference between this provision of the Section 508 Standards and some of the others is that this one is far more general. Provision §1194.22(a) says provide text equivalents for nontext elements. Provision §1194.22(i) says provide titles for frames, but the provision for forms simply says make forms accessible to people using assistive technology. The reason for providing text equivalents for nontext elements is to make those images accessible to people with disabilities, especially those using assistive technology. In the same way, the reason for providing title attributes for frames is to make it possible for people using assistive technology or text browsers to access the information in the frames. The Section 508 provisions for text equivalents and frame titles are very specific in suggesting what web developers should do in order to make their pages accessible to people using assistive technology. Provision §1194.22(n) is not. It is up to us!

Looking to the Web Content Accessibility Guidelines, Version 1.0 (WCAG 1.0) from the World Wide Web Consortium (W3C) Web Accessibility Initiative (WAI), we find a different story. Several checkpoints address accessibility of electronic forms directly; that is, they address the question of what to do to make forms accessible. It has always surprised me that these are only Priority 2 checkpoints, since the issues raised here are critical for a person with a screen reader trying to deal with online forms.

> 10.2 Until user agents support explicit associations between labels and form controls, for all form controls with implicitly associated labels, ensure that the label is properly positioned. [Priority 2]

> 12.4 Associate labels explicitly with their controls. [Priority 2]

The key to accessible forms is that the function of any form control element should be clear to people using a screen reader and they should be able to manipulate the form easily. Knowing the intent of the input element is the purpose of WCAG Priority 2 Checkpoints 10.2 and 12.4. The first checkpoint says position the prompt correctly. The second says that you should programmatically connect the prompt with the input control.

In a form, you might have First Name next to a text-entry field (an input element of type="text"). The text, First Name is what we will call the *prompt* or the *label* of the form element. As another example, the text Send literature next to a check box is the prompt for that check box. The prompt is thus the textual information that explains the purpose of the input control—what the user is supposed to do with it. Sometimes, the prompt is included in the control, as in Cancel on a push button.

So, the main issue with accessibility of forms is whether people who cannot see the screen will know the prompts for all the controls in a form.

Let's look carefully at WCAG Checkpoint 10.2. This is a condition, which says if assistive technology does not support explicit labeling, then use proper positioning. But today, screen readers do support explicit labeling, so Checkpoint 10.2 is satisfied. We don't have to worry about it. It is true that screen readers will pick up the prompts if they are *perfectly* positioned, but depending on positioning for form accessibility is hazardous, because a slight change in layout can render a form element useless for a screen reader user.

The WAI raises other issues. Priority 3 Checkpoint 10.4 addresses the issue of screen readers not being able to find empty text-input controls:

> 10.4 Until user agents handle empty controls correctly, include default, place-holding characters in edit boxes and text areas. [Priority 3]

8

In the past, screen readers literally "read the screen," and so they had difficulty detecting an input field that was blank. This is why Checkpoint 10.4 recommends placing "default place-holding" text in the field. Now that screen readers use Microsoft Active Accessibility (MSAA) or the Document Object Model (DOM) of the browser, they don't generally have this problem anymore. The usefulness of Checkpoint 10.4 has passed, and like Checkpoint 10.2, this requirement is satisfied.

The same is not true for Checkpoint 12.3, which is basically saying that the information should be grouped:

> 12.3 Divide large blocks of information into more manageable groups where natural and appropriate. [Priority 2]

This is especially true for form elements. The intent of Checkpoint 12.3 is clarified by the explanatory text from its guidelines document (www.w3.org/TR/WCAG10):

> For example, in HTML, use OPTGROUP to group OPTION elements inside a SELECT; group form controls with FIELDSET and LEGEND; use nested lists where appropriate; use headings to structure documents, etc.

WCAG 2.0 (as of January, 2006) was clearer on this point:

> SC 4.1.3 The label of each user interface control in the Web content that accepts input from the user can be programmatically determined and is explicitly associated with the control. [Level 1]

Unfortunately, Success Criterion 4.1.3 has been removed, and the Last Call draft of WCAG 2.0 relies on Success Criterion 1.3.1 to cover the labeling of forms:

> SC 1.3.1 Information and relationships conveyed through presentation can be programmatically determined, and notification of changes to these is available to user agents, including assistive technologies. [Level 1]

A form label and the fact that it is associated with some control are information as well as a relationship that must be programmatically determined. But not having any success criteria specifically dealing with forms is a mistake, and I have urged the Working Group to reinstate Success Criterion 4.1.3.

Accessible Forms

In this section, we will look at the techniques for creating accessible forms. They are fairly simple and direct. I'll start with basic form components, then explain how assistive technologies handle forms, and, finally, present best practices for creating accessible forms.

Form Components

Forms consist of a number of possible input or interaction elements, including the following:

- Push buttons: `<input>` elements of type button, submit, and reset
- Graphical buttons: `<input>` elements of type image
- Generalized buttons: `<button>` elements
- Text entry fields: `<input>` elements of type text, password and with no type specified
- Text areas: `<textarea>` elements
- Radio buttons: `<input>` elements of type radio
- Check boxes: `<input>` elements of type checkbox
- Select menus or combo boxes: `<select>` elements

Several of these can be collected in a `<form>` element along with other content, including images and text. Usually, `<form>` elements contain at least one submit button (`<button>` or `<input type="submit">`).

These form elements fall into two subsets: those where the prompting information is included in the control (the buttons) and those where the prompting information is usually outside the control (text-input controls, radio buttons, check boxes, and select menus).

Buttons

Buttons are the easiest for accessibility because the information about what to do with the control is included in the control. The key to nongraphical buttons (input elements of type button, submit, and reset) is the value attribute. The text of the value attribute is what appears visually and also what a screen reader will speak. In evaluating websites and web applications for accessibility, I have never seen one of the following buttons lacking adequate text, because what is visually presented is the same as what a screen reader speaks.

8

Here is the code for these buttons:

```
<input type="submit" >
<input type="reset" >
<input type="submit" value="Skip" >
<input name="b1" type="button" >
```

The first two buttons display the default text for submit (Submit Query) and reset (Reset) buttons, which is the visual display for those kinds of buttons when no value attribute is present. The third button displays the text Skip, which is the value of the value attribute. Finally, the fourth button demonstrates that you are not likely to forget the value attribute on one of those buttons that don't have defaults, because the button will be visually blank. The same thing happens if you place value="". "How silly," you are probably thinking, "no one would do that." But, in fact, that frequently happens for alt-text on image buttons where the error does not change the visual presentation and yet drastically impacts what the screen reader user hears.

Consider these two buttons:

Here is the code for those two examples:

```
<button name="buy" value="buy">
    <img src="new.gif" alt="new">Buy it <em>Now</em>
</button>
<input type="image" alt="Search" src="search.gif" name="search" />
```

The button element permits a push button to contain images and formatted text. In the example here, the text heard by a screen reader (New Buy it Now) is the same as the visible text. An input element with type="image" just displays that image. As you saw in Chapter 6, it is absolutely essential that image buttons include alt-text. That alt-text should almost always be the text on the button; here, it is alt="Search".

> *Make sure that alt-text on image buttons conveys the function of the button and that any images included in button elements have appropriate alt-text.*

Text Input Fields and Text Areas

It is best (and most common) to have a text prompt near any text-input field or text area. The following text input field and textarea have text prompts placed as they should be placed.

Full name: ☐

Please enter your comments:

☐

Full name is the prompt for the first field (<input> with type="text") and Please enter your comments is the prompt for the second field. Although that text is physically close to the corresponding controls, the key concept here is that you want to programmatically tie the prompting text to the corresponding control. This is accomplished with the label element.

```
<label for="name">Full name</label>:
<input name="test" id="name" type="text" size="15"><br />
<label for="comments">Please enter your comments</label>: <br />
<textarea name="comments" cols="25" rows="5" id="comments"></textarea>
```

As you can see from this sample code, the way that programmatic connection is made is that the input control is given an id attribute and the prompt is wrapped in a label element, which has a for attribute matching the id of the control. The text Full name is wrapped in a label with for="name", so that the <input> with id="name" knows its prompt is Full name. Similarly, for the comments text area, the text Please enter your comments is tied to the textarea with id="comments" using the label element with for="comments".

8

> Use the label element to programmatically tie the text prompt with the associated control. The for attribute of the label matches the id attribute of the control.

How Forms Sound

Let's look at an awkwardly coded and inaccessible form to get an idea of the problems faced by those who use screen readers. The form shown in Figure 8-1 is simple (in concept, if not in coding). It includes a text-entry field (<input, type="text">), two radio buttons (<input, type="radio">), a combo box or select menu (<select>), a text area (<textarea>), a check box (<input, type="checkbox">), one submit button (<input, type="submit">), and one reset button (<input, type="reset">).

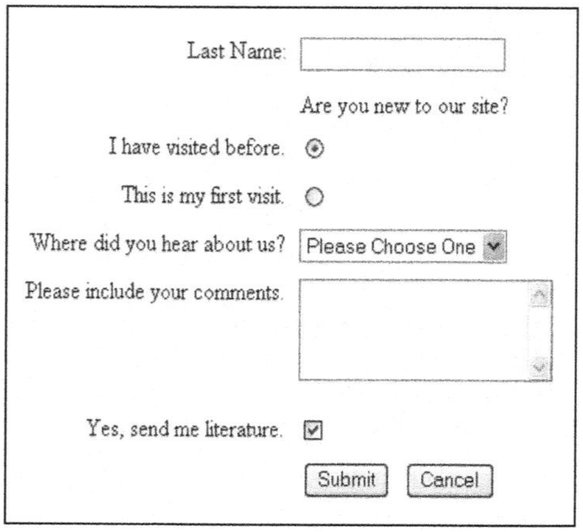

Figure 8-1. A very poorly designed form for illustration

Although the form looks fairly straightforward, the form elements do not speak well with a screen reader. In fact, the whole form does not linearize well because it is laid out using a table with one row and two columns. The first cell of that single row itself contains a table with nine rows, as does the second cell. That first table contains all the prompts, and the second table contains all of the controls—pretty awful coding! This example is presented here to show just how bad the speaking can be for a form and how proper labeling fixes that speaking.

Table 8-1 lists how each of four assistive technologies—Hal, IBM Home Page Reader (HPR in the table), JAWS, and Window-Eyes—speaks the very badly coded form. The form has nine controls. The on-screen prompt and the nature of the control are listed in the second column for each control. Prompting information is highlighted in bold font. So, for example, control 5 has on-screen text, Please include your comments, and it is a text area. The subsequent columns show how each assistive technology speaks the form elements. The italicized words in the Hal column are extra information that Hal gets from the name attributes of the corresponding controls, as explained shortly. The keys to navigate the controls are different for each of the technologies:

- For Hal, I used Tab and Left-Shift+Tab (Hal doesn't have the "letter" keys introduced by Window-Eyes back around 2001).
- For Home Page Reader, I used O and Shift+O.
- For JAWS, I used F and Shift+F (Form).
- For Window-Eyes, I used C and Shift+C (Control).

Table 8-1. How the Assistive Technologies Speak the Poorly Designed Form

Control	The Form	Hal	HPR	JAWS	Window-Eyes
1	**Last name:** text input	*name*, blank line edit area	text	**Yes, send me literature. edit**	edit box
2	**I have visited before.** radio button checked	*visited*, selected radio, use cursor up and down to select	**Are you new to our site?** pressed	**Are you new to our site?** radio button checked, 1 of 2	radio button checked
3	**This is my first visit.** radio button not checked	*visited*, unselected radio, use cursor up and down to select	not pressed	**Are you new to our site?** radio button not checked, 2 of 2	radio button unchecked
4	**Where did you hear about us?** select menu	*referral*, please choose one, use cursor keys to move through the items 1 of 5, pull down list box 5 items	start of select menu with 5 items, collapsed	combo box, please choose one, 1 of 5	please choose one, combo box
5	**Please include your comments.** text area	**Please include your comments.** blank line edit area	text area	edit	edit box
6	**Yes, send me literature.** check box, checked	*literature*, selected check box, press spacebar to toggle	checked	check box, checked	check box, checked
7	**Submit** button	**Submit** button, press spacebar to press	**Submit**, submit button	**Submit** button	**Submit** button
8	**Cancel** button	**Cancel** button, press spacebar to press	**Cancel**, reset button	Cancel button	**Cancel** button

As you can see in Table 8-1, the four technologies use similar names for the form controls, with "line edit area," "text area," "edit," and "edit box" the most divergent.

When I first listened to Hal, whose speech is not familiar to me, it seemed like maybe Hal was doing some "screen reading" because I thought it was picking up some of the prompting information. It was confusing because it seemed to be just a single word from the prompt. But this was not the case. Hal is going that extra step because forms are so often poorly coded. The name attribute of the control is suggestive because that is what the programmer uses to refer to the control. So, the extra words (italicized in the Hal column) are the name attributes of the corresponding controls. This works fairly well, as it is helpful in four out of six cases.

Another interesting point is that JAWS picked up "Yes, send me literature" as a prompt for the first edit field. How could that possibly be? If you move back from the edit field in the HTML source file, you will find that is the first occurrence of text standing by itself. I would argue that JAWS is trying too hard, and that Window-Eyes takes the prize in this contest for finding no prompting text worth conveying to the user for any of the controls.

Both JAWS and Home Page Reader announce the question for the radio buttons when the first one is encountered, and clearly JAWS thinks it is the question, because it is repeated. Note, however, that the question is useless, because you have no idea which radio button goes with each answer. Remember that you are listening to this!

Now, let's see what happens when we use the best accessibility design practices and label the very bad form. By displaying it now, I am showing just how bad this form is! This is the labeled code:

```
<form>
<table border="0"><tr><td>
<table border="0">
    <tr><td height="30" align="right">
       <label for="name">Last Name:</label></td></tr>
    <tr><td height="30" align="right"> </td></tr>
     <tr><td height="30" align="right">
       <label for="old">I have visited before.</label></td></tr>
    <tr><td height="30" align="right">
       <label for="new">This is my first visit.</label></td></tr>
    <tr><td height="30" align="right">
      <label for="refer">
           Where did you hear about us?</label></td> </tr>
    <tr><td height="90" align="right">
       <label for="comments">
           Please include your comments:</label></td></tr>
    <tr><td height="30" align="right">
      <label for="literature">
           Yes, send me literature.</label></td></tr>
    <tr><td height="30" align="right">   </td></tr>
```

```
</table></td><td>
<table border="0">
    <tr><td height="30">
        <input size="20" type="text" id="name" name="Name"></td></tr>
    <tr><td height="30">
         Are you new to our site?</td></tr>
    <tr><td height="30">
        <input type="radio" checked
            id="old" name="visited" value="yes"></td>
    </tr>
    <tr><td height="30">
        <input type="radio"
            id="new" name="visited" value="0"></td></tr>
    <tr><td height="30" valign="top">
        <select name="referral" id="refer">
        <option value="0" selected>Please Choose One</option>
        <option value="1">From a TV show</option>
        <option value="2">On the Internet</option>
        <option value="7">It was a guess</option>
        <option value="3">Other</option>
    </select></td></tr>
    <tr><td height="90">
        <textarea rows="4" cols="20"
            id="comments" name="comments"></textarea>
    </td></tr>
    <tr><td height="30">
        <input type="checkbox" checked id="literature"
                name="literature" value="lit">
    </td></tr>
    <tr><td height="30"> 
        <input type="submit" name="Submit" value="Submit">  
        <input type="reset" name="reset" value="Cancel"></td></tr>
</table></td></tr>
</table>
```

The nested table in the first cell has one column and eight rows containing all the prompts. The second cell contains a table with eight rows containing all the controls.

Remember, the reading order is the source code order, and you can see from the preceding source code that a screen reader will start by reading the first cell, which contains all the prompts, followed by the second cell, which contains all the controls.

Table 8-2 shows how the screen readers deal with the form now that it is correctly labeled.

8

Table 8-2. How the Assistive Technologies Speak the Properly Labeled Form

Control	The Form	Hal	HPR	JAWS	Window-Eyes
1	**Last name:** text input	**Last name:** *name*, blank line edit area	**Last name:** text	**Last name:** edit	edit box, **Last name:**
2	**I have visited before.** radio button, checked	**I have visited before,** *visited,* selected radio, use cursor up and down to select	**I have visited before.** pressed	**Are you new to our site? I have visited before.** radio button, checked, 1 of 2	radio button, checked, **I have visited before.**
3	**This is my first visit.** radio button not checked	**This is my first visit.** visited, unselected radio, use cursor up and down to select	**This is my first visit.** not pressed	**Are you new to our site? This is my first visit.** radio button, checked, 2 of 2	radio button unchecked, **This is my first visit.**
4	**Where did you hear about us?** select menu	**Where did you hear about us?** *referral* please choose one, use cursor keys to move through the items 1 of 5, pull down list box 5 items	**Where did you hear about us?** start of select menu with 5 items, collapsed	**Where did you hear about us?** combo box please choose one, 1 of 5	please choose one, combo box, **Where did you hear about us?**
5	**Please include your comments.** text area	**Please include your comments.** blank line, edit area	**Please include your comments.** text area	**Please include your comments.** edit	edit box, Please include your comments.
6	**Yes, send me literature.** check box, checked	**Yes, send me literature.** *literature,* selected check box, press spacebar to toggle	**Yes, send me literature.** checked	**Yes, send me literature.** check box, checked	check box, checked, **Yes, send me literature.**
7	**Submit** button	**Submit** button, press spacebar to press	**Submit**, submit button	**Submit** button	**Submit** button
8	**Cancel** button	**Cancel** button, press spacebar to press	**Cancel**, reset button	**Cancel** button	**Cancel** button

As you can see, the difference is *dramatic*. All the information is announced perfectly. There are differences between how the technologies handle the available information, but that information *is* available.

Hal continues to announce the name attribute, even though the label is available; that seems like a bad idea. The extra word was confusing to me, but the experienced Hal user would be used to a word (the name) in that position. JAWS is the only technology that repeats the question for the radio buttons. This can be annoying, especially if what JAWS thinks is the question really is not.

Placement of Prompting Text

Now let's consider the placement of the prompting text. Figure 8-2 shows a form that is looking for the same information as the very bad form in Figure 8-1. It has the same controls, but this time with an extremely simple layout without any labeling.

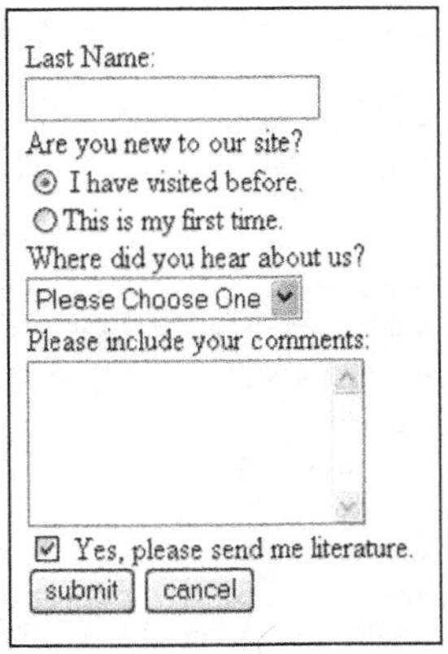

Figure 8-2. A simple form without labels

Here's the code for this form:

```
Last Name:<br />
<input name="lastn" type="text" size="22"><br />
Are you new to our site? <br />
<input name="visited" type="radio" value="" checked>
    I have visited before.<br />
<input name="visited" type="radio" value="">
    This is my first time.<br />
Where did you hear about us?<br />
<select name="referral">
            <option value="0" selected>Please Choose One</option>
            <option value="1">From a TV show</option>
            <option value="2">On the Internet</option>
            <option value="7">It was a guess</option>
            <option value="3">Other</option>
```

8

```
</select><br />
Please include your comments: <br />
<textarea name="comments" cols="20" rows="5"></textarea><br />
<input name="literature" type="checkbox" value="" checked>
    Yes, please send me literature.<br />
<input name="submit" type="submit">
<input name="" type="reset" value="cancel">
```

Table 8-3 shows how the four assistive technologies handle this form.

Table 8-3. How the Assistive Technologies Speak the Form Without Labels

Control	The Form	Hal	HPR	JAWS	Window-Eyes
1	**Last name:** text input	*name*, blank line edit area	**Last name:** text	**Last name:** edit	edit box,
2	**I have visited before.** radio button, checked	*visited*, selected, radio, use cursor up and down to select	**I have visited before.** pressed	**Are you new to our site? I have visited before.** radio button checked, 1 of 2	radio button, checked
3	**This is my first visit.** radio button, not checked	visited, unselected radio, use cursor up and down to select	**This is my first visit.** not pressed	**Are you new to our site? This is my first visit.** radio button not checked, 2 of 2	radio button unchecked
4	**Where did you hear about us?** select menu	*referral*, please choose one, use cursor keys to move through the items, 1 of 5, pull down list box, 5 items	start of select menu with 5 items, collapsed	**Where did you hear about us?** combo box, please choose one, 1 of 5	please choose one, combo box
5	**Please include your comments:** text area	blank line, edit area	text area	**Please include your comments:** edit	edit box
6	**Yes, send me literature.** check box checked	*Literature*, selected check box, press spacebar to toggle	**Yes, send me literature.** checked	**Yes, send me literature.** check box, checked	check box, checked

Control	The Form	Hal	HPR	JAWS	Window-Eyes
7	**Submit** button	**Submit** button, press spacebar to press	**Submit**, submit button	**Submit** button	**Submit** button
8	**Cancel** button	**Cancel** button, press spacebar to press	**Cancel**, reset button	**Cancel** button	**Cancel** button

For this form without labels, but with prompts placed close to their controls, the JAWS screen reader picks up all the prompts; Home Page Reader picks up three out of six of the prompts; and both Hal and Window-Eyes pick up none of the prompts.

It has always been the case that screen readers do their best to provide information for their users, even if that information has not been well presented by the authors of the document or application. In this example, JAWS makes good guesses as to what the prompts are for the form controls. But those guesses can be wrong. As you saw in Table 8-1, JAWS guessed "Yes, send me literature" for the input field whose purpose was "Last Name." Guessing like this is especially serious for input fields in a web form. On top of all the difficulties accessing web information, blind users need to be confident about their interaction—to be able to fill out a form without ambiguity. I think having a text-input field labeled "Yes, send me literature" would tend to shake one's confidence. The point is that any other placement of on-screen prompts would probably cause some screen reader or talking browser to give no information at all or the wrong information to its user.

This example shows that the idea of positioning prompts for screen reader access does not work more than 50 percent of the time. The key is to not depend on positioning of prompts, but to use the label element instead, so that you are certain that screen readers will give the correct information to a blind visitor to your site. Without using the label element, the screen reader can only guess and may be wrong.

Best Practices for Accessible Forms

The conclusion from the experiments described in the previous sections is simple indeed:

- Position prompts carefully for users who interact with your form visually and always programmatically connect the on-screen prompting information to the form control with the label element to accommodate screen reader users.

That is certainly good advice. The fact that all of assistive technologies handled the label element correctly is further evidence that this is the right thing to do. But, of course, there are problems. The following sections describe how to handle those problems.

8

When Labels Won't Work

In many circumstances, there simply is no on-screen text present to enclose in the `label` element. How can that be possible? Frequently, the form has visual clues that are not readily available to the screen reader user. These are visual clues that make a sighted user comfortable filling out a form, but leave a blind visitor at a loss. In these cases, it isn't impossible to move around with the assistive technology and figure out what belongs in the field, but it is awkward and often imprecise.

In online forms, four situations commonly arise where the `label` element cannot or does not work to provide the information to a screen reader user: no on-screen text, prompting information by position, shared prompting information, and forms in tables. Let's take a look at examples of these situations.

No On-Screen Text Often, there is no simple on-screen text, and the information is provided by some other control. The most common situation is where an edit field relates to a button, and the text on the button explains what to do with the input field. The input field for a search on IBM.com shown in Figure 8-3 is an example.

Figure 8-3. The text-entry field is available for search text.

Prompting Information by Position Often, the visual information is given purely in terms of physical position. This is typically found in input fields for U.S. extended ZIP codes (plus 4), phone numbers in three parts, or Social Security numbers in three parts. Part of another IBM.com form illustrates this situation, as shown in Figure 8-4.

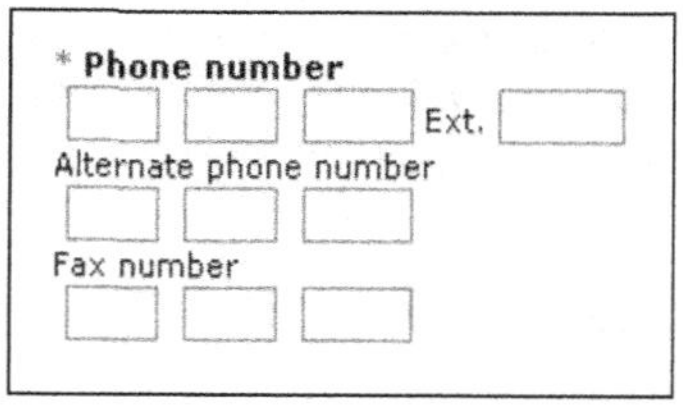

> * **Phone number**
> ☐ ☐ ☐ Ext. ☐
> Alternate phone number
> ☐ ☐ ☐
> Fax number
> ☐ ☐ ☐

Figure 8-4. Position provides information.

Three fields are given for the Phone number, Alternate phone number, and Fax number. What should go in the second and third positions is implied by their relationship to the first field. When a screen reader user lands on the first field, there is no information about the existence of the second and third fields.

Shared Prompting Information Sometimes, text is available but it is scattered, and some of it may apply to several fields. Figure 8-5 shows an example of a Priceline.com form for filling out information in order to search for a rental car.

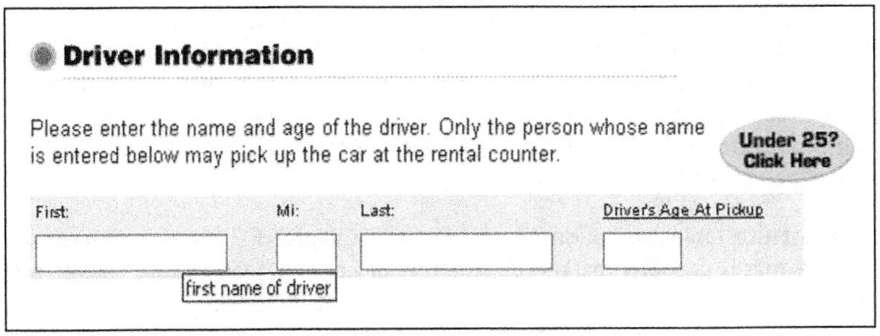

Figure 8-5. The information is distributed, shared, and abbreviated.

In the example in Figure 8-5, the information labeling each form control appears in different places. The heading, Driver Information is shared by all the fields. In addition, each field has a prompt for its specific piece of driver information. Since ids must be unique, and since the label element can specify only one for attribute, it follows that the label element cannot be used to indicate that the shared information goes with each field.

Also in this example, the labeling for each field comes from more than one place. Technically, that can be handled by the label element. You just enclose Driver Information and First in the label element with the same for attribute whose value is the id of the First edit field. Though valid, the results with screen readers are not predictable. On a sample page with two label elements associating prompting text from two different places, Hal picked up the first label, JAWS and Window-Eyes picked up the second, and only Home Page Reader spoke both labels.

Finally, this example has labeling that is visually acceptable (barely) but is not good for a screen reader: First implies first name, one supposes, and that is explained further in the text above the field. Even worse, however is Mi:, read by the screen reader as "me colon," which is confusing at best.

Forms in Tables As a final example of problems that you will encounter using the label element, consider the simple prototype form in Figure 8-6. This form has controls in table cells, and the headings provide the prompting information for someone who can see the form.

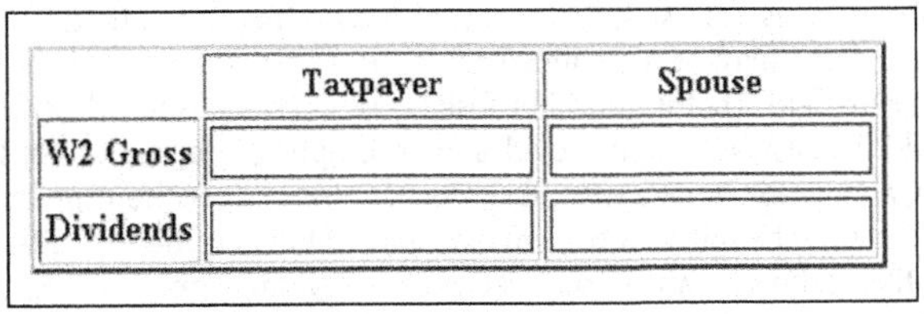

Figure 8-6. A form in a table

8

There are compounded serious problems when the form controls are in table cells. First, the same prompting text applies to more than one input field (each heading applies to two fields in its row or column) and because of the uniqueness of ids, that cannot be done with the label element. Second, prompting information is coming from two places (row and column headers for each cell), and as you saw in the previous example, that situation is not handled well by assistive technology.

So, why not just use table navigation (as discussed in Chapter 6)? When you navigate through a table that is properly marked up, the row or column headers that change are announced. The problem is that screen reader users are not using table navigation when dealing with a form. For a form, a screen reader user employs either the Tab key or the letter keys (F for Jaws, C for Window-Eyes, and O for Home Page Reader) to move from control to control. In that mode of operation, screen readers may not be reading the headings. But there is more. For JAWS and Window-Eyes, when you decide to interact with the form, you enter forms mode (MSAA Mode off in Window-Eyes) by pressing Enter. Then form navigation continues with the Tab key. When in forms mode, JAWS finds *no* prompting information for the text-input fields in the form shown in Figure 8-6, and Window-Eyes prompts with "W2 Gross, Spouse, Dividends, Dividends" (reading in source code order, the first row left to right, then the second row), which is essentially useless information. So, in forms mode, the screen readers provided either no information or the wrong information.

Use the Title Attribute

The good news is that there is a simple solution when the label element is not adequate. The solution is to use the title attribute on the input element itself to say exactly what to do with the control. This is supported by three of the four assistive technologies. The fourth, Hal, claims to support it, but it didn't work for me. (I have explained the problem to Dolphin Systems.) Let's go through the preceding examples and illustrate how the title attribute should be used.

No On-Screen Text The IBM.com search field (Figure 8-3) needs a simple title on the input element; title="search" would work well. Remember that you should not use longer phrases like title="enter search text here" because the "enter" and "here" are redundant (see Chapter 7). When screen reader users land on an edit field, they know that something is to be entered, and they know the prompting text is talking about the current field, "here." A bit longer but also good would be title="Search text".

Unfortunately, IBM.com does not use the title attribute on this search field. The example in Figure 8-3 shows Search form as a tooltip. That is the title attribute of the form element, not on the input field. That is good because Search form does not describe what to do with the edit field. The way IBM.com provides the prompting information for this input field is by including an invisible image with alt="Search for:" near the <input>, which is wrapped in a label element using and the for and id attributes to tie that alt-text to the edit area. I believe this technique was introduced on the IBM site when the title attribute did not have much assistive technology support. But now that the title attribute works well and is supported by the screen readers, there is no reason to use alt-text on an invisible image like this.

Prompting Information by Position It is not completely obvious what title attribute to use on the three fields of a phone number, as shown in Figure 8-4. I am old-fashioned and know the second three digits as the "exchange," so I might say "area code", "exchange", and "number". IBM.com (on invisible images, as described earlier) uses alt attributes with "phone number part 1", "phone number part 2", and "phone number part 3". Instead, the site should use title attributes. On a ZIP code entry with two fields, I would use title="zip code 5 digits" and title="zip code plus 4".

Shared Prompting Information The Priceline.com form (Figure 8-5) uses title attributes, as the tooltip shows: title= "First name of Driver", title="Middle initial of driver", and title= "last name of driver". These title attributes give screen reader users exactly the information they need.

Forms in Tables To solve the problem of forms in tables (Figure 8-6), the title attribute of each input element must include both the column header information and the row header information. I would order the words, with the most important first. The titles I would use are title="W4 Gross, tax payer", title= "W2 Gross, spouse", title="Dividends, tax payer", and title= "Dividends, spouse".

Use the Fieldset and Legend Elements for Sets of Controls

When you land on a control using the Tab key or the form control key (F in JAWS or C with Window-Eyes) and hear the prompting text, you usually know what to do. If the message is "Last name," and you are on an edit field, then you type in your last name. But think about radio buttons: "radio button checked, male." You can guess that the question is "Gender?" As another example, consider "radio button checked, American Express." Again, you can guess that the form wants to know what kind of credit card you are using. How about "radio button checked, yes"? You cannot guess that question. But it is important that a user of your form should *not* have to guess. The correct information must be automatically and correctly provided, so that users can fill out a form on the Web with confidence and certainty, independent of disability.

Note that the question corresponding to a set of radio buttons or check boxes includes the same problem raised by the Priceline.com form in Figure 8-5, where information is common to a set of controls. The problem of the question for a set of radio buttons can be solved in exactly the same way as with the Priceline.com form: by including the question in the title attribute. For example, title="Gender, male" and title="Gender, female" are just fine for a pair of radio buttons whose question is "Gender?" and for which the on-screen text next to the radio buttons is Male and Female.

But there is also a very good programmatic solution: employing the HTML fieldset and legend elements introduced in HTML 4.0. This combination gives what is often referred to as a *group-box* structure for software. The fieldset element encloses the controls in some kind of border. The legend element adds text to that border. The example in Figure 8-7 comes from a site called The Man In Blue (www.themaninblue.com/experiment/InForm/). It includes two fieldset elements. The first has <legend>Payment details</legend>, and the second has <legend>Credit card<legend>.

8

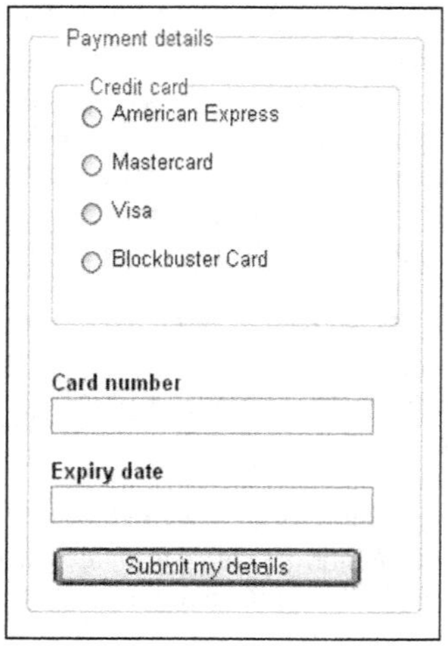

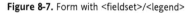

Figure 8-7. Form with <fieldset>/<legend>

Here is the code for the form in Figure 8-7:

```
<fieldset>
    <legend>Payment details</legend>
    <fieldset class="radio">
        <legend>Credit card </legend>
        <input id="card1a" type="radio" name="card1">
            <label for="card1a">American express</label>
        <input id="card1b" type="radio" name="card1">
            <label for="card1b">Mastercard</label>
        <input id="card1c" type="radio" name="card1">
            <label for="card1c">Visa</label>
        <input id="card1d" type="radio" name="card1">
            <label for="card1d">Blockbuster card</label>
    </fieldset>
    <label for="cardnum">Card number</label>
        <input id="cardnum" name="cardnum">
    <label for="expiry">Expiry date</label>
        <input id="expiry" name="expiry">
    <input class="submit" type="submit" value="submit my details">
</fieldset>
```

With this layout, screen readers will read the legend before each control in the fieldset element. So the credit card radio buttons would sound like this: "Credit card, American Express, radio button not pressed."

Today, screen readers read the legend element with every control contained in the corresponding fieldset element. I hope that will improve so that the legend is read on first entry into the fieldset, but is available with some kind of a "Where-Am-I" key after that.

The variation in visual styling of <fieldset>/<legend> markup is especially impressive at The Man in Blue website. For example, Figure 8-8 shows exactly the same <fieldset> code as in the previous example with different CSS styling.

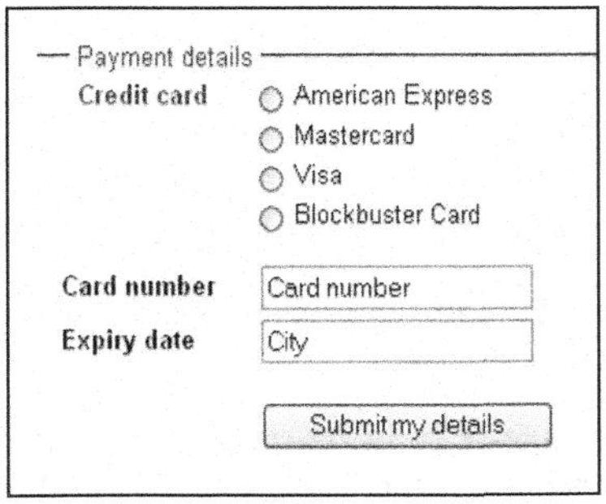

Figure 8-8. Form styled with CSS

A last example of the use of the <fieldset>/<legend> construct combines the requirement of a legend element for a question with the need for title attributes to present information that is visually presented by layout. The form is shown in Figure 8-9.

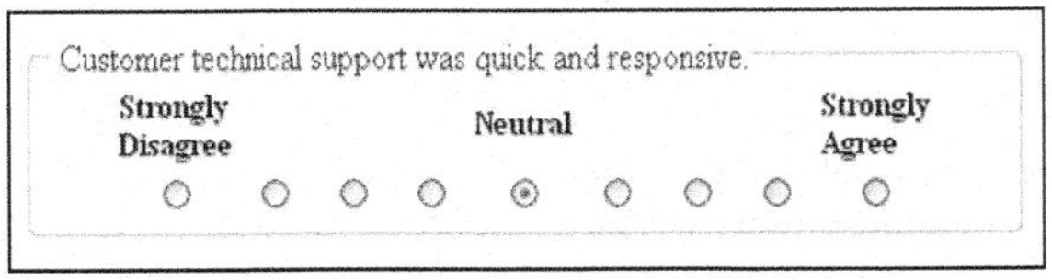

Figure 8-9. Information conveyed by position

The following is some of the code for the form in Figure 8-9:

```
<input type="radio" name="eval" value="1" title="strongly disagree">
<input type="radio" name="eval" value="2" title="disagree 3">
<input type="radio" name="eval" value="3" title="disagree 2">
<input type="radio" name="eval" value="4" title="disagree 1">
<input type="radio" name="eval" value="4.5" checked title="neutral">
<input type="radio" name="eval" value="5" title="agree 1">
<input type="radio" name="eval" value="7" title="agree 2">
<input type="radio" name="eval" value="7" title="agree 3">
<input type="radio" name="eval" value="8" title="strongly agree">
```

I might try to find words to replace agree 1, agree 2, agree 3, and so on, but the important point is that some title text information is needed to convey the relative position of the various radio buttons.

Do Not Use Labels As Containers

The label element can also be used as a *container* of both the on-screen prompt *and* the input control. In WCAG 1.0, this use of the label element is referred to as *implicit labeling* of the control. This could be a considerable savings in code, since it would not require the effort of creating an id for the control and providing the for attribute of the label element matching that id. By the specification of HTML 4.01, the <label> tag can be used as a container only when there is no structural markup intervening between the prompt and the control.

To test whether the assistive technologies support the label element as a container, I used the following code.

```
Text before label
<label>Text in label <input name="lastn" type="text" size="22"></label>
```

The technology will be seen to support using label as a container if it speaks "Text in label" and does *not* speak "Text before label."

Home Page Reader treats this situation correctly, speaking only the on-screen text that is contained in the label container. JAWS ignores the label element altogether and speaks both the preceding and contained text. Hal and Window-Eyes speak no prompt at all.

The conclusion of this experiment is simple:

- Never use the label element as a container of both the prompt and control. Instead, wrap the on-screen text with the label element using the for attribute whose value is the id of the corresponding control.

More Is Not Better

Often, someone new to accessibility wants to do more—with the idea that more must be better. Let's look at an example from my hometown of Austin, Texas.

A wonderful event called the Accessibility Internet Rally of Austin, or AIR Austin (www.knowbility.org/AIR), is held by a nonprofit organization, Knowbility, Inc., for the purpose of promoting accessibility. For this event, teams from high-tech companies (big and small) in the area are trained in best practices for accessibility. Nonprofit organizations in the area apply to be part of the AIR event and are trained in the ideas and process of having a website. On a kickoff day, the tech teams are paired with nonprofit organizations and encouraged to spend time in the next week getting to know each other, reviewing the requirements, and outlining the design and organization of a website (but no coding of the site occurs during that week). Then in a one-day rally, the tech teams build websites for their nonprofit organizations. After the rally, the sites are judged and the winners are recognized at a gala dinner event.

I have been a judge for AIR for a number of years. I was impressed with a form on one of the winning sites in AIR Austin 2005. Part of the form is shown in Figure 8-10.

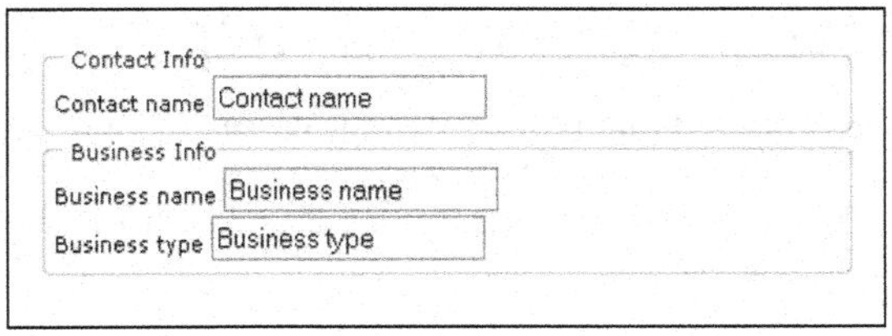

Figure 8-10. An overdone form

I am sure the team who designed the form thought that by adding more accessibility accommodations they would get more points. When I judged this site, the team got points for trying a form, but they lost on providing accessibility. This form is an example of the fact that more is not necessarily better. It uses the following techniques:

- Each text-input field has default text (such as value="Contact name"). As discussed in the guidelines section at the beginning of this chapter, the WCAG Priority 3 checkpoint requiring default text is not applicable anymore because assistive technologies do recognize input fields when they are blank.

- The legend for each fieldset repeats the on-screen prompt. The <legend> tag should be used to enclose groups of controls with a common purpose, such as groups of check boxes or radio buttons where the legend provides the corresponding question. When the size of the group is one, you should reconsider the design.

- The label element is used as a container around both the on-screen prompt and the control. As explained in the previous section, this is not a good idea.

- The label element includes a correctly coded for attribute matching the id of the control. This is the only accommodation that should have been used.

The results of the overkill for the first field in this example are this with JAWS: "Contact info Contact info Contact name edit Contact name." Although it is relatively easy for sighted users to ignore repetitive information as that in the form in Figure 8-10, it is almost impossible for a screen reader user to ignore such repetition. (By the way, I don't know why "Contact info" is repeated twice by JAWS.)

Another common occurrence of overdoing it is by using both the label element and the title attribute. To understand the behavior of assistive technology relative to both title and label, I used code similar to what I used to test the label element as a container:

```
<label for="xx">Text in label </label> Other text
<input name="lastn" id="xx" type="text" size="22" title="last name">
```

If the screen reader recognizes the label element, we should hear "Text in label," and if it recognizes the title attribute, we should hear "Last name." All three screen readers and Home Page Reader speak the contents of the label element and ignore the title attribute. So, the conclusion of this little experiment is clear:

- When labeling forms, use the label element with the for attribute matching the id attribute of the control or use the title attribute on the input element, but do not use both.

8

Mandatory Fields, Errors, and Help for Forms

It is inevitable that people will make mistakes when filling out online forms. Web developers should make it as easy as possible for their visitors by ensuring that mandatory and optional form fields are obvious, and report errors in such a way that it is easy for their visitors to understand and correct.

Mandatory Form Fields

When it comes to indicating mandatory or optional form fields, developers should follow three simple rules:

- Do not rely *only* on color, position, or shape.
- Make sure the information is concise.
- Make sure the information is part of the control's label.

A common mistake for developers is to highlight all mandatory or optional fields using color alone. For example, a typical statement on web forms is All fields in red are required. Color, shape, and position are not reliable methods of conveying information, as this information could be lost for some users. For all visitors to have equivalent access, it is vital that important information is relayed to the visitor as text.

When all fields are mandatory or optional, it is acceptable to indicate this above the form, rather than stating beside each and every form control whether the field is mandatory or optional. When a form contains a mixture of mandatory and optional form controls, this information should be relayed as concisely as possible. If there are more optional fields than mandatory fields, it is better to state that all fields are optional, apart from those indicated as mandatory; conversely, if there are more mandatory than optional fields, it is better to state that all fields are mandatory, apart from those indicated as optional. It is rarely advisable to indicate both mandatory and optional form controls, although that is acceptable and preferable with complex forms.

The information should be concise, but that does not mean encrypted. Symbols are acceptable for indicating mandatory or optional form fields, provided that they have been explicitly explained before the form. But there is nothing wrong with writing in full the words mandatory, optional, or an equivalent within the form control's prompt, as in the following example.

```
<label for="forename">
  Forename (required)
</label>
```

The information can also be relayed using images with appropriate alternative text, which might be a better solution, depending on the design constraints of the form. CSS may be used to help control the presentation, but it is vital that the information is included within the prompt; otherwise, this will not be relayed to some visitors. One simple method is to include the image within the label, as in the following example.

```
<label for="forename">
  Forename
  <img src="/img/required.gif" alt="(required)">
</label>
```

Form Validation

The two basic methods of validating forms are client-side validation and server-side validation. Client-side validation requires a user agent that is capable of executing scripts. As not all user agents are capable of executing scripts, or might have scripting disabled for security reasons, client-side scripting should never be relied on for validation. Client-side validation does have the advantage that the document is not sent to the server for processing, and so is much quicker from the user's perspective, as well as much kinder to your bandwidth allowance. The secret to good form validation is to make sure that form validation is performed on the server, and then use progressive enhancement techniques to replicate the server-side validation with client-side scripting. Using this technique, visitors to your website that have a script-capable user agent will benefit from the speed of the form being validated in their browser; and for those that do not, the form is validated on the server, so no one loses out.

When reporting errors, the two things visitors need to know immediately are how many errors they made and concise details of each error. The simplest method is to provide a list of the errors, with the number of errors reported in a heading above the list. As server-side validation is essential, we will start by investigating a server-side technique.

Server-Side Validation

There are too many server-side languages to consider any one in detail, so we will take a brief look at PHP. The principles can be applied to any server-side language, such as ASP, JSP, and Perl.

The following technique assumes the form is originally posted to itself for validation and sent off for further processing if no errors are found. The error-checking routine simply collects all posted form fields, checking the value of fields that are to be tested to ensure they are valid. If the value for a field is invalid, a message asking the user to correct the error is added to a list of errors, which is presented above the form. Each error in the list is marked up as a link pointing to the form control in error to make it easy for the visitor to fix the problem. If no errors are found, the form is processed as usual.

```
// Set an error count, and start of an error message
$iErrorCount = 0;
$strError = "<ul>\n";
// If the form has been submitted, validate it
if ($_POST) {
  // Read all posted form variables
  $strAge = $_POST["age"];
  // Other form values collected here
  // ---
  // Check each value for possible mistakes
```

```
                 if (!is_numeric($strAge)) {
                   // Write message as a link
                   $strMessage = "<a href=\"#age\">Please enter your age</a>";
                   // Include the message in the error list
                   $strError .= "<li>$strMessage</li>\n";
                   $iErrorCount++;
                 }
                 // Test all other form controls that are required here
                 // ---
                 // If no errors, do what would normally be done here
                 if (!iErrorCount)
                   header("Location: processform.php");
               }
               // Close the error message
               $strError .= "</ul>\n";
               $strMessage = "errors in submission";
               // If there are any errors, add the number of errors to the title, &
               // append the existing errors for reporting at an appropriate point
               if ($iErrorCount > 0)
                 $strError = "<h2>$iErrorCount $strMessage</h2>\n" . $strError;
               // Any preamble before the form here ...
               // If there were errors, report the errors before the form
               if (iErrorCount > 0)
                 echo $strError;
               // Now display the form
               // ---
```

When the user submits the form, any mistakes are presented as a series of links in a list above the form that point to the fields in error. If there are no errors, the form is processed as usual.

Client-Side Validation

Now we have our fallback mechanism in place, we can use progressive enhancement to make the form more usable. This section will not discuss JavaScript in detail, as accessible JavaScript is the topic of Chapter 10. Instead, the focus of this section will be making sure that any errors reported by JavaScript are relayed to assistive technologies, such as screen readers.

By validating on the client, we save bandwidth, and the user saves time as errors can be reported immediately, rather than waiting for the form to be sent to the server for validation, and then sent back for correction should there be errors. The technique is very similar to the server-side solution in that we want a list of errors as links at the top of the form. The difference is that we need to make sure that assistive technology successfully reports the error. If the author doesn't make an effort to report the error, a screen reader typically lets the user know that the page has changed, but not what has changed. For example, when inserting new content into a document with JavaScript, Window-Eyes reports, "Loading Page. Load Done. Looking for visible line." The last visible line is where the user finished, which will be the form control the visitor used to submit the form. A screen reader user might realize from the cue that extra content has been added to the page, but without knowing where the extra content has been inserted, the user is forced to read the whole page again. This cannot be considered an equivalent experience to that of a sighted user who can immediately locate the inserted content.

With server-side validation, reporting errors is not so much of an issue, as we have taken the brute-force approach to validation: we check for errors, and if there are any, the whole page is sent back to the visitor. With client-side validation, we need to force assistive technologies to focus on the part of the page that reports the errors, so that all users can perceive the inserted content.

Unfortunately, only anchors and interface elements can receive focus in HTML. This means that we need to either make the title of our errors an anchor, so that it can receive focus, or give the element a `tabindex` attribute value of `-1`. Negative `tabindex` attribute values are illegal according to the specification, but are, in fact, recognized as being essential for web applications. This issue is being addressed by Web Applications 1.0 (`http://whatwg.org/specs/web-apps/current-work/#tabindex0`), and also by the W3C's Protocols and Formats Working Group in their Dynamic Accessible Web Content Roadmap (`www.w3.org/WAI/PF/roadmap/DHTMLRoadmap040506.html#focus`). A negative `tabindex` value does not put an element into the browser's tab order (the element won't receive focus as the user tabs through the document), but it will be able to receive focus using the JavaScript `focus` method:

```
objAnchor.focus();
```

Once we have a control that can receive focus, either by using an element that can receive focus by default in HTML or by applying a negative `tabindex` attribute value to the element, focus can be given to the element should errors be reported, and screen readers will continue to read from that point. Users can make use of the links to quickly move to the form fields in error.

For a full working example of JavaScript error reporting with a server-side fallback mechanism, see the "DOM and Screen Readers" article (`http://juicystudio.com/article/dom-screen-readers.php`) and the demonstration page (`http://juicystudio.com/experiments/form.php`).

Help for Form Fields

New windows are frowned upon in web development, as visitors to a website expect to receive content, and do not expect the website to interfere with their interaction. If users want to open a link in a new window, they can choose to do so. Similarly, if users want a link to open in a new tab, they can choose to have that happen. When authors decide that a link is to open in a new window, they remove the option for the user to open the link in the current window. Also, pop-up blockers might be used, which means that the page may not successfully open in a new window, and should have a fallback mechanism of opening in the same window.

Help pages in web forms are generally considered an exception. By its very nature, a web form is considered more like a traditional application, as the user is interacting with the document rather than merely receiving content. Opening the help page in the same

8

window could result in visitors losing any data they have entered so far, which is a sure way to lose visitors. If the purpose of your form is for business, this is obviously the last thing you will want to do.

An alternative method to opening help pages in a new window is to structure the document so that the help is included at the end of the document. Next to each form control that has help text, provide a link to the page fragment at the end of the document containing the help text, with a corresponding link back to the form control. With this technique, users will always get the help, regardless of pop-up blocking. As the users never leave the page, the information they have provided is safe. This technique can be further enhanced with JavaScript, so that the help is revealed as and when required. This technique has other advantages, such as providing relevant content for indexing and ranking by search engines. For an example of displaying form help without pop-ups that has been enhanced with JavaScript, see `http://juicystudio.com/article/form-help-without-popups.html`.

PDF Forms

You have probably seen content on the Web that appeared to be a form but didn't have the look and feel of the forms we have been talking about so far.

The part of the form shown in Figure 8-11 (from `www.irs.gov/`) is certainly familiar to readers in the U.S. This is a PDF document, specifically, `www.irs.gov/pub/irs-pdf/f1040.pdf`:

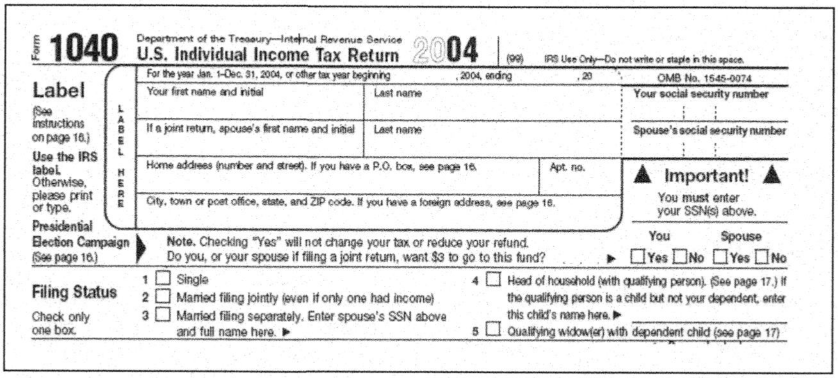
Form 1040 Department of the Treasury—Internal Revenue Service
U.S. Individual Income Tax Return 2004 (99) IRS Use Only—Do not write or staple in this space.
For the year Jan. 1–Dec. 31, 2004, or other tax year beginning , 2004, ending , 20 OMB No. 1545-0074
Label (See instructions on page 16.) Use the IRS label. Otherwise, please print or type.
LABEL HERE
Your first name and initial | Last name | Your social security number
If a joint return, spouse's first name and initial | Last name | Spouse's social security number
Home address (number and street). If you have a P.O. box, see page 16. | Apt. no.
City, town or post office, state, and ZIP code. If you have a foreign address, see page 16.
▲ Important! ▲ You must enter your SSN(s) above.
Presidential Election Campaign (See page 16.) Note. Checking "Yes" will not change your tax or reduce your refund. Do you, or your spouse if filing a joint return, want $3 to go to this fund? ▶ You ☐ Yes ☐ No Spouse ☐ Yes ☐ No
Filing Status
Check only one box.
1 ☐ Single
2 ☐ Married filing jointly (even if only one had income)
3 ☐ Married filing separately. Enter spouse's SSN above and full name here. ▶
4 ☐ Head of household (with qualifying person). (See page 17.) If the qualifying person is a child but not your dependent, enter this child's name here. ▶
5 ☐ Qualifying widow(er) with dependent child (see page 17)

Figure 8-11. Form 1040 (PDF)

PDF stands for Portable Document Format, a format from Adobe (`www.adobe.com`). The whole idea of PDF is to be able to share documents that will *look the same* when printed. The focus of PDF is presentation. In contrast, accessibility must focus on content.

Many PDF documents are just images of printed pages, and thus are totally inaccessible. Up until recently, even those that were not images were generally inaccessible.

Adobe has made significant efforts to incorporate accessibility into its products (see www.adobe.com/accessibility). Now, with the right combination of circumstances, it is possible for someone who is blind to access PDF documents, including forms like the one in Figure 8-11. What do I mean by "the right combination of circumstances"? As with everything we have discussed about web accessibility, the author of the document must take responsibility and design it with accessibility built in; that is, the document must be prepared accessibly.

Beginning with Adobe Acrobat 5, it has been possible to create *tagged forms* so that a screen reader can report the prompt for a form. That capability has been improved with subsequent versions of Acrobat. See Chapter 12 for details on tagging PDF forms.

Accessibility of Forms for People Who Are Deaf

I have always thought of accessibility of the Web as being measured by how well people who have disabilities can use it. Yet, as is obvious, I stress blindness and how well people who are visually impaired can get the information or interact with a website using assistive technology. The reason for that focus is because, in my opinion, 99 percent of the problems with web access are problems that directly affect people who are blind. The remaining 1 percent of the accessibility problems affects people with other disabilities.

If you are deaf or hearing-impaired, you are going to miss out on an audio file or the audio portion of a multimedia presentation. However, at the moment, the Internet is primarily a visual medium rather than an aural one. Also, if you can see the screen but you are deaf, when an audio file begins to play, at least you know exactly what the problem is, because a media player is opened.

During past deliberations of the Web Content Accessibility Working Group, a recommendation was presented by Donald L. Moore. The idea being addressed by Mr. Moore is that when individuals who are deaf fill out a form including a phone number, they have no way to explain that they can't use a regular phone. This is a case, not of accessibility of the web content, but the limitation of the web content to convey or request information that is important for people with disabilities, namely people who are deaf. Banks require a phone number for a loan application, and some mutual fund companies require a phone number when submitting a transfer request. These phone numbers can be critical. If the service provider does not know how to communicate with a deaf customer using a telecommunication device for the deaf (TDD), the transaction could end up being aborted. As shown in Figure 8-12, Mr. Moore's suggestion is simple: add the information specifying the desired form of communication in the typical web form.

8

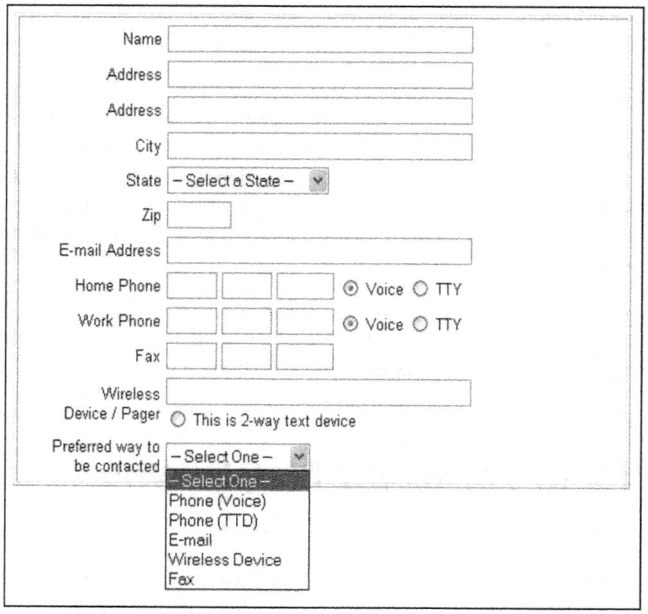

Figure 8-12. A form that specifies the type of phone connection

Timed Responses

Sometimes, it is necessary or useful to require responses from a user of a web page or web application within a certain period of time. A provision in the Section 508 Standards for web accessibility requires special consideration for the fact that some people with disabilities might require more time to complete an action:

> §1194.22(p) When a timed response is required, the user shall be alerted and given sufficient time to indicate more time is required.

Exactly what kinds of situations require a timed response? An example is a certification test where each question must be answered within a specified time. Brainbench (www.brainbench.com) offers certification exams, and each question is allotted 180 seconds (on the test I examined). The technique for accomplishing this is a simple JavaScript script that counts down the 180 seconds. In the test I took at the Brainbench site, the script gives a warning at 30 seconds, and submits the form and moves to the next question at 180 seconds.

I timed speaking an average question in one of those tests. It took 90 seconds with Home Page Reader speaking at its default rate. That rate is, granted, relatively slow for accomplished users, but 90 seconds is half the allotted time. Also, I found that it was often necessary to reread the multiple-choice answers to decide on the correct one. In this example, an alert is provided, but there is no provision for additional time.

The Brainbench alert at 30 seconds replaces the following image above the question:

with another image:

30 Seconds!

Neither of these images have alternative text, making the accessibility issue even worse.

This problem is not restricted to people depending on screen readers. Someone with low vision may be a slower-than-average reader. Just like the Brainbench test, a form on a page may time out before the data-input task is complete. Often when that happens, the data that has been entered is erased. The result is that someone with a disability who is slow to enter data cannot complete the form. That is why the Section 508 provision requires that additional time be allowed.

WCAG 1.0 does not have any item that specifically addresses the issue of timed responses. WCAG 2.0 (Last Call draft) has a guideline relating to timing:

2.2 Allow users to control time limits on their reading or interaction.

The first Level 1 success criterion elaborates on the idea of giving control of timing to the user:

SC 2.2.1 For each time-out that is a function of the content, at least one of the following is true:

- the user is allowed to deactivate the time-out; or
- the user is allowed to adjust the time-out over a wide range which is at least ten times the length of the default setting; or
- the user is warned before time expires and given at least 20 seconds to extend the time-out with a simple action (for example, "hit any key") and the user is allowed to extend the timeout at least 10 times; or
- the time-out is an important part of a real-time event (for example, an auction), and no alternative to the time-out is possible; or
- the time-out is part of an activity where timing is essential (for example, competitive gaming or time-based testing) and time limits can not be extended further without invalidating the activity.

The message of this version of the success criterion is much more constructive than that of the Section 508 Standards provision, recognizing, for example, that timing may be an essential part of the process.

8

When timing of the input or interaction is essential to the function of the page, the warning of a potential time-out must be clear and offered before the timing starts. If possible, you should provide for adjustment of the time or provide contact information so that a user who needs more time can arrange to get it.

When people write about timed responses, they often include automatic page refresh and page redirections. The draft of WCAG 2.0 includes these phenomena as part of the definition of "timed response." Similarly, the Usability.gov Section 508 tutorials (www.usability.gov/web_508/tut-p.html) include page refreshes and redirects as examples of timed responses.

It is true that automatic page refreshes or page redirections can be annoying and frustrating for people with disabilities. For example, some versions of screen readers will start reading a web page from the top when it refreshes. It is also true that page refreshes or page redirections involve timing, but these are not examples of the timed responses that the Section 508 web provision addresses. A timed response is when the website user must complete a specified data interaction or task in a certain amount of time before the form contents are cleared or the form is automatically submitted.

Summary

This chapter discussed how to design forms that are accessible to people with disabilities. You saw how to design forms so that screen readers can identify the appropriate prompt by programmatically associating prompt text with controls using the `label` element. However, in certain situations, an `input` element does not have any prompt text associated with it. You learned how to handle such situations with the `title` attribute of the `input` element (or other control). There are also some subtle problems faced by people who are hard-of-hearing that the designer should consider when designing forms.

To round off the chapter, here is a quick reference checklist for creating accessible forms:

- Use the `label` element with the `for` attribute to explicitly associate on-screen prompts with controls.
- Instead of the `label` element, you may use the `title` attribute on the form control to specify the purpose of the control. This is necessary when the on-screen prompts are not available, are not contiguous, or are not clear.
- Do not use both the `title` attribute and the `label` element.
- Use the `label` element as a container of the on-screen prompt; do not include the control itself within the `label`.
- Use the `fieldset` and `legend` tags to structure complex forms so that they are clearer and simpler to understand.
- Structure your contact information form to specify a desired communication channel (like TDD, pager, e-mail, and so on) for people who are deaf.
- Avoid limiting the amount of time allowed for completing and submitting forms. If that is not possible, explain the timing restrictions and issue an accessible alert before the time-out.

9 **CSS FOR ACCESSIBLE WEB PAGES**

by Richard Rutter

Cascading Style Sheets (CSS) is a style sheet language that allows authors and users to attach styles to structured documents like HTML pages. Style sheets were designed to allow precise control of character spacing, text alignment, object position on the page, font characteristics, color, backgrounds, and so on.

When used to their greatest advantage, style sheets are defined in files completely separate from the HTML documents. By separating style from markup, authors can simplify and clean up the HTML in their documents. This means site-wide changes can be made in just one place, which should decrease maintenance and increase visual consistency across a website.

This chapter discusses the accessibility features of CSS and provides explanations and examples of how to use them. CSS benefits accessibility primarily by separating document structure from presentation, and we'll begin by looking at some examples of how that works.

How Style Sheets Benefit Accessibility

The CSS Zen Garden (www.csszengarden.com/) is a website designed to demonstrate the capabilities of CSS. It has a single HTML document for which hundreds of designers have created style sheets that radically change the layout and presentation. Figures 9-1 through 9-4 show some examples (remember the underlying HTML is identical in each).

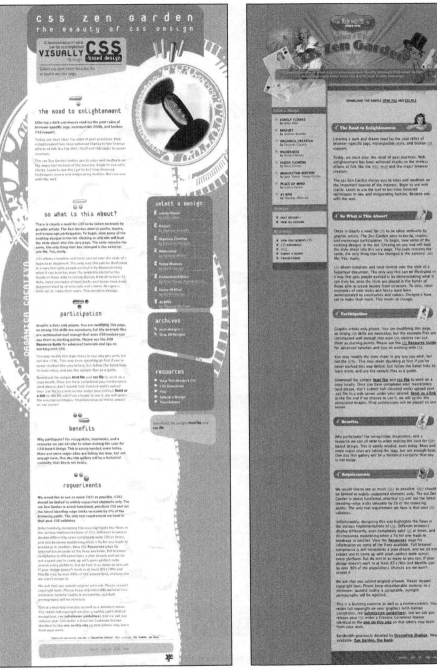

Figure 9-1. CSS Zen Garden design "Organica Creativa" by Eduardo Cesario

Figure 9-2. CSS Zen Garden design "Pinups" by Emiliano Pennisi

9

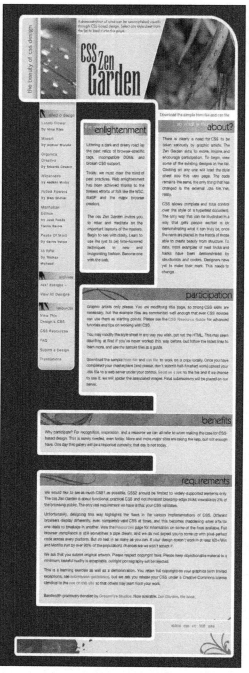

Figure 9-3. CSS Zen Garden design "Obsequience" by Pierce Gleeson

Figure 9-4. CSS Zen Garden design "Invasion of the Body Switchers" by Andy Clarke

Without a style sheet attached, the CSS Zen Garden HTML page looks like Figure 9-5.

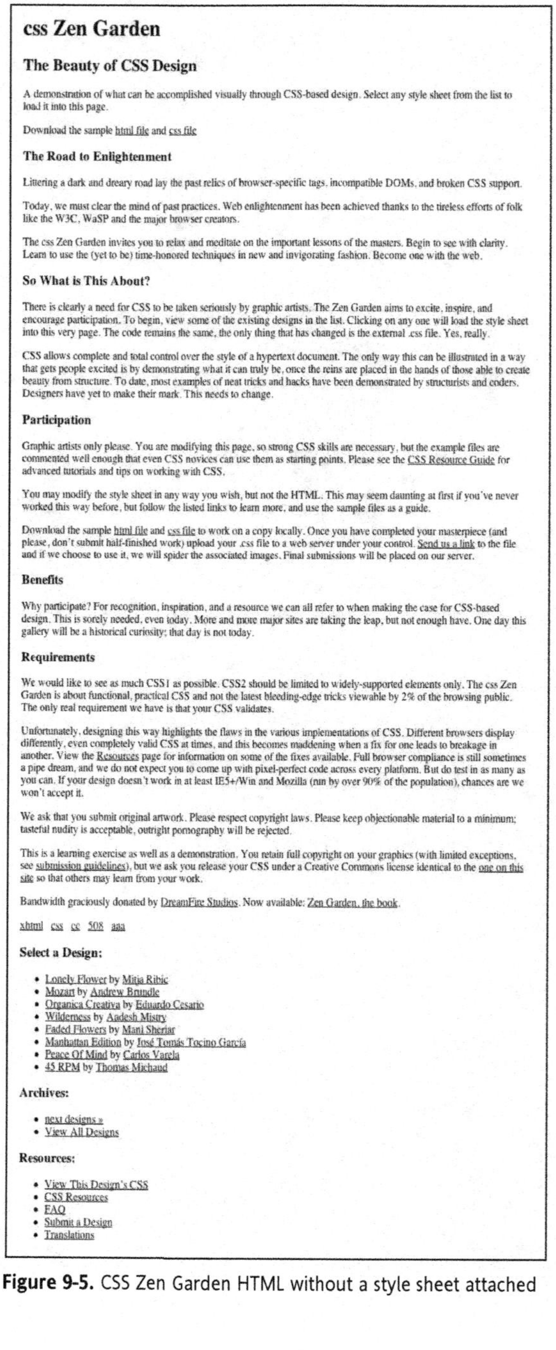

css Zen Garden

The Beauty of CSS Design

A demonstration of what can be accomplished visually through CSS-based design. Select any style sheet from the list to load it into this page.

Download the sample html file and css file

The Road to Enlightenment

Littering a dark and dreary road lay the past relics of browser-specific tags, incompatible DOMs, and broken CSS support.

Today, we must clear the mind of past practices. Web enlightenment has been achieved thanks to the tireless efforts of folk like the W3C, WaSP and the major browser creators.

The css Zen Garden invites you to relax and meditate on the important lessons of the masters. Begin to see with clarity. Learn to use the (yet to be) time-honored techniques in new and invigorating fashion. Become one with the web.

So What is This About?

There is clearly a need for CSS to be taken seriously by graphic artists. The Zen Garden aims to excite, inspire, and encourage participation. To begin, view some of the existing designs in the list. Clicking on any one will load the style sheet into this very page. The code remains the same, the only thing that has changed is the external .css file. Yes, really.

CSS allows complete and total control over the style of a hypertext document. The only way this can be illustrated in a way that gets people excited is by demonstrating what it can truly be, once the reins are placed in the hands of those able to create beauty from structure. To date, most examples of neat tricks and hacks have been demonstrated by structurists and coders. Designers have yet to make their mark. This needs to change.

Participation

Graphic artists only please. You are modifying this page, so strong CSS skills are necessary, but the example files are commented well enough that even CSS novices can use them as starting points. Please see the CSS Resource Guide for advanced tutorials and tips on working with CSS.

You may modify the style sheet in any way you wish, but not the HTML. This may seem daunting at first if you've never worked this way before, but follow the listed links to learn more, and use the sample files as a guide.

Download the sample html file and css file to work on a copy locally. Once you have completed your masterpiece (and please, don't submit half-finished work) upload your .css file to a web server under your control. Send us a link to the file and if we choose to use it, we will spider the associated images. Final submissions will be placed on our server.

Benefits

Why participate? For recognition, inspiration, and a resource we can all refer to when making the case for CSS-based design. This is sorely needed, even today. More and more major sites are taking the leap, but not enough have. One day this gallery will be a historical curiosity; that day is not today.

Requirements

We would like to see as much CSS1 as possible. CSS2 should be limited to widely-supported elements only. The css Zen Garden is about functional, practical CSS and not the latest bleeding-edge tricks viewable by 2% of the browsing public. The only real requirement we have is that your CSS validates.

Unfortunately, designing this way highlights the flaws in the various implementations of CSS. Different browsers display differently, even completely valid CSS at times, and this becomes maddening when a fix for one leads to breakage in another. View the Resources page for information on some of the fixes available. Full browser compliance is still sometimes a pipe dream, and we do not expect you to come up with pixel-perfect code across every platform. But do test in as many as you can. If your design doesn't work in at least IE5+/Win and Mozilla (run by over 90% of the population), chances are we won't accept it.

We ask that you submit original artwork. Please respect copyright laws. Please keep objectionable material to a minimum; tasteful nudity is acceptable, outright pornography will be rejected.

This is a learning exercise as well as a demonstration. You retain full copyright on your graphics (with limited exceptions, see submission guidelines), but we ask you release your CSS under a Creative Commons license identical to the one on this site so that others may learn from your work.

Bandwidth graciously donated by DreamFire Studios. Now available: Zen Garden, the book.

xhtml css cc 508 aaa

Select a Design:

- Lonely Flower by Mitja Ribic
- Mozart by Andrew Brundle
- Organica Creativa by Eduardo Cesario
- Wilderness by Aadesh Mistry
- Faded Flowers by Mani Sheriar
- Manhattan Edition by José Tomás Tocino García
- Peace Of Mind by Carlos Varela
- 45 RPM by Thomas Michaud

Archives:

- next designs »
- View All Designs

Resources:

- View This Design's CSS
- CSS Resources
- FAQ
- Submit a Design
- Translations

Figure 9-5. CSS Zen Garden HTML without a style sheet attached

So, you can see that CSS is extremely powerful. It can provide layout and presentation entirely independent of the HTML document, which is extremely important. If you look at the unstyled version of the CSS Zen Garden page (Figure 9-5), it doesn't look very pretty, but it still makes sense. You can still scan the headings, read the text, and see the lists. This is because the underlying content is in a logical order and marked up with semantic—that is to say, structural and meaningful—HTML.

In the U.S. Access Board's Section 508 Standards, the applicable provision is as follows:

§1194.22(d) Documents shall be organized so they are readable without requiring an associated style sheet.

Similarly, the Web Content Accessibility Guidelines (WCAG) 1.0 says this:

6.1 Organize documents so they may be read without style sheets. For example, when an HTML document is rendered without associated style sheets, it must still be possible to read the document.

To accomplish this, you can think of CSS as a presentation "layer" that you can remove and still be left with readable and understandable content. By moving presentational markup into style sheets, HTML documents are left with clean and semantic markup. This more readily enables people to use a website with devices such as text-only browsers, aural browsers, and screen readers.

CSS can provide a benefit only when used with semantic HTML. You should build the unstyled web page first, paying attention to the order and structure of the pages. As discussed in Chapter 6, remember to mark up all your headings with <hn> elements; all your lists using <dl>, <ul>, or <ol> tags; and so on. You can also wrap related content (such as sidebars) inside <div> elements.

In this chapter, you'll learn how to use various CSS techniques to improve the accessibility of a website. But first, let's review some CSS basics.

CSS Basics

Although many designers are familiar with the basic syntax used in CSS, this section provides a brief overview, with an emphasis on best practices for accessibility. If you need an in-depth guide to CSS, refer to a book dedicated to that subject, such as *CSS Mastery: Advanced Web Standards Solutions* by Andy Budd (1-59059-614-5; friends of ED, 2006).

Style sheets are made up of rules that apply to an HTML document (although style sheets can also be applied to XML documents, this chapter will cover HTML only). Style sheet rules are made up of three parts:

9

- The elements the rule applies to (called the *selector*)
- The property that is being set
- The value of the property

An example of a style sheet rule is shown in Figure 9-6.

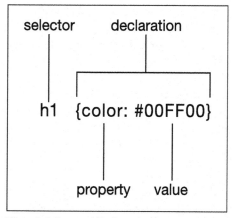

Figure 9-6. An example of a style sheet rule

In the example in Figure 9-6, the selector is h1, the property is color, and the value is #00FF00 (the hexadecimal value for pure green). Together, the property and value form the declaration part of the rule. The selector links the style sheet rule to the HTML. In this case, all h1 elements will be shown in this shade of green.

More than one declaration can be applied to a selector, and more than one selector can be given the same declaration, as in this example:

```
cite, blockquote {font-style:italic; font-family:'Myriad Pro',
Helvetica, Arial, sans-serif}
```

Here, all cite and blockquote elements will be displayed in italic Myriad Pro (or Helvetica or Arial, depending on which fonts are available on the user's computer).

Style sheet rules can be applied to HTML documents in three ways:

- **Inline:** Declarations can be attached inline to individual elements using the style attribute.
- **Embedded:** The rules can be embedded into the HTML document using the <style> element.
- **Linked:** The CSS rules can be written to a separate file, usually with a .css extension, and linked to the HTML document using the <link> element or an @import rule.

Let's look at when it's appropriate to use each of these methods, and then at when user and browser style sheets are applied.

Inline Styles

Inline styles should be used only when the designer needs to specify a particular style in one place in a single document. Here is an example:

```
<p style="border:1px solid purple ">
```

In this piece of code, content (the <p> element) and presentation (the style attribute) are both present. The implication is that inline styles do not separate presentation from content. Therefore, you should use inline styles only in exceptional circumstances.

Even if you require a single element in a document to be given a style, there is an alternative to using an inline style: using an id selector. Give the element a unique id attribute, as in this example:

```
<p id="special">
```

You can then use the id attribute as a selector in your style sheet, like this:

```
#special { border:1px solid purple }
```

If you find yourself repeating the same inline style several times within a document, you should use a class selector. This works in a similar way to the id selector, except it uses a class attribute, like this:

```
<p class="special">
```

Use the class selector in your style sheet like this:

```
.special { border:1px solid red }
```

The main difference between id selectors and class selectors is that an id can be applied only to a single element within an HTML document, whereas class selectors can be applied to as many different elements as you like, although you should limit the use of id and class selectors where possible. One further difference between class and id selectors—from a CSS perspective—is that id selectors are considered to have a higher *specificity*. An id is considered more important than a class, so where rules contradict each other, the id will override the class. For example, consider this HTML code:

```
<p id="veryspecial" class="special">
```

And the corresponding CSS rules:

```
#veryspecial {background: purple}
.special {background: red; font-weight: bold}
```

The paragraph will be displayed in bold, as specified in the class rule. The class rule also specifies a red background, but the id rule says that the background should be purple. As id selectors are more specific than class selectors, the id overrides the class, and the background of the paragraph will be displayed in purple.

9

Embedded Style Sheets

With the embedded method of adding CSS to an HTML document, the CSS rules are enclosed in a `<style>` element, which should be included inside the `<head>` element. Valid HTML requires that you should always include the `type` attribute with the `<style>` element. Here is an example:

```
<style type="text/css">
h1 {
color: #00FF00;
}
#veryspecial {
background: purple;
}
.special {
background: red;
font-weight: bold;
}
cite, blockquote {
font-style:italic;
font-family:'Myriad Pro', Helvetica, Arial, sans-serif;
}
</style>
```

Embedding style sheets in this manner goes one step further in separating content from presentation, as all the style rules are containing within a single element and not intermingled with the HTML. However, embedded style sheets can apply rules to only a single HTML document, so in a site-wide context, the styles are still not very separated from the content. The implication is that embedded style sheets should be used only when rules need to be applied to a single page within a website. For styles that need to be applied to more than one web page (as is often the case), a linked style sheet should be used.

Linked and Imported Style Sheets

By importing or linking to an external style sheet file, the designer can control the presentation of a whole website from one or more style sheets. A style sheet file would normally be named with a `.css` extension and would include style sheet rules like this:

```
h1 {
color: #00FF00;
}
#veryspecial {
background: purple;
}
.special {
background: red;
font-weight: bold;
}
```

```
cite, blockquote {
font-style:italic;
font-family:'Myriad Pro', Helvetica, Arial, sans-serif;
}
```

Notice the rules are exactly the same as with the embedded style sheet, but there is no need for the <style> element. The style sheet file is linked to an HTML page using the <link> element in the <head> of the document, like this:

```
<link rel="stylesheet" type="text/css" href="mystyles.css" />
```

An alternative method is to use @import from within a <style> element, like this:

```
<style type="text/css">
@import url(mystyles.css);
</style>
```

The <link> element is supported by all browsers that support style sheets. However, the @import method is not supported by some older browsers, including Internet Explorer 4 and Netscape Navigator 4 and older. This is often used to the designer's advantage, because the older browsers have very poor support for CSS. Linking to style sheets using the @import method means only capable browsers will be able to use your style sheets. The older browsers will display the unstyled pages, which should still be usable, assuming you have used HTML correctly and marked up the content in a meaningful way. Hence, @import is usually the method of choice for linking to style sheets.

User Style Sheets

So far, I have discussed the use of style sheets created by the author. However, one of the major accessibility features of CSS is that style sheets can be created by users, too. User style sheets are files created by users and stored on their computer. The browser is then configured to apply the user style sheet to all websites that the user visits.

For example, a visually impaired reader may specify a style sheet like this:

```
body {
  color: yellow;
  background: black;
}
```

In this style sheet, the user has set a black background and yellow text for the web page (perhaps because the combination of color makes the text easier to read). The rules in the user style sheet will override rules of an equivalent specificity set by the author. However, if the author sets a more specific rule like this:

```
p.special {background: green;}
```

Then the author's rule will override the user's rule. In this case, the result will be yellow text displayed on a green background for all paragraphs with a class of special, which is clearly undesirable and not at all helpful for the user.

9

257

In order to ensure that users can control styles as they wish, CSS2 defines the !important operator. If a user's style sheet contains !important, it takes precedence over any applicable rule in an author's style sheet. For instance, the rule in the following user style sheet will ensure that every paragraph on the web page is set to the desired colors:

```
p {
    color: yellow ! important ;
    background: black ! important ;
}
```

Authors can also use !important in their style sheets, but it will always be overridden by a user style sheet (although this is only true in Internet Explorer if the user-defined style sheet also contains the !important keyword).

The CSS2 inherit value, which is available for most properties, enables !important style rules that can govern most or all of a document. For instance, the following rules force *all* backgrounds to black and *all* foreground colors to yellow:

```
body {
    color: black ! important ;
    background: white ! important ;
}

* {
    color: inherit ! important ;
    background: inherit ! important ;
}
```

The first rule sets the colors of the <body>, and the second rule uses the * selector to target all elements on the page and the inherit property to inherit the colors from the <body>.

CSS2 also enables further control over the display, including these features:

- System colors (for the color, background-color, border-color, and outline-color properties) and system fonts (for the font property) mean that users may apply their system color and font preferences to web pages.
- Dynamic outlines (using the outline property) allow users to create outlines around content in order to highlight certain information.

For example, to draw a thick blue line around an element when it has the focus, and a thick green line when it is active, the following rules can be used:

```
:focus  { outline: thick solid blue }
:active { outline: thick solid green }
```

These style rules could help some readers with visual difficulties more readily see which element has focus (in a form, for example).

Browser Style Sheets

Even when no user or author style sheet has been specified, browsers still use a style sheet to render HTML with default styling. For example, Firefox uses a file called `html.css` for the default rendering of HTML. Here is an extract showing how Firefox styles level 1 headings:

```
h1 {
    display: block;
    font-size: 2em;
    font-weight: bold;
    margin: .67em 0;
}
```

Browser style sheets have a lower specificity than author and user style sheets.

Color and Backgrounds

CSS allows users with particular presentation requirements to override author styles. This is very important to users who have problems with certain colors and fonts, as CSS allows users to view documents with their own preferences by specifying them in a user style sheet.

Colors are probably the easiest properties to set using CSS, but they can also be the most problematic. In this section, I will highlight the potential problems and provide solutions to specifying color with CSS.

Background and Text Colors

As explained in the "User Style Sheets" section, it is possible for author style sheets and user style sheets to clash. The example I provided had a user specifying yellow text on a black background, with the author using a more specific rule to set the background to green. This resulted in the user seeing green text on a yellow background, which is difficult to read. It is therefore vital that authors specify both a foreground color and a background color so that text will always remain readable.

Color problems can also arise with certain operating system "themes." For example, a designer may want all the form controls to appear with a gray background:

```
input, textarea {background: gray}
```

In most situations, this would be fine. However, form control colors tend to be inherited from the operating system, so an operating system theme with gray text might exist, meaning that the text on the form controls would be invisible. To solve this problem, the designer should specify the foreground color of the form controls as well:

9

259

```
input, textarea {
  background: gray;
  color: black;
}
```

Background Images

CSS also allows designers to set background images. However, it's important to remember that if you do this, you should always set a background color as well:

```
P .special {
  background: red url(bricks.gif);
  color: white;
}
```

By choosing a suitable background color, you can ensure that the text is always readable, regardless of browser settings or any bandwidth problems delaying the downloading of images.

Foreground and Background Contrast

People with low vision often have difficulty reading text that does not contrast enough with its background. This can be exacerbated if the person has a color vision deficiency that lowers the contrast even further. Another group of users affected by low contrast are people using monitors suffering from reflections (perhaps from a window) or screens that have poor contrast. So, following accessibility advice could also benefit people without disabilities.

Designers should ensure that foreground and background colors contrast well. On this subject, WCAG 1.0 states

2.2 Ensure that foreground and background color combinations provide sufficient contrast when viewed by someone having color deficits or when viewed on a black and white screen. [Priority 2 for images, Priority 3 for text].

A very basic test for determining whether color contrast is sufficient to be read by people with color vision deficiencies or by those with low-resolution monitors is to print pages on a black-and-white printer (with backgrounds and colors appearing in grayscale). The important thing to remember is to rely on lightness differences between foreground and background, not to rely on color differences.

For more specific guidance on color contrast, see "Effective Color Contrast" by Aries Arditi, Lighthouse International (www.lighthouse.org/color_contrast.htm), and "Type and Colour" by Joe Clark (joeclark.org/book/sashay/serialization/Chapter09.html). Jonathan Snook has developed an online Color Contrast Checker at www.snook.ca/technical/colour_contrast/colour.html.

Other Means of Conveying Information

I have just stressed the importance of color contrast. It can be inferred that relying on color *alone* is not a reliable method of conveying information and meaning. Indeed, Section 508 states

> §1194.22(c) Web pages shall be designed so that all information conveyed with color is also available without color, for example from context or markup.

As a designer, you should ensure that information and meaning is also conveyed through means that do not depend on the user's ability to differentiate colors. For example, when asking for input from users, do not write "Please select an item from those listed in green." Similarly, do not turn off the underlining of links without providing some other method of visually determining a link. Instead, make sure that information and meaning are available through other style effects, such as bold text or grouped under a heading.

This does not mean that you should not use color to enhance identification of important features. Indeed, color is an extremely important weapon in the designer's arsenal. It does, however, require that some other method of identification, such as text labels, be combined with the use of color.

Text and Fonts

CSS has properties to control font appearance, so authors can avoid using images of text. Using style sheets to style text, rather than creating images of text, makes textual information and meaning far more accessible. Text as text (as opposed to images of text) makes content available to people who use speech synthesizers and Braille displays. It can also more readily be resized and reformatted for visually impaired users or those using alternative devices, such as handhelds and projectors. Another benefit is that the text can be read by other software, such as search engine robots.

In the past, HTML markup was heavily abused and the accessibility implications were ignored in the pursuit of presentational effects. CSS provides many properties for styling text beyond just size, and this opens the door to enabling well laid out pages combined with meaningful, accessible HTML.

Text Sizing

Text size is probably the first font style a designer will need to set. In CSS, this is accomplished with the font-size property:

```
P {font-size:12px}
```

9

This sets all paragraphs to display at a font size of 12 pixels, what the designer may consider the perfect size for paragraph text. However, not all users will agree with that design decision—perhaps they are short-sighted, doing a presentation, using a very-high resolution screen, or simply have tired eyes. The beauty of CSS (and the Web in general) is that users can change settings in their browser to make all the page text proportionately bigger or smaller as they require.

> As a designer, it is important to create web pages that will allow text to be resized without the layout breaking or the design being otherwise compromised. Users can, and will, change the size of text to suit their requirements, and this should always be taken into account.

There is, however, a complication: Internet Explorer for Windows (up to version 6 at the time of writing) will *not* resize text that has been defined in pixels. You could reasonably argue that if users require text to be resized, they should use software that is capable of doing so, such as Firefox and Opera (both of which are free), but not everyone has that choice. Furthermore, WCAG 1.0 has this to say on the subject:

> 3.4 Use relative rather than absolute units in markup language attribute values and style sheet property values. [Priority 2]

In this instance, pixels should be considered absolute units, although they are actually relative to the screen resolution. The alternative to absolute units is relative units, which include percentage, keywords (such as bigger), and for text in particular, ems. Sizing text using ems is slightly more complicated than using pixels, and so warrants further explanation.

The *em* unit of measure is so-called because it approximates the size of an uppercase letter *M*, although 1 em is actually significantly larger than this. In *The Elements of Typographic Style* (0-881-79132-6; Hartley and Marks, 2001), the typographer Robert Bringhurst describes the em as follows:

> The em is a sliding measure. One em is a distance equal to the type size. In 6 point type, an em is 6 points; in 12 point type an em is 12 points and in 60 point type an em is 60 points. Thus a one em space is proportionately the same in any size.

To illustrate this principle in terms of CSS, consider these styles:

```
#box1 {
    font-size: 12px;
    width: 1em;
    height: 1em;
    border:1px solid black;
}
```

```
#box2 {
    font-size: 60px;
    width: 1em;
    height: 1em;
    border: 1px solid black;
}
```

These styles will render as shown in Figure 9-7.

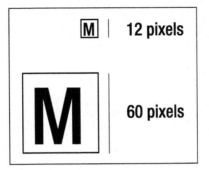

Figure 9-7. Sizing with ems

Note that both boxes have a height and width of 1 em, but because they have different font sizes, one box is bigger than the other. Box 1 has a font-size of 12px, so its width and height are also 12px. Box 2 has a font-size of 60px, and correspondingly, its width and height are also 60px.

To explain how sizing text using ems actually works, consider this extract from a short web page:

```
<body>
<h1>My heading</h1>
<p>A paragraph of text</p>
</body>
```

In this example, the designer wants the heading to be 24px and the paragraph to be 12px. In most browsers, with text set to the default medium size, the font size of the <body> will be 16px. To set the font size of the heading to 24px using ems, you need to apply a little mathematics:

child pixels / parent pixels = child ems

24 / 16 = 1.5

That is to say, the heading is 1.5 times the size of its parent, the body, so you use this rule:

```
h1 {font-size:1.5em}
```

9

Applying the same logic to change the font size of a paragraph, you have 12 / 16 = 0.75, so you use this rule:

```
p {font-size:0.75em}
```

One added complication is that of nested elements. A list might be added to the page like this:

```
<ul>
  <li>Fruit
    <ul>
      <li>orange</li>
      <li>apple</li>
    </ul>
  </li>
  <li>Vegetable
    <ul>
      <li>potato</li>
      <li>carrot</li>
    </ul>
  </li>
</ul>
```

If you also want the list of items to be 12 pixels, you could add the same style sheet rule that you did for paragraphs:

```
li {font-style:0.75em}
```

This will work for Fruit and Vegetable, but orange, carrot, and the other nested list items will be displayed at 9 pixels. Why? Because the rule actually says that any list item should be 0.75 times the size of its parent. So you need another rule to prevent this inherited shrinkage:

```
li li {font-size:1em}
```

This says that any list item inside another list item should be the same size as its parent (the other list item).

For a more detailed explanation of sizing text using ems, see www.clagnut.com/blog/348/.

Text Margins and Indentation

Often, the blockquote element is misused to indent a block of text. This is an unreliable and sometimes harmful approach. It can be harmful because blockquote adds meaning to the text: It tells the browser that the enclosed text has been quoted from a source. If this is not the case, the blockquote would be misleading. It can be unreliable because the indentation may not always be applied. Indentation is simply a common style applied by most browsers, but not necessarily all of them.

If you require a portion of text to be indented, you should apply the `margin` property, which allows you to create space on any or all of the four sides of an element's content. Here is an example:

```
.attention {
  margin-left:2em;
  margin-right:2em;
}
```

Figure 9-8 shows an example of using the `margin` property.

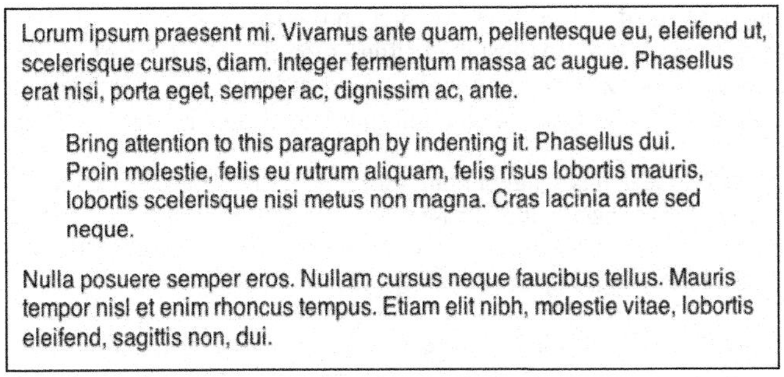

Lorum ipsum praesent mi. Vivamus ante quam, pellentesque eu, eleifend ut, scelerisque cursus, diam. Integer fermentum massa ac augue. Phasellus erat nisi, porta eget, semper ac, dignissim ac, ante.

Bring attention to this paragraph by indenting it. Phasellus dui. Proin molestie, felis eu rutrum aliquam, felis risus lobortis mauris, lobortis scelerisque nisi metus non magna. Cras lacinia ante sed neque.

Nulla posuere semper eros. Nullam cursus neque faucibus tellus. Mauris tempor nisl et enim rhoncus tempus. Etiam elit nibh, molestie vitae, lobortis eleifend, sagittis non, dui.

Figure 9-8. Using the margin property to indent text

As well indenting an entire block of text using margins, CSS also enables you to indent the first line of a block. Instead of using transparent images or multiple   entities to create an indentation, you should use the `text-indent` property. This example of the `margin` property indents the first line of every paragraph by 1em:

```
p {text-indent:1em}
```

A slightly more sophisticated rule using the + adjacent sibling selector would automatically set every contiguous paragraph to be indented:

```
p + p {text-indent:1em}
```

Translating the rule more literally, this says to indent every paragraph that directly follows another paragraph, and would render as shown in Figure 9-9.

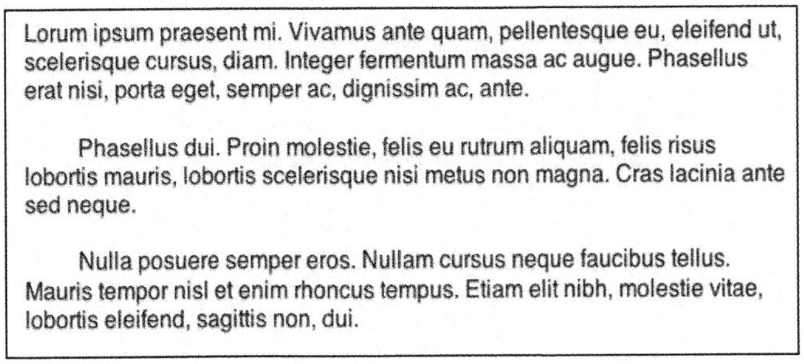

Lorum ipsum praesent mi. Vivamus ante quam, pellentesque eu, eleifend ut, scelerisque cursus, diam. Integer fermentum massa ac augue. Phasellus erat nisi, porta eget, semper ac, dignissim ac, ante.

Phasellus dui. Proin molestie, felis eu rutrum aliquam, felis risus lobortis mauris, lobortis scelerisque nisi metus non magna. Cras lacinia ante sed neque.

Nulla posuere semper eros. Nullam cursus neque faucibus tellus. Mauris tempor nisl et enim rhoncus tempus. Etiam elit nibh, molestie vitae, lobortis eleifend, sagittis non, dui.

Figure 9-9. Using the text-indent property to indent the first line of paragraphs

9

Font Family

Like the deprecated HTML `<font>` tag before it, CSS's `font-family` property provides a way of specifying the display font:

```
body {font-family: Univers, "Helvetica Neue", Arial, Helvetica,
sans-serif}
```

As with HTML, web pages designed with CSS can be displayed only with the fonts installed on the user's computer. So the `font-family` property enables you to provide a list of alternative fonts in order of preference. In this example, the first choice is for the page to be displayed using Univers. If Univers isn't installed on the user's computer, the next preference is Helvetica Neue. If that isn't installed either, then the next choices are Arial, followed by Helvetica, all the way down to a generic sans-serif font family (which will be a font that really is installed on the user's computer and specified in the browser preferences).

There are five generic font families: `serif`, `sans-serif`, `cursive`, `fantasy`, and `monospace`. It is good practice to always specify one of these at the end of your font list so your design will be rendered somewhere close to your original intent. There is more discussion and advice on `font-family` at www.clagnut.com/blog/266/.

CSS1 provides three further font properties: `font-style`, `font-weight`, and `font-variant`. These are well supported across modern browsers and can be used as follows:

```
cite {font-style:italic}
strong {font-weight:bold}
acronym {font-variant:smallcaps}
```

Letter and Word Spacing

Further manipulation of text is available in CSS through the `word-spacing` and `letter-spacing` properties. These can result in some very creative styling without needing to resort to images. Here is an example:

```
letter-spacing: 0.25em
word-spacing: -0.45em
```

Figure 9-10 shows the result.

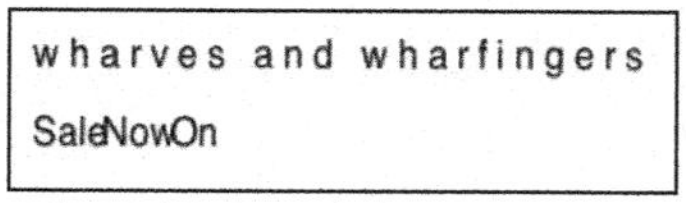

Figure 9-10. Using the letter-spacing and word-spacing properties

Using `letter-spacing` in this manner, as opposed to inserting spaces in between the letters, means the words stay as words. When letters are separated by whitespace characters, they are read as individual letters. For example, if you put spaces between the characters in a word like this:

```
w h a r v e s
```

It will be read by a screen reader as the individual letters—*w*, *h*, *a*, *r*, *v*, *e*, and *s*—rather than the word *wharves*. Text without spaces will be transformed effectively to speech and also be more readily understood by software such as search engines.

Letter Case

When you require words or phrases to be shown entirely in all uppercase letters—for example, in a heading—write the text as you would normally, and then use `text-transform` to change the case:

```
h1 {text-transform:uppercase}
```

If a phrase is an acronym or abbreviation that is normally written in uppercase, such as NASA or IBM, you should still write the word in capital letters, rather than use CSS to transform the word.

Text Direction

This book is written in English and so reads from left to right. Some languages, such as Hebrew, read from right to left. In some cases, you may need to mix together written languages that read in opposite directions. You can use the CSS properties `direction` and `unicode-bidi` to indicate a change in direction of presentation. Here is an example:

```
.hebrew {
  direction: rtl;
  unicode-bidi: bidi-override;
}
```

9

Image Replacement Techniques

As outlined in the previous section, a lot of text effects are available through CSS. While the preferred technique is not to use images of text, many designers will not be satisfied with what can be achieved with CSS alone. Instead, they will resort to images of text to ensure their designs use a certain typeface or treatment. This is fine, provided that the images are marked up correctly with structural HTML and suitable `alt` attributes. For example, as explained in Chapter 6 an image of the heading Introduction should be coded something like this:

```
<h1><img src="introduction.gif" alt="Introduction" /></h1>
```

The disadvantage of this technique is that the text of the heading is accessible only through the alt attribute of the image.

You can use CSS to make text more accessible through background images and positioning properties. These techniques are known as *image replacement* (IR). The CSS Zen Garden examples shown in Figures 9-1 through 9-4 at the beginning of this chapter rely heavily on image replacement techniques for their visual impact, and image replacement has been a major factor in the popularity of CSS.

One such image replacement technique can be applied to the previous example by marking up the heading in the following manner:

```
<h1 id="intro"><span></span>Introduction</h1>
```

To show a designed image instead of real text, you can use the following style rules:

```
#intro {
  width: 300px;
  height: 100px;
  position: relative;
}

#intro span {
  background: url("introduction.gif") no-repeat;
  width: 100%;
  height: 100%;
  position: absolute;
}
```

With these style rules, the image text is inserted by setting the background of the empty span to background:url("introduction.gif"), and then positioning the span on top of the real text (positioning is discussed in the "Layout and Positioning" section later in this chapter). The real text will display if CSS or image loading is turned off in the browser. There are some provisos with this method: An otherwise meaningless <span> element is required, the size of the real text must always be smaller than the size of the text image, and the text image cannot be transparent.

CSS On, Images Off

Many image replacement techniques fail in the situation where CSS is on but images are turned off. This is usually due to CSS rules hiding the real text off screen, such as the Phark technique proposed by Mike Rundle (see phark.typepad.com/phark/2003/08/accessible_imag.html):

```
<h1 id="intro">Introduction</h1>
/* CSS */

#intro {
  text-indent:-100em;
  height:25px;
  background: url("introduction.gif") no-repeat;
}
```

In the Phark technique, the real text is indented by 100 ems, so that it disappears off the screen, leaving just the background image displayed. However if a CSS-enabled browser has images turned off (or perhaps a very slow Internet connection), the image will not be displayed, and neither will the real text, as it is hidden off-screen.

To address this problem, I put together an experiment that uses JavaScript to make image replacement techniques work when CSS is on and images are off, which you can find at www.clagnut.com/sandbox/js-enhanced-IR/.

It's worth noting that the method described at the beginning of this section does work in the situation where CSS is enabled and images are off, as it hides the real text with the image.

Scalable Inman Flash Replacement (sIFR)

One of the more recent image replacement techniques is called scalable Inman Flash Replacement (sIFR), (pronounced "siffer"), developed by Shaun Inman and Mike Davidson. This technique combines CSS and JavaScript to dynamically replace elements (such as headings) with a tiny Flash movie. sIFR allows you to mark up your documents in a standard, meaningful way, without the need for superfluous <img> or <span> elements.

Surprisingly, perhaps, this is one of the most accessible of all the image replacement techniques. If JavaScript, Flash, or CSS is not available, the normal text is shown instead. If readers have their default text size set to large (or some other nondefault size), the Flash movies resize accordingly. This is not something that usually happens with image replacement techniques and is clearly advantageous for visually impaired readers.

The main drawback is that sIFR can slow down the rendering of websites as it is quite resource-intensive (especially if overused on a web page). The sIFR files are free and can be downloaded from www.mikeindustries.com/sifr/.

9

Deprecated Image Replacement Techniques

An early image replacement technique is known as Fahrner Image Replacement (FIR), named after Todd Fahrner, one of the persons originally credited with the idea. Like all image replacement techniques, FIR used a background image for the graphical text, but it also used the display:none property to hide the real text from the browser. This appeared to work well, but was subsequently found to fail in some screen readers (see alistapart.com/articles/fir/ for detailed testing results) as the text was not read aloud. This is because the display property applies to any manifestation, not just visual.

Many image replacement techniques are documented across the Web. Any that use display:none to hide the real text should be avoided, as they are inherently inaccessible. The pros and cons of other methods of image replacement are discussed on Mezzoblue at www.mezzoblue.com/tests/revised-image-replacement/.

What's Wrong with Using an img Tag?

An img tag with suitable alt text will work well in most situations, including the examples cited here. The problem with the alt attribute is that its contents can be only plain text. You cannot add any markup within the alt attribute, so images containing text beyond a few words may not be able to be adequately represented.

This situation is likely to be addressed with the advent of XHTML 2.0. Markup such as the following will be possible:

```
<table src="temperatures.png">
<caption>Average monthly temperatures</caption>
<tr> <th>Jan</th> <th>Feb</th>....
<tr> <td>0</td>    <td>-4</td>...
</table>
```

In this code, a browser that can display images will show the temperatures.png image; all others will display the table. In XHTML 2, the src attribute can be applied to just about any element, so in the future, CSS-based image replacement techniques will not be required.

Image Replacement Abuse

It is vital that you take care not to include important information in images that are displayed through CSS. WCAG 1.0 has this to say on the matter:

> 6.1 Organize documents so they may be read without style sheets. For example, when an HTML document is rendered without associated style sheets, it must still be possible to read the document. [Priority 1]

This means that any background images containing information or text must have the equivalent information in the markup. A real-life example of image replacement abuse is the following code:

```
<p id= "interestrate">The best interest rates available</p>
```

In this example, the paragraph is styled to include an image whose text includes "19.3% Typical Variable." Clearly, this is bad because the important (and possibly legally binding) information that the interest rate is 19.3 percent is available only in an image specified by CSS, making it inaccessible to screen reader users and anyone else without images or CSS.

More examples and discussion of CSS background abuse can be found in the article "Naughty or Nice? CSS Background Images" at 24ways.org/advent/naughty-or-nice-css-background-images.

Layout and Positioning

CSS allows precise control over spacing, alignment, and positioning, allowing authors to avoid markup tricks, such as invisible images and tag misuse. For example, while the <blockquote> and <table> elements in HTML are supposed to be used to mark up quotations and tabular data, they are frequently used to create visual effects, such as indentation and alignment. When specialized browsing software, such as a speech synthesizer, encounters elements that are misused in this way, the results can be unintelligible to the user.

As mentioned in Chapter 6, the <table> element is often misused to lay out pages rather than to mark up and display tabular data, for which it was originally designed. Using the positioning properties of CSS2, designers can control the visual position of almost any element in a manner independent of where the element appears in the document. You should always design documents that make sense without style sheets. This means the document should be written in a logical order, using structural markup to design content that makes sense when CSS is not applied.

Sample Layouts

Page layout with CSS has one of the steeper learning curves. In this section, I will demonstrate methods for creating three simplified layouts and leave you to experiment further.

For more information about CSS layouts, see the Max Design website (www.maxdesign.com.au/presentation/page_layouts/) and the css-discuss wiki (css-discuss.incutio.com/?page=CssLayouts). Also, Alex Robinson has created the One True Layout (www.positioniseverything.net/articles/onetruelayout/), which addresses a multitude of layout issues in CSS (be warned: it covers some very advanced topics).

9

Centered Elastic-Width Column

Figure 9-11 shows the first sample layout. It assumes a simple page with a centered column of text.

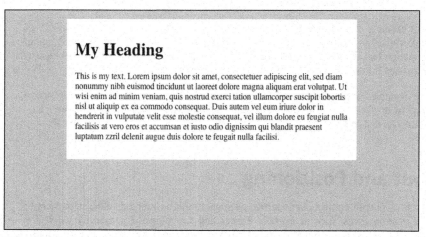

Figure 9-11. Centered elastic-width column layout

Here is the HTML:

```
<div id="content">
<h1>My Heading</h1>
<p>This is my text. Lorem ipsum dolor sit amet...</p>
</div>
```

And here is the CSS to achieve the centered layout:

```
#content {
  width: 33em;
  margin-right: auto;
  margin-left: auto;
  margin-top: 1em;
  padding: 1em;
  background: #fff;
  color: #000;
}
```

The first three properties do all the work in this example. First, the content column is set to 33 ems wide. This gives a comfortable line length for reading. It also means that if users reduce the size of their text, the width of the column will reduce accordingly, thus keeping the text readable with the same number of words on each line. Setting auto as the value for left and right margins has the effect of centering the column.

This type of layout has been coined *elastic*, as it can be said to stretch with the text size. A good example of an elastic layout is Patrick Griffiths's Elastic Lawn design for the CSS Zen Garden (www.csszengarden.com/?cssfile=/063/063.css).

Three Columns Using Absolute Positioning

Figure 9-12 shows the next sample layout. This layout has two sidebars of fixed width and a center column of main content, which fills the remainder of the window.

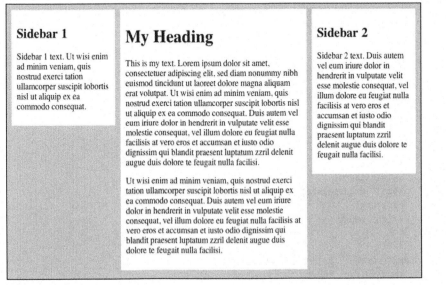

Figure 9-12. Three-column layout

The following is the HTML for the page. Notice the source order has the middle column first, followed by the sidebars.

```
<body>
<div id="maincontent">
<h1>My Heading</h1>
<p>This is my text...</p>
<p>Ut wisi enim ad minim veniam...</p>
</div>

<div id="sidebar1">
<h2>Sidebar 1</h2>
<p>Sidebar 1 text...</p>
</div>

<div id="sidebar2">
<h2>Sidebar 2</h2>
<p>Sidebar 2 text...</p>
</div>
</body>
```

9

Here is the style sheet that performs the layout:

```css
body {
    margin:0;
    background:#ccc;
    color:#000;
}

#maincontent {
    margin-right:220px;
    margin-left:220px;
}

#sidebar1 {
    width:180px;
    position:absolute;
    top:0px;
    left:10px;
}

#sidebar2 {
    width:180px;
    position:absolute;
    top:0px;
    right:10px;
}

#maincontent, #sidebar1, #sidebar2 {
    margin-top: 10px;
    padding:10px;
    background:#fff;
    color:#000;
}
```

Stepping through the rules in order, first the body element is attended to:

```css
body {
    margin:0;
    background:#ccc;
    color:#000;
}
```

Here, any default margin applied to the body by a browser style sheet is removed, and the body background is set to a light gray, remembering to set the color as well. Next the maincontent div is styled:

```css
#maincontent {
    margin-right:220px;
    margin-left:220px;
}
```

The maincontent div, which contains all the content of the center column, is given a large margin to the left and right. This margin is of exactly the right size to fit in the sidebars, which are styled next:

```
#sidebar1 {
  width:180px;
  position:absolute;
  top:0px;
  left:10px;
}

#sidebar2 {
  width:180px;
  position:absolute;
  top:0px;
  right:10px;
}
```

First, both sidebars are given a width of 180px. This will ensure they fit inside the space left by the maincontent margins. Then the sidebars are given a position property of absolute. This takes the sidebars out of the flow of the document and means they can be placed anywhere on the page, including on top of existing content. To place an absolutely positioned element, use a combination of the top or bottom and left or right properties.

Sidebar 1 needs to be positioned in the top-left corner of the page, 10 pixels in from the left edge, so it is set to top:0px and left:10px. Similarly, sidebar 2 needs to be positioned in the top-right corner of the page, 10 pixels in from the right edge, so it is set to top:0px and right:10px.

Visually, the page reads from left to right as follows: sidebar 1, center column, sidebar 2. This is a design decision and has been accomplished in CSS despite the author's chosen logical source order of center column, sidebar 1, sidebar 2. In fact, sidebar 1 and sidebar 2 could be swapped by interchanging the left and right properties of each.

Being able to separate presentation from source order is extremely good for accessibility, as software such as a screen reader follows source order, meaning it can be helpful to have your content first and navigation at the end. There is also the additional benefit that search engines give more credence to content earlier in the source of a page, so if you can code your content before your navigation, this may improve your page rank.

9

A Heading, a Footer, and Two Liquid Columns

The third sample layout is shown in Figure 9-13. It contains a content column and a sidebar, both of which are proportional in width to the size of the user's browser window. This content is topped by a heading and finished off by a footer.

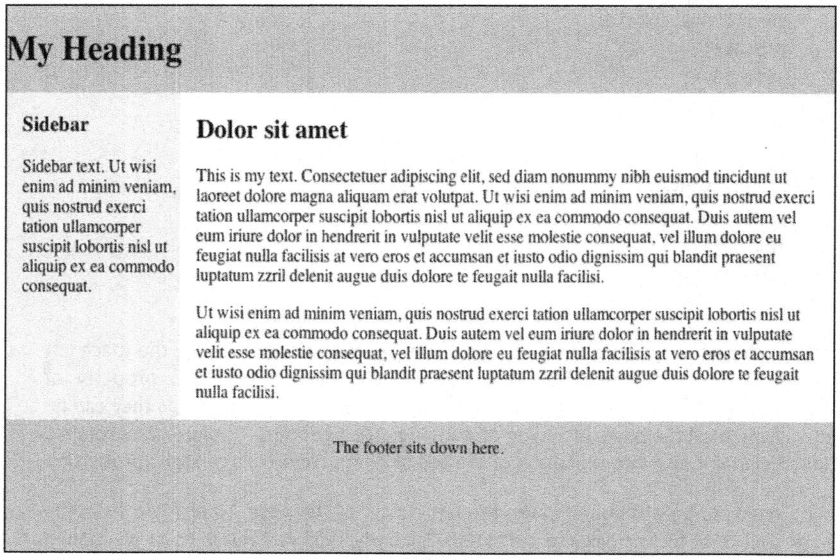

Figure 9-13. Layout with a heading, a footer, and two liquid columns

Here is the HTML for this page:

```
<h1>My Heading</h1>

<div id="content">

<div id="maincontent">
<h2>Dolor sit amet</h2>
<p>This is my text...</p>
<p>Ut wisi enim ad minim veniam...</p>
</div>

<div id="sidebar">
<h3>Sidebar</h3>
<p>Sidebar text...</p>
</div>

</div>

<p id="footer">The footer sits down here.</p>
```

Here is the style sheet that performs the layout:

```
body {
  background:#ccc;
  color:#000;
  margin:0;
}

#maincontent {
  float:right;
  width:75%;
  background:#fff;
  color:#000;
}

#sidebar {
  width:20%;
}

#footer {
  clear:right;
  text-align:center;
}

#content {
  background:#eee;
    color:#000;
  overflow:auto;
}

#maincontent, #sidebar {
  padding:0 1em;
}
```

First, the body is colored and the margins removed, as in the previous layout:

```
body {
  background:#ccc;
  color:#000;
  margin:0;
}
```

Then the maincontent column is positioned:

```
#maincontent {
  float:right;
  width:75%;
  background:#fff;
  color:#000;
}
```

Here, the maincontent column is colored white and given a width of 75%. This width makes the element three quarters the width of its container. In this case, the container is the content div, which stretches the full width of the window—as the window is widened, so is the content. The maincontent element is also given the style float:right. This "floats" the element to the right side and allows any content following it in the source to flow around. This is what enables the sidebar to sit next to the maincontent column.

The sidebar is styled with this rule:

```
#sidebar {
  width:20%;
}
```

The sidebar is given a width of 20% so that it will fit inside the remaining 25% left by the maincontent column.

Next comes the footer:

```
#footer {
  clear:right;
  text-align:center;
}
```

The text-align:center rule makes the text of the footer sit centered on the page. The clear:right rule clears the preceding float of the maincontent column. This means that, instead of sitting next to the maincontent column underneath the sidebar, it sits underneath the maincontent column.

Finally, the content div is styled:

```
#content {
  background:#eee;
  color:#000;
  overflow:auto;
}
```

The content div contains the maincontent and the sidebar. The sidebar is colored light gray. The overflow:auto rule is a little fix that ensures the maincontent column does not flow out of the content div, as floated elements are normally designed to overflow their container.

Navigation Design

Many websites contain a "global navigation" area that provides links to the major section of that website. Often, these global navigation areas run horizontally across the top of the web page, as shown in Figure 9-14.

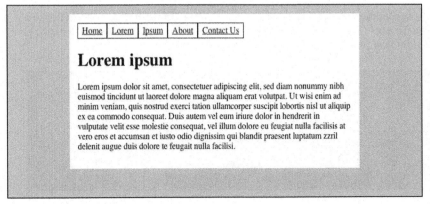

Figure 9-14. A typical global navigation example

Global navigation is simply a list of links, so it follows that an HTML list should be used:

```
<ul id="nav">
  <li><a href="home">Home</a></li>
  <li><a href="lorem">Lorem</a></li>
  <li><a href="ipsum">Ipsum</a></li>
  <li><a href="about">About</a></li>
  <li><a href="contact">Contact Us</a></li>
</ul>
```

By default, an HTML list is rendered vertically and with bullet points, so it wouldn't look at all like the horizontal navigation in Figure 9-14. However, CSS can easily change how the list appears with these rules:

```
#nav {
  margin:0;
  padding:0;
}
#nav LI {
  list-style:none;
  float:left;
  width:auto;
  margin:0;
  padding:0.25em 0.5em;
  border:1px solid #000;
}
```

9

In the first rule, the browser default margins are removed from the nav list. Then for each list item, the bullet point is removed using list-style:none. Next, the list items are floated left, which allows them to line up next to each other in a horizontal row. The width:auto rule is added so the browser knows to make each list item fit its content. Finally, the default margin is removed, some padding is added, and a border is given to each item.

More sophisticated navigation designs using CSS are demonstrated on Max Design's Listamatic page (css.maxdesign.com.au/listamatic/). Figure 9-15 shows a fine example of horizontal navigation based on a list, from SimpleBits (simplebits.com).

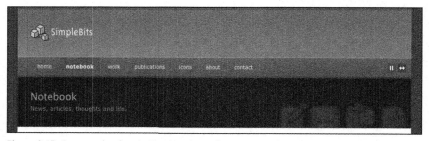

Figure 9-15. An example of navigation based on a list

Invisible Labels for Form Elements

As explained in Chapter 8, it is usually best to include visual labels for all form controls. However, sometimes a visual label is not needed due to the surrounding textual description of the control and/or the content the control contains. For example, consider the search field on the Training and Development Agency for Schools website (www.tda.gov.uk/), shown in Figure 9-16.

Figure 9-16. The search field is labeled with only a Go button.

Despite the fact the search field is labeled with only a Go button on this website, sighted users can intuitively determine the search functionally because it has been placed in the top-right corner, a familiar position for search boxes. Users of screen readers, however, do not have the benefit of seeing the position of forms and need each form control to be explicitly labeled so the intent of the control is well understood when navigated to directly.

To aid users of screen readers, the search form should be fully specified with a label like this:

```
<form action="search.cgi" id="search">
<label for="q">Search</label>
<input id="q" type="text" />
<input type="submit" value="Go" />
</form>
```

You can make the label not display by setting these styles, which set the label as tiny and remove it from the document flow:

```
#search label {
  position:absolute;
  height:0;
  width:0;
  overflow:hidden;
}
```

This technique will prevent the label from being seen by sighted users, but screen readers will speak the label even though it is not displayed. The label will be displayed to all users if CSS is turned off in the browser, which could itself be useful, as the positional context of the form would be lost with CSS unavailable.

Bullet Styles for Lists

Sometimes, the standard discs, circles, and squares available as list bullet styles are not enough for a designer's purposes. Fortunately, CSS provides a method of specifying images as list bullets. This is far preferable to using the <img> element to add bullet images, as it means the list can still be marked up as such. To change the bullet style of unordered list items created with the li element, use the list-style property like so:

```
li { list-style: circle url(bullet.gif) }
```

Notice that a default bullet type, circle, is specified. In situations where the bullet image does not load, this default will be used instead.

9

Empty Table Cells

In some cases, you will need to leave cells in data tables empty. By default, empty data cells do not receive any styling (such as borders). The empty-cells property allows users to leave table cells empty and still display cell borders on the screen or on paper:

```
table { empty-cells: show }
```

A data cell that is meant to be empty should not be filled with whitespace or a nonbreaking space to achieve a visual effect.

Alternative Style Sheets

I mentioned the CSS Zen Garden at the beginning of this chapter as a website that demonstrates that completely different designs and style sheets can be created for the same HTML document. The implication is that a document doesn't need to have a single style sheet. In fact, you can give web pages a default style and also provide any number of alternative choices for the reader.

Alternative Style Sheet Specification

You specify alternative style sheets within the HTML by adding alternate to the rel attribute of the <link> element, for example:

```
<link rel="stylesheet" href="default.css" type="text/css" />
<link rel="alternate stylesheet" href="green.css" type="text/css"
title="Green version" />
```

This code links to the default.css style sheet in the normal way. The second <link> element includes alternate in the rel attribute and points to the green.css style sheet. When the document is first loaded, the default.css style sheet is used to display the page, and green.css is ignored. However, the reader could then choose the green.css alternate style sheet instead, and default.css would subsequently be ignored.

The title attribute on the alternative style sheet is *required*, as groups of links with the same title are automatically combined into one style sheet. To include extra style sheets, simply add more <link> elements in the header, with the right rel and title attributes.

Style Sheet Switching

How the reader can select the alternatives depends on the browser. Not all browsers currently offer a menu item for it, but in Firefox, for example, you can find all the styles by selecting View ➤ Page Style, as shown in Figure 9-17.

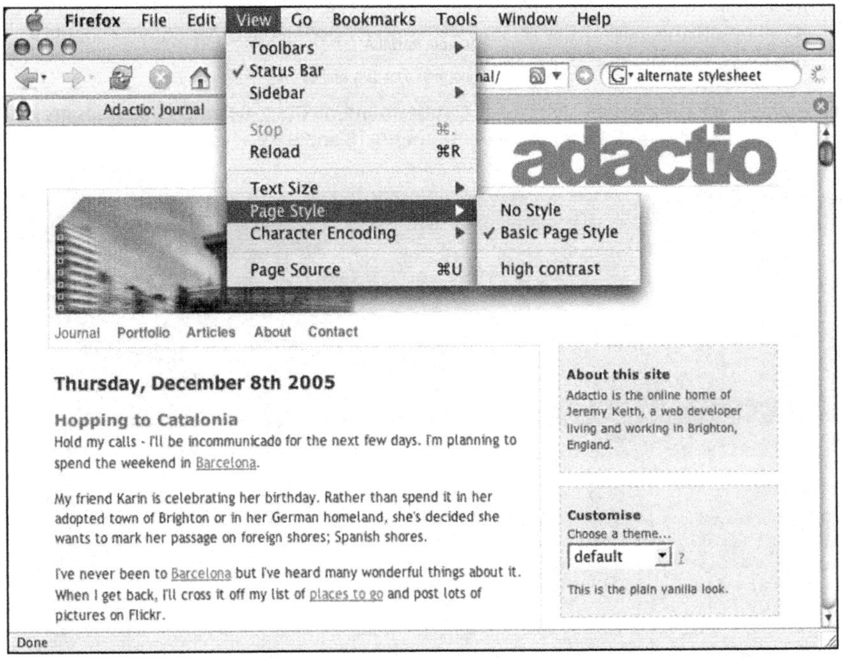

Figure 9-17. The adactio.com website has a Basic Page Style style sheet and an alternative high contrast style sheet, which you can switch to using the View ➤ Page Style option in Firefox.

You can also use JavaScript or server-side scripting to create a style-switcher widget that sits within the web page. This is discussed by Paul Sowden at www.alistapart.com/articles/alternate/. Dustin Diaz has developed an Ajax style sheet switcher, which combines JavaScript and server-side scripting to create the widget; see www.dustindiaz.com/udasss/ for details.

Zoom Layouts

A particular sort of alternative style sheet was suggested by Joe Clark in his article "Big, Stark & Chunky," at www.alistapart.com/articles/lowvision/. Clark notes that with the advent of CSS, more could be done to address the needs of low-vision users. Low-vision users have particular design requirements (most obviously, large fonts), and so an alternative style sheet specifically for them would seem a perfect solution. A low-vision design should do the following:

9

283

- Switch to a big font.

- Invert the screen. Many visitors will want light-colored text and a dark background.

- Customize colors. Bright white on flat black will not work for everyone; it's too bright. Try using green, yellow, or blue on black or dark brown, or the old WordPerfect 5.1 default of white on blue.

- Rearrange content. In order to accommodate large fonts and to prevent content scrolling off the side of the screen or the user's perimeter of vision, you should rearrange your site into one column.

A fine example of a low-vision style sheet can be found at Doug Bowman's Stopdesign, located at www.stopdesign.com, as shown in Figures 9-18 and 9-19.

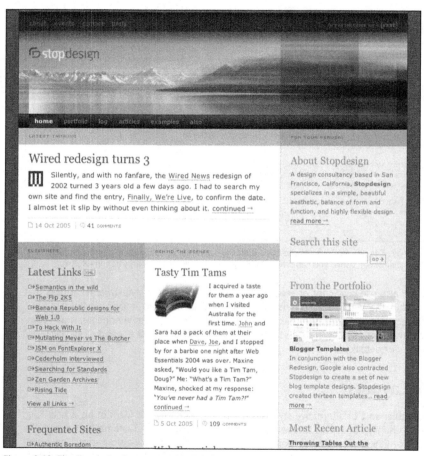

Figure 9-18. The Stopdesign homepage with default styling

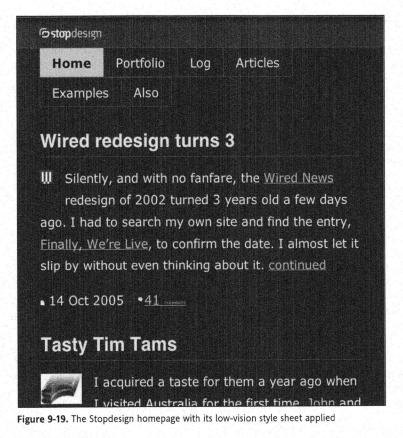

Figure 9-19. The Stopdesign homepage with its low-vision style sheet applied

As a further mechanism of identifying an alternative zoom style sheet as such, you can add the rev attribute to the <link> element, as follows:

```
<link rel="alternate stylesheet" href="zoom.css" media="screen"
type="text/css" title="high contrast zoom" rev="zoom" />
```

Indeed, there may come a time when a general consensus is reached that a professionally designed, standards-compliant, accessible site isn't complete without a zoom layout alternative style sheet.

Nonscreen Media

Style sheets can be specified for different media (such as screens, Braille readers, or print), and alternative style sheets can be created to help specific groups of people to use a website in graphical browsers.

All the CSS I have discussed so far has involved styling web pages for visual display on screens. However, CSS also provides properties for media other than screens.

Auditory CSS

CSS2's aural cascading style sheets provide information to nonsighted users and voice-browser users, much in the same way fonts provide visual information. These include properties such as volume, azimuth, pause, cue, speech-rate, and voice-family. However, these properties were never implemented by any screen reader or any other software, so in CSS 2.1, aural style sheets moved to an appendix.

The hope for aural style sheets now is the CSS3 speech module. The World Wide Web Consortium (W3C) has created a voice browser working group to study and formulate this recommendation, but for the time being, auditory CSS remains largely theoretical. At the time of writing, the only implementation of aural style sheets is Fire Vox, a Firefox plug-in developed by Charles L. Chen. Fire Vox is free and open source, and can be downloaded from clc-4-tts.cjb.net.

Paged Media

CSS 2.1 has a number of properties specifically for the printed page (www.w3.org/TR/CSS21/page.html). Support for these properties is fairly patchy across browsers; however, the page-break-before and page-break-after properties are well supported. For example, this rule forces each h1 to start on a new page:

```
h1 {page-break-before:always}
```

The A List Apart article "Printing a Book with CSS: Boom!" (www.alistapart.com/articles/boom) covers some of the advanced paged media properties of CSS2 and CSS3 in more detail.

Media-Specific Style Sheets

Entirely separate style sheets can be specified for different media. For example, you could create one style sheet for use on screen and another for use in print. You could link a document to those style sheets through the media attribute of the <link> element or within the @import rule:

```
<link rel="stylesheet" type="text/css" media="screen" href=
  "screen.css" />
<link rel="stylesheet" type="text/css" media="print" href=
  "print.css" />

@import url("screen.css") screen;
@import url("print.css") print;
```

In these cases, the screen style sheet would be completely ignored when printing, and likewise the print style sheet would be ignored when displaying the web page on screen.

The @media rule allows authors to embed styles for different media within one style sheet, as in this example:

```
@media print {
  body { font-size: 10pt }
}
@media screen {
  body { font-size: 13px }
}
@media screen, print {
  body { line-height: 1.2 }
}
```

The following are the recognized media types:

- all: Suitable for all devices.

- braille: Intended for Braille tactile feedback devices.

- embossed: Intended for paged Braille printers.

- handheld: Intended for handheld devices (typically small screen, limited bandwidth).

- print: Intended for paged material and for documents viewed on screen in print preview mode.

- projection: Intended for projected presentations, for example projectors.

- screen: Intended primarily for color computer screens.

- speech: Intended for speech synthesizers.

- tty: Intended for media using a fixed-pitch character grid (such as teletypes, terminals, or portable devices with limited display capabilities). Authors should not use pixel units with the tty media type.

- tv: Intended for television-type devices (low-resolution, color, limited-scrollability screens, sound available).

Testing and Validation

Style sheets can become as large and complicated as HTML documents. I therefore recommend CSS validation as a part of your development and testing routine. The W3C offers a free online testing service at jigsaw.w3.org/css-validator/, which will test an online style sheet, let you upload one for testing, or test some directly inputted style rules.

Chris Pederick's Web Developer Extension toolbar is a free extension for Firefox and should really be in every web developer's toolbox. You can download the latest version from chrispederick.com/work/webdeveloper/. Microsoft has recently developed a similar toolbar for Internet Explorer, which you can download from tinyurl.com/8rwb8. Figure 9-20 shows the CSS components of the Web Developer Extension toolbar.

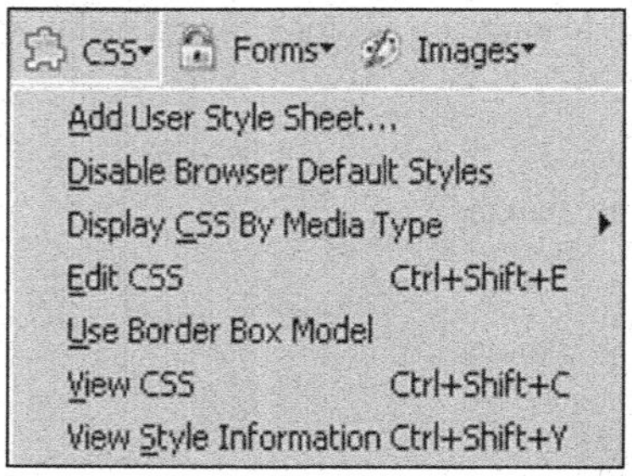

Figure 9-20. Web Developer Extension toolbar for Firefox

The Web Developer Extension toolbar provides a raft of features than can help you test your style sheets and accessibility in general, including one-click validation and more important, the ability to disable style sheets altogether. By reverting to the default browser styles, you can verify that your website will be understandable without style sheets.

If you have moved all the presentational information to your style sheets and ordered your content logically, marking it up correctly with headings, lists, tables, and so on, this will be evident when style sheets are turned off. And if you do achieve that, you will have successfully separated content and structure from presentation, which is the main goal of using style sheets.

Summary

I hope to have demonstrated in this chapter that CSS can contribute greatly to accessibility. However, it is no panacea. CSS is open to abuse and misuse, as with any other web technology. I have already discussed abuse of image replacement techniques, but equally fundamental is the importance of maintaining semantics within your document.

With CSS, it is perfectly possible to style all your headings by marking up your web page with `<p class="header">`, but that would render your headings meaningless when CSS is unavailable. Remember to start off with the correct HTML for the job and add style afterwards. It is also helpful to avoid presentational class names such as `class="bigred"`. This won't affect the accessibility of your web pages, but it will hinder maintenance of your style sheets, especially when the time comes for that text to be small and blue.

CSS is admittedly difficult to become expert in, although in fairness, a lot of the steep learning curve is due to browser inconsistencies and bugs. Many CSS beginners end up littering their web pages with superfluous divs and classes. However, if they use meaningful HTML, accessibility will still be improved through their use of CSS. But it is well worth learning the intricacies of CSS, such as advanced selectors and properties, and the power of CSS will become ever more evident.

10 ACCESSIBLE JAVASCRIPT

by Christian Heilmann

It is a common myth that JavaScript and accessibility don't go well together. This bad reputation is largely due to the very obtrusive manner in which JavaScript is generally applied, and not the fault of the language. JavaScript is a tool—a means to achieve a goal. If you use a knife as a tool, you could slice bread with it or cause bodily harm. It is not the knife that determines how it is used.

Accessible JavaScript is a misnomer, as we cannot expect all user agents to support JavaScript—from a usability perspective, not from a guideline point of view. Modern user agents are expected to support scripting, and the upcoming Web Content Accessibility Guidelines (WCAG) 2.0 will have a concept of baseline technologies that include scripting. However, designing with accessibility in mind means that we don't assume that visitors have scripting enabled. They might be stuck with old technology that does not support scripting and have no way to upgrade. Or it might be their company's policy not to allow any scripting for security reasons. This means that we don't rely on JavaScript, but instead use it to enhance the experience when and if JavaScript is enabled. The common term for this is *unobtrusive JavaScript*—JavaScript that helps instead of blocking the way of visitors.

We are currently at a crossroad in JavaScript design. As a web developer, you should be aware that there is a constant change in best practices and ideas in web development. Something that makes perfect sense now might be outdated in a week's time. At the end of the chapter, you will find a list of online resources you can check frequently to keep up-to-date with what's hot and what's not. In this chapter, I will concentrate on some examples of how to approach accessibility when developing JavaScript and what outdated practices and pitfalls to avoid. But first, let's take a look at the big picture.

The JavaScript Saga

JavaScript has been around for quite a while. It was not really an issue or even obvious to web users until Dynamic HTML (DHTML) was born. DHTML never was a World Wide Web Consortium (W3C) standard, or even a stand-alone technology. It was a buzzword—marketing speak—for HTML, Cascading Style Sheets (CSS), and JavaScript interacting to make web pages more dynamic. While that sounds like a really good idea, the implementation of DHTML was not necessarily there to help guide web users, but more often than not, driven by excitement for what new browsers could do.

The drivers of DHTML were overly enthusiastic developers and marketing people. It was used to "wow" visitors and reinvent navigation and basic usability concepts in a more complex and, in most cases, less accessible way (similar to the type of use that gave Flash a bad reputation). The wow effect of DHTML got more people interested in JavaScript, but as fast as it got into the limelight, it also lost its zing. It is cool to see parts of the page move, unfold, and zoom the first time you visit it. When the same movement makes you wait the next time you load the web page, it becomes an annoyance rather than a cool feature.

JavaScript gave pages more life; the times of boring linked text documents were over. However, as accessibility was not obvious as a legal requirement and far down on the "to care" list of web designers, no one bothered to test for it before applying the code. Visitors without JavaScript were treated as lower-class citizens, or even left out—no shirt, no tie, no navigation.

The very impractical upshot of sites with JavaScript navigation was that they also blocked out search engines. This meant fewer visitors. When the dot-com boom was over and the money ran out, many business stakeholders started cleaning up the sites rigorously. JavaScript got dismissed as something tried and failed. It had to go, along with the 600KB Flash intro, the animations, and the cool and groovy text that was great marketing but didn't tell users much (for example, "LOOT!" instead of "your shopping basket"). What we need now is successful sites. We want to create sites that draw customers, satisfy their needs, and keep them coming back for more—thus keeping a stream of revenue flowing instead of venture capital vanishing.

Our new money-driven design made business stakeholders reconsider another aspect of JavaScript: It can be used to give a visitor immediate feedback—for example, when a form field is filled out the wrong way—without the need for a page reload. This saves the site visitor time and saves the site maintainer server traffic, and traffic costs money. Therefore, JavaScript is still lingering around in the development cycle as something that can help save money and make some things easier for the user.

However, the need to create clean, maintainable, and unobtrusive JavaScript is not very obvious. Web development costs money, so why not just use what is already out there? Why bother reinventing the wheel?

One reason for JavaScript of the obtrusive kind is money. Advertisements only make sense when visitors see and click them. Advertisers will not give you money unless you can show them a lot of hits and leads in return. Therefore, it can happen that marketing dictates using JavaScript to push ads in the visitor's direction via pop-ups, interstitials, and overlays. The mere existence of hundreds of ad-blocking and pop-up blocking software should indicate that this is not what visitors want or see as something worthy of clicking. But, in the end, the business dictates what will be on the site, and the money earned also includes your wage. Luckily though, this is changing. Newer browsers have out-of-the-box pop-up blocking technology, and the legal requirement for accessibility makes unobtrusive JavaScript a bit more interesting again. The old scripts don't work any longer and need replacement. We now have the chance to replace outdated and obtrusive scripts with modern ones.

10

Why JavaScript Has a Bad Reputation

JavaScript has a bad reputation because it has been used in a very obtrusive manner. When you surf the Web, you will encounter a lot of annoyances only possible with JavaScript, such as unwanted pop-up windows, scripts that turn off your context menus (no right-click menu), pages that don't work without JavaScript, and browser-sniffing scripts telling you that your browser is outdated and that you should upgrade to Microsoft Internet Explorer 6—even if your browser was developed a year after Internet Explorer 6.

All of these give the impression that scripting is used against visitors, rather than as a tool to enhance their experience. Subsequently, this leads to accessibility guidelines and company standards that discard JavaScript as "bad" before even considering its merits.

Another reason for prejudice against JavaScript is the sorry state of some of the code available on the Web. JavaScript has one big advantage over other technologies like Java, C#, PHP, and Perl: It is very easy to learn, and you don't need to install any major development environment to start writing it. A text editor and a browser are all you need, and those come free with every operating system. This is also its biggest disadvantage. Higher programming languages that need assembling before execution, rather than relying on a browser, come with proper debuggers, a much stricter syntax, and test tools. JavaScript lives in the wild, and good JavaScript debugging tools have been available only in the past few years. Add very forgiving browsers and software vendors who claim you don't need to understand scripts (just use the prebuilt ones that come with the editor), and you have a recipe for disaster.

If you were to believe the software promotional material, there is no need to learn anything about web development: Handy, what you see is what you get (WYSIWYG) editors promise interactive websites at the click of a button. No need to fulfill the hard, confusing, and tiring task of learning the tools of the trade. It is true that these tools are getting better every year, and they can perform annoying repetitive tasks for you, but that is where their usefulness ends. They cannot optimize your product for you or make it work in an environment as diverse as the Web. You can paint a picture with a paint-by-numbers kit, but you will have trouble explaining how the harmonies of the picture were achieved and if there is a special meaning in the use of a certain color.

Back when the Web was still relatively young, the ease of developing JavaScript, its subsequent boom, and the fact that the letters *DHTML* on your resume made the interviewer's eyes shine brightly led to another problem: A mass of ready-made scripts on the Web in so-called script archives, DHTML catalogs, or even cross-browser libraries. These were developed in a time when browsers just started to properly support CSS and the Document Object Model (DOM), and in a lot of cases, "cross-browser" meant that the scripts worked for both Netscape 4.x and Internet Explorer 5, and not according to any standard.

> *If you plan on using ready-made scripts, make sure to check their date. See if they were updated at all in the last few years when browsers turned from marketing machines to something you can use to surf the Web and optimize to your needs. Later in this chapter, I'll list outdated techniques to test scripts against. If a script uses many of those techniques, don't touch it. Much like a car you get really cheap from a junkyard, it might work nicely, but it will pollute the environment unnecessarily and cost you a bundle in repair costs.*

JavaScript Considerations

JavaScript was never bad for your visitors; however, bad implementation was—and still is—bad for your visitors. Let's leave browser security holes and their misuse by malicious scripts and cross-server-scripting (XSS) aside, and concentrate on how we still use

JavaScript to deter visitors rather than invite and help them. Here are some of the main JavaScript evils users suffer on the Web:

- Changes to the browser, like spawning new windows without informing users or hijacking the status bar
- Changes to basic browser functionality (such as right-click prevention scripts, and simulated site navigation in one page and the associated breaking of back button functionality)
- Preventing visitors from surfing to the site (browser sniffing and automatic redirects)
- Crucial content or functionality that expects JavaScript to be enabled

A lot of these are based on an archaic view of websites as a medium and scripting as a technology. We assumed in the past that the website is ours and we define how it looks. We thought that the visitors have the same likes and dislikes we have and want content in the same format that we do. And we assumed that visitors don't know what they want and need us to guide them.

The Web has been around for quite a while now, and our visitors have gotten more versed in its ways and how to use their browsers. Browsers have become better and now allow users to customize them to their needs. Our visitors have also become a lot more diverse. The times of the Web consisting basically of technology-crazy geeks and kids are over. The web population has aged, and visitors with disabilities are not uncommon.

> *Of course, your audience also varies with the type of web product. You will get fewer pensioners on a fan portal for the latest game console craze than on a council site. However, let's not forget that not only those who use a product are the ones who buy it.*

10

Now that even business stakeholders (probably with a possible lawsuit in mind) start thinking about accessibility and see the benefits of usable websites rather than force-feeding visitors the brand and offers, you should always keep some ideas in the back of your mind:

- You cannot assume—or dictate—that the user has JavaScript enabled.
- There is no JavaScript protection that is not hackable by a good scripter.
- The browser, its settings, and its functionality belong to the visitor, and are not yours to dictate or remove.
- With the media reporting almost weekly new viruses and security issues, visitors and their technical administrators might see JavaScript as evil first and helpful second.

Remember that the browser configuration and window dimensions are set for a reason: to make it as easy and comfortable as possible for the user to surf with this browser. If you override some of the functionality or change the window size to dimensions your design needs, you might make it impossible for the user to interact with your page. Avoid spawning new browser windows. You cannot expect users to be able to deal with several windows or their setup to allow for them. If your solution really needs to spawn a new window, tell the users about it, so they can make amendments and be prepared for it. Don't hijack the status bar. The status bar gives information about linked documents and other information about the document. It shows a status of how things are, not what you would like them to be.

What Visitors Need

The first question you should consider before you start any web development is what the visitors need. It is tempting to create a web product to your likings and needs, but in the end, you won't be the one using it or, even worse, you might end up being the only person using it.

Tutorials explaining that accessibility does not interfere with design are deluded; the design has to cater as much to the needs of the visitors as the technology does. The only way you will be able to deliver usable and accessible sites is by getting to know your audience and thinking about their needs first, and then what you want to give them.

In the case of disabled users, this means you need to anticipate what they might use to surf the Web and how it impacts your design. The following list is a start; however, some people have more than one disability or different varieties.

- **Blind users:** In older accessibility tutorials, you might have read that a text browser with JavaScript turned off is a good simulation of how blind users experience the Web. This is not fully the case, as most screen readers do support JavaScript and render changes in the DOM—inconsistently between different ones for added confusion. It is pretty easy to set up a testing environment for different browsers; however, testing on different screen readers is not that common.

> *A screen reader is an output device that provides feedback on users' interaction with their computer, in the same way that a monitor is an output device that helps users interact with their computer. Screen readers read out anything that happens when you interact with the operating system, other applications, in browsers, and eventually in your website. Screen readers are complex tools, and their functionality differs from vendor to vendor. This is a big problem. It is the sequel of the browser wars, when we had to consider different browsers supporting different DOMs to make our applications work. The differences are that the user group affected is not as huge and the software involved is not free in Windows environments. There are free screen readers included in Mac OS X and Solaris 10, and there are free screen readers for Linux.*

- **Visually impaired visitors:** The website experience for these visitors is limited to a screen space that is a lot smaller than the one we normally have at our disposal. Menus and other interactive elements that assume a certain screen size to be available—like multilevel drop-down menus expanding when you hover the mouse over them—are almost impossible for visually impaired visitors to use.

- **Visitors with dexterity impairments:** Any script that is dependent on a mouse to hover in a very coordinated way over an element or has very small interactive elements will render the page unusable to visitors who cannot move their hands in a controlled fashion (or at all). Interactive elements should have an ample amount of space in between them. Furthermore, any element that is not interactive by default and is used to trigger an effect is most likely to be inaccessible to this group, as the browser does not allow for keyboard access to it. You could also offer keyboard access via scripting, but you might overwrite necessary keyboard settings and shortcuts of other assistive technology. Instead of making elements like DIVs or headings clickable, it is a lot more logical to create a link inside these elements and apply your functionality both for keyboard users and mouse users.

Accessibility concerns are not limited to meeting the needs of people with disabilities. Depending on the theme of your web product and the intended audience, the range of abilities and environments of your visitors can be quite mind-boggling. You will encounter the high-tech, young visitor on a 1600 × 1200 resolution monitor and an 8 Mbps broadband connection, who considers the Web his real home. You might also encounter the grandfather with the thick glasses and the unsteady hand accessing the Web with a 56 Kbps modem and a very outdated browser ("It works, so why should I change it?"). Even the high-tech visitor might not share your enthusiasm for JavaScript and see every use of it as a potential security risk.

Does this mean you need to limit yourself to a lowest common denominator and create boring websites? Yes, if you see diversity as a blocker; no, if you see it as a challenge. Diversity can be a good thing; for example, the loudspeaker was invented to help hard-of-hearing people, and we all benefit from its invention today.

Guidelines for Dynamic JavaScript

The environment in which your JavaScript is executed is totally unknown. You cannot assume anything about the user agent or the hardware on which it runs. Knowing what can go wrong makes planning for it easier. The following issues are just some of those that can make your life harder.

- The visitor might not have JavaScript turned on.

- Some other software (like firewalls, proxy servers, or site metrics software) might add dynamic scripts to your site and mess with global variables.

- The user agent might get things wrong or won't update the document properly without a reload.

- The connection could be flaky and not load your script completely before trying to access parts of it.

- The content maintainer might not create the HTML on which your script depends.

- The visitor may need a certain keyboard shortcut for her assistive technology that you are also using for your application, so they conflict.

- The visitor's impairment might make it impossible for him to use your product; for example, if you use a drag-and-drop interface without backing it up with an easier way of selecting an item.

10

Any of these are less of a problem when you stick to the following guidelines when writing JavaScript.

Follow Standards, Not Browsers

If you want to ensure that your code will work with future user agents and assistive technology, you need to stick to the W3C standards. Unless there is a really good reason, there is no need to use browser-specific extensions to the web standards.

Modern browsers all support the W3C DOM, as described at www.w3.org/DOM/. To test for this, all you need to do is to determine if the document.getElementById object is available. However, as some browsers (like older versions of Opera) do support this but fail to implement it, you also need to check for document.createTextNode. Instead of wrapping your whole script in a condition, it is easier to check if the W3C DOM is available and not apply any more JavaScript if that is not the case.

```
if(!document.getElementById || !document.createTextNode){return;}
// other code
```

The return statement exits JavaScript and simply keeps the page as it is, if the script was called when the page was loaded, or follows a link or button if the script was executed when the user interacted with that element.

Essential Markup Should Not Rely on JavaScript

HTML created via JavaScript won't be available when JavaScript is turned off, effectively rendering the page less usable or even completely unusable. Therefore, don't create HTML that is absolutely necessary, such as the navigation, via JavaScript.

There is a practical side effect of following this rule: Not creating HTML via the DOM makes the product a lot easier to maintain. Non-JavaScript-savvy colleagues won't need to try to deal with something they are not sure about to change the document. This is especially important in distributed development environments or when the client becomes the maintainer.

Generated HTML Follows the Same Rules As Written HTML

An accessible site should start with a semantically correct, well-structured HTML document. Using the DOM gives you a lot of control over the document. You can generate any HTML you want—even invalid HTML—and automated validation of the document would still report no issues. However, the final user agent will need to try to render this code, and may choke on it.

We stopped using CSS to make elements look like headers instead of using real header elements. The same applies to the DOM. Redundant HTML elements to fix a design or add a design feat is—well, redundant, no matter what technology was used to add it.

This is also true for server-side scripting. Just because you can create and maintain inline mouseover and mouseout handlers easily in a loop doesn't make them a good idea. For starters, they unnecessarily bloat the document.

Be Aware of Visitor and User Agent Restrictions

DOM JavaScript allows you to turn almost any page element into something interactive. The question is whether the visitors using their user agents can reach the interactive element. A common mistake is to make elements react only to mouseover events rather than onclick. A visitor dependent on a keyboard will never be able to activate those. Even if you use onclick handlers on elements, they may not be reachable via keyboard or voice recognition. When you develop accessible interactive pages, the keyboard is your friend. Elements that can be reached via tabbing are very likely to be available to other assistive technologies.

JavaScript allows you to come up with your own keyboard events. If you want to use those, try to make sure that they won't interfere with necessary keyboard shortcuts of the user agent, and make it clear to the visitors what the shortcuts are.

Sometimes Less Is More

You can do a lot to enhance websites via JavaScript; however, sometimes less is more. It is very tempting to add a lot of scripts with the best of intentions, but in regard to accessibility, it is always a good idea to lean back and reflect: Does this script help visitors to reach a goal faster or overcome a problem, or is it just there because it is flashy or trendy?

A good example is the use of font-resizing tools that depend on JavaScript and cookies. These are seemingly very helpful to visitors suffering from low vision, but simply resizing the font inside the browser is not enough to help them. A person with low vision will need to have the whole operating system in larger fonts or have the whole screen magnified, not only the current web page. A lot of font-sizing widgets simply simulate what browsers do out of the box anyway: Give the user an option to resize the font. Nearly every browser has that feature, some more prominently than others. Even worse, badly implemented resizing widgets expect JavaScript and cookies to be enabled, which is not necessarily a given in the user's computer setup. The browser functionality keeps the font size choice and applies it to all websites. A font-sizing widget would not give that option, and users would be expected to use one of those on every page they visit. In essence, you use a solution that may fail to work around a problem that was solved by user agents already and only became an issue because the initial font size of your page is too small.

> Browsers have options for resizing the fonts. In Firefox, press Ctrl++ (plus) and Ctrl+- (hyphen) to increase and decrease the font size, respectively. In Safari, press Apple++ and Apple+-. In Internet Explorer, choose View ➤ Text Size. Internet Explorer 7 has a zoom feature that magnifies the whole document, including images. Opera has had such a zoom feature for a while.

Don't Break Too Many Conventions

JavaScript can make web pages behave completely differently from how you expect them to behave. This can confuse visitors or make it impossible for them to use your products. You cannot expect visitors to read instructions on how to use your site; a good product is intuitively usable. This might even mean that it should follow conventions that are cumbersome and appear inefficient.

10

A holy war debate in the web development community centers around whether the browser controls as we know them in HTML are enough. For example, a slider control is more intuitive to nontechnical visitors, as it is a real-life control we use every day. However, on the Web, the slider control is not available out of the box (a scrollbar does not change a value; therefore, it is not a slider) and may not be usable via keyboard or voice control, or indicate the current value to a blind user.

User testing can help. If your users hit the back button repeatedly and thereby lose the state of the application, it might not be as intuitive as you originally thought it was.

Test Everything You Access

One of the biggest causes for buggy code and websites that don't work is that their developers tried to access methods, elements, or objects that were not available. While some browsers will allow you to try to access attributes of a nonexistent element, others will throw an error and show it to the visitor. For example, the following works only when the object o is available and will throw an error if it isn't.

```
function addclass(o,c)
{
  o.className+=o.className?' '+c:c;
}
```

Testing for the object before trying to access its attributes is safer. This code will not execute unless the object is available:

```
function addclass(o,c)
{
  if(o)
  {
    o.className+=o.className?' '+c:c;
  }
}
```

Keep Everything Separated

A lot of scripts hailing from the times of the DHTML craze use global variables to store information and expect them to be available at all times. This can lead to problems when more than one script is used on the page or some third-party software adds extra scripts to the document. Instead of relying on global variables, you can keep the variables in the scope of the function or even use object attributes.

Another big mistake is to use the style attribute collection of an object to define its visual representation. The definition of how something should look in a user agent is the job of CSS. Instead of mixing CSS and JavaScript, you can add and remove classes from the element in question and keep the maintenance of the look and feel in the style sheet. This is not always possible—for example, with drag-and-drop interfaces that need to constantly change the element coordinates via the style attributes—but can help you solve a lot of problems. It also means that you don't necessarily need to know CSS and can leave its complexities to the designer.

Unobtrusive JavaScript

JavaScript is a wonderful tool to give your websites more life, to make them appear a lot more dynamic, and to prevent visitors from suffering unnecessary page reloads. This might seem redundant in a time where broadband is considered the norm (at least in the Western world), but page reloads are more than just transmission of page data. The page needs to be rendered by the browser on every reload and that can—depending on the speed of the computer, available RAM, or the system load—take much longer than the actual loading of the page.

The main rule of creating unobtrusive JavaScript, or indeed any accessible web design, is separation of the different development layers. The structure (defined in the HTML), the presentation (defined in the CSS), and the behavior (defined in JavaScript) all need to make sense and be maintainable without impacting the others. There might be overlaps, like CSS classes needed to achieve a certain effect or HTML elements with the correct IDs, but good documentation can take care of these issues. An accessible website needs to be accessible to all, regardless of user agent, operating system, connection speed, display size, and other factors. Predicting all of these is next to impossible, and the only thing you can do is stick to standards and make sure that you don't rely on anything that might be unavailable.

Writing proper unobtrusive JavaScript is an ever-changing skill. As a developer, you cannot have all user agents at your disposal, and you cannot possibly emulate every environment in which your code might be viewed. What you can do is make sure your code does not assume any givens and watch for publications on the Web discussing the newest techniques and practices. Sometimes, you need to consider and weigh the consequences: Should I make sure my code is spot-on, totally unobtrusive and bloated, or should I keep it simple and make it achieve what is necessary for this particular problem?

> *Every so often, some hard-core programmers will come up with the JavaScript library to end all JavaScript libraries. Often, these scripts are based on practices that make sense in Java or Perl but don't apply so well to JavaScript. The difference is that JavaScript is executed on the client side, and this is unknown territory. Therefore, it is sometimes wiser to keep it short and sweet and add some appropriate comment, rather than to use the 140KB JavaScript include file, following regular programming practices. After all, the turnaround and changes in the web design area are a lot quicker than those on the server side.*

10

In this section, we'll look at JavaScript's role in web development, and then some examples of unobtrusive Java coding. Finally, I'll list some outdated scripting methods and their replacements. The code examples in this chapter are available from the friends of ED website (www.friendsofed.com), in the code download section.

JavaScript As the Behavior Layer

One of the basic concepts of accessibility-aware web development is to realize that a document on the Web is not what meets the eye on your monitor. Most web pages are not visual constructs; they are basically text. It's true that some websites make sense only when you can see them—like Flickr or Google Maps—but these are web representations of applications. In most cases, you'll want to deliver information that is in text format.

The text features embedded HTML tags that define the document structure and tell the user agent what it contains. CSS defines how the user agent should render these elements. Last but not least, languages like JavaScript can access this text or the HTML elements via the DOM. The DOM offers you the document as a collection of nodes and attributes and allows for programmatic changes to the document structure. For example, the following HTML is rendered in the browser as a form:

```
<form action="send.php" method="post" id="contactform">
  <h1>Contact Us</h1>
  <p><span class="required">*</span> Indicates a mandatory field</p>
  <p>
    <label for="name">Name:</label>
    <input type="text" name="name" id="name" size="30" />
  </p>
  <p>
    <label for="email">Email:<span class="required">*</span></label>
    <input type="text" name="email" id="email" size="30" />
  </p>
  <p>
    <label for="Message">Message:<span class="required">*</span>
    </label>
    <textarea name="Message" id="Message" cols="30" rows="5">
    </textarea>
  </p>
  <p class="submit">
    <input type="submit" name="send" id="send" value="send message" />
  </p>
</form>
```

Once executed within a browser, you should see a form like the one shown in Figure 10-1.

Figure 10-1. A form rendered by the browser

The DOM representation of the same HTML is a collection of nodes, attributes, and values, as you can see in the Mozilla DOM Inspector, shown in Figure 10-2.

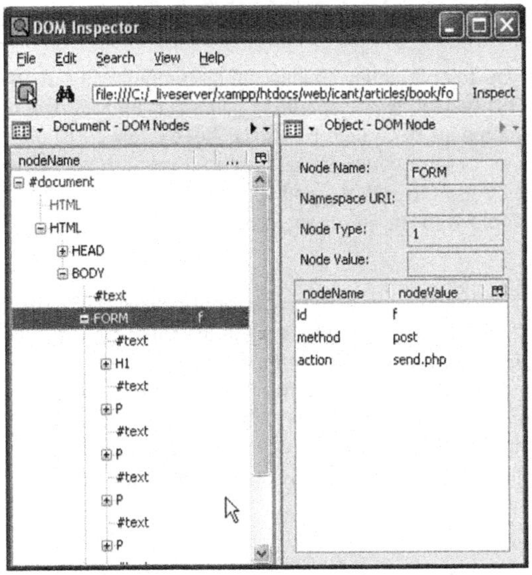

Figure 10-2. The DOM representation of an HTML document

10

You can completely change documents via the DOM and a programming language (which is usually JavaScript, but as the DOM is language-independent, you can also use it with Java, PHP, and many other languages). You can access all items in the document, change them, read their values, rearrange them, delete them, or even create new ones. For example, if you wanted to change the action of the form when JavaScript is available, you could use the getElementsByTagName method together with the setAttribute method:

```
var f=document.getElementsByTagName('form');
if(f.length>0)
{
  var ourform=f[0];
  ourform.setAttribute('action','otherscript.php');
}
```

In plain English, this would be "Define f as a list of all the form elements in the document. If this list has entries—which means there is at least one—get the first form element (computers start counting at 0) and set its attribute with the name action to otherscript.php."

As this HTML has a defined ID with the value contactform, you could also use the getElementById method, which saves you defining the variable ourform:

```
var f=document.getElementById('contactform');
if(f)
{
  f.setAttribute('action','otherscript.php');
}
```

Using the DOM allows you to completely change the document, without any need to mix HTML and JavaScript. This technique of separating JavaScript into its own document and harnessing the DOM as a means to change HTML has been lately christened the *behavior layer* and crops up sooner or later when the talk is about modern web development and scripting. It means that by using the DOM, you turn JavaScript into a separate and independent layer in the whole web development process and stop treating it as an HTML add-on.

We stopped using font tags and presentational attributes like align and bgcolor, and defined all these settings using CSS. The defined styles are then applied to any HTML document that utilizes the CSS file. That way, we defined the HTML as a *structure layer* and the CSS as a *presentation layer*. We now stop mixing JavaScript and HTML, and put all JavaScript in a separate file and define yet another layer—the behavior layer. JavaScript describes how a document behaves, the same way as CSS describes how the document is rendered. Figure 10-3 illustrates the three levels of web development.

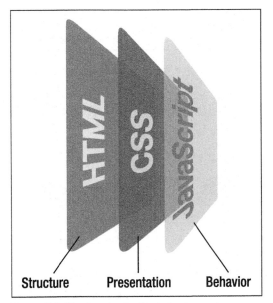

Figure 10-3. The three levels of web development

The question the web development community is arguing over right now is what constitutes behavior. Is it everything that changes when the user interacts with it? By that argument, a hover effect that changes a link's color should be implemented in JavaScript and not in CSS. What about hiding and showing elements? Is that to be done with CSS or JavaScript? The answer is simple: Whatever fits. Both are tools, and from an accessibility point of view, neither CSS nor JavaScript is trustworthy.

The following are some points in favor of JavaScript:

- It allows for programming logic: conditions, loops, functions, methods, objects, attributes, and so on.
- It allows for functionality independent of the input device.
- It allows for timers; for example, to delay the hiding of an element.
- It is much more supported across different user agents than CSS2 or CSS3.
- You can programmatically suppress JavaScript functionality; you cannot turn off CSS from within CSS, unless you depend on browser hacks.

JavaScript and CSS can both access elements of the HTML, as shown in Table 10-1. The support information is based on the majority of current browsers, including Internet Explorer 6. Firefox, Opera, and Safari support more CSS2, and some even support more CSS3 than Internet Explorer 6 does.

10

Table 10-1. DOM and CSS Access to HTML

Task	CSS	JavaScript and DOM
Get all paragraph elements	p { }	document.getElementsByTagName ('p');
Get the paragraph with the ID mypara	#mypara { }	document.getElementById ('mypara')
Get the third paragraph of the document		document.getElementsByTagName ('p')[2]
Get the next element following the third paragraph		document.getElementsByTagName ('p')[2].nextSibling
Get the element before the third paragraph		document.getElementsByTagName ('p')[2].previousSibling
Get the first element inside the third paragraph		document.getElementsByTagName ('p')[2].firstChild

When it comes to generating content, JavaScript and DOM leave CSS far behind. While CSS2 has the :before and :after pseudo selectors that can add content before and after an element, this content is limited to generating text content, displaying attributes, numbering, adding quotation marks, or embedding media. JavaScript and DOM have a lot more to offer, as shown in Table 10-2.

Table 10-2. JavaScript and DOM Content Generation

Command	Effect
createElement(element)	Creates a new element
createTextNode(string)	Creates a new text node with the value string
setAttribute(attribute,value)	Adds a new attribute with the value to the element or alters the current attribute
appendChild(child)	Adds the child node as the last child to the element
cloneNode(bool)	Makes a copy of the current node; if bool is true, it includes all child nodes (the clone is simply a copy of the HTML and does not include any JavaScript functionality you might have applied to the element beforehand)

Command	Effect
hasChildNodes()	Returns true if the element already has child nodes
insertBefore(newchild,oldchild)	Inserts the node newchild before oldchild
removeChild(child)	Removes the child node
replaceChild(newchild,oldchild)	Replaces oldchild with newchild
removeAttribute(attribute)	Removes the attribute from the element

Once you have reached an element, either via getElementsByTagName or getElementById, you can navigate the node tree via other attributes, as listed in Table 10-3.

Table 10-3. JavaScript Attributes for Node Tree Navigation

Attribute	Meaning
childNodes	An array of all the childNodes of an element. If you don't know how many nodes are in another node, you can loop through this array. There are also shorter notations for the first and the last child: firstChild instead of childNodes[0] and lastChild instead of childNodes[this.childNodes.length-1].
parentNode	The node the current one is contained in.
nextSibling	The next node on the same level as the current one.
previousSibling	The previous node on the same level as the current one.

10

Every node you reach has a range of attributes and methods, as listed in Table 10-4.

Table 10-4. JavaScript Node Attributes and Methods

Attribute	Meaning
attributes	Array of all the attributes of the node
data	Returns or sets the textual data of the node
nodeName	Returns the name of the node (in HTML, the element name)

Continued

307

Table 10-4. *Continued*

Attribute	Meaning
nodeType	Returns the type of the node (in HTML, this is 1 for element, 2 for attribute, or 3 for text)
nodeValue	Returns or sets the value of the node; this is the text when the node is a text node, the attribute value when it is an attribute node, and null when it is an element
getAttribute(attribute)	Retrieves the attribute value

Interactivity

Event handlers are what make things click, sometimes quite literally. Many event handlers are available, and some of them hint at the chance to create really sexy, rich user interfaces with JavaScript. In terms of accessibility, there is a danger that you can go in a direction that simply cannot be accessible to all.

Event handlers execute a script when the user agent detects a certain action. For example, the click event handler triggers a function when the visitor clicks an element (or presses Enter after tabbing to the link), mouseover is executed when the mouse pointer hovers over the element, and mouseout is triggered when the mouse pointer leaves the element.

Accessible websites need to be device independent, and the WCAG demands the use of device-independent event handlers for your scripts:

> Otherwise, if you must use device-dependent attributes, provide redundant input mechanisms (i.e., specify two handlers for the same element):
>
> Use "onmousedown" with "onkeydown"
>
> Use "onmouseup" with "onkeyup"
>
> Use "onclick" with "onkeypress"

Users who depend on keyboard browsing do normally have a key set up to simulate clicking (either the Enter key or spacebar), and that key triggers the click event. By using keypress, you might hijack other keyboard functionality the user needs. Examples are the type-ahead functionality of Mozilla, which automatically jumps to text or links containing the word you enter, Opera's extensive keyboard shortcuts (like the A key for next link), or the JAWS keyboard controls. While it is true that all of these are the issues the browser developers should tackle, it is your visitors who will suffer the problems they cause. This means that by following the WCAG, you might create a less accessible script. In practice, click typically does not need an extra "fallback" event handler.

So, how should you handle event handlers? Consider a drag-and-drop interface. This works fine for a visual user with good mouse skills, but you cannot assume that visitors who depend on voice recognition or screen readers will be able to use it—although their assistive technology does support this event! It doesn't hurt to add a click handler as well, thereby making everyone happy.

You can add event handlers in several ways, the least appropriate being inline:

```
<a href="index.html" onmouseover="doJSMagic()"➥
onclick="doJSMagic();return false" id="home">Home</a>
```

The less obtrusive way is to use a function to add handlers via the DOM Level 1 direct assignment:

```
function addMagic()
{
  // check if DOM is available
  if(!document.getElementById || !document.createTextNode){return;}
  // check if there is a link with the id home
  var hl=document.getElementById('home');
  if (!hl){return;}
  // apply the event handlers calling the function
  hl.onmouseover=doJSMagic;
  hl.onclick=function(){doJSMagic();return false}
}
```

The problem with this approach is that you can add only one handler at a time. If you want to call more than one function, you need to add it inside the anonymous function assignment:

```
function addMagic()
{
  // check if DOM is available
  if(!document.getElementById || !document.createTextNode){return;}
  // check if there is a link with the id home
  var hl=document.getElementById('home');
  if (!hl){return;}
  // apply the event handlers calling the function
  hl.onmouseover=doJSMagic;
  hl.onclick=function()
  {
    doJSMagic();
    moreSpells();
    return false;
  }
}
```

This is not really an issue when you use one script, but when you are developing more complex JavaScript applications, you might have different functions trying to assign event handlers to the same object, especially the window.

10

A clever developer named Scott Andrew came up with a function to dynamically add event handlers to an element. This is a much cleaner way, but the downside is that you need to do a lot of object detection and code forking to make it work in newer browsers and the ones that are getting a bit rusty now, like Internet Explorer 6.

```javascript
function addEvent(elm, evType, fn, useCapture)
// cross-browser event handling for IE5+, NS6+ and Mozilla/Gecko
// By Scott Andrew
{
  if (elm.addEventListener) {
    elm.addEventListener(evType, fn, useCapture);
    return true;
  } else if (elm.attachEvent) {
    var r = elm.attachEvent('on' + evType, fn);
    return r;
  } else {
    elm['on' + evType] = fn;
  }
}
function addMagic()
{
  // check if DOM is available
  if(!document.getElementById || !document.createTextNode){return;}
  // check if there is a link with the id home
  var hl=document.getElementById('home');
  if (!hl){return;}
  // apply the event handlers calling the function
  addEvent(hl,'mouseover',doJSMagic,false);
  addEvent(hl,'click',doJSMagic,false);
  addEvent(hl,'click',moreSpells,false);
}
```

This demonstrates the power of addEvent. With it, you can easily add several functions to a single event handler. If the visitor now clicks the element with the ID home, both the functions doJSMagic and moreSpells will be triggered without having to use an anonymous function, as in the earlier example. Using addEvent also means that your scripts will never be in the way of other scripts, as you don't hijack the event for your script exclusively. In the case of an element, that is never that much of a problem. In the case of the window and its onload handler, it could be fatal for other scripts.

Using addEvent makes it easier to use several different scripts on a page without having to amend them to work together. However, it also has its drawbacks. The biggest drawback is browser support. If you need to support older browsers like Internet Explorer 5 on the Mac or Netscape 4.x on the PC, you cannot use addEvent exclusively. Another annoying problem is that addEvent does not allow for the object that was activated to be sent to a script. With onclick, it is easy to get the object that was activated, using the this keyword. Consider this image example:

```
<p><img src="robot_tn.gif" alt="Battery powered Toy Robot" /></p>
<p><a href="robot.jpg" onclick="showPic(this.href);return false">
Large Image</a></p>
```

JavaScript:

```
function showPic(picurl){
  var picwin = window.open(picurl,'picwin','
                    [… window attributes …]      ')
  return false;
}
```

This will work, as picurl is submitted. If you add showPic via addEvent however, you cannot send the parameter, and you'll need another function to recognize which element has been activated to read out the href attribute. Furthermore, you'll also need a third function to stop the link from being followed, as return false does not stop the execution of the script when it is applied via addEvent.

> *Event handlers are a very vast and large field when it comes to developing JavaScript and different browsers, plus their lack of support of the W3C standards can prove to be quite a headache. Fortunately, enthusiastic web developers find problems and their solutions almost every week. Access Matters (www.access-matters.com/) has a JavaScript section that explains the problems of event handlers in detail (www.access-matters.com/results-for-javascript-part-1-navigating-links/).*

Look and Feel

The definition of the look and feel of a document is best kept in a separate CSS file. However, it is possible in JavaScript to access the style attribute collection of an element directly, and you might encounter older scripts that do that a lot, making it hard for you to change the look and feel of the effect they produce. For example, you could simulate a CSS rule completely in JavaScript, as in the following example.

CSS:

```
#specialOffer {
  border:1px solid #000;
  background:#cfc;
  color:#060;
  font-size:1.3em;
  padding:5px;
}
```

10

JavaScript:

```
var special=document.getElementById('specialOffer');
if(!special){return;}
special.style.border='1px solid #000';
special.style.background='#cfc';
special.style.color='#060';
special.style.fontSize='1.3em';
special.style.padding='5px';
```

The difference is that you can not only set the styles in JavaScript, but you can also read them. That way, it is easily possible to write a function that shows and hides an element by setting its display property to none when the page loads and read it when another element is activated. You might have encountered functions like this:

```
function showhide(o)
{
  // check if the object exists
  var obj=document.getElementById(o);
  if(!obj){return;}
  // if the object display setting is 'none',
  // set it to 'block' and vice versa
  obj.style.display=obj.style.display=='none'?'block':'none';
}
```

There are several problems with this type of function. First, elements that get a display property of none or visibility of hidden are not read by some screen readers. Second. if there are more changes to the look and feel of the hidden and the shown element, you need to add more and more style-changing lines to the function, or some third-party developer or designer will have to go through the JavaScript code to change the look and feel, which is neither safe nor easy on the maintenance time budget.

A better way is to change the className attribute of the element you want to change, thus applying a class to it that can be maintained by a CSS developer without any scripting aspirations. A script that turns an unordered list into a dynamic navigation could allow for different styles by adding a class. You can then create a rule in your CSS to display the navigation differently when JavaScript is available and when it is not.

```
<ul id="nav">
  <li><a href="index.php">Home</a></li>
  <li><a href="about.php">About Us</a></li>
 [… more options …]
  <li><a href="portfolio.php">Portfolio</a></li>
  <li><a href="contact.php">Contact</a></li>
</ul>
```

```
function initmenu()
{
  var n=document.getElementById('nav');
  if(!n){return;}
  n.className='dynamic';
  [... more code ...]
}
```

When JavaScript is available, the `<ul>` will get the class `dynamic`, which allows you or a future maintainer to define different styles for the plain menu and the one that is enhanced via scripting:

```
/* plain menu */
ul#nav{
  [… settings …]
}
/* scripting enhanced menu */
ul#nav.dynamic{
  [… settings …]
}
```

However, if you simply change the `className` attribute, you might overwrite already existing classes. The `class` attribute allows for several values, separated by a space. That is why you need to check if there is already a class applied and add the new one preceded by a space.

```
function initmenu()
{
  var n=document.getElementById('nav');
  if(!n){return;}
  n.className=n.className?n.className+' dynamic': 'dynamic';
  [... more code ...]
}
```

You run into the same issues when you want to remove classes that have been added dynamically, as some browsers don't allow for spaces before the first class or after the last class. This can be pretty annoying, and it is easier to reuse a function that does this for you:

```
function cssjs(a,o,c1,c2)
{
  switch (a){
    case 'swap':
      o.className=!cssjs('check',o,c1)? ➥
      o.className.replace(c2,c1):o.className.replace(c1,c2);
    break;
    case 'add':
      if(!cssjs('check',o,c1)){o.className+=o.className?' '+c1:c1;}
    break;
```

```
         case 'remove':
           var rep=o.className.match(' '+c1)?' '+c1:c1;
           o.className=o.className.replace(rep,'');
         break;
         case 'check':
           return new RegExp("(^|\\s)" + c1 + "(\\s|$)").test(o.className)
         break;
       }
     }
```

This function uses four parameters. a is the action you want it to perform: swap, add, remove, or check. swap replaces one class name with another, add adds a new class, remove removes it, and check tests if the class was already applied to the element. o is the object/element to which you want to apply the class. c1 and c2 are the two different classes. c2 is necessary only when the action is swap.

If you apply this tool function to the menu example, you get the following:

```
function initmenu()
{
  var n=document.getElementById('nav');
  if(!n){return;}
  cssjs('add',n,'dynamic');
  [... more code ...]
}
```

You will see more examples of this function in the "Element Visibility" section later in this chapter.

New Windows

Opening links in new browser instances or windows is a big usability and accessibility dilemma. On the one hand, you might need to do so; on the other hand, you cannot assume that the user agent supports several windows. For example, text browsers like Lynx do not support multiple windows.

Unsolicited opening of new windows—so-called pop-up windows—has been a marketing practice ever since browsers supported it, and is not the issue here. Let the plethora of pop-up blocking software out on the market deal with that. Sadly enough, badly developed pop-up blocking software might even interfere with windows that were opened with the user's consent. There is not much we can do about this, except for hoping users will spot that software mistake and tell the vendors about it. Another, maybe even more important, issue is that due to the constant misuse of pop-ups for unsolicited advertising, visitors are likely to see all new windows as a nuisance and close them before even glancing at their content.

An example of a reason to open a new window is to link to extra information on a third-party page or a lengthy terms and conditions page. This makes sense to show in a pop-up window, as you don't force the visitors to leave the document and thereby lose all the data they might have entered in a form already. However, if you have the chance to store this data in a session or database before going to the other document and reinstate it when going back, do so—it is the safest and most accessible way.

Guidelines for Opening Windows

The following general rules apply to opening new windows:

- Do not rely on them being available. Provide a link back to the previous page in any case.

- Opening of new windows in a controlled manner—for example, defining the window dimensions—is dependent on JavaScript; therefore, add this functionality via JavaScript.

- Try to avoid interaction of windows—for example, sending data back from the pop-up window—especially in environments with strict accessibility guidelines or needs.

- Add JavaScript-dependent content (for example, close this window links) via JavaScript to avoid promising the user functionality that is not available.

Opening the linked document in a new browser instance is possible in HTML, via the target attribute. The target attribute can be the name of a frame inside the document or the name of another window. It can also be one of the generic terms blank, top, or parent preceded by an underscore. The _parent and _top values make sense only inside a frameset pointing to one frameset above the one the document was opened in or the main browser window. The _blank value will open a new browser instance, if the visitor hasn't disabled this option (some browsers allow you to do that).

The following code opens a new browser window in an accessible manner using HTML exclusively. The only drawbacks are that target is a deprecated attribute for modern HTML derivatives and that users who cannot open new windows will get a confusing message saying that the link opens in a new window:

```
<a href="http://www.example.com" target="_blank">➡
visit our example client (opens in new window)</a>
```

Visitors should be notified that this link opens in a new window inside the text of the link. A lot of accessibility tutorials state it is enough to add a title attribute with that information. However, not all assistive technologies support title attributes, and users tend to turn them off, as titles have been abused for extraneous text because of their tooltip representation in visual browsers. The information contained in titles will also be hidden from keyboard users; with visual user agents, only hovering over the element with the mouse pointer reveals the title.

10

Fans of strict XHTML frown upon the target attribute, as the strict derivatives of XHTML and HTML do not allow it. If you want to use strict markup derivatives, and you still want to have pop-up windows for visitors with JavaScript enabled, you can use either the rel attribute or CSS classes in conjunction with an appropriate script. Without JavaScript, the page will open in the same browser window.

```
<a href="example.html" rel="popup">help</a>
<a href="example.html" class="popup">help</a>
```

The class method has its merits, as it also allows you to style the links accordingly. The problem is that the styling makes sense only when CSS and scripting is enabled. Therefore, if you go the CSS classes route, you should apply the extra styling only when JavaScript is available. The rel method indicates link relationships, and a pop-up is a link relationship—one that is made up and not supported by browsers. You could also use the profile attribute of the head element to make this relationship obvious to user agents.

JavaScript allows you to open a new window with certain measurements and turn off parts of the browser. The latter is particularly popular with design agencies, as the designer's nightmare—not being able to control the size of the canvas—can be avoided by opening a pop-up window with fixed dimensions.

To open a new window in JavaScript, you use the open method of the window object. This method comes with various window attributes in a rather uncommon syntax:

```
newwindow = window.open("document.html", "windowname",➡
"attribute1=value,attribute2=value,attribute3=value");
```

The third parameter is a comma-separated list of attribute and value pairs. The attributes and their meaning are legion. You can find a good list of them, including browser support, on the German site SelfHTML (http://de.selfhtml.org/javascript/objekte/window.htm#open).

One bad practice that is commonly used on the Web is to make a pop-up link dependent on JavaScript:

```
<a href="javascript:window.open
('example.html','','width=400,height=400,➡
location=no,menubar=no,resizable=no,scrollbars=no')">➡
help</a>
```

Without JavaScript, this help will not be helpful, as nothing happens when the frustrated visitor activates this link. Even worse, if the visitor has JavaScript enabled and gets a pop-up window, the restrictions of the window defined in the attributes might render it useless. A low-vision user who needs to have a large font size might not be able to read the content, as it has been cut off and the user will not be able to reach it because both scrolling and window resizing have been turned off. It is much safer and more user-friendly to keep the browser as it is. You simply cannot predict all the needs of your visitors.

Using an onclick handler on the link also ensures that there is no dependency on JavaScript:

```
<a href="example.html" onclick="window.open(this.href,'',➡
'width=400,height=400,resizable=yes,menubar=yes,➡
scrollbars=yes');return false">help</a>
```

A couple items here might be confusing and need clarifying. The first mystery might be this.href. The magic word this always refers to the element that is activated. The href attribute is what the link points to. Using this.href saves you a needless repetition of example.html as the document location of the pop-up window. Second, the return false statement at the end of the onclick command ensures that the link is not being followed in the main window; otherwise, example.html would be opened both in the pop-up window and the main window.

If you want to make sure that a new browser window will be opened regardless of JavaScript availability, you can add a target attribute and inform the visitor about it:

```
<a href="example.html"  target="_blank"➡
onclick="window.open(this.href,'','width=400,height=400,➡
resizable=yes,menubar=yes,scrollbars=yes');return false">➡
help (opens in a new window)</a>
```

As explained earlier in the "Interactivity" section, this example will make automated testing choke and is a violation of the WCAG 1.0 guidelines, unless you add an onkeypress handler. This handler would do more bad than good, unless it also tests which keys were pressed and takes appropriate action. As developing proper keypress-handling scripts in JavaScript can be tricky, you need to rethink your pop-up windows as a whole if you want the site to be accessible and pass automated validation.

A Reusable Pop-Up Script

One thing is for certain: Pop-up windows need JavaScript to get their full effect. With that in mind, the most logical solution is to shift all the pop-up functionality to JavaScript and stick with the plain-vanilla HTML link opening the document in the same window. For the window-opener links, you can use the rel="next" attribute, and for the closing ones, you can use the rev="prev" attribute. These are normally used for pages inside a collection of pages, like a book, linking to the next and previous chapters. If you want to use them as they were intended, you can also come up with your own "poptrigger" and "popup" values.

Let's say that you want a help document to open in a pop-up window. The most basic example—assuming the worst—would be a link to the help in the document that should spawn the pop-up window and a link back to the previous page in the pop-up document.

```
<a href="help.html" rel="popup">help</a>
<a href="form.html" rev="poptrigger">back to previous page</a>
```

This works in any case. If you were to use a target attribute, the link back wouldn't be possible, as you cannot close windows without JavaScript. The help.html document might open in a new window, but open the form in the new window when the visitors activate the link back to the previous page.

10

Now, if JavaScript is available, you want the pop-up link to open a new window—and tell the visitor about it—and the back link should close the current window. You could do this with inline event handlers, inline JavaScript, and noscript:

```
<!-- on the opener page -->
<a href="help.html"
onclick="window.open(this.href,'','width=400,height=400,➡
resizable=yes,menubar=yes,scrollbars=yes');➡
return false" rel="popup">help</a>
<script type="text/javascript">➡
document.write('(opens in a new window)');</script>

<!-- in the pop-up -->
<a href="form.html" onclick="window.close();➡
return false" rev="poptrigger">
<noscript>back to previous page</noscript>
<script type="text/javascript">document.write('close window');</script>
</a>
```

Not a nice sight to behold, a nightmare to maintain, and—depending on the user agent and the HTML version—a source of various failures and validation errors.

Let's develop an unobtrusive script that triggers the same functionality without mixing HTML and JavaScript. The script should do the following:

- Check if the DOM is available.
- Grab all links in the document.
- Test if there is a window.opener object, which indicates that the current document is open in a pop-up window.
- If there is a window.opener object, loop through all the links and test if they have a rev attribute of "poptrigger". If so, replace the link text with the "close window" message and attach a function that will close the window when the link is activated.
- If there is no window.opener object, loop through all the links and test if they have either a target attribute or a rel attribute of "popup". If so, add the "opens in a new window" message and attach a function that will open a window when the link is activated.

This translates to the following reusable JavaScript functions:

```
function popuptools()
{
  // test if DOM is available
  if(!document.getElementById || !document.createTextNode){return;}
  // define variables
  // target to indicate popup link
  var triggerTarget='_blank';
  // rel to indicate popup link
  var triggerRel='popup';
  // rev to indicate closing link
```

```
  var backRev='poptrigger';
  // message to add to a link with a popup rev but no target
  var openMessage=' (opens in a new window)';
  // message to replace back links with
  var closeMessage='Close window';
  // links to loop over (it is a good idea to constrain this further)
  var links=document.getElementsByTagName('a');
  // If the window is a popup window (there is a opener window)
  if(window.opener)
  {
    // define new regular expression to test for the rev attribute
    var check = new RegExp("(^|\\s)" + backRev + "(\\s|$)");
    // loop over all links
    for(var i=0;i<links.length;i++)
    {
      // if there is no appropriate rev attribute, skip this link
      if(!check.test(links[i].getAttribute('rev'))){continue;}
      // if the closing message is not empty,
      //replace the link text with it
      if(closeMessage!=''){links[i].firstChild.nodeValue=closeMessage;}
      // close the window when the link is activated
      addEvent(links[i],'click',dealwithwin);
    }
  // if the window is not a popup
  } else {
    // loop over all links
    for(var i=0;i<links.length;i++)
    {
      // if the link has no appropriate rel or target attribute, skip
it
      if(links[i].getAttribute('rel')!=triggerRel &&
      links[i].getAttribute('target')!=triggerTarget)
      {continue;}
      // if the link has no target, add the open message
      if(!links[i].target)
      {
        links[i].appendChild(document.createTextNode(openMessage));
      }
      // open a new window with the defined attributes when the
      // link gets activated and set the focus to the window.
      addEvent(links[i],'click',dealwithwin);
    }
  }
}
function dealwithwin(e)
{
  // define name and attributes of the popup window
  var popupname='popup';
  var windowAttributes='width=400,height=400,scrollbars=yes, ➡
```

10

319

```
     resizable=yes,menubar=yes';
     // if this function was not called in a popup window,
     // try to open a window
     if(!window.opener)
     {
       var popup=window.open(this.href,popupname,windowAttributes);
       // if the popup was sucessfully opened,
       // set the focus to it and don't follow the initial link
        if(popup)
        {
          popup.focus();
          // do not follow the link and open the document,
          // in the same window
          if(e.returnValue){e.returnValue = false;}
          if(e.preventDefault){e.preventDefault();}
          return false;
        }
      // otherwise, close this window
      } else {
        window.close();
      }
   }
   function addEvent(elm, evType, fn, useCapture)
   // cross-browser event handling for IE5+, NS6+ and Mozilla/Gecko
   // By Scott Andrew
   {
     if (elm.addEventListener) {
       elm.addEventListener(evType, fn, useCapture);
       return true;
     } else if (elm.attachEvent) {
       var r = elm.attachEvent('on' + evType, fn);
       return r;
     } else {
       elm['on' + evType] = fn;
     }
   }
   addEvent(window,'load',popuptools,false);
```

If you add these functions to both the opening document and the one being opened in the pop-up, the links are automatically converted. First, add them to the document triggering the pop-up window:

```
<!DOCTYPE HTML PUBLIC "-//W3C//DTD HTML 4.01//EN"➡
"http://www.w3.org/TR/html4/strict.dtd">
<html dir="ltr" lang="en">
<head>
  <meta http-equiv="Content-Type"➡
  content="text/html; charset=iso-8859-1">
  <title>Pop-up Window Examples - Parent page</title>
```

```
    <style type="text/css"></style>
    <script type="text/javascript" src="popuptoolbox.js"></script>
</head>
<body>
<p><a href="popup.html" rel="popup">Help</a></p>
</body>
</html>
```

And then add them to the document opened in the pop-up window:

```
<!DOCTYPE HTML PUBLIC "-//W3C//DTD HTML 4.01//EN"➡
"http://www.w3.org/TR/html4/strict.dtd">
<html dir="ltr" lang="en">
<head>
    <meta http-equiv="Content-Type" content="text/html;➡
charset=iso-8859-1">
    <title>Popup window example</title>
    <style type="text/css">
      </style>
    <script type="text/javascript" src="popuptoolbox.js"></script>
</head>
<body>
<a href="popupparent.html" rev="poptrigger">Go back</a>
<h1>This is the popup window</h1>
<p><a href="popupparent.html" rev="poptrigger">Go back</a><p>
</body>
</html>
```

This is as accessible and unobtrusive as you can get when it comes to pop-up windows. A legitimate use might be when you need to display a third-party site or a lengthy legal text.

Another solution to this problem would be using an IFRAME and giving it a proper summary in its title. However, this is deprecated in strict HTML 4.01 and XHTML transitional, so out of the question if you use these.

For smaller portions of text, it might be better to use a technique called *layer-ad* (at least in advertising). Using this technique, you add the text to the document, hide it dynamically, and show it when the visitors interact with another element.

Element Visibility

Showing/hiding page elements is probably one of the most common JavaScript tricks. In regards of accessibility, it can make or break the page. On the one hand, it is nice not to overwhelm the visitors with options and content, but instead offer them the choice to expand and collapse what they want. On the other hand, hiding things does not make them disappear, and users without JavaScript will need to take in all the elements at once. In a visual browser, this might not seem that taxing, but visitors who depend on a screen reader will need to listen to a lot of content that may not be of any interest to them at the moment. A classic example is a navigation menu that has all pages of the site available.

10

For a visitor who can see and use a mouse, this might be a handy shortcut, but listening to dozens of links with no connection to the current page is not fun. A good rule of thumb is to design the page with all options available, test it with real users, and then start enhancing via JavaScript.

You can hide page elements in a variety of ways. For example, you can set their display property to none, set their visibility property to hidden, or position them off the screen. Other methods involve text-indent, clip, negative Z-indexes, hidden overflow, margins, and line-height. A Google search for "image replacement technique" gives you all the ideas developers have come up with from the CSS side of things.

Setting the display or visibility property can cause problems, as they could hide your content not only to the sighted visitors, but also to those using assistive technology, depending on the software used and its configuration.

One common technique to show and hide elements that works for all user agents is called *off-left*, as it positions the element off the screen but still keeps it readable for nonvisual user agents:

```
.hide{
    position:absolute;
    top:-9999px;
    left:-9999px
    overflow:hidden;
}
```

In the past, you might have encountered some code examples like this one:

```
<h4><a href="#address" onclick='showstuff('address')'>Our Address:</a>
</h4>
<address id="address" class='hide' >
<strong><a name="address">Company Name</strong><br />
  House<br />
  Street<br />
  Post Code<br />
  City<br />
  County<br />
  United Kingdom<br />
</address>
<p>More content</p>
```

The problem with this example is that you rely on JavaScript being available. Visitors with CSS enabled and JavaScript turned off will never be able to see the address. It is much safer to add the class and the functionality via JavaScript using the aforementioned cssjs and addEvent functions. All that remains in the HTML are two IDs to ease the process of finding the elements to apply the functionality.

```
<h4 id="addresstrigger">Our Address:</h4>
<address id="address">
  Company Name<br />
  House<br />
```

```
    Street<br />
    Post Code<br />
    City<br />
    County<br />
    United Kingdom<br />
</address>
<p>More content</p>
```

The script itself needs to check for these two IDs and create the rest of the elements necessary to show and hide the address.

```
addEvent(window,'load',initaddress,false);
function initaddress()
{
  if(!document.getElementById || !document.createTextNode){return;}
  var adt=document.getElementById('addresstrigger');
  var add=document.getElementById('address');
  if(!adt || !add){return;}
  // add the link to the heading
  var newa=document.createElement('a');
  newa.href='#address';
  var txt=adt.firstChild.nodeValue;
  newa.appendChild(document.createTextNode(txt));
  adt.replaceChild(newa,adt.firstChild);
  addEvent(newa,'click',showhideaddress,false);
  // add the named anchor to address
  newa=document.createElement('a');
  newa.setAttribute('name','address');
  txt=add.firstChild.nodeValue;
  newa.appendChild(document.createTextNode(txt));
  add.replaceChild(newa,add.firstChild);
  cssjs('add',add,'hide');
}
```

The actual showing and hiding is achieved by removing or adding the hide class.

```
function showhideaddress()
{
  var add=document.getElementById('address');
  if(cssjs('check',add,'hide'))
  {
    cssjs('remove',add,'hide');
  } else {
    cssjs('add',add,'hide');
  }
  return false;
}
```

10

By using two different IDs, you take the easy way out, as you don't need to loop through elements and try to find the ones to hide. Too much looping and checking can slow down your scripts and should be avoided if possible. When dealing with generated content though, you might not have the chance to create unique IDs but need to rely on element names. For example, say you have an FAQ page you want to make collapsible. Your code might be as follows:

```
<div id="faq">
  <h2>Question 1</h2>
  <div>
    <p>Answer 1</p>
  </div>
  <h2>Question 2</h2>
  <div>
    <p>Answer 2</p>
  </div>
  <h2>Question 3</h2>
  <div>
    <p>Answer 3</p>
  </div>
  <h2>Question 4</h2>
  <div>
    <p>Answer 4</p>
  </div>
</div>
```

With the following code, you can make the question headings clickable and expand and collapse the answers.

```
function initfaq()
{
  if(!document.getElementById || !document.createTextNode){return;}
  // check if the FAQ element exists
  var f=document.getElementById('faq');
  if(!f){return;}
  // grab all headings level two
  var h2s=f.getElementsByTagName('h2');
  var tohide
  // loop through all the headings
  for(var i=0;i<h2s.length;i++)
  {
  // find the next sibling element and make sure
  // it is an element and a div
    tohide=h2s[i].nextSibling;
    while(tohide.nodeType!=1 && tohide.nodeName.toLowerCase!='div')
    {
      tohide=tohide.nextSibling;
    }
    cssjs('add',tohide,'hide');
    h2s[i].tohide=tohide;
```

```
      addEvent(h2s[i],'click',setElement(h2s[i]),false);
    }
  }
  function faqcollapse(e,targetElement)
  {
    // find the element that was activated
    var el = window.event ? targetElement : e ? e.currentTarget : null;
    if (!el) return;
    // check if the element stored in the tohide attribute is already
    // hidden or not and hide or show it by adding or removing
    // the hide class
    if(cssjs('check',el.tohide,'hide'))
    {
      cssjs('remove',el.tohide,'hide');
    } else {
      cssjs('add',el.tohide,'hide');
    }
  }
  // tool functions
  function setElement(node) …
  function cssjs(a,o,c1,c2) …
  function addEvent(elm, evType, fn, useCapture) . . .
  addEvent(window,'load',initfaq,false);
```

Your FAQ can now be expanded and collapsed, but there is one mistake. Using only a keyboard to navigate the page, visitors will never be able to expand the answers. They cannot reach and activate the headings. The remedy is to add links around the headings and anchors inside each <div>.

```
  function initfaq()
  {
    // . . . code removed for legibility . . .
    for(var i=0;i<h2s.length;i++)
    {
    // find the next sibling element and make sure it is an element and
    // a div
      tohide=h2s[i].nextSibling;
      while(tohide.nodeType!=1 && tohide.nodeName.toLowerCase!='div')
      {
        tohide=tohide.nextSibling;
      }
    // create a target and a link pointing to it
        newtarget=document.createElement('a');
        newtarget.name='faqtarget'+i;
        newlink=document.createElement('a');
        newlink.href='#faqtarget'+i;
        // insert the target in the FAQ answer
        tohide.insertBefore(newtarget,tohide.firstChild);
        // read the content of the FAQ question
```

```
                h2content=h2s[i].firstChild.nodeValue;
                // add a link around the question
                newlink.appendChild(document.createTextNode(h2content));
                h2s[i].replaceChild(newlink,h2s[i].firstChild);
            cssjs('add',tohide,'hide');
            h2s[i].tohide=tohide;
            addEvent(h2s[i],'click',setElement(h2s[i]),false);
        }
    }
```

You can enhance this example to show different styles when the heading is activated and for the closed and open FAQ items by adding and removing more classes. You could also easily make the headings react when the mouse hovers over them, but that can result in unsightly jumping of the page.

Another necessary evil is that the whole page content is visible until the page has finished loading and the hide script has executed. There is no clean way around that issue, but there is a hack, and it is the only justifiable use of document.write. Adding a small script that writes out the necessary hiding class to the document ensures that when the elements get rendered, they will be hidden. However, this fix comes with the dangers of document.write, as explained in the next section, so avoid it if possible.

Probably the biggest virtue when it comes to showing and hiding elements is restraint. It is tempting to make the whole page collapse and expand. It is a sexy feature, invites user engagement, and makes your sites look a lot more like applications. However, unless you rely a lot on JavaScript or use buttons as the interactive elements—to send the state changes to the back end for storage—you won't be able to offer the same functionality that real applications give the user. The more interactivity a page offers, the more likely users are to expect it to behave like a real application. An application stores the state of all windows, menu bars, and custom settings when you close them, and reinstates them when you open the application again. Can you be sure to offer that to your visitors safely?

Outdated Techniques and Replacements

When you use scripts downloaded from the Web or from older tutorials, you are likely to encounter some outdated techniques. There might be conditions where their use is still a necessity—say to support very old browsers—but, in general, you will create much slicker and easier to maintain scripts when you stop using them and concentrate on their replacements, as described in this section.

document.write

If you use document.write, you write out content to the HTML document, inside the body of the document and mixed with the markup. This is not only a maintenance issue, but it can also lead to browsers not rendering the page or visitors retrieving JavaScript code instead of the content.

The solution is to identify the page element you want to add content to via getElementById or getElementsByTagName, create your elements via createElement or createTextNode, and insert them via appendChild or insertBefore. This will also ensure that the created elements are well-formed—something that is a responsibility of the developer if you use document.write. If you use XHTML documents and you serve them as application/XHTML plus XML on the server, document.write will not work anyway, as it is deprecated.

There is one exception, which is a cosmetic issue: If you hide or rearrange page elements by applying classes, you can get an unsightly shifting of the page when the document loads. Writing out the style sheet link with document.write makes sure that the necessary classes are defined before the changes occur, and the page load will look a lot smoother, as mentioned in the previous section.

<noscript></noscript>

The noscript directive tells the user agent what to render when there is no scripting support enabled. You will encounter it a lot in accessibility tutorials, where it is advertised as a way for every visitor to use your site. What it means is that you are relying on JavaScript to be available and trying to find a clean way out by adding a "Sorry, but you really need JavaScript" message. Instead of using noscript, you can leave the "no scripting" message in the document and replace it only when scripting is available.

```
<p id="nojs"><strong>Warning:</strong>
  You need JavaScript enabled to use this application.
  If there is no way for you to enable JavaScript, please
<a href="contact.php">contact us</a> to find a way around this problem.
</p>

function replacenoscript()
{
  // check if DOM is available
  if(!document.getElementById || !document.createTextNode){return;}
  // check if there is a "No JavaScript" message
  var nojsmsg=document.getElementById('nojs');
  if(!nojsmsg){return;}
  // create a new paragraph and link to the application and replace
  // the non-JavaScript message with it.
  var newp=document.createElement('p');
  var newtxt='A test of your browser configuration found no errors. ';
  newp.appendChild(document.createTextNode(newtxt));
  var newa=document.createElement('a');
  newa.setAttribute('href','application.html');
  newtxt='Proceed to the application';
  newa.appendChild(document.createTextNode(newtxt));
  newp.appendChild(newa);
  nojsmsg.parentNode.replaceChild(newp,nojsmsg);
}
```

This function, executed when the page loaded, will test if there is a paragraph with the ID nojs and replace it with a message stating that the browser configuration was successfully tested. It also creates a link pointing to the document that needs JavaScript enabled—

10

in this case, `application.html`. You might argue that you could automatically transfer the user to the other document via JavaScript and the `window.location.href` directive, but this can be prevented in modern browsers as it was abused for unsolicited advertising and other malicious code. Furthermore, telling the visitor that the following product must have JavaScript enabled might make it less confusing when the product behaves differently than a plain HTML/CGI solution.

href="javascript: . . ." and onclick="javascript:"

There is no such thing as a JavaScript protocol on the Web. Links use protocols like `http://` or `https://` to connect documents. By using `javascript:` as a protocol, you make yourself dependent on scripting being available. If you need a link that exclusively points to a function, generate the link via the DOM and assign an event handler to it instead.

One common use of this outdated technique is for links that point to a full-size version of an image in a pop-up window, something like this:

```
<p><img src="robot_tn.gif" alt="Battery powered Toy Robot" /></p>
<p><a href="javascript:showPic('robot.jpg');return false">
Large Image</a></p>
```

This link will do nothing when JavaScript is not available. Instead of using the pseudo protocol, you could link to the image with a normal link and use an event handler to call the script:

```
<p><img src="robot_tn.gif" alt="Battery powered Toy Robot" /></p>
<p><a href="robot.jpg" onclick=" showPic(this.href);return false">
Large Image</a></p>
```

Notice that you don't even need to repeat the image URL twice. You just read the `href` attribute of the link via `this.href`.

If, for some reason you want to show the link only when JavaScript is available, you can use the DOM to replace a caption with a link:

```
<p><img src="robot_tn.gif" alt="Battery powered Toy Robot" /></p>
<p id="caption">Toy robot</p>
```

JavaScript:

```
// grab the element with the ID caption
var cap=document.getElementById('caption');
// create a new link element
var newlink=document.createElement('a');
    // set the link's href attribute to the large picture
newlink.setAttribute('href','robot.jpg');
// call showPic when the user clicks on the link
newlink.onclick=function(){
  showPic(this.href);
  return false;
```

```
}
// read the text content of the caption
var capText=cap.firstChild.nodeValue;
// set the link text to this
newlink.appendChild(document.createTextNode(capText);
// replace the text inside the caption with the link
cap.replaceChild(newlink,cap.firstChild);
```

You might wonder why you don't skip setting the `href` attribute and send the image name as a parameter to `showPic` directly. The reason is that the link would not be styled as a link if it doesn't have an `href`, and it is helpful for the visitor to know where the link points.

onclick="void(0)" and Other "Do Nothing" Commands

Why put effort into creating something that by definition is not doing anything? The only time you will see this is when someone created a not-too-clever script and tries to gloss over the problems it causes. If you point a link to a JavaScript function and you don't want it to be followed once the function has executed, end the function with a `return false`.

document.all, document.layers, and navigator.userAgent

Unless your project environment is Internet Explorer 5.0 and Netscape Communicator 4.x (my condolences if it is), there is no need for `document.all`, `document.layers`, and `navigator.userAgent` any longer. Object detection is better than trying to guess what the browser in use is, and the W3C DOM is more likely to be used in future user agents than the earlier Netscape or Microsoft ones. If you don't know what I am talking about or you haven't ever encountered `document.layers` and `document.all` before, just believe me that everything with `document.getElementById` is much more stable and future-proof than the other two.

If you use browser sniffing, by reading the `userAgent` or testing for the different DOMs, you expect the user agent to identify itself, which may not be the case. Opera, for example, identifies itself as Internet Explorer (because the amount of websites testing for Internet Explorer exclusively was staggering and the Opera developers didn't want their users to be blocked out), unless the user changes that. Browser sniffing makes you dependent on a certain user agent, and that is one of the biggest *faux pas* in accessible web development. Testing for objects, on the other hand, only means that you check if what you apply can be understood—much like checking the depth of the water before jumping in head-first.

Functions with a Lot of Parameters

Functions with a lot of parameters like `onmouseover="myCall('I','pity','the','foo', 1233,'I aint going on no plane')"` are hard to maintain, confusing, and—if used as in this example—add unnecessary page weight to the document. Anything crucial to the user experience that your script needs has to be in the document anyway, for users without JavaScript. Reusing this markup is a lot easier, cleaner, and more maintainable than sending a lot of parameters. If there is any reason to send parameters, a simple `this` (or detecting the current element via the DOM event) does the trick in most cases, as `this` sends the object you clicked on to the script and you can navigate from there.

10

innerHTML

Creating complex HTML constructs can be quite a task when you use the DOM. Say you want to tell the visitors that there is more functionality on the page than normal HTML would give them. You could do this by adding a paragraph with the text "This document has enhanced functionality. Read more about the enhancements and how to use them." and link the second sentence to a document explaining the changes, named jshelp.html. Let's further assume that the page has a main content element that is a DIV with the ID content. With pure DOM methods, you could do that as follows:

```
function addjsinfo()
{
  // check if DOM is supported
  if(!document.getElementById || !document.createTextNode){return;}

  // define all the variables
  var contentId='content';
  var s1='This document has enhanced functionality. ';
  var s2='Read more about the enhancements and how to use them.';
  var helpurl='jshelp.html';

  // if the content element exists
  var con=document.getElementById(contentId);
  if(!con){return;}
  // create a new paragraph, and add
  // the first sentence as a new text node
  var helpp=document.createElement('p');
  helpp.appendChild(document.createTextNode(s1));
  // create a new link, point it to the help document
  // and add the second sentence as a new text node
  var helplink=document.createElement('a');
  helplink.setAttribute('href',helpurl)
  helplink.appendChild(document.createTextNode(s2));
  // add the new link to the paragraph
  helpp.appendChild(helplink);
  // add the paragraph before the first child element of the content
  con.insertBefore(helpp,con.firstChild);
}
```

Using the nonstandard innerHTML attribute, things get a lot easier:

```
function addjsinfoinner()
{
  if(!document.getElementById || !document.createTextNode){return;}
  var con=document.getElementById('content');
  if(!con){return;}
  var jsmsg='<p>This document has enhanced functionality.
  <a href="jshelp.html">Read more about how to use the enhancements</a>
  </p>';
  con.innerHTML=jsmsg+con.innerHTML;
}
```

However, the issue with `innerHTML` is that you mix JavaScript and HTML syntax. Instead of properly constructing your markup (and thereby leaving a trail of variables that can be reused later), you define HTML as a string of text and offer maintainers the option to create invalid HTML that might break the page rendering.

What `innerHTML` is really good for is testing your scripts. Together with the `window.alert` method, it allows you to see what you have assembled in your DOM script easily (another option is the View Generated Source option of Mozilla). Depending on the browser, and the `DOCTYPE`, browsers will give you invalid markup though: elements in uppercase and attributes without quotation marks.

Accessible Forms and JavaScript

Forms make the Web truly interactive. Links allow visitors to go from one page to another. You can add rollover effects and drag-and-drop functionality. But only forms allow the visitor to enter text, send it off to the server, and see what happens with it. (It is possible to create a drag-and-drop interface that also sends information to the server via Ajax, but that is hardly accessible.) Filling out a long form can be quite an annoying experience though, especially when it has been badly designed or enhanced via JavaScript without testing it first.

By now, many people have realized that you can jump from form element to form element by hitting the Tab key, thus making the data-entry process a lot quicker. You don't have to point your mouse to the text field and activate it; you simply press Tab once and start typing. Depending on the data you need to enter, you might not even look at the screen. Instead, you might look at a paper document to find a reference number, the address to transfer a payment to, and how much you have to pay. This process becomes all the more frustrating when you realize after entering the third number that the form is still stuck in the first text field, and a JavaScript alert with all the charm and grace of a charging rhino is displayed on the screen to tell you that something is wrong, as shown in Figure 10-4.

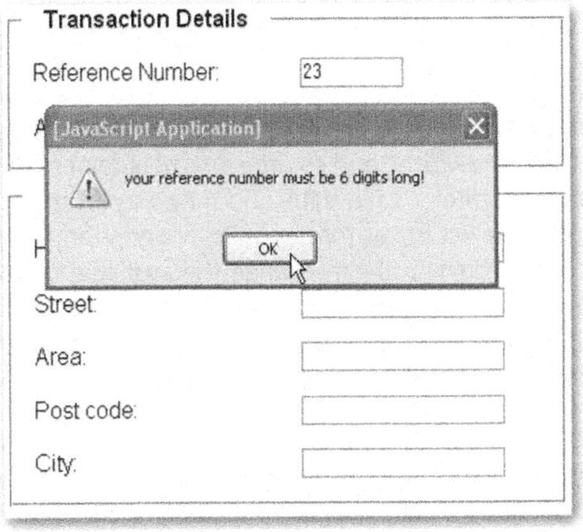

Figure 10-4. How not to tell the user that something went wrong

Forms are the *enfant terrible* of web page elements. They refuse to be styled consistently or at all, they can be a good entry point for hackers if they are not developed securely, and they are annoying to fill out. If you have many forms on your web product, make sure to assign a lot of usability testing time to those.

The better you plan the forms, the easier it will be for the end users to fill in those forms. Does every element have a proper label? Is it clear what syntax is required for the data? Did you choose the right form element for the job (why have two radio buttons stating yes and no when one check box does the same thing)?

When developing for the Web these days, forms feel cumbersome and dated. Faster computers, slicker and richer operating systems, and application interfaces make the old HTML/server interaction appear too slow and annoying to use. This has become especially obvious in the past year or so, when more and more applications installed on the operating system started talking to the Web. These fat client applications follow different rules than websites and offer a richer interface with more widgets than HTML offers, such as sliders, calendars, combo boxes, and contextual menus. All of these come with keyboard shortcuts, and many are customizable to the user's needs. The problem with web applications and websites is that they are already running inside at least two different applications—the operating system and the browser—both of which take up a lot of the available keyboard shortcuts.

As a JavaScript developer, you can enhance web applications written in HTML enormously. However, while it is possible to simulate rich client applications with JavaScript and HTML, it is not necessarily a good idea, especially when you want to stay accessible to all users.

Form Enhancements

As JavaScript developers, we love the power this language gives us, and it is very tempting to reinvent the wheel or enhance anything we see to function better than the boring old HTML controls. This is not necessarily bad, but it can be dangerous. A lot of usability testing and research has gone into the out-of-the-box HTML controls, and once web surfers have become used to them, they do not have to think twice when confronted with them again.

However, there are some things that are too good to be left out for the sake of accessibility and usability. One of them is the date picker. Date fields in forms can be a really frustrating experience, both for the visitor and for the site maintainer. There are simply too many conventions on how to enter a valid date, and they vary from country to country. The worst solution is to offer select boxes for day, month, and year, for the simple reason that not every month has 31 days. You can change the available options of the day drop-down list dynamically via JavaScript, but you cannot assume that a blind visitor will be notified about that change. The most accessible way is a free text-entry field with a sample value and an explanation in the label.

A very high-end solution to the date field problem is a date picker or a pop-up calendar. There are many scripts available, and the newer ones offer clean code and easy style changes. However, none of these are really accessible, as they are a pain to use via keyboard, voice recognition, or screen reader. This does not mean that you should not use them—they do enhance form usability greatly. Rather, it means that they should be applied only when JavaScript is available, and the form should be editable regardless of their function.

This applies to any form enhancement. If you want to offer interacting select boxes to allow for sorting two lists, you can do so; however, make sure that all the buttons and fields that require JavaScript are also created via JavaScript. Sometimes, the fallback server-side also needs to become a different interface—one that offers easier selection when pages must be reloaded. With interacting select boxes, this might be a list of check boxes.

> For some web applications, the form controls HTML provides out of the box might not be enough, and the functional specifications ask for richer controls like sliders and Microsoft Excel-like spreadsheets. A lot of development frameworks like Microsoft's .NET have these, but the accessibility of them is rather poor in most of the cases. Instead of trying to roll your own solutions and bearing the whole testing and development on yourself, it might be a good idea to take a leaf out of the book of Mozilla, who has worked together with Sun on a set of rich controls that are keyboard accessible and released under the creative commons license. You can find the current releases and documentation at www.mozilla.org/access/dhtml/.

Form Validation

You can do a lot of validation and form enhancement via JavaScript and also automatically change values when the user goes to the next field, but you cannot rely solely on JavaScript; you need to back it up with a server-side script. This means double maintenance of validation rules: once in the JavaScript and a second time in the server-side script. Any change to the rules means that both scripts need to be updated. On top of that, you also need to tell the user explicitly what data is expected in the form label or initial value.

This does not mean that you shouldn't do any JavaScript validation—far from it. A reload spared is a good thing for both your visitors and your server traffic. Rather, it means that your validation should follow some rules:

- The validation should not interfere with the natural flow of filling out the form— no alerts or extra links.
- The validation should not rely on a certain input device (onblur/onfocus instead of onmouseover/onmouseout).
- The validation error message should provide links to the elements that have an issue to make it easy to amend them.

The cleanest way to validate a form is to do so when it is submitted, instead of validating every element and giving immediate feedback. Nothing is more annoying than a form that keeps changing while you use it, even if that change was meant to prevent the visitor from making errors. After submitting the form, you can create a list of elements that have erroneous data and provide links pointing to the respective field. That way, keyboard, mouse,

10

and screen reader users can spot and reach the fields that need amending. This less dynamic way of validation also spares you assigning event handlers to each element, which might be a slow and memory-intense process, depending on the complexity of your form.

There are several ways to identify a form element that is mandatory or needs validation. You can have a list of mandatory element names in a hidden field, you can add a special CSS class to the fields that need to be validated, or you can just have a JavaScript array with all the field names. All options have the "double maintenance" issue.

Clever scripts maintain the validation rules in a shared back-end script that, depending on how it is triggered, writes out the necessary JavaScript or just validates what has been sent to the server. Examples of these are the PHP Pear package HTM_QuickForm (http://pear.php.net/manual/en/package.html.html-quickform.php) or Manuel Lemos's formsgeneration class (www.phpclasses.org/formsgeneration).

As you should tell the user, regardless of technology, which form field is a mandatory one, you could also reuse this information to tell your script which fields need its attention. You do rely on proper HTML in this case, but it seems to be the cleanest solution of them all. Let's say you have a name field. A common way to indicate that it is a mandatory field is to add an asterisk after the field and explain before the form starts that asterisks indicate a mandatory field.

```
<p>
    <label for="name">Your Name:</label>
    <input type="text" id="name" name="name" size="20" />
    <span class="mandatory">*</span>
</p>
```

Your validation script could now check all input, textarea, and select elements inside the form and test if their next sibling is a span with the CSS class mandatory. Then it could validate the field, checking for a value or the checked attribute, respectively, depending on whether the field is a text field or check box/radio button. Further validation rules could be applied depending on the field's ID.

If you want to use this functionality, make sure to keep a note of that in your web product's maintenance documents; otherwise, a web designer might change the location of the span and prevent your script from validating.

Summary

This chapter can only be a teaser of what JavaScript and the DOM have to offer and how it can clash with accessibility. Even the code examples here will change, and it is a good idea to revisit the book's homepage from time to time.

The following are some good JavaScript resources:

- The DOM Scripting Task Force (http://domscripting.webstandards.org/), which is always up-to-date on what needs to be done to use JavaScript in a modern fashion

- Unobtrusive JavaScript (www.onlinetools.org/articles/unobtrusivejavascript), a self-training course on unobtrusive JavaScript (which I wrote) and its follow up "From DHTML to DOM Scripting" (http://www.icant.co.uk/articles/from-dhtml-to-dom/), comparing the two methods by generating the same example in each method

- The Access Matters JavaScript section about event handlers (www.access-matters.com/results-for-javascript-part-1-navigating-links/)

- Sun and Mozilla's Accessible DHTML examples and tutorials (www.mozilla.org/access/dhtml/)

- *DOM Scripting: Web Design with JavaScript and the Domain Object Model* by Jeremy Keith (1-59059-533-5; friends of ED, 2005)

- My book, *Beginning JavaScript with DOM Scripting and Ajax* (1-59059-680-3; Apress, 2006)

10

11 ACCESSIBLE FLASH

by Bob Regan and Andrew Kirkpatrick

This chapter is for web designers who wish to make accessible, interactive rich media. It's a guide to creating accessible Adobe Flash content that assumes no previous knowledge of accessibility or assistive technology. This chapter covers the following topics:

- User requirements for users with disabilities
- The base set of technical requirements for developing accessible Flash content
- Key concepts common to computer programming that are relevant to developing accessible Flash content
- Best practices for creating accessible design in Flash

User Requirements

For many Flash designers, the single greatest challenge to understanding accessibility is how to best appreciate the experience of people with disabilities. Web designers' inherent talent is an ability to perceive the world in a unique visual way. The skill of web designers allows them to view, conceptualize, and translate visual information into layout and graphics. This is a fundamental and powerful way of seeing and understanding the world that should not be taken for granted.

First, we'll look at some of the key questions to ask to consider the user's perspective, and then we'll consider some use case scenarios in which fictional characters provide a framework for understanding users with disabilities.

Key Questions

To understand accessibility and implement it in practice is to ask designers to set their visual skills aside. The first thing to do when addressing accessibility is to step outside your frame of reference and consider the perspective of users with disabilities. Key questions such as the following arise:

- What are the specific issues that prevent users from accessing content?
- What are the tools used by people with disabilities to navigate the Internet?
- What techniques and interfaces are used to make working with the Web easier?

Use Case Scenarios

The following descriptions of fictional characters illustrate common issues for people with disabilities and may be helpful when planning your design project. The list is certainly not exhaustive but does illustrate the broad range of disabilities and highlights the unique issues, challenges, techniques, and tools associated with them. What is important here is that a consistent set of use case scenarios becomes an integral part of the plan, build, and test phases of your accessible Flash web design project.

John

John, 53, a user who is blind,

- Uses the Window-Eyes 5.0 screen reader
- Uses the keyboard exclusively for input and navigation
- Does not use the mouse
- Relies on audio cues to let him know if something has happened on the screen

John is a university professor who uses the computer for all of the same tasks as his colleagues, who are not visually impaired. He writes e-mail and research papers, and reviews student work.

John is part of a dance troupe in town and uses the Web extensively to read up on a wide range of topics. He is easygoing, most of the time, but he really finds it frustrating when websites of interest do not make their content accessible.

Ava

Ava, 30, a user who is visually impaired (with 20/300 vision),

- Relies heavily on the keyboard for input
- Uses a mouse, but only when she can't use the keyboard
- Uses ZoomText, a screen magnifier to receive information about Flash content
- Uses JAWS with ZoomText when there is a lot of text

Ava is a developer for a small consulting firm. She can see, but only with significant magnification or when objects are held very close. She uses the computer every day for work to review and write code for her clients. She uses ZoomText most of the time but will occasionally use a screen reader to read long text passages.

Ava loves music and is a fan of Stevie Wonder. Ironically, Stevie Wonder's site, a Flash site, is completely inaccessible. She has been waiting for the new album and checks the site from time to time for information but finds it frustrating that she is left out.

Jeff

Jeff, 22, a user who is color-blind,

- Needs visuals that are usable given specific color limitations

Like 10 percent of all men, Jeff is color-blind and cannot distinguish between certain colors. Generally, he does not have much trouble using the Web. However, trouble arises on sites where red buttons are placed on a green background, or where red and green buttons are next to one another to "start" and "stop" actions. This lack of contrast in foreground and background colors and red and green combinations can be frustrating for users who are color-blind.

11

Makoto

Makoto, 48, a user with a mobility impairment,

- Uses only the keyboard to navigate web content

Makoto was involved in an auto accident and lost the use of his hands. He relies on a mouth stick (a long stick in his mouth with a small rubber pointer tip on the end) to navigate web pages and applications via the keyboard. He uses the Tab and Enter keys to move between objects on the screen, as well as the Windows StickyKeys tool to create key combinations.

Makoto works at a local rehab center with other adults with disabilities. He uses his computer to complete paperwork for clients and file weekly reports. A devoted New York Yankees fan, Makoto takes a few minutes each day to check the online baseball scores. His favorite baseball page is The Sporting News. However, accessing this page can be a tedious experience due to the many navigational links he must tab through to get to the day's top stories.

Karen

Karen, 29, a user who is deaf,

- Receives information from the Flash content in a visual form

Deaf since birth, Karen is an art teacher at the local high school. She needs to maintain her teaching license. With two young children at home, Karen decided to take the required courses online. Accessing the course was no trouble for Karen; however, a problem arose concerning some instructional video content. While most of the videos used in the coursework contained closed captioning, a few did not. In the cases where no captioning was available, Karen had to request a full transcript from student services, which often took more than a week to be delivered. As a result, Karen fell behind in her course work.

Technical Requirements

Web accessibility can be broadly described as the capacity of any user, regardless of disability, to access the same content and information. With regard to accessible Flash web content, obstacles for users with disabilities have two sources: issues associated with design and issues associated with assistive technologies. In this section, we'll investigate the technical requirements and review assistive technologies. The next section discusses the techniques for successful, accessible Flash design.

Developers creating accessible Flash sites must design content to work with the following, as a minimum:

- Macromedia Flash Player 6 or later
- Windows 98, 2000, or XP
- Microsoft Internet Explorer 5 or later

- Screen readers:
  - GW Micro Window-Eyes 4.2 or later
  - Freedom Scientific JAWS 4.5, 6.1, or later
  - IBM Home Page Reader 3.04
  - Dolphin HAL 6.50
  - KDS PC Talker (Japan)

Flash Player Version

The release of Macromedia Flash MX and Flash Player 6 marked the first accessible versions of the Flash platform. This version of the player serves as a minimum requirement for accessible Flash content. The current version of the Flash Player is available at http://www.macromedia.com/software/flashplayer/.

Platform and Browser

All accessible Flash content must be tested on the Microsoft Windows platform. While there have been recent improvements to the Apple Mac OS X 10.4 release (Tiger), including a built-in screen reader called VoiceOver, the Flash Player does not support this screen reader.

All accessible Flash content must be tested using Microsoft Internet Explorer. At the time of writing, Internet Explorer was still the only browser to which the Flash Player exposes accessibility information. The Mozilla Project has made improvements with the Firefox browser, and now both JAWS and Window-Eyes users can use Firefox. However, the version of the Flash Player that runs in Firefox is not yet accessible.

Designers often question the wisdom of testing accessible content using only one browser and one platform. While the future of cross-platform and cross-browser accessibility looks promising (with the recent improvements made by Apple and Mozilla), the reality is that today, assistive technology users are almost exclusively using Windows with Internet Explorer. For now, designers should feel comfortable testing their content using only this configuration.

Screen Reader

As part of your development, production, and testing phases for accessible Flash content, you should rely on a minimum of one screen reader. While Flash content does not behave exactly the same in all screen readers, it is generally true that an application that functions properly in one screen reader will likely work in another. If you're designing an application with greater complexity or a wide range of users, you should plan to test using more than one screen reader.

11

Flash uses Microsoft Active Accessibility (MSAA) to deliver information about Flash movies to screen readers and other assistive technologies. MSAA operates as the go-between for the Flash Player and the screen reader. The Flash Player creates a list of objects on the screen and records them on the MSAA "data tree." The screen reader will then read this list as it encounters Flash content. As changes are made to the screen, the MSAA data tree is updated. Changes to the movie prompt the screen reader to return to the top of the movie and start reading through the list again.

By default, text objects in a Flash movie are read by screen readers. Screen readers are also able to identify buttons and movie clips with attached scripts. Screen readers, however, cannot look at a graphic element on the screen and determine its meaning. It is up to the designer to assign a text description of any graphic or animated elements in a Flash movie. This information can be assigned via either the Accessibility panel or ActionScript. Some properties, such as the `forceSimple` property (used to toggle the accessibility of child objects), have no counterpart in HTML. Designers will need to rely on information in this chapter as well as information found on the Adobe Accessibility Resource Center site (`www.adobe.com/accessibility/`) to learn more about these properties and the associated techniques.

Screen readers and MSAA shape the experience of Flash content for users with visual disabilities in ways that are often quite unfamiliar to sighted designers. Given that screen readers always start from the top of the movie and can read only one thing at a time, there are some complex forms of Flash content that simply cannot be made accessible. For example, many simulations require users to attend to several objects at the same time. Users must make decisions based on multiple factors and relay them back to the simulation quickly. This type of multitasking activity may be easy to do in the real world for someone who is blind, but can pose a real challenge while using a screen reader.

Key Concepts for Accessible Flash Design

For accessible design, you need to consider how users manipulate objects within Flash. User interaction is through controls. It is important to create accessible controls that work both in a technical sense (are accessible to a screen reader) and in a practical sense (controls that are familiar and work as expected). In other words, the user should be able to understand how a control functions without significant effort or help from someone else.

Flash allows designers to create simple objects that can be used as a number of different controls. Take this simple circle for example.

If we add a label and a script to this circle, it becomes a button.

Another slight change, and it becomes a slider.

Yet another alteration, and this same circle is now a dial.

Visually, it may be obvious what these controls are and how to operate them. However, to a screen reader user, it may not be apparent. For simple buttons, no extra effort is required. Yet as controls become increasingly sophisticated, additional information about the control is required.

This is where Flash accessibility begins to approach the accessibility of desktop applications. HTML offers only 12 different types of controls. The screen reader knows how to handle them, and an experienced screen reader user understands how the controls work. Windows has 76 different types of controls (such as sliders, spin buttons, and so on) and an infinite variety of custom objects. Some screen reader users may not understand how a complex control works, and combinations of controls can add greater levels of difficulty to an application.

Flash allows authors to create these types of controls in ways that other applications simply can't. While technologies such as Scalable Vector Graphics (SVG) and Ajax have generated interest in the past couple of years, work to develop accessible controls in Ajax has only just started. (See Chapter 4 for an overview of Ajax and SVG accessibility.) When accessibility is a priority, developers should use these technologies with care and in a manner that degrades gracefully, if at all possible.

11

Now, let's look at what makes an accessible control in a Flash movie, reviewing labels, roles, states, and structure. These will help you understand how a user with disabilities manipulates objects within Flash content.

Control Labels

The label for a control answers the question, "What is this thing?" Every control in a movie should have a label that describes the purpose of the control. Labels should be concise and read immediately before the control or together with the control. In this simple example, the label for the button is clearly displayed as text inside the button. It is important that the screen reader also reads the label.

When the label for a control is an icon, designers should provide a text equivalent for the label as a text equivalent for the button. For example, the following button shows a commonly used icon for "play." It is up to the designer to make sure this button has a label associated as a text equivalent.

If the function of the control changes, so should the label. The next example shows a pause button from a movie controller. Typically, play and pause are included in the same button. If the user chooses play, the button transforms to a pause button. As the user activates this button, the label should update as well.

Control Roles

The role of a control answers the question, "What does this thing do?" As shown previously, a simple control made of a circle can be a button, a slider, a dial, or any number of possibilities. Flash automatically assumes that if a script is attached to an object, that control is a button. The designer can formally specify a role in MSAA using the Flash component architecture. However, this is a significant amount of effort and well beyond the scope of all but the most complex development projects. Instead, the role can be exposed using simple text objects that provide hints to the user.

The role helps the user to understand how a control operates. If a control is defined as a combo box, then the users will naturally assume it will behave similarly to other combo boxes they have come across in the past. The role provides a quick and easy method of explaining to a user how a control is operated.

Control States

The state of a control answers the question, "Is this thing on or off?" or "Is it at level 1, 2, or 3?" and so on. Many controls have multiple settings. Think of a dial that sets a skill level in a game using this control:

In this case, there are three possible settings: level 1, level 2, and level 3. The position of the arrow lets us know visually that level 2 is selected. However, screen readers have no way of knowing anything about the arrow or how many levels are possible.

In controls with multiple settings, designers need to let the user know how many possible states exist for a control and what state is selected. In the game control example, you might use a text object or even the name property to read, "Level 2 of 3 is selected."

Control Structure

The structure of a control answers the question, "How does this thing relate to the other things on screen?" It is important that individual elements within a control not be read separately from the rest of the control. In Flash, this is generally a matter of controlling the reading order. In the example in the previous section, it is crucial that the designer ensure that the text "level 3" is read right after the text "level 2." In some cases, Flash reading order can get jumbled based on the position on screen. Mixing up elements of content and controls can result in a terribly confusing experience for the user.

Flash Accessibility Best Practices

When developing accessible Flash content, you should adhere to the following basic rules:

- Provide text equivalents
- Provide context
- Control reading order

11

- Control animation
- Ensure keyboard access
- Use progressive disclosure
- Enable component accessibility
- Provide captions
- Provide control over audio playback
- Use color wisely
- Support users with low vision
- Embed Flash accessibly

This list is not intended to be fixed, nor is it comprehensive. It is up to designers to make decisions about individual applications and whether they meet the requirements as outlined in the use case scenarios.

The following sections describe how to follow these best practices.

Provide Text Equivalents

Screen readers are not able to discern the meaning of graphic or animated elements on the stage. As a result, designers must provide a brief text description of graphic elements. You can provide text equivalents for an entire Flash movie, a single object within a movie, or a group of objects within a movie.

Providing Text Equivalents for an Entire Movie

You should provide text equivalents for an entire movie when the movie can be conveyed using a single text equivalent. Examples of this include movies that show a simple animation or banner ads. You also may need to do this for complex movies that cannot otherwise be made accessible.

When you use a single text equivalent for an entire movie, you should make the child objects inaccessible. This will prevent animations within the movie from causing frequent updates to the screen reader. It will also facilitate automated testing of the content for accessibility.

You can assign the text equivalent using the Accessibility panel. Place the text equivalent in the Name field. It is generally advisable to make the contents of the Name field short and focused in order to describe the function of the movie. The Description field can be used for longer descriptions. However, be aware that both JAWS and Window-Eyes read this content automatically rather than upon user request. As a result, long descriptions can result in a tedious listening experience.

Figure 11-1 shows the text equivalent "Moon orbiting a planet" in the Name field of the Accessibility panel, along with the movie to which the name applies.

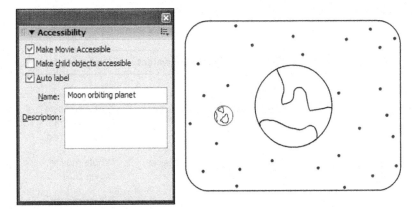

Figure 11-1. Assign text equivalents in the Name field in the Accessibility panel.

You can also provide a text equivalent using ActionScript, by creating a new object for each instance and then assigning the accessibility information. Once the name value has been assigned, the accessibility objects must be updated. This is done once for all objects when a change is made. It is not necessary to update each instance of the object. Here is an example of using ActionScript to provide a text equivalent:

```
_root._accProps = new Object();
_root._accProps.name = "Moon orbiting planet";
_root._accProps.forceSimple = true;
Accessibility.updateProperties();
```

> Adobe Flash Player 9 uses ActionScript 3, which includes some minor changes in the way that accessibility is handled. The _accProps object and global property are replaced by the AccessibilityProperties class and the accessibilityProperties property, but the usage is similar. For example, the preceding example would be written as follows:
>
> ```
> // assumes a movieclip with an instance name of 'moon_mc'
> moon_mc.accessibilityProperties = new AccessibilityProperties();
> moon_mc.accessibilityProperties.name = "Play";
> moon_mc.accessiblityProperties.forceSimple = true;
> Accessibility.updateProperties();
> ```
>
> Flash Player 9 is still capable of interpreting ActionScript 2 content, such as that created in Flash 8, but Flash 9 content will use ActionScript 3.

11

This example includes a line to create the new object for the entire movie. Next, the value is assigned for the `name` property, and then the child objects are made inaccessible using the `forceSimple` property. Table 11-1 shows a complete list of the ActionScript properties, along with the corresponding fields on the Accessibility panel.

Table 11-1. Accessibility Properties in ActionScript

Property	Type	Accessibility Panel Equivalent	Applicable Items
`silent`	Boolean	Make Movie Accessible/ Make Object Accessible (inverse logic)	Whole movies, buttons, movie clips, dynamic text, input text
`forceSimple`	Boolean	Make Child Objects Accessible (inverse logic)	Whole movies, movie clips
`name`	String	Name	Whole movies, buttons, movie clips, input text
`description`	String	Description	Whole movies, buttons, movie clips, dynamic text, input text

Making Objects Inaccessible

Unlike HTML, not every movie clip or button in a Flash movie requires a text equivalent. For example, elements that are purely decorative, are repetitive, or convey no content should be made inaccessible.

You can make a movie clip "silent," or inaccessible, through the Accessibility panel by deselecting the Make Object Accessible option, as shown in Figure 11-2. This is the Flash equivalent of a purely decorative image in HTML that requires a null `alt` attribute value.

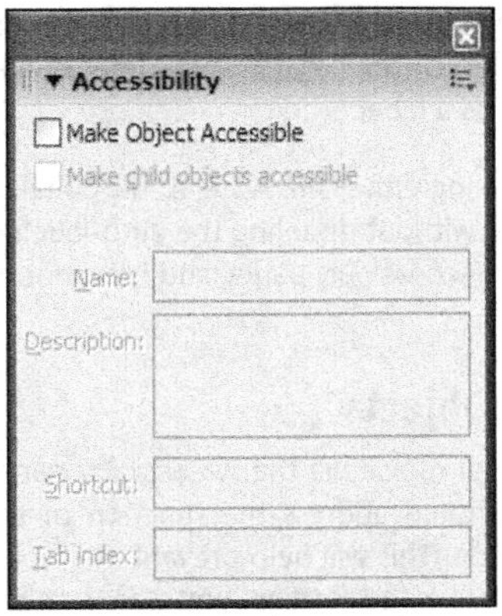

Figure 11-2. Deselect the Make Object Accessible option in the Accessibility panel for elements that should remain silent.

To set the object to be inaccessible with ActionScript, use the silent property, as in this example:

```
logo_mc._accProps = new Object();
logo_mc._accProps.silent = true;
Accessibility.updateProperties();
```

Using Auto-Labeling

Flash includes an Auto Label option, as shown in Figure 11-3. If a text object is used within a button, the Flash Player will assume that text object is the label for the button. The same holds true for movie clips used as buttons. In these cases, the child objects of the movie clip *should be* accessible. It is important to keep in mind that only a single text object can be used as a label, and the text object must fit completely within the hit area of the button.

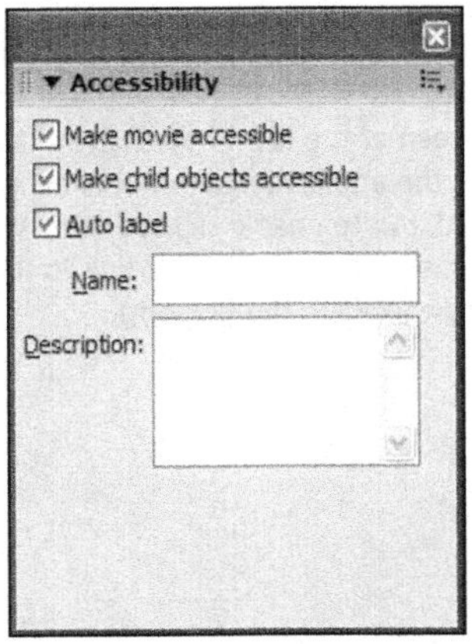

Figure 11-3. The Accessibility panel includes an Auto Label option.

Auto-labeling also works for movie components such as radio buttons and list boxes. The Flash Player will assume text objects above or to the left of the control should be used as the label. Again, only a single text object will be used as a label.

If a text equivalent is assigned via the name property using either the Accessibility panel or ActionScript, that value will override the auto-labeling without disabling the auto-labeling completely. You can turn off auto-labeling only via the Accessibility panel, and it cannot be changed dynamically once set.

Assigning Text Equivalents for Single Objects

You can assign a text equivalent for a single object in a movie via the Accessibility panel. The text equivalent should be relatively short and should address the function of the object, rather than a longer or more detailed description. This will help prevent the movie from becoming verbose and tedious to navigate. As noted earlier, you can use the Description field for longer descriptions. However, JAWS and Window-Eyes will both read this field by default. As a result, there is no advantage to using this field at this time.

Provide Context

Screen readers are not able to provide clues to a screen reader user about the layout or structure of a Flash movie, or about individual controls within that movie. Complex movies should provide descriptions about the movie itself, as well as about its important parts and controls. Determining when a movie is sufficiently complex to merit a description or when a control requires additional cues is up to each designer.

Describing the Movie

You should provide a description of the movie at the root level to let the user know what the movie or application is about. This description should help the user get oriented to the application quickly and understand the key controls and shortcuts used.

You can provide the movie description in a number of ways. For example, you might place it on a separate screen in the Flash movie or on a separate HTML page. If you use an HTML page, you should place a link to the information screen at the top of the page in a button titled site info. Using this short title will help prevent the application from becoming overly verbose. This site info button can be hidden if desired, but to enable sighted users with disabilities to access the same information, it is recommended that a second link to the same information be placed elsewhere on the screen (most likely at the bottom).

Exposing State

Flash allows designers to create an infinite variety of controls. In cases where the user is provided visual cues about the state of a control or a screen within the movie, this information should also be made available via a dynamic text field that is updated as the control is activated.

Consider the example shown in Figure 11-4. In this case, the movie uses tabs that drop down to indicate which screen is the active screen. While this is a helpful visual cue, this information is not available to screen reader users with standard Flash content (there are tab navigator components in Adobe Flex that do expose information correctly to screen readers).

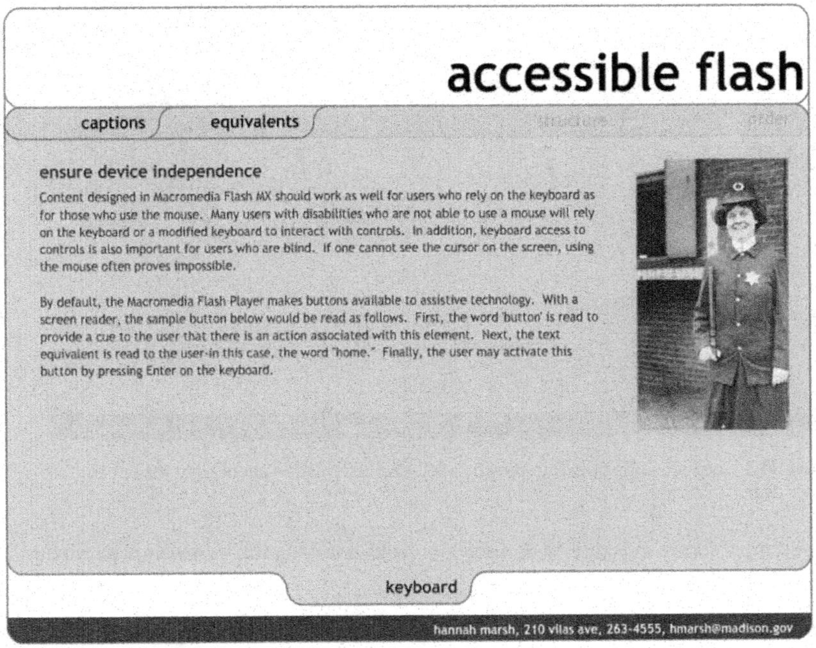

Figure 11-4. Visual clues, such as tabs, to expose state do not work with screen readers.

To provide a cue for the screen reader user, a text field is hidden under the banner (see the circled area in Figure 11-5, where the hidden text is made available). Since it is intended to provide information for screen reader users, it does not need to be visible. As the user moves between screens, the contents of this field can reflect the active screen.

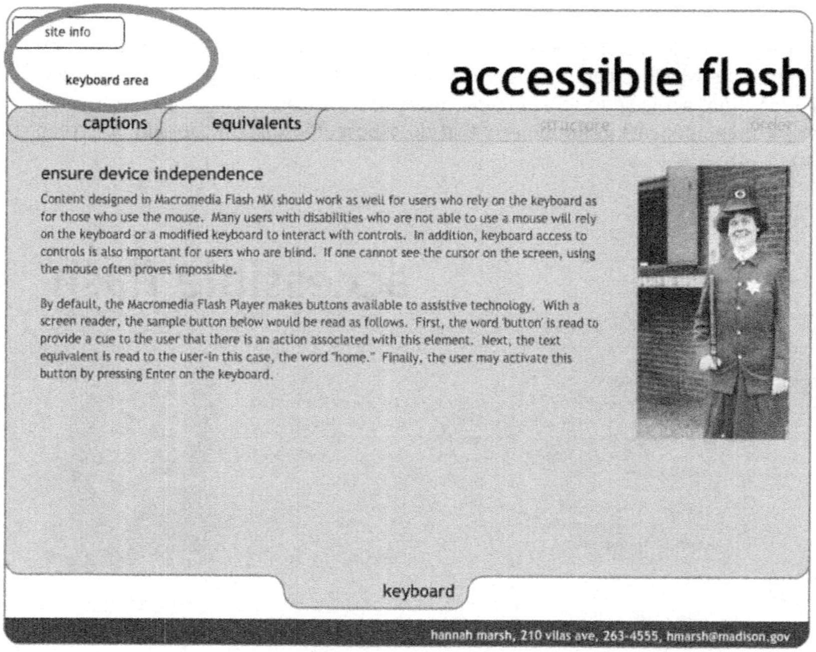

Figure 11-5. Use hidden text fields to provide additional information about state for screen reader users.

In the example shown in Figure 11-5, a screen reader accessing this as a web page would read the following:

- Accessible Flash
- Site info button
- Keyboard area
- Captions button
- Equivalents button

Within each area of the site, the text keyboard area will update to reflect the active area.

Control Reading Order

The default reading order of a Flash movie does not follow a predictable left-to-right, top-to-bottom order. As a result, contents of a Flash movie can be difficult to understand. Take the example shown in Figure 11-6. Based on the visual presentation of the alphabet in three rows, it would be natural to expect the reading order to follow alphabetical order.

Figure 11-6. You might expect the reading order to be alphabetical.

However, the actual reader order jumps between letters in each row. The resulting order illustrated in Figure 11-7 shows why you need to control the reading and tab order for Flash movies.

Figure 11-7. Actual reading order

With the release of Adobe Flash Player 8, handling issues with the reading order has been significantly simplified. In previous releases, a designer had to specify values for all objects in a movie. Missing one would cause the reading order to revert to the default. This made setting the reading order a tedious and time-intensive task. In Flash Player 8, the reading order can be partially specified. You need to list only the objects that you want to control. The remaining objects will follow the default reading order after the specified values.

It is still important to consider the reading order of a movie from the beginning of the development process. It is certainly more work to retrofit for proper reading order after the movie has been completely built. Therefore, using a screen reader to evaluate the movie during an ongoing development process can definitely make finding and fixing problems much easier.

11

Reflecting the Screen Structure

The key to creating an appropriate reading order is to ensure that the order reflects the structure of the screen. At a high level, the elements of the screen should be reading in a reasonable and consistent order from one screen to the next. For example, you would expect that the title of the site would be followed by the navigation, followed by the content. Placing the title of the application at the end of the reading order might create confusion.

The reading order should also ensure that elements from each of these higher level groups are not mixed together. For example, the title of the application should not be read between buttons on the navigation bar or pieces of the content on screen. To extend this concept, buttons at one level of a navigation bar should not be read mixed in with buttons on the next level.

You can use two strategies to control reading order. The simplest is to keep the physical size of the movie small. A small Flash movie that is less than 300 pixels wide and consists of a single column or a single row of objects usually will not require any specific control over the reading order. Examples might include small animations or applications that pop up in a separate window, a navigation bar that consists of a single row, or an application that consists of a single column. The second strategy requires controlling the reading order using the Accessibility panel or ActionScript.

Using Tab Index Values

The most precise means for controlling reading order is to use tab index values, which you can assign using the Accessibility panel or ActionScript. Using the Accessibility panel, you simply assign each object a value that reflects the desired reading order, as shown in the example in Figure 11-8. Objects within a Flash movie that are assigned a tab index value are then placed at the end of the reading order, following the default order.

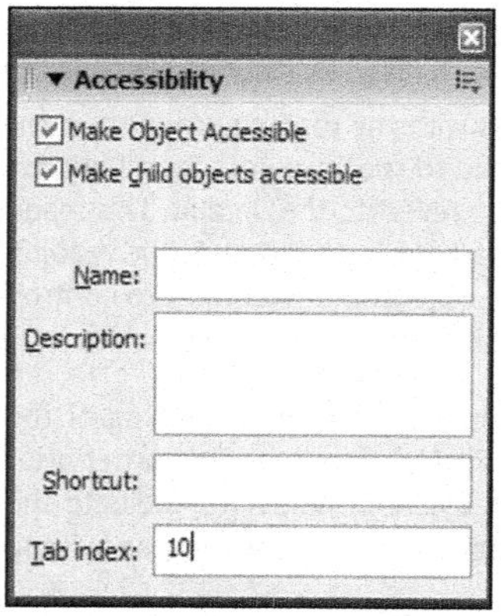

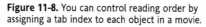

Figure 11-8. You can control reading order by assigning a tab index to each object in a movie.

Tab index values need not be sequential. In fact, the order should usually *not* be sequential, to allow designers to add objects into the movie at a later time. Intervals of 10 should be sufficient.

Assigning a Reading Order Using ActionScript

In cases where the reading order is dynamic or objects are created on the fly, you will need to use ActionScript to assign tab index values. All objects in ActionScript have a tabIndex property. You do not need to create an accessibility object to assign a tab index value.

Consider the simple example shown in Figure 11-9, which has three circles with the text Third, Second, and First displayed on screen.

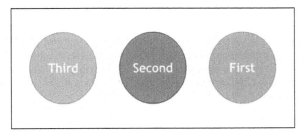

Figure 11-9. An example for reversing the reading order

When the following ActionScript is added to the movie, the reading order reverses to read First, Second, Third.

```
first_mc.first_txt.tabIndex = 10;
second_mc.second_txt.tabIndex = 20;
third_mc.third.txt.tabIndex = 30;
```

In general, it is best practice to place the ActionScript controlling the reading order at the root level of the movie in the first frame. This makes it easy to locate the code when changes are needed and ensures that the script is loaded at the very start of the movie.

When controlling the reading order using ActionScript, the tabIndex property value must be assigned to the text object itself, not to the parent. In the example, the tabIndex property is assigned to the text objects in the circle movie clips. The values of the parent are not inherited by the child. Thus, assigning the tabIndex property values to the circles would not result in the reversed reading order.

It is not possible to provide an instance name to static text objects. As a result, it is not possible to assign a .tabIndex property to a static text object, so you cannot control the reading order of static text objects.

In cases that do require precise control over the reading order, designers are encouraged to use dynamic text objects. This will have implications for the font used in the application and potentially impact the overall file size. To learn more about handling font symbols in Flash, visit www.adobe.com/cfusion/knowledgebase/index.cfm?id=tn_15403.

In cases where a series of child SWF files are loaded into a parent movie, the list of tabindex values must be listed in the child movie clip. However, the values list in the reading order of each child SWF must be unique. For example, if two child movies are loaded into a parent movie, and each has three elements with tabindex values of 1, 2, and 3, the

11

screen reader will read the first value of the first movie loaded, then the first value of the second movie loaded. Next, the screen reader will read the second value of the first movie clip loaded, then the second value of the second movie clip loaded, and so on. In order to read the contents of the first movie followed by the contents of the second movie, the list of `tabindex` values for the first movie should be 1, 2, 3 while the list of values for the second move should be 4, 5, 6. These values do not need to be sequential, but they should be unique.

Removing Objects from the Reading Order

You may want to hide elements from the user and remove them from the reading order temporarily. Realize that objects placed behind another object or tucked just off stage are not necessarily removed from the reading order. Screen readers have no concept of whether one object is in front of another or whether it is just barely on stage or completely off stage. You need to more formally hide objects if you wish to remove them from the reading order.

The easiest means of removing an object from the reading order is to move it completely off the stage. The bounding rectangle of the object needs to be more than 1 pixel off the stage. Even if the visible object itself is off the stage, the bounding rectangle is what matters. Consider the example shown in Figure 11-10. Circle One is off the stage. However, you can see that the blue bounding rectangle is still on the stage. As a result, this object will be read by the screen reader. Circle Two's bounding rectangle is completely off the stage, and this object will not be read by the screen reader.

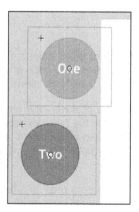

Figure 11-10. The bounding rectangle of the object needs to be more than 1 pixel off the stage to remove the object from the reading order.

A more formal way to make sure a screen reader does not read an object is to set the `_visible` property to false or the silent property to true.

Referring back to this example in Figure 11-9, the circles labeled Third and Second can be temporarily removed from the reading order by using the `_visible` property, as follows:

```
second_mc._visible = false;
third_mc._visible = false;
```

When the `_visible` property is set to false, the circles are not read by the screen reader. However, they are not visible either.

Using the silent property ensures that the screen reader will not read these objects without affecting the visibility of these objects.

```
second_mc.silent = true;
third_mc.silent = true;
```

Detecting Screen Readers

Since this case is intended to benefit screen reader users alone, this method is frequently used in conjunction with screen reader detection. Flash has a unique advantage over JavaScript in that it is able to use MSAA to detect the presence of a screen reader. The method Accessibility.isActive() will return a value of true if a screen reader is present and it is currently focused on the Flash content. It is important that this method not be called in the first moments in the timeline of the movie, or it could return a false negative. Rather than calling this method in the first frame of a movie, one strategy is to attach this method to the first button in the movie.

Control Animation

While Flash is now much more than an animation tool, it is still commonly used to create and deliver animations for a variety of purposes. Three key issues to consider when using animations in Flash are hiding child objects, avoiding constant motion, and avoiding blinking.

Constant changes to the screen can cause a screen reader to refresh continually. This can be very frustrating to screen reader users when they are trying to read through content and the screen reader is repeatedly returning to the top of the page. To prevent constant screen reader refreshes, hide the child objects of the movie clips that contain animation. This can be accomplished via the Accessibility panel by deselecting Make Child Objects Accessible. Using ActionScript, set the forceSimple property to true to hide the child object.

Avoid constant motion on the screen when the user is expected to read text on the screen. For users with certain learning and cognitive disabilities, moving objects or patterns on the screen can be a distraction. It is acceptable to use motion together with text, but the screen must settle after a moment or two.

You should also avoid blinking for more than a second across a large viewable area of the screen. Photosensitive epilepsy can be triggered by blinking at specific rates if viewed at close quarters across a significant portion of one's field of vision. There is no way to predict a flicker rate precisely because it is dependent on the end user's machine. Subsequently, it is important to avoid flicker completely.

Ensure Keyboard Access

All controls that can be manipulated via the mouse should also be accessible via the keyboard. This is intended to support screen reader users as well as users with mobility impairments. The Flash Player facilitates keyboard access on its own by automatically making mouse-defined events accessible via the keyboard. However, two specific techniques

11

commonly used among Flash designers should be avoided. In addition, you should add keyboard shortcuts to facilitate keyboard access in complex applications. Finally, designers should be aware of an issue with the Flash Player 6 and earlier in pages that blend HTML and Flash content.

Avoiding Techniques That Prevent Access

Consider the following script that might be used to open a web page:

```
on (click) {
    getURL(index.html);
}
```

It is directly associated with the instance of the movie clip used as a button. This script should instead be placed in a frame, likely the first frame, of the movie. The revised script could be as follows:

```
home_mc.onRelease = function () {
    getURL(index.html);
}
```

Another common technique is to use hit areas, which are empty button clips with a shape defined in the hit state. These allow designers to reuse single library objects repeatedly by placing them over text objects and varying only the scripts used. However, screen readers may find a problem with this technique. The screen reader assumes that if the button clip up state is empty, then it is not a button at all. The solution to this issue is quite simple. By placing a transparent movie clip in the up state, screen readers will recognize the button and allow the user to activate it.

Assigning Keyboard Shortcuts

In complex applications with multiple controls, it is extremely helpful for users to navigate the application using keyboard shortcuts. For many users with mobility impairments, pressing keys may be very difficult. Using keyboard shortcuts helps reduce the number of keystrokes required to perform important tasks.

Using the Shortcut field on the Accessibility panel or the shortcut property in ActionScript is not sufficient for this purpose. Creating a keyboard shortcut requires you to define a listener event and associate a script with that listener. The Shortcut field merely announces a shortcut value via MSAA. It does not create the listener. Moreover, as of this writing, no screen readers support this feature.

Use Progressive Disclosure

One of the greatest challenges for screen reader and keyboard users in navigating a complex site is moving from the top of the screen to the content they are trying to access. Sites with numerous controls or links can result in a time-consuming and tedious experience for the user. As a result, the best user interface for someone who relies on a screen reader or a keyboard is one that is very narrow, offering a limited number of options at the top and increasingly more as the user drills down.

A tactic increasingly used in Flash content is to hide multiple controls under a single control. As the user requests more information, additional controls are progressively revealed to the user. For example, consider the control shown in Figure 11-11. A phone with many buttons is placed near the top of a Flash application. Quite a few key presses would be required to get past it. If it reappears on other screens, then it would require additional key presses on each of these screens just to progress further.

Figure 11-11. A complex control with many buttons

To reduce the complexity of this control, the phone object is grouped into a single movie clip with the name property Pick up Phone. By default, the silent property for each of the buttons is set to true. The screen reader user hears only one button.

If the user presses the button to pick up the phone, four things happen:

- The individual buttons are exposed.
- The Pick up Phone button is temporarily hidden.
- All of the other content on screen outside the phone is hidden. This allows the user to focus on just the phone for a brief period of time.
- A slight change is made to the Hang Up button. It not only disconnects the call, but it reverts the phone to its default state, hiding the individual buttons, revealing the Pick up Phone button and exposing other content on screen.

The advantage of this technique is that it allows designers to create interfaces that are narrow for users with disabilities without making significant changes to the layout. In general, this technique can be applied quickly with a few extra lines of code. The only consideration is how to use movie clips to strategically group objects and facilitate the showing and hiding of content.

Enable Component Accessibility

With the release of Macromedia Flash MX 2004, the following accessible components were included with the application:

- Simple Button
- Check Box
- Radio Button

11

- Label
- Text Input
- Text Area
- Combo Box
- List Box
- Window
- Alert
- Data Grid

For each component, you can enable the accessibility object by using the command enableAccessibility(). This includes the accessibility object with the component as the movie is compiled. Because there is no simple means of removing an object once it has been added to the component, these options are turned off by default. It is therefore very important that you enable accessibility for each component. This step needs to be done only once for each component; it is not necessary to enable accessibility for each instance of a component. Here is the sample code added for the Label component:

```
import mx.accessibility.LabelAccImpl;
LabelAccImpl.enableAccessibility();
```

Again, this code is added only once for each component. It is best to attach this script to the first frame in the movie to ensure that the script is executed immediately and for easy access. The code required for each of the components is shown in Table 11-2.

Table 11-2. Code to Enable Accessibility for Components

Component	Code
Simple Button	`import mx.accessibility.ButtonAccImpl;` `ButtonAccImpl.enableAccessibility();`
Check Box	`import mx.accessibility.CheckBoxAccImpl;` `CheckBoxAccImpl.enableAccessibility();`
Radio Button	`import mx.accessibility.RadioButtonAccImpl;` `RadioButtonAccImpl.enableAccessibility();`
Label	`import mx.accessibility.LabelAccImpl;` `LabelAccImpl.enableAccessibility();`
Combo Box	`import mx.accessibility.ComboBoxAccImpl;` `ComboBoxAccImpl.enableAccessibility();`

Component	Code
List Box	`import mx.accessibility.ListAccImpl;` `ListAccImpl.enableAccessibility();`
Window	`import mx.accessibility.WindowAccImpl;` `WindowAccImpl.enableAccessibility();`
Alert	`import mx.accessibility.AlertAccImpl;` `AlertAccImpl.enableAccessibility();`
Data Grid	`import mx.accessibility.DataGridAccImpl;` `DataGridAccImpl.enableAccessibility();`

No additional code is required for the text input and text area components. The player implements the accessibility for these components automatically.

There is a known bug with screen readers and Flash Player 7. Information following the Combo Box, List Box, and Data Grid components is not passed on to screen readers without entering forms mode.

Provide Captions

Flash is frequently used to deliver audio and video content. Any audio used to deliver substantive content should include a synchronized text equivalent in the form of captions. Three key strategies for including captions are by importing previously captioned audio content, by placing text objects directly on the stage, or by streaming caption data via XML.

Importing Captioned Content

A simple if rather limited approach to captioning in Flash is to import content that has been captioned in another application. The limitation of this solution is that it restricts the design options and flexibility of the application. By building the caption tool directly into Flash, the designer has an increased number of options in terms of formatting and the user interface.

Placing Text Directly on the Stage

A second strategy for captioning Flash content relies on placing text objects directly on the stage. This method is the most precise in terms of synchronizing audio content with the captions, yet it is the most tedious in terms of the effort required on the part of the designer. One particular advantage of this method is that it allows for captions to be positioned on the stage to indicate different speakers, as well as to convey emphasis and emotion.

11

Using third-party tools, you can deliver captions by placing text objects directly on the stage. The single greatest challenge in delivering captions is creating the transcript of the audio. While voice-recognition software has improved tremendously, it still is not a reliable means of converting speech to text automatically.

Once the transcript is available, three commonly used tools for creating captions are Captionate from the Manitu Group (http://buraks.com/captionate/), Hi-Caption SE from Hi-Software (www.adobe.com/products/flash/extensions/hicaption/), and MAGpie from the National Center for Accessible Media (http://ncam.wgbh.org/webaccess/ magpie/). These tools help designers break the transcript into individual screens of text and then set the timing for each of those screens. Hi-Caption SE has the additional advantage of being able to convert this information directly into text objects on the timeline. This is particularly useful in situations where use of XML can result in sandbox violations, such as a Macromedia Breeze presentation.

Streaming XML Caption Data

A straightforward means of delivering caption data in a Flash movie is to stream caption data at runtime. This is possible with both Hi-Caption SE and MAGpie. Both create a custom XML file with caption data that Flash can use. This file strips down XML data included in captioning standards such as Synchronized Accessible Media Interchange (SAMI) for improved performance in the Flash Player.

Hi-Caption SE includes a component that imports this XML file and delivers it via a prebuilt closed-captioning interface. The designer may modify the look and feel of the icon as well as the text used to deliver the captions. MAGpie requires that the developer write code to parse and display the caption data themselves.

Captionate doesn't operate by adding text to the stage or by streaming XML caption data. Rather, it uses Flash Video (FLV) file cue points to display caption information at predefined times.

Provide Control Over Audio Playback

Music and audio that play as the site loads present a serious challenge to screen reader users. The audio from a Flash movie can interfere with the end user's ability to hear the contents of a movie using a screen reader. Therefore, you should make sure that the user is given control over when music is played.

The simplest strategy for handling audio playback is simply to allow the end user to control audio with play and pause buttons, as shown in Figure 11-12. Allowing the end user to initiate audio provides the experience of the audio without creating additional hurdles.

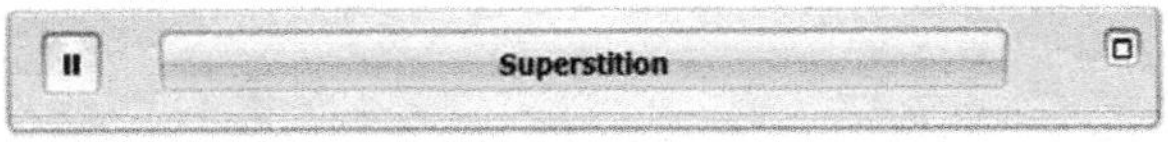

Figure 11-12. Provide play and pause buttons to give users control over audio playback.

A more advanced strategy for controlling playback relies on the use of keyboard shortcuts. Providing global keystrokes that allow the user to control the audio can greatly enhance the experience for end users. Here are several controls to consider:

- **Play/Pause:** Play and pause are typically controlled using a single keystroke, such as the letter *P*, as a toggle. The first time the button is pressed, the audio starts to play. The second time the button is pressed, the audio is paused.

- **Mute:** A mute control, such as the letter *M* or the number 0, silences but does not stop the audio. This provides the screen reader user the opportunity to listen to the screen reader temporarily without stopping the audio.

- **Volume:** Volume controls allow the user to quietly play the audio in the background while still listening to the screen reader. This is most appropriate in cases where the audio does not require the focused attention of the user, as in the case of a music stream.

Use Color Wisely

When you're selecting from the wide range of colors available to Flash designers, you must consider issues for people with color deficits and low vision. This means that color should not be the sole means of providing information. For example, you should never say, "Click the red button to move forward and the green button to move back." It is acceptable to reference color, but a second indicator should be used at the same time. The same example would be fine if you added a reference to position as well, "Click the red button on the right to go forward and the green button on the left to go back."

A second issue related to the use of color is to ensure that foreground and background colors have sufficient contrast to ensure readability. One way to think of this is by asking the question, "If the application were displayed on a black-and-white television, would the colors be readable?" Colors that lack contrast can make it very challenging to read elements on the page.

11

A helpful tool in making decisions about the use of color is the ColorDoctor from Fujitsu, shown in Figure 11-13. This free tool simulates grayscale as well as three different types of color blindness. The ColorDoctor can be found at http://design.fujitsu.com/en/universal/assistance/colordoctor/.

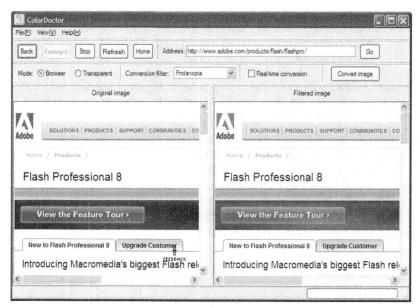

Figure 11-13. The ColorDoctor is helpful for making color decisions.

Support Users with Low Vision

One of the most complicated situations in accessible Flash design is that of a person with low vision who does not rely on the use of a screen magnifier. Users with moderate to severe low vision rely on the use of a screen magnifier to view content on the screen. Magnifiers, such as ZoomText from AI Squared, not only make the contents of the screen larger but also move the point of focus to the center of the screen to make working with content easier. Many magnifiers also include functionality that allows users to view content in a variety of contrast modes and include screen reader functionality. Screen magnifiers are based on very similar technologies to screen readers. As a result, content that reads well in a screen reader will also tend to read well with a screen magnifier.

However, many people with low vision do not rely on screen magnifiers but instead use the browser settings to change the font size. The Adobe Flash Player does not currently support browser settings for font size. As a result, designers need to take additional steps to consider and support users with low vision. Applications built in Flash should incorporate options that allow users to modify the text size of an application when possible. The simple example shown in Figure 11-14 demonstrates one technique. It allows the user to globally increase the text size from 12 points to 18 points by clicking a button on the homepage of the application.

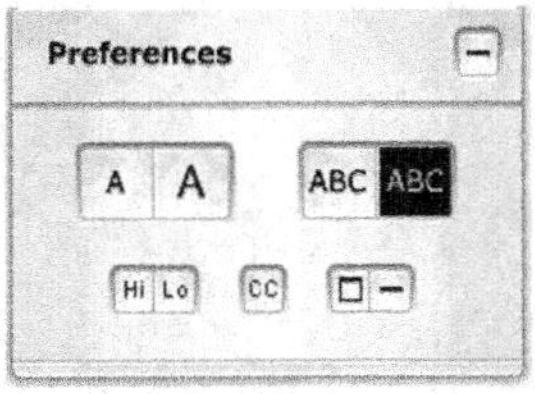

Figure 11-14. Allow users to modify text size.

Embed Flash Accessibly

Several strategies exist to include Flash in a web page. The Flash authoring tool uses a tried-and-true method that employs an HTML object element with an HTML embedded element inside the object as a fallback for browsers that don't support the object. Some developers dislike this approach because it breaks page validation, but the alternatives all have shortcomings. Drew McLellan popularized an approach he titled Flash Satay (www.alistapart.com/articles/flashsatay/), which produces valid code, but has the unfortunate limitation of not working for JAWS screen reader users due to a limitation of JAWS. A comparison of the various techniques is available at http://weblogs. macromedia.com/accessibility/archives/2005/08/in_search_of_a.cfm.

Another issue to be aware of is when using the wmode parameter in the object element. There are three settings for wmode: window (the default), transparent, and opaque. The Flash Player sends information to screen readers only when wmode is set to window. If you need the Flash to be accessible, don't specify the wmode parameter at all, or use <param name="wmode" value="window" />.

Summary

If you are a web designer new to Flash accessibility, it is best to keep in mind that the biggest challenge to creating accessible rich media may not be the technical aspect, but rather the mental. Understanding how people with disabilities use web applications and what makes a great web experience requires designers to revisit their assumptions about user interfaces and interactivity. Designers must create and revisit their use case scenarios regularly, while continuing to test and review using assistive technologies. Getting to know and understand these use cases will help designers develop the instincts they need to build applications that are not only accessible but truly usable for people with disabilities.

The techniques reflected in this chapter are neither technically advanced nor aesthetically challenging. Building a great Flash movie depends on designers developing an instinct for how all users, including those with disabilities, use content and making sound design and development decisions along the way.

For more information, refer to the Adobe Accessibility Resource Center at www.adobe.com/accessibility/ and the accessibility blog at http://blogs.adobe.com/ accessibility/.

11

12 PDF ACCESSIBILITY

by Andrew Kirkpatrick

Adobe Portable Document Format (PDF) is a popular format for publishing and delivering documents on the Web. Authors like to use PDF because PDF document creation is simple, the format preserves the appearance of the original document for printing and viewing, and it offers additional security on the document contents. Unfortunately, many authors deliver documents in PDF because of the ease of creating the file, and often the file is created without regard to accessibility. However, PDF documents can be highly accessible to users with various disabilities, sometimes with little additional effort on the part of the document author.

The single largest drawback to PDF is that authors need to focus additional attention on the document to ensure accessibility. Fortunately, Adobe Reader is getting better at analyzing and repairing PDF documents that lack accessibility information, but the need for the author to attend to accessibility remains important. The most important ingredients of an accessible PDF are a well-structured, well thought-out source document and the correct settings on the program used to create the PDF from the source document.

In this chapter, you will learn how users with disabilities can use PDF documents and how to create accessible PDF documents. The intent of this chapter is not to provide information about every possible method of authoring and viewing PDF files, but to focus on authoring and remediating PDF documents for accessibility. For most examples and discussion, I'll be referring to Adobe Reader 7.0, Adobe Acrobat 7.0 Professional, and the Adobe Acrobat PDFMaker plug-in for Microsoft Word (and to a lesser extent, Acrobat 6.0 and Adobe InDesign CS2). Unfortunately, the accessibility story for PDF creation largely centers around Adobe's own products. As of the time of writing, only two non-Adobe products (Open Office and the Microsoft Office 12 beta) are able to create PDF documents with tags.

Accessibility Features in Adobe Reader

Adobe Reader offers a significant amount of support for users with a variety of disabilities. Some features enable an author to provide more accessible content, but others require little or no effort from the author and are available for the user if needed.

Changing Document Colors

Many users benefit from the ability to adjust colors used to display documents. Adobe Reader provides a means to modify colors used within a PDF in the Accessibility section of the Preferences dialog box, as shown in Figure 12-1.

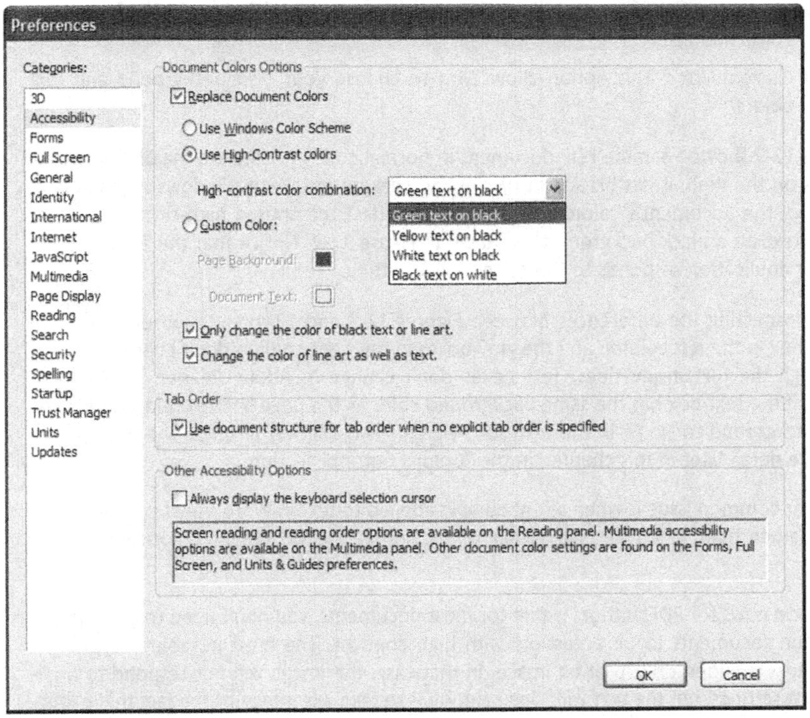

Figure 12-1. The Accessibility section of the Adobe Reader Preferences dialog box

When you check the Replace Document Colors check box in the Document Colors Options group, you have three choices of how Adobe Reader should effect the change:

- Use Windows Color Scheme: Adobe Reader will use the settings in the Windows Accessibility Control Panel. To modify the display setting, select the Display tab in the Accessibility Options dialog box and check Use High Contrast. Several styles are available in the Settings for High Contrast dialog box, as shown in Figure 12-2. This option is available only in the Windows version of Adobe Reader.

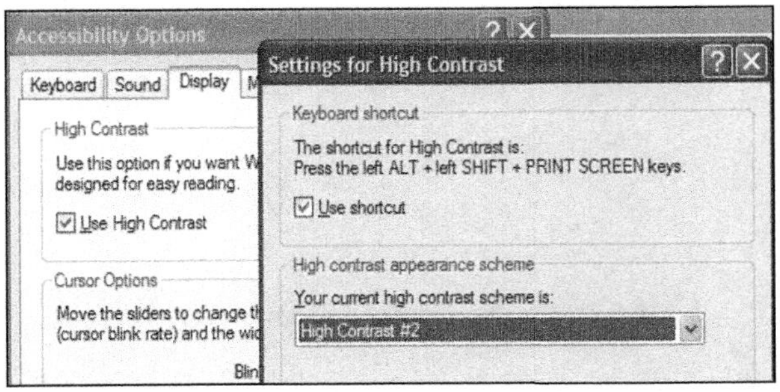

Figure 12-2. Windows Settings for High Contrast dialog box

- Use High-Contrast colors: This option allows you to choose from a few high-contrast combinations.
- Custom Color: This option allows you to choose your own background and text colors.

Figure 12-3 shows a sample PDF document in normal contrast. Like the majority of documents on the Web, it has black text on a white background. With Windows high contrast enabled, the document's colors are modified to reflect the chosen high-contrast style of green text on a black background, as shown in Figure 12-4. Notice that the entire Adobe Reader application responds to this system-wide setting.

Upon inspecting the differences between Figures 12-3 and 12-4, you'll observe that the white box in the left column and the gray boxes in the right column don't change in color, although the text inside does. Text boxes don't change in Adobe Reader. In Microsoft Word, if the text box has the same background color as the page background, set the text box background to No Fill in the text box's Borders and Shading settings. This is discussed in more detail later in this chapter, in the "Color Contrast" section.

Another common issue is when a font color is applied to text in Word. Any text with a font color other than Automatic will retain that color in the document color-replacement process.

The good news for PDF authors is that for most documents, you don't need to do anything for your documents to be accessible with high contrast. The most notable exception is when text is added on top of an image. In that case, the image will not respond to high-contrast settings, but the text will. One solution is to take advantage of the fact that explicitly colored text in Word doesn't change color and to apply a high-contrast color in Word (something that you would probably do anyway when placing text over an image). Another possible solution is to make the text part of the image and add the text to the image's Alternative Text field, which we'll review later in this chapter, in the "Images" section. The main downside to this second solution comes into play when the document is resized, which we'll examine next.

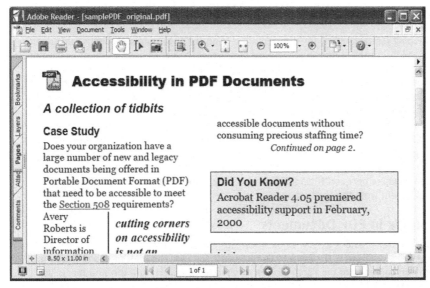

Figure 12-3. A sample document with normal contrast

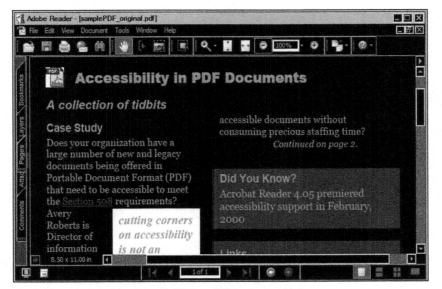

Figure 12-4. A sample document with Windows high contrast enabled

12

Resizing Documents

Developing digital content for users who are blind tends to dominate discussions about accessibility, but this is due to the level of involvement required by the authors and is not proportional to the prevalence of blind users. In fact, users who can see but prefer to increase the size of the content are far more numerous. A 2003 Forrester Research report (*The Market for Accessible Technology—The Wide Range of Abilities and Its Impact on Computer Use*, www.microsoft.com/enable/research/phase1.aspx) found that 16 percent, or 27 million, working-age adults have mild visual difficulties or impairments; 11 percent, or 18.5 million, working-age adults have severe visual difficulties or impairments; and among computer users in the same group, about 25 percent have some form of visual difficulty or impairment. Given how ubiquitous PDF documents are, it seems safe to assume that somewhere between 16 and 27 percent of the working-age readers of your document would benefit from the ability to increase the size of the text.

Zooming in PDF Documents

Adobe Reader provides a very simple zooming feature. By using the keyboard shortcuts Ctrl++ (plus) and Ctrl+- (hyphen) to increase and decrease the level of zoom, selecting a zoom percentage from the Zoom toolbar, or choosing Zoom To from the View menu, users can magnify a PDF until the text is a readable size.

Figure 12-5 shows the sample PDF document with the zoom level set to 200 percent. Since the whole document is being zoomed, even scanned text and images of text get larger, although these types of text will suffer pixelation issues at high zoom levels.

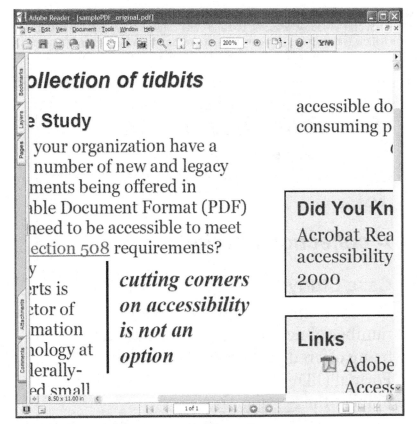

Figure 12-5. A sample document zoomed to 200 percent

Eliminating Horizontal Scrolling

Zooming often renders a document substantially less readable because it introduces the need to scroll in two dimensions as lines of text stretch off the left and right page margins, as you can see in the zoomed example in Figure 12-5. Adobe Reader offers a feature called Reflow, which the user can activate by selecting Reflow from the View menu.

Zoom To...	Ctrl+M
Actual Size	Ctrl+1
Fit Page	Ctrl+0
Fit Width	Ctrl+2
Fit Visible	Ctrl+3
Reflow	Ctrl+4

12

The Reflow feature prevents the need for horizontal scrolling by redrawing the page at the available width of the window, wrapping text and other content as needed. The best thing about the Reflow feature is that it requires no intervention from the author to enable it. Figure 12-6 shows the sample PDF zoomed to 200 percent with Reflow enabled.

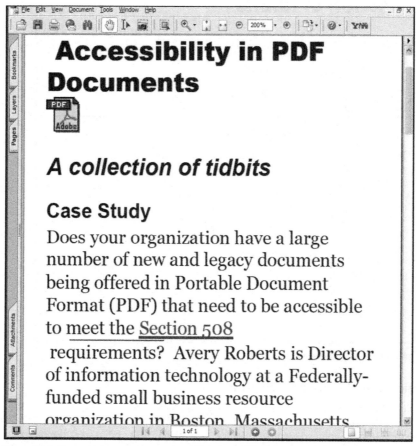

Figure 12-6. A sample document zoomed to 200 percent with Reflow enabled

In addition, the Reflow feature limits zooming for images and untagged content, so that zooming stops once the content reaches the edges of the window. One effect of this is that scanned documents, which are often a series of large images of the scanned pages, will generally not zoom much. Users can turn off the Reflow feature, but then they will need to scroll horizontally and vertically.

In the case of an image with text placed on top of it, the text resizing is limited by the size of the image. If the text is on an image that is as wide as the page, very little magnification will result. With Reflow turned off, the quality of the text in the image will degrade as the image pixelates.

Self-Voicing

Adobe Reader has a Read Out Loud feature that provides basic access to PDF documents. To activate this feature, the user selects Read Out Loud from the View menu.

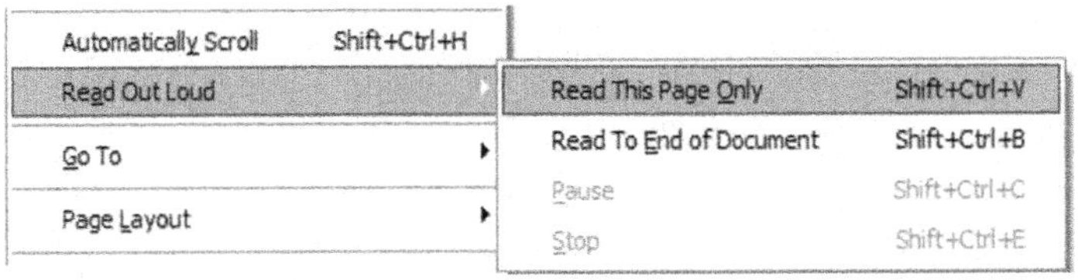

Reading options can be set in the Reading section of the Preferences dialog box, as shown in Figure 12-7.

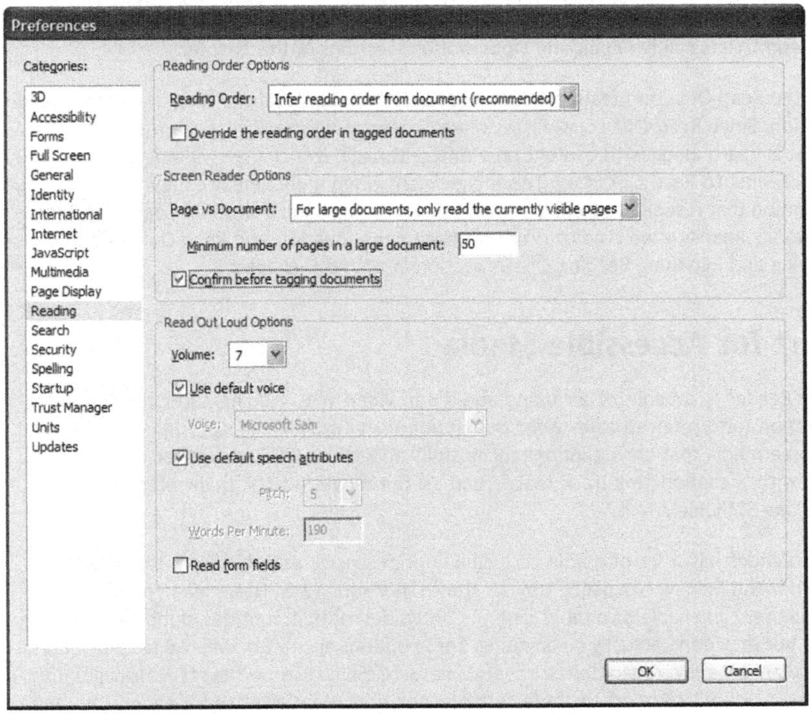

Figure 12-7. The Reading section of the Adobe Reader Preferences dialog box

A blind user is unlikely to find the Read Out Loud feature satisfactory for access to PDF documents. The Read Out Loud feature reads, but it doesn't communicate structure or links, nor does it allow the user to navigate through the document or the tables it contains. If you save a PDF as text (File ➤ Save As Text), the output created is the same as what is voiced in Read Out Loud.

Since not all users will download the PDF document to read in the full version of the Adobe Reader, it is important to note that it is not immediately apparent that the Read Out Loud feature is available for a document viewed in the browser. However, the Read Out Loud feature can be used by users who know the keyboard shortcuts to activate this feature. The shortcuts should be featured in the browser-based player user interface, but until that happens, the shortcuts are as follows:

- Read This Page Only: **Shift+Ctrl+V**
- Read To End of Document: **Shift+Ctrl+ B**
- Pause Reading: **Shift+Ctrl+C**
- Stop Reading: **Shift+Ctrl+E**

The Read Out Loud feature works best with previously tagged PDF documents. The reading order is usually based on the tag structure if it exists, so if the tags are in the correct order, the document will be read in the correct order. If the tags are jumbled, the user will probably find the document very confusing. If there are no tags in the document, the reading order is inferred by Adobe Reader. Tagging is discussed in detail in the "Tagged PDFs" and "Accessibility Repair and Optimization" sections of this chapter.

While the Read Out Loud feature follows a document's tag structure, there is one notable exception. Since Read Out Loud always reads a page at a time, if tags are moved so that content is heard along with content on a different page, this change will not be heard by users listening to Read Out Loud. This is significant when a document contains a block of information that is separate from the main flow of the text and that spans pages. We'll discuss modifications to the reading order for both screen readers and Read Out Loud in the "Verifying and Repairing Reading Order" section later in this chapter.

Support for Accessible Media

Adobe Reader is capable of including audio and video files. Adding captions and audio description (also referred to as *video description*) is more challenging. Truth be told, I've yet to see media that plays captions successfully added to a PDF, except for a QuickTime movie with a caption text track that is part of the movie (rather than referenced via a QuickTime SMIL file).

Adobe Reader has a set of media accessibility preferences, available from the Multimedia section of the Preferences dialog box, as shown in Figure 12-8. These lead you to believe that the user can enable or disable captions, audio description, subtitles, dubbing, and language, but they don't actually *do* anything. These options align with SMIL 2.0 test attributes (systemCaptions, systemAudioDesc, systemOverdubOrSubtitle, and systemLanguage), but RealPlayer doesn't respond to these settings, nor does Windows Media. QuickTime and Flash have no player-level preferences related to captions, let alone audio descriptions, subtitles, or dubbing, so these media types don't stand a chance of responding to the preferences.

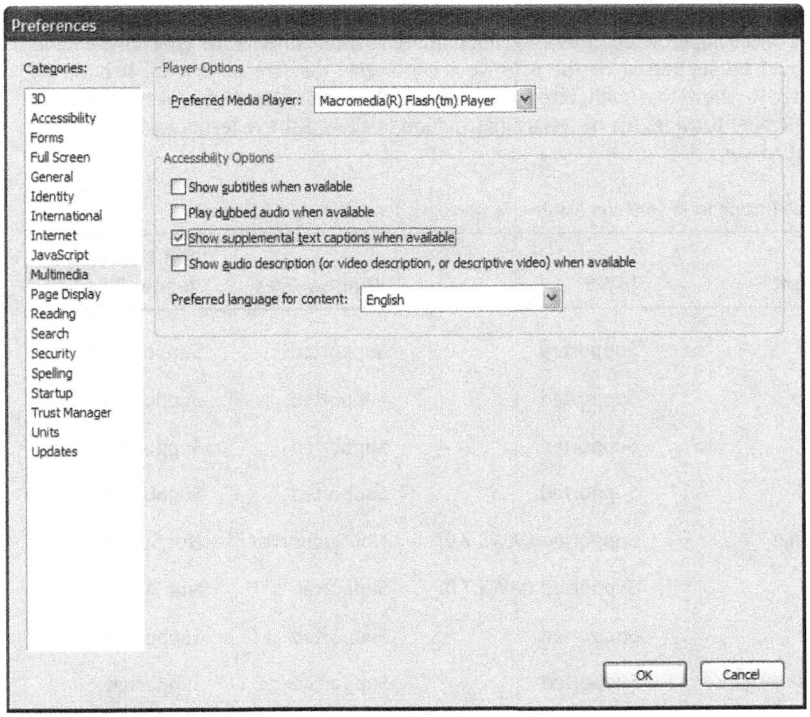

Figure 12-8. The Multimedia section of the Adobe Reader Preferences dialog box

To view examples of PDF files with captioning, visit the National Center for Accessible Media's Beyond the Text project. At the project site, you'll find a prototypes page (http://ncam.wgbh.org/ebooks/prototypes.html) with several examples of PDF documents containing captioned media created as part of an investigation into e-book accessibility.

If you are providing media that must be captioned or described, use QuickTime and add the caption track to the movie directly (this requires QuickTime Pro). If this is not possible, provide a separate link to the media so that it opens in the stand-alone media player.

Assistive Technology Support

Adobe Reader provides access to document information for assistive technologies, starting with the Accessibility plug-in available with Acrobat Reader 4.05 in February 2000. In the past few years, support for (and coordination with) assistive technologies has improved. Adobe Reader now supports a level of interaction with PDF documents using screen readers that compares favorably to the interaction experience with an HTML document.

12

Table 12-1 shows common elements and whether they are supported by popular screen readers or talking browsers. This list is not comprehensive, either in the types of elements that could be supported or the assistive technologies that are compared. It is simply intended to show that with three popular English-speaking tools for Windows users, Adobe Reader provides the necessary information to allow assistive technologies to deliver content to users.

Table 12-1. Support in Common Assistive Technologies for Selected PDF Elements

Element	JAWS	Window-Eyes	IBM HomePage Reader 3.04
Text	Supported	Supported	Supported
Images	Supported	Supported	Supported
Links	Supported	Supported	Supported
Tables	Supported	Supported	Supported
Headings	Supported (JAWS 7.0)	Not Supported	Not Supported
Lists	Supported (JAWS 7.0)	Supported	Not Supported
Forms	Supported	Supported	Supported
Paged navigation	Supported	Supported	Supported

Adobe also makes versions of Adobe Reader for Mac OS X and Unix that function with screen readers on those platforms:

- VoiceOver on Mac OS X 10.4 (www.apple.com/macosx/features/voiceover/), which is not supported yet by Adobe Reader
- Gnopernicus for Unix (www.baum.ro/gnopernicus.html)

Adobe Reader delivers information to a few platforms via Accessibility application program interfaces (APIs):

- Microsoft Active Accessibility (MSAA) (http://msdn.microsoft.com/library/default.asp?url=/library/en-us/msaa/msaastart_9w2t.asp) and also through the Document Object Model (DOM)
- GNOME Accessibility API (http://developer.gnome.org/projects/gap/)
- Apple's Accessibility API (http://developer.apple.com/documentation/Cocoa/Conceptual/Accessibility/index.html#//apple_ref/doc/uid/10000118i)

PDF documents must be tagged in order to correctly communicate information about document structure and functionality to the Accessibility APIs. Adobe Reader will add tags to any untagged document that it opens, with mixed results, as discussed in the next section. In order to deliver the most accessible PDF documents possible, some work is required on the part of a PDF author to modify the PDF tags.

Here are a few links for more information about PDF accessibility:

- Acrobat 7.0 Family and Accessibility:
  www.adobe.com/enterprise/accessibility/acrobat70.html

- PDF Reference:
  http://partners.adobe.com/public/developer/pdf/index_reference.html

- Adobe Acrobat Voluntary Product Accessibility Template (VPAT):
  www.adobe.com/products/server/vpat_livecycle_doctsec.html

- Planet PDF's Accessibility Learning Center:
  www.planetpdf.com/learningcenter.asp?ContainerID=1505

Tagged PDFs

PDF tags are comparable to HTML elements. If you are familiar with HTML headings, anchors, tables, lists, paragraphs, forms, and headings, you'll catch on quickly. Other PDF tags exist, such as Article and Annotation, and authors can define new tags for their own purposes. However, for our purposes, we will stick to the predefined tags and focus on the tags that are supported by assistive technologies.

Tags do not affect the initial visual appearance of PDF documents, so you may not be immediately aware whether any specific PDF document is tagged. A quick check in the Document Properties dialog box will make this apparent, as shown in Figure 12-9.

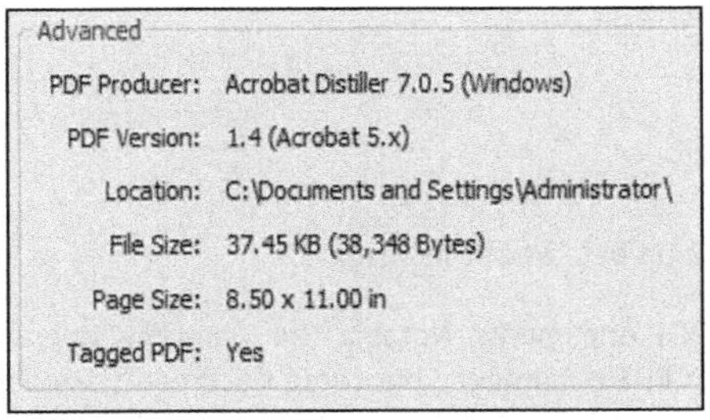

Advanced

PDF Producer: Acrobat Distiller 7.0.5 (Windows)

PDF Version: 1.4 (Acrobat 5.x)

Location: C:\Documents and Settings\Administrator\

File Size: 37.45 KB (38,348 Bytes)

Page Size: 8.50 x 11.00 in

Tagged PDF: Yes

Figure 12-9. The Document Preferences dialog box indicates whether a PDF document is tagged.

12

Tags are needed for a few accessibility features in Adobe Reader:

- Screen readers and other assistive technologies use the tags to convey document structure and content.

- The Reflow feature depends on tags in order to redraw the PDF page to fit the existing window width, but reflows content within only a single page at a time.

- The Read Out Loud feature uses tags to determine the reading order, although this is user-configurable. As mentioned earlier, Read Out Loud uses the tags, but for each page, only tags that are connected to objects on the page being read are voiced. Tags from other pages moved in between other tags on the page being read are not voiced.

Tagging a PDF document does come with a price. Adding tags to a PDF document may increase the file size by 50 percent or more. You can reduce the file size using the Reduce File Size option on the Acrobat File menu without any negative effect on the tags, but the file size will still be larger than the untagged version.

You can also resize documents using the PDF Optimizer tool available from the Advanced menu (and also from the Tools menu under Print Production). When using the Optimizer tool, make sure that the Discard document structure check box in the Discard Objects Settings area of the Optimizer dialog box is unchecked; if that option is checked, Adobe Acrobat will remove all tags upon optimization.

If a document is untagged, Adobe Reader will add tags to it unassisted, but this process is not perfect. Good tagging translates directly to a higher-quality experience for disabled users reading and interacting with PDF files. Leaving the tagging up to Adobe Reader will mean that images are lacking equivalents, structural headings are probably not indicated, and the reading order in multiple-column documents is most likely incorrect.

Tagged PDF documents can be created using a handful of tools, mostly Adobe products:

- Adobe Acrobat
- Adobe Acrobat Capture
- Adobe Acrobat Messenger
- Adobe InDesign CS2
- Adobe Acrobat PDFMaker plug-in for Microsoft Office (Windows only)
- Adobe LiveCycle Designer
- Adobe FrameMaker
- Adobe PageMaker
- OpenOffice
- Microsoft Office 12 (in beta as of this writing)

Many other tools create PDF documents. Notably, the Mac OS X operating system has a built-in, easy way to create PDF documents, but these documents are not tagged and will require some attention to be accessible. Mac owners can create tagged PDF documents using Adobe Acrobat or other tools in the preceding list.

Here, we'll look at two common ways to create tagged PDF documents: using the Adobe Acrobat PDFMaker plug-in with Microsoft Word and using Adobe InDesign CS2.

Creating Tagged PDFs in Microsoft Word

In Microsoft Word 2000 and newer, Adobe Acrobat PDFMaker is installed along with Adobe Acrobat. This tool makes it easy to create tagged PDF documents.

To create a tagged PDF from a Word document, first select Adobe PDF ➤ Change Conversion Settings. In the Acrobat PDFMaker dialog box, make sure that the Enable accessibility and reflow with Tagged PDF check box is checked, as shown in Figure 12-10. If it is not checked, no tags will be added. This setting is persistent, so it doesn't need to be set every time.

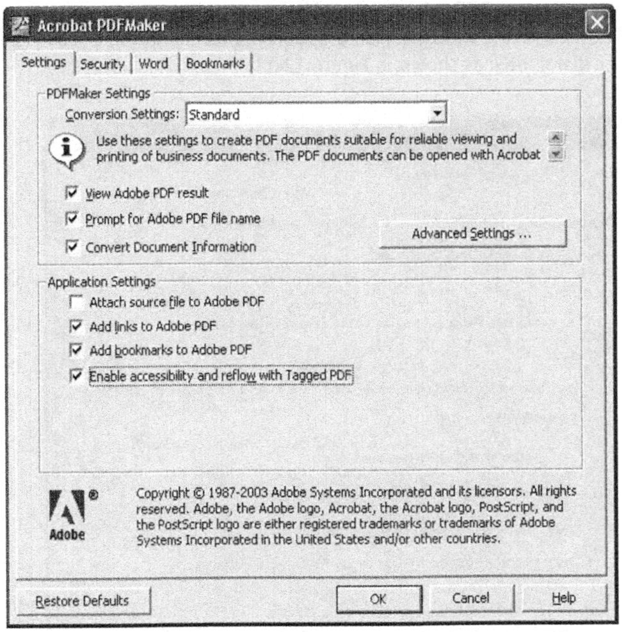

Figure 12-10. Make sure Enable accessibility and reflow with Tagged PDF is selected in the Acrobat PDFMaker dialog box.

Next, choose Adobe PDF ➤ Convert to Adobe PDF. You will be prompted for the filename and save location for the tagged PDF.

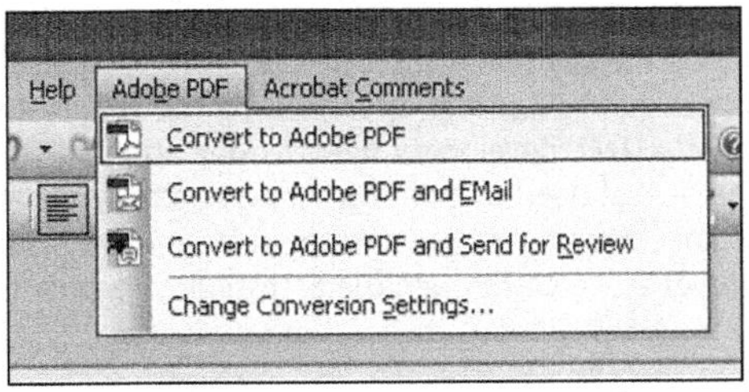

You can create PDF documents by choosing File ➤ Print *and choosing the* Adobe PDF *printer, but this will not result in tagged PDFs.*

If you're enabling document security, you also need to make sure that this does not impact the PDF's accessibility. PDF documents can be locked in a variety of ways. Document authors can set a document password that prevents page modifications or even the ability to copy and paste content. In versions of PDF earlier than PDF 1.4 (Acrobat Reader 5.0), adding the security necessary to prevent copying and pasting of text and images also meant blocking access for screen readers. If you are adding security to your PDF files, make sure that you are using PDF 1.4 or newer. Also make sure that the Enable text access for screen reader devices for the visually impaired option is checked in the Security tab of the Acrobat PDFMaker dialog box, as shown in Figure 12-11.

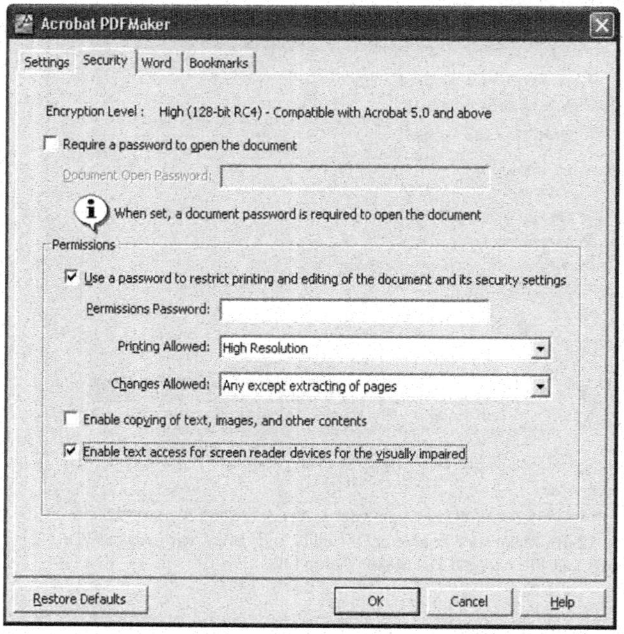

Figure 12-11. Make sure Enable text access for screen reader devices for the visually impaired is selected in the Acrobat PDFMaker dialog box.

There is a short list of important tips that will result in a more accessible PDF document and fewer issues to resolve in Adobe Acrobat after creating the PDF. Not surprisingly, the tips are similar to tasks that HTML developers need to pay attention to when creating accessible websites. The areas that need attention are images, structure, tables, hyperlinks, lists, reading order, and color contrast. We'll review the sample Word document shown in Figure 12-12 (samplePDF.doc) as we go through the accessibility recommendations.

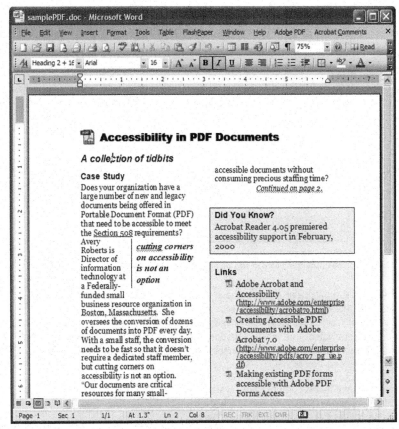

Figure 12-12. A sample PDF created in Microsoft Word

Images

Graphics, photographs, and other images inserted into Word need to have text equivalents. You can easily add text equivalents using the Format Picture dialog box, shown in Figure 12-13. To open this dialog box, either right-click an image and select Format Picture or select an image and choose Format ➤ Picture. In the Format Picture dialog box, choose the Web tab, and enter the alternative text that represents the content of your image.

12

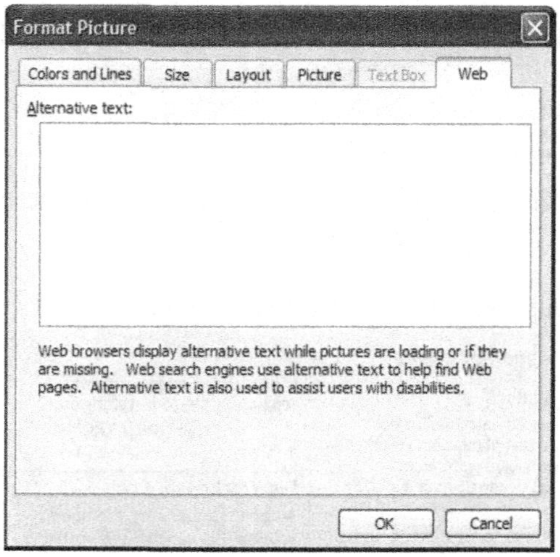

Figure 12-13. The Web tab in Word's Format Picture dialog box provides a way to add text equivalents to images.

If you do not want a particular image to have a text equivalent, leave the Alternative text box blank. This is the PDF equivalent of HTML's alt="" for null images. For example, in the sample document (samplePDF.doc), the image at the top of the page could have "Adobe PDF" as the text equivalent, but in this situation, the image doesn't really carry any information—it just serves as a visual reinforcement for the adjacent text. So, it makes sense to leave its Alternative text box blank.

If you have an image that is composed of several individual parts, make sure to use Word's Group option, available from the Draw menu on the Drawing toolbar. That way, you will need to write only one text equivalent for the image.

Structure

Conveying structure in a PDF document is very important. In HTML, you add h1 through h6 headings to provide structure, and the process is similar for a PDF file. Word provides document styles to make document formatting easier. The key to easily adding structure to PDF documents that originate in Word is to use styles to structure your document with headings, as shown in Figure 12-14.

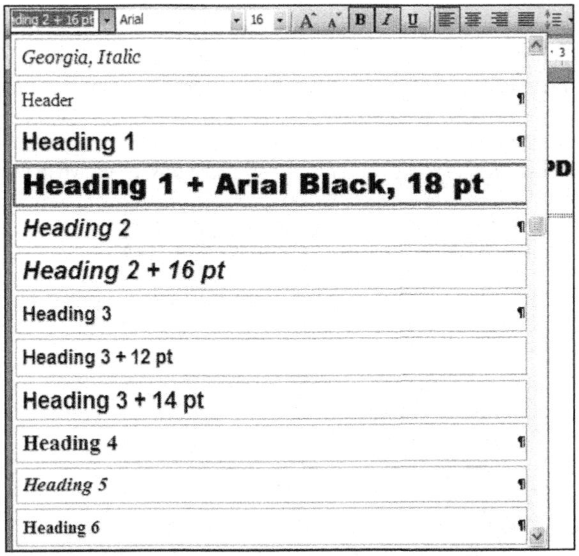

Figure 12-14. Use Word's document styles to add headings to Word documents before converting documents to PDF.

When converted to PDF, Word headings are tagged as headings in the PDF document. The headings will be used by JAWS 7.0 when reading and navigating a PDF document. Additionally, the headings can be used as bookmarks in the PDF document to ease navigation for all users, not just those using JAWS.

In the sample document (samplePDF.doc), Word headings are used to create a basic heading structure, as shown in Figure 12-15.

At the time of writing, only JAWS 7.0 can access headings in PDF documents, and only when Adobe Reader version 7.0 or newer is used. It seems likely that other screen readers will add this support in the future. However, many users would benefit from additional navigational abilities. One way to handle this when using Microsoft Word as the PDF source document is to add a table of contents at the beginning of the document, and include clickable reference links (using Word references, found on the Insert menu) that take the user directly to major sections of the document. This may be easier for some users than opening and navigating the Bookmarks panel in Adobe Reader.

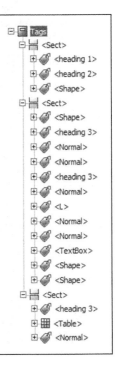

Figure 12-15. The unmodified tag structure, including headings, as viewed in Acrobat after converting samplePDF.doc to a PDF

12

Tables

Basic tables are simple to handle in Word. When creating a table in a Word document, always use Word's Table feature rather than using tabs to align columns and drawing lines for cell boundaries. As in HTML, it is important to identify headings in tables. To do this, select the row containing headings, choose Table ➤ Table Properties, and check Repeat as header row at the top of each page in the Table Properties dialog box, as shown in Figure 12-16.

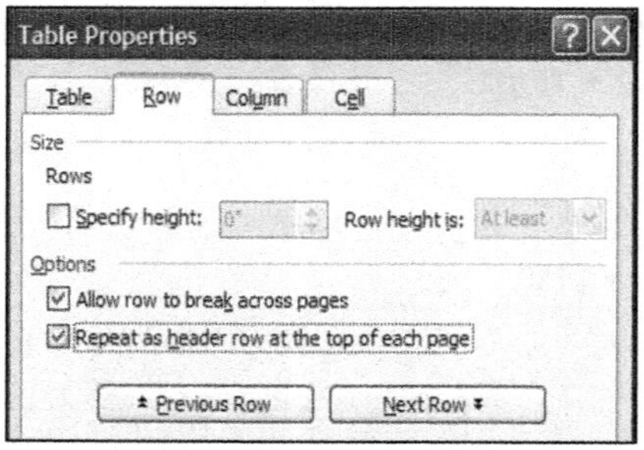

Figure 12-16. Mark rows containing headings in the Table Properties dialog box.

The result of marking table rows in this way is not entirely satisfying, but clearly distinguishes the headings. The rows marked as headings in Word are placed in a <THEAD> tag, but the cells are marked as <TD> tags, not <TH>. See Figures 12-17 and 12-18 for a comparison of the treatment of identified and unidentified row headings.

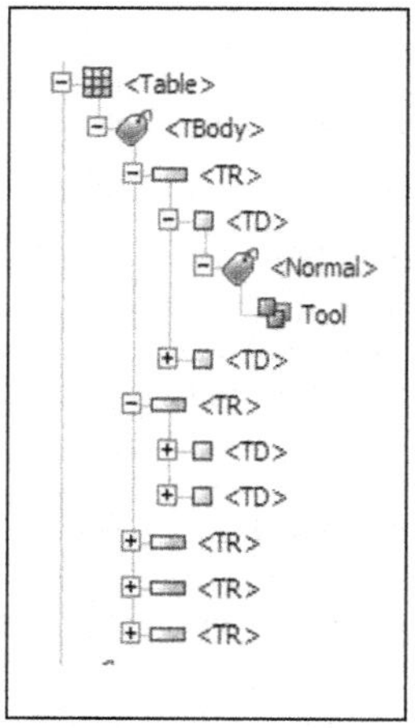

Figure 12-17. Table tag structure when table heading row is not identified

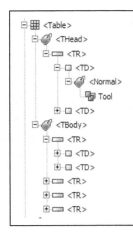

Figure 12-18. Table tag structure when table heading row is identified

For a simple table with headings only in rows, this is adequate to identify the headings. Tables that require headings for rows as well as columns will need to be modified in Adobe Acrobat, as explained in the "Verifying and Repairing Tables" section later in this chapter.

For tables with multiple levels of headings, such as the one shown in Figure 12-19, cells are merged in Word so that they span multiple columns or rows. When converted to PDF, these cells are correctly indicated in the PDF tag structure, although it is not immediately apparent. The tag structure for the table appears to be ambiguous with regard to which heading cell aligns with others, as shown in Figure 12-20, but drilling into the properties for the table cells in question reveals that attributes for rowspan and colspan are created. To check these attributes, view the properties for the table cell and click Edit Attribute Objects to open the Attributes dialog box, as shown in Figure 12-21.

| | JAWS | | Window-Eyes | |
	Version 4.5	Version 7.0	Version 4.0	Version 5.0
Text	Supported	Supported	Supported	Supported
Images	Supported	Supported	Supported	Supported
Headings	Not Supported	Supported	Not Supported	Not Supported

Figure 12-19. A table with multiple levels of headings

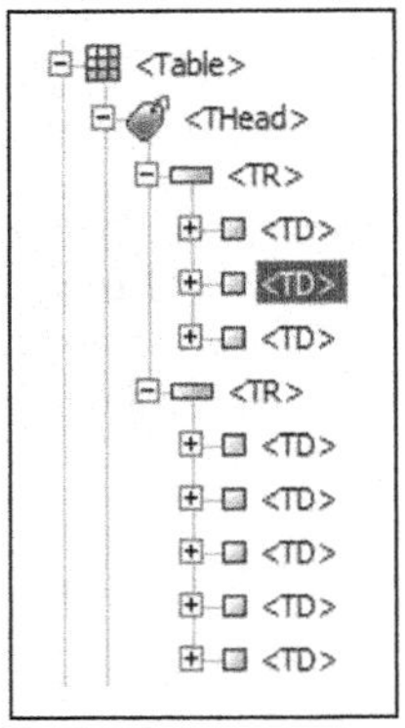

Figure 12-20. Table tag structure for a table with multiple level headings

12

387

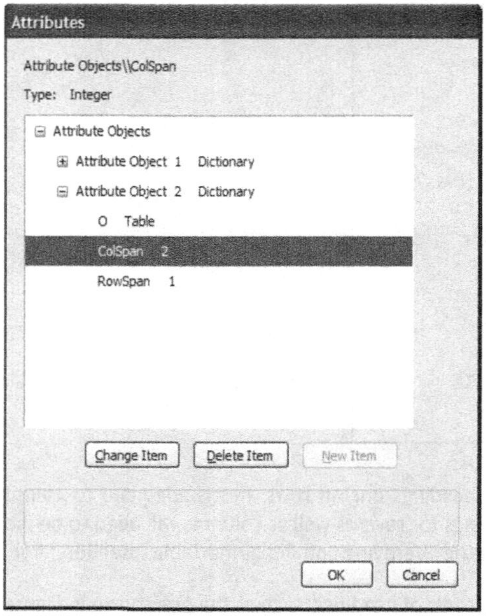

Figure 12-21. Examine the attributes for a table tag to verify that colspan attributes are used.

It merits mention that support for complex tables is not a strong suit of screen readers. If you have multiple levels of headings on both columns and rows, users will not have particularly positive experiences accessing the information, even though it may be technically accessible. Screen readers are improving in this area, but you should make sure to test your complex tables with assistive technologies.

Hyperlinks

Word hyperlinks are converted accurately by Acrobat PDFMaker. The issue is in ensuring that the link text makes sense out of context, which is largely editorial. Make sure that your links are short and to the point. If your link text is a URI, try to make it appear on a single line, because Adobe Reader will break the link into separate parts for each line. This is fixed if the document is reflowed, but presents some difficulties when the document is not reflowed.

Lists

Ordered and unordered lists can be identified as lists by assistive technologies as long as they are tagged as lists. Acrobat PDFMaker will tag lists that are created using Word's bullets and numbering feature. This is not generally a problem (often it is more difficult to *not* make a list in Word). In general, if Word thinks that you made a list, so will PDFMaker.

Reading Order

In most cases, there is little ambiguity about the order in which text in a document should be read. The main exceptions are when authors add text boxes to a document and when columns are used.

Columns can be constructed several ways in Word. The best way to make accessible PDFs with columns is using Word's column-formatting feature (Format ➤ Columns). PDFMaker creates the tags in the correct order consistently when this feature is used, but is unable to do so reliably when columns are created using text boxes or by setting a tab stop in the middle of the page.

Text boxes in Word are used for more than columns, as in samplePDF.doc. In this file, the callout text "cutting corners on accessibility is not an option" is in a text box. As you will see when we discuss repairing PDF files, this text is not in the best logical location in the tag structure and needs to be adjusted.

Headers and footers in Word are not part of the reading order when exported using the PDFMaker utility. If you need to include this information, you must add it manually in Acrobat or include it as part of the document body, rather than in the header or footer region. In many cases, the document footer indicates the page number, which is functionality that Acrobat Reader provides for the user.

Color Contrast

PDF authors should make sure that adequate contrast is provided in the content. Adobe Reader handles most color contrast issues for you, but text boxes present a problem. The problem is that Adobe Reader is capable of changing text and background colors in a PDF document, but the background color of text boxes is not changed even though the text is changed.

Text boxes often have a background color, and even if the color is white to match the usual page background, this color is often explicitly specified in Word, as shown in Figure 12-22. The result can be black text on a white text box turning into white text on a white text box. For text boxes that have the same background color as the page, you can set the text box background to No Fill, so that changes to the page color will show through the text box.

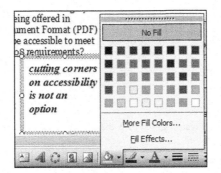

Figure 12-22. Be careful when using a text box with a background color. Use No Fill whenever possible.

12

Creating Tagged PDFs in InDesign CS2

Adobe InDesign CS2 allows document authors to add tags to their documents, but the process for creating a structured and tagged PDF is not completely obvious.

InDesign provides two ways to create tagged PDF documents:

- Documents can be marked for tagging in the File Export dialog box on an individual basis.
- Tagging can be turned on by default so that all exported files are tagged.

To verify that tagging is enabled for all documents in InDesign, select File ➤ Adobe PDF Presets ➤ Define. Click each preset to determine if tags are enabled (this feature is enabled in the High Quality Print preset by default). Click New to define a new preset. In the New PDF Export Preset dialog box, make sure that the Create Tagged PDF check box is checked, as shown in Figure 12-23.

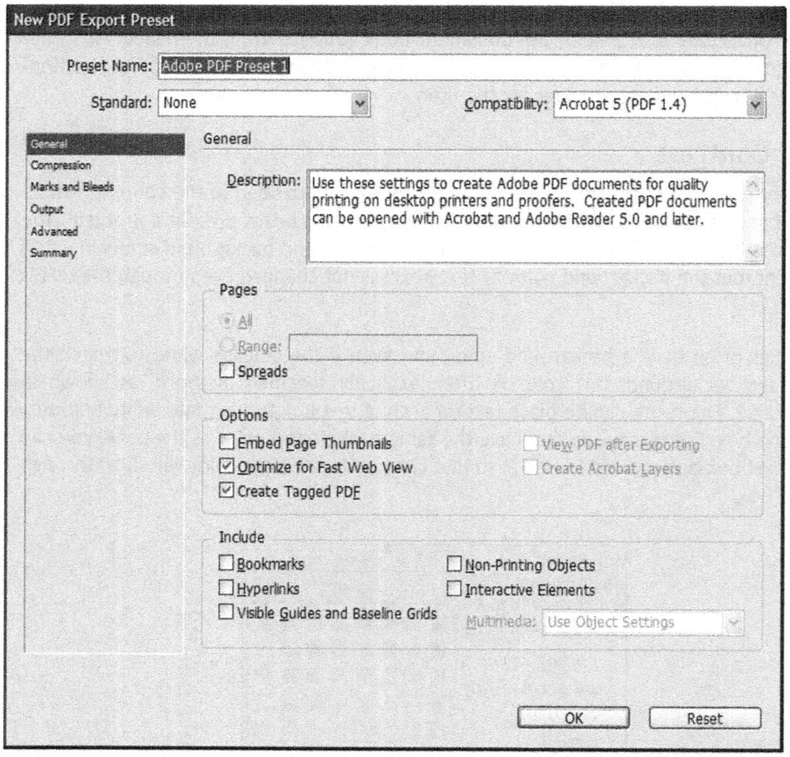

Figure 12-23. Make sure that Create Tagged PDF is checked when creating a new PDF export preset in InDesign.

390

InDesign does create tags for PDF documents, but to get the tags to be recognized as semantic structures such as headings by screen readers, you need to use styles that are named appropriately. The style names are used in creating the tag structure, so a style named h1 will result in JAWS identifying the contents as a level one heading, but other names will not have the same effect.

InDesign provides a Structure panel (select View ➤ Structure ➤ Show Structure), which is similar to the Tags tab in Acrobat (discussed in the next section). You can move tags around in the overall structure, and the resulting PDF document will reflect these changes. It is possible to tag an element in the Structure panel as one of a selected few tags (H1 through H6, P, Artifact, and so on), but it is important to note that these changes appear only in InDesign's XML output, not the PDF. It is possible to tag a text block as an H1 heading, but this change does not affect the exported PDF.

You can add text equivalents to images in InDesign by right-clicking the image's tag in the Structure panel and choosing New Attribute. In the New Attribute dialog box, enter **Alt** in the Name field (it's case-sensitive, so make sure to capitalize the **A** in **Alt**) and the text equivalent in the Value field.

In most cases, you will need to edit accessibility tags in Acrobat Professional after publishing a PDF document from InDesign in order to include other semantic elements such as links and lists, and to identify changes in the primary language of the PDF document text. This type of repair is the subject of the next section.

Accessibility Repair and Optimization

Automated tagging—whether in Acrobat PDFMaker, Acrobat Professional, or Adobe Reader—is imprecise, and errors and misinterpretations are inevitable. Documents with incorrect tags need to be repaired in Acrobat. Repair in Acrobat can be a time-consuming task when the document is very long or untagged.

Older Adobe Acrobat versions support tag repair, but Acrobat 7.0 Professional makes the repair process ten times easier (in my estimate). Acrobat 7.0's TouchUp Reading Order tool alone makes the upgrade worthwhile.

The first step in repairing PDF files for accessibility is to verify whether they are already tagged. Once Acrobat takes its best shot at tagging, the repair process begins. Here, we'll look at how to deal with untagged documents, and then how to repair tags.

Dealing with Untagged Documents

PDF documents must be tagged in order to be accessible. As mentioned earlier in this chapter, Adobe Reader will add tags to untagged documents automatically, but this process is imperfect. Let's look at an example. The samplePDF.doc file (shown earlier in Figure 12-12) was converted to PDF by PDFMaker, but with the tagging disabled, so it is not tagged PDF. When you open this document in Adobe Reader 7.0, a dialog box indicates that the document is to be tagged, as shown in Figure 12-24.

12

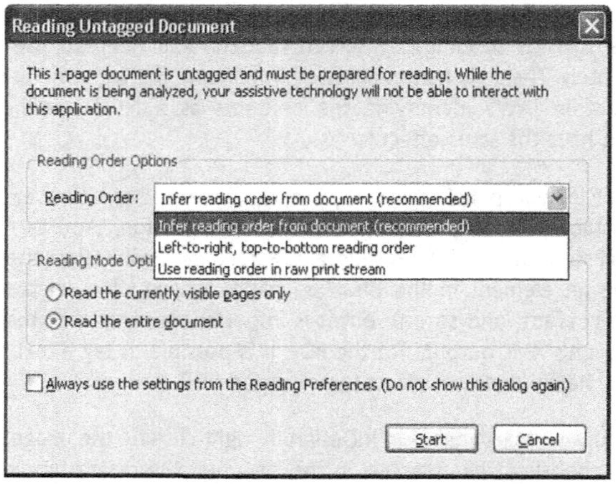

Figure 12-24. The Reading Untagged Document dialog box indicates that a PDF lacks tags.

Once the tagging is done by Adobe Reader, you read the document in JAWS 7.0, with the following results:

- No headings are found.
- There are 13 links.
- No lists are found.
- No tables are found.
- The callout text is read, but after the list of links, which is well after the paragraph that contains it.
- The footer is read.

If ideally tagged, this same PDF would be read by the screen reader with the following results:

- Six headings are found.
- There are nine links.
- One list of three items is found.
- One table with headings is found.
- The callout text is removed from the reading order. (This might not always be the right decision for callout text, but in the `samplePDF.pdf` document, I believe it is.)
- The footer is read.

Adobe Reader did a decent job of defining tags resulting in a readable document, but several important features of the document were omitted. Depending on the complexity of your documents and the version of Adobe Reader that you are using, the accuracy of the PDF tags created will vary.

In Acrobat 7.0 Professional, you use the Tags tab to work with tabs. To display this tab, select View ➤ Navigation Tabs ➤ Tags. The Tags tab will appear as either a floating tab or a docked tab, as shown in Figure 12-25.

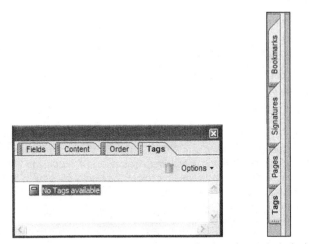

Figure 12-25. The Tags tab may appear as a floating tab or a docked tab.

If the Tags tab is floating, you can add it alongside the docked tabs by clicking and dragging the tab title to the Navigation pane. This is highly recommended as it keeps the document and the Tags tab out of each other's way and makes the Tags tab as tall as the document. You'll want the space.

> *The* Options *menu in the* Tags *tab has options and context-sensitive items similar to those found on the* Advanced *menu, under* Accessibility.

Untagged PDF documents, however they are created, are easy to add tags to in Adobe Acrobat. Simply open the untagged PDF in Adobe Acrobat. In the Tags tab, you'll see that the document is untagged.

Select Advanced ➤ Accessibility ➤ Add Tags to Document. After a few seconds (depending on the document length), the Tags tab indicates that the tags have been created by showing a fully collapsed tree control that is named Tags.

12

Let's take a look at what happened. If you expand all tree nodes (click the tree and press the asterisk key), you'll find the following tags:

- Nine headings
- Thirteen links
- No lists
- No tables, nor text within the table
- Callout text, but interwoven with the text from the adjacent paragraph (clearly not a desirable outcome)
- A footer

> *If the same Word document is saved as a PDF on a Mac OS X system and then brought to a Windows machine for tag repair (a legitimate scenario: PDF documents created on a Mac and made accessible on a Windows machine), the results are similar, but different. When Adobe Acrobat tags the PDF that originated on the Mac, it finds one less heading and no links. It does find and tag the table correctly (but still no table headings), and it has the same difficulty with the callout box text.*

Your document is now tagged PDF. You're a step closer to a really accessible PDF document. Don't forget to save the document!

In general, adding tags is easy to do, but the results will vary. We'll leave it up to Adobe to continually improve the automatic tagging process, but until tagging happens accurately and retains intended semantic information, you need to spend some time repairing the tags.

Making Scanned Documents Accessible

A common method for creating PDF files is to scan paper documents. This is often cited as a concern for PDF documents, particularly when a significant court case is underway, since U.S. courts create a lot of PDF documents by scanning.

Scanning turns the whole PDF into an image. The way to make the image accessible is to perform Optical Character Recognition (OCR) in Adobe Acrobat. To do this, with the scanned PDF open, select Document ➤ Recognize Text Using OCR and choose Start. The Recognize Text dialog box opens and provides information about how the OCR process will proceed, as shown in Figure 12-26.

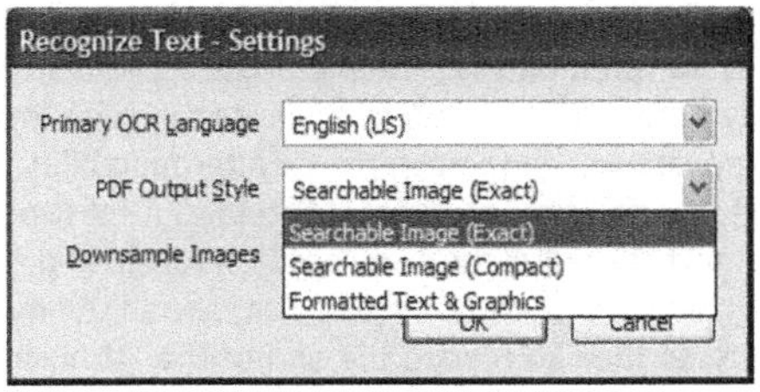

Figure 12-26. Choosing the PDF Output Style setting

Of particular interest is the PDF Output Style setting. This setting determines whether OCR-recognized text replaces scanned text or sits behind it. You can change this setting by clicking the Edit button and choosing the style. As shown in Figure 12-26, you can choose one of the following output styles:

- Formatted Text & Graphics: If the scanned document uses regular fonts, is straight on the page, and in clear high-contrast text, try the Formatted Text & Graphics setting. This will replace the image of the document with text. Remember that OCR is not 100 percent accurate, so if there are many words or characters that can't be determined by OCR, the document may end up with a mix of fonts, or it will take significant extra work on the PDF author's part to repair.

- Searchable Image: If the scanned document is not from a clear copy or uses obscure fonts, the OCR process will have more difficulty. In this case, it may be better to select the Searchable Image setting. This creates a set of tags behind the image and retains the current appearance.

The scanned document now has text in one form or another. The next step is to add tags as described in the previous section, and then begin the repair process, as discussed in the next section. You should expect that the repair process will take longer for scanned documents—just how long depends on the quality of the scan and how easy it is for OCR to find the text.

Correcting Tagging Issues

In order to address issues in a systematic manner, we'll use the following list as a guide to making a PDF document accessible:

1. Verify and repair reading order.
2. Add missing text.
3. Verify and add headings.
4. Add text equivalents for images.
5. Verify links.
6. Verify and repair tables.

12

The list can also be used to help prioritize PDF repair. If you have only five minutes to repair a document, there is no question that reading order is the first order of business. Reading order affects many different users due to accurate tagging's impact on the Read Out Loud feature, reflow appearance, and screen reader interoperability, and the potential for completely jumbling all or part of a document. Therefore, it must be at least verified. Headings and images are next, because they are easy to repair and have a significant impact on users. Links and tables are important, but these take a little more time to repair and are less common errors, so they go toward the end of the list, even though they are by no means unimportant.

> *As you become familiar with making PDF documents accessible, you will likely work through the document from start to finish, addressing different kinds of issues in parallel.*

Verifying and Repairing Reading Order

Repairing the reading order is absolutely critical. As you saw earlier in this chapter, Adobe Reader doesn't always get the reading order correct on its own. Whether two whole columns are mixed together or a single callout quote is intertwined with the paragraph text, the outcome is content that is somewhere between difficult to understand and incomprehensible.

As a first step, you should verify the reading order, correct content that is out of order, and remove items that are not needed. You can use two main methods to modify the reading order: the TouchUp Reading Order tool and the Order tab. As noted earlier (in the "Dealing with Untagged Documents" section), you'll always use the Tags tab to work with tags in Adobe Acrobat.

Checking the Reading Order To verify the reading order, set up your Adobe Acrobat window so that you can see the Tags tab as well as the page being edited, as shown in Figure 12-27 (from the samplePDF.pdf document). At this time, you may find that the ability to view the entire page is as important, if not more important, than the ability to easily read the content. When I'm repairing PDF document order, I like to be able to see at least a whole page at a time, and sometimes wish for more since it is not uncommon for tags to be created on page 3 of a document when they belong on page 1.

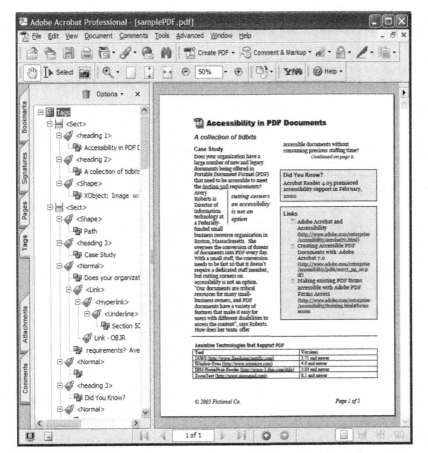

Figure 12-27. The Acrobat window, set up for examining reading order with a whole page in view at once

Next, enable the Highlight Content option in the Tags tab's Options menu. Enabling this option means that clicking any part of the Tags tree will highlight the tag's position in the document.

Now start at the top of the tree (I sometimes expand the whole tree by pressing the asterisk key) and move down through the tree items, watching the position of the highlighting as you do so.

Figure 12-28 shows three examples of the movement of the highlight as I move down through the Tags tree. Notice that the highlight doesn't follow the expected reading order.

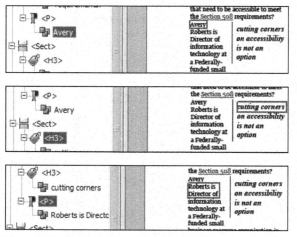

Figure 12-28. Checking the reading order of the tags

If everything is in the order you expect, great. If not, you need to move the tags around.

Using the Touchup Reading Order Tool Moving tags around is simple. You can either click a tag or the tag content and drag it to a new location in the tree, or you can select the node with the keyboard and cut and paste. When you move a node, all subnodes move with it. One way to handle this issue is to use the TouchUp Reading Order tool. This tool will save you hours of work.

To access this tool, select Accessibility ➤ Advanced ➤ TouchUp Reading Order. As shown in Figure 12-29, the TouchUp Reading Order tool allows you to select sections of the document and click a button to change their tags.

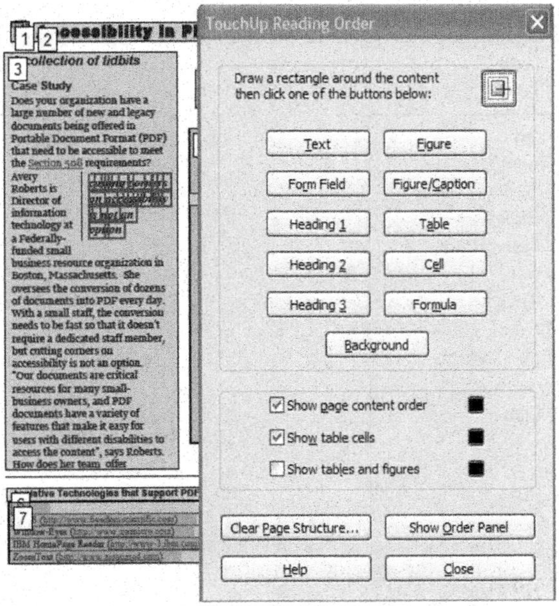

Figure 12-29. The TouchUp Reading Order tool with a selected block of text

After selecting a block of text (Figure 12-29 shows the callout text being selected), click the type of tag that the content should be enclosed within. In this case, Text was chosen, and the callout text was placed within a single paragraph tag, as shown in Figure 12-30. Now the text can easily be moved or deleted.

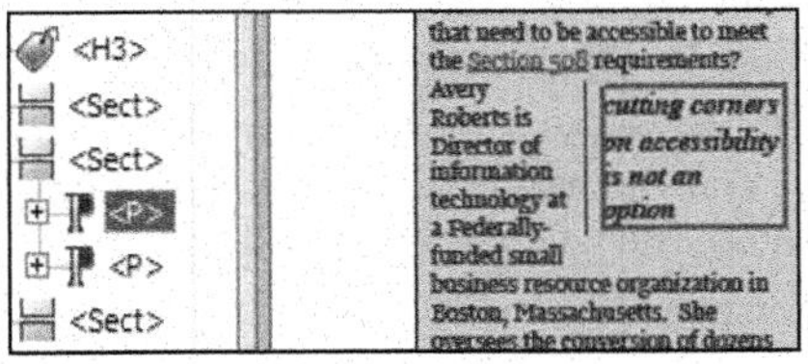

Figure 12-30. The TouchUp Reading Order tool creates a new paragraph for the callout.

12

Move the text within the paragraphs and other tags, so that the text that goes together resides in the same tag, as shown in Figure 12-31. Then the extra, now empty, tags can be deleted.

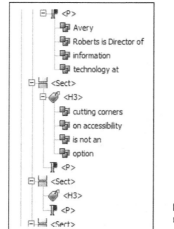

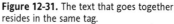

Figure 12-31. The text that goes together resides in the same tag.

Since, in this case, the callout text is redundant to the story and mainly serves to break up the page visually, you might decide to delete it. All you need to do is locate the tags containing only the callout content and hit the Delete key for each. This clearly is not the solution for every situation, particularly not when two columns of text need to be separated.

The following are a few caveats regarding using the TouchUp Reading Order tool:

- Try to avoid touching up text that contains hyperlinks. Hyperlinks require a few extra steps to re-create, and if you select a block of text containing a link and define it as text with the TouchUp Reading Order tool, the links are removed.

- The Show tables and figures option of the tool is very useful, but tends to get in the way, particularly on a crowded page. You should get comfortable with what information it provides and enable it only when needed.

- Save often. There is no undo feature.

- Sometimes using the TouchUp Reading Order tool to modify tags results in a changed order of the paragraphs.

Using the Order Tab The Order tab offers another method that you can use to reorder the content. To open it, select View ➤ Navigation Tabs ➤ Order. You'll see the Order tab, as shown in Figure 12-32.

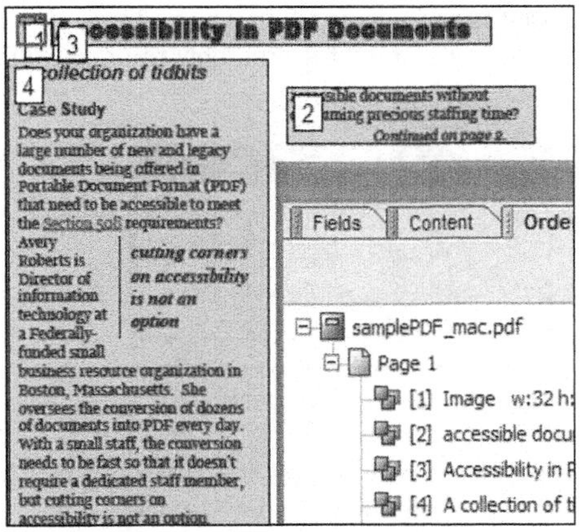

Figure 12-32. The Order tab allows you to drag-and-drop blocks of text to change the order.

In the Order tab, click and drag (or cut and paste) content blocks to move them to their new locations. Highlighting on the page helps make this process intuitive.

When you're using the Order tab to modify the reading order, blocks of text will automatically combine. Sometimes, this is a good feature because it reduces the overall number of items you need to put in order or check. However, it can be viewed as a loss of control over the individual blocks on the page.

Another important point to realize is that the order of the content blocks in the TouchUp Reading Order tool and in the Order tab is not necessarily the same as what exists in the Tags tab. Moving a block in the Order tab does also change the tag structure, but changing the tag structure *does not* change the order of the content blocks in the Order tab or the TouchUp Reading Order tool view. Recognizing this difference makes the repair process much more understandable if you use both methods for reorganizing the reading order.

Some authors like to start accessibility repair with the Order panel; others prefer to make exclusive use of the Tags panel to make changes. Ultimately it is up to you to decide which method you prefer for your workflow.

Adding Missing Text

The most common reason for adding text to a PDF is to provide a text equivalent for an image. For example, if the text in a scanned image can't be recognized, you may need to add tags manually.

To add a tag manually, follow these steps:

1. In the Tags tree, select the node that you want to precede the new node.

2. Choose New Tag from the Tags tab's Options menu to open the New Tag dialog box.

12

3. Locate the tag you want to add (Figure 12-33 shows a Paragraph tag selected). The Title field is not used in any output; it is used only to provide information in the Tags tree view.

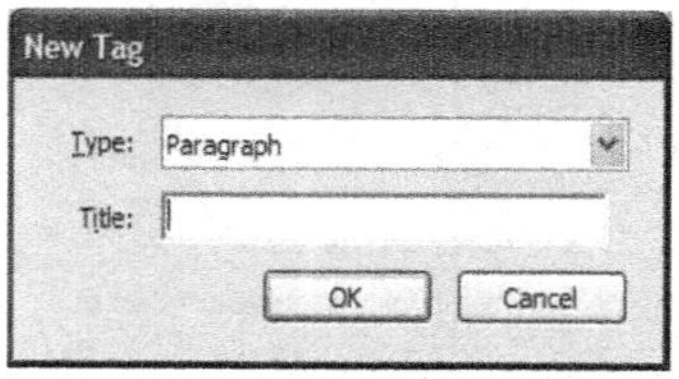

Figure 12-33. The New Tag dialog box

4. With the new tag selected, choose Properties from the Tags tab's Options menu and enter the text for the new tag in the Alternative Text field.

Adding alternative text is legal for all tags, but it will cause all content inside a tag to be hidden in favor of this value. In this case, this is the desired behavior. If there are any inline tags that need to be included in the text (for example, a hyperlink), the text will need to be split among multiple new tags to allow for the link without creating redundant text. You can't add a link within alternative text.

The big downside to including text in a PDF in this way is that it won't zoom with actual text. This is a drawback, but this technique is still preferable to not having the text available at all.

Verifying and Adding Headings

Headings are easily viewed by scanning through the Tags tree. Whether you identify a heading that shouldn't be one or want to make text or images into headings, the process is basically the same. Choose from one of the following methods:

- **Use the TouchUp Reading Order tool:** Highlight a block of text, images, or a combination, and click the Heading button in the TouchUp Reading Order tool. If you want an H4 heading, choose a different level in the tool (only levels 1 through 3 are available) and then redefine the tag.

- **Redefine a tag:** To redefine an existing heading or paragraph, select the tag in the Tags tree and choose Properties from the context menu or the Tags tab's Options menu. In the TouchUp Properties dialog box, choose the tag you want from the Type drop-down list. This method will not disrupt the structures within a particular tag, so if you need to turn an existing heading that contains a hyperlink into a paragraph, this method is easiest since it leaves the link intact.

Adding Image Equivalents

It'll be a fine day when images get tagged with the alternative text automatically, but don't hold your breath waiting for it. Tagging images is simple to do using either of the following two methods:

- Locate the image in the Tags tree and open the Properties menu option from the Tags tab's Options menu. Add the text equivalent in the Alternative Text field. If you don't want the image to be heard at all, you can delete the tag containing the image from the Tags tree.

- Locate the image and right-click it. If you don't see a context menu with an Edit Alternative Text option, open the TouchUp Reading Order tool and try again. You'll see the Alternate Text dialog box, as shown in Figure 12-34. Specify the alternative text here.

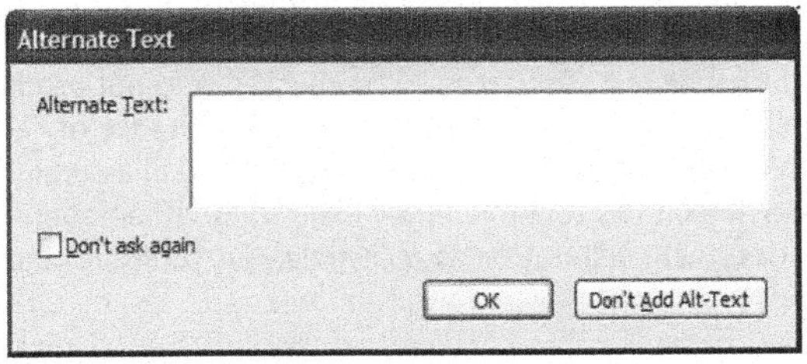

Figure 12-34. The Alternate Text dialog box for providing text equivalents for images

Verifying and Repairing Tables

Repairing tables is probably the most time-consuming PDF repair activity. The basic goal is for the Tags tree structure for the table to look similar to the structure of an HTML table. Within a table tag, you need table rows; within rows, you need table header cells and table data cells; within table header and table data cells, you need content.

The TouchUp Reading Order tool is a tremendous help because you can select whole tables or table cells and create tags. If the table is simple enough, you may be able to select the whole table with the TouchUp Reading Order tool and click the Table button. If you are fortunate, the table, table row, and cells will be created. However, there will be times when it is necessary to select individual cells and click the Cell button. In this case, you may be able to move the newly created TD tags into an existing table tag. If not, you will need to create a table and table rows in the Tags tree to have places to move the new cells.

To create a new element in the Tags tree, select the tag that you would like to precede the new tag and choose New tag from the Tags tab's Options menu. You can then drag tags and content into this new container. Don't forget to redefine the TD cells that should be TH tags as such.

Repairing complex tables is more difficult, as discussed earlier in the chapter, in the "Tables" section. Many complex tables can be correctly identified when rowspan and colspan attributes are used, as shown in Figure 12-21 earlier in the chapter.

12

Using Acrobat's Accessibility Checker

If you've already gone through the process of repairing the document as detailed in the preceding section, the results of Adobe Acrobat's accessibility checker (accessed from the Advanced ➤ Accessibility submenu) shouldn't be too much of a surprise. Acrobat's testing tool is useful as a verification that no images have been missed, the table structure is correct, form controls are in the document tag tree, and a few other criteria have been met.

The accessibility checker, like accessibility checking tools for websites such as Bobby and Lift, is unable to determine anything about the accuracy of the structure for the document or the quality of the alternative text. The accessibility checker does not produce a positive verification of accessibility; it checks for only the presence or absence of certain types of errors. As with other testing tools, there is the risk that people will assume that it checks everything. If you are relying on this tool to identify issues rather than examining the document manually, your document will not be as accessible as it could be, and it might not be accessible enough.

Accessible PDF Forms

Adobe Acrobat is capable of adding basic form controls to PDF documents. In addition, Adobe LiveCycle Designer, an application that comes with Acrobat 7.0 Professional, allows for the creation of more sophisticated forms that are delivered as XML and rendered and processed by Adobe Reader.

Acrobat is able to insert text fields, radio buttons, check boxes, combo boxes, list boxes, and buttons, and all of these elements can be made accessible to assistive technologies. To insert form controls, open the Advanced Editing toolbar from the Tools menu. From this toolbar (or within the Advanced Editing menu under Tools), choose the type of form control, and then draw a rectangle on the PDF document where the field should reside. Immediately, a Properties dialog box opens for the specific control type, as shown in Figure 12-35.

In this dialog box, make sure that you add a tooltip for each control. This text will be used by assistive technologies to describe the control.

After you've added form controls, you need to tag the PDF document. If it is already tagged, the form controls need to be introduced into the Tags tree using the TouchUp Reading Order tool. To do this, select the control and click the Form Control button. Once this step is done, the form control tags need to be moved within the Tags tree to the appropriate location to ensure a correct reading order.

Making form controls accessible is straightforward and relatively simple, and PDF forms, properly designed, can be used by users with disabilities. One major limitation of PDF interactive forms is that reflowing the document is not possible, which can cause some difficulty for low-vision users.

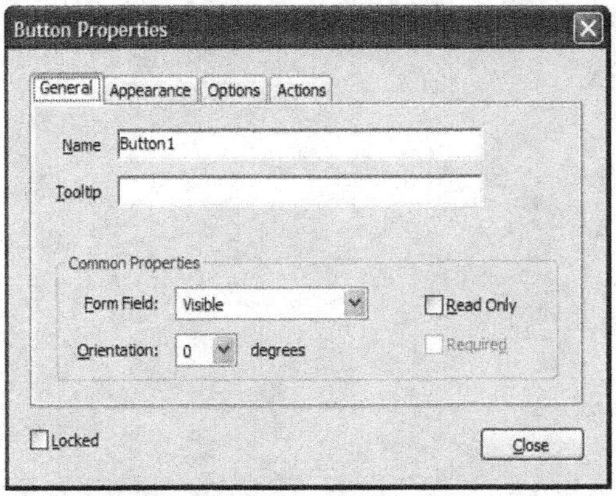

Figure 12-35. Add information for assistive technologies in the form control's Properties dialog box.

Summary

The PDF format has come a long way in the past five years, from prompting legal threats to its current position as a format for which many accessibility issues have been resolved. Even though there are accessibility solutions in place for many PDF features, it is apparent that Adobe continues to pay attention to accessibility issues within PDF documents. Additional awareness and resources for developers of PDF documents are always needed to improve the average level of accessibility within PDF documents on the Internet, but today PDF documents are more accessible than ever. Creating PDF documents that meet accessibility requirements is not just possible, it's getting easier all the time.

12

13 ACCESSIBILITY TESTING

by Jim Thatcher

A large number of sophisticated software tools can be used to check for web accessibility. U.S. federal agencies and corporations are spending millions of dollars on tools that claim to test websites for accessibility. But what actually can and cannot be tested with these tools?

Any accessibility testing must be viewed as a process that combines automated software tools with human judgment. There is no tool that you can run against your website (or web page, for that matter) in order to assert that it is accessible and/or complies with the Section 508 provisions or the Web Content Accessibility Guidelines (WCAG)—no matter how much you are willing to pay. When a website claims Section 508 conformance or WCAG conformance verified by some tool or other (and many do), the most it can mean is that the site (or page) passed all of the *automatic* Section 508 or WCAG tests. Having said that, software-testing tools can help you find out if your site is *not* accessible or does *not* comply with WCAG or Section 508, by testing for the absence of valid required elements and/or attributes.

The first part of this chapter discusses the extent to which you can rely on software tools to check your web content for accessibility compared to how much you must rely on human evaluation. The next part of this chapter looks at six commercial accessibility testing tools and their performance on a set of test files.

What Testing Is Possible?

We are going to look at each Section 508 provision in turn and discuss the two aspects involved in testing for compliance with the provision. I will call these two parts of the job the *algorithmic* part and the *judgment* part. Algorithmic testing generally verifies the presence of a valid element or attribute, such as the `alt` attribute or the `label` element. Judgment comes in with questions, such as whether or not the value of the `alt` attribute conveys the function of an active image or the information in an inactive image.

This will be a fairly open-ended discussion. The algorithmic section addresses which parts of the accessibility testing *could* feasibly be automated. We will not be looking at particular tools, but what tools could do. The judgment section points out things that you, as an expert, can evaluate and then decide whether a given page passes or fails.

As noted at the beginning of the chapter, the next part of this chapter will review specific accessibility checking tools. For reviewing those tools, I devised a set of tests that cover accessibility issues, which are described in the "Test Suite" section later in this chapter. When there are specific tests in the test suite that relate to the Section 508 provision, I list them in the section on algorithmic testing. For example, the section on text equivalents refers to two tests (tests 1 and 4) relating to the presence of `alt` attributes.

Text Equivalents

The following is the Section 508 provision for text equivalents:

§1194.22(a) A text equivalent for every non-text element shall be provided (for example, via "alt", "longdesc", or in element content).

Algorithmic

A computer program can verify the presence of alt attributes on elements where they are required, including img, area, and input with type="image" (tests 1 and 4). You can algorithmically check whether the alt attribute is actually present and whether it consists of a text string (test 2). This includes the null string alt="", which is desirable on formatting images but never valid on an input element with type="image" or on any link where there is no text as part of the anchor (tests 22, 23, and 24). These restrictions can also be checked.

Common errors or violations, such as the use of filenames for alt-text, can also be detected. Words like *spacer, go, click*, and *null*, and an alt attribute consisting of a space are also errors that software could detect or highlight for examination. Several of the tools covered in the "Accessibility Checking Software" section of this chapter allow you to add suspicious words or phrases and other characteristics of the alt-text that should raise errors or warnings (tests 2 and 5).

I think tools should distinguish between the kinds of alt-text failure. Active images—like image links, image buttons, and image-map areas—need alt-text (test 6). When the alt-text for these items is missing, that is a very serious error. On the other hand, although small images (formatting images that are less than 10 pixels in either dimension) need alt-text, if they don't have it, that is just not a big deal. These images are required to have an alt attribute to be valid XHTML, and they should have alt="", which tells a screen reader to ignore the image. But ignore the image is exactly what the screen readers do if the alt-text is missing.

The only tool to make distinctions between the types of images is LIFT Machine. Unfortunately, it identifies 11 different types of images, including banner, bullet, composition, decorative, thumbnail, repetitive, and five more.

It is certainly possible for a software program to raise the question of whether or not a longdesc attribute belongs on an image for, say, images larger than a predetermined size. This doesn't seem very helpful to me, but many software tools do raise this question for any nontrivial image. Furthermore, the presence of certain file types should trigger questions about the existence of text equivalents. These include (but are certainly not limited to) the various media file types, such as .wav, .ra, .rm, and .ram files.

13

Judgment

Judgment comes in when evaluating the *quality* of the text equivalents—whether a text string serves as a textual equivalent to the nontext element. More specifically, you need to ask:

- Does the alt-text convey the function of the image when the image is active?
- Does the alt-text convey the information of the image in the case the image is not active and when the image is conveying information?

You should use alt="" for images that do not convey information, like formatting images.

There is some disagreement about the finer details. For example, I would say that graphical "bullets" in front of items in a list should have alt="", while others might argue for using alt="bullet". Of course, such lists should be coded as HTML unordered lists (<ul>), with CSS specifying a list-style image referencing those graphical bullets. However, the basic rules still apply, and either choice for alt-text complies with §1194.22(a), regardless of which side of this particular argument you take.

You may also need to visually inspect for the presence of text equivalents for audio and multimedia elements. In addition, in order to decide whether or not a transcript is appropriate, someone will need to actually read through the text to check that it actually matches the audio presentation.

If alt-text or object content is used for applets or objects (test 3), that text must be compared with the applet or object for equivalence. Consider an applet that acts as a ticker application for displaying stock prices. Alt-text or object content that says, Applet displays current stock prices, (as suggested by the U.S. Access Board guide to the Section 508 Standards, www.access-board.gov/sec508/guide/1194.22.htm) is not actually an equivalent, since it does not enable the user to obtain the current stock prices. Some more imaginative way of presenting the equivalent data must be found, and deciding whether that equivalence is achieved requires human judgment.

Judgment is also required in determining which images require long or in-line descriptions, like charts and graphs, as discussed in Chapter 6, and whether a long description is adequate in conveying the information of the image.

Synchronized Multimedia

The following is the Section 508 provision for synchronized multimedia:

§1194.22(b) Equivalent alternatives for any multimedia presentation shall be synchronized with the presentation.

Algorithmic

The existence of multimedia content can be detected by file extension in an anchor or contents of an `object` element. For some multimedia formats (`.smi`, for example), it may be possible to determine algorithmically whether or not captioning is included. I think the most important role for software testing relative to this provision of the Section 508 Standards is to highlight the places where multimedia appears, so that humans can examine the accessibility accommodations of that content.

Judgment

It is not possible to determine the existence of captions for all media formats. Therefore, human evaluation is required just to determine whether the synchronized equivalents are present. Then there is the question of the accuracy of the captions. Also the multimedia content must be studied to determine whether audio descriptions are necessary, and if they are necessary, are the audio descriptions adequate?

These questions must be answered to determine compliance with this provision of the Section 508 Standards on web accessibility.

Color Coding

The following is the Section 508 provision for color coding:

> §1194.22(c) Web pages shall be designed so that all information conveyed with color is also available without color, for example from context or markup.

Algorithmic

Automated software could be used to check for color specifications in the style sheet and corresponding elements in the web page, and deduce any color changes in the page that way. If there are no color changes through HTML or CSS on a web page, the page automatically complies with §1194.22(c) as far as *text* is concerned. However, images on the page could still be color-coded (images used as links, for instance). If the image color conveys important information, it raises accessibility issues.

Moreover, if there *were* color changes in the page, it would be difficult to detect algorithmically whether information was being conveyed by color *alone*. For example, a simple search for "color words" in a page's source code might turn up phrases from the page content, such as "the books in green are available for checkout," which might suggest non-compliance, but still requires a human evaluation.

Judgment

A general evaluation of the page is necessary to determine if information is conveyed by color alone. Most sources that discuss testing for this provision recommend that human testing be done by viewing the page in black and white. I think that is wrong. It is much easier to check for the use of color-conveying information when color is available to the person addressing the question.

13

Style Sheets

The following is the Section 508 provision for style sheets:

> §1194.22(d) Documents shall be organized so they are readable without requiring an associated style sheet.

Algorithmic

An algorithm can detect the presence of style sheets, style elements, and style attributes. If they don't exist, the page complies with §1194.22(d) vacuously. A testing tool could determine if style sheets are present and if there is no CSS positioning in those styles. In that case also, this provision is probably met. Beyond these boundary conditions, human judgment is needed to study how the document looks with style sheets disabled. In particular, it is necessary to evaluate background images to be sure that they do not convey any information, or if information is conveyed in background images, that it is also available by other means. All of this is important because screen readers generally operate on a page as if style sheets were disabled.

Judgment

Pages should be viewed using a browser with style sheets turned off to determine whether the reading order of the page makes sense. It is also a judgment call whether there are structural elements, such as lists and headings, being presented just with stylistic changes instead of using HTML markup.

Redundant Text Links

The following is the Section 508 provision for redundant text links with server-side maps:

> §1194.22(e) Redundant text links shall be provided for each active region of a server-side image map.

Algorithmic

If no server-side maps are present (img with the ismap attribute), the page obviously passes this provision (test 7). If a server-side map is found (img with the ismap attribute and no valid usemap attribute), the question is whether or not redundant text links are available. A program could be written to click on every pixel of the map, record the new URL, and compare it with all href values on the page. That sort of overkill would be kind of silly though!

Software can at least detect the presence of server-side maps and flag them for subsequent human evaluation.

Judgment

If a server-side map is found, it must be evaluated for the availability of text links for all the active regions of the map.

Use Client-Side Image Maps

The following is the Section 508 provision for requiring client-side image maps:

§1194.22(f) Client-side image maps shall be provided instead of server-side image maps except where the regions cannot be defined with an available geometric shape.

Algorithmic

If there is no server-side map on the page, it obviously complies with §1194.22(f) (test 7). If there is one, see §1194.22(e).

Since all regions can actually be defined with polygons, the page should fail if a server-side map is used. All areas of the client-side map must have a valid alt attribute (test 6). The ismap attribute should never be used on an input element with type="image" (an "image button").

Judgment

My interpretation of this provision is that the page does not comply with §1194.22(f) when a server-side map is found. The absence of a server-side map means that the page is compliant. Since this is an either/or requirement, no human judgment is required.

Table Headers

The following is the Section 508 provision for table headers:

§1194.22(g) Row and column headers shall be identified for data tables.

Algorithmic

If a page has no tables at all, this provision is vacuously satisfied. I believe it is possible to devise sophisticated heuristic algorithms to separate data tables from layout tables with adequate certainty (test 32). Since almost all tables are layout tables, and since many websites still use layout tables, it would be especially advantageous if software could successfully separate out tables that are data tables. There are many issues involved in achieving this. The use of images in cells would suggest a layout table, whereas uniformity of cell content suggests a data table, and so on. Nested tables are almost certainly not data tables. Once an accessibility checker has determined that a table is probably a data table, the question of compliance comes down to whether or not row and column headers have been identified.

13

Having detected a data table, the tool could assert compliance if all row and column heading cells (column 1 and row 1) are marked with th elements or if only the first column or the first row of cells is marked with th.

The tool's capacity to identify data tables should extend to determining that accessible table markup (th, headers, summary, scope, caption) is being used when it should not be used (test 33).

Judgment

No matter how sophisticated the algorithm to detect data tables is, every page must be checked for their presence because the heuristics cannot be guaranteed to find data tables in every case. Once a table is determined to be a data table, the validity of its headings specification must be verified by examining the HTML source code for headings markup.

Complex Tables

The following is the Section 508 provision for complex tables:

§1194.22(h) Markup shall be used to associate data cells and header cells for data tables that have two or more logical levels of row or column headers.

Algorithmic

Although a tool could probably determine which tables on a site are data tables (albeit with some degree of uncertainty), I cannot imagine any way of algorithmically determining whether or not a given table is complex in the sense that it has two or more logical levels of row or column headers. However, if all data cells in the table have valid header attributes, the table conforms to this provision—whether or not it is complex.

Judgment

Again, the situation is similar to that for the previous provision. Any page must be searched for data tables. When one is found, it requires human judgment to determine whether or not there are two or more logical levels of row or column headers. If there is *at most* one row heading and *at most* one column heading for each data cell, and these are in the same row and column as the cell, respectively, then the table is not complex. Judgment is required to determine whether or not the headers markup that is required by this provision is adequate. This can be verified by human testing with assistive technology or careful analysis of the HTML code.

Frames

The following is the Section 508 provision for frames:

§1194.22(i) Frames shall be titled with text that facilitates frame identification and navigation.

Algorithmic

Software can check whether the `frame` elements in a `frameset` have valid `title` attributes (tests 8, 34, and 40). Exception can be taken in some cases when `title` attributes are inadequate, similar to considerations of suspicious alt-text (test 9).

Judgment

Human judgment will determine whether or not the frame `title` attributes are useful for the purposes of identification and navigation. For example, `title="frame10078"` and `title="frame10077"` are not useful ways of identifying a frame to convey its purpose.

Flicker Rate

The following is the Section 508 provision for flicker rate:

> §1194.22(j) Pages shall be designed to avoid causing the screen to flicker with a frequency greater than 2 Hz and lower than 55 Hz.

Algorithmic

Software can detect whether or not there are technologies present on a web page that *might* cause flickering in the hazardous range. Java, Flash, and JavaScript qualify as potential culprits. Furthermore, any animated GIF on the page could cause flickering. Animation and the frequency of frame transitions also could be detected algorithmically, but a frame rate in the hazardous range does not necessarily mean that the screen will be flickering at this rate; it is the change from light to dark that causes flickering. Taking the requirement beyond specific flicker rates, software can certainly flag moving text with the deprecated `blink` and `marquee` elements (tests 35 and 36).

Judgment

You must inspect any page that has potential "flickering technology" on it to check whether or not flickering is occurring. If so, you need to determine whether the frequency is in the range disallowed by this provision and rectify matters if that is the case.

Text-Only Page

The following is the Section 508 provision for a text-only page:

> §1194.22(k) A text-only page, with equivalent information or functionality, shall be provided to make a web site comply with the provisions of this part, when compliance cannot be accomplished in any other way. The content of the text-only page shall be updated whenever the primary page changes.

13

Algorithmic

While it is possible to detect algorithmically some references to text-only pages, it is impossible to evaluate the equivalence of content or frequency of update of a text-only page. This provision mandates the use of a text-only page only in circumstances where compliance cannot be accomplished in any other way. The fact that a page cannot be made accessible in the first place obviously cannot be determined algorithmically.

Judgment

There are two parts to evaluating a web page for compliance with this provision:

- Is it really impossible to make the page accessible in some other way?
- If it is impossible, is there a text-only page readily available and, if so, is it accessible?
  - Does it meet all the other Section 508 provisions for web access?
  - Does the text-only version offer equivalent functionality and information to the original?
  - Is it kept up-to-date with the same frequency as the original page?

These are all difficult questions to answer, making this one of the most daunting of the Section 508 provisions for compliance testing.

Scripting

The following is the Section 508 provision for scripting:

§1194.22(l) When pages utilize scripting languages to display content, or to create interface elements, the information provided by the script shall be identified with functional text that can be read by assistive technology.

Algorithmic

If a page uses scripts to modify attributes for visual effect, this is fine from an accessibility standpoint, since it does not affect the user's ability to interact with the site. In some cases, this could be determined with a software accessibility checker since (in principle) an algorithm could be devised to check if the fly-over submenu links are available on the page opened by the main menu item link. However, this is a pretty complex task. It is, in effect, one program trying to evaluate another.

Judgment

The criterion here should be simply whether someone using assistive technology can handle the page and its interactions. This requires testing using the screen readers or a talking browser like Home Page Reader. Without access to assistive technology, you can evaluate items such as fly-over menus by testing whether redundant text links are readily available for all submenu links; that is, is the enhancement provided by the script simply visual?

Applets and Plug-Ins

The following is the Section 508 provision for applets and plug-ins:

§1194.22(m) When a web page requires that an applet, plug-ins, or other application be present on the client system to interpret page content, the page must provide a link to a plug-in or applet that complies with §1194.22(a) through (l).

Algorithmic

It is possible for software accessibility checkers to detect whether or not applets, plug-ins, or other applications are required or opened on a page. They might be able to determine if corresponding links are present on the page at least for a few common examples, like Adobe Reader for PDF files.

Judgment

Human involvement and significant further testing may be required in determining whether or not a link is present to open or obtain the plug-in, applet, or application and whether or not that plug-in, applet, or application meets the Section 508 provisions for software in §1194.21(a)–(l).

Online Forms

The following is the Section 508 provision for online forms:

§1194.22(n) When electronic forms are designed to be completed online, the form shall allow people using assistive technology to access the information, field elements, and functionality required for completion and submission of the form, including all directions and cues.

Algorithmic

A testing tool can check that every input element of type text, password, checkbox, radio, and file has an id attribute matching the for attribute of a label element enclosing text, which is the prompt for that input element (tests 10 and 12–16). If there is no such label, the tool can check if there is a valid title attribute on the form control (test 11). The same checking applies to textarea elements and select menus (tests 17 and 18).

There can be algorithmic checks on the quality of both the title and the label. For example, a tool could verify that neither is empty (test 20).

In addition, input elements of type image must have a valid alt attribute, but that is an alt-text problem, not a form problem.

13

Judgment

Human judgment comes in verifying that the prompts (labels) and titles are appropriate. Keyboard access should be checked as well.

Skip Navigation

The following is the Section 508 provision for skip navigation:

> §1194.22(o) A method shall be provided that permits users to skip repetitive navigation links.

Algorithmic

If there were a reliable algorithm to determine the position of the main content, and what to skip over, then screen reader developers would include that in their products, and so no skip navigation link would be needed! In fact, screen readers include jumps like this, but they are still heuristic and quite likely to miss the mark. For each large block of links (greater than, say, five), software could check if there is a link to a local anchor that skips over those links (test 29). In a similar way, a tool could check for the presence of headings markup that could serve instead of skip links (test 30). If either of these tests turn out positive, the page complies with §1194.22(o). The page probably also complies if there is no large block of links. The page also complies with this provision if it uses frames that comply with 1194.22(i) and that separate main content from navigation.

Judgment

Examine the page to determine whether there are large blocks of "repetitive navigation links" and use assistive technology to verify that a skip navigation link works in helping users bypass those links.

Timed Responses

The following is the Section 508 provision for timed responses:

> §1194.22(p) When a timed response is required, the user shall be alerted and given sufficient time to indicate more time is required.

Algorithmic

If there are no `meta refresh` tags, no forms, and no scripting, then there are no timed responses. There may be heuristics to help decide if a timed response is required, but it is difficult to imagine an algorithm that could further decide whether or not sufficient time has been allowed.

Judgment

Check all form submissions to determine if timed responses are required and if it is possible to request more time if they are. If the meta refresh tag is used, check whether the time allowed is sufficient or if the user is given the option of requesting more time.

Accessibility Checking Software

The Web Accessibility Initiative (WAI) Evaluation and Repair Tools working group lists more than 90 software tools in three categories: Evaluation, Repair, and Transformation. Here, we will look at only the following six commercial web accessibility testing tools. *These brief descriptions are drawn from their corresponding websites*:

- **Bobby:** Watchfire's Bobby (www.watchfire.com/products/webxm/bobby.aspx, $299) spiders through a website and tests on a page-by-page basis to see if it meets several accessibility requirements, including readability by screen readers and the provision of text equivalents for all images, animated elements, and audio and video displays. Bobby can see local web pages, as well as web pages behind your firewall. It performs more than 90 accessibility checks.

- **InFocus:** InFocus Desktop (http://ssbtechnologies.com, $1,795 for corporate customers), from the SSB BART Group, was the first commercial web accessibility software and remains the market leader. It offers more than 115 accessibility tests, encompassing all major accessibility standards, with a high level of automation.

- **LIFT Machine:** LIFT Machine (http://usablenet.com, LIFT Online, $999), from UsableNet, is a server-based application that automatically scans internal and external websites for more than 140 quality, accessibility, and usability issues. It then generates a variety of web-based reports for both executives and individual content creators.

- **Ramp Ascend:** Deque's Ramp Ascend (http://deque.com, $1,499) includes full capabilities for adding SMIL captioning to multimedia, ensures web animations are safe, and provides comprehensive table remediation to even the most complex, n-dimensional tables. It includes plug-ins for Macromedia Dreamweaver, Microsoft FrontPage, and Mercury Interactive TestDirector 8.

- **WebKing:** Parasoft's WebKing (www.parasoft.com, contact info@parasoft.com for prices) allows users to record critical user click paths by following them in a browser. Then it automatically configures and executes functional/regression tests that verify paths and page contents while ignoring insignificant differences. WebKing's static analysis identifies client-side code that does not comply with Section 508 accessibility rules, as well as pages with broken links, XML problems, and spelling errors.

- **WebXM:** Watchfire's WebXM (www.watchfire.com, contact sales@watchfire.com for prices) provides software and services to identify, measure, and prioritize accessibility and compliance risks that exist on corporate web properties.

13

To review these tools, I went through a simple process of evaluating about 70 files, looking for specific errors in about half the cases and for the *absence* of specific errors in roughly the other half. This is not a complicated spidering problem. Once errors were found, I was not interested in repair (remediation), which is provided by both InFocus and Ramp Ascend. LIFT Machine, WebKing, and WebXM offer tests for usability—we aren't looking at those tests. For the latter two, accessibility checking is only a recent addition to features involving site maintenance, integrity, and security

After the first pass on the tests, I submitted the results to each of the product owners to verify that I had interpreted the tools' results correctly and to make a case for improvements in the testing algorithms. Both Deque (Ramp Ascend) and Parasoft (WebKing) made changes in their tool's algorithms, and with those revised tools, I reran the tests. Both tools improved their scores, and Deque provided access to the beta version of Ramp Ascend version 6.0, which I tested late in the process. With that version, Ramp Ascend achieved the highest score.

When I first ran these tests, I included two additional tools that are not covered here. One was aDesigner, a beta version of a tool from IBM Tokyo Research Center, available from IBM AlphaWorks. I hadn't remembered that the public version of the tool did not have any spidering, so it was not acceptable for the task. The other tool I dropped from the process was PageScreamer because the company (Crunchy Technologies) seems to be out of business. aDesigner had one of the best scores on the first round; PageScreamer had the worst.

The following descriptions of these testing tools go through the four simple steps of setting up the tests to be performed, analyzing the files, examining the results, and obtaining the reports. Generally, I tried to use WCAG AA conformance together with the Section 508 Standards. Brief descriptions of the test files and a summary of the results from all the tools are presented in the "The Test File Set and Results" section later in this chapter.

Bobby 5.0

Bobby, from Watchfire, is the best known accessibility checker because it has been around for the longest time. Bobby was first released by the Center for Applied Special Technology (CAST, www.cast.org/) as a free downloadable tool in September 1996. Bobby was acquired by Watchfire in 2002. In 2003, Watchfire produced Version 5.0, with improved spidering and reporting. My understanding is that the testing algorithms for the previous version, Bobby Worldwide (Version 4.0), are the same.

Choose the Tests to Be Used—Bobby

To choose tests in Bobby 5.0, you need to create a project and associate the choice of tests with that project. So once Bobby is started, open the project Properties dialog box (Tools ➤ Project Properties). Choose a name for the project, say STEP Tests, and select Accessibility from the list on the left side of the project Properties dialog box, as shown in Figure 13-1.

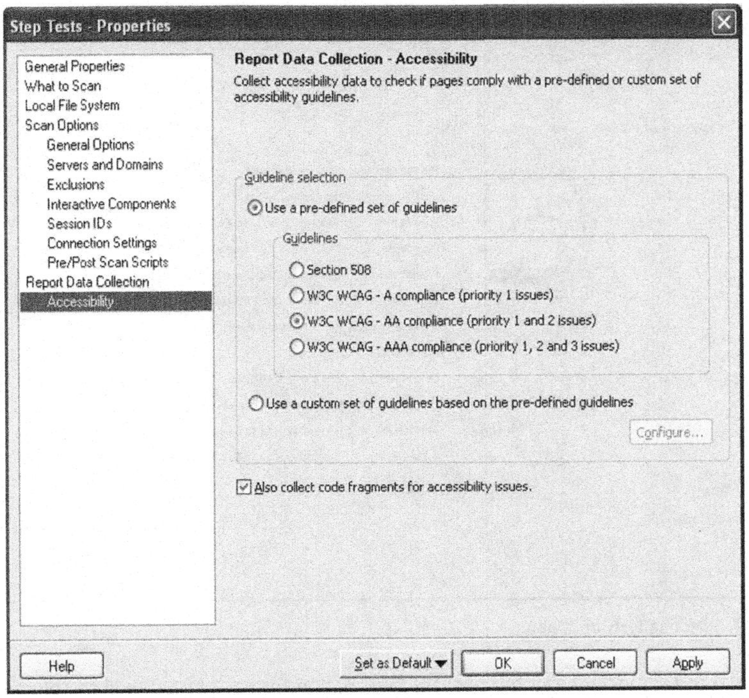

Figure 13-1. Choosing guideline sets in Bobby 5.0

The Guidelines section of this Properties dialog box allows the choice of Section 508 Standards or WCAG with A, AA, or AAA compliance (most of the tools offer these choices). Notice that you cannot select Section 508 *and* WCAG Priority 1 and 2 (this is also the case with WebXM). So, you will create a custom set of guidelines that combines the two.

Notice the check box to collect code. If you want the code fragments included in the reports, check this box.

To create custom guidelines, select that radio button and click the Configure button. You will see the Configure Custom Guidelines dialog box, as shown in Figure 13-2.

13

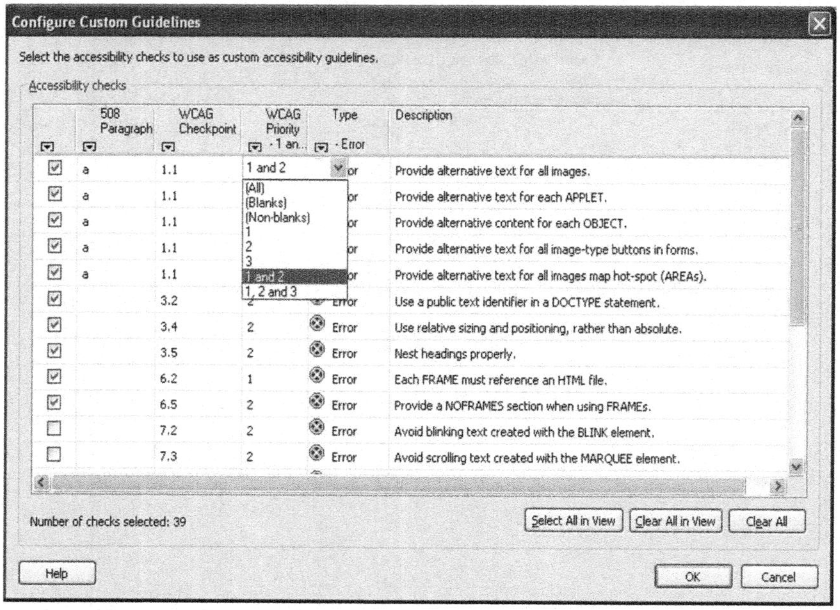

Figure 13-2. Selecting tests in Bobby

This Bobby interface includes all the relevant information for each test. The Type column indicates whether or not the test raises an error or a warning. For each test, the corresponding WCAG checkpoint and priority is listed. If relevant, the paragraph of the Section 508 Standards appears there, too.

Using this interface, if you want all WCAG Priority 1 and 2 sure-fire tests (no warnings), restrict the Type column to Errors and the WCAG Priority column to 1 and 2, using the pull-down menus shown in Figure 13-2. Then select the Select All in View button, and each of the check boxes will be checked. Well, that should work, but it doesn't. What happens as a result of the sequence just described is that all Priority 1 and Priority 2 tests are checked, including the warnings. You need to sort through the tests and uncheck the warnings you don't want.

Analyze the Files—Bobby

The project Properties dialog box is also where you set up Bobby to analyze the site. Select What to Scan from the list on the left to see the dialog box shown in Figure 13-3.

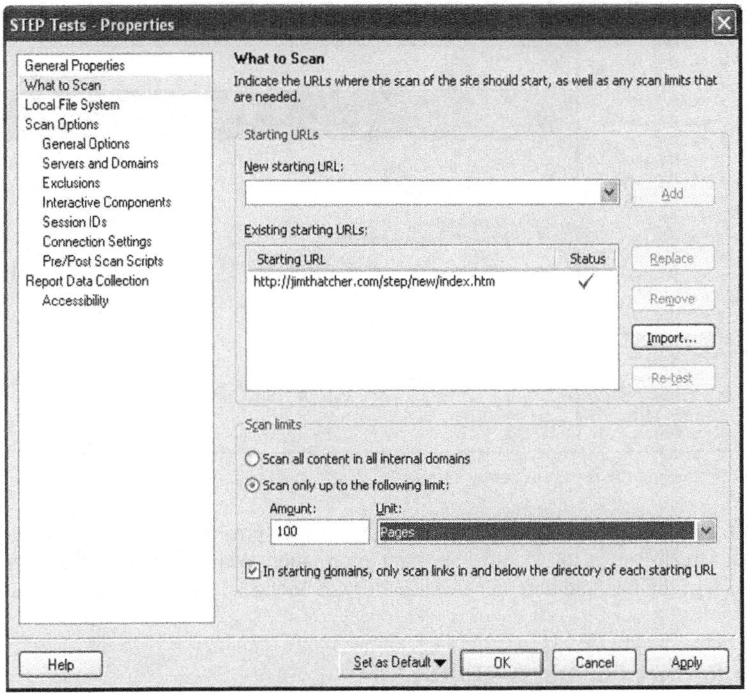

Figure 13-3. Specifying files to scan in Bobby

The Scan limits portion of this dialog box is disappointing. Rather than a click depth, only the number of pages (or directories) is allowed to limit the scan. That's not a problem for our test files, but for a site with more complicated structure, the numeric limit may be very different from the click-depth limit. It would seem that if the process of analysis is multi-threaded, even successive runs might end up with different sets of files. And depending on the algorithm for finding the 100 files, the selected files might all be down one branch of the site's tree, as opposed to sampling broadly across all branches (which is what click-depth constraints do).

Select the OK button, and back in the main window, use the menu to scan the entire site (Scan ➤ Scan Entire Site) or click the green arrow to the right of the URL entry field at the top of the window.

Examine the Results—Bobby

Like Ramp, WebKing, and InFocus, Bobby lists files in the left pane of the user interface, as shown in Figure 13-4. When any file is selected, the report is displayed on the right. In the right pane, you can choose to see the raw HTML of the page, a preview of the page, and a list of pages associated with the current highlighted item.

13

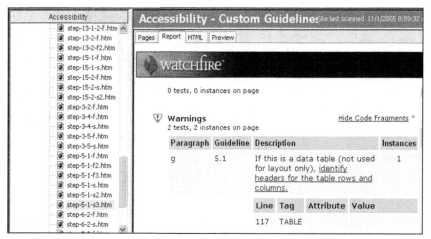

Figure 13-4. Examining the results in Bobby

The report has a lot of unnecessary formatting (the Watchfire logo and widely spaced tables) that actually serves to hide the important information. With patience, you can step through each of the files and determine whether or not Bobby 5.0 passes the various issue tests.

Choose Report Formats—Bobby

Report formats in Bobby 5.0 are disappointing. There is no way to view the results of the Bobby 5.0 analysis except by viewing reports in the Bobby user interface. There is no way to save the report or share it with someone—well, almost no way.

It is possible to obtain an XML report, but first you must edit the Windows registry key HKEY_LOCAL_MACHINE\SOFTWARE\Watchfire\WebXM\2.0\WFScan, adding a string value with name BobbyLog and a value that is the path and filename for the XML output file. I used C:\bobby.xml for simplicity. Be sure to copy that file to some other place (or to some other name), because the next time you run Bobby 5.0, the XML file will be overwritten. Before you edit the Windows registry, be sure to make a backup (see http://support.microsoft.com/kb/322756).

InFocus

I used InFocus Version 4.2.2 for these tests. SSB offers an InFocus Enterprise product, and I was told that the analysis engine is the same for the two tools.

Choose the Tests to Be Used—InFocus

After starting InFocus, open the Testing Control dialog box (Configuration ➤ Testing Control). As shown in Figure 13-5, the Testing Control dialog box offers a welcome option: Manual Checks OFF. After reading the caution to not use color alone to convey information on every page for 100 pages, you get very tired of the advice. It is important not to use color alone to convey information, but we are smart enough (I hope) to not need to be reminded of that fact at every turn—well, on every page. InFocus is the only tool that provides a single option to turn off all those tests.

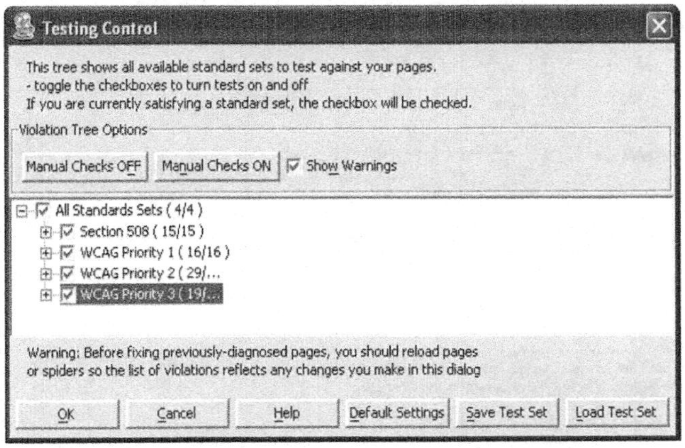

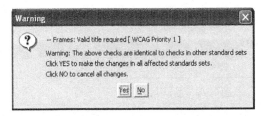

Figure 13-5. Choosing tests in InFocus

The simplest way to select all Section 508 and WCAG Priority 1 and 2 (nonmanual) tests is to make sure that all tests are checked. Then uncheck WCAG Priority 3 and select Manual Checks OFF.

The Show Warnings check box next to the Manual Checks buttons has nothing to do with the tests themselves, and that is confusing at first. These are warnings that appear as you turn on or off selected tests.

For example, if you turn off the check for frame titles in Section 508, you are warned that this is also turning off the frame test in WCAG, as shown in Figure 13-6. You can decide that you don't want to be bothered by those warnings by unchecking the Show Warnings check box. This decision is superior to the one found in, for example, LIFT Machine, where it is necessary for you to manually turn off all occurrences of any given test.

Figure 13-6. A warning about rules shared between
Section 508 and WCAG

This is only the beginning of tailoring your test procedure with InFocus. Many of the tests take parameters. For example, the test for valid alt-text excludes alt-text that is too long or contains certain words. These options are set in the Test Settings Editor dialog box (Configuration ➤ Test Settings), as shown in Figure 13-7.

13

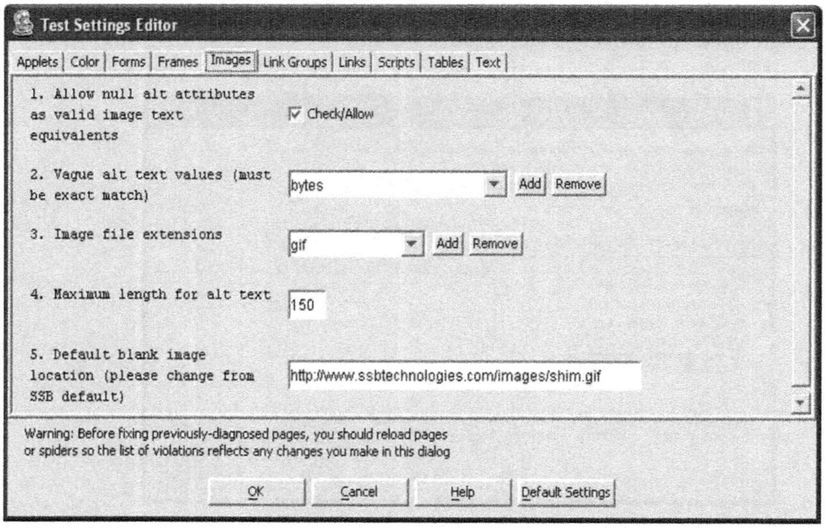

Figure 13-7. Test settings for InFocus

Many of the tests depend on settings like the ones shown in Figure 13-7. One of the most interesting pages in this dialog box is the one that determines which table elements will be considered to be data tables.

Analyze the Files—InFocus

After choosing the tests to be used, you want to set up the test file analysis. If you want to check a single file, just enter it in the URL field at the top of the main window and press Enter.

For the sample test files, you need to spider to depth 1 for the test files. To do this, click the spider icon or choose Edit ➤ Create Spider from the menu. The Create Spider Wizard has seven steps:

1. Enter the URL in the first step, as shown in Figure 13-8.

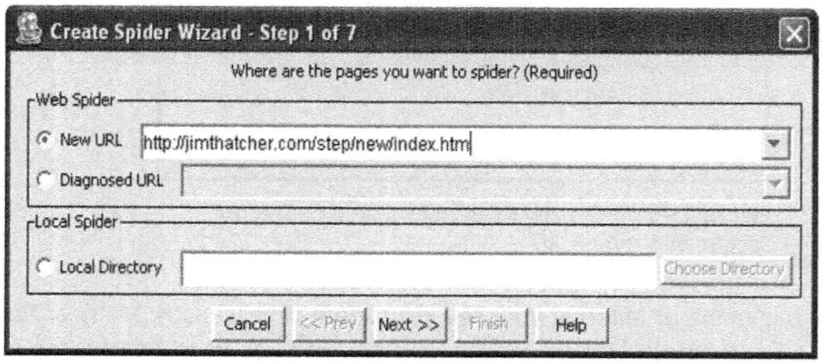

Figure 13-8. Setting up the spider in InFocus

2. The wizard provides the opportunity to enter a user ID and password if authentication is required for the site you are testing.

3. Choose the report format and report location, as shown in Figure 13-9. The options for report format are XML, Evaluation and Repair Language (EARL), XLS (Microsoft Excel spreadsheet), or HTML. In this dialog box, be sure to check Add Generated Pages to History (it is not checked by default). With this setting, you can check out the errors using the InFocus interface, which is much easier than using one of the reports.

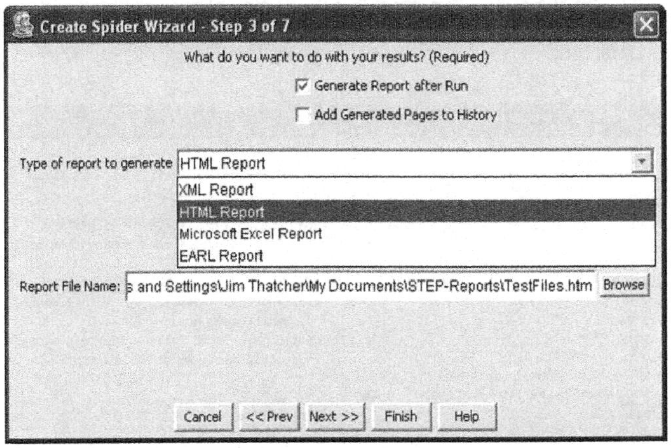

Figure 13-9. Choosing report options with InFocus

4. Choose how to determine the number of files to be analyzed, as shown in Figure 13-10. It is recommended that you keep this number relatively small—less than 100. If you want to scan more than that, you probably need to consider using the InFocus Enterprise product instead. InFocus uses the term "page depth" for what I think of as "click depth"—the number of mouse clicks or links followed from the start page you specified in Step 1 to the analyzed page. You can also specify the maximum number of pages and the maximum page size.

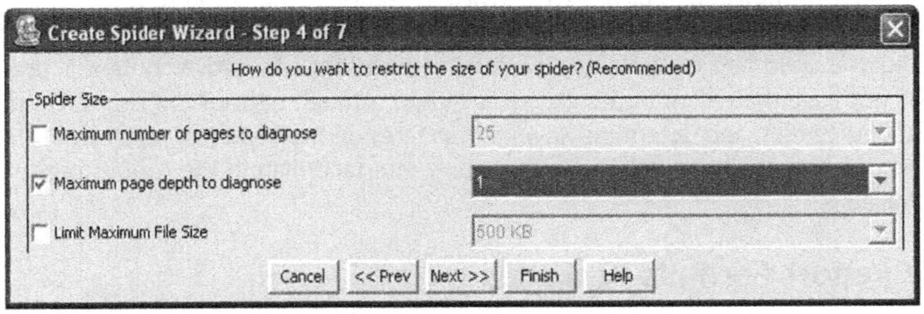

Figure 13-10. Choosing the extent of the scan with InFocus

5. Filter file types to diagnose.

6. Choose whether the followed URLs must be in the same folder or on the same host. For this example, choose the same host.

7. Choose the speed of the spider. (I always leave the default setting.) Then select Finish. You'll go to a window that will display the progress of the scan after you select Start.

Examine the Results—InFocus

It is especially easy to run through the test file results with the InFocus user interface. Most issues require looking at two files: the good one and the bad one, so to speak. As shown in Figure 13-11, you can highlight the two files in the tree view on the left and open the tree to list the errors detected.

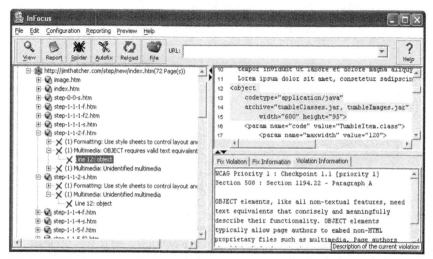

Figure 13-11. Examining errors in InFocus

The issue being examined in the example in Figure 13-11 is "Object requires default content" (test 3). The two files are step-1-1-2-f.htm (the failing file—with an error) and step-1-1-2-s.htm (the successful file—no error). In Figure 13-11, the tree is opened at those two files. The one that should fail (no default content) does indeed invoke an error: "OBJECT requires valid text equivalent." The file in which that alternative content is provided does not have that error. In this way, you can go through each of the issues, check the corresponding files, and determine how InFocus fares on the tests. It is much easier to make these comparisons here with the InFocus user interface than in the various reports that are available.

Choose Report Formats—InFocus

If, during Step 3 of the spider definition (Figure 13-9), you specified a report type and location, the InFocus report will be there when the analysis completes. You can create additional reports by going to the main menu and choosing Reporting ➤ Generate Reports. The Generate Report dialog box allows you to select individual files or spidered directories as the subject of the report, as shown in Figure 13-12.

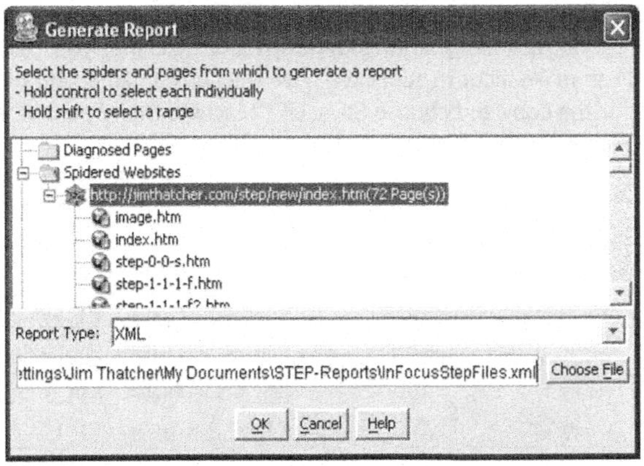

Figure 13-12. Selecting reports in InFocus

The options for the report type are HTML, XML, Microsoft Excel, or EARL. InFocus is the only tool to include EARL as a report format option.

LIFT Machine

LIFT Machine is a server-based testing tool from UsableNet. You log on to the LIFT Machine server to set up scans of desired websites. You can be notified by e-mail when a job finishes, or you can just wait. Depending on the size of the scan, it may not take very long.

Before Deque and Parasoft modified their tools (and improved their scores), LIFT Machine had the best score of 27 out of 40, or 68 percent.

LIFT Machine has a wide range of configurability, which I consider to be very valuable. But there were a number of issues in that configuration process that were distracting.

Choose the Tests to Be Used—LIFT

LIFT Machine offers many choices for sets of tests. The main window has a set of tabs, as shown in Figure 13-13.

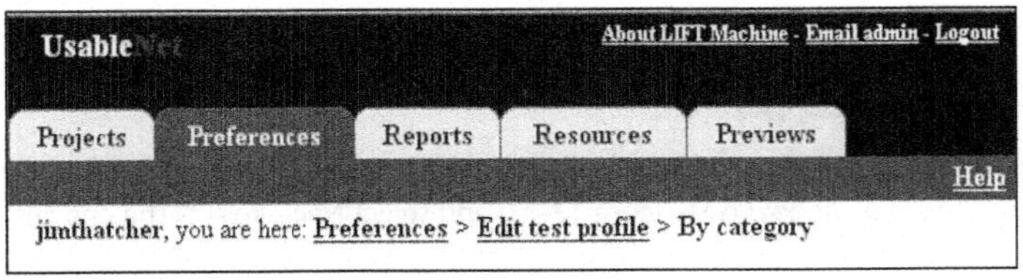

Figure 13-13. The tabs for the LIFT Machine user interface

Choose the Preferences tab. The Preferences page has four groups of settings: Test profiles, Spider profiles, User interface settings, and Account settings. We are interested in the test profiles. Expand that section and select Duplicate for the W3C/WCAG 1.0 priority 1 & 2 profile. Since that test profile is shared among users of LIFT Machine, you cannot edit it directly. Instead, you can make a copy (duplicate), give the copy a name, and then edit the copy. Select a name for the copy and choose Save. LIFT Machine then opens screen to edit the copy you have created, as shown in Figure 13-14.

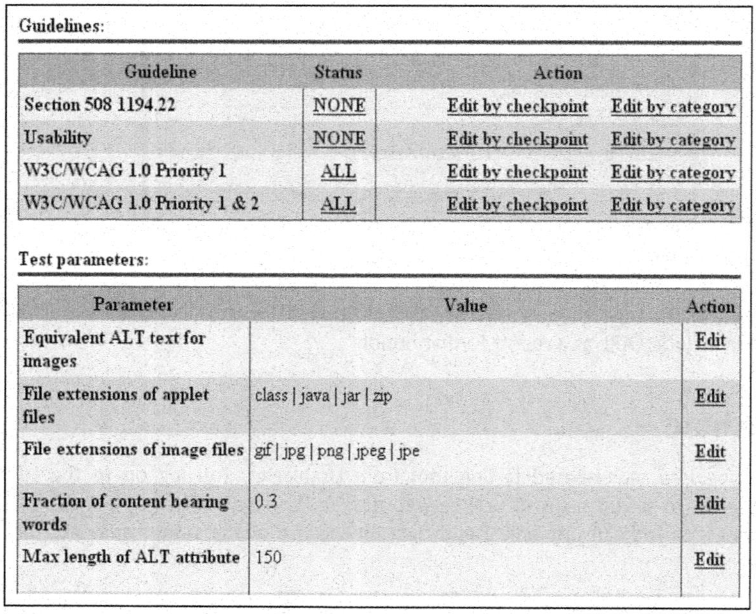

Guidelines:

Guideline	Status	Action	
Section 508 1194.22	NONE	Edit by checkpoint	Edit by category
Usability	NONE	Edit by checkpoint	Edit by category
W3C/WCAG 1.0 Priority 1	ALL	Edit by checkpoint	Edit by category
W3C/WCAG 1.0 Priority 1 & 2	ALL	Edit by checkpoint	Edit by category

Test parameters:

Parameter	Value	Action
Equivalent ALT text for images		Edit
File extensions of applet files	class | java | jar | zip	Edit
File extensions of image files	gif | jpg | png | jpeg | jpe	Edit
Fraction of content bearing words	0.3	Edit
Max length of ALT attribute	150	Edit

Figure 13-14. LIFT choices for editing a test profile

In Figure 13-14, notice that all of the WCAG Priority 1 and 2 tests are included, and none of the Usability or Section 508 1194.22 tests are selected. If you were to choose all of the Section 508 tests now (just click NONE, and it will change to ALL), many tests will be duplicated. As an alternative, select Edit by checkpoint on the Section 508 line, and then change NONE to ALL on both 508 (n) Forms and 508 (o) Skip Menus. Then return to the test profile editor by selecting the Edit test profile link at the top of the main page (see Figure 13-13).

This process creates a new test profile, which you can now use in the analysis of the test files.

Analyze the Files—LIFT

To analyze the files, you should set up a project (as with the other tools). Choose the Projects tab in the main window (see Figure 13-13) and select New Project. The choices are quite simple, as shown in Figure 13-15. But be careful. If you decide to edit the spider profile, for example, when you come back to the project page, some of your choices will have disappeared.

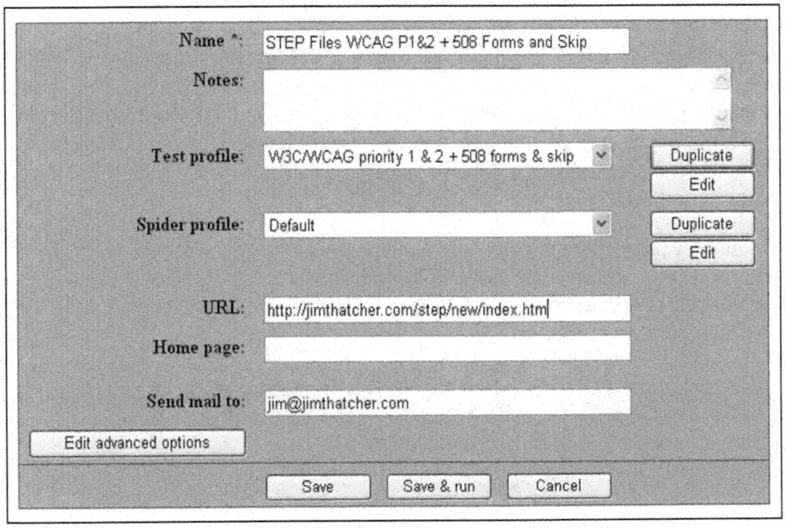

Figure 13-15. The choices for a LIFT project

Be sure to pick a name that will distinguish this project from other projects, because only the name appears elsewhere in the process.

Choose the test profile W3C/WCAG priority 1 & 2 = 508 forms & skip, which was created when you chose the tests. The default spidering profile is unlimited in click depth but limited to 250 files. That will easily cover the test files. Don't forget to add the starting URL (http://jimthatcher.com/step/new/index.htm). This could be part of the spider profile or not, as you wish. Since you are using the default spider profile, you must add the URL here.

When the parameters are set, choose Save & run. This submits the job to LIFT Machine. You will receive an e-mail when the job is done, or you can sit on the project page and wait, hitting refresh (F5) occasionally. For large projects, I would not advise that process.

In my case, the progress indicator specifying the total number of pages completed got stuck at 23 pages (a minor bug), so that the progress read 45 of 22 pages, 55 of 23 pages, 67 of 23 pages, and then finally completed 70 pages. Figure 13-16 shows the final status report. The testing took less than two minutes.

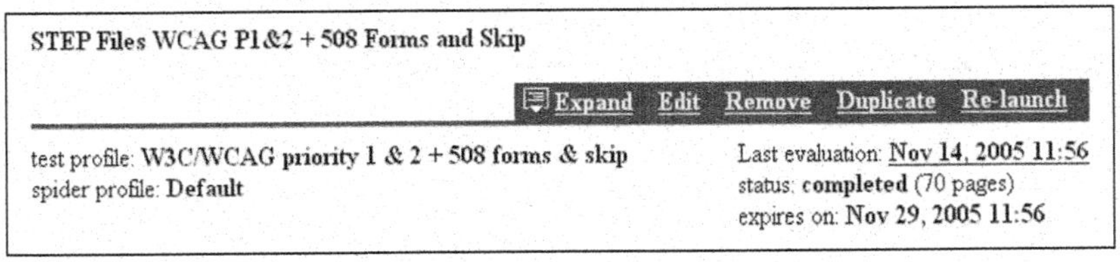

Figure 13-16. The item on the projects page for the completed project

13

431

Examine the Results—LIFT

Now let's find the results of this evaluation. The date of the last evaluation, Nov 14, 2005 11:56, as shown in Figure 13-16 is a link. Follow that link to display a summary of the overall status, indicating how many pages had errors and how many did not. Our test pages did not fare well. The summary page indicated that there was only one page without any problems (in fact, it wasn't even a page, but rather something called SITE LEVEL ISSUES, which I haven't figured out yet).

From the summary page, there is a link, view failed pages, and that is what you want. Then from the list of failed pages, you can examine the individual reports for each of the files to determine whether or not the tool passed each test. A sample individual report for the file step-0-0-0.htm is shown in Figure 13-17.

Test	Type	Checkpoint	Priority	Issues	Actions
Clarify natural language usage	?	WCAG 04.1: Language Changes	1	1	Hide
Divide information into appropriate manageable groups	?	WCAG 12.3: Divide Blocks	2	4	Hide
Mark up quotations	?	WCAG 03.7: Mark up Quotations	2	1	Hide
Provide information about site organization	?	WCAG 13.3: Site Map	2	1	Hide
Provide metadata to pages and sites	⚠	WCAG 13.2: Metadata	2	1	Hide
Use clear language for site's content	?	WCAG 14.1: Clear Language	1	1	Hide
Use header elements according to specification	⚠	WCAG 03.5: Headers	2	1	Hide
Use last appropriate W3C technologies	?	WCAG 11.1: W3C Technologies	2	1	Hide

Figure 13-17. LIFT sample report for a single page

The subject file has no errors, several manual checks, and two warnings. A neat feature in looking at the reports here, rather than downloading them, is that you can decide to hide issues and they won't appear when you look at subsequent pages. If you made a mistake in setting up the tests, you may get duplicate rules—one coming from Section 508 and one from WCAG. It seems to me that there should be one rule that belongs to both the Section 508 set and the WCAG set, but if you end up with such duplicate rules, you can hide them here and they will not appear on subsequent pages.

Choose Report Formats—LIFT

Choose the Reports tab in the main window (see Figure 13-13) to move to the Reports page of LIFT Machine. Then choose the New report link, just under the tabs. The Reports page offers several options, both in format and in detail, as shown in Figure 13-18.

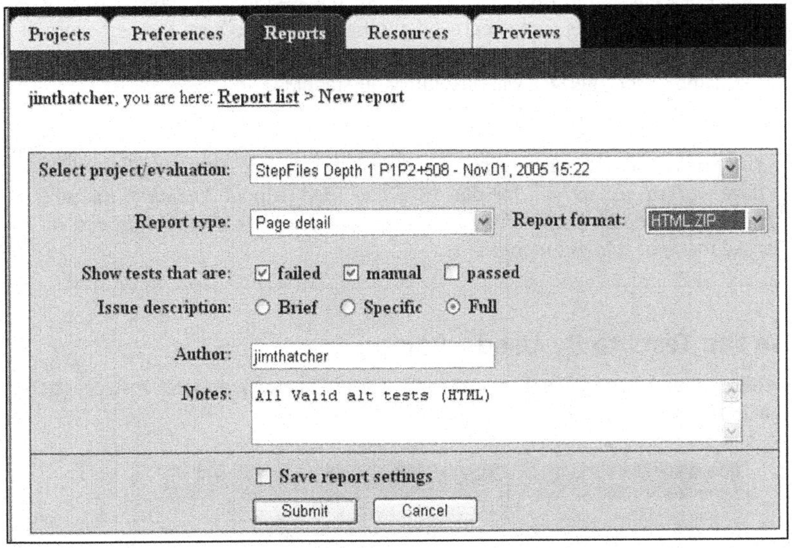

Figure 13-18. Choosing report details in LIFT

The report type can be either detailed or an executive summary. The format can be HTML or XML. Other choices include whether or not to include manual checks, passed tests, and failed tests, and whether the issue descriptions should be brief, specific, or full.

After you submit the request, LIFT Machine creates the report. It usually takes a couple of minutes, and, as with the scan, you can wait for an e-mail notification or just refresh the page after a minute or two. The format is a single zip file, called getreport.zip as a default. When the report has been prepared, the report name (project name plus date) becomes a link (similar to the situation when the scan was finished, as you saw in Figure 13-16), which you can activate to download getreport.zip. I suggest changing the name at this point (in the Save As dialog box), so that you don't risk overwriting a different report from LIFT Machine.

13

Ramp Ascend

Ramp Ascend is an accessibility testing and remediation tool from Deque Systems, Inc. I first tested with Ramp Ascend 4.0 and reported my results to Deque Systems. The next version of this testing tool, Ramp Ascend 5.0, improved over their previous version by 7 points, or 25 percent. Ramp Ascend Version 6 was released in May 2006. With a beta copy of that version, the tool's score improved another 7 points to have the best score of 38 out of a possible 40. The company's response to the challenges of the tests and to comments about Ramp's user interface was absolutely outstanding.

> *Ramp is also available without the repair function, called Ramp Grade for $279, which would have worked just as well for our tests, and then without spidering, RampPE (Personal Edition) for $79. Deque also has an enterprise version, called Worldspace. All versions use the same analysis algorithms.*

Choose the Tests to Be Used—Ramp

After opening Ramp Ascend, open the Accessibility Options **dialog box** (Tools ➤ Accessibility Options) **and choose the** Analysis **tab, as shown in Figure 13-19.**

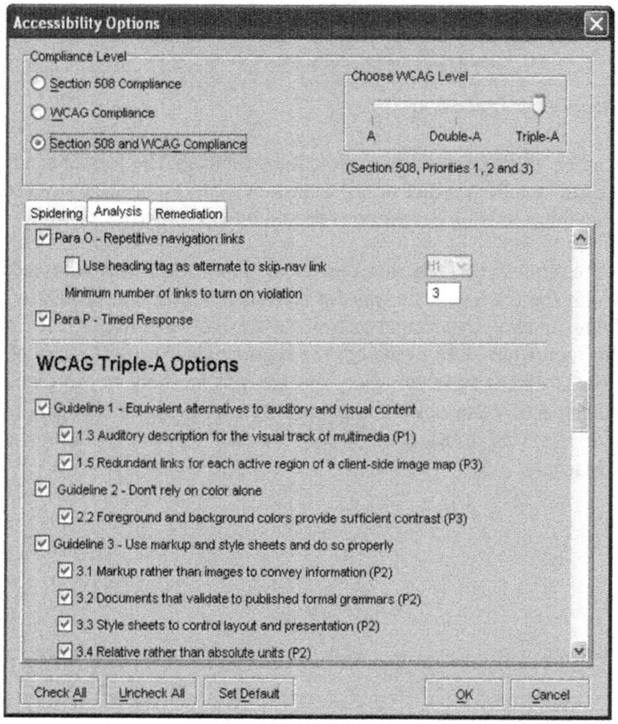

Figure 13-19. Choosing the tests in Ramp Ascend

In Ramp 4.0, you could choose only Section 508 or Web Content Accessibility Guidelines Priority 1, Priority 1 and 2, or Priority 1, 2, and 3. As with Bobby, the compliance selections were alternatives (radio buttons), so you could select either Section 508 or WCAG, but not both. In order to get the Section 508 tests and the WCAG AA tests, it was necessary to make two runs. That has changed in Ramp 6.0, as indicated in Figure 13-19.

Another disappointing aspect of Ramp 4.0 was the fact that the WCAG compliance level was not accurately represented in the detailed list of checkpoints/tests. But that, too, has changed in Ramp 6.0, as also indicated in Figure 13-19.

To eliminate the "manual checks," I went through and unchecked those items that I thought would result only in warnings, like "Clearest and simplest language," Checkpoint 14.1. Another improvement that Ramp might make is to add an option to eliminate manual tests, as is available with InFocus.

Analyze the Files—Ramp

Having chosen the tests, it is a simple matter to check the test files. All you need to do is enter the URL in the text box at the top of the main user interface window, select 1 for the Link Level (left of the URL field), and select Analyze, as shown in Figure 13-20.

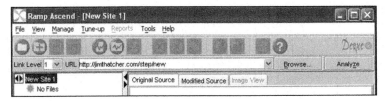

Figure 13-20. The Ramp specification of parameters for the analysis

You can also set up the analysis using the Analyze Web Application dialog box (File ➤ Analyze Web Application). There were no significant advantages to going that route in what I wanted to do. However, when set up that way, a web application can be respidered with no input required from the user, because session and state values are stored in the web application script and used automatically.

Examine the Results—Ramp

The method of examining test files is similar to what is available with InFocus. The user interface includes a list of files, and each can be highlighted to expose the source code and a list of violations in the right panel of the user interface. However, Ramp has one important addition: an Interactive Checks section at the bottom-right side of the window, as shown in Figure 13-21.

13

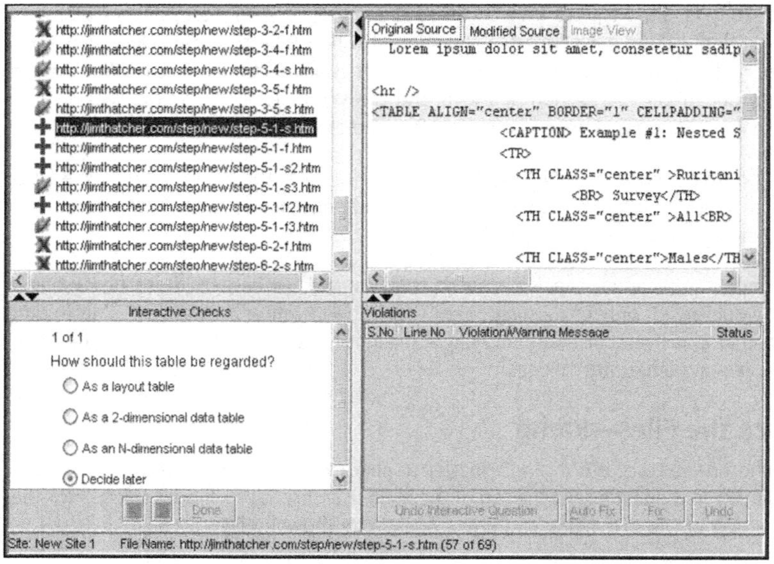

Figure 13-21. The Ramp interface for examining errors

The presence of these interactive checks for a given file is indicated by a plus (+) icon in the file list. Errors are present in files marked with a red X, and a clean bill of health is shown with a green checkmark. With the interactive checks, the tool is asking for help to clarify the role of certain features of the page. All four files with interactive checks shown in the example in Figure 13-21 are files with data tables. The check is to confirm (or deny) that they are data tables—even to decide between a simple table (two-dimensional table) and a complex data table (n-dimensional table).

My test case for data tables was specifically designed to see if the tools recognize data tables or can distinguish data tables from layout tables, at least in what I would call "obvious" cases. Although Ramp is looking for confirmation, the tool has drawn the distinction. The file with a layout table (step-5-1-s3.htm) is *not* called out for an interactive check, whereas the files with data tables require the interactive confirmation. In other words, Ramp is raising the interactive check for tables in just those cases where the tables were, in fact, data tables.

The downside to the interactive check idea is that you may need to interact too often. If you chose all the Priority 1 WCAG tests, you will get the interactive check "Are there foreign words/phrases used in this document?" on *every* file. That user check seems to be the first, so you need to answer it before others in the queue. You may quickly realize that it is best to uncheck that test in the Accessibility Options dialog box. On the other hand, that seems to be the only interactive check elicited on every file. These interactive checks provide a valuable addition to the process with some costs in user involvement. According to Deque, its enterprise product streamlines this process significantly.

The process of examining the files is simple. The errors are displayed on the right, as is the source code, as shown in Figure 13-22.

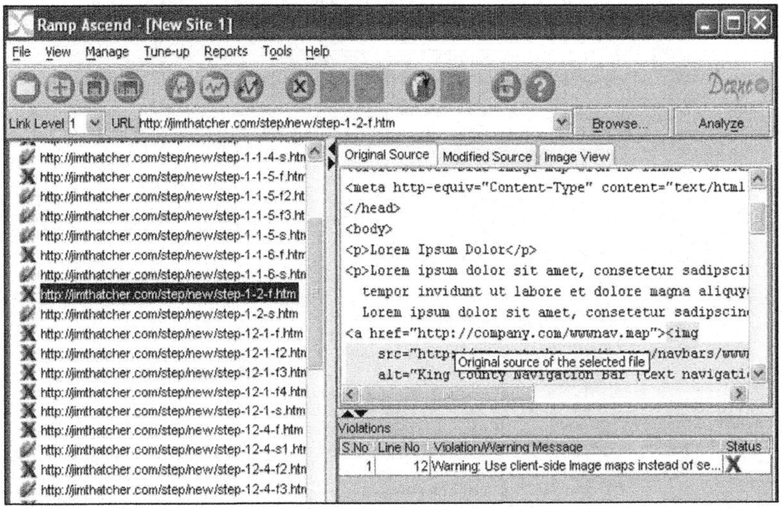

Figure 13-22. Examining the results with Ramp

Choose Report Formats—Ramp

The reports are available in XML and HTML formats. For the XML report, select Reports ➤ Generate XML Report from the main menu. Be sure that the site, not one of the files, is highlighted (selected). Each report opens in a Ramp window, but you can view it in the browser (Report ➤ View in Browser) or save it as HTML.

All the HTML reports are derived from the XML output. They range in detail from a site synopsis to a listing of all violations together with code (Reports ➤ Violations Code All Files). Ramp includes a Report Wizard (Reports ➤ Report Wizard), which lets you choose the tests you want to include.

WebKing

WebKing Version 5.1, from Parasoft, Inc., is much more complex and powerful than any of the other tools discussed so far. Testing for accessibility is only a very small part of its function. As with the other products, you can modify which tests are to be used, but with WebKing, you can also write your own tests or modify the ones provided, and the results are available across several platforms.

13

Choose the Tests to Be Used—WebKing

To see the basic choices for existing rules, select Tools ➤ Customize, and then select Check Web Accessibility on the left side of the Customize Tools dialog box, as shown in Figure 13-23.

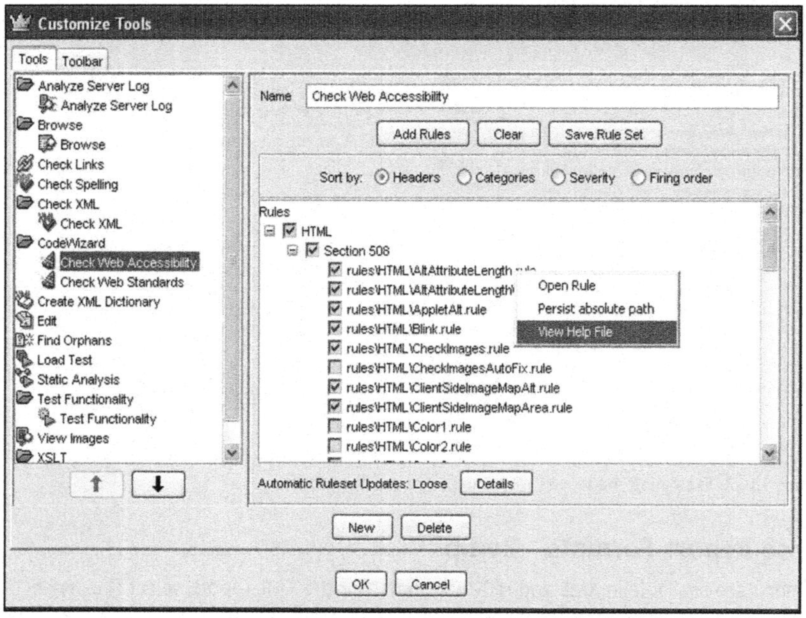

Figure 13-23. Choosing tests in WebKing

The rules tree in the Customize Tools dialog box has two nodes under HTML: Section 508 and WAI Guidelines. Under each of those two is a list of check boxes for rules to be included. The text for each rule is actually the filename of the rule, like `rules\HTML\Blink.rule`. If you right-click any rule, the context menu (see Figure 13-23) includes options to open the rule (note that it opens in the main window behind the dialog box) or to view the help file, which describes the function of the rule. Rules can be sorted by Headers information (Section 508 and WAI), by Categories (accessibility, navigation, and presentation), by Severity, or by the order in which the rules are applied by WebKing (Firing Order).

The sorting by Section 508 (as partially shown in Figure 13-23) and by the WAI Guidelines is misleading because rules are listed only once. The rules listed under Section 508 are not repeated under WAI Guidelines. The rules that appear under WAI Guidelines are only the ones that support WCAG checkpoints that are not found in Section 508. For example, the CheckImages.rule rule listed under Section 508 (Figure 13-23) is the one that checks for alt-text and thus implements WAI Checkpoint 1.1, but it appears in the Section 508 list, not in the WAI list.

Analyze the Files—WebKing

To begin testing for accessibility, you need to create a project. Select File ➤ New ➤ Project and select the Project tab to give a name to the project. Then use the Source tab to specify the parameters of the scan, as shown in Figure 13-24.

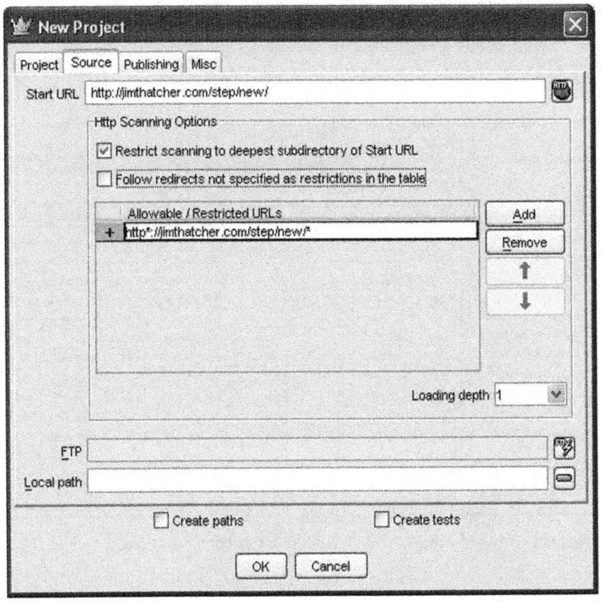

Figure 13-24. Creating a new project in WebKing

Enter the URL in the Start URL field (http://jimthatcher.com/step/new/ in the example). The Loading depth (click depth) setting defaults to 1, which is what we want for the test files. Select OK, and then WebKing will load the site with user intervention for entering data in form controls. The first time I was given that opportunity, I chose skip all for the forms, which meant that further user intervention was not required. Note that this process does *not* perform any analysis on the files; it does only the specified spidering and loads the files.

Once the project files are loaded, they are represented in the project tree on the left side of the user interface. From this project tree, you can perform analysis and transformation operations on files or, more generally, on subtrees of the project tree.

13

Highlight the root of the project tree, and then select Tools ➤ Code Wizard ➤ Check Accessibility. This will evaluate WebKing accessibility rules against all the files in the tree and produce the results displayed on the right panel of the user interface, as shown in Figure 13-25.

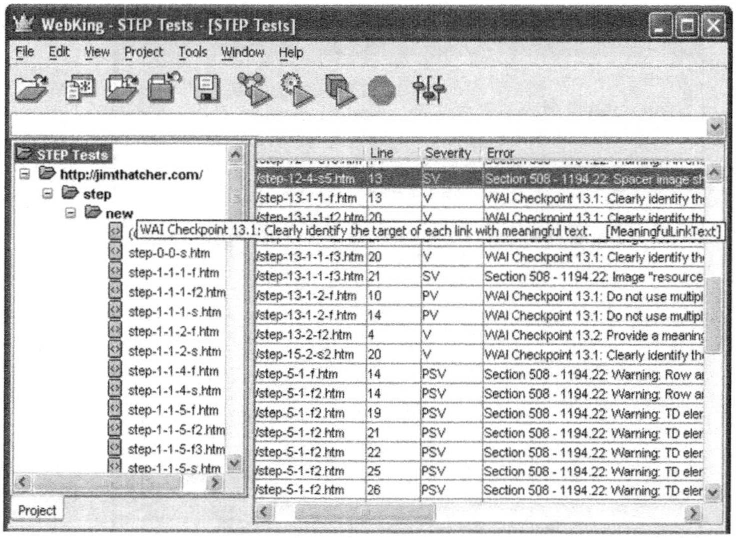

Figure 13-25. Results of the WebKing Check Accessibility tool

Examine the Results—WebKing

The results window (see Figure 13-25) lists all the errors and warnings. For our process, we just check if an error has been raised when it should be raised, and when necessary, check that no error has been found for the comparison files.

When I first ran these tests with WebKing version 4.0, the tool received the lowest score of 18. With version 5.1, WebKing's score is 34, the second highest—almost doubling its performance.

Choose Report Formats—WebKing

To see the report format choices, make sure that the Check Web Accessibility results are in the right pane of the WebKing window. (If you changed the contents of that pane, you can return to the accessibility results by selecting Window ➤ Windows, choosing Check Web Accessibility, and then choosing Show.) The reports are not available from the main menu. Instead, right-click the results window and select Save As. As shown in Figure 13-26, your choices are HTML, text, XML, binary, or CSV format.

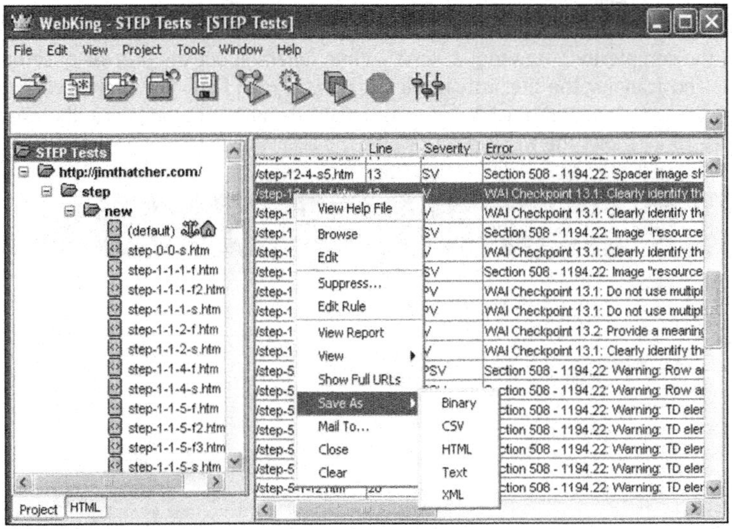

Figure 13-26. Choosing a report format

The report is saved as a single file with the same contents as those that appear in the Check Web Accessibility panel (right side) of the interface.

WebXM

WebXM, from Watchfire, is a server-based tool like LIFT Machine. It is very sophisticated, with many functions, as indicated by this quote from the Watchfire site:

> WebXM is the only Online Risk Management platform to automate the scanning, analysis and reporting of online security, privacy, quality, accessibility and compliance issues across corporate web properties. WebXM ensures visibility and control by delivering executive dashboards that are used to identify, assign and track the issues impacting your online business.

There is much more to WebXM than accessibility. In fact, accessibility was added in 2003, after Watchfire acquired Bobby.

13

Choose the Tests to Be Used—WebXM

Because of the complexity of the tool, I won't go into details about the process of setting up the tests and scanning the site; instead, I'll just tell you what I did. The project concept for WebXM is a "webspace" in which the user sets many defaults for scan jobs in that webspace. Figure 13-27 shows the window for picking the accessibility tests.

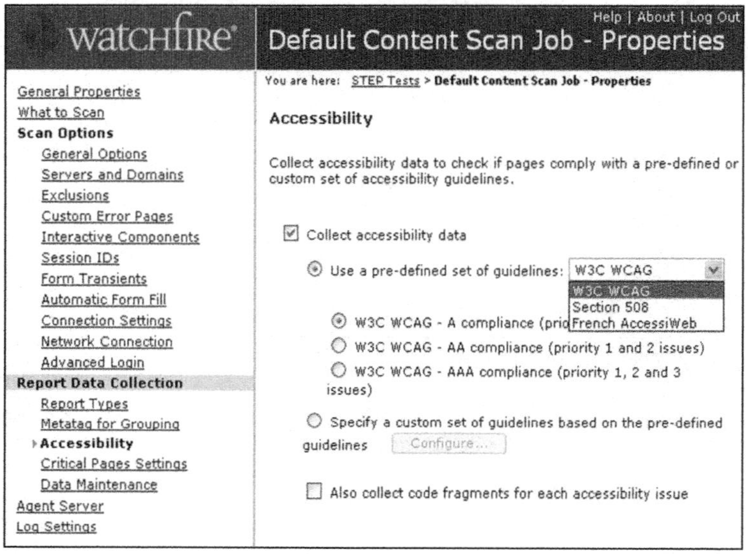

Figure 13-27. Setting default job properties in WebXM

The Accessibility dialog box is one of many that can be opened from the list on left side of the Scan Job – Properties window. The process for choosing tests is hauntingly similar to that for Bobby 5.0. You can choose from three guideline sets: W3C WCAG (A, AA, or AAA conformance), Section 508, and French AccessiWeb (Bronze, Silver, or Gold conformance). Alternatively, you can select to define a custom set, and you will be shown a list of all tests from which to choose, as shown in Figure 13-28.

I am not certain what technique is the best for choosing tests in this window. I wanted to use the Section 508 tests plus WCAG Priority 1 and Priority 2 tests. Then I wanted to go through those to eliminate any tests that would just clutter the reports. The way I did that was to first select All in the combo box, and then uncheck everything. Then I selected Section 508 and checked those. Then I selected W3C WCAG – Priority 1 and 2 (AA Compliance) and checked those. However, that left many of the interesting AccessiWeb tests (http://accessiweb.org) unchecked.

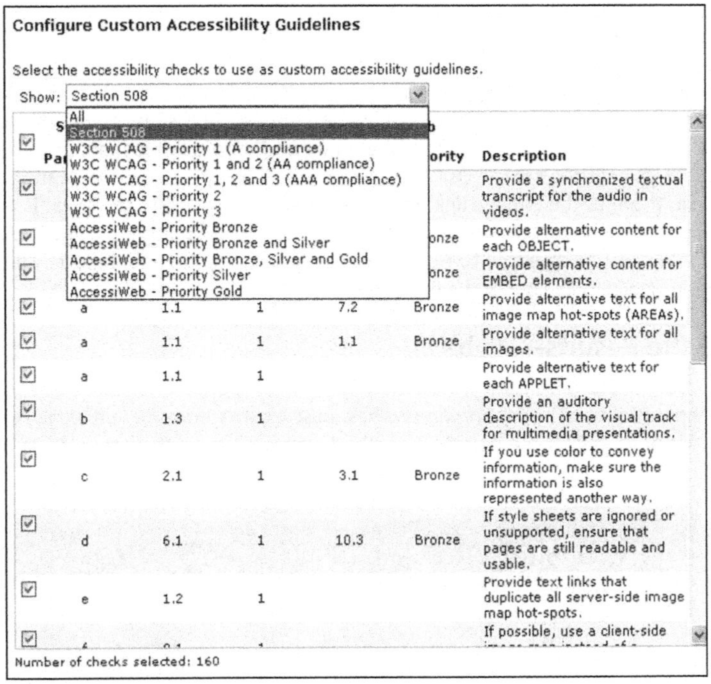

Configure Custom Accessibility Guidelines

Select the accessibility checks to use as custom accessibility guidelines.

Show: Section 508

All					
Section 508					
W3C WCAG - Priority 1 (A compliance)					
W3C WCAG - Priority 1 and 2 (AA compliance)				Description	
W3C WCAG - Priority 1, 2 and 3 (AAA compliance)				Provide a synchronized textual	
W3C WCAG - Priority 2				transcript for the audio in	
W3C WCAG - Priority 3				videos.	
AccessiWeb - Priority Bronze				Provide alternative content for	
AccessiWeb - Priority Bronze and Silver			nze	each OBJECT.	
AccessiWeb - Priority Bronze, Silver and Gold				Provide alternative content for	
AccessiWeb - Priority Silver			nze	EMBED elements.	
AccessiWeb - Priority Gold				Provide alternative text for all	
a	1.1	1	7.2	Bronze	image map hot-spots (AREAs).
a	1.1	1	1.1	Bronze	Provide alternative text for all images.
a	1.1	1			Provide alternative text for each APPLET.
b	1.3	1			Provide an auditory description of the visual track for multimedia presentations.
c	2.1	1	3.1	Bronze	If you use color to convey information, make sure the information is also represented another way.
d	6.1	1	10.3	Bronze	If style sheets are ignored or unsupported, ensure that pages are still readable and usable.
e	1.2	1			Provide text links that duplicate all server-side image map hot-spots.
					If possible, use a client-side

Number of checks selected: 160

Figure 13-28. Setting up testing in WebXM

Analyze the Files—WebXM

The What to Scan option is in the collection of navigation links on the left side of the Scan Job - Properties window (see Figure 13-27). On the What to Scan page, you just enter the start URL and the usual options about what to scan. As with WebKing and Bobby 5.0, you cannot specify a (click) depth for the scan, but you can limit the scan by number of pages. The Watchfire technical contact explained this as follows:

> Since WebXM is optimized for enterprise scanning, a given scan job is usually performed by multiple "scan agents" that can even be installed on different servers. Those scan agents operate completely independently. Whenever one finds a URL in a link, they check the database and if it hasn't already been stored, adds it to the queue for later scanning. When an agent finishes scanning a page, it pops whatever URL happens to be on the top of the list and scans that, even though a different agent may have put that URL on the list.

13

But the technical contact also explained that there is considerable interest in the option of limiting the scan by click depth and that it may be available in a later version of the product.

The process so far established default job settings and options. In the webspace, you now create a job (choose Create Scan Job from the menu on the left), which inherits all the default settings established so far. Use the Create and Continue link at the bottom of the page. Next, move to the Reports link on the left of the Create Job Page (which is very similar to Figure 13-27), and choose the Create and Package All button. Finally, choose Finish. Then a link will be available to Run the job. After running the job, reports will be available in the Report Pack area of the webspace.

Examine the Results—WebXM

Select the Report Packs tab in the workspace. There, the report will be listed as a link, which you should follow. The report window has a list of links down its left side. These provide various ways to view the report. Figure 13-29 shows Pages with Section 508 Issues selected.

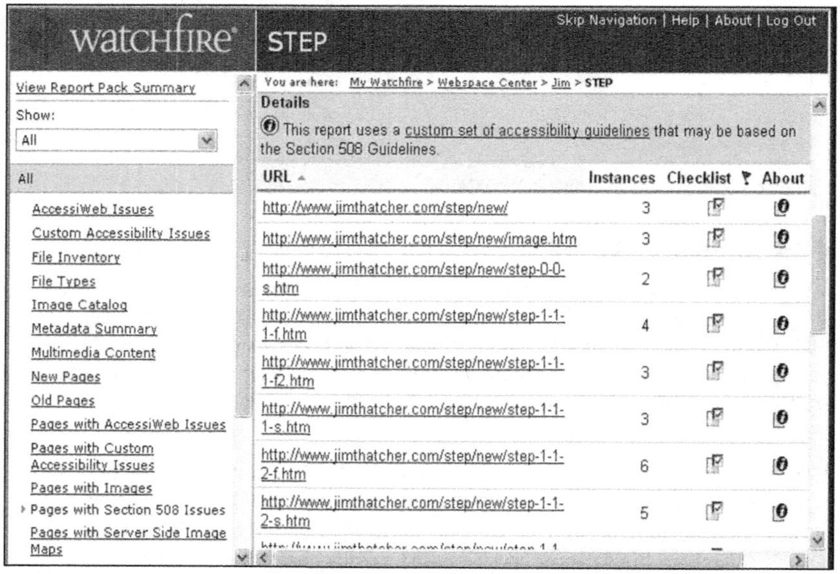

Figure 13-29. The list of files with errors in WebXM

Since I wanted to study each file, I sorted the list of files by URL, by clicking URL at the top of the list. Each file can then be analyzed by looking at its report, as shown in the example in Figure 13-30.

Figure 13-30. WebXM report format

That report format shown in Figure 13-30 is reminiscent of the report format in Bobby 5.0 (see Figure 13-4). It is necessary to scroll down the report to find the errors and warnings of interest.

Choose Report Formats—WebXM

When you open a report, you'll see an Export All Report Data link near the top of the page. That link will download the data of the current view as an XML file. Alternatively, the Printer Friendly link opens the current data as an HTML file in your web browser, and you can save the report from there. The views include the summary for each of the options shown on the left in Figure 13-29, and the individual reports for specific files. I was not able to find a way of downloading a report that had both the list of files for a set of issues and the specific errors found with each file, although I am sure that this is possible.

13

The Test File Set and Results

When I started looking for test files to use to compare accessibility testing tools, I was attracted to tests developed by Chris Redpath at the Adaptive Technology Resource (ATR) Centre at the University of Toronto (http://atrc.utoronto.ca/). Those tests consist of about 220 files (http://checker.atrc.utoronto.ca/), including at least one file and often several files for each of the WCAG 1.0 checkpoints. Although still in working draft form, there are also tests for WCAG 2.0.

My main concerns with the ATR tests were that there were so many files and that many of the test files are nearly empty. For example, some files relating to object elements had merely <object /> in the code; I think a checker could—maybe even should—recognize that this is an empty object and raise no warning or error.

So I decided to create a much smaller and more manageable set of files (covering many fewer conditions), in which each file contains more content and generally there are pairs of files to compare the tool's response for the error condition and the error condition corrected. Sometimes the ATR files are paired: one file with the error condition and the other *without* the error condition—not with the error corrected.

The Test Suite

The test suite is arranged by issues, not by files. So there is the "Alt-text" issue (test 1) with two files associated with it: one in which the image has no alt-text (step-1-1-1-f.htm) and essentially the same file with the alt attribute added (step-1-1-1-s.htm) with respectable alt-text. The file-naming system stems from an earlier version of the ATR tests. The filename includes the WCAG guideline number, test number for that guideline, and an f for failure or s for success.

You can find a list of all the files at http://jimthatcher.com/step/new. All the files referred to in the following descriptions are available in that directory, too; for example, http://jimthatcher.com/step/new/step-1-1-1-f.htm, which I refer to as just step-1-1-1-f.htm.

1. **Alt-text:** Every image element, img, must have an alt attribute. No alt-text (step-1-1-1-f.htm) is an error, and there should be no error when alt-text is present (step-1-1-1-s.htm).

   Results: All of the tools passed this test—no surprise here.

2. **ASCII art for alt-text:** If alt-text is ASCII art, like alt="-->", a screen reader would speak "hyphen hyphen greater than," which is not meaningful. It is an error when alt-text consists of ASCII art (step-1-1-1-f2.htm).

   Results: On my first appraisal of the results of this test, I thought that InFocus caught the error. I was concerned because the error was "Alt text required," which means that the alt attribute is missing. When I tried different ASCII art, namely alt=":-)", InFocus did not pick it up as an error. From the highlighting of the source code in the original case (alt="-->"), it turned out that InFocus was prematurely terminating the img tag with the ">" at the end of the value of the alt attribute, and did not actually catch this error.

For each of its alt-text errors, LIFT had both "image should have valid alt" and "image should have equivalent alt." Lacking valid alt-text is an error, while the equivalent alt message is a human review warning saying it is necessary to compare the image with the alt-text. Since that warning is raised on any significant image, it would seem that LIFT would need to say that the ASCII art for alt-text is not valid, but it did not do that. Compare this with test 5, where LIFT declares alt-text longer than 150 characters to be "not valid."

WebKing and Ramp were the only tools to pass this test, and both did so with later versions; they failed the test the first time through.

3. **Object requires default content:** An object element should have content that is available if the object/plug-in is not supported (step-1-1-2-s.htm). Though this is a requirement of WCAG 1.0, it is not widely supported by assistive technology. A testing tool scores on this issue if there is no warning or error on the good file (step-1-1-2-s.htm) and there is a warning or error on the bad one (step-1-1-2-f.htm), which has no default content.

Results: All of the tools passed this test.

4. **Image button:** Every image button (input element with type="image") must have alt-text that specifies the purpose of the button (step-1-1-4-s.htm, step-1-1-4-f.htm).

Results: Technically, all six tools caught this error, but WebXM received a failing grade because of the way it presented the issue. WebXM raised the form-labeling error for this test: "Explicitly associate form controls and their labels with the <label> element." That error is not raised for the file that has alt-text on the image button (step-1-1-4-s.htm). In this version, WebXM considers the alt-text on an image button to be a form-labeling problem, not an alt-text problem.

Both test files have an input element with type="text", which is correctly labeled. InFocus raises the error "Label should be placed next to input" whenever there is an input element; even when the prompt (label) is perfectly placed and labeled. This stems from WCAG 1.0 Checkpoint 10.2:

Until user agents support explicit associations between labels and form controls, for all form controls with implicitly associated labels, ensure that the label is properly positioned.

But a testing tool should be able to estimate positioning and raise this issue only when it is really necessary, especially because user agents *do* support explicit associations between labels and form controls.

5. **Long alt-text:** Alt-text should be short, succinct, and to the point. How long is too long? I chose 151 characters (step-1-1-5-f.htm) as the break-off point that should raise an error. There is also a file with 102 characters of alt-text (step-1-1-5-f2.htm), which I think should be an error, too.

Results: All of the tools caught the error of alt-text longer than 150 characters. None of the tools raised an error for 102 characters. Several tools (InFocus, Ramp, and LIFT) allow user specification of the maximum length, along with other characteristics of acceptable alt-text.

13

InFocus raises the violation "Valid alt attribute required." As mentioned in the description of test 2, LIFT also raises an error about validity of the alt-text. What is troubling is that the alt-text at 151 characters is certainly valid, but too long. The detailed explanation of the InFocus violation softens this concern with "This image has an invalid or suspicious alt attribute." On the other hand, Bobby warns, "Alt text > 150 characters, consider providing a separate description," making the statement of the error/warning perfectly clear.

6. **Image map areas:** Every `area` element of a `map` for a client-side image map needs to have alt-text. The sample file (`step-1-1-6-f.htm`) has one `<area>` tag that has no alt-text. For comparison, `step-1-1-6-s.htm` has alt-text on all the `area` elements.

   Results: All of the tools passed this test. WebXM did fine on this test, but I noticed that the test itself, "Provide alternative text for all image map hot-spots," is also listed in the section of the report called Passed Evaluations. The reason the test appears in the list of evaluations that passed is that there are several image map area elements that do have alt-text, and for those elements, the evaluation passed. I think that the idea should be that the page passes the "image map hotspot" test if all image map hotspots have appropriate alt-text, and it fails if any one does not.

7. **Server-side image maps:** I believe that a server-side map (`img` with `ismap` attribute) should never be used, so any page with a server-side map should raise an error. There are two test files: one with the server-side map and no text links (`step-1-2-f.htm`) and, just for interest, `step-1-2-s.htm` is coded with text links provided for each server-side hotspot. The tools get this right if they raise an error or warning for the server-side map (on either or both files).

   Results: All of the tools got this right, but usually by raising a warning. Bobby has a warning, "Provide text links that duplicate all server-side image map hot-spots." It is a warning because the tool can't tell whether or not the duplicate links are available. I think that this should be an error, or at least a stronger statement about the problem with server-side image maps. Checkpoint 9.1 of WCAG and §1194.22(e) of Section 508 use the same wording concerning the use of server-side maps:

   Provide client-side image maps instead of server-side image maps except where the regions cannot be defined with an available geometric shape.

   It may be impractical to use client-side image maps, but all regions can be defined by available geometric shapes. Ramp's response is also a warning, but the wording is better: "Use client-side image maps instead of server-side maps."

8. **Frame titles:** Each `frame` in a `frameset` needs a title attribute indicating the purpose of the frame. In the sample file (`step-12-1-f.htm`), the frame elements do not have `title` attributes. For comparison, `step-12-1-s` has adequate `title` attributes. (`iframe` is treated separately in test 40.)

   Results: All of the tools passed this test.

9. **Quality of frame titles:** The `title` attributes on the `frame` elements must be meaningful. Here (`step-12-1-f2.htm`), the sample frames have `title="top"`, `title="left"`, and `title="right"`, which are not meaningful—they do not specify the purpose of the frame.

Results: On the first round of tests, only InFocus go this right. With updated versions of the products, Ramp and WebKing raised errors here. Again, as with test 5, some tools allow personalizing the words or phrases that will *not* be allowed in the title attributes of the frame elements.

10. **Input element needs label:** The first form example (step-12-4-f.htm) is just a text input field (type="text") with neither a title attribute nor an associated label element. This condition should raise an error. The same form using the label element (step-12-4-s.htm) is correct and should not raise the error.

    Results: All of the tools passed this test.

11. **Use of title attribute for form control:** Another way to explicitly specify prompting text for a text input field is to use the title attribute on the input control. This is illustrated in step-12-4-s4.htm. There should be no error or warning for this file.

    Results: Only three of the six tools—InFocus, Ramp, and WebKing—got this right. This is disappointing. As argued in Chapter 8, there are situations where the title attribute is the only reasonable way to precisely label a form control.

12. **Text intervenes between label and control:** The text that is enclosed by the label element does *not* need to be right next to the control. Here, the label element encloses text, but there is intervening text before the control is encountered. This file (step-12-4-s3.htm) should *not* raise an error or warning.

    Results: InFocus insists that prompting text must be properly placed. Using the label element frees the developer from that requirement by programmatically connecting the prompt with the control, at least for people using assistive technology. For others with cognitive impairments or low vision, the positioning can be critical. Unfortunately, InFocus raises this warning even if the prompt is perfectly placed. Since I wanted to find out if the tool accepts a label coming from a place that is *not* next to the control, I concluded that InFocus failed this test. The other tools passed.

13. **Prompting text from two places:** Not only does the labeling text not have to be adjacent; it can come from two places. It is perfectly legitimate to have two label elements with the same for attribute, as this file (step-12-4-s6.htm) demonstrates. As you learned in Chapter 8, assistive technology support for two labels is spotty at best, but this should *not* be an error.

    Results: All of the tools passed this test. I suspect that the tools didn't even notice that there were two labels. Since support by screen readers for this situation is so poor, this probably should be deemed an error.

14. **An invisible GIF holds the prompting text:** A common phenomenon on http://www.ibm.com is to use an invisible GIF with alt-text as the prompt for the search form text-entry field. This technique was introduced by IBM at a time when few tools recognized the title attribute (see test 11). Although this technique is acceptable—it is not an error—the title attribute is much better (see Chapter 8). The file, step-12-4-s5.htm, uses an invisible GIF with alt-text in the label container. It should not raise an error.

13

Results: All of the tools got this right, but there were two minor problems. InFocus continued to warn that prompting text must be properly placed, and WebKing raised the error that a spacer image requires alt="". When it is clear that the "spacer image" is conveying information, as is the case here, that warning should be turned off.

15. **Label that matches no control:** This form example, step-12-4-f2.htm, has a label element, but the for attribute does not match any id. This is an error.

    Results: All of the tools passed this test.

16. **Two input elements with same id:** In this case (step-12-4-f3.htm), there are two input elements with the same id. Not only is this an accessibility error, but it is also invalid XHTML (using the same id on any two elements).

    Results: Surprisingly, on the first testing pass, this was detected only by LIFT. The newer versions of WebKing and Ramp now find this error. So, LIFT, WebKing, and Ramp passed this test.

17. **Textarea needs label or title:** This file, step-12-4-f8.htm, contains a textarea with no label element or title attribute. This test is just like test 10, except it uses a textarea field instead of an input field with type="text".

    Results: All of the tools passed this test.

18. **Select menu needs label or title:** This file, step-12-4-f9.htm, contains a select menu with no label element or title attribute. This test is just like test 10, except it uses a select menu instead of an input field with type="text".

    Results: All of the tools passed this test.

19. **Inaccessible select menu:** This file, step-12-4-f10.htm, contains a select menu that is open (size="4") and has an onChange event handler that opens a new page. This menu is not accessible because it cannot be operated with the keyboard. As soon as you press the down arrow when the menu has focus, it fires and the new page is opened. This is an error, but the tool scores here only if it does not flag step-12-4-s10.htm as an error. That file is the same, except the select menu is not open (size="1"), which can be handled from the keyboard using Alt+down arrow, and then the up and down arrow keys.

    Results: Ramp raises an error on both files. Only WebKing got it right.

20. **Empty label:** This file (step-12-4-f11.htm) has a properly coded label element, but the contents of that label element are empty. This is an error.

    Results: It is surprising that apparently only two tools (WebKing and WebXM) were looking at the "quality" of the label on the first pass through the tests. Version 6.0 of Ramp now looks at that aspect of form labeling, so three tools passed this test.

21. **Inadequate link text:** The link text is click here (step-13-1-1-f.htm), which is an error.

    Results: InFocus and LIFT missed this. Bobby flags an *error* for the click here link: "Create link phrases that make sense when read out of context." The same message appears as a warning (see test 22) any time links are present.

22. **Image link with empty alt-text:** An extreme case of inadequate link text, this file has an anchor containing only one image, and that image has empty alt-text, alt="" (step-13-1-1-f2.htm).

Results: InFocus is the only tool to fail this test (and test 23). Ramp lists the violation as "invalid text equivalent for image." It would seem that if the text equivalent were invalid, it would be invalid in test 24, which it is not. I think this error should be "invalid (empty) link text."

WebXM raises the error "Create link phrases that make sense when read out of context" for the situation of an image link in which the alt-text is empty and also for the case when the alt-text is just spaces (test 23). The error description is directly from the WCAG, but these situations seem to me to be worse than the inability to read out of context. There is no link text! On the other hand, when there is no link text, JAWS reads the image source filename, which in this case is Resources, giving good information about the link. One certainly should not count on that.

Bobby raises the error "Provide alternative text for all images" for this file, and also the warning (not error, as in test 21) "Make sure that all link phrases make sense when read out of context." This warning is raised for all files that have links. In this case, the image has alt-text. Bobby's response is not adequate.

23. **Image link with spaces for alt-text:** Very similar to test 22, this file, step-13-1-1-f3.htm, has an anchor element (a) that contains just one img element and the alt-text on that is alt="   " (quote four-spaces quote).

Results: InFocus failed this test, and the other tools passed (WebKing got it right even though it failed test 22).

24. **Link with empty alt-text but also text:** This file, step-13-1-1-s2.htm, represents a common situation: there is an image in the anchor with alt="", but there is also text in the anchor. This file should pass, but a tool gets a score here only if it passes this file and fails the file in test 22. The issue here is distinguishing between empty link text and nonempty link text.

Results: Two tools failed this test: Bobby and InFocus. Bobby raised the same errors for this file as for the one with empty alt-text and no text in the anchor.

25. **Link text; "click here" with title attribute:** This file (step-13-1-1-s3.htm) has an anchor element (a) containing the text click here, which is inadequate (see test 21). But there is also a title attribute on the anchor that specifies the target of the link. This is not an error. A tool scores here only if this file passes and test 21 fails.

Results: Two tools got this right: Ramp and WebKing. Watchfire informed me that WebXM has an option to look for the title attribute on links, but that is switched off in the default settings that I used.

26. **Same link text, different targets:** If two links have the same link text but different targets (href), then the links cannot be distinguished in a list of links. This file, step-13-1-2-f.htm, has two links with the same text but different href. It is an error.

Results: All of the tools passed this test.

13

27. **Page title:** The content of the `title` element of a page is what appears in the title bar of the browser, and it is spoken by a screen reader when the page opens. Every page should have a nonempty `title` element. This file, `step-13-2-f.htm`, has no `title` element, which is an error.

   Results: InFocus and WebKing were the only tools that did not raise an error in this case. The other four tools passed this test.

28. **Inadequate page title:** This test is similar to test 27, but here the title is Title— the code looks like this: `<title>Title</title>`. The file, `step-13-2-f2.htm`, should raise an error.

   Results: Only Ramp got this right on the first testing pass. The newer version of WebKing joined the circle of winners after the second test run. Four tools failed this test.

29. **Skip link:** The two files both have links at the top of the page followed by text. The file that fails has neither headings nor a skip link after the "navigation links" (`step-15-2-f.htm`). The file that is okay has a skip link (`step-15-2-s2.htm`). A tool scores on this test if it raises an appropriate error on the file with no skip link, `step-15-2-f.htm`, and does not raise that error on `step-15-2-s2.htm`, which has the skip link.

   Results: Three tools got this right: InFocus, LIFT, and Ramp.

30. **Heading for skipping to content:** This is exactly like test 29, except that the successful file (`step-15-2-s.htm`) has headings, especially a level 1 heading at the beginning of the main content.

   Results: I was disappointed that, on the first pass through the tests, none of the tools that were looking for skip techniques at all recognized headings as such a technique. Now Ramp Ascend 6.0 sees a heading after a block of links as a technique for skipping those links. This test can be turned on and off in the Accessibility Options of Ramp. I hope more tools will recognize this option, because headings markup provides a much better technique for addressing page navigation than skip links (see Chapter 7).

31. **Layout table that won't resize:** When a layout table uses pixel widths, it won't resize with either a larger window or larger text. This file, `step-3-4-f.htm`, uses fixed widths in pixels. The response by the tool needs to be compared with that for a file that uses percentage widths instead of pixel widths (`step-3-4-s.htm`). The tool is successful if it raises an error for the table with fixed widths and does not raise an error on the table with percentage widths.

   Results: All of the tools got this right, although Ramp failed on the first pass through the tests.

32. **Data tables:** The issue I wanted to check was whether the tools checked for data tables—distinguishing them from layout tables. The data table (`step-5-1-s.htm`) is quite obviously such and marked up properly. A tool scores here if there is no data table error or warning on the good table or on the layout table (`step-5-1-s3.htm`) and there is a table markup warning or error on the one that does not use th (`step-5-1-f.htm`).

Results: Four tools got this right. Bobby and WebXM failed. Ramp raised an inter-active check for the user to confirm that a table is a data table. But Ramp is successful because it is raising that test when it suspects a table is a data table, and *not* on all tables. So, it raised the interactive check on the data tables and not on the layout tables.

33. **Layout table with a summary:** It is an error for a layout table (step-5-1-f3.htm) to have a summary attribute and/or th markup.

    Results: Only Bobby and Ramp got this right. Bobby raised a warning, "If this table is used for layout only, do not use structural markup to achieve formatting effects," and it does not raise that warning when a layout table does not have structural markup. Ramp raised two errors: one for the summary attribute ("Tables used for layout should not have summary") and one for the table head (th) markup ("Tables used for layout should not use headings to create formatting effects").

34. **Frame source must be HTML:** This file (step-6-2-f.htm) has a frame page (frameset) in which the first frame directly references an image (.gif). The src attributes of frame must be an HTML page.

    Results: Only LIFT failed this test. The wording of the InFocus error in this case was awkward: "use markup file as source." But the tool definitely caught the problem.

35. **Blink element:** This file, step-7-2-f.htm, uses the blink element. This is an error because the result is blinking text and also because the blink element is deprecated.

    Results: All of the tools passed this test.

36. **Marquee element:** This file, step-7-3-f.htm, uses the marquee element. As with test 35, this is an error because text is moving and because the marquee element is deprecated.

    Results: All of the tools passed this test.

37. **Auto-refresh:** This page (step-7-4-f.htm) has an auto-refresh every six seconds, which is an error.

    Results: All of the tools except InFocus and WebXM raised an error for the auto-refresh.

38. **Keyboard access:** The issue with this file, step-9-3-f.htm, is keyboard access. It contains a JavaScript function that requires a double-click (onDoubleclick), and it doesn't work from the keyboard. A tool scored here if it raised a scripting error on this file (no keyboard access) but not on step-9-3-s.htm, where onKeyDown is used for the same function.

    Results: Only Bobby passed this test.

39. **Structure of headings markup:** WCAG suggests that headings should be used according to specification. There are two files for testing the use of headings. The correct one, step-3-5-s.htm, has the headings (in order) h1, h2, h2, h3, h1. The error file, step-3-5-f.htm, has h4, h1, h2, h5, h1. There are two errors here: the transition h4 (starting) to h1, and h2 followed by h5. The use of headings is crucial for page navigation, so errors like these are not important, in my opinion.

13

Results: LIFT and WebKing failed this test. Deque pointed out that Accessibility Evaluation and Repair Tools (AERT) techniques (www.w3.org/TR/2000/WD-AERT-20000426) specify that the requirement on header nesting to be that "Header levels must not increase by more than 1 level." So there is only one error in the subject file, step-3-5-f.htm, which is the transition from h2 to h5, by this specification.

For pages with no headings markup whatsoever, LIFT warns, "Use header elements according to specification." Yet neither of the pages with headings markup (step3-5-s.htm and step3-5-f.htm) got that warning. It seems totally backwards to me.

40. **Title for in-line frame:** This is another frame issue—an iframe without a title attribute (step-12-1-f3.htm).

Results: All the tools, except InFocus, got this right.

Results Summary

Table 13-1 summarizes the results of these tests. Refer to the previous section for details.

Table 13-1. Results of the Accessibility Checker Tool Tests

Test	Correct	Bobby	InFocus	LIFT	Ramp	WebKing	WebXM
1. Alt-text	6	Yes	Yes	Yes	Yes	Yes	Yes
2. ASCII art as alt-text	2	No	No	No	Yes	Yes	No
3. Object requires default content	6	Yes	Yes	Yes	Yes	Yes	Yes
4. Image button	5	Yes	Yes	Yes	Yes	Yes	No
5. Long alt-text	6	Yes	Yes	Yes	Yes	Yes	Yes
6. Image map areas	6	Yes	Yes	Yes	Yes	Yes	Yes
7. Server-side image maps	6	Yes	Yes	Yes	Yes	Yes	Yes
8. Frame titles	6	Yes	Yes	Yes	Yes	Yes	Yes
9. Quality of frame titles	3	No	Yes	No	Yes	Yes	No
10. Input element needs label	6	Yes	Yes	Yes	Yes	Yes	Yes
11. Use of title attribute for form control	3	No	Yes	No	Yes	Yes	No

Test	Correct	Bobby	InFocus	LIFT	Ramp	WebKing	WebXM
12. Text intervenes between label and control	5	Yes	No	Yes	Yes	Yes	Yes
13. Label text from two places	6	Yes	Yes	Yes	Yes	Yes	Yes
14. Invisible GIF holds prompt	6	Yes	Yes	Yes	Yes	Yes	Yes
15. Label matches No control	6	Yes	Yes	Yes	Yes	Yes	Yes
16. Two controls with same id	3	No	No	Yes	Yes	Yes	No
17. Text area needs label	6	Yes	Yes	Yes	Yes	Yes	Yes
18. Select menu needs label	6	Yes	Yes	Yes	Yes	Yes	Yes
19. Inaccessible select menu	1	No	No	No	No	Yes	No
20. Empty label	3	No	No	No	Yes	Yes	Yes
21. "Click here"	4	Yes	No	No	Yes	Yes	Yes
22. Image link with empty alt-text	4	Yes	No	Yes	Yes	No	Yes
23. Image link with spaces for alt-text	5	Yes	No	Yes	Yes	Yes	Yes
24. Link with text and image with empty alt-text	3	No	No	Yes	Yes	No	Yes
25. "Click here" plus title	2	No	No	No	Yes	Yes	No
26. Same link text; different URLs	6	Yes	Yes	Yes	Yes	Yes	Yes
27. Page title	4	Yes	No	Yes	Yes	No	Yes
28. Adequate page title	1	No	No	No	Yes	No	No

Continued

13

455

Table 13-1. *Continued*

Test	Correct	Bobby	InFocus	LIFT	Ramp	WebKing	WebXM
29. Skip link	3	No	Yes	Yes	Yes	No	No
30. Headings for skipping	1	No	No	No	Yes	No	No
31. Layout table won't resize	6	Yes	Yes	Yes	Yes	Yes	Yes
32. Data table	4	No	Yes	Yes	Yes	Yes	No
33. Layout table with summary	2	Yes	No	No	Yes	No	No
34. Frame source must be HTML	5	Yes	Yes	No	Yes	Yes	Yes
35. Blink	6	Yes	Yes	Yes	Yes	Yes	Yes
36. Marquee	6	Yes	Yes	Yes	Yes	Yes	Yes
37. Auto-refresh	4	Yes	No	Yes	Yes	Yes	No
38. Keyboard access	1	Yes	No	No	No	No	No
39. Headings structure	4	Yes	Yes	No	Yes	No	Yes
40. Inline frame title	5	Yes	No	Yes	Yes	Yes	Yes
Totals		**28**	**23**	**27**	**38**	**34**	**26**

Summary

A large number of sophisticated software tools are designed to facilitate checking web content for accessibility. The basic products range in price from $50 to over $2,500, and enterprise-level products are also available. According to the lists of customers on the suppliers' websites, it is clear that federal agencies and corporations are buying into the idea of using these tools to test their sites for accessibility.

In this chapter, we barely scratched the surface of the accessibility testing tools. For looking at our test files, the six tools that we examined are remarkably similar. In a recent post to an e-mail list, Glenda Sims, Senior Systems Analyst at the University of Texas (UT) and member of the UT Web Team, had this to say about one of the tools we evaluated in this chapter:

WebXM is perfect for our decentralized needs. I work on a campus with 1000+ webmasters. Yes, it is like trying to herd cats. WebXM gives us a delicious dashboard that lets me quickly see the "health" of our entire site with a quick overview of which subsites within `www.utexas.edu` *are the best and the worst.*

We didn't even look at the dashboard. The point is that although the tools are similar in the task we undertook, they are radically different regarding other tasks and features, such as usability, security, integrity, scalability, reporting, and scheduling.

These tools are inherently limited in what they can do. Most aspects of web accessibility require some human evaluation, and the best that can be asked of the software tools is that they facilitate the human review process. On the other hand, software accessibility checkers can do something human evaluators cannot do: examine dozens (even millions, for some tools) of pages to find missing `alt` attributes or `label` elements. Humans are not so good at such exhaustive and tedious examination. Detectable errors like these include some of the most important concerns for accessibility and generally are symptomatic of more serious mistakes.

An important aspect of carrying out these tests was the way the tool developers reacted. All were supportive and responsive, and that was very reassuring. Of course, some were more responsive than others. Two stand out because not only were they helpful, but they also made significant changes in their products in response to this process. Parasoft (WebKing) and Deque (Ramp Ascend) made major improvements in their accessibility checking tools to end up in second and first place, respectively. Ramp went through two versions during this review process, and its current "winning" score of 38 out of 40 is for the newest version, Ramp Ascend 6.0.

13

14 INTRODUCTION TO WCAG 2.0

by Mark Urban and Michael R. Burks

The Web Content Accessibility Guidelines 2.0 (WCAG 2.0) Working Draft (www.w3.org/TR/WCAG20/) is a new set of guidelines for making the content on websites accessible to people with disabilities. This Working Draft evolved from the current WCAG 1.0 (www.w3.org/TR/WCAG10/), which was published in 1999. WCAG 2.0 is an attempt to make the guidelines more robust, measurable, and technology-independent. In addition, more supporting information is incorporated into WCAG 2.0 than was present in WCAG 1.0.

These guidelines are being developed by a group representing industry, government, educational, and nonprofit interests. The official name of the group is the Web Content Accessibility Guidelines Working Group (WCAG WG), which is part of the World Wide Web Consortium (W3C) Web Accessibility Initiative (WAI). Since WCAG 2.0 is a Last Call Working Draft, it is still under development and can be commented on and contributed to at the time of the publication of this book. Modifications can be expected up until it is officially accepted by the W3C, so some of the details contained within this chapter are likely to have changed by the time it is published.

The purpose of this chapter is to give you a good understanding of how WCAG 2.0 is organized and how you might use the guidelines effectively. It will explain the differences between WCAG 1.0 and WCAG 2.0, the purpose of the various elements of WCAG 2.0, and its attendant documentation and resources. The chapter is not an exhaustive analysis of WCAG 2.0, a full reference, or a complete tutorial on every detail. It is a roadmap to assist you in getting acquainted with the guidelines. We thought it best to present the information like this, and generalize somewhat, because it is still subject to change.

These guidelines are for producing accessible content delivered using web-based technology. Although many consider them standards, they are not. It is appropriate to have a short discussion of the difference between standards and guidelines, so we'll begin by making that distinction.

Standards vs. Guidelines

Standards are repeatable, measurable, and testable specifications that can be used as normative technical requirements. An example of a standard is IEEE 802.11b, the Institute of Electrical and Electronics Engineers standard for 10Mbps Wireless Local Area Networking. Any device claiming to conform to this standard can be tested by any lab and found to either meet or not meet the standard.

Guidelines, such as WCAG, are literally *guidance*. An example of a guideline might be "To stay healthy, a person should exercise at least 20 minutes a day." But what constitutes "healthy"? Does this mean optimum health, a state of homeostasis, or just "better than poor health"? The point is that guidelines are open to interpretation. (WCAG 2.0 tries to break this mold somewhat; all the "success criteria" are written as testable statements, with the aim of making the guidelines more testable.)

So, why do people keep pointing at the various WAI guidelines as standards?

The answer is that industry and governments use standards all the time, as mechanisms to ensure normative activity. What this means in real life is that governments and industry need to have a measurable, testable way to ensure that accessibility exists in a given web document, and to what extent.

When accessibility advocates note that accessibility is a quality, not a quantity, and therefore not measurable except to an individual's unique needs, one of two things happen:

- Eyes roll and people say "Of course, I understand now," and then they go and use the automated tool and accept whatever comes out as a test and measure.
- People agree, and then in frustration, a specific user community (for example, blind folks using the JAWS for Windows screen reader) is used as the metric for accessibility.

So, the issue here for both regulators and implementers is that the WAI has consistently failed to write measurable, testable standards for the web technologies within the W3C purview. The guidelines are, by definition, a "best practice" for any document on the Web in any form. What is needed is an accessibility standard for HTML, XHTML, and so on that is specific, testable, and measurable. Such a standard would be ideally submitted to the International Organization for Standardization (ISO) or the American National Standards Institute/International Committee for Information Technology Standards (ANSI/INCITS) for fast-track incorporation. Regulators and industry could then reference the standard, making it easy to keep pace with changes in technology.

WCAG 2.0 from 50,000 Feet

WCAG 2.0 is voluminous—more than 600 printed pages. As one commenter noted:

> Part of my concern is that it is really huge. As a developer, I could go through WCAG 1.0 and find the relevant information that I needed to make sure I had what I needed in my website. It is all there in WCAG 2.0 in amazingly rich detail. That amazingly rich detail is just so much information to parse.

This is why it is good to start off by reading the "Understanding WCAG 2.0" document (www.w3.org/TR/UNDERSTANDING-WCAG20/), which provides a more manageable overview. As you'll see in this chapter, there are also annotated checklists for developers to follow to quickly determine which items apply, and how they are applicable to the technology they are using. So, digesting WCAG 2.0 isn't actually as nightmarish as you might first think. The other place you should visit straight away to get better acquainted with WCAG 2.0 is the "Overview of WCAG 2.0 Documents" page, located at www.w3.org/WAI/intro/wcag20.php.

WCAG 2.0 is organized in a completely different manner from WCAG 1.0. WCAG 1.0 consists of guidelines, each of which includes a set of checkpoints that explain how the guideline applies to web development. The checkpoints (www.w3.org/TR/WCAG10/full-checklist.html) are prioritized as Priority 1, 2, and 3. In contrast, WCAG 2.0 is organized by principles, guidelines, and success criteria. Additionally, the success criteria are not prioritized, but instead are ranked by levels. These components of WCAG 2.0 are described in the next section.

14

The new guidelines are more technology-independent and address web-based accessibility issues in a more general manner than WCAG 1.0. This is at least in part because of the changing nature of the Web and the technologies that are being used to produce and present web content. The WAI is trying to make sure that the guidelines can address these changing and evolving technologies, and that they will be useful in determining the accessibility of web pages produced with methods and technologies not yet developed.

While the guidelines and principles are more general, a great deal of material is being supplied on how to achieve conformance. This material is specific and helpful. It is also still under development, so those who are involved in the accessibility arena are encouraged to make contributions.

What's in WCAG 2.0?

Here, we'll look at the contents of the WCAG 2.0 Working Draft, including the principles, guidelines, and the three levels of success criteria that form the guidelines. A good understanding of these elements and how they are used is critical in understanding WCAG 2.0 as a whole.

Principles and Guidelines

The WCAG 2.0 is organized around four design principles of web accessibility (www.w3.org/TR/2005/WD-WCAG20-20051123/intro.html#overview-design-principles):

1. Content must be perceivable.
2. Interface elements in the content must be operable.
3. Content and controls must be understandable.
4. Content must be robust enough to work with current and future technologies.

The following are the guidelines for each principle. These are not for the most part technology-specific. They tell you what to do, not how to do it. For a more detailed list of the guidelines and their subparts, refer to www.w3.org/TR/WCAG20/appendixB.html.

Principle 1

The first principle is that content that cannot be perceived in some way or another by web visitors is not serving its purpose.

Principle 1: Content must be perceivable

Four guidelines help those designing and building websites to make content perceivable to the largest number of people possible.

Guideline 1.1 Provide text alternatives for all non-text content

Providing text alternatives for nontextual content makes it possible for people with different abilities using different devices to perceive the content of web-based resources.

Guideline 1.2 Provide synchronized alternatives for multimedia

Where multimedia is presented on the Web or using web-based technology, alternatives such as synchronized captioning with audio and video presentations should be presented.

Guideline 1.3 Ensure that information and structure can be separated from presentation

It is necessary to ensure that information, structure, and functionality can be separated from presentation (the way the content looks or sounds). Using structural markup correctly ensures that standards-compliant user agents can determine how the content should be presented, even when the user agent must adapt the presentation to meet the needs of people with disabilities. Conversely, *incorrect* use of structural markup—for example, to create visual effects that are not related to the organization and meaning of the content—may create unintended obstacles for users with disabilities.

Guideline 1.4 Make it easy to distinguish foreground information from its background

Principle 2

The second principle is that any elements on the web page must be usable by all persons, regardless of disability.

Principle 2: Interface elements in the content must be operable

Five guidelines are associated with this principle.

Guideline 2.1 Make all functionality operable via a keyboard interface

Guideline 2.2 Allow users to control time limits on their reading or interaction

Guideline 2.3 Allow users to avoid content that could cause seizures due to photosensitivity

Guideline 2.4 Provide mechanisms to help users find content, orient themselves within it, and navigate through it

Guideline 2.5 Help users to avoid mistakes and make it easy to correct mistakes that do occur

14

Principle 3

The third principle is that all content (be it text, images, and so on) and controls (for example, navigation elements) must be readable by all users, whether or not they are sighted.

Principle 3: Content and controls must be understandable

This principle has two guidelines.

Guideline 3.1 Make text content readable and understandable

Guideline 3.2 Make the placement and functionality of content predictable

Principle 4

The fourth principle is that all content should be designed so that it will not break in the future; for example, when viewed in future user agents.

Principle 4: Content should be robust enough to work with current and future user agents (including assistive technologies)

Two guidelines support the fourth principle.

Guideline 4.1 Support compatibility with current and future user agents (including assistive technologies)

Guideline 4.2 Ensure that content is accessible or provide an accessible alternative

Success Criteria

Success criteria are defined as "testable statements that are not technology-specific" (www.w3.org/TR/WCAG20/). These criteria indicate what must be done to achieve success at various levels of conformance. They are used to determine if a "web unit" conforms to WCAG 2.0.

> Web unit *is a collective term for a collection of information on the Internet, not necessarily a single web page, but accessed through a single uniform resource identifier (a URL, for example.). A set of web pages, plus some images and a style sheet, accessed through a single URL would count as one web unit.*

The success criteria have been organized into three separate levels of conformance. Each level has its own criteria, as follows (www.w3.org/TR/2005/WD-WCAG20-20051123/intro.html#overview-design-principles):

- Level 1 success criteria:

    1. Achieve a minimum level of accessibility through markup, scripting, or other technologies that interact with or enable access through user agents, including assistive technologies.

    2. Can reasonably be applied to all Web resources.

- Level 2 success criteria:

    1. Achieve an enhanced level of accessibility through one or both of the following:

        a. markup, scripting, or other technologies that interact with or enable access through user agents, including assistive technologies

        b. the design of the content and presentation

    2. Can reasonably be applied to all Web resources.

- Level 3 success criteria:

    1. Achieve additional accessibility enhancements for people with disabilities.

    2. Are not applicable to all Web resources.

Note: Some guidelines do not contain level 1 success criteria, and others do not contain level 2 success criteria.

This method of grouping success criteria differs in important ways from the approach taken in WCAG 1.0. In WCAG 1.0, each checkpoint is assigned a "priority" according to its impact on accessibility for users. Thus Priority 3 checkpoints appear to be less important than Priority 1 checkpoints. The Working Group now believes that all success criteria of WCAG 2.0 are essential for some people. Thus, the system of checkpoints and priorities used in WCAG 1.0 has been replaced by success criteria grouped under Levels 1, 2, and 3 as described above.

The Working Group believes that all success criteria should be testable. Tests can be done by computer programs or by people who understand this document. When multiple people who understand WCAG 2.0 test the same content using the same success criteria, the same results should be obtained.

In analyzing the success criteria levels, it is clear that they do not point to a specific technology but are more general in nature, so they can be applied with a variety of technological solutions. This is a strong point for the guidelines.

14

Techniques Documents

As we just mentioned, the guidelines and success criteria in WCAG 2.0 are presented in a way that is not technology-specific. However, as you go deeper into the documentation linked to the success criteria, the techniques for specific technologies begin to emerge. This information is found in the "techniques" documents for the different W3C technologies. These guides are indispensable for WCAG 1.0, and will probably be more so in WCAG 2.0, due to its size and complexity. For example, the following documents are available for WCAG 1.0:

- Core Techniques for Web Content Accessibility Guidelines 1.0 (www.w3.org/TR/WCAG10-CORE-TECHS/)
- HTML Techniques for Web Content Accessibility Guidelines 1.0 (www.w3.org/TR/WCAG10-HTML-TECHS/)
- CSS Techniques for Web Content Accessibility Guidelines 1.0 (www.w3.org/TR/WCAG10-CSS-TECHS/)

The following are also available for WCAG 2.0:

- Techniques for WCAG 2.0 (www.w3.org/TR/WCAG20-TECHS/)
- HTML Techniques for WCAG 2.0 (www.w3.org/TR/WCAG20-HTML-TECHS/)

Example of Using the WCAG 2.0 Guidelines

One problem with WCAG 2.0 is that the guidelines are so general that it is sometimes difficult to determine which guideline or guidelines apply to a specific technique or situation. Using tables to format a page is a good example of this. The following is the guideline dealing with tables:

Guideline 1.3 Ensure that information and structure can be separated from presentation.

This is all well and good; however, the guideline does not mention tables (or other website constructs) specifically. But that's the point—it is deliberately structured so that it deals in general with all of the issues that make the collision of structure and presentation lead to inaccessible web pages. This way, the guideline will be relevant to future technologies as well as current ones.

Let's have a look at the success criteria that appear under this guideline (there are no Level 3 criteria for this guideline):

Level 1 Success Criteria for Guideline 1.3

1.3.1 Information and relationships conveyed through presentation can be programmatically determined, and notification of changes to these is available to user agents, including assistive technologies.

1.3.2 Any information that is conveyed by color is also visually evident without color.

1.3.3 When the sequence of the content affects its meaning, that sequence can be programmatically determined.

Level 2 Success Criteria for Guideline 1.3

1.3.4 Information that is conveyed by variations in presentation of text is also conveyed in text, or the variations in presentation of text can be programmatically determined.

1.3.5 Information required to understand and operate content does not rely on shape, size, visual location, or orientation of components.

Looking at these success criteria, it is not hard to figure out that all of these could be applied to tabular data. When you get used to how WCAG 2.0 works, it can be quite effective. When you've identified which guidelines apply to a particular problem, find those guidelines on the W3C site, and then follow the How to meet. . . links to find out how to meet the success criteria.

Let's compare this to the WCAG 1.0 guidelines, checkpoints, and priorities for making tables accessible (www.w3.org/TR/WAI-WEBCONTENT/). Guideline 5 is the main one related to tables:

Guideline 5. Create tables that transform gracefully.

5.1 For data tables, identify row and column headers. [Priority 1]

5.2 For data tables that have two or more logical levels of row or column headers, use markup to associate data cells and header cells. [Priority 1]

5.3 Do not use tables for layout unless the table makes sense when linearized. Otherwise, if the table does not make sense, provide an alternative equivalent (which may be a linearized version). [Priority 2]

5.4 If a table is used for layout, do not use any structural markup for the purpose of visual formatting. [Priority 2]

5.5 Provide summaries for tables. [Priority 3]

5.6 Provide abbreviations for header labels. [Priority 3]

Checkpoint 10.3 also applies to tables:

10.3 Until user agents (including assistive technologies) render side-by-side text correctly, provide a linear text alternative (on the current page or some other) for *all* tables that lay out text in parallel, word-wrapped. [Priority 3]

14

These checkpoints look much more obvious to try to follow, at least, at this level (WCAG 2.0 does have technology-specific support documents, but the guidelines themselves are technology-independent).

Even someone who is familiar with WCAG 1.0 may find it difficult to figure out which WCAG 2.0 guidelines and success criteria apply to a particular situation, such as tables. The document "Mapping of WCAG 1.0 checkpoints to WCAG 2.0 success criteria" (www.w3.org/WAI/GL/2005/11/23-mapping.html) can be very useful in this situation.

> *Sometimes a particular situation can exist that is covered by multiple guidelines. This will be more complicated than having to deal with only one guideline, but the same techniques outlined here apply.*

Also, many users find the WCAG 2.0 Checklist (www.w3.org/TR/WCAG20/appendixB.html) to be a good quick reference for the guidelines.

WCAG 2.0 Advantages and Concerns

In this section, we outline the apparent advantages and concerns that have been raised about the WCAG 2.0 guidelines.

Advantages

The following are the advantages of WCAG 2.0:

- **It's outcome-based, not based on just using the right element.** Since the focus of these guidelines is the product, not which elements are used to achieve the results, there is more flexibility incorporated in how the goals are achieved. However, in taking this approach, the guidelines themselves have become much more complex and understanding them has become more difficult.

- **It addresses more than just markup language issues.** The guidelines seek to address issues that are more than just those involved with markup languages such as HTML or XHTML.

- **It's a work in progress, so contributions are still possible.** It is important to note that those interested in web accessibility should look closely at these guidelines and make comments as soon as possible. As of the time this book went to press, final comments were being accepted. However, it should be noted that, as with any W3C Recommendation, there is nothing to prevent the formulation of a WCAG 2.1. Such a thing can come to pass only with the support of the development community at large, rather than the small "accessibility" community that normally participates in the WAI Working Groups.

- **It seeks to be technology-independent.** There is no question that the technology used to produce websites is changing and evolving at a rapid pace. In order to address this concern, the WCAG 2.0 guidelines are more technology-independent and seek to be written in a way that can be applied to technology that has not been invented yet.

- **It's more general than WCAG 1.0.** Because the WCAG 2.0 guidelines are more general than the WCAG 1.0 guidelines, they can be applied to new technologies in the future without having to be rewritten.

- **Usability issues are incorporated into the guidelines.** A large number of the guidelines and success criteria have incorporated usability issues. This is a very positive development and will help make websites more usable by everyone—people with and without disabilities.

Concerns

The accessibility community is not unified in support of either the approach or the claimed effectiveness of WCAG 2.0. Some of the expressed concerns are discussed in the following sections.

Not Completely Measurable

At this time, the guidelines do not appear to be completely measurable. This was one of the original aims. One of the most common aspects of any technical standard is its ability to have compliance be *measurable*. That is, such a standard must have metrics—ways to measure a particular product's compliance that can be compared objectively with other products. Much of WCAG 2.0 contains subjective, rather than objective, measurements.

For example, how does one measure an "appropriate alternative text for a non-text element"? Obviously, an art historian would feel that a book would need to be written to express the *Mona Lisa*, whereas someone who had no opinion or appreciation might have "painting of a smiling lady" as their alternative text. Which is right? Which is better? WCAG 2.0 leaves this to the testers' own interpretation. In no other endeavor do the authors of works have such ability to be their own "critics." This should be improved by the time the final version comes out.

Revolutionary Rather Than Evolutionary

WCAG 2.0 is a revolutionary rather than evolutionary standard. Development has been proceeding worldwide that utilizes the practices and examples of WCAG 1.0. Much of the significant expenditure in this regard may need to be supplemented by organizations choosing to implement WCAG 2.0. As a revolutionary standard, many of the techniques and mechanisms (such as validation tools) that have been developed will need to be reexamined one by one, potentially with significant costs. Due to long product cycles, this could take years.

14

The impact of not having an evolutionary standard is well understood by standards organizations. The International Committee on Information Technology Standards has a policy discussion of the factors involved in balancing standards evolution. This document (available at www.ncits.org/sd9_feb2002.htm#_Toc514030136) was developed by INCITS (then X3), who took more than ten years to examine this one issue. The committee's findings—that standards need to ensure some effective, retrospective, progression—underscore the challenges in this area that WCAG 2.0 presents to specific consumers of the guidelines.

Some examples follow, illustrating different points of view from the various parties involved.

- **Web developers:** Several considerations apply to website developers:
  - It is always a challenge to keep the hard-working and often-stretched web development community apprised of changes in standards. Keeping them engaged when their knowledge of WCAG 1.0 is no longer market-worthy will be challenging.
  - Changing requirements cost developers and clients that use the standards money and time. Often, more advanced, customizable off-the-shelf products have development cycles of years, making the investment in WCAG 1.0 significant in both time and money.
  - What happens to multinational companies that might have to develop to meet Section 508, WCAG 1.0, and now WCAG 2.0?
- **Toolmakers:** Many companies have invested significant capital and time into developing conformance tools for WCAG 1.0. This includes tools for testing, as well as tools for accessible development. How much more capital and time they will need to invest in WCAG 2.0 compliance remains to be seen.
- **Assistive technology developers:** Probably the hardest hit group will be developers of assistive technologies. Many of these are products with slim margins and small development staff. Often, it takes years for assistive technology to catch up with changes in mainstream IT. Making assistive technology work with the changes in WCAG 2.0 may be more than some of the smaller companies can bear. Think of how assistive technology will respond to the programmatic interruptions allowed for in Success Criterion 2.2.5 ("Interruptions, such as WCAG 2.0 updated content, can be postponed or suppressed by the user, except interruptions involving an emergency"), even if justified!

Baselines and Conformance

WCAG 2.0 concepts such as *baselines* and *scoping* are complex and have not yet been fully developed. A *baseline* is defined as follows (www.w3.org/WAI/WCAG20/baseline/):

A "baseline", as used in WCAG 2.0, is the set of technologies that an author assumes are supported and turned on in accessible user agents. Authors must ensure that all information and functionality of the Web content conform to WCAG 2.0 even when a user agent supports and uses only the technologies in the baseline.

Using this definition, baselines are most useful in a controlled environment where the technology used by the end user is limited. In a public environment, which is much harder to control, it will be more difficult for baselines to be useful and helpful to the user or the developer. Since they have such a wide reach, it will be difficult. Scoping of conformance may help, but it is too early to tell.

Conformance means meeting the WCAG 2.0 success criteria. The success criteria levels explain what is expected to achieve conformance. In order to define and explain how *scoping* is used in conformance, a definition is required. Here is the definition from the W3C (www.w3.org/TR/WCAG20/conformance.html#conformance-reqs):

> Conformance claims can be limited, or "scoped," to pertain to only some parts of a Web site. Scoping by URI to exclude sections of a site is allowed so that authors can make claims for just some parts of a site. . . . Scoping cannot exclude a particular type of content (for example, images or scripts) since it would allow exclusion of individual success criteria.

The positive aspect of this is that parts of sites can be clearly marked as accessible or inaccessible. The negative aspect is that the exclusion of parts of websites can cause major problems when it is decided that certain parts of a site do not "need" to be prioritized for accessibility to people who have disabilities—scoping shouldn't be considered an excuse to leave some sections of the website inaccessible. At best, it would be considered an admission of failure.

Other Concerns

The following are some other concerns related to WCAG 2.0:

- **Extremely complex:** Parts of the guidelines are very simple, but as you drill deeper into the success criteria, they become more specific and more complex.

- **Language:** Rather than using plain language, the guidelines are couched in academic terms and difficult for many to understand. There are many terms that are specific to the guidelines.

- **Testing:** Some criteria can be tested only by human beings. This always leaves room for differences.

- **Government acceptance:** The W3C WAI guidelines weren't wholly accepted by the U.S. government. There is a significant amount of background linked to the WCAG 1.0 guidelines and the U.S. Section 508 Standards, and why the U.S. government ended up devising its own legislation to enforce web accessibility, which is not really equivalent to the W3C's work. The U.S. government accepted WCAG 1.0, but required the checkpoints to be written as testable statements for legislation. The U.S. government wanted to incorporate only issues that caused significant barriers, so Section 508 Section 1194.22 is similar to WCAG 1.0 Level A.

14

Section 508 and WCAG

Section 508 covers all Electronic and Information Technology (EIT). Our discussion will be limited to Subpart B – Technical Standards, Section 1194.22 of the Section 508 Standards (see Appendix B of this book for an excerpt of this part).

There are close matches between WCAG 1.0 and Section 508 1194.22 paragraphs (a) through (l). Beyond that, the mappings diverge.

Section 508 covers more than just web-based technology. Plus it was meant to be more precise and measurable than the WCAG guidelines that existed at the time. The desired effect was to cover a wide range of technologies, including Flash, PDF, and Java. This suggests that Section 508 is a bit closer to WCAG 2.0 than the original WCAG 1.0.

Several mappings are useful in understanding the relationship between Section 508 and WCAG 1.0 and WCAG 2.0, formulated and written by Jim Thatcher:

- WCAG 1.0 to 508: www.jimthatcher.com/sidebyside.htm
- WCAG 2.0 to 508: www.jimthatcher.com/508wcag2.htm

Leaning more towards how Section 508 works, WCAG 2.0 concentrates on the result, aiming to be more outcome-based. The guidelines themselves emphasize the final result that is achieved. As noted earlier in this chapter, at their highest level, the guidelines are technology-independent. Only as you go deeper into the success criteria and documentation on how to achieve those criteria do the technology-specific techniques begin to appear. The technological restrictions on achieving the goal are not as onerous as they were under WCAG 1.0, and there are more ways to achieve compliance.

If WCAG 2.0 could be made "regulatory friendly" with adoption as a worldwide accessibility regulatory standard, it would make it easier to maintain and enforce accessibility. However, implementation of this goal can be perceived as culturally unfriendly. Not all situations in all cultures are going to be covered, and this can produce unwanted situations. This is obviously a delicate situation, and a middle ground must be found to benefit the largest number of people.

The focus of regulatory compliance is often at odds with technical compliance. This is seen often in the U.S. with the Section 508 Standards. The legal requirement of compliance with the regulatory standards creates confusion in developers, who simply want to know the answer to "How do I code this?" or "How do I use a tool to check the code?" Since the "standards" are regulatory rather than technical, there are no easy mechanisms to ensure technical compliance, and U.S. companies have fought furiously to prevent standardized metrics that would allow easy comparison between products. Such comparisons could result in millions of dollars in windfalls and losses, based on how the final metrics are determined.

WCAG 2.0 tries to walk this line better than 1.0. However, the fundamental issue—that regulatory standards require a functional compliance and technical standards require a measurable, testable compliance—is not solvable without involving standards organizations such as ISO in the process, something that W3C is understandably loath to consider at this time.

Summary

Looking at all the concerns, it is fair to say that the jury is still out on WCAG 2.0. Ultimately, whether WCAG 2.0 will be the accessibility standard of the future will be decided by developers, their clients, and the governments of the world. And their awareness will be the responsibility of the W3C's WAI (www.w3.org/wai).

The WCAG 2.0 guidelines are organized in a way that is radically different from WCAG 1.0's organization. While the concepts are to some degree evolutionary, the organization of the guidelines is definitely revolutionary. This will require a good deal of work on the part of those who are used to the WCAG 1.0 guidelines.

Since the guidelines are outcome-based, many of the old restrictions no longer exist. The goals are designed so that new technology that has not yet been developed can achieve them without imposing the many restrictions that exist in the WCAG 1.0 guidelines.

Due to the fragmentary nature of the W3C process, there are varying degrees of consistency in the quality of the implementation practices that have been developed. Many of the sample markup fragments in the "how to meet" documents advocate practice that is not consistent with WCAG 1.0 best practice, such as not clearly identifying headers in a table. These sections are informative rather than normative; however, many developers generally do not have the time to review the arcane language in the guidelines document itself, and will simply refer to the "how to meet" sections when attempting to write or determine compliant code.

14

15 RETROFITTING CASE STUDY: REDESIGN OF A UNIVERSITY WEBSITE

by Patrick H. Lauke

My first real contact with accessibility came when I started in my position as Web Editor at the University of Salford in January 2001. As part of the responsibilities of my new job, I started researching some of the legal requirements involving educational websites in the UK, inevitably coming across the Special Educational Needs and Disabilities Act (SENDA) and the wider-reaching Disabilities Discrimination Act (DDA). From there, I delved further into the area of web accessibility. It soon became obvious that the University's site, which had undergone a year-long redesign process just before I started, presented some fundamental accessibility concerns that urgently needed to be addressed.

This chapter covers the process I went through in redesigning the University of Salford's website, with an eye on increased accessibility and the adoption of web standards. These techniques should be of use to you if you're faced with the challenge of retrofitting, or completely rebuilding, a site in order to make it more accessible.

The Original Site

Figure 15-1 shows the original homepage for the University of Salford. Purely from a graphic design point of view, the site was compliant with the University's corporate identity guidelines. However, the additional visual elements of the design—the heavy use of large, rounded corners and the complementary blue/orange color scheme (which, to this day, prompts people to refer to it as the "blueberry-and-custard" site)—were based on the University's recent designs for its print campaign.

The Problems

Subjectively, I would say that the rounded corners, both in the overly large header and footer, were too strong a design element in their own right. Because of their size, they often overpowered the actual content presented on each page. In addition, many people (including myself) often criticized the look of the template for being fairly dated; even in 2001, the "rounded-corners" trend had been gone for a few years.

The design choices for any further visuals on a page were severely restricted. Images with straight edges looked out of place, often requiring them to be "rounded off" first, simply to make them visually fit within the overall feel of the template. An extreme case in point: When asked to include a permanent new feature on the homepage (to advertise the fact that the University had just been awarded a prestigious prize), I ended up having to construct a whole new rounded section as part of the page footer, as shown in Figure 15-2.

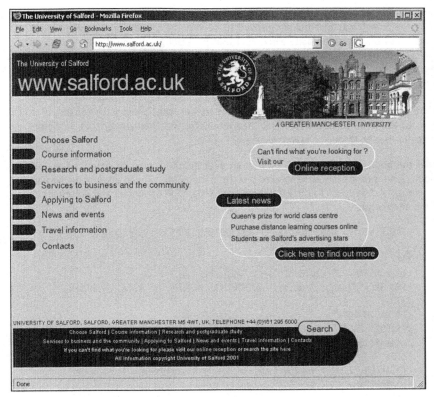

Figure 15-1. The University of Salford homepage in 2001

Figure 15-2. More rounded edges to make additional graphics fit with the overall design

15

As for usability, one of the major pieces of feedback received from users in the weeks following the launch was that the site proved to be very confusing. This sort of problem would have been identified quite early on in usability testing, but unfortunately, no tests were carried out before the launch in December 2000 (apart from a series of focus groups, mainly concentrating on the visual aspects of the site). Because of the drop down–based navigation and the absence of any indication as to where the current page was situated within the context of the overall site (apart from a simple image in the top-right corner with the generic name for the current section), users were simply lost and often forced to return to the homepage just to orient themselves. This was particularly true of visitors coming to the site through a search engine.

Under the hood, the markup was what, even back in 2001, could be described as "old school." Any visual aspects were handled directly in the HTML, with no attempt on the part of the original developers to carry out some basic separation of content and presentation. Here is an excerpt:

```
<TABLE WIDTH="98%" BORDER="0" CELLPADDING="0" CELLSPACING="0">

<TR>
<TD ROWSPAN="4" WIDTH="1%">
<IMG SRC="/images /dot.gif" WIDTH="30" HEIGHT="1" ALT="-" BORDER="0">
</TD>
<TD WIDTH="99%">
<P><FONT FACE="arial,helvetica" SIZE="4" COLOR="#0000CC">
Academic enterprise</FONT></P>
</TD>
<TD ALIGN="RIGHT" VALIGN="TOP" WIDTH="35%"></TD>
<TD ROWSPAN="4" WIDTH="5%"> </TD>
</TR>

<TR>
<TD COLSPAN="2">
<!--MAIN BODY OF PAGE-->
<TABLE WIDTH="100%" BORDER="0" CELLPADDING="0" CELLSPACING="0">
<TR>
<TD VALIGN="TOP"><FONT FACE="arial,helvetica" SIZE="2">
Salford has always had a reputation for enterprising initiatives
... </FONT>
...
```

With no use of Cascading Style Sheets (CSS) in sight, each table cell, paragraph, list item, and so on featured a <font> tag to set the basic typeface, size, and color.

The entire layout was based on a series of convoluted tables, using rowspan/colspan and set cell dimensions (although, to the designers' credit, they did use a combination of pixel and percentage values, making the layout halfway elastic). Due to their construction, these tables also didn't linearize in a sensible way, which I swiftly demonstrated to management by running the site through the Lynx text-only browser. (See Chapter 6 for an explanation of table linearization.)

Plain HTML does not lend itself well to a design based predominantly on rounded corners. To "fake" the rounded-design elements demanded by the University's print campaign, a lot of extra markup had been added to the already complex table layout, as shown in Figure 15-3.

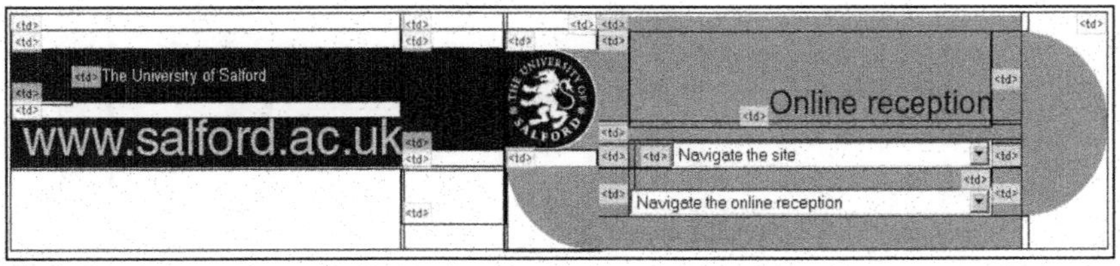

Figure 15-3. Faking rounded corners with tons of table-based markup

Because of the cluttered table markup and the abundance of table cells used purely for spacing and presentation, the resulting code was unnecessarily cumbersome to work with.

This layout was not just used on the University's core site, but also employed across the whole range of departmental sites. With the decentralized web management structure at the University, individual departments have their own web authors looking after their particular site. The experience and skill level of these web authors can vary considerably across the institution, ranging from fairly web-confident technicians to administrative staff and lecturers with little or no knowledge of HTML. Particularly for this latter group, the overly convoluted code of the templates proved difficult to understand. This can often lead to a vicious circle in development. With an increasingly complex maze of markup, web authors who are not too confident in working directly with HTML will rely more and more on the use of what you see is what you get (WYSIWYG) editors. Although these editors hide the complexity of a page's underlying markup, they often introduce even further bloated code, thus compounding the problem. Then, when things go wrong and for some reason a page's layout falls apart at the seams, it's increasingly difficult to fix the problem at the HTML level.

To achieve the rounded-edges look, the original designers used a mixture of table cell backgrounds for solid areas of color and image elements for the corners. This presented an interesting problem when pages were printed.

By default, browsers will print images present in the markup, but omit any background colors (unless users explicitly set this option in their print settings). The result, as indicated in Figure 15-4, was that our pages looked very odd on paper, with a mixture of text content and isolated images of rounded corners set against the white background of the page.

15

Figure 15-4. Print preview of a typical page from the old site, with rounded-corner images clearly visible

For this reason, many of the core pages (for instance, all of our online course information) needed a separate "printer-friendly" version, as in the example in Figure 15-5. Luckily, many of the pages were already database-driven, so I only had to create a new page that pulled the content from the database and presented it without any of the surrounding site template that was causing the problems. But this solution was inelegant and still left the remainder of static pages on the site looking shabby when put on paper.

Figure 15-5. Detail of an events page, showing the printer-friendly version link

Another problem area was the site navigation. As shown in the following code, classic Dreamweaver "jump menu" drop-downs were used to provide the navigation for all major site areas and subpages within the current section.

```
<SCRIPT LANGUAGE="Javascript">
<!--
function gotoPage(number) {
  i=document.navform.elements[number].selectedIndex;
  parent.location.href=➥
  document.navform.elements[number].options[i].value;
}
// -->
</SCRIPT>


<SELECT NAME="choose" onChange="gotoPage(0)">
  <OPTION VALUE="#">Navigate the site</OPTION>
  <OPTION VALUE="#">.......................................</OPTION>
  <OPTION VALUE="http://www.salford.ac.uk/">Homepage</OPTION>
  <OPTION VALUE="http://www.salford.ac.uk/reception/">Online
reception➥
  </OPTION>
  <OPTION VALUE="http://www.salford.ac.uk/choose/">Choose Salford➥
  </OPTION>

...

</SELECT>
```

In the very first version of the site, these navigation menus were completely reliant on client-side scripting. Simply marked up as a couple of `<select>` elements, not contained inside any `<form>` and certainly lacking a conventional submit button, these menus relied on the `<select>` element's onchange event to load a new page whenever the user changed the current selection.

Apart from making the navigation unusable when client-side scripting is unavailable or disabled, this makes keyboard access (with or without assistive technology) tricky. Using default cursor keys to move through the available options triggers the script. Effectively, this makes it impossible for keyboard users to move beyond the first `<option>` unless they are aware of work-arounds built into their browser or assistive technology.

> *An example of a work-around for keyboard users in Internet Explorer is using Alt+cursor keys to "open" the* `<select>` *menu—a concept that certainly doesn't translate well to the nonvisual realm. This suppresses any* onchange *event until the* `<select>` *menu is closed by either pressing the Enter key or tabbing away from it.*

15

The worst use of these jump menus was the Online Reception page, shown in Figure 15-6. This was a one-stop-shop page used in lieu of a proper index or site map, which had no less than six <select> elements to provide quick links to the majority of the University's top-level pages and departmental sites.

Figure 15-6. The University's Online Reception page, featuring a total of six JavaScript-driven jump menus (excluding the main navigation)

Some of the drop-downs on the Online Reception page also nicely demonstrate another shortcoming of <select> elements: the difficulty with providing effective levels of grouping and subcategorization. Although HTML does offer the ability of grouping individual <option> elements inside an <optgroup>, support for this element was (and still is, in certain browsers) flaky or nonexistent. Therefore, the designers used a variety of visual tricks to "fake" the semblance of hierarchy and structure within the <select> elements by introducing empty spacer <option> elements and prefixing subpages with a simple dash— a purely visual subterfuge. Figure 15-7 shows an example.

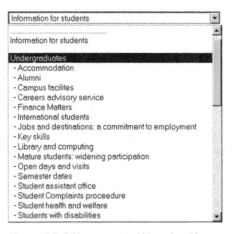

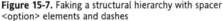

Figure 15-7. Faking a structural hierarchy with spacer
<option> elements and dashes

The following is the code that creates the menu in Figure 15-7:

```
<SELECT NAME="choose" onChange="gotoReceptionPage(2)">
    <OPTION VALUE="..." SELECTED>Information for students</OPTION>
    <OPTION VALUE="#">......................................</OPTION>
    <OPTION VALUE="...">Information for students</OPTION>
    <OPTION VALUE="#"></OPTION>
    <OPTION VALUE="...">Undergraduates</OPTION>
    <OPTION VALUE="...">  - Accommodation</OPTION>
    <OPTION VALUE="...">  - Alumni</OPTION>
    <OPTION VALUE="...">  - Campus facilites</OPTION>
    <OPTION VALUE="...">  - Careers advisory service</OPTION>
    <OPTION VALUE="...">  - Finance Matters</OPTION>
    ...
</SELECT>
```

Other than inconveniencing, or outright excluding, certain users, this type of navigation also had a noticeable impact on the University's search engine rankings. With hardly any real links in the markup, content was effectively hidden from search engine spiders. Even our own internal search engine needed to be explicitly pointed to specific URLs to index in order to keep search results relevant.

Along with these problems were the usual suspects of inaccessible sites: a proliferation of click here links, extensive use of graphical buttons, inappropriate use of markup to achieve a certain type of visual presentation, and so on.

15

In short, the site that I had inherited was a mess. Unfortunately, the University had just launched its new design (after a considerable investment of money and time), and many departments across the institution had already started the process of painstakingly transferring their content into the new cumbersome layout. It was therefore decided that, rather than embarking on yet another redesign so soon after the last one, just the most obvious accessibility issues should be fixed.

The Initial Fixes

A small retrofit in its own right, my initial "damage limitation" exercise concentrated mainly on the two biggest problems: making the table-based layout linearize properly and making the drop-down navigation at least workable for non-JavaScript users.

Paradoxically, to fix some of the linearization issues of the template, the tables themselves had to be broken down into further nested tables, thus adding even further "scaffolding" markup to the already convoluted code.

To make the navigation work even without client-side scripting, I implemented a rudimentary server-side fallback mechanism. The two separate <select> elements in the header (as well as the six jump menus on the Online Reception page) were each wrapped in a proper <form> element, and a discreetly designed image-based submit button was included. When submitted, the destination's URL was passed to a simple PHP script, whose only purpose was to redirect the user's browser to the desired target page. This approach was not very elegant, as it added an unnecessary round-trip to the server and made it impossible to gather any useful page-referrer information within the site (although, admittedly, the PHP code could have been further expanded to separately log this type of information). Nonetheless, this fallback at least meant that users without JavaScript would be able to navigate the site. Figure 15-8 shows the new menu.

Figure 15-8. Tweaked jump menu, now wrapped in a form element with an unobtrusive image-based submit button to the right

The following is the HTML that creates the tweaked jump menu shown in Figure 15-8:

```
<form action="/redirect.php" method="post">
    <select name="select" onchange="MM_jumpMenu('document',this,1)">
        <option value="#" selected="selected">Navigate the site➡
        </option>
        <option value="#">_____</option>
        <option value="http://www.salford.ac.uk/">Homepage</option>
        <option value="#">_____</option>
        <option value="http://www.salford.ac.uk/about/">➡
        About the University</option>
        <option value="http://www.salford.ac.uk/faculties-schools/">➡
        Faculties and Schools</option>
```

...

```
</select>
<input type="image" border="0" name="submit"➡
    src="/images/common/go.gif" alt="Go" width="11" height="11">
</form>
```

And the following is the corresponding server-side code to handle the redirection:

```php
<?php
// expects a value for 'select' either GET or POST
if (isset($_REQUEST['select'])&&(!($_REQUEST['select']=="#")))
{
    // redirect user to selected page
    header('Location: '.$_REQUEST['select']);
} else {
    // default behaviour - go back from whence you came
    header('Location: '.$_SERVER['HTTP_REFERER']);
}
?>
```

Initially, to address the keyboard access problems for users that *did* have JavaScript, I also removed the client-side scripting completely. However, this change immediately prompted a barrage of messages from users and management, reporting that suddenly the navigation was "broken." Grudgingly, I had to take the pragmatic decision to reintroduce the JavaScript-based functionality (on top of the server-side fallback) in order to make the fundamentally flawed navigation scheme usable for the majority of users, while acknowledging that keyboard users would still be faced with some difficulties.

The Redesign

At the start of 2003, the University undertook a review of its corporate identity guidelines. A new design agency was tasked with expanding the existing guidelines (which were quite minimal, mainly centered around the appropriate use of the University logo, our two core corporate colors, and the right choice of typeface) to provide additional color combinations and a modular set of templates for print and electronic formats. Although the agency didn't specifically look at guidelines related to the Web, I worked closely with the designers to ensure that it would be possible to interpret and adapt the revised identity for online use.

In contrast with the comparatively lax previous corporate identity, the new guidelines introduced a set of tighter restrictions. For instance, they prescribed the top-left position of the logo (which was also slightly altered to now include the University name and the "A Greater Manchester University" slogan in a set configuration next to the original logo roundel) and a limited palette of primary and secondary colors that could be used.

As these new guidelines applied to our site as well, it was clear that the blue-and-orange color scheme and the general page header would have to be revised. So, after two years

15

of "blueberry-and-custard," we were faced with a fundamental choice: Should we simply apply a new facade to the University's web presence, changing only visual aspects of the markup while maintaining the rest of the underlying, table-based structure? Or should we learn from past mistakes, be mindful of the fundamental accessibility problems present in the current site, and make a fresh start?

Clearly, a complete rebuild would have involved a considerable amount of work, with every page of the site having to be recoded. However, remember the complete absence of separation of content and presentation? Because the colors and general layout were hard-coded into the presentational HTML, even superficial changes would have required work on each page. I therefore decided to seize the opportunity of this corporate identity review to radically change the University site for the better, rather than awkwardly carrying on with small fixes and tweaks to the existing markup.

Unlike many other web managers in charge of corporate sites, I was fortunate that management allowed me a certain level of flexibility in making these kinds of decisions autonomously. Apart from a series of briefings to key groups of internal stakeholders, centered mainly on the need to redesign from a corporate identity point of view, I did not have to do a "hard sell" to convince the University to move toward a web standards–based approach. None of these briefing sessions ever actually mentioned web standards or layouts without tables in any technical detail. I merely put the point across that the redesign would follow modern web development best practice. Similarly, for the accessibility side of the redesign, I did not enter into any lengthy explanation of the Web Content Accessibility Guidelines (WCAG), assistive technology, or people with disabilities. I merely reassured management that, in adopting the proposed best practice strategies, the University's site would fall in line with legal requirements with regard to SENDA.

> Web managers who are having more difficulty in convincing their bosses or clients of the value of a web standards–based approach may be interested in the documents put together by the Making A Commercial Case for Adopting Web Standards (MACCAWS) research group, at www.maccaws.org.

Decisions in Early Planning Stages

A number of decisions had to be made during the early planning stages of the redesign. Some of the important ones were to design to web standards, to use XHTML, and to use CSS rather than table-based layouts. The following sections look at these decisions in some detail.

Why Web Standards?

Nowadays, the majority of web professionals should at least have heard of web standards, thanks in no small part to the ongoing efforts of grassroots movements such as the Web Standards Project (www.webstandards.org), the increased availability of valuable online and paper-based resources on the subject, and excellent examples of large corporate sites that have made the switch to valid, table-free, structural markup.

At the time of the University of Salford website redesign, however, these resources were few and far between. Designing with web standards, thoroughly separating content from presentation, and abandoning tables in favor of pure CSS solutions were still the exceptions. However, the fundamental benefits of a web standards–based approach were already becoming evident:

- Coding to official World Wide Web Consortium (W3C) specifications and abandoning proprietary markup (more often than not aimed squarely at Internet Explorer) ensures that pages work in the majority of browsers, without the need for separate versions or the risk of shutting out a percentage of your visitors.

- The separation of content and presentation results in "lighter" web pages, devoid of presentational clutter, that load and display considerably faster and are easier to maintain.

- Thinking beyond this particular design, with an eye on the possibility that the University's branding or visual guidelines may change in future, having all aspects of the presentation neatly centralized in a handful of CSS files allows for a quick way to radically alter the look and feel of an entire site, without needing to amend each individual page.

As at the time the University's central web team was composed of only myself (a team of one), all of these benefits certainly would have helped in "working smarter, not harder" and giving me better control over the institution's site.

Why XHTML Rather Than HTML?

Generally, many developers assume that "designing with web standards" implies the need to switch to XHTML. Of course, that's not necessarily true. It is perfectly possible to use HTML 4.01 (preferably following the Strict DOCTYPE) to create lean, semantically structured sites. With enough "personal discipline"—consciously avoiding presentational language elements such as bold, italic, and <font> tags in favor of structural equivalents and CSS—you can follow the principles of web standards (valid, semantic code and the separation of content and presentation) without the need for XHTML.

> *Purists will argue that the only real benefits of XHTML can be reaped when combining it with other XML-based technologies (for example, mixing XHTML and MathML). But in order to do this, pages need to be sent with an XML MIME type (such as* application/xhtml+xml*), which Internet Explorer does not understand. This is a fact that purists will often use as proof positive that, for general-purpose web pages that do not mix XML technologies, there is no reason to use anything other than plain HTML.*

The decision to move the University site to XHTML was dictated not so much by any intrinsic advantage of XHTML over HTML, but by the need to make life easier for myself when it comes to testing and quality assurance. Because the majority of presentational markup has been removed from XHTML (with a few debatable exceptions like the sub/sup elements), running pages through the W3C markup validator quickly brings to light any use of presentational elements and attributes. This is a particularly useful first test when checking pages developed by departmental web authors or third-party suppliers. Of course, it's still

15

possible to create completely nonsemantic and inaccessible documents that are completely valid XHTML/CSS, so this sort of testing needs to be followed up by a proper look at the markup. Nonetheless, it can be helpful as a very superficial initial assessment.

Another thought at the back of my mind when choosing XHTML was the planned adoption of a content management system (CMS) by our IT department a few years further down the line. With the possibilities opened up by simple, readily available technologies such as XSLT and the use of XML-based languages for data import into such systems, it would be possible to repurpose web pages by transforming XHTML into a format suitable for inclusion into the CMS. Further potential applications, such as print-on-demand systems where XML content can be loaded directly into a desktop publishing package such as Adobe InDesign or Quark Xpress, further influenced this decision.

Why Move Away from Tables?

The syntax of XHTML still allows the use of tables, and rightly so, as the table construct is ideally suited to mark up the complex relationships of headings and values of tabular data. In that respect, it's obvious that tables are not purely presentational. However, web designers have traditionally relied on table markup for exactly that: defining a visual layout. Even stretching the definition, there is usually no relationship being defined in a table-based layout other than "I want these two columns of text to sit next to each other."

> *If you're ever in doubt about whether or not something could be considered "tabular data," ask yourself if you would put this information in an Excel spreadsheet. This method isn't foolproof though, as over the years, I've come to know many managers who treat Excel like a poor man's layout tool. Incidentally, these are usually also the people who think PowerPoint is a web design tool in its own right and proudly hand over their mock-ups with an "I've already done the layout of my pages for you as well" remark.*

The original definition for tables from the HTML 4.01 specification (www.w3.org/TR/html401/struct/tables.html#h-11.1) is slightly vague on the subject.

> The HTML table model allows authors to arrange data -- text, preformatted text, images, links, forms, form fields, other tables, etc. -- into rows and columns of cells. [...] Tables should not be used purely as a means to layout document content as this may present problems when rendering to non-visual media. [...] authors should use style sheets to control layout rather than tables.

Even WCAG 1.0 mentions the use of tables for layout, but fails to actually prohibit their presentational use (www.w3.org/TR/WCAG10/wai-pageauth.html#gl-table-markup).

5.3 Do not use tables for layout unless the table makes sense when linearized. Otherwise, if the table does not make sense, provide an alternative equivalent (which may be a linearized version). [Priority 2]

5.4 If a table is used for layout, do not use any structural markup for the purpose of visual formatting. [Priority 2]

Regardless of wooly definitions in the HTML specification and get-out clauses so readily provided in the WCAG, staying true to the idea of separating content from presentation means abandoning table-based layouts in favor of CSS.

There are obvious advantages to CSS-driven layouts. Externalizing all of a site's presentation (layout, colors, typeface definitions, and so on) to style sheets provides an excellent way of keeping control over the look and feel of a site at a central location. When rigorously applied to all pages, CSS provides an excellent means of maintaining a consistent layout and presentation across a site. It also gives a certain measure of future-proofing. For example, if the University's corporate colors or choice of overall design were to change, a large part of the redesign would involve nothing more than a change to the styles, rather than requiring a complete recoding of each individual page.

Another advantage of CSS is the ability to define different presentation styles for a variety of delivery channels. Through the use of @media directives or the media attribute for style sheet <link> elements you can specify how a document should look on the screen or in print, making a separate printer-friendly version unnecessary.

> *There are still edge cases in which a printer-friendly version may be required. One example would be a lengthy document that was split into separate pages for easier reading. A designer may want to provide the same document as a single, albeit long, page.*

See Chapter 9 for details on using CSS for accessible web pages.

Site Structure—Taking Stock

A complete redesign is a good opportunity to not only change the appearance of a site, but to also take a critical look at a site's structure and content. Sites can grow in a very organic fashion. Despite an initially defined information architecture, new pages and sections that don't quite fit the original structure are added at a later date. It's often surprising how much legacy content is still present, often carried from one redesign to the next.

Before embarking on a redesign, it is therefore useful to start with a completely blank slate. For the University of Salford website redesign, the first phase involved a meticulous inventory of any content available on the old site. Working with the respective content owners, outdated content was pruned and amended. To work out the new site's overall structure, I enlisted the help of various stakeholders across the University, including a sample of current students, in order to carry out simple taxonomy and card-sorting.

15

Card-sorting is a user-centered design method in which users sort a series of cards, each representing a particular piece of content or functionality of a site, into groups that make sense to them. Card sorting can help in understanding the users' mental models, thus allowing you to organize your content in a way that matches their expectations.

It's usually possible to make smaller design or structural changes directly on a live site. However, as this redesign involved a complete restructuring and rebuilding, I requested a new development server to be set up centrally by the University's IT department. Even if, as was the case with this redesign, you're the only developer working on a new site, there are many advantages to this approach over simply setting up a local development server on your own workstation. Chief among them is the ability to let management and other interested parties across the institution keep an eye on the work in progress. Coupled with a simple feedback form, this can give them the opportunity to have their say and effectively take a certain amount of ownership of the redesign (be careful to manage their expectations, though; otherwise, they will expect any single suggestion to be implemented immediately).

Based on the new information architecture, I prepared the development server by basically setting up an equivalent directory structure. I then proceeded to copy the relevant existing pages, plus any additional pieces of amended information (mostly provided by the content owners as Word documents) into their respective new folders.

So, with a new streamlined site structure and up-to-date content, it was time to get down to the nitty-gritty of the actual build.

Building Page Templates

In an ideal web standards workflow, the task of creating a site template can be broken down into two distinct phases:

- Content—creating the page structure in (X)HTML
- Presentation—applying a style and layout to the structure (CSS)

As shown in Figure 15-9, these phases would normally be carried out in sequence, practically in isolation. Reality, however, is never quite as structured as this ideal model.

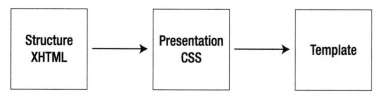

Figure 15-9. Ideal web standards workflow as a one-way process: first create the structure, then the presentation

Planning the Page Structure

Web designers (as opposed to developers) are often intrinsically visual people. Even at the earliest stages—planning the purpose of a site, what content it will present, what functionality it will offer users—they're likely to already form a mental picture of the kind of layout and style that would be most appropriate for the finished site. As difficult as it may be, when planning the page structure and how it could best be represented in markup, designers need to try to put their visual interpretation to one side. At this point, it's not important to dwell on how things will look. Wearing a content editor's hat, you should first decide which structural blocks will need to be present in a page and in what logical order they should be placed in the markup.

Stylistic decisions should not influence your choice of HTML. When checking the unstyled markup (or rather, styled purely with the browser's default style sheet), don't worry if things looks slightly bland or disproportionate. That overly large <h1> or those bunched up form elements will be dealt with in the styling phase.

So, concentrating purely on the "functional" blocks that I envisaged for our pages, I decided on a structure that included the following:

- Branding (logo)
- Search box
- Navigation
- Breadcrumb trail
- Content
- Footer

HTML is fairly limited in terms of the elements that make up the language. Many of these elements are only vaguely defined in the official HTML specification, and the majority are very generic and open to interpretation. There are no ready-made, specific markup constructs to define certain common page elements such as breadcrumb trails, footers, or navigation bars.

For this reason, choosing the most semantically appropriate way to mark up a page's structure is not always straightforward, and it is a subject of much debate among web standards "purists." Unless designers have an inclination to engage in pedantic discussions, they need to make a pragmatic judgment call, with an eye on current best practices (such as John Allsopp's "Web Patterns" initiative; see www.webpatterns.org for more information).

> The extensibility of XHTML 1.0, as well as the modular nature of XHTML 1.1 and the upcoming XHTML 2.0 specifications, allow web developers to include other XML vocabularies in their documents, even to the point of creating their very own specialized set of additional markup elements. However, it's worth remembering that user agents (including browsers and assistive technologies) still need to be able to interpret the markup in order to present it to users in a sensible and structured way.

15

Translating my simple page outline directly into markup, I ended up with the first draft for the new document template. The following listing shows the general code structure of the site.

```
<div>
    <a href="/"><img src="/images/logo.gif" ➥
    alt="University of Salford - A Greater Manchester University" /></a>
</div>
<form>...</form>
<div id="navbar">...</div>
<div id="breadcrumbs">...</div>
<div id="content">...</div>
<div id="footer">...</div>
```

Following a best practice example that was emerging and gaining momentum at the time of the redesign, I opted for an unordered list of links as the most appropriate way in which to mark up the site navigation itself. Or rather: I started off with the idea of a simple unordered list, only to get tangled up in an almost philosophical debate with myself on how to best represent subgroupings within the navigation. I ended up with a structure that, in hindsight, is a rather inelegant mixture of divs and unordered lists (see the "Problems Along the Way—Lessons Learned" section later in this chapter for more on that problem).

```
<div id="navbar">
    <div class="navgroup">
        <ul>
            <li><a href="/">University Home</a></li>
        </ul>
    </div>
    <div class="navgroup">
        <ul>
            <li><a href="...">About the University</a></li>
        </ul>
    </div>
    <div class="navgroup">
        <ul>
            <li><a href="...">Study at Salford</a></li>
            <li><a href="...">Course Finder</a></li>
            <li><a href="...">Research</a></li>
        </ul>
    </div>

    ...

</div>
```

With the rough structure completed, I devoted some time to adding a few additional touches of markup for accessibility and usability purposes.

As the template markup included a fairly long navigation bar before the area containing the actual page content, a skip to content link was included directly after the main logo. As at the time I was primarily concerned with screen reader users, I implemented this as an unobtrusive link wrapped around a single 1-pixel transparent GIF.

```
<a href="#content" accesskey="2">
    <img src="/images/transparent.gif" alt="skip to content" ➡
    width="1" height="1" />
</a>
```

As already hinted at in the previous code sample, I also added an abridged and slightly modified set of access keys, based on the UK Government accesskeys standard (mandated by the Cabinet Office's e-Government handbook, www.cabinetoffice.gov.uk/e-government/resources/handbook/html/2-4.asp):

- Access key 1 - Homepage
- Access key 2 - Skip to content
- Access key 4 - Set focus to search box
- Access key 0 - Help

Access keys are mentioned as an HTML technique in WCAG 1.0 (www.w3.org/TR/WCAG10/wai-pageauth.html#tech-keyboard-shortcuts):

> 9.5 Provide keyboard shortcuts to important links (including those in client-side image maps), form controls, and groups of form controls. [Priority 3]

Over the past few years, though, access keys have come under much criticism. Some argue that it is not the place of document authors to prescribe which key combinations are available to users (leaving this instead in the hands of users themselves and their respective user agent/assistive technologies). Beyond this (possibly academic) discussion, however, it's certainly true that the concept of access keys is good, but their implementation in many browsers is flawed. Taking the common example of Internet Explorer under Windows, access keys are triggered via the Alt+access key combination. Unfortunately, the Alt key is also used to enable keyboard access to browser menus, to enter characters in their numerical key code format (for example, Alt+0228 for an *ä*), and, in some situations, to activate certain options of assistive technologies or other helper applications running in the background. Therefore, it is almost impossible to find any reasonable set of access key definitions that don't have the potential of conflicting with, or outright overriding, other system shortcuts on which a user may be relying. For this reason, web designers should carefully consider whether or not to implement even a minimal set of access keys in their pages. For my own part, I am now considering dropping access keys from the next version of the site.

Before proceeding to the next phase, I made sure that the final HTML validated. Badly formed markup can have unforeseen consequences when it comes to styling. In fact, it's good practice to get into the habit of regularly validating your markup, particularly after

15

any major changes have been carried out. Nothing can get more frustrating, particularly in the later stages of the design, than a small validation error being carried around in the template.

Styling the Template

Once the markup for the overall structure of the template was finished, I proceeded to create the general style sheet that would determine how the functional blocks of a page would be laid out on the screen. Tentatively putting my "design" hat back on, I decided on a classic layout, as shown in Figure 15-10.

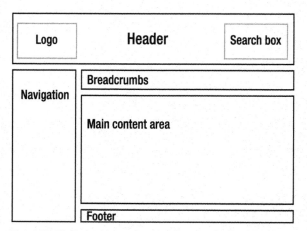

Figure 15-10. Planned layout for the University of Salford website template

Different web designers will have their preferred method of creating a site's style sheet. Personally, I find the "top-down" approach most useful, tackling the very general areas first (rough position of elements) before moving on to the finer details (setting margin and padding, adjusting line spacing, and so on). Creating the style sheet for the template probably took longest in the overall build, as I experimented with a variety of positioning schemes before arriving at a layout that proved reasonably robust in different browsers and under different text sizes.

As per the ideal web standard workflow, there should be no need at this stage to make any further changes to the markup. If the HTML is structured correctly and sufficiently conveys the intended semantics, it should simply be a case of working on the styling of this structure. However, because many browsers have still not fully implemented the full CSS specification, and because of limitations in the actual specifications themselves, it is still necessary on occasion to revisit the markup created in the previous phase, as illustrated in Figure 15-11.

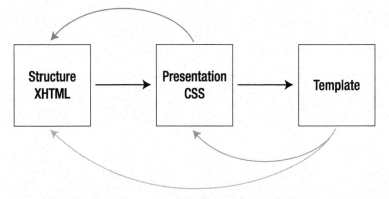

Figure 15-11. In a break with the ideal workflow, requirements in the template or desired presentation effects may require the CSS or even the XHTML to be revisited at a later stage.

This process often involves adding further HTML to group certain functional blocks together or to add additional "hooks" (such as id or class attributes) to facilitate the styling process. However, this should still be done with an eye towards logical structure, and not purely as a styling device. For instance, you should choose id and class names that are representative of the function and purpose of the elements they're applied to, rather than names that imply their intended visual appearance. For instance, as an id, "navigation" makes more sense than "leftcolumn" and won't cause confusion if the navigation is moved to the right side of a layout at a later date. See the W3C Quality Assurance tip "Use class with semantics in mind" for further examples (www.w3.org/QA/Tips/goodclassnames).

To achieve the layout I had in mind for the University template, I ended up needing to add two blocks in the markup: a "header" div, containing the logo and search form, and a "container" div to hold the navigation, breadcrumb trail, and main content area in place. Additionally, the footer was moved inside the actual "content" block.

```
<div id="header">
    <a href="/"><img src="..." alt="University of Salford - A Greater➡
    Manchester University" /></a>
    <form></form>
</div>
<div id="container">
<div id="navbar"></div>
<div id="breadcrumbnav"></div>
<div id="content">
    <div id="footer"></div>
  </div>
</div>
```

15

Yes, it could well be argued that, by making those changes, I've tainted the structural purity of the template. I won't dispute that some of these changes were made mainly with an intent to facilitate visual styling. Pragmatically, though, they are far from the excesses of presentational markup, and the resulting document structure still follows a logical order.

Creating complete table-free layouts, or even working on a few subtle visual tweaks, can be a frustrating experience when faced with different browsers and the variety of inconsistencies and bugs related to their particular CSS capabilities. Nothing is worse than working perfectly in accordance with official W3C CSS specifications, only to realize in testing that a particular browser behaves erratically due to certain combinations of markup and style or seemingly unrelated CSS rules. During the styling phase for this particular template, I encountered some classic issues (such as Internet Explorer's faulty box model implementation, or the notorious "3-pixel jog"). Due to the sometimes haphazard nature of these problems, it's impossible to give a definitive answer as to how they can be avoided. To avoid chasing your own tail when it comes to compensating for these issues, I would suggest the following methodology:

- Write your styles according to the specifications.
- Test them during development with reasonably standards-compliant browsers.
- Once you're happy with the result, run them through less CSS-capable browsers, applying documented hacks and work-arounds (such as conditional comments for Internet Explorer, if you don't mind tarnishing your clean markup with some proprietary code masquerading as a simple HTML comment) where absolutely unavoidable.

Even more problematic than current browsers with a few CSS bugs are old browsers with very incomplete CSS implementations. These browsers try, but usually fail miserably, to parse complex style sheets, resulting in page layouts that aren't just strange-looking, but are also outright unusable (with symptoms such as overlapping text columns and unclickable links, for instance). Netscape 4.x, and to a smaller extent Internet Explorer 5 for Mac, fall in this particular category. To protect these browsers from their own shortcomings, I split the style sheets for the University template into a series of separate files, called with the following <link> elements:

```
<link rel="stylesheet" href="salford_basic.css"➡
type="text/css" />
<link rel="stylesheet" href="salford_advanced.css"➡
 type="text/css" />
```

As the name implies, the first style sheet contains the majority of basic style rules, defining things like overall typeface, colors, and so forth. These styles do not generally cause any problems, even in the oldest of CSS-aware browsers.

The advanced style sheet, however, takes care of most of the "heavy lifting," with all the various layout positioning and media-specific styles. As these rules *do* cause havoc to the likes of Netscape 4.x, I took advantage of a series of well-documented shortcomings in those problematic browsers (see the CSS filter list at www.centricle.com/ref/css/filters/ for further details). The advanced style sheet is, in fact, only a "wrapper" that calls further CSS files via a couple of @include directives. As these are not parsed by the offending browsers, these style sheets remain effectively hidden from them, circumventing any problems they may have caused.

```
@import "salford.css";
@import 'salford_print.css';
```

As I've mentioned, CSS allows designers to specify different styles of presentation for different media. Although the majority of my time was spent tweaking and perfecting the on-screen look and feel of the University site, I did add a simple print style sheet. Due to the way I chose to implement styling (not specifically setting the main style sheets to be screen-specific, but rather to apply to *any* medium), the purpose of the University's print style is to mainly remove certain page elements, which are unnecessary on paper, from the printed version. This includes the search box and the main site navigation. In addition, the print style sheet also displays the href attribute of links as additional text on the page, to clearly indicate their destination in the printed version. CSS offers different methods for including media-specific style sheets into pages (@media directives and the <link> element's media attribute). As the print styles for the University template are called in a roundabout way, via the @import in salford_advanced.css, I opted for the @media route. The following is a simplified version of the print style sheet:

```
@media print {
    #header form { display: none; }
    #navbar { display: none; }
    a { text-decoration: underline; color: #000; }
    #content a:link:after {
        content: " (" attr(href) ") ";
        font-size: 90%;
        color: #000;
    }
}
```

Bringing in the Content

With the template completed both in terms of structure and general style, it was finally time to start putting the new site together.

Taking pages from the existing site as a starting point, this was mostly a case of copying the content (plus any amendments identified during the "taking stock" inventory phase) into the new template, setting appropriate page titles and breadcrumb trails, and placing the resulting new page into the right directory on the development server.

For simple content pages, the content was simply copied "naked": opening the existing page in a browser, copying the (almost exclusively text-based) content, pasting the text into the new template, and manually tagging it as appropriate (headings, paragraphs, list, and so on). This avoided a lot of grief in terms of cleaning up any existing markup (such as <font> tags and surrounding table cells).

This process of tagging the content was similar to the way the template structure was constructed: focus on the content's semantics, rather than any desired visual presentation, and mark up things according to their structure and function within the document, pragmatically choosing the HTML element that most closely fits the bill.

15

Again, in an ideal workflow, at this stage, it should not be necessary to touch any of the template's underlying HTML or CSS, as shown in Figure 15-12.

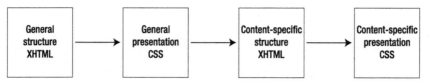

Figure 15-12. In the ideal one-way workflow, first the markup and style of the template are created. After that, the specific content is marked up, with additional styles being created if necessary, and inserted into the template.

It's certainly easy to create wonderful CSS-driven layouts when the actual markup and content are "frozen" and known well in advance. Showcase sites, such as the seminal CSS Zen Garden (www.csszengarden.com) clearly demonstrate the limitless possibilities offered by a pure CSS layout. However, it's important to note that, as beautiful as many of the "garden" designs are, the underlying markup is artificial. It's immutable, and strewn with a variety of ready-made class names and id attributes designed specifically for the purpose of styling.

Real-world content, however, is rarely predictable. It can offer interesting challenges from a markup point of view (again, because there is often no right way of marking up certain types of content), which cannot always be foreseen when designing a site template. These content types can often completely break a table-free layout that doesn't take them into account from the start.

As a result, the actual web standards workflow may, on occasion, make it necessary to go back to the overall template style sheets, or even the underlying template structure itself, as illustrated in Figure 15-13. Good planning and experience can help to minimize this, but during the University website redesign, there were a few instances where I needed to make subtle tweaks.

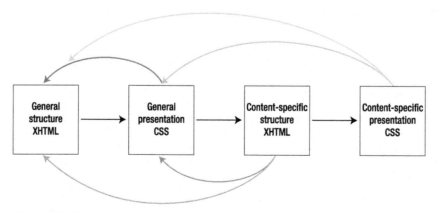

Figure 15-13. Occasionally, unforeseen content may require changes to the template styles or even the fundamental structure of the template itself.

A proper templating system would have helped considerably in this phase. Without any CMS (forgetting for a moment that most, if not all, current CMSs are far from web standards or accessibility friendly in their own right) centrally controlling the University site, this was certainly the most tedious part of the redesign process. Changes to the overall template this late in production often meant revisiting and amending any pages created up until that point. Even when these previously completed pages did not present any particular problems in their current state, it was best to change them in accordance with the revised template structure. You never know how content on those pages might change in the future, so having a consistent template avoids unpleasant surprises further down the line.

Getting Dynamic

In addition to static HTML pages, the University site also features a series of simple, database-driven areas, such as news, events, and the online equivalent of the prospectus, the "course finder."

By design, database-driven pages already have a certain degree of separation of content (stored in the database) and presentation (server-side scripts used to display the content). Carrying these sections over to the new design was mostly a matter of making some minor modifications to the server-side scripts' output. Where necessary, the scripts were further altered to "massage" or postprocess the content to make sure that things like unescaped special characters stored in the database would not introduce validation problems in the final HTML output.

Historically, some of our database fields (for instance, the main body of text for each news item) already contained a certain amount of basic HTML—mainly `<br>` line breaks. Again, to avoid problems with invalid markup, these chunks of HTML were replaced with their valid XHTML equivalents directly in the database with a series of simple UPDATE statements, effectively running the database equivalent of a "find and replace" on any existing entries.

To try to solve the problem at the root and prevent any future data entered into the database from being malformed or invalid, I made changes to the relevant web-based administration pages for these systems, replacing any "free-form" `<textarea>` elements that could contain markup with a basic WYSIWYG editor. This made the process of data entry far more intuitive and usable for the majority of staff working with those systems, while guaranteeing a consistent quality of data going into the database.

It's worth noting that the Java-based WYSIWYG applet I originally used was itself completely inaccessible. To make the administration pages at least halfway usable, I provided a mechanism for staff to revert back to a plain `<textarea>`, and complemented this with a server-side cleanup routine (through a PHP implementation of Dave Raggett's TIDY utility to correct simple markup errors; see www.w3.org/People/Raggett/tidy/) to make sure that anything going into the database would be reasonably valid.

In the past year, the inaccessible Java applet was replaced with a slightly better alternative. XStandard (www.xstandard.com), shown in Figure 15-14, is a plug in–based WYSIWYG editor, currently available only for Windows (a Mac OS X version is scheduled for release).

15

Although far from perfect, it does offer keyboard access and reportedly works reasonably well with assistive technologies such as screen readers.

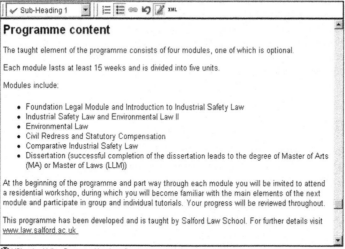

Figure 15-14. XStandard WYSIWYG plug-in

To cover situations in which the plug-in may not be available, I took advantage of the built-in fallback functionality of the <object> element:

```
<object type="application/x-xstandard" ... name="[name_of_input]">
    <textarea name="[name_of_input]">...</textarea>
</object>
```

If the browser fails to launch the XStandard plug-in, it will once again revert back to a simple <textarea>. See my XStandard integration experiment (www.splintered.co.uk/experiments/78/) for further details.

Testing and Site Launch

In all, the redesign process took approximately six months to complete. At various points throughout the redesign, both the "naked" template and a selection of completed pages were thoroughly checked for cross-browser compatibility. I conducted small, informal user testing (involving a selection of colleagues and students across the institution), mainly to inform certain decisions with regard to the site's information architecture and the overall usability of key areas such as the course finder.

From an accessibility point of view, I employed a combination of automated checkers (particularly HiSoftware's "Cynthia Says," www.contentquality.com, checking against WCAG 1.0, aiming for Level AA or better) and informed common sense.

Having already worked with the JAWS for Windows screen reader a few months prior to the redesign (albeit, at a basic level), I was able to carry out a minimal amount of testing with it myself. It's worth noting, though, that simply giving web designers a copy of a screen reader is not always the best idea. Without appropriate training, and an understanding of the various customizable settings of a complex program such as JAWS and how real blind and visually impaired people actually use it, there is a danger that designers may draw the wrong conclusions from their testing. It may even lead to changes in a site's code aimed exclusively at "fixing" issues encountered in one particular piece of assistive technology.

Of course, wherever appropriate and in line with semantically correct markup, you should strive to create pages that work well with screen readers and other assistive technologies. But, as these assistive technologies, just like browsers, often behave very differently from each other, optimizing a site to work purely in JAWS, for example, may well make the experience worse for other users, and is no different from the old days of "best viewed in Netscape." The whole idea of designing with web standards aims to overcome these types of limitations.

After a final round of validation, accessibility checks, and browser testing, the site was finally launched in September 2003. Apart from "flicking the switch," effectively turning the development site into the live site, this process also entailed setting up an extensive list of server-side redirections and URL rewrite rules, to ensure that visitors trying to access content from the old "blueberry-and-custard" were transparently redirected to the most appropriate location on the relaunched site. Of course, it was also helpful to keep a close eye on the server's error logs for the first few weeks following the launch, just to check that no old URL had slipped through the net.

Does the Design Solve the Original Problems?

Figure 15-15 shows the current University of Salford website. Looking back at the list of problems present in the original site, let's see if the redesign addresses the major issues.

From a visual design point of view, the site now falls in line with the revised corporate identity guidelines with regard to the use of color and the correct position of the new logo.

Far from presenting a dominant design feature in its own right, the overall layout is now fairly neutral. This gives increased flexibility for individual departments, and even campaign-specific sections of the main University site, to adopt their own individual identity and design while remaining within the framework of the template.

15

Figure 15-15. The current University homepage and a typical first-level page (despite a few design changes, we're still using the basic structure of the 2003 templates)

In sharp contrast with the criticism faced by the visual appearance of the old site, the redesigned University site—although admittedly a bit dry and conservative in certain text-heavy pages—has often been commended for its "professional" appearance.

Informal user testing carried out both before and after the launch confirmed that, thanks to the breadcrumb trail and the revised navigation, users were not feeling "lost" within the site, as was the case with the previous design.

From a technical point of view, adopting the separation of content and presentation inherent in designing with web standards yielded the results expected at the outset. By moving all layout and visual aspects to central CSS files, the HTML markup for each individual page was reduced on average by 20 to 30 percent. For the most part, working with the new "lighter" templates became a lot easier both for myself and the various departmental web authors (although some of those who had become quite adept at wrangling nested tables for their particular layout purposes were initially quite unimpressed by the need to learn a "new" way of realizing their designs).

Thanks to the print-specific style sheets, pages now look reasonable on paper, without the need for any printer-friendly pages, as shown in Figure 15-16.

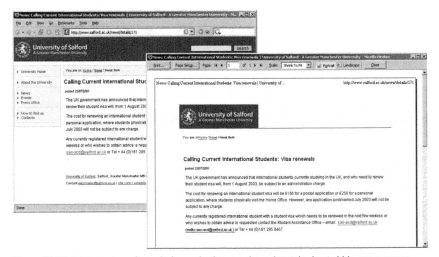

Figure 15-16. Print preview of a typical page in the new site; print style sheets hide unnecessary elements and reformat the content without the need for additional printer-friendly pages.

With any reliance on client-side scripting removed, the simple list of links that makes up the site navigation should not present any problems to keyboard users or those lacking JavaScript.

In the course of the redesign, I had the good fortune to discuss accessibility issues with Adrian Higginbotham, a blind web developer and proficient JAWS user who worked at the University of Salford at the time (later, in August 2004, he took a position as accessibility and inclusion adviser at the British Educational Communications and Technology Agency). Adrian helped to identify some of the major access problems present in the old site and give feedback on proposed changes. Commenting on the redesigned site, he wrote:

> The drop-down navigation [on the old site] was poorly implemented—as soon as you highlighted an item, the navigation jumped. Not only did this make the "go" buttons redundant, but it made using the drop-down navigation with a screen reader very complex—impossible if you didn't take advantage of some of the more advanced functions of the screen reader. It required four different single- or multi-key keystrokes to manipulate the drop-down box, not including the arrowing through the options.

15

With so many layout elements on each page, there was plenty for the screen reader to hook into for navigation. For example, I know that the main content always begins in the sixth table, so I can use screen reader features to skip from table to table. However, this meant that there was also lots of noncontent-related information being read out when reviewing pages, meaning that it took significantly longer to read a page than it should—poor, as listening is already slow enough compared to visually scanning. And this was the situation for someone who was very familiar with the site, as I used it several times a week (if not daily)—not at all good for someone (e.g., a prospective student) unfamiliar with the site.

Advantages of the new site: mainly the opposites of all the above. Using the quick navigation actually became "quick" rather than something to fight with when I couldn't find what I was looking for via the textual navigation. Reading became quicker, as the volume of data my screen reader had to process was significantly reduced, but the in-page navigation remained good, as the structural elements were in place for the screen reader to hook into.

Problems Along the Way—Lessons Learned

The majority of issues encountered during the redesign were largely due to my initial inexperience with XHTML/CSS. As I was effectively learning the concepts of designing with web standards along the way, I often found myself adding further changes and tweaks to the templates and pages in line with emerging best practices. This, combined with the fact that the redesign happened in parallel with the day-to-day maintenance and development on the old site, certainly contributed to the overall length of the redesign process.

As I've mentioned, choosing the semantically most appropriate elements when marking up structure and content in HTML is not always a straightforward process. It's often a case of making an informed and pragmatic judgment call. Looking back now at the final code I produced, there are a few areas where I feel I could have taken my markup decisions a bit further. For instance, the breadcrumb trail was marked up as a simple div, with no further structure within:

```
<div id="breadcrumbs">
You are in: <a href="/">Home</a> / <a href="/about/">➡
About the University</a> / Virtual tours
</div>
```

Although web standards developers' opinions differ on how to best mark up breadcrumb trails (some proposing quite convoluted solutions such as recursively nested unordered lists, vehemently proclaiming them to be "the only semantically valid way"), I would now tend to favor the view that a breadcrumb trail is an ordered list of steps to get from the site's homepage to the current page, and probably mark it up as such:

```
<div id="breadcrumbs">
    <p>You are in:</p>
    <ol>
        <li><a href="/">Home</a></li>
        <li><a href="/about/">About the University</a></li>
        <li>Virtual tours</li>
    </ol>
</div>
```

Similarly, the complex markup I ended up with for the navigation bar could certainly be streamlined into a single list:

```
<ul id="navbar">
    <li><a href="/">University Home</a></li>
    <li><a href="...">About the University</a></li>
    <li>
        <ul>
            <li><a href="...">Study at Salford</a></li>
            <li><a href="...">Course Finder</a></li>
            <li><a href="...">Research</a></li>
        </ul>
    </li>

    ...

</ul>
```

Adding the skip to the content link as a transparent 1-pixel image with appropriate alt-text may have made the redesigned site easier to navigate for screen reader users, but it still didn't help another user group that could benefit from this sort of feature: sighted keyboard users. For this reason, I recently changed the skip link on the University site, as shown in Figure 15-17.

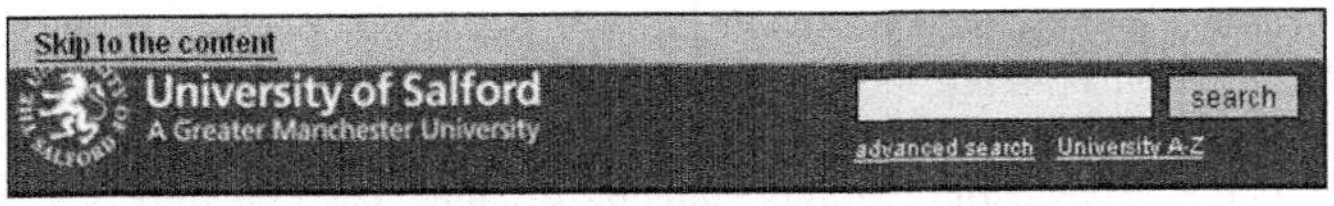

Figure 15-17. New skip to the content link, now also visible to sighted keyboard users

In the markup, the skip link now appears as a standard link in the header:

```
<div>
<a href="#content" accesskey="2" id="skipper">Skip to the content</a>
</div>
```

15

Through CSS, the link is hidden from normal view, but becomes clearly visible when a user tabs to it (for example, when the link itself receives focus):

```
#header #skipper {
    position: absolute;
    top: 0; left: 0;
    margin: 0; padding: 0;
    text-indent: -600em;
    color: #fff;
    background: transparent;
}

#header #skipper:focus,
#header #skipper:hover,
#header #skipper:active {
    display: block;
    width: 100%;
    text-indent: 1em;
    background: #ced318;
    font-weight: bold;
    color: #000;
}
```

Some developers will say that skip links should always be visible, so that users who may benefit from them are aware of their presence. Again, this is a pragmatic decision that strives to strike a balance between the site's overall aesthetics and its accessibility features. As the skip link on the University site appears in a logical position and almost immediately at the beginning of the tab order, I would argue that keyboard users (including those using screen magnifiers) will still be able to notice and take advantage of this feature.

It could be argued that skip links themselves are really a stop-gap solution, to compensate for the fact that most user agents still offer fairly rudimentary keyboard controls to navigate a website. Certainly, the onus should be on browser developers to natively provide more powerful functionality, such as the ability to skip entire block-level elements (for example, navigation marked up as lists) or moving directly between structural headings within the page—features that are already available to the majority of screen reader users. It is hoped that a future revision of the W3C User Agent Accessibility Guidelines (UAAG) might place more emphasis on this issue.

Not quite trusting my ability at the time to completely abandon any presentational markup, the redesign was carried out with an XHTML 1.0 Transitional DTD, which still allows a handful of those elements and attributes. As it turns out, the jump from the Transitional to the Strict XHTML DOCTYPE is far less traumatic than I originally anticipated. Any pages I have produced in the past few years have gone directly for the Strict DOCTYPE, and this would certainly be my preferred choice if I had to start over with any new templates today.

Even during late stages in the redesign, it was occasionally necessary to make amendments to the overall template, which then had to be reintroduced to any pages already converted up to that point. The problem was alleviated in part through a certain level of modularization in the template itself. By further splitting up the template into a series of common PHP include files, it was possible to change specific parts such as the page footer in a relatively painless fashion.

Although far from ideal, in the absence of a complete templating solution (such as a fullblown CMS or the integrated PHP Smarty template engine—see `http://smarty.php.net/`), it would have probably been worth exploring the client-side (from a developer's point of view) template functionality of Dreamweaver.

> *Even to this day, I mainly use Dreamweaver as a glorified text editor with built-in FTP capabilities. I prefer to work directly in the code view, and use the WYSIWYG preview as a general way of quickly moving to different parts of the markup.*

The Implementation of the New Design

As a single developer, solely in charge of all phases of the conversion of the core University site, the redesign was comparatively easy. The hard part came after the relaunch of the main site: getting all the departmental web authors, with their varying skill levels, to also adopt the new, standards-based templates.

Detailed Web Publishing Guidelines, easy to understand templates, and a focus on staff development and education all played a key role in this process. Just as accessibility does not simply involve the rote mastery of all WCAG 1.0 checkpoints, but first and foremost an awareness of what the underlying issues are (*why* things have to be done a certain way), it was important to bring web authors on board with the concept of designing with web standards. From a pragmatic point of view, even with the tightest quality assurance processes in place, the current decentralized model of web management at the University cannot guarantee that, on occasion, a page or two will present some invalid markup, such as an unescaped ampersand or an apostrophe that was copied and pasted straight from Word and now appears in the wrong character encoding. These small errors can always be fixed (and arguably don't immediately translate into an accessibility hurdle). The important thing is that web authors understand the benefits of the web standards approach.

Summary

This case study gave a general (albeit personal) overview of the process involved in retrofitting a fairly large site from an inaccessible and inflexible mess to a functionally accessible site, in line with modern web standards practices.

15

Apart from the fundamental problems with the way it was originally coded, the University of Salford site did not present complex accessibility issues such as the heavy use of Flash or audio/video files. I'll also be the first one to admit that there are still certain unresolved issues with the current site, particularly when it comes to the occasional untagged PDF file, but overall, the site's accessibility has improved considerably thanks to the redesign.

No great truths of web standards development were uncovered along the way, but a series of stumbling blocks that asked for some pragmatic decisions were identified. Overall, though, the process worked successfully, making this one of the first university sites in the UK to switch to web standards.

Since its launch in 2003, the site has undergone further changes and tweaks, with an upcoming rebranding planned for the upcoming academic year. With a few exceptions, though, the underlying structure of the template and site has remained the same.

Using web standards, and particularly moving to XHTML, does not automatically guarantee that a site becomes more accessible in the process. It's true that more recent document types like XHTML 1.0 Strict deprecate presentational attributes and elements that used to be present in HTML 4.01, as well as mandate things like alt attributes for every image, which can help in identifying potential accessibility issues through simple code validation. However, XHTML and CSS are not magic bullets, and it is still possible to create highly inaccessible sites while sticking to valid, standards-compliant code. Developers still need to understand the potential problems that users can face.

Nonetheless, separating content from presentation, using CSS rather than tables for layout, and correctly marking up a document's structure to identify the purpose of each element certainly constitute a first step on the road to an accessible site—a solid foundation on which to build.

PART 3 **ACCESSIBILITY LAW AND POLICY**

16 U.S. WEB ACCESSIBILITY LAW IN DEPTH

by Cynthia D. Waddell

Through the American disability rights tradition, access to electronic and information technology has emerged as a civil right. As technology advanced, it was only a matter of time before a federal law would establish accessible design specifications for a broad class of electronic and information technology. Today, there are significant legal incentives for ensuring that Internet and intranet websites designed for U.S. entities meet accessible web requirements.

Ever since the passage of the 1964 Civil Rights Act prohibiting discrimination on the basis of race, legal protections for persons with disabilities have emerged and expanded through a patchwork of civil rights laws prohibiting discrimination on the basis of disability (for more, see *The Accessible Future*, National Council on Disability, June 21, 2001, at www.ncd.gov/newsroom/publications/2001/accessiblefuture.htm).

The Americans with Disabilities Act of 1990 (ADA), Section 255 of the Telecommunications Act of 1996, and Sections 504 and 508 of the Rehabilitation Act of 1973 form the basis for discussion in this chapter. These federal laws and accompanying regulations, interpretative guidance, and case law, are only a few of many U.S. disability rights laws impacting technology and access to information. As such, this body of law is complex and cannot be fully addressed in a chapter on accessible web design. In fact, I do not believe it would necessarily be helpful for web design technologists to delve into this complexity.

This chapter introduces the current state of U.S. accessibility law as it pertains to the design of a website. All decision makers—whether they are web developers, their clients, or policy makers—need to understand the legal reasons for designing accessibly and the legal liability for ignoring the issue. This is especially important since ignorance of the law is not a defense. We will examine the ADA accessible web case, and briefly discuss Section 504 of the Rehabilitation Act and Section 255 of the Telecommunications Act. The meat of this chapter, however, concerns the U.S. legislation addressing accessible web design in Section 508—the Electronic and Information Technology Accessibility Standards. We will then take a look at how to decide when to apply the World Wide Web Consortium (W3C) Web Content Accessibility Guidelines (WCAG) as opposed to a Section 508 accessible web design rule. Finally, an in-depth chapter would not be complete without discussing current legal hot topics for accessible web design and challenges ahead.

As Lawrence Lessig commented in *Code and Other Laws of Cyberspace* (0-46503-912-X; Basic Books, 1999), "We can build, or architect, or code cyberspace to protect values that we believe are fundamental, or we can build, or architect, or code cyberspace to allow those values to disappear. There is no middle ground."

This chapter is an introduction to U.S. web accessibility law in depth. It is not intended to be a complete discussion of the complex legal issues involved, nor does it intend to be the final word regarding the changing regulatory and technological environment. Comments in this chapter should not be construed as legal advice or opinion on specific facts. Particular legal questions can best be answered by seeking the advice of legal counsel.

Americans with Disabilities Act and the Internet

This year, the U.S. celebrates the sixteenth anniversary of the passing of that landmark civil rights legislation, the Americans with Disabilities Act of 1990 (ADA). When former President Bush signed the ADA, it marked a watershed moment. Now persons with disabilities would have access to facilities, programs, services, and employment just like any other person.

One major goal of the ADA is to remove barriers in society, both physical and programmatic, to improve the quality of life of people with disabilities. This effort has created side benefits for those beyond the community of persons with disabilities, but that topic is reserved for another time. Many Americans are aware that one of the most significant impacts has been the establishment of a building code specifying the accessible elements for designing buildings, public pathways, and parking lots. Members of the construction industry, building code societies, and disability organizations came to the table to draft this important regulation after the ADA was enacted. At that time, many people did not understand why there were no persons with mobility disabilities in inaccessible buildings. They would say, "Why should we remove barriers in construction? I don't see anyone needing access!" Similarly, many who do not understand the subject of this book have said the same about accessible web design.

Another significant impact of the ADA has been the use of technology in the workplace. Technology has enabled people with disabilities to demonstrate their ability to perform the essential functions of the job, leading many to become independent and self-reliant. This is done through the "reasonable accommodation" process, along with the requirement that "effective communication" and "auxiliary aids and services" be provided. These ADA concepts will be discussed later in this chapter when we look at ADA web cases.

> The ADA is a complex law, and so this chapter only touches the surface of important issues. For more information, visit the U.S. Department of Justice ADA homepage at www.usdoj.gov/crt/ada/adahom1.htm.

Section 504 of the Rehabilitation Act of 1973

The granddaddy of the ADA is the Rehabilitation Act of 1973, which established the fundamental civil rights protections for individuals with disabilities. Today, entities subject to Section 504 of the Rehabilitation Act—such as government entities, schools, colleges, and universities receiving federal financial assistance—are prohibited from discrimination on the basis of disability in public and private programs and activities. In 1973, Congress determined that the penalty for discrimination on the basis of disability would be the revocation of federal funding.

In 1990, Congress expanded civil rights protections by enacting the ADA and extended civil rights protections beyond entities receiving federal financial assistance. For the first time, the private sector, including commercial businesses, became subject to prohibitions against discrimination on the basis of disability. The ADA is a landmark civil rights law that impacts employment, state and local government, and the private commercial sector.

Eight different federal agencies are responsible for enforcing the ADA, and this responsibility is assigned according to the function of each agency. The U.S. Department of Education, Office for Civil Rights (OCR), is the enforcer of educational entities subject to Section 504 and has required educational institutions to develop and maintain accessible websites. The U.S. Department of Justice (USDOJ) requires State and local governments subject to Section 504 and the ADA to implement accessible websites as part of its Project Civic Access effort.

Accessible Web ADA Myths

Perhaps this is a good time to point out four myths or erroneous views that have found their way into ADA legal literature:

- Accessible web requires the cost-prohibitive use of streaming audio and high bandwidth.
- Accessible web requires two versions of the same website—one text and one graphical.
- Accessible web is required only if you are an entity that receives federal funding.
- Web developers cannot be held liable if their client told them to ignore accessible web design.

The first myth that accessible web requires expensive streaming audio and high bandwidth comes from not understanding how a screen reader or voice browser operates when viewing web pages. I have observed legal arguments against accessible web design built upon this myth—all the way from Congressional law and policy memoranda to law review articles! To the contrary, accessible web not only enables people with disabilities to have access, it also means that people with slow modems can turn off images and quickly reach web content. This fact has been a very important cost-savings issue for Internet users in developing countries.

As to the second myth, in certain cases there may be the need to show two versions of website content, but technology has now brought us to the point that we have the knowledge and the means to design accessibly without segregation and without driving up the cost for implementation and maintenance. In my opinion, having two versions of a website is not a best practice. We have markup solutions to enable someone using a text browser, such as Lynx, to reach the content of a graphical web page. In fact, the W3C Web Accessibility Initiative (WAI) FAQ states that having two versions is counterproductive and not necessary (see www.w3.org/1999/05/WCAG-REC-fact#text).

The third myth—that accessible web is required only if you are an entity that receives federal funding—is also incorrect. This is true because liability under the ADA does not require the covered entity to be a recipient of federal financial assistance. In some cases,

16

however, the issue may be moot because some entities are covered under both the ADA and Section 504. For example, a government entity or a school district, college, or university that accepts federal funding, such as federal financial assistance for its students, can be found liable for discrimination under Section 504 of the Rehabilitation Act of 1973 if its website is not accessible. Under Section 504, all programs at a school or college are covered, and this means that participants in the program—including parents, students, and employees—are protected from discrimination.

The fourth myth—that web developers cannot be held liable for inaccessible web design due to client instructions and pocketbook limitations—is not true. Under the ADA, architects of buildings subject to new construction or remodeling have been held liable for failure to design and construct accessible facilities, although courts have not been consistent in their findings. In fact, the USDOJ has consistently maintained that architects can be held liable for violating the ADA. For more information, see *Legal Rights of Persons with Disabilities: An Analysis of Federal Law*, by Bonnie Poitras Tucker and Bruce A. Goldstein (0-93475-346-6; LRP Publications, 1991).

Similarly, it is now highly likely that web developers could also be held liable, both for the construction of a website and any time they modify it. This is because the ADA imposes an ongoing duty to remove barriers, maintain accessible features, and provide effective communication in a timely manner.

Even though the ADA requires the removal of barriers to programs, services, and facilities, it provides no technical guidance on how to design accessible websites. Now that Section 508 Electronic and Information Technology Accessibility Standards is law, the ADA is informed about what it means to design accessible websites. In fact, the 2003 ADA guidance provided by the USDOJ for state and local government websites points to Section 508. And to make matters further complicated (or easier, depending on your point of view), all states now have a policy, statute, or set of guidelines related to accessible web design. So, even though Section 508 directly impacts federal agencies, there is also an indirect impact on nonfederal entities for a variety of reasons. For some guidance through this maze, see the "When Does a Web Developer Follow Section 508 Rules?" section later in this chapter.

> *Prior to Section 508 being enacted, the only legal guidance on accessible web was the 1996 USDOJ policy ruling that the ADA applied to the Internet. This is why it was so significant that I implemented the first accessible web design standard for local government in 1995, as discussed in Chapter 2. ADA website complaints were being filed, people with disabilities needed access, and there was no standard to follow. This early web standard contributed to the eventual passage of Section 508. As noted by The National Council on Disability (an independent federal agency that monitors the implementation, effectiveness, and impact of the ADA and advises the President and Congress), "These [Waddell] standards were important for two reasons: first, because they constituted an acknowledgment of the legitimacy of claims by people with disabilities for access to the web; and second, because they demonstrated that objective and workable criteria for vindicating these rights could be devised (see* When the ADA Goes Online: Application of the ADA to the Internet and the Worldwide Web, *National Council on Disability, at* www.ncd.gov/newsroom/publications/2003/adainternet.htm).*

Now that the Section 508 Electronic and Information Technology Accessibility Standards have become law, these standards inform ADA entities on how to create accessible websites and services, including the help desk and all product documents. As a result, web developers may be liable, as discussed later in this chapter in the "Section 508 Overview" section.

I attribute these myths to lawyers not understanding technology and what it means to design accessibly. But we should not discount the possibility that these lawyers consulted the technical community, or that these erroneous views may have originated from the technical community. So watch out for variations of these myths!

Applying the ADA to the Internet

Under the ADA, covered entities are required to furnish appropriate auxiliary aids and services where necessary to ensure effective communication with individuals with disabilities, unless doing so would result in a fundamental alteration to the program or service, or an undue burden. Auxiliary aids include taped texts, Brailled materials, large-print materials, captioning, and other methods of making audio and visual media available to people with disabilities.

On September 9, 1996, the USDOJ issued a policy ruling applying the ADA to the Internet. Under the rationale of "effective communication," the USDOJ states that state and local governments (ADA Title II), as well as public accommodations (nongovernmental) and commercial facilities (ADA Title III), must provide effective communication whenever they communicate through the Internet.

"Public accommodations" include private entities that offer goods and services to the public, such as the following:

- Sales or rental establishments
- Service establishments
- Places of exhibition or entertainment, public gatherings, recreation, and education

The policy ruling stated that:

> Covered entities under the ADA are required to provide effective communication, regardless of whether they generally communicate through print media, audio media, or computerized media such as the Internet. Covered entities that use the Internet for communications regarding their programs, goods, or services must be prepared to offer those communications through accessible means as well.

The USDOJ continued in the policy ruling by discussing a variety of ways to provide accessibility. These included a text-only page or the provision of accessible instructions on the web page, so that a person with a disability could request the same web information in an accessible format such as Braille, large print, diskette, or audiotape.

Prior to the prevalent use of the Internet, entities met ADA requirements by providing accessible information in alternative formats such as those suggested by the USDOJ. My office quickly experienced a cost saving of staff time and alternative format expenses when we began to provide accessible information through the Internet.

In addition, the definition of "effective communication" was eventually further refined to be a three-pronged definition including "timeliness of delivery." It would no longer be an option to design an inaccessible website and post instructions on how to request the same web content in an accessible format. Stay tuned for the California Community College case, as discussed in the "OCR Letter of Resolution, Docket No. 09-97-6001" section later in this chapter.

> It is interesting to note that the policy ruling came as a result of a letter initiated by a web designer who also was a lawyer. He was knowledgeable about the ADA, the prohibition against discrimination against persons with disabilities, and wanted "to do the right thing." He wrote to his senator, who then made an inquiry to the USDOJ. The policy ruling was in response to the inquiry by Senator Harkin on behalf of this web designer. So web designers can make a difference! (See the United States Department of Justice Policy Ruling, 9/9/96: ADA Accessibility Requirements Apply to Internet Web Pages at 10 NDLR 240 or at www.usdoj.gov/crt/foia/tal712.txt, for more on the inquiry from a web designer.)

The policy ruling includes a list of resources on how to design accessible web pages. Visitors to the Center for Information Technology Accommodation of the U.S. General Services Administration were pointed to resources, including my accessible web design standard at the City of San José, California (www.icdri.org/CynthiaW/city_of_san_jose_world_wide_web_.htm).

Accessibility of State and Local Government Websites

In 2003, the USDOJ issued guidance on accessible websites for state and local governments and cited the legal obligations under the ADA and the Rehabilitation Act. Helpful guidance is found in this document at www.usdoj.gov/crt/ada/websites2.htm, including the following Action Plan for Accessible Websites:

- Establish a policy that your web pages will be accessible and create a process for implementation.
- Ensure that all new and modified web pages and content are accessible:
  - Check the HTML[1] of all new web pages. Make sure that accessible elements are used, including alt tags, long descriptions, and captions, as needed.
  - If images are used, including photos, graphics, scanned images, or image maps, make sure to include alt tags and/or long descriptions for each.
  - If you use online forms and tables, make those elements accessible.

1. Web pages are written using a language called HTML (or "hypertext markup language"). HTML is a "markup language" that tells a computer program (called a "browser") how information will appear or will be arranged on a computer screen. HTML tags are specific instructions understood by a web browser or screen reader.

- When posting documents on the website, always provide them in HTML or a text-based format (even if you are also providing them in another format, such as Portable Document Format (PDF)).

- Develop a plan for making your existing web content more accessible. Describe your plan on an accessible web page. Encourage input on improvements, including which pages should be given high priority for change. Let citizens know about the standards or guidelines that are being used. Consider making the more popular web pages a priority.

- Ensure that in-house staff and contractors responsible for web page and content development are properly trained.

- Provide a way for visitors to request accessible information or services by posting a telephone number or E-mail address on your home page. Establish procedures to assure a quick response to users with disabilities who are trying to obtain information or services in this way.

- Periodically enlist disability groups to test your pages for ease of use; use this information to increase accessibility.

Introduction to the ADA Complaint Process

In the U.S., disability rights cases are complaint-driven and are either administrative or filed in court. If an entity refuses to remediate the website upon inquiry from a person with a disability, then a complaint must be filed in order to remedy the problem. Also, under the ADA, a person with a disability need not hold American citizenship to file the complaint.

At times, the USDOJ will initiate a lawsuit, but only after it has first unsuccessfully attempted to settle the dispute through negotiations. However, the USDOJ may file lawsuits to enforce the ADA and may obtain court orders including compensatory damages and back pay to remedy discrimination. Under Title III (applicable to public accommodations and commercial facilities), the USDOJ may also obtain civil penalties of up to $55,000 for the first violation and $110,000 for any subsequent violation.

Another way an ADA federal enforcement agency might become involved would be to initiate a compliance review that included the correction of a website deficiency. You will see an example of this activity when we look at the California Community College case, in the "OCR Letter of Resolution, Docket No. 09-97-6001" section later in this chapter.

> *Members of the legal profession may not necessarily be knowledgeable about civil rights and accessible web liability, since disability rights law is not a bar exam requirement. Because of my concern for educating the business and legal community about inaccessible technologies and their impact, I have authored a number of papers and articles currently posted at* www.icdri.org/CynthiaW/cynthia_waddell.htm. *One such paper, "Applying the ADA to the Internet: A Web Accessibility Standard"* (www.icdri.org/CynthiaW/applying_the_ada_to_the_internet.htm), *was requested by the American Bar Association in 1998 because of the need for education. This paper has been frequently cited in legal literature, as well as in reports to the U.S. President and Congress, such as* The Accessible Future (www.ncd.gov/newsroom/publications/2001/accessiblefuture.htm).

Current ADA Case Law

Since at least 1995, many ADA web cases have been filed, and the results have been mixed. In addition, many parties have entered into settlement agreements. Some of these agreements are available to the public; others are private and confidential. Here, we will look at some of the more recent public cases.

Martin v. Metropolitan Atlanta Transportation Authority

In November 2001, six plaintiffs, including Fulton County Magistrate Judge Stephanie Davis, filed a class action in federal court against the Metropolitan Atlanta Rapid Transit Authority (MARTA). Three plaintiffs were blind, one had cerebral palsy and required a wheelchair for mobility, and two plaintiffs were quadriplegics who required wheelchairs for mobility.

The complaint contained a long list of ADA violations, including the problem that the agency failed to make information available to people with disabilities through accessible formats and technology. For example, MARTA's web developer testified by affidavit that the website at www.itsmarta.com provided the general public with extensive information on the routes and schedules for its fixed-route services. However, it was not formatted in such a way to make it accessible to blind persons who use screen reader software. Plaintiffs sought injunctive and declaratory relief under the ADA and Section 504 of the Rehabilitation Act of 1973.

On the issue of accessible web, the federal district court in Georgia held in favor for the plaintiffs, finding that the website was not accessible and violated the ADA. This was the first ADA Title II case for state and local government directly on point concerning the issue of whether or not the ADA applied to websites. You can read the decision at www.gand.uscourts.gov/documents/1001cv3255TWTinj.pdf.

Access Now v. Southwest Airlines

Shortly after the <u>Martin v. Metropolitan Atlanta Transportation Authority</u> decision was issued, another district court in Florida dismissed a lawsuit brought against Southwest Airlines for the inaccessibility of the website at www.southwest.com, on the grounds that the website was not a place of public accommodation under Title III of the ADA. See the court order at www.bytowninternet.com/southwest.html, published in October 2002.

One of the difficult issues before this court was the fact that airlines such as Southwest are generally not covered under the ADA, but by another disability access statute, the pre-ADA Air Carrier Access Act. Another problem with this case was that the judge did not have the correct facts regarding standards for accessible web design. The judge concluded that the W3C WCAG were not a generally accepted authority on accessibility. In Footnote 1 of the District Court opinion, the judge wrote:

> Although it appears that no well-defined, generally accepted standards exist for programming assistive software and websites so as to make them uniformly compatible, Plaintiffs provided the Court with a copy of the Web Content Accessibility Guidelines 1.Q, W3C Recommendation 5-May-1999, produced by the Web Accessability[sic] Initiative See Web Content Accessibility Guidelines 1.0, at http://www.w3.org/TR/WCAG 10/ (Last visited Oct, 16, 2002). While "these guidelines explain how to make Web content accessible to people with disabilities," the guidelines further note that they do "not provide specific information about browser support for different technologies as that information changes rapidly." Id. Moreover, not only are these guidelines over three-years old, but **there is no indication that the Web Accessibility Initiative**, which "pursues accessibility of the Web through five primary areas of work: technology, guidelines, tools, education and outreach, and research and development," **is a generally accepted authority on accessibility guidelines.** See About WAI, at http://www.w3.org/WAI/about.html, Last visited Oct. 16, 2002)

www.bytowninternet.com/southwest.html (emphasis added)

Upon appeal, the U.S. Court of Appeals did not reach the issue of whether or not ADA Title III entities providing online services needed to be accessible. The court simply dismissed the case due to procedural issues. This case has generated a number of misleading articles in the U.S. and abroad, which said that the court upheld the lower court ruling. Contrary to what was reported, the court did not rule on the merits of the case and did not uphold the lower court ruling.

However, even though the U.S. Court of Appeals declined to evaluate the merits of the Southwest Airlines case, the court found that the legal questions are significant. The court stated that, "The Internet is transforming our economy and culture, and the question whether it is covered by the ADA—one of the landmark civil rights laws in this country—is of substantial importance" (see http://caselaw.lp.findlaw.com/data2/circs/11th/0216163p.pdf).

Because the judge wrote that the WAI was not a generally accepted authority on accessibility guidelines, you may be interested in reading the response of the W3C when the case was appealed. Two Amicus (or Friend of the Court) briefs were filed in support of the appeal in March 2003: the W3C Amicus Brief filed at www.icdri.org./legal/w3c_amicus_brief.htm and the Disability Community Amicus Brief filed at www.icdri.org./legal/swa_amicus_brief.htm.

The issue as to whether airlines must have accessible websites may be moot given that the U.S. Department of Transportation has initiated rulemaking on this issue. See the "U.S. Department of Transportation Notice of Proposed Rulemaking" section later in this chapter for further discussion.

Hooks v. OKBridge

For an interesting read about accessible web and playing online bridge, see this USDOJ appellate brief outlining the ADA enforcement agency position. On June 30, 2000, the USDOJ filed a friend of the court appellate brief in <u>Hooks v. OKBridge</u> arguing that ADA Title III applied to the Internet. See *Hooks v. OKBridge, Inc. 99-50891* (5th Cir.2000); also see the USDOJ Amicus Curiae brief at www.usdoj.gov/crt/briefs/hooks.htm.

OKBridge is a commercial website where customers can play bridge and participate in online discussion groups regarding the game for a fee. The USDOJ argues that a commercial business providing services over the Internet is subject to the ADA's prohibition against discrimination on the basis of disability because:

A. The Language Of The ADA Does Not Limit It To Services Provided At A Company's Physical Facility

1. Services "Of" A Place Of Public Accommodation Need Not Be Provided "At" The Place Of Public Accommodation

2. The Definition Of "Public Accommodation" Is Not Limited To Entities Providing Services At Their Physical Premises

3. The Absence Of Specific Mention In The ADA Of Services Provided Over The Internet Does Not Restrict The ADA's Coverage

B. This Court Has Already Rejected The View That The ADA Is Limited To Services Performed At A Physical Place

www.usdoj.gov/crt/briefs/hooks.htm.

The USDOJ points out that a growing number of services are being provided over the Internet, creating modes of commerce that are replacing physical buildings. In addition, many businesses provide services at places other than their premises, and they are not relieved from the prohibition from discriminating on the basis of disability; for example, services provided over the telephone or through the mail, such as travel agencies, banks, insurance companies, catalog merchants, and pharmacies. The USDOJ also points out that many other businesses provide services in the homes or offices of their customers, such as plumbers, pizza delivery, moving companies, cleaning services, business consulting firms, and auditors from accounting firms.

In short, it is the USDOJ's position that the entertainment or recreation services provided by OKBridge make it a place of public accommodation. However, the Fifth Circuit Court ruling in this case did not reach the question of whether or not the ADA applied to the Internet.

Other ADA Cases

As for whether or not the ADA applies to private websites—and not government websites like the Martin case—the courts are currently split on this issue. The First and Seventh Circuit Courts have suggested that websites can be considered public accommodations and thus subject to the ADA. On the other hand, the Sixth, Third, and Ninth Circuit Courts have held otherwise and require a physical place.

The problem is that current case law finds courts disagreeing as to whether or not the ADA definition of "place of public accommodation" is limited to actual physical structures. In Carparts Distribution Center v. Automotive Wholesalers Association of New England, the First Circuit Court held that places of public accommodation are not limited to physical facilities—see 37 F.3d 12 (lst Cir. 1994). The court based its conclusion on legislative history and the purpose of the ADA and stated:

> It would be irrational to conclude that persons who enter an office to purchase services are protected by the ADA, but persons who purchase the same services over the telephone or by mail are not. Congress could not have intended such an absurd result.

> www.harp.org/carparts.txt (p. 19 of the decision)

Similarly, the Seventh Circuit Court in Doe v. Mutual of Omaha Insurance Company stated in its discussion that websites are a place of public accommodation. In Doe, the court said:

> The core meaning of this provision, plainly enough, is that the owner or operator of a store, hotel, restaurant, dentist's office, travel agency, theater, **web site**, or other facility (**whether in physical space or in electronic space**) that is open to the public cannot exclude disabled persons from entering the facility and, once in, from using the facility in the same way that the non-disabled do.

> http://lw.bna.com/lw/19990615/984112.htm, cited as 179 F.3d 557
> (7th Cir. 1999)(emphasis added and citations omitted)

On the other hand, the Third, Sixth, and Ninth Circuit Courts have held that the ADA does not cover services outside a physical location. See Ford v. Schering-Plough Corporation, 145 F.3d 601, 614 (3d Cir. 1998); Parker v. Metropolitan Life Insurance Company, 121 F. 3d 1006 (6th Cir. 1997), and Weyer v. Twentieth Century Fox Film Corp., 198 F.3d 1104 (9th Cir. 2000).

Selected ADA Accessible Web Complaints

Many ADA accessible web complaints have been filed, both administratively and in court, and many have been settled. Some of the settlements are private, but some are public. Let's take a look at the public settlements, mediations, and legal compliance reviews underway, in chronological order.

Office for Civil Rights, U.S. Department of Education

Each year, the OCR receives approximately 5,000 complaints claiming discrimination on the basis of race, color, national origin, sex, disability, and age. These complaints involve some of the most important issues affecting equal access to good-quality education. For example, the disability discrimination issues range from accessibility of school facilities and programs to auxiliary aids and accessible web design.

Access to the learning environment is a critical, front-line issue requiring immediate resolution. Library reference services are being transformed by the application of Internet access to information systems and search engines. Professors are teaching long-distance learning courses over the Internet, and even if a student is physically in class, homework assignments and resources are being posted on classroom web pages. Yet, even if a library terminal has assistive computer technology installed for students or visitors with disabilities, Internet research is not possible with inaccessible web page design.

The following is a summary of four California OCR, U.S. Department of Education Letters of Resolution, which impact Internet accessibility.

OCR Letter of Resolution, Docket No. 09-95-2206 (January 25, 1996) This case concerned a student complaint that a university failed to provide equivalent access to the Internet. A student with a visual disability was required to make appointments with personal reader attendants as the exclusive mechanism for access to the Internet. The University also failed to complete the "Self-Evaluation Plan" as required by ADA Title II (see www.icdri.org/legal/sjsu.htm). According to the finding:

> The issue is not whether the student with the disability is merely provided with access, but rather the extent to which the communication is actually as effective as that provided to others. Title II of the ADA also strongly affirms the important role that computer technology is expected to play as an auxiliary aid by which communication is made effective for persons with disabilities. OCR notes that the "information superhighway" is fast becoming a fundamental tool in post-secondary research.

> Letter of Resolution, pp. 1-2; 38 C.F.R.§35.160(a)

OCR Letter of Resolution, Docket No. 09-97-2002 (April 7, 1997) This case concerned a student complaint that a university failed to provide access to library resources, campus publications, open computer laboratories, training on adaptive computer technology, and computer test-taking (see www.icdri.org/legal/csula.htm). According to the finding:

Title II of the Americans with Disabilities Act (Title II) requires a public college to take appropriate steps to ensure that communications with persons with disabilities "are as effective as communications with others" [28 C.F.R. § 35.160(a)]. OCR has repeatedly held that the term "communication" in this context means the transfer of information, including (but not limited to) the verbal presentation of a lecturer, the printed text of a book, **and the resources of the Internet**. Title II further states that, in determining what type of auxiliary aid and service is necessary, a public college shall give primary consideration to the requests of the individual with a disability [28 C.F.R. § 35.160(b)(2)].

In further clarifying what is meant by "effective communication," OCR held that the three basic components of effective communication are, "timeliness of delivery, accuracy of the translation, and provision in a manner and medium appropriate to the significance of the message and the abilities of the individual with the disability" (Letter of Resolution, p. 1).

The first prong of the definition, "timeliness of delivery," strengthened the legal requirement for accessible web design. Previous practices of posting information on the website to tell people with disabilities that they could get the web content in an accessible format by phoning or e-mailing a request no longer met the ADA definition of "effective communication." While one person could access the content of a website within seconds, another, with a different disability, might need to make a phone call and have the content snail-mailed to him in an accessible format. The "timeliness of delivery" prong of the definition was now going to play an important role in the civil right to information.

We also see the emergence of policy that later became law in Section 508: an accessible technology plan. In this Letter of Resolution, OCR points out that the courts have held that a public entity violates its obligations under the ADA when it responds on only an ad-hoc basis to individual requests for accommodation. There is an affirmative duty to develop a comprehensive policy in advance of any request for auxiliary aids or services—see Tyler v. City of Manhattan, 857 F. Supp. 800 (D.Kan. 1994). Moreover, according to OCR, "[a] recognized good practice in establishing such a comprehensive policy is to consult with the disability community, especially those members most likely to request accommodations" (Letter of Resolution, p. 2).

The bottom line, according to OCR, is that effective communication imposes a duty to solve barriers to information access that the entity's purchasing choices create. Whenever existing technology is "upgraded" by a new technology feature, it is important to ensure that the new technology either improves accessibility or is compatible with existing assistive computer technology. Web-authoring software programs that erect barriers in their coding of web pages fall under this scrutiny.

Lastly, OCR states that when an entity selects software programs and/or hardware equipment that is not adaptable for people with disabilities, "the subsequent substantial expense of providing access is not generally regarded as an undue burden when such cost could have been significantly reduced by considering the issue of accessibility at the time of the initial selection" (Letter of Resolution, p. 2).

When applied to accessible web design, there is all the more reason to ensure that the initial design and any subsequent "updates" meet with accessibility requirements. If the problem of accessibility is not addressed at this stage, then the money to address the burden of expense afterwards may not be available. Therefore, all technology improvements must take into account the removal of existing barriers to access and ensure that new ones do not occur. Covered entities preparing to retrofit their websites need to be aware of this requirement.

OCR Letter of Resolution, Docket No. 09-97-6001 (January 22, 1998) Because OCR recognizes that not all illegal discrimination situations can be addressed by relying on complaints filed from the public, OCR conducts agency-initiated cases, or compliance reviews. According to OCR, these compliance reviews "permit OCR to target resources on compliance problems that appear particularly acute, or national in scope, or which are newly emerging" (see www.ed.gov/about/offices/list/ocr/AnnRpt99/edlite-how.html).

In March 1996, the OCR notified the California Community Colleges that it was about to begin a statewide compliance review under Title II of the ADA. The purpose of the review and subsequent OCR Report was to assess how 106 California Community Colleges meet their obligations to students with visual disabilities in providing access to print and electronic information. In OCR's letter dated January 22, 1998, the comprehensive review suggested nine strategies to address (see www.icdri.org/legal/ocrsurltr.htm):

- Cost-effective approach to purchasing adaptive technology
- Adaptive technology training
- Access guidelines for distance learning and campus web pages, as well as tools for training faculty and staff
- Inclusive language in the distribution of standard technology grants/funds addressing college responsibility to ensure technology access and compatible upgrades
- Print materials translated into alternative formats such as electronic text and Braille
- Central registry of textbooks in alternative formats
- Library technology initiatives for access to both students and patrons with disabilities
- Follow-up to OCR survey initiated on September 18, 1996, to determine compliance progress
- Annual reviews of Disabled Student Programs and Services to include attention to the removal of barriers in electronic technology

The Community College Chancellor agreed to implement OCR's recommendations to help the colleges meet their obligations under the ADA and Section 504 of the Rehabilitation Act (see March 9, 1999, Letter from Ralph Black, General Counsel for the California Community Colleges, to Paul Grossman, Chief Regional Attorney, U.S. Department of Education, OCR re: Case Docket No. 09-07-6001).

Whereas the assistive computer technology training, support, and services for students with disabilities were once limited to staff exclusively working with the Office of Disabled Student Programs, a systematic plan is now required for mainstreaming this knowledge campus-wide: "Technology access, like architectural access, must be addressed institutionally as an integral part of the planning process" (Letter of Resolution, p. 5).

Just as the removal of architectural barriers requires a plan for implementation, the removal of technological or digital barriers in programs and services requires a comprehensive institutional plan impacting every campus office. You will again see this concept of a plan for accessible technology in the discussion of Section 508 later in this chapter.

Today, a standard for long-distance learning has been established by the California Community Colleges as a direct result of this compliance activity. The 1999 "Distance Education: Access Guidelines for Students with Disabilities" (www.htctu.net/publications/guidelines/distance_ed/disted.htm) are considered a model for the nation.

OCR Letter of Resolution, Docket No. 09-99-2041 (April 20, 1999) This was a student complaint that the university failed to provide access to the College of Business curriculum and other educational programs, including computer laboratories and classes in the College of Business (see www.icdri.org/legal/lbeach.htm). OCR noted that, although the academic community has heavily relied upon centralized units on campus to house and maintain assistive computer technology:

> [S]uch sole reliance upon a single centralized location (when not limited to adaptive technology training, but instead used for instructing disabled students in course subject matter) may run counter to the strong philosophy embodied in [ADA] Title II and Section 504 regarding the importance of fully integrating students with disabilities into the mainstream educational program, unless such services cannot be otherwise effectively provided [see 34 C.F.R. § 104.4(b)(iv); 28 C.F.R. § 35.130(b)(iv).] Thus, OCR assumes that in most cases computer access will be effectively provided to the student with the disability in an educational setting with his or her non-disabled peers and classmates at the various computer laboratory sites scattered throughout the campus.

OCR went on to point out that by April 1, 1999, the University provided OCR with a voluntary resolution plan, which resolved the issues raised in this case. The plan included the following commitments by the University:

- Develop and implement a written procedure describing which campus units are responsible for installing and maintaining adaptive workstations situated in college and central computer laboratories.
- Develop and implement a systematic method for ensuring that the issue of accessibility to persons with disabilities, particularly persons who are blind, is taken into account when colleges purchase computer technology (software and hardware).
- Develop and implement a systematic method for informing campus employees who design/select web pages for use by students to make sure the web pages are in accordance with principles known to maximize accessibility to users with disabilities, including visual impairments.

As a result, the mainstreaming of students with disabilities created the need for appropriate technology tools for access to the learning environment. And as students with disabilities move into the workforce as employees, employers, and consumers, accessible web design, accessible web-authoring tools, and an accessible Internet platform remain significant issues to be addressed. In other words, overcoming barriers in web design requires appropriate policies, technology tools, and education for accessible design and implementation.

America Online

In November 1999, the National Federation of the Blind (NFB) filed a suit against America Online, Inc. (AOL), charging that AOL's proprietary browser and Internet website was inaccessible to consumers who were blind. According to the complaint, screen readers were encountering accessibility barriers to AOL services due to the use of unlabeled graphics, keyboard commands that had to be activated through a mouse, customized graphical controls, and channels hidden within unlabeled graphics. Some of the web design barriers included the following:

- An inaccessible AOL service sign-up form that was not designed to inform the user as to the content requested for each blank field

- A Welcome screen with features such as favorites, parental control, and chat rooms, where the text was hidden within graphics

- The required use of browser software designed to operate so that screen readers did not know when the browser was operating, thus making it very difficult for users who are blind to enter a keyword search, a web address, or even tab through the links

- Barriers to the ADA requirement of "effective communication," where the user could not benefit from a significant number of AOL service features

According to the complaint, service features that the user could not use included the following:

- Electronic mail services

- Buddy list feature

- Public bulletin boards

- Public and private chat rooms and auditorium events

- AOL's 19 channels providing informational content

- Commerce and community opportunities relating to news, sports, games, finance, shopping, health, travel, kids, and other subjects

- AOL's personalization and control features for users, such as those for updating stock portfolios or blocking their children's access to inappropriate websites

On July 26, 2000, NFB and AOL announced that the first ADA Internet complaint against an Internet service provider had been dismissed by mutual agreement. It was no accident that the joint press release was released on the tenth anniversary of the ADA. As I reviewed the Agreement, I found that although the complaint was dismissed without prejudice, NFB expressly reserved its rights to renew their ADA action against AOL. This means that the Agreement should not be regarded as a settlement.

However, the Agreement set forth a number of remedies to assist AOL in addressing accessibility. For example, AOL committed to an Online Accessibility Policy, now found on the AOL website at `www.corp.aol.com/accessibility/inclusiveness.html`. AOL's Online Accessibility Policy has three components:

- Raising employee awareness of information technology accessibility issues

- Taking responsibility for developing accessible products and services

- Collaborating with the disability community for input and feedback on AOL products and services

> *I have further discussed this case in several articles. These include "Suit Targets Cyberspace for ADA Compliance," National Disability Law Reporter, Highlights, Volume 16, Issue 5, December 16, 1999; "The National Federation of the Blind Sues AOL," Human Rights, Volume 27, No. 1, Winter 2000, American Bar Association Magazine for the Section of Individual Rights and Responsibilities (www.abanet.org/irr/hr/winter00humanrights/waddell2.html); and "Will the National Federation of the Blind Renew Their ADA Web Complaint Against AOL?" National Disability Law Reporter, Volume 18, Issue 5, August 24, 2000.*

Online Banking Settlements

If you have ever wondered why a bank ATM has Braille labels on LCD displays, you are not alone. Although the ADA Accessibility Guidelines requires this "accessibility feature," few members of the blind and low-vision community can benefit from this feature, since it does not tell them what content the window displays.

In response to this problem, disability advocates and consumers, led by Attorney Lainey Feingold, are spearheading structured negotiations to persuade major banking institutions not only to install talking ATM machines for people with visual disabilities, but also to set up accessible bank websites. To date, institutions such as Bank of America, Fleet, Washington Mutual, First Union/Wachovia, Bank One, Citizens Bank, and Sovereign Bank have entered into agreements that include commitments for accessible online banking.

As early as March 2000, a settlement was reached between the California Council of the Blind and Bank of America (see `www.icdri.org/ATMs/bank_of_america_atm_settlement_a.htm`). Bank of America not only agreed to install more than 2,500 talking ATMs in Florida and California, but also to design their websites to be in conformance with Priority 1 and 2 levels of the W3C WCAG 1.0.

This was the beginning of a series of talking ATM settlements that has continued today. A February 28, 2001, press release announced an agreement by Fleet National Bank to install talking ATMs and ensure accessible online banking services. According to the agreement, Fleet was to use its best efforts to design its web pages to comply with Priority 1 of the

W3C WCAG 1.0 by June 1, 2001, and to eventually comply with Priority 2 of the WCAG by December 31, 2001. For more agreements to date involving Sovereign Bank and Citizens Bank, see www.dlc-ma.org/News/atm/index.htm.

These agreements contain various enforcement mechanisms to keep disability advocates and attorneys apprised of the banks' progress toward meeting the settlement requirements. Take a look at some of the clauses from the June 2003 Bank One settlement at www.icdri.org/Assistive%20Technology/ATMs/bank_one_settlemen.htm. It includes web accessibility provisions requiring conformance with WCAG 1.0, third-party content, and the publication of web accessibility information on the bank website for customers:

6. Web Accessibility.

6.1 Priority 1. Bank One will use its good faith efforts to design and generate each page of www.bankone.com, online.bankone.com, cardmemberservices. firstusa.com, onlinefirstusa.com and www.firstusa.com so that each substantially complies with Priority 1 of the Web Content Accessibility Guidelines found at www.w3c.org.TR/WCAG10 (hereinafter "Guidelines"), by June 30, 2003.

6.2 Priority 2. Bank One will use its good faith efforts to design and generate each page of www.bankone.com, online.bankone.com, cardmemberservices. firstusa.com, onlinefirstusa.com and www.firstusa.com so that each substantially complies with Priority 2 of the Guidelines by December 31, 2003.

6.3 Reports. Bank One will, during the term of this Agreement, report to Claimants on a semi-annual basis beginning June 30, 2003, regarding the progress made toward compliance with Sections 6.1 and 6.2. Claimants may submit to Bank One, within thirty (30) days of receipt of each such report, written questions regarding the report, and Bank One will, within thirty (30) days of receipt of such questions, provide answers to Claimants.

6.4 Information to the Public Regarding Web Accessibility. No later than September 30, 2003, Bank One will add one or more pages to www.bankone.com and www.firstusa.com describing the Bank's efforts to make the Bank One websites accessible to Persons with Vision Impairments or Blindness. The page(s) will include information as to how users can contact Bank One and/or Bank One, Delaware, NA concerning website accessibility issues.

6.5 Third Party Content on Bank One Websites. Bank One will use good faith efforts to include web accessibility as one of its criteria in relevant requests for proposals and other procurement documents involving third party content, which is web pages that are directly linked to pages of www.bankone.com, online.bankone.com, cardmemberservices.firstusa.com, and www.firstusa.com within sixty (60) days of the Effective Date.

6.6 Limitation of Remedies. A breach of this Section 6 shall occur only where Claimants can establish that Bank One has engaged in a pattern or practice of non-compliance with Section 6. The Parties agree that if a web site contains Accessibility Errors from time to time that are inconsistent with the Priority levels described in this Section 6, or other access problems from time to time, such occurrences will not necessarily constitute a breach of this Agreement. However, the Parties recognize that repeated Accessibility Errors of the same or similar type may be evidence of a pattern or practice of non-compliance. Furthermore, Claimants will not assert a breach of Section 6 unless a mutually agreed upon web consultant, hired by Bank One, has determined that the challenged web page or portion thereof, does not substantially comply with the applicable Priority 1 or 2 Guidelines. No breach of contract claims related to Bank One's obligations under Section 6 of this Agreement may be maintained by persons who are not Parties to this Agreement.

Online Voting

In March 2000, the Arizona Democratic Presidential Primary was conducted online for the first time. Members of the blind community went to the polls expecting to vote for the first time independently and in private, but found that the website ballot was not accessible to screen readers.

> *A now-defunct website posted information about this incident, and so I interviewed a number of the complainants in order to understand the scope of the voting accessibility problem. In fact, I had predicted this very outcome the previous year in a paper commissioned by the U.S. Department of Commerce and the National Science Foundation for the first national conference on the impact of the digital economy. I had noted that Fortune 500 companies were already using the Internet as an option for shareholder participation in annual or special business meetings and appeared to be unaware of the accessibility problems of their website ballots. I had pointed out that this problem should be a reminder for governments that Internet voting for local, state, or national elections requires accessible web design to prevent the disfranchisement of people with disabilities. (See* The Growing Digital Divide in Access for People with Disabilities: Overcoming Barriers to Participation, *by Cynthia D. Waddell, at* www.icdri.org/CynthiaW/the_digital_divide.htm.*)*

www.election.com had provided the Internet voting website for the Arizona Democratic Presidential Primary. In response to the complaints, top-level www.election.com officials issued a press release in April 2000 stating that they would "take definite steps toward greater accessibility for blind voters" (previously posted at www.election.com/us/pressroom/pr2000/0419.htm but as of December 2005, www.election.com no longer maintains a website).

The following year, a U.S. government federal agency, the U.S. General Accounting Office, issued a report in October 2001 entitled *Voters with Disabilities: Access to Polling Places and Alternative Voting Methods*, GAO-02-107. This report pointed out that one advantage for Internet voting was that voters who are blind could vote independently when the web ballot is designed according to Section 508 standards (see www.gao.gov/new.items/d02107.pdf).

Online IRS Tax Filing Services Settlement

April 2000 also brought an announcement by the Connecticut Attorney General's Office and the NFB that four online tax filing companies had agreed to make their Internet sites accessible to the blind. Four companies—HDVest, Intuit, H & R Block, and Gilman & Ciocia—agreed to implement changes to conform to the W3C WCAG by the 2000 tax-filing season (see www.cslib.org/attygenl/press/2000/health/blind.htm). The popular online tax-filing services had been listed on the Internal Revenue Service's official website as online partners.

Credit Card Company Monthly Statements

In the USDOJ April–June 2001 report, *Enforcing the ADA-Update*, it was reported that a successful ADA mediation was concluded between a credit card company and a blind person from Colorado (www.usdoj.gov/crt/ada/aprjun01.htm). The credit card company agreed to change its practice when a customer who was blind complained that the large-print credit card statement routinely provided by the company was too small to read. The credit card company agreed to maintain an accessible website and worked with the complainant so he could access the website to enlarge and print his monthly statements in a format usable by him. The credit card company also paid the complainant's attorney's fees.

Suffice it to say that the Internet has made transactions so transparent that it is now very obvious to the community of people with disabilities when they cannot access the content of a website due to inaccessible design. In my opinion, the emergence of Section 508 Electronic and Information Technology Accessibility Standards was a logical step in an evolution of disability rights. It seeks to level the playing field in access to the powerful tools that information and technology have become in our global economy.

Websites and Tax Fraud

In May 2004, USDOJ announced that a federal court in Las Vegas, Nevada, had issued permanent injunctions against Oryan Management and Financial Services, ADA Adventure and four individuals, barring them from marketing bogus accessible websites. According to the complaint, the defendants marketed bogus websites with links to particular products and merchants. Each purchaser was offered a separate website virtual mall business, which could be "modified" in order to comply with the ADA.

In reality, each "business" was merely an account on one website. The "business" required no payment up front. Instead, each purchaser agreed to provide the website designers with a stated percentage of the commissions earned from the website. The cost for the accessible web modification was $10,475 ($2,495 cash, plus a $7,980 promissory note). This scheme was said to entitle the purchaser to claim a $5,000 Disabled Access Credit and a $5,475 business-related deduction.

The USDOJ estimated that the abusive accessible web tax scheme allegedly cost the U.S. Treasury about $99 million. Read more about it at www.usdoj.gov/opa/pr/2004/May/ 04_tax_309.htm.

Websites and USDOJ Project Civic Access

Through Project Civic Access, the USDOJ has entered into more than 135 settlement agreements with counties, cities, towns, and villages to ensure that they comply with the ADA. Frequently, these government jurisdictions have entered into settlement agreements that require them to implement accessible websites. For an example of an agreement requiring an accessible website, see the City of Sedona agreement, posted at www.usdoj.gov/crt/ada/civic2005.htm, which includes the following:

WEB-BASED SERVICES AND PROGRAMS

22. Within 3 months of the effective date of this Agreement, and on subsequent anniversaries of the effective date of this Agreement, the City will distribute to all persons—employees and contractors—who design, develop, maintain, or otherwise have responsibility for content and format of its website(s) or third party websites used by the City (Internet Personnel) the technical assistance document, "Accessibility of State and Local Government Websites to People with Disabilities," which is Attachment E to this Agreement (it is also available at www.ada.gov/ websites2.htm).

23. Within 6 months of the effective date of this Agreement, and throughout the life of the Agreement, the City will do the following:

A. Establish, implement, and post online a policy that its web pages will be accessible and create a process for implementation;

B. Ensure that all new and modified web pages and content are accessible;

C. Develop and implement a plan for making existing web content more accessible;

D. Provide a way for online visitors to request accessible information or services by posting a telephone number or e-mail address on its home page; and

E. Periodically (at least annually) enlist people with disabilities to test its pages for ease of use.

www.ada.gov/suffolkva.htm

Travel Websites Settlement Agreements

In August, 2004, New York Attorney General Eliot Spitzer announced settlements with two major travel websites to make the sites more accessible to visitors with visual disabilities. The websites, www.ramada.com and www.priceline.com, agreed to implement accessibility standards and to pay the State of New York $40,000 and $37,500, respectively, for the cost of the investigation. According to the press release, once the companies were notified of the accessibility issues by the Attorney General, they worked with his Internet Bureau to correct the issues. According to the press release:

> Under the terms of the agreements, the companies will implement a range of accessibility standards authored by the Web Accessibility Initiative ("WAI") of the World Wide Web Consortium ("W3C"), an organization that recommends Internet standards. For instance, graphics and images must have comprehensible labels, tables must have appropriately placed row and column headers, and edit fields (boxes where the Internet user inputs information) which must be labeled to indicate which information is requested.

> www.oag.state.ny.us/press/2004/aug/aug19a_04.html

This public settlement closely followed a private settlement by Ramada in another case where I served as an expert witness on accessible web design.

Section 255 of the Telecommunications Act of 1996

The Telecommunications Act of 1996 was the first major revision of our nation's communications policy in 62 years. Section 255 requires that manufacturers of telecommunications and customer premises equipment, as well as vendors of telecommunications services, make their products and services accessible to, and usable by, persons with disabilities, unless it is not "readily achievable" to do so (see the February 1998 *Telecommunications Act Accessibility Guidelines* at www.access-board.gov/telecomm/rule.htm).

This is not a federal procurement law, and it has a lower burden for compliance than Section 508, because "readily achievable" means without significant difficulty or expense. It also has one major limitation in that Section 255 does not cover every function or service in the scope of the telephone network.

This was the first product design law to attempt to drive the market to create accessible products. It is not a traditional civil rights law, since it is an accessible design law that does not depend on the filing of a complaint for its requirements to be enforced. Although persons with disabilities can file a complaint with the Federal Communications Commission (FCC), this law does not provide for damages, and lawsuits are not authorized.

On September 22, 2000, the FCC reminded manufacturers and providers of voice mail and interactive products that they were subject to Section 255 (for more on this, see www.fcc.gov/eb/Public_Notices/da002162.html). As we watch the boundaries blur between the Internet and telecommunications, web developers should be reminded that interactive voice response (IVR) features on websites need to meet the accessibility requirements of Section 508. Let's discuss Section 508 next.

Electronic and Information Technology Accessibility Standards (Section 508) Overview

Understanding that technology was becoming integral to the quality of life for persons with disabilities, former President Clinton signed the 1998 Amendments to the Rehabilitation Act into law. By strengthening Section 508 of the Rehabilitation Act, it provided an enforcement mechanism for the procurement of accessible electronic and information technology. I call this significant law the "ADA of Cyberspace."

A week before Section 508's effective date, June, 25, 2001, President George W. Bush visited the Pentagon's Computer/Electronic Accommodations Program Technology Evaluation Center and spoke about these new rules:

> I'm pleased to announce that when Section 508 . . . becomes effective for all federal agencies next Monday, there will be more opportunities for people of all abilities to access government information . . . Increasingly, Americans use information technology to interact with their government. They rely on thousands of government web pages to download forms, learn about federal programs, find out where to turn for government assistance, and communicate with elected officials, such as the President. And because of Section 508, government web sites will be more accessible for millions of Americans who have disabilities. Section 508 will also make the federal government a better employer, as roughly 120,000 federal employees with disabilities will have greater access to the tools they need to better perform their jobs. This is one example of the successful public-private partnerships that are removing barriers to full community participation by Americans with disabilities. I thank the leaders of the technology industry who are with us today for your innovation and your ongoing cooperation.

> www.whitehouse.gov/news/releases/2001/06/20010619-1.html

For the first time in U.S. history, we have a procurement law that prohibits federal agencies (with limited exceptions) from developing, purchasing, using, or maintaining electronic and information technology that is inaccessible to persons with disabilities. Broad in scope, it requires functionality in the design of electronic and information technology including hardware, software, operating systems, web-based intranet and Internet information and applications, phone systems, video and multimedia products, and self-contained products such as fax machines, copiers, hand-helds, and kiosks. It covers both products and services.

On December 21, 2000, the U.S. Access Board published the *Electronic and Information Technology Accessibility Standards* (www.access-board.gov/sec508/standards.htm), which are now part of the federal government's procurement regulations. Provisions in the standards identify what makes these products accessible to persons with disabilities, including those with vision, hearing, and mobility impairments. The Board includes technical criteria specific to various types of technologies, as well as performance-based requirements, which focus on a product's functional capabilities.

As the world's largest consumer of electronic and information technology, the federal government is required to use the power of the purse to push the electronic and information technology industries to design accessible products. All vendors, whether they are U.S. or foreign, must design according to Section 508 if they want to participate in the federal government market.

Section 508 seeks to create a marketplace incentive to design for accessibility. In fact, vendors may protest the award of a contract to other vendors if they believe their product or service is more accessible. In addition, an agency can terminate a vendor's contract for noncompliance or require the vendor to provide a compliant version of the product or service. Lastly, a growing number of state governments are adopting Section 508 policies or legislation, since they also want their products and services to reach the widest possible audience.

With respect to legal liability, compliance with the accessibility standards is required except where it would pose an "undue burden" or where no complying product is commercially available. *Undue burden* is defined as "significant difficulty or expense." Certain technologies related to national security are exempt. The law allows federal employees and members of the public with disabilities to file a complaint with the appropriate federal agency concerning access to products procured after the effective date. Alternatively, individuals may file suit against an agency seeking injunctive relief and attorneys' fees alleging noncompliance with the accessibility requirements.

In addition, web developers should not need to be reminded that if they knowingly misrepresent compliance with accessibility standards, they may find themselves subject to a False Claims Act (FCA) violation. Under the FCA, the government may impose penalties up to $10,000 for each false "claim" and recover treble damages. (A false claim could constitute each invoice for accessible web design services.) In addition, the FCA permits individuals to file whistle-blower actions on behalf of the government. Such actions would enable the individual to receive up to 30 percent of the government's recovery. The operative word here is "knowingly" misrepresenting compliance with Section 508, a definition that includes deliberate ignorance or reckless disregard of the truth. So there is all the more reason to read this book!

State of Federal Accessibility Report to the President

Implementation of Section 508 requires periodic compliance reviews and reports. Under the leadership of the USDOJ, every federal agency will periodically evaluate the accessibility of its electronic and information technology. In addition, the USDOJ will also evaluate agency responses to Section 508 discrimination complaints.

The first report, *Information Technology and People with Disabilities: The State of Federal Accessibility*, was presented to the President and Congress in April 2000. All executive agencies and departments, including the United States Postal Service, were required to conduct self-evaluations to determine the extent to which their electronic and information technology is accessible to persons with disabilities. One theme that emerged, which was discussed earlier in this chapter, in the "Office for Civil Rights, U.S. Department of Education" section, was that the USDOJ has determined that accessibility issues cannot continue to be addressed exclusively on an "ad hoc" or "as needed" basis. A systematic accessibility plan must be in place for electronic and information technology.

According to the April 2000 U.S. Attorney General report on the state of federal accessibility:

> Data provided by the agencies suggest that the majority of agencies continue to handle IT accessibility issues exclusively on an "ad hoc" or "as needed" basis, instead of integrating accessibility into the development and procurement of their mainstream IT products. Many IT officials hold the mistaken belief that persons with disabilities can always be accommodated upon request by using widely available assistive technology devices (for example, screen readers, screen enlargers, volume control apparatuses, pointing devices that serve as alternatives to a computer mouse, voice recognition software, etc.) in conjunction with mainstream technology applications. Indeed, the goal of section 508 is to ensure that the agency will always be able to provide reasonable accommodations. Without adequate planning, however, the possibility of providing an accommodation to persons with a disability may be foreclosed. See, for example, the discussions of accessibility barriers created by certain uses of Adobe Acrobat's Portable Document Format, in section III, n. 19. Use of an "ad hoc" or "as needed" approach to IT accessibility **will** result in barriers for persons with disabilities. A much better approach is to integrate accessibility reviews into the earliest stages of design, development, and procurement of IT. Once an accessible IT architecture is established, then and only then can persons with disabilities be successfully accommodated on an "as needed" basis.

> April 2000 Report of the U.S. Attorney General Information Technology and People with Disabilities: The Current State of Federal Accessibility, Section II, General Findings and Recommendations, p. 7, at www.usdoj.gov/crt/508/report/intro.htm

U.S. Access Board Guide to the Standards

The Electronic and Information Technology Accessibility Standards, 36 CFR Part 1194, contain four subparts:

- Subpart A: General
- Subpart B: Technical Standards
- Subpart C: Functional Performance Criteria
- Subpart D: Information, Documentation, and Support

In particular, web developers should become familiar with Subparts B and D. Subpart B includes "1194.21 Software applications and operating systems" and "1194.22 Web-based intranet and Internet information and applications" (among others). Subpart D includes "1194.41 Information, documentation, and support."

The U.S. Access Board provides technical assistance for the implementation of Section 508, and web developers should first review and apply this information before inserting their own independent interpretations on the application of each rule. It is expected that additional guidance will be made available as the implementation moves forward.

There are two approaches to compliance with Section 508. First, a website would be in compliance if it met §1194.22(a) through (p). Second, a website would also be in compliance with Section 508 if it met the WCAG 1.0, Priority 1 checkpoints *and* 1194.22(l), (m), (n), (o), and (p) of these standards. See 36 Part 1194, page 80510.

Because WCAG 1.0 was not developed within the U.S. regulatory enforcement framework, it was not possible for the U.S. Access Board to adopt it as a standard for accessibility. However, the U.S. Access Board acknowledged that at the publication of the Section 508 Electronic and Information Technology Accessibility Standards, the WAI was developing the next version, WCAG 2.0. The U.S. Access Board stated that it plans to work with the WAI in the future on the verifiability and achievability of WCAG 2.0 when the time comes to revise the Section 508 web technical requirements.

Appendix B of this book covers the specific guidance provided by the U.S. Access Board for the implementation of the Subpart B web-based rules. The accessibility rules for software applications are also included. This is because the Section 508 web-based rule at 1194.22(m) requires plug-ins, applets, or other applications to meet all of the software application accessibility standards at 1194.21(a) through (l).

At the time of this writing, the U.S. Access Board has not provided Subpart D rule guidance. However, web developers should be aware that if their website contains product support documentation or help desk services for a federal agency, they must meet the requirements under Subpart D.

According to the U.S. Access Board, the first nine rules in §1194.22, (a) through (i) incorporate the exact language recommended by the WAI in their comments to this rulemaking, or they contain language not substantially different from WCAG 1.0, supported by the WAI. Rules §1194.22(j) and (k) were meant to be consistent with WCAG 1.0, but the U.S. Access Board needed to use language consistent with enforceable regulatory language. Rules §1194.22(l), (m), (n), (o), and (p) are different from WCAG 1.0 due to the need to require a higher level of access or prescribe a more specific requirement. The U.S. Access Board commented on certain WCAG priority one checkpoints and the reason for not adopting them (see Electronic and Information Technology Accessibility Standards; Final Rule; 36 CFR Part 1194, p. 80510):

- **WCAG 1.0 Checkpoint 4.1 (natural language):** Not adopted due to the fact that only two assistive technology programs could interpret such coding or markup and that the majority of screen readers utilized in the U.S. do not have the capability of switching to the processing of foreign-language phonemes.
- **WCAG 1.0 Checkpoint 14.1 (clearest and simplest language):** Not adopted because it is difficult to enforce since a requirement to use the simplest language can be very subjective.

- **WCAG 1.0 Checkpoint 1.3 (auditory description of visual track):** Not adopted in the web rules because a similar provision was adopted in the video and multimedia product rules.
- **WCAG 1.0 Checkpoint 6.2 (dynamic content):** Not adopted because "the meaning of the provision is unclear."

When Does a Web Developer Follow Section 508 Rules?

So now we have two sets of technical specifications for accessible web design: the W3C WCAG 1.0 and the federal Electronic and Information Technology Accessibility Standards. Which should a web developer apply?

The answer depends on who owns the website. If it is a U.S. federal agency, or if the website is a vendor website that is accessed as a part of a help desk or vendor product documentation for federal agency services, then Section 508 applies.

If the website is for a state or local government agency, then it will depend on whether or not that agency has adopted Section 508. According to the study, *State IT Accessibility Policy: The Landscape of Today* (www.rit.edu/~easi/itd/itdv09n1/golden.htm), authors Diane Cordry Golden and Deborah V. Buck report that every state in the union, including the District of Columbia, has now adopted a web accessibility measure. They note that between 1996 and 2000, the number of states that adopted and formalized web accessibility practices flourished. This is reflected in various mechanisms such as state statutes, executive orders, policies, or technical standards. Some states have adopted Section 508, some have adopted W3C WCAG, and some have compiled standards of their own mix.

For this reason, it is very likely that local government agencies, such as counties, cities, and towns, may also have some form of web accessibility policy or practice in place. For example, in the State of California, Government Code 11135 requires that if local government agencies and higher education entities receive State funding, they must comply with Section 508, and this includes the accessible web technical requirements. The same is true for nonprofit organizations that receive State funding.

Here are some steps to follow:

- Find out if the organization you are developing web pages for (your client) has an accessibility policy or practice and implementation plan.
- Find out if your client has already set up a style guide and templates.
- Ask your client what technical standards you should follow. Ultimately, it is the client's responsibility to tell you, and this step provides you with some protection. If for some reason your client does not know, tell your client to ask the organization's lawyer or compliance officer. A best practice would be to have the technical standards specified by the client in your contract for web development services.

And here is a list of people to talk to about what standards to follow:

- Federal government: Agency Section 508 Coordinator and/or Agency CIO
- State government: State ADA Compliance Officer and/or IT Department Head

- County/City government: ADA Compliance Officer and/or IT Department Head
- Higher Education: ADA/504/508 Compliance Officer or Affirmative Action Officer
- Corporation: Corporate Counsel or IT Department Head

But remember, Section 508 technical standards are *minimum* standards for accessibility, and this means that you can also implement additional accessibility standards from W3C WCAG.

It is my opinion that state and local government agencies should implement Section 508 since they are subject to the ADA and Section 504 of the Rehabilitation Act of 1973. This is because the ADA requires accessible websites for "effective communication," and Section 508 tells us how to design accessible websites. This does not mean that an entity cannot also implement additional W3C WCAG to maximize accessible design. Many states have already adopted W3C WCAG for ADA-compliance reasons, and so now Section 508 provides the minimal legal requirements for accessibility.

In California, some education institutions had already adopted Section 508 prior to the State adoption by statute because of the federal Tech Act requirements. For example, the California Community Colleges took steps to ensure that information technology and services procured, leased, or developed with State or federal funding met the Section 508 requirements (see the June 11, 2001, Legal Opinion at www.resna.org/taproject/goals/education/cccc508letter.doc). This included long-distance learning as well as campus websites. This was because the Tech Act of 1998, which was scheduled to sunset in September 2004, and then was continued by Congress through the Assistive Technology Act of 2004, required that states receiving federal Tech Act money must comply with Section 508. However, as of the writing of this chapter, the 2006 budget being presented by President Bush eliminates state funding for Tech Act projects. Compliance because of Tech Act requirements may now be moot. Today, there are reasons other than the Tech Act for designing accessible websites.

And what about everyone else? If you are an employer, you may be subject to the employment provisions of the ADA. Any of your employees protected under the ADA could request your intranet or Internet to be accessible as a "reasonable accommodation" in order for them to do their work. The bottom line is that it is a "best practice" to follow Section 508 in addition to W3C WCAG. This is because Section 508 informs entities covered under the ADA and Section 504 of the Rehabilitation Act on what it means to design accessible websites for satisfying the "effective communication" mandate for nondiscrimination.

Legal Hot Topics for Web Developers and Policy Makers

In this section, we will look at proposed rulemaking addressing web accessibility, as well as some of the most common website features that cause problems for web users in their access to web content and services. After all, accessible web design enables your website to reach the widest possible audience, including older adults, people with disabilities, and people using alternative Internet access devices. Web developers need to be especially careful when designing these features, and policy makers need to be knowledgeable of the features and functionality required for enabling access to content and services.

U.S. Department of Transportation Notice of Proposed Rulemaking

In November 2004, the U.S. Department of Transportation issued a Notice of Proposed Rulemaking asking for comments on proposed rules by March 5, 2005. According to my communications with the agency, the final rules are expected to be published in mid-2006.

The proposed rulemaking is to revise its regulations that implement the Air Carrier Access Act of 1986 and to require accessible websites. The agency noted that in Access Now v. Southwest Airlines, the lower court found that ADA Title III required a physical place for a public accommodation and that a website was not such a place. But the agency noted that "the Air Carrier Access Act contains no such limitation" and that:

> The ACAA requires that all airline services to the public be accessible to persons with disabilities and provided in a nondiscriminatory manner. This applies whether the service is provided in person, over the phone, or on the internet.
>
> *Federal Register*, Volume 69, No. 213, p. 64369, or http://a257.g.akamaitech.net/ 7/257/2422/06jun20041800/edocket.access.gpo.gov/2004/04-24371.htm

According to the rulemaking, new websites going online after the effective date of the new rules would need to be accessible. Existing websites would have two years to comply. Websites serving as affiliates, agents, or contractors for a number of carriers, such as Orbitz, Expedia, and Travelocity, would be required to be accessible. Airline carriers, both domestic and foreign, are subject to this rulemaking. Websites of foreign carriers would need to make accessible those portions of their websites that contain information on flights beginning or ending at a U.S. airport.

The agency also sought comments as to whether there should be additional or specific requirements added concerning online travel agencies (for example, websites that provide schedule and fare information and ticketing services for many air carriers).

Electronic Forms

One positive impact of e-government has been the streamlining of governmental transactions through the use of electronic forms. Because of the prevalence of forms used by governmental agencies, it should not be a surprise that electronic forms are specifically addressed in Section 508. Frequently, an electronic form is posted on the Web to be printed and completed offline. Even if online submittal is not an option, enabling the form to be completed online would be of great benefit to many people. Web developers should note that regardless of whether the form is to be submitted online, it is important that the form be designed so that a person using assistive technology can fill it out and understand the directions for completing and submitting it. For this reason, Section 508 covers electronic forms under both the software and web technical standards at §1194.21(l) and §1194.21(n).

As noted in previous chapters, there are accessibility issues with the portable document format (PDF). Until PDF issues are fully resolved, I (and the USDOJ) highly recommend that if web developers post PDF electronic forms, they should also post accessible electronic forms complying with Section 508 rules.

Applets, Plug-ins, and Applications

One of the most frustrating experiences for persons with disabilities has been the requirement at various websites to use applets, plug-ins, or other applications to access the content of the web page. Plug-ins can interfere with the functionality of assistive technology and can even cause the application to crash. Plug-ins may also have features and functionality that are inaccessible by design.

Section 508 addresses the problem by requiring that web developers using these applications meet the software standards at §1194.21. It is very important to note the guidance at §1194.22(m) from the U.S. Access Board: "This provision places a responsibility on the web page author to know that a compliant application exists, before requiring a plug-in."

This means that web developers must not use plug-ins that do not meet the Section 508 software accessibility requirements. Likewise, applets and applications are subject to the Section 508 software technical requirements for accessibility, so be sure to become familiar with the U.S. Access Board material in Appendix B.

PDF and Posted Documents

Since this is a chapter about legal requirements, this is not the place to discuss the various methods for creating PDF documents and how to minimize accessibility problems in their creation (see Chapter 12 for advice on authoring accessible PDFs). Remember that it was the posting of City Council documents in PDF that brought an ADA complaint to the City of San José. Today, although Adobe has taken great strides to ensure that a PDF document has structure for assistive technology to access, there are still difficulties, especially in the conversion of complex documents to accessible HTML. Recognizing that there are benefits to having a print version of a document in PDF, the USDOJ recommends that if a document is posted in PDF, that an accessible version be posted as well:

> Agencies should also test the accessibility of their pdf documents using screen readers before posting them to their web sites. Adobe's accessibility site includes includes [sic] the latest recommendations for making pdf files accessible (http://access.adobe.com). Finally, agencies should be careful that non-text content be accompanied by text descriptions in pdf files. Agencies that choose to publish web-based documents in pdf should simultaneously publish the same documents in another more accessible format, such as HTML.

www.usdoj.gov/crt/508/web.htm

Therefore, a good practice is to not rely solely on the user to use plug-ins and PDF conversion tools to convert a PDF document to an accessible format. Setting aside the issue of accessibility for people with disabilities, imagine the frustration experienced by people using alternative Internet access devices such as cell phones and personal digital assistants who encounter documents that they cannot access. The USDOJ recommendation for web developers to do the conversion to ensure accessibility should be followed until we solve this problem. Moreover, it is essential that organizations review their processes for document creation and formatting as part of their overall strategy for addressing accessibility. At this time, it may very well be that the only way to ensure that a stand-alone PDF is accessible is to follow strict procedures to produce tagged PDFs, and then post them only after user testing.

Multimedia, Audio Broadcasts, and Captioning

Prior to Section 508, one web design technique to meet the ADA requirement for access to the President's State of the Union video clip was to post the text version of the speech. As a result, people who were deaf or hard-of-hearing could watch the video, not understanding what was said, and then read the static transcript.

Today, Section 508 requires that text equivalents be provided for sound and that these be synchronized with multimedia presentations (see §1194.22(a) and (b)). Excellent free software tools such as Media Access Generator (MAGpie) are available to the web developer to make multimedia accessible to persons with disabilities (see http://ncam.wgbh.org/webaccess/magpie/index.html).

Yet another challenge for web developers is the requirement that audio broadcasts be captioned so that the deaf and hard-of-hearing community can have equal and timely access to the content. According to the U.S. Access Board guidance found in Appendix C for rule §1194.22(a), it might appear that the guidance is correct when it says, "If the presentation is audio only, a text transcript would meet this requirement." This is in error.

In response to my request to the U.S. Access Board for clarification concerning this rule and live audio broadcasts that do not contain video, I received the following communication:

> If an audio file is on a web site, it is considered a non-text element and therefore needs a text alternative such as a transcript. If the audio instead of being a file, is an audio feed of a live event, even if it is only audio, the audio should be captioned as that is the only way to provide an equivalent alternative. A text transcript posted after the live session would mean that while the session was taking place, there would be no text equivalent and the web site would be in violation of 1194.22(a).
>
> E-mail dated January 22, 2002, from Doug Wakefield, U.S. Access Board

Remember that audio is a nontext element that is required to be just as accessible as images. Many governmental agencies have been broadcasting public meetings on the Internet without realizing that they had failed to provide access to people who are deaf or hard-of-hearing. Government employees or members of the public who are required to listen to audio broadcasts for their work or for appearance before legislative hearings may need real-time captioning. The web developer should be aware that real-time captioning services might need to be contracted to meet accessibility requirements. In some cases, governmental agencies may also need to arrange for the display of captioning on a screen in the public hearing room so that people present at the meeting, as well as those on the Internet, can have access to the content of the audio. At this time, real-time captioning services are required for this functionality, since the voice-input-to-text-output technology solution is not at a level where it can be applied to meet this type of need.

This should be a reminder that accessible web design is a cross-disability issue. Accessible web solutions based solely on one sensory mode (such as speech output for hearing) may be helpful for the blind and low-vision community who may use a screen reader to hear the web page. But this solution will not meet the needs of those who are deaf or hard-of-hearing. So remember that technologies such as interactive voice response may not be the complete solution to accessible web design, especially if any of the interactive voice response content and service is not available on the website.

And since we are on the topic, interactive multimedia has its own challenges for accessibility. For example, Macromedia (now Adobe) has made a commitment to make Flash more accessible, as well as to make the Flash Player accessible to assistive technology.

Links to Inaccessible Content Off-Site

Now that there are legal requirements for accessible web design in the U.S., it is my opinion that web developers should consider ways to indicate to the user when the content is not their own. This prevents your client from being drawn into an ADA or a Section 508 complaint process by the complainant. One method is to signal to the user at the link that they are leaving the website. However, if the website significantly relies on the content of an inaccessible website, the web developer should consider seeking legal counsel.

Summary

In summary, the ADA and Section 508 principles tell us that entities must adopt accessible web design policies and procedures for consistent implementation:

- A comprehensive policy must be implemented so that staff members do not continue to respond to access issues on an ad hoc basis.
- Web developers and managers must receive training, design tools, and resources.
- There must also be a process within all organizations to handle and monitor website access concerns and complaints.
- The community of people with disabilities must be consulted as we address challenges ahead.

One impact of Section 508 is that it seeks to prevent proprietary extensions of accessibility in technology. Although technology changes, civil rights do not. We have now defined the commons where everyone can work and play through effective communication. But as technology evolves, it will be important to continually assess the state of accessibility for our electronic and information technology. Without accessibility, we cannot have effective governance.

Section 508 places the U.S. on the threshold of building accessibility into our Internet and intranet environments. Amidst all the technical and legal maze of requirements, standards, and guidelines, it is important to keep one fact clear: accessible web design offers opportunities to provide services to the widest possible audience, to the greatest extent possible, in ways that have been inconceivable until now.

The economic, political, and ethical benefits far outweigh the cost of this effort. The cost of being inaccessible—missing the boat on the coming age of thin clients, failing to serve our most needful citizens and employees, and legal liability—can be incalculable.

This millennium offers unprecedented opportunities for efficient, effective governance. The Internet should be accessible to all. It is the right thing to do.

17 WORLDWIDE ACCESSIBILITY LAWS AND POLICIES

by Cynthia D. Waddell

The U.S. is not the only country that has an accessible web design law. This chapter takes a look at web accessibility efforts around the world and highlights those countries that have adopted and implemented an accessible web design policy or law.

Many countries have adopted the World Wide Web Consortium (W3C) Web Content Accessibility Guidelines (WCAG) 1.0 or a variation, along with rules particular to that jurisdiction. Some countries, such as Australia and Denmark, have also adopted the U.S. Section 508 web requirements. Many quality marks or labels certifying accessibility are also covered in this chapter, including a project of the European Union (EU) Web Accessibility Benchmarking (WAB) Cluster to recommend a uniform quality mark for all countries implementing certain accessible web design criteria in the EU.

If you are a web developer, manager, information technology (IT) professional, IT lawyer, or decision maker, you should be aware of the legal requirements affecting websites. Consult this chapter if you are entering into a contract to provide web development services within any of these countries. Although legal sanctions are discussed whenever provided under the law—such as civil and even criminal penalties for not designing accessibly—this chapter should not be considered legal advice. Specific legal questions can best be answered by seeking the advice of legal counsel.

As of the writing of this chapter, 25 countries or jurisdictions have web design laws and policies, including Australia, Austria, Belgium, Brazil, Canada, Denmark, European Union, Finland, France, Germany, Hong Kong, Ireland, Italy, Japan, Korea, Luxembourg, The Netherlands, New Zealand, Norway, Portugal, Singapore, Spain, Sweden, Thailand, and the UK. If your country does not have an accessible web law or policy, perhaps you might use this chapter as leverage to encourage legislation (a suggestion from a web designer in Asia).

Australia

After reading about the Maguire v. Sydney Organising Committee for the Olympic Games web accessibility case in Chapter 2, it should not be a surprise to hear that the Internet Industry Association (IIA, Australia's national Internet industry organization) issued a press release with the headline, "IIA Warns SOGOC: Decision Puts Business on Notice" (see www.independentliving.org/docs5/sydney-olympics-blind-accessibility-decision-press-release.html).

The Disability Discrimination Act

As you learned in Chapter 2, the Australia Disability Discrimination Act (DDA) of 1992 requires that all online information and services be accessible (see Section 24 of this Act at www.austlii.edu.au/au/legis/cth/consol_act/dda1992264/). According to the Human Rights and Equal Opportunity Commission (HREOC), the body charged with ensuring the accessibility of website content under the DDA, the DDA applies to any individual or organization developing a web page in Australia or placing or maintaining a web page on an Australian server. More specifically, the HREOC states

This includes pages developed or maintained for purposes relating to employment; education; provision of services including professional services, banking, insurance or financial services, entertainment or recreation, telecommunications services, public transport services, or government services; sale or rental of real estate; sport; activities of voluntary associations; or administration of Commonwealth laws or programs.

World Wide Web Access: Disability Discrimination Act Advisory Notes,
www.hreoc.gov.au/disability_rights/standards/www_3/www_3.html

Therefore, all Australian web developers should be familiar with the HREOC document titled *World Wide Access: Disability Discrimination Act Advisory Notes* (www.hreoc.gov.au/ disability_rights/standards/www_3/www_3.html). Although this document does not have direct legal force, the Advisory Notes indicate that agencies can consider them when dealing with inaccessible website complaints. HREOC also commented that implementing the Advisory Notes "make[s] it far less likely that an individual or organization would be subject to complaints about the accessibility of their web page."

Of interest are the following Advisory Notes comments on the Portable Document Format (PDF):

The Portable Document Format (PDF) file system developed by Adobe has become widely used for making documents available on web pages. Despite considerable work done by Adobe, PDF remains a relatively inaccessible format to people who are blind or vision-impaired. Software exists to provide some access to the text of some PDF documents, but for a PDF document to be accessible to this software, it must be prepared in accordance with the guidelines that Adobe has developed. Even when these guidelines are followed, the resulting document will only be accessible to those people who have the required software and the skills to use it. The Commission's view is that organisations who distribute content only in PDF format, and who do not also make this content available in another format such as RTF, HTML, or plain text, are liable for complaints under the DDA. Where an alternative file format is provided, care should be taken to ensure that it is the same version of the content as the PDF version, and that it is downloadable by the user as a single document, just as the PDF version is downloaded as a single file.

The Advisory Notes also contain a warning on the use of Macromedia Flash in Section 2.4, "Access to New and Emerging Technologies":

[W]ork is currently underway to make Macromedia's Flash technology accessible to people who use screen-reading software. While some positive progress has been made, it will be a considerable time before most users will benefit, and even then, Flash may be accessible only in certain specific circumstances. It is certainly wrong for web designers to assume that improvements in the accessibility of a technology mean that it can be used indiscriminately without regard for the principles of accessible web design.

Government Website Standards

On June 30, 2000, the Online Council issued a press release announcing the adoption of the W3C WCAG as the minimum website access standards by all Australian governments (see www.dcita.gov.au/Article/0,,0_4-2_4008-4_15092,00.html).

The *Guide to Minimum Website Standards* was designed to assist Australian Government departments and agencies to implement the Government's minimum website standards. Originally published in 2000, the guide was updated in April 2003 and is found at www.agimo.gov.au/practice/mws.

For additional resources on Australian website policies for the States of Australian Capital Territory, New South Wales, Northern Territory, Queensland, South Australia, Tasmania, Victoria, and Western Australia, see the W3C Web Accessibility Initiative (WAI) Policies Page at www.w3.org/WAI/Policy/AU-States.html.

Banking and AIMIA Websites

If you are developing a website for a bank, be sure to follow the *Australian Bankers' Association Industry Standard*, which, was developed with the cooperation of the HREOC. The standard is available at www.bankers.asn.au/ArticleDocuments/Web%20Standard.htm. You will find this standard includes W3C WCAG technical specifications in addition to U.S. Section 508 requirements.

If you are developing a website for a member of the Australian Interactive Multimedia Industry Association (AIMIA), you need to know that the IIA and the AIMIA have jointly developed an *Accessibility Web Action Plan* (see www.iia.net.au/index.php?option= com_content&task=view&id=91&Itemid=35). This is the industry's first plan for encouraging web accessibility awareness and helping members to develop and maintain accessible websites. As with other action plans developed under the DDA, this plan has no copyright or commercial confidentiality restrictions. However, adoption or attribution to IIA/AIMIA requires permission from the Taskforce Chair. The plan includes key performance indicators to ensure that it is regularly evaluated and effective.

Austria

Web accessibility legislation under the E-Government Act was voted by the Austrian Parliament in February 2004 and entered into force on March 1, 2004. The Act serves as the legal basis for the instruments used to provide a system of e-government and for closer cooperation among all authorities providing e-government services. According to the November 26, 2004, official report, titled *The Information Society in Austria*:

> Programmes for challenged persons: Websites of public authorities must be made accessible to everybody regardless of any physical or technical obstacles. Barrierfree websites can be set up in accordance with the so-called "Web Accessibility Initiative" (WAI)-guidelines. By 1 January 2008 all websites of public authorities must be set up to comply with the needs of challenged persons.

For the English text of the E-Government Act addressing accessible websites, take a look at Part I: Paragraph 3 at http://europa.eu.int/idabc/servlets/Doc?id=21448. For the German version of the E-Government Act, see www.parlament.gv.at/pls/portal/docs/page/PG/DE/XXII/BNR/BNR_00149/fname_014980.pdf.

Belgium

Although Belgium has no federal legislation that specifically requires accessible websites, the obligation to develop accessible websites is being interpreted as a requirement based on the Anti-Discrimination law of 2003. The legislation was voted on February 25, 2003, and published in the *Official Journal* on March 17, 2003.

According to the EU Information Society portal on policies (http://europa.eu.int/information_society/policy/accessibility/web/wa_belgium/index_en.htm), one of the main clauses of the Anti-Discrimination law is that "[a]ny lack of reasonable adjustments for people with disabilities will be considered as a form of discrimination." The Dutch-adapted version of W3C WCAG is posted at the portal site.

The BlindSurfer Project

Since 2000, the Belgium BlindSurfer Project has received the support of public entities and has established an accessibility label that enables a website visitor with visual disabilities to know that the website has met an adapted version of W3C WCAG requirements. The label is now distributed by two Belgian organizations: Blindenzorg Licht en Liefde and Oeuvre Nationale des Aveugles. According to Marc Walraven (Project Manager of ASCii's Web Accessibility and Usability Department), the BlindSurfer label has been proposed as the official quality mark for accessible websites. BlindSurfer is a member of the EuroAccessibility Consortium, which is committed to work with the Guidelines and Techniques developed by the WAI. See the January 2005 presentation entitled "E-Accessibility Initiatives Undertaken in Belgium and on the Demand of European Institutions in the Field of E-Accessibility" at www.braillenet.org/colloques/policies/walraven_paper.html.

Here is the BlindSurfer accessibility screening process:

A candidate Website sends its screening application to the BlindSurfer evaluation team via a special screening application form. The site URL is then provided to at least two experts, a blind person and a person with good vision who will screen the site. The site is then examined on the basis of a thirteen-point checklist in order to determine if it meets the accessibility conditions. This list is based on the Web Content Accessibility Guidelines (WCAG) published by the Web Accessibility Initiative (WAI) that is part of the World Wide Web Consortium (W3C). These directives are acknowledged as a world standard and have been accepted by many public authorities. The evaluation results are then collected and a screening protocol is written. This protocol contains, if necessary, a certain number of explanatory comments in order to facilitate finding solutions for possible remaining accessibility problems. If the screening is positive, the site owner is awarded the BlindSurfer label. If the site is not perfectly accessible, the BlindSurfer team is ready to provide any available information and suggestions for realizing the needed adaptation works. Websites that receive the BlindSurfer label are asked to respect the usage conditions of the label of which we remind the most important ones:

- in principle, the label must be located on the site homepage
- the label must be present with its indissociable alt-tag complement which contains the "BlindSurfer" text
- the label must include a hyperlink towards our BlindSurfer site
- the label may not be modified

As the label owner, BlindSurfer reserves itself the right to withdraw the label from a site that, owing to a transformation, would not meet the accessibility directives any more. This is why checks are performed from time to time.

"The BlindSurfer accessibility screening process,"
www.blindsurfer.be/bsindexE.htm.

Figure 17-1 shows the BlindSurfer label.

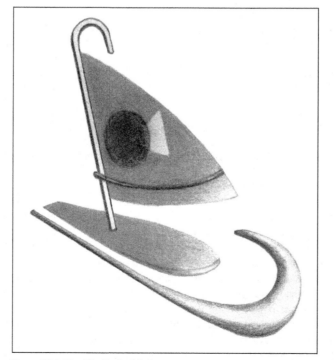

Figure 17-1. The BlindSurfer label

Flanders Plan for Accessible Websites

In a June 11, 2004, plan called TOEWEB (an abbreviation of *Toegankelijke Websites*, which means *Accessible Websites*), the Flemish Government decided that websites and related online services of its institutions—including Flemish Parliament, the Flemish Government, the Ministry of the Flemish community, and the Flemish public institutions—should be made accessible. Target dates were for the Internet websites to be accessible by the end of 2007 and intranet websites by 2010.

According to the plan, websites and any related online services should be made accessible to people with disabilities and the elderly within a reasonable time frame and within the available budgets. It anticipated that the first results would be visible before June 30, 2005, for websites that could easily be made accessible. Priority is given to websites and services related to employment, welfare, and mobility, and those explicitly addressing people with disabilities and the elderly.

Before the end of 2005, each webmaster was to provide a clear Action Plan for the period 2006–2010 to the Flemish Parliament. These Action Plans were to include clear indications on timing, budgetary impact, and a proposal for long-term quality assurance measures. See www2.vlaanderen.be/ned/sites/toegankelijkweb/ (in Dutch) for more information.

Walloon Government

In June 2001, the Walloon Government set up and adopted the *Wall-On-Line Project* (http://egov.wallonie.be/accessibilite/index.htm, in French) to establish a multiple-purpose and accessible online portal for all local services. Oeuvre Nationale des Aveugles is responsible for the technical aspects, and a list of priority sites was established and made available online in 2004. These sites were expected to be made accessible by the end of 2005.

According to Marc Walraven, on February 20, 2003, the Walloon Region in Belgium decided to actively start addressing the problems of the region's inaccessible websites. On April 10, 2003, measures were adopted to improve the accessibility of the majority of public websites.

Brazil

In Brazil, the Law on Accessibility (L. 10.098) enacted in 2000 requires accessibility in communication and barrier removal and expressly guarantees the right of persons with disabilities to information and communication. In 2004, Decree 5.296 provided more detailed provisions for implementation and requires all governmental Internet websites to be accessible to persons with disabilities (see https://www.planalto.gov.br/ccivil/_ato2004-2006/2004/decreto/d5296.htm for the Portuguese version). This decree provides that all governmental websites—local, state, and federal—are to be accessible within 12 months and that a symbol indicating Internet accessibility will be posted on those sites that are accessible to people with disabilities. As of the writing of this chapter, I was not able to verify the extent of compliance with this decree. (Many thanks to Mary Barros-Bailey for the English translation.)

According to the *International Disability Rights Monitor Project Americans 2004 Report* (www.cirnetwork.org/idrm/index.cfm), the Brazilian Technical Standards Association (ABNT) has created a working team for the development of a technical standard on accessibility to Internet content. However, technical standards were not available at the time this chapter was written.

Canada

In May 2000, the government of Canada adopted a policy for all federal government organizations that requires conformance to W3C WCAG Priority 1 and 2 Checkpoints. In September 2005, the *Common Look and Feel Standards and Guidelines for the Internet* (CLFI) was updated (see www.tbs-sct.gc.ca/clf-nsi/pc-cp_e.asp). According to the Secretary of the Treasury Board, it enables institutions to be confident that Canadians can use websites and that website design is in "full accord with Government of Canada legislation and policies." English and French versions of the CLFI are available at www.tbs-sct.gc.ca/clf-nsi/default.asp.

Instead of creating policy, the Province of Ontario moved forward to adopt legislation in 2005 that is broad in scope and includes the requirement that both public institutions and private businesses provide accessible websites. Effective June 14, 2005, the *Accessibility for Ontarians with Disabilities Act* (AODA) established the Accessibility Standards Advisory Council for developing proposed standards that must be implemented within five years. This rule-making process requires the Council to submit developed standards to the Minister, who will make the standards public for receiving comments. After considering the public comments, the Council may make any changes and will then provide the Minister with the proposed accessibility standard. The Minister will decide within 90 days whether or not to recommend the proposed standards for adoption by regulation. Once the standard has been adopted as a regulation, all affected persons and organizations will be required to comply within the timelines set out in the standard. In addition, organizations will be required to file accessibility reports to confirm compliance. Spot audits will verify the reports, and there are tough penalties for noncompliance. Read about the AODA at www.e-laws.gov.on.ca/DBLaws/Statutes/English/05a11_e.htm.

Jutta Treviranus, expert witness for the Maguire v. Sydney Organising Committee for the Olympic Games case, was appointed to the Advisory Council on December 13, 2005. According to an e-mail communication I received from Ms. Treviranus, she is serving on the Information, Communications and Technology standards committee and will be covering web accessibility standards (WCAG, ATAG, and UAAG). At the time this chapter was written, the committee had not made an accessible web design standard recommendation. You can follow the progress of this effort at the web page of the Accessibility Directorate of Ontario at www.mcss.gov.on.ca/accessibility/index.html.

Denmark

Although there is no national law in Denmark requiring web accessibility, there are guidelines about accessibility for government agencies. The Interoperability Framework includes accessible web design standards and serves as a guideline for public agencies as they develop information technology plans and projects. It contains descriptions and recommendations of selected standards, technologies, and protocols for implementation of e-government in Denmark. Both W3C WCAG and the U.S. Electronic and Information Technology Accessibility Standards (Section 508) are incorporated into the guideline.

Seeking to ensure that the knowledge society will be more accessible to all, the National IT and Telecom Agency has established the Competence Center IT for All (KIA). KIA was established according to the action plan *Disability No Obstacle*, published by the Minister for Science Technology and Innovation in January 2003.

KIA participates in the eAccessibility expert group, which is providing advice to the eEurope Advisory Group in the area of eInclusion as part of the eEurope 2005 Action Plan. This Action Plan seeks to ensure a true and universal information society involving all social groups. For more information, follow the English link at www.oio.dk/.

KIA has launched the Public Procurement Toolkit in order to make it easy for public authorities to include accessibility requirements in public procurement, as well as in the development and purchase of digital solutions. A web-based tool, the Public Procurement Toolkit contains a large database of functional accessibility requirements. It offers concrete specifications on how to make accessible solutions, guidance on why the authorities must provide accessible solutions, and a review of the challenges caused by inaccessible solutions. Four guidelines form the core of the Toolkit:

- An accessible software solution (this includes software applications and operating systems)
- An accessible website (this includes web-based information and web applications)
- An accessible hardware solution
- An accessible integrated hardware solution (which is typically stand-alone hardware with integrated software)

For each guideline, two documents provide technical specifications and guidance. The technical document supporting an accessible website contains a list of the technical specifications needed to design accessibly. The specifications include the U.S. Section 508 and W3C WCAG. The guidance document provides information on the benefits of accessible solutions and the obstacles that inaccessible websites cause. This document explains the levels in the specifications and guidance on the problems each specification solves. It is here that users of the Toolkit can read why they should include a specification and what would be the effect if it is not included.

The Toolkit is designed for the public procurement process with the specifications identified so they can be easily placed in the Calls for Tender or Request for Proposals. For more information see www.oio.dk/it_for_alle/udbudsvaerktoejskassen and www.braillenet.org/colloques/policies/documents/Shermer.doc.

European Union

As early as 1994, the EU has recognized the importance of web accessibility through various action projects.

eEurope and i2010 Initiatives

In December 1999, the *eEurope—an Information Society for All* initiative was launched by the European Commission to bring the benefits of the Information Society to all Europeans.

In June 2000, the Feira European Council adopted the *eEurope Action Plan 2002*, which included steps to address access to the Web for people with disabilities.

The September 2001 communication from the Commission to the Council, The European Parliament, The Economic and Social Committee, and The Committee of Regions, "eEurope 2002: Accessibility of Public Web Sites and their Content," emphasized that

> Public sector web sites and their content in Member States and in the European institutions must be designed to be accessible to ensure that citizens with disabilities can access information and take full advantage of the potential for e-government.
>
> http://europa.eu.int/eur-lex/en/com/cnc/2001/com2001_0529en01.pdf, page 7

On February 27, 2002, a press release announced that the European Economic and Social Committee (ESC) had welcomed the Commission's communication on the accessibility of public websites and their content, as referenced in the preceding paragraph. According to the press release,

> The ESC also took the opportunity to rebut some misunderstandings relating to the time and cost involved in making public web sites compatible with the needs of disabled and elderly people. 'In many Member States the objection has been raised that the process of implementation of the WAI (web accessibility initiative) guidelines will constitute an excessive financial engagement. This assumption is simply wrong, because implementing the accessibility guidelines from the first is only a little more expensive than not implementing them,' says the opinion, which suggests that national funding be earmarked for implementation of the communication's provisions.

Also according to the press release, the ESC indicated that work was needed to make the new version of their website, Europa II, accessible in time for the 2003 European Year of Disabled People. For the entire report on the accessibility of websites, see Opinion CES-189(2002) published on February 20, 2002, at http://europa.eu.int/information_society/policy/accessibility/web/wai_2002/a_documents/ces_opinion_web_wai_2002.html.

On June 13, 2002, the European Parliament adopted a resolution to support the importance of web accessibility in EU institutions and Member States. The resolution states that the W3C WCAG 1.0 (Priority 1 and 2 levels) and future versions should be implemented on public websites. In addition, it called for all EU Institutions and Member States to also comply with the W3C Authoring Tools Accessibility Guidelines by the year 2003. See EP (2002) 0325 by visiting www.europarl.eu.int/ and following the links English ➤ Parliament ➤ Access to Documents ➤ Register of Documents ➤ Search, and entering "eEurope 2002 Accessibility."

17

The eEurope 2005 Action Plan continues to monitor the progress of accessibility for the EU public sector websites. See http://europa.eu.int/information_society/policy/accessibility/web/index_en.htm for more information.

Promoting an inclusive society is one of the primary policies of the EU effort, as seen in the June 1, 2005, European Commission launch of *i2010: European Information Society 2010*. The objective of i2010 is to boost the digital economy by fostering growth and jobs and to promote an inclusive society. See http://europa.eu.int/information_society/eeurope/i2010/inclusion/index_en.htm for more information.

On September 15, 2005, the European Commission issued an eAccessibility Communication calling for more coordinated action to ensure the accessibility of information and communication technologies accessible to all citizens. According to the press release,

> While continuing to support ongoing measures such as standardisation, Design for All (DFA), Web accessibility and Research & Technology Development, the Commission proposes the use of three policy levers available to Member States:
>
> to improve the consistency of accessibility requirements in public procurement contracts in the ICT domain,
>
> to explore the possible benefits of certification schemes for accessible products and services.
>
> to make better use of the "e-Accessibility potential" of existing legislation
>
> http://europa.eu.int/information_society/policy/accessibility/com_ea_2005/index_en.htm.

As for the Europa server, the European Commission has adopted level A (Priority 1) of the W3C WCAG 1.0 for conforming new and updated websites. The Europa web accessibility policy web page states that although some top-level Europa sites already meet level A, the European Commission is continuing to move forward to achieve conforming for the existing pages. For the pages that conform to WCAG 1.0, the WAI conformance logo is being utilized. See http://europa.eu.int/geninfo/accessibility_policy_en.htm for more information.

EU Web Accessibility Benchmarking Cluster

The Web Accessibility Benchmarking (WAB) Cluster is a cluster of European projects to develop a harmonized European methodology for evaluation and benchmarking of websites. More than 20 partners are working together on an assessment methodology based on W3C WAI that will support the expected migration from WCAG 1.0 to WCAG 2.0. The first draft of the *Unified Web Evaluation Methodology* (UWEMO.5) is online at www.wabcluster.org/uwem05/.

Other WAB Cluster projects include the development of a quality mark or website label for accessibility, as well as the development of test suites for evaluation tools and integration of testing modules in content management systems. For more information, see www.wabcluster.org/.

Finland

The W3C WCAG 1.0 has been adopted as part of the Finnish Government Public Administration Recommendations in the *JHS 129 Guidelines for Designing Web Services in the Public Administration*, Ministry of the Interior, December 2000. According to the JHS English abstract, the recommendation provides public authorities with guidance on how to plan, implement, and purchase online services. It describes the process for producing online services and implementing a user interface designed especially for end users that addresses usability and accessibility. The recommendation also includes application guidelines for online services with regard to the use of metadata as described in the JHS 143 recommendation. For more information, see www.jhs-suositukset.fi/ (follow the In English ➤ Search: links and enter "JHS recommendation abstracts").

As early as 1993, the *Nordic Guidelines for Computer Accessibility* provided guidance on the design of accessible information and communication technologies, including websites. It was updated in 1998 by the Nordic Cooperation on Disability, an organization under the Nordic Council of Ministers composed of the governments of Denmark, Finland, Iceland, Norway, and Sweden. See http://trace.wisc.edu/docs/nordic_guidelines/nordic_guidelines.htm for more information.

France

On February 11, 2005, French legislation was published requiring all web services of the public sector to conform to the international guidelines for web accessibility. W3C WCAG is indirectly referenced in Law n° 2005-102, article 47, providing for "equal rights and opportunities, participation and citizenship of people with disabilities." Web services of the public sector have a deadline of three years to become accessible. Sanctions for noncompliance will be defined in the Code of Practice of the law.

According to the EU Information Society report on web accessibility in France, the Ministry of People with Disabilities drafted the law, and guidelines for implementation were prepared by the e-Administration ADAE (Agence pour le Développement de l'Administration Electronique, www.adae.gouv.fr/spip/index.php3). The ADAE web accessibility guidelines are based on the AccessiWeb criteria developed by the BrailleNet Association (see www.braillenet.org/) and include usability criteria based on the work of Jacob Nielsen. The Code of Practice of the law will define the web accessibility rules as set forth in the ADAE guide.

Although the BrailleNet Association has developed the AccessiWeb label (bronze, silver, or gold), shown in Figure 17-2, and provides evaluation and certification of websites, as of the writing of this chapter, public websites are not legally required to submit to the BrailleNet Association AccessiWeb evaluation. See the report at http://europa.eu.int/information_society/policy/accessibility/web/wa_france/index_en.htm.

Figure 17-2. The AccessiWeb label

Previously, the Prime Minister published standards for accessibility of public websites on October 12, 1999. These administrative guidelines (circulaire) were known as the *Mission pour les Technologies de l'Information et de la Communication* (MTIC). This action sought to promote documentation and tools for public sector webmasters, and these were available on MTIC's website formerly at www.atica.pm.gouv.fr/interop/accessibilite/index.shtml (no longer available):

- The *circulaire* on Internet sites of public services and administrations
- The recommendation of the W3C on the Guidelines
- The white paper of BrailleNet entitled "Towards a More Accessible Web"
- The free web browser Braillesurf
- Tools to verify the accessibility of websites
- The existing labels
- The recommendations of the Council of Europe

Germany

On April 27, 2002, the German legislature passed the *Act on Equal Opportunities for Disabled Persons*. Subsequently, at the federal level, the *Ordinance on Barrier-Free Information Technology* was established July 24, 2002. This ordinance, referred to as BITV, is found at www.einfach-fuer-alle.de/artikel/bitv_english/.

According to the EU Information Society report on web accessibility in Germany (http://europa.eu.int/information_society/policy/accessibility/web/wa_germany/index_en.htm), the BITV is based on W3C WCAG 1.0 with the following changes:

WCAG Priorities A and AA are integrated into Priority I of the German BITV;

WCAG Priority AAA corresponds to Priority II of the German BITV; and

Checkpoint 2.2 of WCAG 1.0 which already had 2 priorities assigned has now been divided into checkpoints 2.2 (color contrast in images) and 2.3 (added- color contrast for text) of the German BITV

In addition, the report states that the federal BITV

Applies to All Federal Administration authority websites and pages including their publicly accessible websites and pages and IT based graphic user interfaces that are publicly accessible;

Applies to All private web-pages of private companies covered under the BITV;

Directs that private companies have the obligation to begin negotiations with registered organizations for people with disabilities to produce "targeted agreements" for implementing accessible web; and

Provides that only the obligation for negotiation is mandatory whether or not an agreement is reached.

In his presentation "E-Accessibility in Germany: Act and Ordinances, Outcome of Benchmarking and Activities," dated January 31, 2005, Rainer Wallbruch points out that the BITV annex contains requirements and checkpoints that incorporate WCAG 1.0 as much as possible. He points out that "every public internet page has to reach WAI conformance level AA and in addition to this, every public central navigation page should reach WAI conformance level AAA" (see www.braillenet.org/colloques/policies/wallbruch_paper.html).

As for sanctions, although no precedent has been set, the BITV gives registered organizations for people with disabilities the right to take legal actions on behalf of people with disabilities who experience discrimination by federal information technology that is not compliant.

The EU Information Society report also discusses web accessibility efforts at the State level. References to WCAG for web accessibility are not uniform because some States adopt the federal BITV and others adopt different subsets and definitions. For a review of the various State efforts on accessible web, see the link identified in the report at www.wob11.de/gesetze/landesgleichstellungsgesetz.html (German only).

Currently, various organizations and private companies provide a range of quality labels based on BITV. The German standardization authority, DIN-CERTCO, is working on developing a national label, as well as several national certification centers. See www.din-certco.de/en/index.php for more information.

Hong Kong

The Hong Kong government has established internal web accessibility guidelines for both Internet and intranet web pages, entitled *Guidelines on Dissemination of Information through Government Homepages* (www.info.gov.hk/digital21/eng/knowledge/guide/ch1.htm). The guidelines are based on the W3C WCAG 1.0 as well as input from the industry and organizations such as the Hong Kong Blind Union.

As early as 1999, the Hong Kong government began to revise all government websites according to web accessibility guidelines. This revision was accomplished in early 2003 according to the *E-Government Roadmap Report* (www.info.gov.hk/digital21/e-gov/eng/roadmap/a.htm).

The Digital 21 Strategy website (www.info.gov.hk/digital21/eng/knowledge/access_main.html) includes tips on accessibility as well as web accessibility education and training in Hong Kong since 2001.

For further information, see the WebAim collection of links posted at www.webaim.org/coordination/law/hongkong.

Ireland

According to the National Disability Authority (NDA), Irish public policy includes requirements for government department websites to conform to Priority Levels 1 and 2 of the W3C WCAG 1.0 (see www.accessit.nda.ie/policy_and_legislation.html).

On October 5, 2005, the President of Ireland, Mary McAleese, officially launched the Excellence through Accessibility Award program. This program, developed by the NDA in partnership with the Department of Justice, Equality and Law Reform, acknowledges departments and agencies that have made their services more accessible. Through this award, NDA seeks to support the achievement of maximum accessibility of all public services for people with disabilities in Ireland. For more information, see www.nda.ie/cntmgmtnew.nsf/accessibilityHomePage?OpenPage.

In June 2002, the NDA issued the *Irish National Disability Authority IT Accessibility Guidelines* for web, telecommunications, public access terminals, and application software. The guidelines for web accessibility adopt W3C WCAG 1.0 (see www.accessit.nda.ie/guidelineindex_1.html).

In addition, recent legislation in Disability Act 2005 (www.oireachtas.ie/documents/bills28/acts/2005/a1405.pdf) requires access to information and provides for a complaint-filing process effective December 31, 2005. Section 28 of the legislation states in part

> Where a public body communicates in electronic form with one or more persons, the head of the body shall ensure, that as far as practicable, that the contents of the communication are accessible to persons with a visual impairment to whom adaptive technology is available.

Companies who have received directly or indirectly loans or funding from the government also fall under the definition of "public body."

The NDA is charged with the development of codes for practice for Disability Act 2005, and the October 4, 2005, Code of Practice draft points to the accessible web requirements of the NDA IT Accessibility Guidelines as well as Level AA conformance with the W3C WCAG 1.0. It is interesting that in a footnote within the draft Code of Practice, the NDA noted that the Department of the Taoiseach's "New Connections—A Strategy to realize the potential of the Information Society" stated that "all public websites are required to be WAI (level 2) compliant by end 2001" (see www.nda.ie/ and follow the links Standards ➤ Code of Practice ➤ Draft Code of Practice on Accessibility of Public Services and Information provided by Public Bodies).

Italy

This summary of the current state of accessible web laws and policies in Italy is based on the unofficial English translation provided by the Information Systems Accessibility Office at CNIPA (National Organism for ICT in the Public Administration) accessed in January 2006 at www.pubbliaccesso.gov.it/english/index.htm. Refer to this site for English links to the law and regulations discussed here. (Many thanks to Dr. Patrizia Bertini, Senior E-Accessibility Advisor and Researcher of the European Internet Accessibility Observatory, for her assistance.)

On January 9, 2004, national legislation was enacted by Law 4, setting in motion provisions to support access to information technologies for people with disabilities and the accessible design of public websites. The law applies to public administrations, private firms that are licensees of public services, regional municipal companies, information and communication technologies (ICT) services contractors, public assistance and rehabilitation agencies, and transport and telecommunication companies where the State has a prevalent interest. Article 11 of Law 4 directed that the following steps be established through a decree by the Minister for Innovation and Technologies:

> Guidelines for the different accessibility levels and technical requirements; and

> Technical methodologies for verifying the accessibility of Web sites as well as assisted evaluation programs that can be used for this purpose.

Subsequently, the Decree of the President of the Republic, March 1, 2005, No. 75, provided the implementation regulations, and the Ministerial Decree of July 8, 2005, provided the technical methodologies and evaluation programs that became effective August 2005. The Ministerial Decree of July 8, 2005, contains the following:

- The Decree
- Annex A: Technical assessment and technical accessibility requirements of Internet technology-based applications
- Annex B: Methodology and criteria for the subjective accessibility assessment of Internet technology-based applications
- Annex C: Technical accessibility requirements of desktop and laptop personal computers
- Annex D: Technical accessibility for operating system, applications and retail products
- Annex E: Accessibility logo for Internet technology-based websites and applications (see the extract at the end of this section)
- Annex F: Maximum amounts private parties must pay for accessibility evaluation of their website and the amount owed should an inspection determine that the level of accessibility is not as indicated by the logo used

The scope of the accessibility effort in Law 4 is broad, and it also provides a benchmark for public administrations in the following areas:

- Vendor bidders for the provision of IT goods and services shall be granted preferential status if they meet the accessibility requirements and their offer is equivalent in all other conditions per Article 4(1).
- Contracts for the creation and modification of websites must meet these accessibility requirements or be considered void per Article 4(2).
- Contract renewals, amendments, or novations of any contract already in force on the date of the decree will be voided if the accessibility requirements are not met per Article 4(2).
- Government public grant awards for the purchase of IT goods and services used by workers with disabilities or the public, including the installation of telework stations, must comply with the accessibility requirements per Article 4(3).

The *Digital Administration Code* was adopted as a Legislative Decree on March 7, 2005, and provides the legal framework for the development of e-government and the removal of "virtual barriers." It came into force on January 1, 2006, and requires all government websites to be accessible within two years. The law is available in Italian at www.padigitale.it/home/testodecreto.html.

The Italian technical requirements take into account the following sources:

- W3C WAI WCAG 1.0
- U.S. Section 508 - 36 CFR Part 1194.22 for the Web

- International Organization for Standardization technical specifications
- Experience gained by the Italian government through the implementation of the Authority for Information Technology in Government, which is now the Centre for Information Technology in Government (CNIPA) concerning the gov.it domain (www.pubbliaccesso.gov.it/normative/circolare_aipa_20010906.htm, in Italian)

According to Article 9 of Law 4, failure to comply with the provisions of the law implies both executive responsibility and disciplinary action, and can also include possible criminal prosecution and civil liability.

The scheme for certifying website accessibility includes both a technical evaluation performed by experts using a variety of techniques and a subjective evaluation conducted by end users, including users with disabilities. The evaluation is to be carried out independently of the government by assessors that will register on a list held by the CNIPA for private sector operators. Evaluators are expected to be announced in the coming months. Should the evaluation validate accessibility, then the private sector operators can request the accessibility logo for their website from the Department of Innovation and Technologies. The CNIPA will verify whether websites and services continue to meet accessibility requirements.

Regarding the accessibility logo, the following is an extract of Annex E of the *Italian Ministerial Decree of July 8, 2005* (www.pubbliaccesso.gov.it/normative/DM080705-E-en.htm):

Annex E
Accessibility logo for Internet technology-based web sites and applications

1. Logo without asterisks

This consists of the sienna-coloured outline of a personal computer, together with three stylised human forms which, from the left, are sky-blue, blue and red respectively, coming out of the screen with open raised [arms]. This logo corresponds to level one accessibility, associated with conformity with the requirements laid down for the technical assessment.

2. Logo with asterisks

This consists of the same design described above, with the addition of asterisks. This guarantees conformity with the requirements of the technical assessment and the next level of quality achieved by the site, following a positive outcome of the subjective assessment, in accordance with the provisions of Annex B(1). This level of quality is indicated by one, two or three asterisks in the part of the logo showing the keyboard of the personal computer. In particular:

a) Logo with one asterisk in the part showing the keyboard:

corresponds to the level of accessibility certifying that the technical assessment has been passed and that, on conclusion of the subjective assessment, an average overall value greater than 2 and less than 3 has been attributed.

b) Logo with two asterisks in the part showing the keyboard:

corresponds to the level of accessibility certifying that the technical assessment has been passed and that, on conclusion of the subjective assessment, an average overall value greater than or equal to 3 and less than 4 has been attributed.

c) Logo with three asterisks in the part showing the keyboard:

corresponds to the level of accessibility certifying that the technical assessment has been passed and that, on conclusion of the subjective assessment, an average overall value greater than or equal to 4 has been attributed.

Japan

Japan is a leader in seeking international standardization in the accessibility of technology. In 1998, in response to a proposal from Japan, the Committee on Consumer policy of the International Organization for Standardization (ISO) at its general meeting adopted a resolution to set up a task force. The ISO task force was charged with developing a policy statement on general principles and guidelines for the design of products and the environment to address the needs of older persons and persons with disabilities. The working group, led by Japanese members, actively carried out the task and finalized the general principles in early 2002 as the ISO/IEC Guide 71—*Guidelines for standards developers to address the needs of older persons and persons with disabilities.*

> *I would like to especially thank Kaoruko M. Nakano, Vice President and Secretary of Pacific, Prologue Corporation of San Jose, California, and Masaya Ando of Allied Brains, Inc., Tokyo, Japan, for providing source documentation and various translations for this section on the accessible web effort in Japan.*

JIS X 8341-3 Standard

In June 2004, the Japanese Standards Association (JSA) established JIS X 8341-3 as an official Japanese industrial standard for web content information accessibility. The standard is based on ISO/IEC Guide 71 (JIS Z 8071)—*Guidelines for standards developers to address the needs of older persons and persons with disabilities.* In fiscal year 2003, the working group that developed JIS X 8341-3 was dissolved, and a new working group, Web Accessibility International Standards Research Working Group, was launched in fiscal year 2004. The objectives of the new working group are international standard harmonization with W3C WAI WCAG and other guidelines around the world and to promote JIS X 8341-3 in Japan.

According to a 2005 CSUN presentation entitled "Japanese Industrial Standard of Web Content Accessibility Guidelines and International Standard Harmonization" (which I attended), JIS X 8341-3 was developed by taking into consideration W3C WCAG 1.0 and specific Japanese issues. Presenters Takayuki Watanabe, Tatsuo Seki, and Hazime Yamada explained that WCAG 1.0 was not directly adopted because WCAG 1.0 was known to have some drawbacks and that W3C WAI was working on WCAG 2.0. For further information about the concerns discussed at this presentation, see `www.csun.edu/cod/conf/2005/proceedings/2162.htm`. For a comparison between JIS X 8341-3 and the WCAG, see the CSUN 2004 presentation at `www.comm.twcu.ac.jp/~nabe/data/JIS-WAI`. The JIS Web Content Guideline can be purchased online at the JSA web store at `www.webstore.jsa.or.jp`.

Accessible web design efforts appear to have had a positive impact on businesses in Japan. For example, since 2002, Fujitsu Limited has been seeking to improve web accessibility and should be commended for including accessibility as part of brand development. According to Mr. Kosuke Takahashi, Manager, Corporate Brand Office, Fujitsu Limited,

> Fujitsu has considered that one of the vital roles of an information technology (IT) company is to popularize its accessibility improvement activities in society and make the fruits of its efforts freely available to the public. This philosophy is based on Fujitsu's mission of continually creating value and enhancing mutual beneficial relationships within our communities worldwide. Improvement of Web accessibility should not be implemented just by individual companies; instead, it should be achieved through society-wide collaborative activities.

Fujitsu's Efforts to Improve Web Accessibility,
`www.itpapers.com`

Japanese Policy Development

A web accessibility guideline for the removal of information barriers was first announced in May 1999, by the Telecommunication Accessibility Panel. This guideline contained some of the rules from the W3C WCAG. Members of the panel included the Ministry of Posts and Telecommunications and the Ministry of Health and Welfare (see *The Guidelines to Make Web Content Accessible,* `www.soumu.go.jp/joho_tsusin/policyreports/japanese/group/tsusin/90531x51.html`, in Japanese).

The following year brought a report from the same panel recommending that a web accessibility evaluation tool (J-WAS) be developed in order to promote accessible web design. Issued on May, 23, 2000, the report noted that the nature of Japanese language characters as well as the popular use of cell phones for the Web warranted attention to this matter. The report also noted the importance of including the opinions of the elderly and people with disabilities in the system planning (see "The plan to assist the use of the information and communication technology, and secure the web accessibility for elderly and disabled individuals," `www.soumu.go.jp/joho_tsusin/pressrelease/japanese/tsusin/000523j501.html` in Japanese, and `www.icdri.org/Asia/japanpress.htm`).

According to Masaya Ando of Allied Brains, Inc., one of the accessibility difficulties unique to the Japanese language is mispronunciation by screen readers. For example, one Kanji (the Chinese-based characters of Japanese) can be pronounced in several different ways. It is also difficult to complete a sentence with Kanji that can be understood by everyone. This is because the Japanese language consists of three different kinds of characters—Kanji, Katakana, and Hiragana—and although there is a standard for Kanji used in everyday Japanese life, the individual's comprehension level will vary with age, generation, and education. Moreover, in the Japanese writing system, words are not separated by spacing, and so the screen reader will not pronounce a word correctly when a space exists within the word.

By November 6, 2000, the government declared that websites of all ministries and the national public sector should apply the web accessibility guideline. At this Joint Meeting of the IT Strategy Council and the IT Strategy Headquarters (The Fifth Conference), it was also decided that the web accessibility evaluation tool (J-WAS) should be developed and used by government organizations to increase the accessibility of their web pages after April 2001 (see www.kantei.go.jp/jp/it/goudoukaigi/dai5/5siryou7-1.html, in Japanese).

In addition, November 2000 also brought Japanese legislation impacting IT law entitled *Basic Law on the Formation of an Advanced Information and Telecommunications Network Society*. Also known as *Basic IT Law*, Article 8 provided the basis for addressing accessible web design (see www.kantei.go.jp/foreign/it/it_basiclaw/it_basiclaw.html):

> Article 8. In forming an advanced information and telecommunications network society, it is necessary to make active efforts to correct gaps in opportunities and skills for use of information and telecommunications technology that are caused by geographical restrictions, age, physical circumstances, and other factors, considering that such gaps may noticeably obstruct the smooth and uninterrupted formation of an advanced information and telecommunications network society. Approved by the Japanese Diet on 29 November 2000, the law became effective 6 January 2001.

The e-Japan Policy program for barrier-free access has resulted in significant policies impacting the accessible web. On March, 29, 2001, the government IT Strategy Headquarters announced a number of policies, such as the following (see www.kantei.go.jp/foreign/it/network/priority-all/8.html, VII. Crosscutting Issues, 2. Closing the Digital Divide, subpart 2) Overcoming Age and Physical Constraints):

- Websites of ministries and agencies shall be accessible so that government information on the Web can be easily utilized by people with visual disabilities.
- Official Gazettes distributed over the Web will be tailored to the needs of people with visual disabilities.

- So that people with visual and hearing disabilities can enjoy broadcast services just like people without disabilities, R&D activities on production technologies for broadcast programming will be conducted with the costs of programming for closed captions, explanatory narration, and sign languages to be subsidized.

- School environments for children who are blind or deaf and with other disabilities will be addressed so that computers can be utilized by the students.

- R&D activities will be conducted to provide children in hospitals with the ability to study through the Web.

- Technologies will be developed to enable the elderly and people with disabilities to use the Internet easily, an accessibility checking system of websites will be created, and verification experiments will be conducted for the promotion of a barrier-free environment of information access.

Ongoing work for the development of J-WAS (the web accessibility evaluation tool) continued until it went public on the Web with a trial experiment in September 2001. The September 2001 trial experiment, found at www.jwas.gr.jp/activity/event/contents/jimukyoku.pdf (in Japanese), resulted in the findings shown in Figure 17-3.

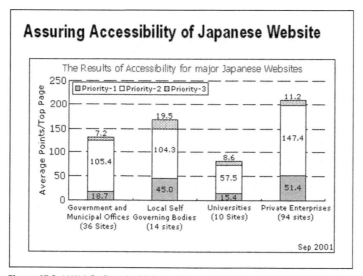

Figure 17-3. J-WAS findings (published with permission from Uchida, H., Ando, M., Ohta, K., Shimizu, H., Hayashi, Y., Ichihara, Y.G., and Yamazaki, R., "Research And Improving Web Accessibility in Japan," Slide 7, Internet Imaging III Proceeding of SPIE, Vol. 4672, 2002, pp. 46-54)

Korea

Korea has information laws that provide people with disabilities and older adults with the rights to use and access information equally without any assistance. In 2002, Article 7 of Korea's law on bridging the digital divide was revised to require government, local autonomous bodies, and public organizations to consider establishing policies so that people with disabilities and older adults could use ICT services.

According to information I received from Mr. Ki-Hoon Kim (Manager of the Standards Coordination Team for the Standardization Department of Telecommunications Technology Association), the implementing ordinances recommended that the Minister of Information and Communications (MIC) develop a guideline to encourage accessibility. As a result, in 2002, the MIC established the *Guideline for Fostering ICT Accessibility of the Senior and Disabled People*. Also in 2002, the agency for technology and standards developed a Korean Industrial Standard entitled *Guidelines for standards developers to address the needs of the senior and persons with disabilities* based on the ISO/IEC Guideline 71.

As for the Web, in 2004 the Telecommunications Technology Association (TTA), a private ICT standardization organization, established the *Web Contents Accessibility Guidelines 1.0* as a TTA standard based on the W3C WCAG. Published on December 23, 2004, the Korean Web Contents Accessibility Guidelines are Standard Number TTAS.OT-10.0003. In 2005, the web standard was adopted as a Korean Information and Communications Standard. TTA is also establishing *Korean Authority Tools Accessibility Guidelines* and *Korean User Agent Accessibility Guidelines* based on the W3C standards.

Mr. Ki-Hoon Kim also reported to me that in 2005, the MIC carried out a survey on whether or not public institutions observed web accessibility standards and subsequently distributed the results and recommendations to each public institution so that the institutions could make their websites more accessible. As of the writing of this chapter, the MIC is planning to seek mechanisms for improving web accessibility awareness, including the use of a web accessibility certification system.

Luxembourg

Although Luxembourg does not have a national law in force requiring the accessible design of websites, there are mandatory guidelines for all public institutions that create and maintain a website. The official standardization document, *Charte de normalization de la presence sur Internet de l'état*, was published May 30, 2002, and was approved by the National Commission for Information Society. The following are the main goals of this effort:

- Develop a corporate identity for all public portals and websites of the Grand Duchy of Luxembourg.
- Create public websites that meet quality criteria such as usability and accessibility.
- Ensure quality by strict project management.

Service eLuxembourg (SEL) is tasked to validate websites according to the standardization document prior to the web pages being launched online. SEL is a government service in charge of planning and coordinating e-government in Luxembourg. See the EU Information Society web page at http://europa.eu.int/information_society/policy/accessibility/web/wa_luxembourg/index_en.htm for details.

The Netherlands

In the Netherlands, under the *Act on equal treatment on the grounds of handicap or chronic illness*, there is an obligation to produce accessible websites. The Act (Stb. 2003, 206) was published in December 2003 and contains no references to the WCAG.

In 2001, *Drempels Weg* (literally meaning "away with barriers") was started as an initiative of the Ministry of Health, Welfare and Sport. Four national ambassadors took on the task of education and outreach about barriers created by inaccessible websites. In 2002, the National Accessibility Agency took charge of the project. See www.drempelsweg.nl/smartsite.dws?id=51 for more information.

Beginning in 2005, Drempels Weg was replaced by the *Quality Mark drempelvrij.nl*. This quality mark is based on the WCAG 1.0 Priority 1 checkpoints, as shown in Figures 17-4 and 17-5. Details about the assessment, costs, and user complaint procedure for visitors who believe that a website does not meet the quality mark standards can be found at www.accessibility.nl/toetsing/waarmerkdrempelvrij. An official quality mark register is maintained at www.drempelvrij.nl/waarmerk (in Dutch).

Figure 17-4. Quality mark drempelvrij.nl for meeting all 16 checkpoints

Figure 17-5. Quality mark drempelvrij.nl for meeting 13 out of 16 checkpoints

The Bartimeus Accessibility Foundation is the first certified inspection organization. For further information see www.accessibility.nl/ (in Dutch).

New Zealand

New Zealand policy development began in 2000, when the Government Information Systems Manager Forum (GOVIS) started adapting the UK Government's Web Guidelines to the New Zealand environment. According to the December 2003 Cabinet Paper for Web Guidelines, the UK Guidelines were chosen because they were based on the W3C WCAG 1.0. The *New Zealand Government Web Guidelines* have undergone a number of revisions. The current version is 2.1.3 as of the writing of this chapter (see www.e.govt.nz/ standards/web-guidelines/web-guidelines-v-2-1).

The New Zealand Government Web Guidelines specify in Section 6.3.2 that content developers apply the W3C WCAG 1.0 as follows:

Must satisfy priority 1 checkpoints (see exemption below)

Should satisfy priority 2 checkpoints

May satisfy priority 3 checkpoints

An exemption: The WAI requirement to identify changes in natural language with the lang attribute (http://www.w3.org/TR/WCAG10/#gl-abbreviated-and-foreign) does not extend to the Māori language in these Guidelines, while support for correct rendering in screen readers also does not extend to the Māori language.

The Guidelines also recommend that

Since a number of the priority 2 and 3 checkpoints are not especially onerous to implement, agencies should aim to go beyond the requirements of priority 1 where this can be done economically.

CAB Min (03) 41/2B, dated December 15, 2003, directed all Public Service departments, the New Zealand Police, the New Zealand Defence Force, the Parliamentary Counsel Office, and the New Zealand Security Intelligence Service to implement the Guidelines as follows:

All new or revised content produced for existing non-Guideline compliant websites after 1 April 2004 should comply with the Guidelines as closely as possible

Existing websites should become compliant with version 2.1 of the Guidelines on the Next Occasion of a complete website redevelopment occurring before 1 January 2006

All websites must comply with at least version 2.1 of the Guidelines by 1 January 2006

All websites must comply with subsequent versions of the Guidelines produced after 1 January 2006.

17

For more information, see the Minute of Cabinet decision at www.e.govt.nz/standards/web-guidelines/cabinet-minute-200402/.

The Cabinet Paper for Web Guidelines points out that the Web Guidelines enable agencies to be in compliance with law and government policy. The Guidelines assist agencies to meet their obligations under the Official Information Act 1992; the Human Rights Act 1993; the Policy Framework for Government-held Information; and the E-government, New Zealand Disability, and Māori Language strategies (see www.e.govt.nz/standards/web-guidelines/cabinet-paper-200402).

More specifically, agencies would fail to meet certain legal obligations if they did not implement the Guidelines. For example, the Official Information Act 1992 requires government to increase the availability of official information and provide each person with proper access to it as part of good government. The Human Rights Act 1993 requires nondiscrimination in access to public places and facilities, including government websites, and in the provision of public goods and services. Noncompliant websites could result in breach of either of these Acts.

If you are involved in the development of web pages in New Zealand, you should also know that the Guidelines in Section 1.8 specifically recommend that the following people read the document:

- Senior managers (sections 2–4 particularly)
- Business managers (sections 2–8 particularly)
- Website managers (sections 2, 5–8 particularly)
- Communications and IT support people (sections 2, 5–7 particularly)
- Vendors tendering for government Internet service requirements (sections 2, 5–8 particularly)

Section 6.3.3 of the Guidelines addresses web document markup and requires valid HTML 4.01 Transitional. If an agency wishes to adopt XHTML, rather than HTML, the agency must seek an exemption from this requirement from the E-government unit. Section 6.3.3 further states that

> Although deprecated tags are part of the HTML 4.01 specification and therefore will not make a web document invalid HTML, you should avoid their use in favour of newer methods of achieving the same thing. The tags deprecated in the HTML 4.01 specification are <applet>, <basefont>, <center>, <dir>, <font>, <isindex>, <menu>, <s>, <strike>, <u>. You must not use proprietary tags like <layer> and <comment>.

Section 6.3.4 of the Guidelines addresses style sheets and requires that text be properly marked up to signify document semantics (headings, lists, emphasis, and so on), rather than using styles to change appearance alone. In particular, it states

> You should use style sheets to define the visual appearance of pages. You should not rely on custom styles to denote document structure. You should use HTML structural tags (<h1> to <h6>, <ol>, <ul> etc) instead, so that people are not disadvantaged using non-visual browsers or browsers that ignore style sheets. You may use selectors, properties and values that are defined in CSS2, but only where you are sure they will degrade gracefully in browsers that don't correctly interpret CSS2 or do so poorly.

Section 6.3.5 of the Guidelines addresses scripting and requires websites using scripting to degrade gracefully, so that the site remains fully functional if scripting is ignored. All information and services on a government website must be available whether or not scripting is available to the user. It goes on to say that

> You should use scripting languages only where required and ensure text-based alternatives are available. Where active scripting is used, it should conform to the ECMAScript standard, rather than a proprietary standard, and should use the W3C Document Object Model (DOM), which is a platform- and language-neutral interface that will allow programs and scripts to dynamically access and update the content, structure and style of documents.

Norway

The Ministry of Government Administration and Reform (formerly the Ministry of Modernisation) has published new web accessibility goals for public websites in Norway. The *eNorge 2009: the Digital Leap* plan states that by 2007, 80 percent of all official government websites will comply with Norge.no's quality criteria on accessibility (see http://odin.dep.no/filarkiv/254956/eNorway_2009.pdf).

As of the writing of this chapter, the new criteria for the 2007 assessment has not been formulated (according to Mr. Haakon Aspelund of the Directorate for Health and Social Affairs). It is expected that the W3C WAI will be used as a reference in the new guidelines. The Norge.no official government portal quality criteria involve three parts: accessibility, user friendliness, and useful information. It is posted at www.norge.no/kvalitet/kvalitet2005 (in Norwegian).

Previously, the ICT strategy for 2004 through 2005 was that public websites must be user friendly and compliant with the W3C WAI international standards. According to Harald Jorgensen, Department of IT Strategy and Statistics for the Norwegian Directorate for Health and Social Affairs, since June 13, 2003, it has been official government policy that public information on the Internet must be compliant with the W3C WAI standards (see www.w3.org/WAI/EO/2004/02/policies_eu.html).

In addition, the Norwegian government has introduced a national quality mark for public websites (see the EU Information Society Report on Norway at www.eu.int/information_society/policy/accessibility/web/wa_norway/index_en.htm). Mr. Haakon Aspelund reported to me that Norge.no has made four manual assessments of all public websites in Norway, and the last assessment, which included more than 700 websites, was completed in autumn 2005. The quality mark is star-based, and the assessment information on the accessibility of the websites can viewed by the number of stars (one through six), by the accessibility score, by the average score, and so on (see www.norge.no/kvalitet/kvalitet2005/sok.asp, in Norwegian).

Of interest is the ongoing EU project by the European Internet Accessibility Observatory (EIAO), which is carried out at the Agder University College in Norway. The observatory will consist of a web-crawling robot that is planned to automatically assess approximately 10,000 European websites on a regular basis, storing assessment data in a data warehouse for statistics and information retrieval, and provide a basis for decision making (see www.eiao.net for more information).

For additional background documents about web accessibility efforts in Norway, see the following (all in Norwegian):

- Norwegian Internet Policy (www.dep.no/odinarkiv/norsk/dep/nhd/2002/publ/024101-990129/index-hov008-b-n-a.html): Official Internet pages must be user friendly and comply with international guidelines for universal design (W3C/WAI) (eNorway 2005).

- 25 criteria for quality of the Internet pages (Statskonsult, www.kvalitetpaanett.net/Krit_fase2.htm).

- ICT-Strategy in the Public Sector, 2003–2005 (www.odin.dep.no/aad/norsk/publ/handlingsplaner/002061-990025/index-dok000-b-n-a.html): About web services (page 31).

Portugal

Portugal was one of the early pioneers in national legislation for accessible web. The Portuguese Special Interest Group (PASIG), a nonprofit, nongovernment organization, established an International Accessibility Board consisting of well-known accessibility experts (I was a member of the Board). Working with PASIG, the Board compiled Internet accessibility guidelines that were submitted to the Portuguese parliament on February 17, 1999. This petition resulted in a national law requiring accessible websites: *Accessibility of Public Administration Web Sites for Citizens with Special Needs (Resolution of the Council of Ministers Number 97/99)*, also referred to as RCM97/99 (see www.acesso.umic.pcm.gov.pt/acesso/res9799_en.htm).

Article 1 of this law requires the following entities to implement accessible websites: general directorates and similar agencies, departments, or services, as well as public corporations. This includes universities, schools, and State corporations such as television, radio, and banks.

The accessible web requirement language is broad:

> The methods chosen for organizing and presenting the information . . . must permit or facilitate access thereto to all citizens with special needs (art. 1; point 1.1. of RCM97/99) . . . . The accessibility referred to in article 1.1 above shall apply, as a minimum requirement, to all information relevant to the full understanding of the contents and for the search of same (art. 1; point 1.2) . . . . To achieve the goals referred to in the previous article, the organizations mentioned therein must prepare both the written contents and the layout of their Internet pages so as to ensure that: a) Reading can be performed without resorting to sight, precision movements, simultaneous actions or pointing devices, namely mouse. b) Information retrieval and searching can be performed via auditory, visual or tactile interfaces. (art 2, of RCM97/99)

In addition, the law requires an accessibility quality mark or label fixed to the homepage to indicate that the website complies with accessibility requirements. (art 3, of RCM97/99).

The Codes of Practice in the *Accessibility Requirements* provide minimum requirements for accessibility and include a recommendation to conform to the accessibility requirements of W3C WCAG 1.0 (see www.acesso.umic.pcm.gov.pt/acesso/vis_en.htm). They also promote the use of the U.S. National Center for Accessible Media's Web Access Symbol, found at http://ncam.wgbh.org/webaccess/symbolwinner.html and shown in Figure 17-6. Websites that have the accessibility label fixed at the homepage are listed at the Accessibility Gallery at www.acesso.umic.pcm.gov.pt/galeria.htm.

Figure 17-6. NCAM Web Access Symbol

As for quality monitoring, the law requires that the Minister for Science and Technology monitor and evaluate the enforcement of this act and inform the government regularly on the progress of its application (art 5, of RCM97/99). Two reports have been produced: one in February 2002 and the second in December 2003.

The Knowledge Society Agency (UMIC) accessibility program, called ACESSO, performs evaluations and consultation. The main UMIC portal in English is at www.infosociety.gov.pt/. The UMIC provides resources such as Portugal's *Best practices guide for the construction of the web sites of the state administration* and *Guide for software*, which addresses issues of concern for the accessibility of products and services (www.umic.gov.pt/UMIC/CentrodeRecursos/Publicacoes/guia_boas_praticas.htm, in Portuguese).

Singapore

On July 15, 2003, the Deputy Prime Minister Lee Hsien Loong announced the launch of a three-year *e-Government Action Plan II* for 2003–2006. According to the description of the plan, the goal is to "transform the Public Service into a Networked Government that delivers accessible, integrated and value-added e-services to our customers, and helps bring citizens closer together" (see the *Infocomm Development Authority of Singapore Factsheet* under section E at www.ida.gov.sg/idaweb/marketing/MktFactSheetHome.jsp).

According to Mr. Leonard Cheong of the eGov Policies and Programmes Division of the Infocomm Development Authority of Singapore, web content accessibility efforts were implemented as a set of guidelines under the Website Interface Standards (WIS) for the Singapore Government on August 18, 2004. His team is responsible for the effort. WIS aims to establish a set of standards and guidelines for Singapore Government websites and online services to meet the following goals:

- Facilitate ease of navigation, retrieval of information, and access to online services within and across Singapore Government websites.

- Ensure a consistent and smooth online experience when one navigates from one government website to the next.

Singapore Government agencies have been given a three-year grace period to adopt WIS. As for the W3C WCAG, Mr. Cheong reported (in an e-mail exchange with me in February 2006) that agencies were given the flexibility to make the judgment call depending on the needs of the customers they served. A good example is the Senior Citizen Portal (http://seniors.gov.sg/) under the Family & Community Development category in the eCitizen portal (www.eCitizen.gov.sg). A visit to the eCitizen portal finds the W3C WCAG 1.0 Level A badge or quality mark on the website.

Further, in following W3C WCAG 1.0, Mr. Cheong explained the process:

> The checklist provided by W3C will be referenced by agencies seeking to make the websites WCAG compliant. The process, as recommended by WCAG, is to ensure that the recommendations in the checklist are adhered to before placing the logo on the website. We are aware that a version of WCAG 2.0 is in the midst of development. Our team tracks this closely and will make the necessary recommendations during our policy review once the WCAG 2.0 is officially released.

Spain

Spain has four national laws related to accessibility in general:

- Law 34, June 11, 2002—Information Society and Electronic Commerce Services Act
- Law 51, December 2, 2003—regarding equality of opportunities, nondiscrimination, and universal accessibility for people with disabilities
- Royal Decree 209, February 21, 2003—regarding registries and the telematic notifications
- Law 59, December 19, 2003—regarding electronic signature

Law 34 includes an obligation to fulfill generally recognized accessibility criteria and does not mention W3C WCAG. Also referenced as LSSICE, Law 34 specifies that all public administration websites and all websites financed by public funds must be accessible before December 31, 2005. Article 8 provides sanctions that include the removal of the data from the website.

Royal Decree 209 discusses the W3C WCAG guidelines for obtaining Priority Level AA.

For further information about web accessibility efforts in Spain, including the national laws in Spanish, see the EU Information Society report at http://europa.eu.int/information_society/policy/accessibility/web/wa_spain/index_en.htm.

Sweden

In support of the March 2000 national disability law, the national action plan for disability policy, *From patient to citizen* (1999/2000:79), requires Swedish government authorities to ensure that their premises, activities, and information are accessible to people with disabilities. Individual action plans, including the implementation of accessible public sector websites, were required to be submitted by December 21, 2001, and to be implemented no later than 2005.

Supporting *Guidelines for Websites, Version 2*, were published in June 2004 and incorporate material from all WCAG 1.0 checkpoints. For further information about the effort, see the EU Information Society report at http://europa.eu.int/information_society/policy/accessibility/web/wa_sweden/index_en.htm.

Thailand

At the Tenth Asia Pacific Telecommunity Forum in October 2005, Ms. Wantanee Phantachat, Director of the Assistive Technology Center of the National Electronics and Computer Technology Center (NECTEC), reported on "Thai Developments in Usability and Accessibility" (see www.aptsec.org/meetings/2005/ASTAP10/default.htm).

17

Published in 2003, *A Guideline on ICT Accessibility for Persons with Disabilities* sought to promote accessibility of ICT. In 2004, it became the policy of the Ministry of Information and Communication Technology to promote web accessibility in e-government. The action plan calls for all departments in all Ministries—more than 280 organizations—to have their websites conform to the W3C WCAG 1.0. Both the NECTEC and the Ministry of Information and Communication Technology conduct surveys on website development, including web accessibility and usability. In 2004, 2 websites out of the 280 websites were in partial conformance with WCAG 1.0. A second survey in 2004 found that 5 websites were in partial conformance with WCAG 1.0. It is interesting to note that IBM launched its Thai-speaking web browser, Home Page Reader, in 2003.

United Kingdom

Although web accessibility is not specifically mentioned in the UK disability rights legislation, it is mentioned in the Code of Practice that provides a guide as to what might or might not be considered unlawful.

Readers should be aware of two primary pieces of legislation:

- Disability Discrimination Act 1995, also known as the DDA
- Special Educational Needs and Disability Act 2001, legislation that amended the DDA to provide obligations for both pre- and post-16 education.

Effective May 27, 2002, the *Code of Practice: Rights of Access to Goods, Facilities, Services and Premises* under the DDA specifically references web accessibility:

- Section 2.2 (page 7): The Act makes it unlawful for a service provider to discriminate against a disabled person:
    - by refusing to provide (or deliberately not providing) any service which it provides (or is prepared to provide) to members of the public; or
    - in the standard of service which it provides to the disabled person or the manner in which it provides it; or
    - in the terms on which it provides a service to the disabled person.
- Section 4.7 (page 39): From 1 October 1999, a service provide has had to take reasonable steps to change a practice, policy or procedure which makes it impossible or unreasonably difficult for disabled people to make use of its services;
- Sections 2.13–2.17 (pages 11–13): What services are affected by Part III of the Act [DDA]? An airline company provides a flight reservation and booking service to the public on its website. This is a provision of a service and is subject to the Act;

- Section 5.23 (pages 68–69): For people with hearing disabilities, the range of auxiliary aids or services which it might be reasonable to provide to ensure that services are accessible might include . . . accessible websites; and

- Section 5.26 (page 71): For people with visual impairments, the range of auxiliary aids or services which it might be reasonable to provide to ensure that services are accessible might include . . . accessible websites.

The e-Government Unit, which is housed within the UK Government Cabinet Office, has posted web accessibility guidelines that "are a comprehensive blueprint of best practices for building and managing well designed, usable and accessible websites" at www.cabinetoffice.gov.uk/e-government/policy_guidance/. In Section 2.4, entitled "Building in universal accessibility + checklist," the guidelines require that UK websites conform to the W3C WCAG 1.0 Priority Level 1 "A" standard.

The Disability Rights Commission (DRC) was established in April 2000 by an Act of Parliament. Part of the DRC's duties include monitoring the DDA. The DRC has the power to conduct formal investigations, and in 2003, it launched an investigation into UK website accessibility. The DRC 2004 formal investigation report can be found at www.drc-gb.org/newsroom/newsdetails.asp?id=633&section=1.

One outcome of the formal investigation has been for the DRC to commission the British Standards Institution (BSI) in April 2005 to produce formal guidance on web accessibility. The guidance to be developed is to be a *Publicly Available Specification—PAS 78: Guide to Good Practice in Designing Accessible Websites*. According to the DRC, this step is necessary in part because of the knowledge gap of web developers and the prevalence of web-authoring tools that do not make W3C-compliant code. See the DRC press release at www.drc-gb.org/newsroom/newsdetails.asp?id=805&section=4. See Appendix C of this book for more information about PAS 78.

Summary

This chapter introduced the accessible web design policies and laws around the world. You learned that at least 25 countries or jurisdictions implement W3C WCAG 1.0, a combination of W3C WCAG 1.0 and U.S. Section 508 web requirements, or another variation of rules particular to that jurisdiction. In addition, you learned that in some countries, sanctions or penalties are available for noncompliance—with Italy providing for criminal sanctions as well as civil liability. You also learned that a number of website quality marks or labels have been developed for certifying accessibility based on varying criteria.

You now have a core understanding of some of the international issues and practices supporting accessible web design policies and laws. This chapter should serve as a key resource whenever you are contemplating web development work for clients within any of the countries covered by this chapter.

A **GLOSSARY OF TERMS**

A

Accessibility Task Force (ATF)

A subgroup of the Web Standards Project (WaSP) focusing on accessibility, assistive technology, and standards support.

ADA

See *Americans with Disabilities Act*.

Ajax

A combination of technologies that allows bits of a web page to be refreshed from the server without refreshing the whole page, which gives the user a more responsive, seamless experience. It is a good buzzword, but a lousy acronym for Asynchronous JavaScript and XML (because it doesn't require XML). Ajax currently is most often seen in Google Maps, Google's Gmail, and the like. Many accessibility problems have yet to be addressed. A similar result, without using JavaScript, may be achieved using Flash or even HTML frames.

alt-text

A generic term describing descriptive text attached to certain objects on a web page that can be read aloud by a screen reader, so that a person with a visual impairment can know the nature of such objects, too. Alt-text is therefore an accessible alternative to a potentially inaccessible item of content. For example, the object element may use text embedded within it as a fallback mechanism.

The most common alternative text is found as an attribute of the `<img>` element, and it describes the function of an image, or is blank in the case of purely decorative images.

It is evil and wrong to refer to this as an alt *tag* (there is no alt element in (X)HTML), and many hope that WCAG 3.0 will mandate the death penalty for such incorrect nomenclature.

Americans with Disabilities Act (ADA)

A U.S. law passed in 1990 that prohibits discrimination against people with disabilities.

applet

A Java program or application that provides interactivity not offered by (X)HTML and designed to be embedded in, and invoked from, a web page. In many cases, Flash has superseded applets as the means to achieve extra interactivity.

assistive technology

Equipment or software that assists people with disabilities in performing everyday activities. Examples include screen readers and voice-input software.

ATAG

See *Authoring Tools Accessibility Guidelines*.

ATF

See *Accessibility Task Force*.

Authoring Tools Accessibility Guidelines (ATAG)

Published by the W3C in 2000 to assist authoring tool developers in "designing authoring tools that produce accessible Web content and to assist developers in creating an accessible authoring interface" (www.w3.org/TR/ATAG10/). In other words, your blogging tool or CMS should not only *produce* accessible pages, but also be accessible itself so that users with disabilities can *create* content.

B

baseline

In WCAG 2.0, a set of technologies assumed to be supported by, and enabled in, user agents in order for web content to conform to WCAG 2.0. Some examples of entities that may set baselines include authors, companies, customers, and government entities.

Bobby

A free website accessibility assessment tool developed by CAST (www.cast.org/), and then acquired by Watchfire (www.watchfire.com/). The free version of Bobby was discontinued in April 2003.

Bobby had some utility in checking for things like missing alt-text, but, unfortunately, it lulled site owners into a false sense of security, as they believed that "passing Bobby" guaranteed accessibility. There are many other online "validators," such as Cynthia Says and the WAVE. Gez Lemon has a salutary article about the usefulness of such programs at http://juicystudio.com/article/invalid-content-accessibility-validators.php.

browser

The software on a computer that allows websites to be rendered so they can be displayed to users. There are two types of visual browsers. Internet Explorer, Firefox, Opera, Safari, and the like render all content including the latest technologies. Others, like Lynx, are text-only. But many other types of browsers exist, some of which produce voice output, such as IBM Home Page Reader.

C

Cascading Style Sheets (CSS)

A means of applying styling/formatting to markup (for example, XML or HTML). This has many advantages over using HTML formatting tags, such as <b> and <font>. For a start, CSS formatting is more powerful and allows more flexibility. If you want to change a style, you need only change its definition in the style sheet, rather than changing every instance of it in the HTML. CSS has great uses for accessibility. For example, you can use an alternative style sheet to make the text on a website bigger for the benefit of people with visual impairments. See Chapter 9 of this book for more details.

CMS

See *content management system*.

content management system (CMS)

A program that allows users to create and manage web pages and other content. CMSs are often browser-based. They can range from free blogging tools, such as WordPress, to expensive systems that can run a whole enterprise site, such as TeamSite or Vignette. They are generally template-driven and promise (with varying success) to turn user's text-based input into HTML. Many spit out horribly inaccessible code, and most do not conform to ATAG and are therefore unable to be used by people with disabilities to produce sites. It's always important to ask vendors about their conformance to ATAG before purchasing a CMS.

CSS

See *Cascading Style Sheets*.

D

DDA

See *Disability Discrimination Act*.

design for all

See *universal design*.

Disability Discrimination Act (DDA)

A name shared by two laws passed in Australia (1992) and the United Kingdom (1995, extended 2005). They both prohibit discrimination against people with disabilities.

D-LINK

A link that takes the form of a capital *D* near an image. It provides a longer description of the image or its purpose than is feasible using the alt attribute. It's basically a hack, because most browsers don't cope with longdesc well.

Document Object Model (DOM)

A view of a document (HTML, XHTML, or XML) that can be parsed and manipulated to add new content, amend styles, and change behavior after a web page has loaded—generally via JavaScript, as this is built into most browsers. See Chapter 10 of this book for more details.

Document Type Definition (DTD)

A file that defines the relationships and constraints for elements and attributes used in the markup language in the form of a schema. For example, a DTD may define whether an attribute is required for a particular element. Effectively, it's the grammatical rules for the language.

DOM

See *Document Object Model*.

DTD

See *Document Type Definition*.

dyslexia

A language-based learning disability that is often characterized by difficulties with understanding written language and being more attuned to a graphical or an object-based learning style.

E

ECMAScript

The standardized version of JavaScript (JScript in Internet Explorer) that can be used effectively to manipulate the DOM, validate forms, and control Ajax, or uselessly to produce effects such as pictures of unicorns following the mouse pointer. ActionScript (found in Adobe's Flash) is also a flavor of ECMAScript (and is equally good with unicorns).

Extensible Hypertext Markup Language (XHTML)

Defined by the W3C as "a reformulation of the three HTML 4 document types as applications of XML 1.0. It is intended to be used as a language for content that is both XML-conforming and, if some simple guidelines are followed, operates in HTML 4 conforming user agents" (www.w3.org/TR/xhtml1/#xhtml).

XHTML is very much like HTML with a few extra rules. There are three main flavors. XHTML 1.0 Transitional allows many deprecated tags, and as the name suggests, was designed to help developers make the transition from HTML. XHTML 1.0 Frameset allows frames and therefore has attendant accessibility issues. XHTML 1.0 Strict is, well, strict (when compared with traditional HTML).

The idea that XHTML is "better" than HTML is subject to ferocious (but rather futile) debate, as it is largely a matter of personal preference, understanding the difference, and using the right tools for the job.

Extensible Markup Language (XML)

A language specification from the W3C that allows users to develop their own markup languages (often called vocabularies), and format their documents using style sheets to be presented on a browser if desired. XML has a very strict set of rules that must be adhered to, allowing a lot of control over document format. XML is most useful, however, as a completely language/platform-agnostic data format.

Extensible Stylesheet Language (XSL)

A W3C specification that contains three parts: Extensible Stylesheet Language Transformations (XSLT) for changing the formatting and structure of markup according to a set of rules, Extensible Stylesheet Language Formatting Objects (XSL-FO) for applying a strong set of rules to a document to ensure reliable formatting when printed, and XPath to select the elements required by XSLT.

F

Firefox

An open source browser available for all main operating systems, developed by the Mozilla Corporation. The good (but not perfect) standards support and availability of community-written extensions makes it the browser of choice for many web developers.

Flash

The name given to the product by Adobe (formerly Macromedia) that allows moving graphics to be displayed in a web page. It refers to the Flash Player, which plugs in to the browser, as well as (more generally) the program and effects. Flash can be made accessible on Windows machines via MSAA, and some of the most widespread screen readers can access the content. Although Flash has gotten bad press from some accessibility advocates, it has proved very helpful in delivering accessible content to people with cognitive disabilities.

FLEX

A product from Adobe (formerly Macromedia) that allows a developer to create a rich, interactive web page that can update with the server in real time, with Ajax-like results.

frames

A feature of (X)HTML that allows a web author to divide a page into two or more separate windows. If the frame does not have a `<title>` element, or the `<title>` element is not meaningful, this can cause accessibility issues. In addition, some browsers do not support frames.

H

HTML

See *Hypertext Markup Language.*

Hypertext Markup Language (HTML)

The markup language that is used to create the vast majority of web pages. The standards for HTML are controlled by the W3C.

I

image map

An area of an image on a web page that has links to other areas of the Web. For example, an image map could take the form of a map of Europe, in which clicking the map of England could open a page about warm beer, rain, and world-renowned cuisine; whereas the area corresponding to Belgium takes you to a page about great beer and a list of household names from all fields of human endeavor.

There are two types of image maps: client-side and server-side. In Chapter 7 of this book, you will read "If you want to use an image map, make it a client-side image map." A List Apart has a good article on building an accessible, standards-compliant image map at www.alistapart.com/articles/imagemap.

J

Java

An object-oriented programming language developed by Sun Microsystems. Java was specifically designed for the distributed environment of the Web and can be used to create applications that can run on a single computer or distributed among several computers in a network. It can also be used to write applets (small, stand-alone programs) or animations, although Flash is more commonly used for these.

JavaScript

A scripting language often used on web pages. It's a type of ECMAScript. See Chapter 10 for a discussion of JavaScript and accessibility.

JScript

The Microsoft variant of JavaScript found in Internet Explorer web browsers.

L

linearization

The process of removing the cellular structure from a layout table and checking the cells' contents in their linear (source) order, left to right, top to bottom. Linearization takes the contents of row 1 column 1, then row 1 column 2, and so on. If any cells contain a nested table, all of those cells are linearized before proceeding to the next cell of the original table. The Lynx browser or Web Developer plug-in for Firefox is a good way to see the linearized structure. See Chapter 6 for a full discussion of how table linearization works.

The purpose of linearization is to see if the content still makes sense, as the linearized order is the order in which a screen reader will voice the web page to the user. If it does still make sense (and it generally does), both WCAG 1.0 and 2.0 say your layout is accessible. But no one has professionally used tables to lay out web pages since Mozart fell off his penny-farthing during a stegosaurus hunt.

Lynx

A text-only browser that was popular among UNIX users and sometimes used by people with disabilities and those in low-bandwidth areas. Lynx can be downloaded from http://lynx.isc.org/release/. A Lynx emulator is also available at www.delorie.com/web/lynxview.html, and it useful for testing how tables linearize.

A

M

Microsoft Active Accessibility (MSAA)

A layer in all modern Windows systems that allows assistive technologies to hook into applications. It is how screen readers "know" what is on the screen.

MSAA

See *Microsoft Active Accessibility*.

multimedia

Using a computer to present multiple types of media simultaneously, in an integrated manner. Media can include sound, graphics, video, text, animation, or any other form of information representation. For the purposes of WCAG 2.0, multimedia refers to combined audio and video presentations, as well as audio-only and video-only presentations that include interaction.

O

on-screen keyboard

A keyboard that appears on the screen. Users who cannot use their hands can use assistive technology (such as a head pointer) to enter keyboard input via the on-screen keyboard.

outcome-based

In WCAG 2.0, refers to the determination of the application of a process. What were the results of the application of a specific guideline? Were the success criteria achieved?

P

PAS 78

The Publicly Available Specification from the British Standards Institution (BSI), titled "Guide to Good Practice in Commissioning Accessible Websites," released in March 2006. See Appendix C of this book for more details.

PDF

See *Portable Document Format*.

plug-in

A module (either hardware or software) that adds a special feature to a larger system or program; for example, a program to play movies on a browser or the plug-in that allows browsers to display Flash content.

Portable Document Format (PDF)

Developed by Adobe Systems Inc. as a way to publish documents electronically, with good formatting for printing and document security (documents are generally read-only). Originally, it was in an image format, and this presented major accessibility issues. Recently, however, Adobe has made large strides in making the PDF format accessible to people with disabilities, although it's generally more complex to navigate a PDF file or to make a PDF file accessible than doing so with an equivalent HTML document. See Chapter 12 of this book for details on PDF accessibility.

programmatically determined

In WCAG 2.0, means something can be recognized by user agents, including assistive technologies, that support the technologies in the chosen baseline. For our purposes, it seems to mean marking up documents semantically, so a program (like a JavaScript favelet, screen reader, or search bot) can tell what's a list, what's a heading, and so on, without having to rely on context.

R

refreshable Braille display

An assistive device that turns information into raised Braille characters electromechanically, by raising small pins up through holes in a plate, which can be sensed by users placing their fingers on the plate.

S

Scalable Vector Graphics (SVG)

A language for vector graphics coded in XML. XML documents can have these graphics placed directly into the document, with many advantages. SVG produces graphics that are smaller, transmit more quickly, are scalable without loss of resolution, can have searchable text labels, and can be interactive. SVG is being developed by the W3C.

scope

In WCAG 2.0, refers to limiting conformance claims to pertain to only some parts of a website. Scoping allows authors to claim conformance to WCAG 2.0 for all URLs in one part of a site and exclude other parts of the site. "Scoping cannot exclude a particular type of content (for example, images or scripts) since it would allow exclusion of individual success criteria" (www.w3.org/TR/WCAG20/conformance.html#conformance-reqs).

screen magnifier

A device (or software) that will make images and text on a screen larger for the benefit of visually impaired users. Many Microsoft Windows machines have a simple screen magnifier built in (available from the Start ➤ Programs ➤ Accessories ➤ Accessibility menu).

screen reader

A computer program that reads the screen to a user. It can be used to surf the Web, to write a spreadsheet or document, or just to read pages. It is closely related to voice output. In many ways, screen reader is a misnomer; most modern screen readers actually read the text in source-code order, regardless of the positions of the various elements in the visual layout. Examples of screen readers are JAWS for Windows, Window-Eyes, and VoiceOver on Mac OS X version 10.4.

Section 508

A common name for Section 508 of the Rehabilitation Act. This is an amendment to a U.S. law that basically says all electronic and information technology purchased or developed by the U.S. government must be accessible to people with disabilities. See Appendix B for details.

SMIL

See *Synchronized Multimedia Integration Language*.

spacer image

Small, transparent image placed on a page, usually in a table-based layout, also called spacer GIF. Spacer images are an old-fashioned way to position text and images on the page for a good visual effect. These should be found only in legacy pages, and should have null alt-text (alt="").

style guide

A document that sets out the rules for your website. All your developers must follow your style guide, and the webmaster should enforce it. Accessibility rules and standards can be included in this style guide. This is a good idea, as when a style guide is implemented, accessibility becomes part of the basic parameters for your website and becomes much less of an issue.

style sheet

See *Cascading Style Sheets* and *Extensible Stylesheet Language*.

success criteria

In WCAG 2.0, testable statements that will be either true or false when applied to specific web content (see www.w3.org/TR/UNDERSTANDING-WCAG20/).

SVG

See *Scalable Vector Graphics*.

Synchronized Accessible Media Interchange (SAMI)

An HTML-like language used to embed captions in Windows Media files.

Synchronized Multimedia Integration Language (SMIL)

A markup language developed by the W3C that allows developers to separate multimedia content into distinct files and transmission streams such as text, images, audio, and video. These can then be sent to the user's computer separately, reassembled, and displayed as intended. SMIL 2.1 became a recommendation in December 2005.

T

table linearization

See *linearization*.

text equivalent

A term used to describe the technique of providing a text alternative that will be the same in both content and function as a nontext object on a web page, such as an image map.

text-only browser

A browser that does not show images. It does not have images turned off; rather, it just doesn't display them. An example of a text-only browser is Lynx.

U

UCD

See *user-centered design*.

universal access

The idea that all things on the Internet should be accessible by the largest audience possible, regardless of disability, location, device, or speed of connection to the Internet. It therefore differs from accessibility, which is solely concerned with access for people with disabilities.

universal design

Designing for the largest audience possible, regardless of disability or ability to speak the native language. This is a process rather than an end in itself.

usability

The idea that a website or web page is easily used by a web user.

user agent

A term used by the W3C as a generic description for "any software that retrieves and renders Web content for users" (www.w3.org/TR/WAI-USERAGENT/glossary. html#def-user-agent). A browser, mobile phone, screen reader, plug-in, or search engine's web crawler may be considered a user agent.

User Agent Accessibility Guidelines (UAAG)

A document that provides guidelines for designing accessible user agents (browsers, assistive technologies, media players, and the like), published by the W3C in 2002. See www.w3.org/TR/WAI-USERAGENT/ for more information.

user-centered design (UCD)

The design process that places the user at the center of the design rather than the object to be designed. It is a philosophy and process rather than an end in itself.

UAAG

See *User Agent Accessibility Guidelines.*

V

voice input

Software that recognizes voice commands and responds accordingly.

voice output

Software that reads the necessary information to the user, in a synthesized voice.

voice recognition software

Software that can be trained to recognize a person's voice and either execute commands or turn the voice into text or other forms of media, such as sign language for the deaf.

VoiceXML

A type of XML that allows the user to interact with a web page using voice recognition software.

voicing browser

A browser that uses a synthesized voice as a means to communicate with the user. IBM Home Page Reader is an example. It differs from a screen reader in that a voicing browser is purely a web browser, whereas a screen reader reads any screen.

W

W3C

See *World Wide Web Consortium.*

WAI

See *Web Accessibility Initiative.*

WaSP

See *Web Standards Project.*

WAT-C

See *Web Accessibility Tools Consortium.*

WCAG

See *Web Content Accessibility Guidelines.*

Web Accessibility Initiative (WAI)

Started by the W3C and its members, an organization that addresses web accessibility issues. See www.w3.org/WAI/ for more information.

Web Accessibility Tools Consortium (WAT-C)

Described as a consortium that "provides a collection of free tools to assist both developers and designers in the development and testing of accessible web content." See www.wat-c.org/ for more information.

Web Content Accessibility Guidelines (WCAG)

Guidelines developed by the W3C/WAI to address issues in building accessible web pages. WCAG 1.0 was published as long ago as 1999; WCAG 2.0 is "coming soon."

Web Standards Project (WaSP)

Described as a project that "was formed in 1998 with the goal of promoting core web standards and encouraging browser makers to do the same, thereby ensuring simple, affordable access for all." See http://webstandards.org/about/ for more information.

World Wide Web Consortium (W3C)

An international consortium of companies and organizations involved with the Internet and the World Wide Web, responsible for maintaining web technology standards, such as HTML and CSS. See www.w3.org/ for more information.

X

XHTML

See *Extensible Hypertext Markup Language*.

XML

See *Extensible Markup Language*.

XSL

See *Extensible Stylesheet Language*.

B **GUIDE TO THE SECTION 508
STANDARDS FOR ELECTRONIC AND
INFORMATION TECHNOLOGY**

This appendix is an excerpt from the *Guide to the Section 508 Standards for Electronic and Information Technology, Subpart B – Technical Standards, Section 1194.22*. This is the only section that is relevant to web developers/designers. The whole guide is available at www.access-board.gov/sec508/guide/index.htm.

Web-Based Intranet and Internet Information and Applications (1194.22)

Updated: June 21, 2001

These provisions of the standards provide the requirements that must be followed by Federal agencies when producing web pages. These provisions apply unless doing so would impose an undue burden.

The key to compliance with these provisions is adherence to the provisions. Many agencies have purchased assistive software to test their pages. This will produce a better understanding of how these devices interact with different coding techniques. However, it always should be kept in mind that assistive technologies, such as screen readers, are complex programs and take extensive experience to master. For this reason, a novice user may obtain inaccurate results that can easily lead to frustration and a belief that the page does not comply with the standards.

For example, all screen reading programs use special key combinations to read properly coded tables. If the novice user of assistive technology is not aware of these commands, the tables will never read appropriately no matter how well the tables have been formatted.

A web site will be in compliance with the 508 standards if it meets paragraphs (a) through (p) of Section 1194.22. Please note that the tips and techniques discussed in the document for complying with particular sections are not necessarily the only ways of providing compliance with 508. In many cases, they are techniques developed by the Board, the Department of Education, and the Department of Justice that have been tested by users with a wide variety of screen reader software. With the evolution of technology, other techniques may become available or even preferable.

(a) Text Tags	(b) Multimedia Presentations
(c) Color	(d) Readability (style sheets)
(e) Server-Side Image Maps	(f) Client-Side Image Maps
(g) & (h) Data Table	(i) Frames
(j) Flicker Rate	(k) Text-Only Alternative
(l) Scripts	(m) Applets and Plug-Ins
(n) Electronic Forms	(o) Navigation Links
(p) Time Delays	

B

1194.22(a) A text equivalent for every non-text element shall be provided (for example via alt or longdesc attributes, or in element content).

What is meant by a text equivalent?

A text equivalent means adding words to represent the purpose of a non-text element. This provision requires that when an image indicates a navigational action such as "move to the next screen" or "go back to the top of the page," the image must be accompanied by actual text that states the purpose of the image. This provision also requires that when an image is used to represent page content, the image must have a text description accompanying it that explains the meaning of the image.

HTML Source Code: `<img src="art/logo-green.gif" alt="Access Board Logo">`

http://www.access-board.gov/

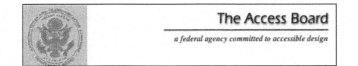

597

How much information actually needs to be in the text equivalent?

The text information associated with a non-text element should, when possible, communicate the same information as its associated element. For example, when an image indicates an action, the action must be described in the text. The types of non-text elements requiring actual text descriptions are limited to those elements that provide information required for comprehension of content or those used to facilitate navigation. Web page authors often utilize transparent graphics for spacing. Adding a text description to these elements will produce unnecessary clutter for users of screen readers. For such graphics, an empty alt attribute is useful.

Example of source code: `<img src="transparent.gif" alt="">`

What is meant by the term, non-text element?

A non-text element is an image, graphic, audio clip, or other feature that conveys meaning through a picture or sound. Examples include buttons, checkboxes, pictures and embedded or streaming audio or video.

HTML Source Code: `<img src="art/logo-green.gif" alt="Access Board Logo">`

How should audio presentations be treated?

This provision requires that when audio presentations are available on a multimedia web page, the audio portion must be captioned. Audio is a non-textual element, so a text equivalent of the audio must be provided if the audio is part of a multimedia presentation, Multimedia includes both audio and video. If the presentation is audio only, a text transcript would meet this requirement.

What are ways of assigning text to elements?

There are several ways of providing textual information so that it can be recognized by assistive technology devices. For instance, the `<img>` tag can accept an alt attribute that will enable a web designer to include text that describes the picture directly in the `<img>` tag.

HTML source code:

```
<img src="image/ab_logo1.gif" alt="The Architectural and➡
   Transportation Barriers Compliance Board emblem-Go to Access➡
   Board website">
```

Similarly, the `<applet>` tag for Java applets also accepts an alt attribute, but it only works for browsers that provide support for Java. Often, users with slower Internet connections will turn support for Java applets off. A better alternative for providing textual descriptions is to simply include the alternative text between opening and closing `<applet>` or `<object>` tags. For instance, if a web designer wanted to include an applet called MyCoolApplet in a web page, and also include a description that the applet shows a stock ticker displaying the current price of various stocks, the designer would use the following HTML coding for example:

```
<applet code="MyCoolApplet.class" width="200", height="100">
// This applet displays current stock prices for many popular stocks.
</applet>
```

Finally, yet another way of providing a textual description is to include it in the page in the surrounding context:

```
<p> Below is a picture of me during my great vacation!</p>
<img src="pictureofme.jpg">
```

1194.22(b) Equivalent alternatives for any multimedia presentation shall be synchronized with the presentation.

What are considered equivalent alternatives?

Captioning for the audio portion and audio description of visual information of multimedia presentations are considered equivalent alternatives. This provision requires that when an audio portion of a multimedia production is captioned, as required in provision (a), the captioning must be synchronized with the audio. Synchronized captioning would be required so someone reading the captions could also watch the speaker and associate relevant body language with the speech.

If a web site offers audio files with no video, do they have to be captioned?

No, because it is not multimedia. However, since audio is a non-text element, a text equivalent, such as a transcript, must be available. Similarly, a (silent) web slide show presentation does not need to have an audio description accompanying it, but does require text alternatives to be associated with the graphics.

If a Federal agency official delivers a live audio and video webcast speech, does it need to be captioned?

Yes, this would qualify as a multimedia presentation and would require the speech to be captioned.

Example:

National Endowment for the Humanities: www.neh.gov/media/scottcaptions.ram

National Center for Accessible Media (NCAM): http://main.wgbh.org/wgbh/access/dvs/lion.ram

1194.22(c) Web pages shall be designed so that all information conveyed with color is also available without color, for example from context or markup.

Why is this provision necessary?

When colors are used as the sole method for identifying screen elements or controls, persons who are color-blind as well as those people who are blind or have low vision may find the web page unusable.

Does this mean that all pages have to be displayed in black and white?

No, this provision does not prohibit the use of color to enhance identification of important features. It does, however, require that some other method of identification, such as text labels, must be combined with the use of color. This provision addresses not only the problem of using color to indicate emphasized text, but also the use of color to indicate an action. For example, a web page that directs a user to "press the green button to start" should also identify the green button in some other fashion than simply by color.

This Illustration is a variation of the actual image published by the U.S. Access Board. To view the published illustration, visit www.access-board.gov/sec508/guide/1194.22.htm#(c).

Is there any way a page can be quickly checked to ensure compliance with this provision?

There are two simple ways of testing a web page to determine if this requirement is being met: by either viewing the page on a black and white monitor, or by printing it out on a black and white printer. Both methods will quickly show if the removal of color affects the usability of the page.

1194.22(d) Documents shall be organized so they are readable without requiring an associated style sheet.

What are the potential problems posed by style sheets?

Style sheets can enable users to define specific viewing preferences to accommodate their disability. For instance, users with low vision may create their own style sheet so that, regardless of what web pages they visit, all text is displayed in an extra large font with white characters on a black background. If designers set up their pages to override user-defined style sheets, people with disabilities may not be able to use those pages. For good access, therefore, it is critical that designers ensure that their web pages do not interfere with user-defined style sheets.

In general, the "safest" and most useful form of style sheets are "external" style sheets, in which the style rules are set up in a separate file. An example of an external style sheet is:

Example of source code: <link rel="stylesheet" type="text/css" href= "section508.css">

1194.22(e) Redundant text links shall be provided for each active region of a server-side image map.

How do "image maps" work?

An "image map" is a picture (often an actual map) on a web page that provides different "links" to other web pages, depending on where a user clicks on the image. There are two basic types of image maps: "client-side image maps" and "server-side image maps." With client-side image maps, each "active region" in a picture can be assigned its own "link" (called a URL or "Uniform Resource Locator") that specifies what web page to retrieve when a portion of the picture is selected. HTML allows each active region to have its own alternative text, just like a picture can have alternative text (see §1194.22(a)). By contrast, clicking on a location of a server-side image map only specifies the coordinates within the image when the mouse was depressed. The ultimate selection of the link or URL must be deciphered by the computer serving the web page.

Why is this provision necessary?

When a web page uses a server-side image map to present the user with a selection of options, browsers cannot indicate to the user the URL that will be followed when a region of the map is activated. Therefore, the redundant text link is necessary to provide access to the page for anyone not able to see or accurately click on the map.

1194.22(f) Client-side image maps shall be provided instead of server-side image maps except where the regions cannot be defined with an available geometric shape.

Why do client-side image maps provide better accessibility?

Unlike server-side image maps, the client-side image map allows an author to assign text to image map "hot spots." This feature means that someone using a screen reader can easily identify and activate regions of the map. An explanation of how these image maps are constructed will help clarify this issue.

Creating a basic client-side image map requires several steps:

- Identify an image for the map. First, an image must be used in a client-side image map. This image is identified using the <img> tag. To identify it as a map, use the usemap attribute.
- Use the <map> tag to identify "areas" within the map. The <map> tag is a container tag that includes various <area> tags that are used to identify specific portions of the image.

601

■ Use <area> tags to identify map regions. To identify regions within a map, simply use <area> tags within the <map> container tags. Making this client-side image map accessible is considerably easier to describe: simply include the alt attribute and area description inside each <area> tag. The following HTML demonstrates how to make a client-side image map:

```
<img src="navbar.gif" border="0" usemap="#Map">
<map name="Map">
   <area shape="rect" coords="0,2,64,19" href="general.html"
         alt="information about us">
   <area shape="rect" coords="65,2,166,20" href="jobs.html"
         alt="job opportunities" >
   <area shape="rect" coords="167,2,212,19" href="faq.html"
         alt="Frequently Asked Questions">
   <area shape="rect" coords="214,2,318,21" href="location.html"
         alt="How to find us">
   <area shape="rect" coords="319,2,399,23" href="contact.html"
         alt="How to contact us">
</map>
```

1194.22(g) Row and column headers shall be identified for data tables.

1194.22(h) Markup shall be used to associate data cells and header cells for data tables that have two or more logical levels of row or column headers.

Why are these two provisions necessary?

Paragraphs (g) and (h) permit the use of tables, but require that the tables be coded according to the rules of the markup language being used for creating tables. Large tables of data can be difficult to interpret if a person is using a non-visual means of accessing the web. Users of screen readers can easily get "lost" inside a table because it may be impossible to associate a particular cell that a screen reader is reading with the corresponding column headings and row names. For instance, assume that a salary table includes the salaries for federal employees by grade and step. Each row in the table may represent a grade scale and each column may represent a step. Thus, finding the salary corresponding to a grade 9, step 5 may involve finding the cell in the ninth row and the fifth column. For a salary chart of 15 grade scales and 10 steps, the table will have at least 150 cells. Without a method to associate the headings with each cell, it is easy to imagine the difficulty a user of assistive technology may encounter with the table.

Section 1194.22 (g) and (h) state that when information is displayed in a table format, the information shall be laid out using appropriate table tags as opposed to using a preformatted table in association with the <pre> tag. Web authors are also required to use one of several methods to provide an association between a header and its related information.

How can HTML tables be made readable with assistive technology?

Using the Scope Attribute in Tables – Using the scope attribute is one of the most effective ways of making HTML compliant with these requirements. It is also the simplest method to implement. The scope attribute also works with some (but not all) assistive technology in tables that use colspan or rowspan attributes in table header or data cells.

Using the Scope Attribute – The first row of each table should include column headings. Typically, these column headings are inserted in <th> tags, although <td> tags can also be used. These tags at the top of each column should include the following attribute:

```
scope="col"
```

By doing this simple step, the text in that cell becomes associated with every cell in that column. Unlike using other approaches (notably id and headers attributes) there is no need to include special attributes in each cell of the table. Similarly, the first column of every table should include information identifying information about each row in the table. Each of the cells in that first column are created by either <th> or <td> tags. Include the following attribute in these cells:

```
scope="row"
```

By simply adding this attribute, the text in that cell becomes associated with every cell in that row. While this technique dramatically improves the usability of a web page, using the scope attribute does not appear to interfere in any way with browsers that do not support the attribute.

Example of source code – the following simple table summarizes: the work schedule of three employees and demonstrates these principles.

```
<table>
  <tr>
    <th> </th>
    <th scope="col">Spring</th>
    <th scope="col">Summer</th>
    <th scope="col">Autumn</th>
    <th scope="col">Winter</th>
  </tr>
  <tr>
    <td scope="row" >Betty</td>
    <td>9-5</td>
    <td>10-6</td>
    <td>8-4</td>
    <td>7-3</td>
  </tr>
  <tr>
    <td scope="row">Wilma</td>
    <td>10-6</td>
    <td>10-6</td>
    <td>9-5</td>
    <td>9-5</td>
```

603

B

```
      </tr>
      <tr>
        <td scope="row">Fred</td>
        <td>10-6</td>
        <td>10-6</td>
        <td>10-6</td>
        <td>10-6</td>
      </tr>
    </table>
```

This table would be displayed as follows:

	Spring	Summer	Autumn	Winter
Betty	9-5	10-6	8-4	7-3
Wilma	10-6	10-6	9-5	9-5
Fred	10-6	10-6	10-6	10-6

The efficiency of using the scope attribute becomes more apparent in much larger tables. For instance, if an agency used a table with 20 rows and 20 columns, there would be 400 data cells in the table. To make this table comply with this provision without using the scope attribute would require special coding in all 400 data cells, plus the 40 header and row cells. By contrast, using the scope attribute would only require special attributes in the 40 header and row cells.

Using the "ID" and "Headers" Attributes in Tables

Unlike using the scope attribute, using the id and headers attributes requires that every data cell in a table include special attributes for association. Although its usefulness for accessibility may have been diminished as browsers provide support for the scope attribute, the id and headers attributes are still very useful and provide a practical means of providing access in smaller tables.

The following table is much more complicated than the previous example and demonstrates the use of the id and headers attributes and then the scope attribute. Both methods provide a means of complying with the requirements for data tables in web pages. The table in this example includes the work schedules for two employees. Each employee has a morning and afternoon work schedule that varies depending on whether the employee is working in the winter or summer months. The "summer" and "winter" columns each span two columns labeled "morning" and "afternoon." Therefore, in each cell identifying the work schedule, the user needs to be told the employee's name (Fred or Wilma), the season (Summer or Winter), and the shift (morning or afternoon).

```
<table>
  <tr>
    <th> </th>
    <th colspan="2" id="winter">Winter</th>
    <th colspan="2" id="summer">Summer</th>
  </tr>
  <tr>
    <th> </th>
    <th id="am1">Morning</th>
    <th id="pm1">Afternoon</th>
    <th id="am2">Morning</th>
    <th id="pm2">Afternoon</th>
  </tr>
  <tr>
    <td id="wilma" >Wilma</td>
    <td headers="wilma am1 winter">9-11</td>
    <td headers="wilma pm1 winter">12-6</td>
    <td headers="wilma am2 summer">7-11</td>
    <td headers="wilma pm2 summer">12-3</td>
  </tr>
  <tr>
    <td id="fred">Fred</td>
    <td headers="fred am1 winter">10-11</td>
    <td headers="fred pm1 winter">12-6</td>
    <td headers="fred am2 summer">9-11</td>
    <td headers="fred pm2 summer">12-5</td>
  </tr>
</table>
```

This table would be displayed as follows:

	Winter		Summer	
	Morning	Afternoon	Morning	Afternoon
Wilma	9-11	12-6	7-11	12-3
Fred	10-11	12-6	9-11	12-5

B

Coding each cell of this table with id and headers attributes is much more complicated than using the scope attribute shown below:

```
<table>
  <tr>
    <th> </th>
    <th colspan="2" scope="col">Winter</th>
    <th colspan="2" scope="col">Summer</th>
  </tr>
  <tr>
    <th> </th>
    <th scope="col">Morning</th>
    <th scope="col">Afternoon</th>
    <th scope="col">Morning</th>
    <th scope="col">Afternoon</th>
  </tr>
  <tr>
    <td scope="row">Wilma</td>
    <td>9-11</td>
    <td>12-6</td>
    <td>7-11</td>
    <td>12-3</td>
  </tr>
  <tr>
    <td scope="row">Fred</td>
    <td>10-11</td>
    <td>12-6</td>
    <td>9-11</td>
    <td>12-5</td>
  </tr>
</table>
```

This table would be displayed as follows:

	Winter		Summer	
	Morning	Afternoon	Morning	Afternoon
Wilma	9-11	12-6	7-11	12-3
Fred	10-11	12-6	9-11	12-5

Is the summary attribute an option?

Although highly recommended by some web page designers as a way of summarizing the contents of a table, the summary attribute of the <table> tag is not sufficiently supported by major assistive technology manufacturers to warrant recommendation. Therefore, web developers who are interested in summarizing their tables should consider placing their descriptions either adjacent to their tables or in the body of the table, using such tags as the <caption> tag. In no event should web developers use summarizing tables as an alternative to making the contents of their tables compliant as described above.

1194.22(i) Frames shall be titled with text that facilitates frame identification and navigation.

Why is this provision necessary?

Frames provide a means of visually dividing the computer screen into distinct areas that can be separately rewritten. Unfortunately, frames can also present difficulties for users with disabilities when those frames are not easily identifiable to assistive technology. For instance, a popular use of frames is to create "navigational bars" in a fixed position on the screen and have the content of the web site retrievable by activating one of those navigational buttons. The new content is displayed in another area of the screen. Because the navigational bar doesn't change, it provides a stable "frame-of-reference" for users and makes navigation much easier. However, users with disabilities may become lost if the differences between the two frames are not clearly established.

What is the best method for identifying frames?

The most obvious way to accomplish this requirement is to include text within the body of each frame that clearly identifies the frame. For instance, in the case of the navigation bar, a web developer should consider putting words such as "Navigational Links" at the beginning of the contents of the frame to let all users know that the frame depicts navigational links. Providing titles like this at the top of the contents of each frame will satisfy these requirements. An additional measure that should be considered by agencies is to include meaningful text in the <frame> tag's title attribute. Although not currently supported by major manufacturers of assistive technology, the title attribute is part of the HTML 4.0 specification and was intended to let web developers include a description of the frame as a quote-enclosed string. Demonstrating the use of the title attribute requires a basic understanding of how frames are constructed. When frames are used in a web page, the first page that is loaded must include a <frameset> tag that encloses the basic layout of the frames on the page. Within the <frameset> tag, <frame> tags specify the name, initial contents, and appearance of each separate frame. Thus, the following example uses the title attribute to label one frame "Navigational Links Frame" and the second frame "Contents Frame."

```
<frameset cols="30%, 60%">
  <frame src="navlinks.html" name="navlinks"➡
    title="Navigational Links Frame">
  <frame src="geninfo.html" name="contents_page"➡
    title="Contents Frame">
</frame>
```

B

While assistive technology does not yet widely support the title attribute, we recommend including this attribute in web pages using frames.

Example: ADA Technical Assistance Program – the use of frames with "No Frames Link"

www.adata.org

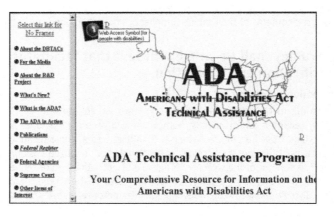

1194.22(j) Pages shall be designed to avoid causing the screen to flicker with a frequency greater than 2 Hz and lower than 55 Hz.

Why is this provision necessary?

This provision is necessary because some individuals with photosensitive epilepsy can have a seizure triggered by displays that flicker, flash, or blink, particularly if the flash has a high intensity and is within certain frequency ranges. The 2 Hz limit was chosen to be consistent with proposed revisions to the ADA Accessibility Guidelines which, in turn, are being harmonized with the International Code Council (ICC)/ANSI A117 standard, "Accessible and Usable Buildings and Facilities," ICC/ANSI A117.1-1998 which references a 2 Hz limit. An upper limit was identified at 55 Hz.

How can flashing or flickering elements be identified?

Flashing or flickering elements are usually added through technologies such as animated gifs, Java applets, or third-party plug-ins or applications. Java applets and third-party plug-ins can be identified by the presence of <applet> or <object> tags. Animated gifs are images that download in a single file (like ordinary image files), but have content that changes over short periods of time. Like other images, however, they are usually incorporated through the use of the <img> tag.

1194.22(k) A text-only page, with equivalent information or functionality, shall be provided to make a web site comply with the provisions of these standards, when compliance cannot be accomplished in any other way. The content of the text-only page shall be updated whenever the primary page changes.

What must a text-only page contain to comply with this provision?

Text-only pages must contain equivalent information or functionality as the primary pages. Also, the text-only page shall be updated whenever the primary page changes.

Example: Disability.gov displays a text-only page on home page.

HTML source code:

```
<div ID="textonly">
  <p>
    <a HREF="../textonly/default.asp">Text Only</a>
  </p>
</div>
```

Link: http://www.disability.gov/

B

1194.22(l) When pages utilize scripting languages to display content, or to create interface elements, the information provided by the script shall be identified with functional text that can be read by assistive technology.

What accessibility problems can scripts cause?

Web page authors have a responsibility to provide script information in a fashion that can be read by assistive technology. When authors do not put functional text with a script, a screen reader will often read the content of the script itself in a meaningless jumble of numbers and letters. Although this jumble is text, it cannot be interpreted or used.

How can web developers comply with this provision?

Web developers working with JavaScript frequently use so-called JavaScript URLs as an easy way to invoke JavaScript functions. Typically, this technique is used as part of <a> anchor links. For instance, the following link invokes a JavaScript function called myFunction:

```
<a href="javascript:myFunction();">Start myFunction</a>
```

This technique does not cause accessibility problems for assistive technology. A more difficult problem occurs when developers use images inside of JavaScript URLs without providing meaningful information about the image or the effect of the anchor link. For instance, the following link also invokes the JavaScript function myFunction, but requires the user to click on an image instead of the text "Start myFunction":

```
<a href="javascript:myFunction();"><img src="myFunction.gif"></a>
```

This type of link, as written, presents tremendous accessibility problems, but those problems can easily be remedied. The <img> tag, of course, supports the alt attribute that can also be used to describe the image and the effect of clicking on the link. Thus, the following revision remedies the accessibility problems created in the previous example:

```
<a href="javascript:myFunction();">
  <img src="myFunction.gif" alt="picture link for starting myFunction">
</a>
```

Another technique advocated by some developers is to use the title attribute of the <a> tag. For instance, the following example includes a meaningful description in a title attribute:

```
<a title="this link starts myFunction" href="javascript:myFunction();➥
"><img src="myFunction.gif"></a>
```

This tag is supported by some but not all assistive technologies. Therefore, while it is part of the HTML 4.0 specifications, authors should use the alt tag in the enclosed image.

Finally, the browser's status line (at the bottom of the screen) typically displays the URL of any links that the mouse is currently pointing towards. For instance, if clicking on an anchor link will send the user to http://www.usdoj.gov, that URL will be displayed in the status line if the user's mouse lingers on top of the anchor link. In the case of JavaScript

URLs, the status line can become filled with meaningless snips of script. To prevent this effect, some web developers use special "event handlers" such as onmouseover and onmouseout to overwrite the contents of the status line with a custom message. For instance, the following link will replace the content in the status line with a custom message "Nice Choice."

```
<a href="javascript:myFcn();" onmouseover="status='Nice Choice';➡
    return true;" onmouseout="status='';">
  <img src="pix.gif">
</a>
```

This text rewritten into the status line is difficult or impossible to detect with a screen reader. Although rewriting the status line did not interfere with the accessibility or inaccessibility of the JavaScript URL, web developers should ensure that all important information conveyed in the status line also be provided through the alt attribute, as described above.

JavaScript uses so-called "event handlers" as a trigger for certain actions or functions to occur. For instance, a web developer may embed a JavaScript function in a web page that automatically checks the content of a form for completeness or accuracy. An event handler associated with a "submit" button can be used to trigger the function before the form is actually submitted to the server for processing. The advantage for the government agency is that it saves government resources by not requiring the government's server to do the initial checking. The advantage for the computer user is that feedback about errors is almost instantaneous because the user is told about the error before the information is even submitted over the Internet.

Web developers must exercise some caution when deciding which event handlers to use in their web pages, because different screen readers provide different degrees of support for different event handlers. The following includes recommendations for using many of the more popular event handlers:

- onClick – The onClick event handler is triggered when the user clicks once on a particular item. It is commonly used on links and button elements and, used in connection with these elements, it works well with screen readers. If clicking on the element associated with the onClick event handler triggers a function or performs some other action, developers should ensure that the context makes that fact clear to all users. Do not use the onClick event handlers for form elements that include several options (e.g. select lists, radio buttons, checkboxes) unless absolutely necessary.

- onDblClick – The onDblClick event handler is set off when the user clicks twice rapidly on the same element. In addition to the accessibility problems it creates, it is very confusing to users and should be avoided.

- onMouseDown and onMouseUp – The onMouseDown and onMouseUp event handlers each handle the two halves of clicking a mouse while over an element – the process of (a) clicking down on the mouse button and (b) then releasing the mouse button. Like onDblClick, this tag should be used sparingly, if at all, by web developers because it is quite confusing. In most cases, developers should opt for the onClick event handler instead of onMouseDown.

611

- onMouseOver and onMouseOut – These two event handlers are very popular on many web sites. For instance, so-called rollover gifs, which swap images on a web page when the mouse passes over an image, typically use both of these event handlers. These event handlers neither can be accessed by the mouse nor interfere with accessibility – a screen reader simply bypasses them entirely. Accordingly, web designers who use these event handlers should be careful to duplicate the information (if any) provided by these event handlers through other means.

- onLoad and onUnload – Both of these event handlers are used frequently to perform certain functions when a web page has either completed loading or when it unloads. Because neither event handler is triggered by any user interaction with an element on the page, they do not present accessibility problems.

- onChange – This event handler is very commonly used for triggering JavaScript functions based on a selection from within a <select> tag. Surprisingly, it presents tremendous accessibility problems for many commonly used screen readers and should be avoided. Instead, web developers should use the onClick event handler (associated with a link or button that is adjacent to a <select> tag) to accomplish the same functions.

- onBlur and onFocus – These event handlers are not commonly used in web pages. While they don't necessarily present accessibility problems, their behavior is confusing enough to a web page visitor that they should be avoided.

1194.22(m) When a web page requires that an applet, plug-in, or other application be present on the client system to interpret page content, the page must provide a link to a plug-in or applet that complies with §1194.21(a) through (l).

Why is this provision necessary?

While most web browsers can easily read HTML and display it to the user, several private companies have developed proprietary file formats for transmitting and displaying special content, such as multimedia or very precisely defined documents. Because these file formats are proprietary, web browsers cannot ordinarily display them. To make it possible for these files to be viewed by web browsers, add-on programs or "plug-ins" can be downloaded and installed on the user's computer that will make it possible for their web browsers to display or play the content of the files. This provision requires that web pages that provide content such as Real Audio or PDF (Adobe Acrobat's Portable Document Format) files also provide a link to a plug-in that will meet the software provisions. It is very common for a web page to provide links to needed plug-ins. For example, web pages containing Real Audio almost always have a link to a source for the necessary player. This provision places a responsibility on the web page author to know that a compliant application exists, before requiring a plug-in.

How can plug-ins and applets be detected?

Plug-ins can usually be detected by examining a page's HTML for the presence of an <object> tag. Some plug-in manufacturers, however, may require the use of proprietary tags. Like plug-ins, applets can also be identified by the presence of an <object> tag in the HTML source for a web page. Also, an <applet> tag may signal the inclusion of an applet in a web page.

1194.22(n) When electronic forms are designed to be completed on-line, the form shall allow people using assistive technology to access the information, field elements, and functionality required for completion and submission of the form, including all directions and cues.

Why do electronic forms present difficulties to screen readers?

Currently, the interaction between form controls and screen readers can be unpredictable, depending upon the design of the page containing these controls. HTML forms pose accessibility problems when web developers separate a form element from its associated label or title. For instance, if an input box is intended for receiving a user's last name, the web developer must be careful that the words "last name" (or some similar text) appear near that input box or are somehow associated with it. Although this may seem like an obvious requirement, it is extremely easy to violate because the visual proximity of a form element and its title offers no guarantee that a screen reader will associate the two or that this association will be obvious to a user of assistive technology.

The following form demonstrates these problems. Visually, this form is part of a table and each field is carefully placed in table cells adjacent to their corresponding labels (n.b. formatting forms with tables are by no means the only situation presenting the accessibility problems inherent in forms; tables merely illustrate the problem most clearly).

While the relationship between the titles "First Name" or "Last Name" and their respective input boxes may be obvious from visual inspection, the relationship is not obvious to a screen reader. Instead, a screen reader may simply announce "input box" when encountering each input box. The reason for these difficulties is revealed from inspecting the HTML source for this table. The following code is a simplified version of this table.

```
<form>
  <table>
    <tr>
      <td><b>FIRST NAME: </b></td>
      <td><input type="text" name="firstname"> </td>
    </tr>
    <tr>
      <td><b>LAST NAME: </b></td>
      <td><input type="text" name="lastname"> </td>
    </tr>
  </table>
<p></p>
<input type="submit" value="submit">
</form>
```

The two pairs of form elements are indicated in bold above. The problem created by laying out form elements inside of this table is now clear – the form elements are separated from their labels by the formatting instructions for the table.

How can developers provide accessible HTML forms?

The first rule of thumb is to place labels adjacent to input fields, not in separate cells of a table. For the web developer who does not wish to place form elements immediately adjacent to their corresponding titles, the HTML 4.0 specification includes the `<label>` tag that lets web developers mark specific elements as "labels" and then associate a form element with that label. There are generally two ways to use the label tag: explicit labels and implicit labels.

"Explicit Labels" Work Well

Experience has shown that explicit labeling works extremely well with all popular assistive technology and is recommended in all but the very simplest of tables. We recommend that all agencies ensure that their web developers are familiar with these important concepts. Using "explicit" labels involves two distinct steps:

- Use the `<label>` tag and associated `for` attribute to tag labels. In other words, identify the exact words that you want to use as the label for the form element and enclose those words in a `<label>` tag. Use the `form` attribute to uniquely identify that element.

- Use the `id` attribute in the associated form element. Every form element supports the `id` attribute. By setting this attribute to the identifier used in the `form` attribute of the associated `<label>` tag, you "tie" that form element to its associated label. For instance, we have rewritten the HTML code for our simple form-inside-a-table to include explicit labels below. The new HTML for the explicit labels is indicated in bold:

```
<form>
  <table>
    <tr>
      <td><b><label for="first"> first name:</label> </b></td>
      <td><input type="text" name="firstname" id="first"></td>
    </tr>
    <tr>
      <td><b><label for="last"> last name:</label> </b></td>
      <td><input type="text" name="lastname" id="last"></td>
    </tr>
  </table>
<p></p>
<input type="submit" value="submit">
</form>
```

In a nutshell, that's all there is to making HTML form elements accessible to assistive technology. Experience has shown that this technique works extremely well in much more complicated and convoluted forms and it should work well in all agency HTML forms.

Avoid Using "Implicit Labels"

In "implicit" labels, the form element and its associated label are contained within an opening <label> tag and a closing </label> tag. For instance, in the table above, an implicit label to associate the words "First Name" with its associated input cell, we could use an implicit label as follows:

```
<label>
  <tr>
    <td><b>first name:</b></td>
    <td><input type="text" name="firstname"></td>
  </tr>
</label>
```

Experience has shown that implicit labeling should be avoided for two reasons. First, implicit labeling is not reliably supported by many screen readers and, in particular, does not work well if explicit labels are simultaneously used anywhere on the same web page. Often, the output can be wildly inaccurate and confusing. Second, if any text separates a label from its associated form element, an implicit label becomes impractical and confusing because the label itself is no longer easily identified with the form element.

1194.22(o) A method shall be provided that permits users to skip repetitive navigation links.

Why do navigational links present impediments to screen readers and other types of assistive technologies?

This provision provides a method to facilitate the easy tracking of page content that provides users of assistive technology the option to skip repetitive navigation links. Web developers routinely place a host of routine navigational links at a standard location – often across the top, bottom, or side of a page. If a nondisabled user returns to a web page and knows that he or she wants to view the contents of that particular page instead of selecting a navigation link to go to another page, he or she may simply look past the links and begin reading wherever the desired text is located. For those who use screen readers or other types of assistive technologies, however, it can be a tedious and time-consuming chore to wait for the assistive technology to work through and announce each of the standard navigational links before getting to the intended location. In order to alleviate this problem, the section 508 rule requires that when repetitive navigational links are used, there must be a mechanism for users to skip repetitive navigational links.

B

Example: USDA Target Center and DOL web sites use Skip Repetitive Navigational Links.

http://www.usda.gov/oo/target.htm

http://www.dol.gov/dol/odep/

1194.22(p) When a timed response is required, the user shall be alerted and given sufficient time to indicate more time is required.

Why do timed responses present problems to web users with disabilities?

Web pages can be designed with scripts so that the web page disappears or "expires" if a response is not received within a specified amount of time. Sometimes, this technique is used for security reasons or to reduce the demands on the computer serving the web pages. Someone's disability can have a direct impact on the speed with which he or she can read, move around, or fill in a web form. For instance, someone with extremely low vision may be a slower-than-average reader. A page may "time out" before he is able to finish reading it. Many forms, when they "time out" automatically, also delete whatever data has been entered. The result is that someone with a disability who is slow to enter data cannot complete the form. For this reason, when a timed response is required, the user shall be alerted via a prompt and given sufficient time to indicate whether additional time is needed.

Example: Thrift Savings Plan

www.tsp.gov

B

C OVERVIEW OF PAS 78 GUIDE TO GOOD PRACTICE IN COMMISSIONING ACCESSIBLE WEBSITES

by Bruce Lawson

On March 8, 2006, the British Standards Institution (BSI) launched a Publicly Available Specification (PAS) as a guide to good practice in commissioning accessible websites. The document was commissioned by the UK's Disability Rights Commission, which describes itself as "an independent body established in April 2000 by Act of Parliament to stop discrimination and promote equality of opportunity for disabled people."

The BSI develops and owns the copyright for PAS 78. It costs £30 plus sales tax and is available in a variety of formats, including accessible PDF, from www.bsi-global.com/ICT/PAS78/.

The Background of PAS 78

In April 2004, the UK Government-funded Disability Rights Commission (DRC) conducted a formal investigation into the state of web accessibility in the UK, discovering that 81 percent of sites failed to uphold the simplest World Wide Web Consortium (W3C) Web Content Accessibility Guidelines (WCAG) recommendations.

Based on the DRC's findings, the authors of the *Formal Investigation: The Web: Access and Inclusion for Disabled People* report (in conjunction with City University) offered some additional advice to developers:

- Reduce the number of links and ensure that genuine and necessary links are clearly identified as such.

> *Why reduce the number of links? Skip navigation is an excellent idea, but removing links seems almost anti-Web. And what is an "unnecessary" link?*

- Avoid site fragmentation: navigation mechanisms should be consistent (for example, in appearance and behavior), the relative importance of different sections (across the site and within pages) should be apparent, and markup languages should be used to indicate the structure of pages.
- Preserve links to the homepage.
- Improve search design.

> *These are not particularly helpful. At least define what is inadequate about (presumably) all of the searches surveyed, so we can deduce what might constitute "improvement."*

- Eradicate excessively deep site structures, and ensure that page titles are informative.

> *With shallow and wide site structures, one would assume more links on each level's navigation menus, surely contravening the first instruction to reduce the number of links.*

The report also courts controversy with Finding 5:

> Nearly half (45%) of the problems experienced by disabled users when attempting to navigate websites cannot be attributed to explicit violations of the Web Accessibility Initiative Checkpoints. Although some of these reflect shortcomings in the assistive technology used, most reflect the limitations of the Checkpoints themselves as a comprehensive interpretation of the intent of the Guidelines.

The W3C responded (www.w3.org/2004/04/wai-drc-statement.html), claiming that the report's authors didn't really understand the guidelines:

> W3C/WAI's examination of the DRC data available as of 14 April 2004 shows that 95% of the barriers reported are indeed covered by existing checkpoints in WAI Guidelines . . . Essentially, the interpretation of the data in the report fails to account for the role of browser and media player accessibility, and the role of interoperability with assistive technologies, in ensuring that people with disabilities can use Web sites effectively.

The fact that none of these questionable technical recommendations are repeated in PAS 78 suggests that the DRC no longer stands by them (and rightly so, in my opinion).

The DRC report is quasi-available at http://www.drc-gb.org/library/webaccessibility. asp. Ironically, however, the DRC seems incapable of publishing it in HTML, so Joe Clark has converted it and hosts it at http://joeclark.org/dossiers/DRC-GB.html.

After the formal investigation into accessibility, the DRC decided that businesses needed some guidelines on how to begin making accessible websites, which eventually became the PAS.

This specification was initially authored by Julie Howell, an accessibility campaigner who works for the Royal National Institute for the Blind, and a Steering Group consisting of representatives of groups like the BBC, UK Cabinet office, IBM, Tesco, University College London, and the Usability Professionals' Association. It was then reviewed by a large team of stakeholders (including this author), and launched on March 8, 2006.

621

What PAS 78 Is Not

It is important to stress that PAS 78 is *not* a British Standard. Standards take a long time to develop because they require unanimity from all participants. A PAS is reviewed every two years, and may therefore be amended if circumstances change. In the fast-moving pace of the Web, this isn't a bad thing.

The DRC's announcement explains:

> A PAS is not a full British Standard but is developed using the same rigorous processes. We are supporting a PAS on website accessibility as it can be introduced more quickly than a British Standard which can often take several years to be introduced. The other advantage of supporting a PAS is that it can be updated frequently.

A further cause of confusion is the audience for PAS 78. While it was originally intended for developers, the terms of reference were changed early in the process. The PAS is intended to help people who *commission* web design, rather than developers themselves. There's little in the PAS that an experienced web professional who has read this book wouldn't know. It is written as a document that commissioners can understand and can use to discuss accessibility issues with web design project managers. Thus, PAS 78 is *not a technical document*, although reference is made to Web Accessibility Initiative (WAI) guidelines, usability testing, automated checking tools, and so on.

It is also vital to note that PAS 78 is *not compulsory*.

The Guidance in PAS 78

The PAS makes various recommendations regarding commissioning accessible websites, which I'll briefly summarize here (numbers refer to the paragraph of the PAS, which I can't quote, as the copyright belongs to the BSI).

The PAS states that developers should follow the lead of the W3C and WCAG 1.0 (7.1.1). It also explicitly advises the use of Cascading Style Sheets (CSS), as a way to separate content from presentation (7.1.2–4).

The PAS notes that PDF and Flash are proprietary (but published) formats that have significantly increased their accessibility in recent releases (4.2.2.2). The PAS recommends that PDF/Flash only be used to benefit the end user, *not* the content authors. It is generally accepted that well-thought-out Flash can benefit some users with cognitive disabilities, so this is a point well made. However, a common reason for using PDFs is to quickly repurpose printed documents to be on the Web, without all that tedious HTML coding. Additionally, some organizations favor PDFs because they believe that format can preserve branding, corporate typefaces, and the like. These particular reasons are perceived to benefit the originating organization, but generally are of no benefit over HTML to the end users, regardless of their disability.

The PAS draws the distinction between technical accessibility and real, usable accessibility, and advises involvement of users at all stages of the design process. It advocates the publication of an accessibility policy prominently on the site (6.1.1). The policy should be a working document that can form the basis of contracts with third-party suppliers (6.1.4). It should also explain the level of accessibility supported, who to contact with problems, and an honest statement of what is inaccessible, along with a reasonable estimate of when the repairs will be made and how people with disabilities can access this information or these services via alternative means (6.2.4).

Refreshingly, the PAS cautions against overreliance on automated accessibility testing suites, noting that they assist checking for technical accessibility (8.3.1), but manual checks should always be undertaken and nothing replaces actual user testing (4.3.1–2). Throughout the document, considerable emphasis is placed on involving people with disabilities at all stages of design and testing, using a user-centered design methodology.

Therefore, like the authors of this book, the PAS recommends designing for accessibility wherever possible, rather than attempting to retrofit a website after it's built (8.1.6) and that the site, once built, should be regularly checked (8.5.1). All organizations, large or small, should make certain that it's not only the developers who do the testing.

Not all the responsibility for accessibility is placed on the author, however. Annex G is a checklist for those purchasing authoring tools to ensure that it is even possible for proposed off-the-shelf content management systems to separate the content and styling, add alt-text, and so on. Suppliers are referred to an organization's accessibility policy (Annex C3), and it is suggested that suppliers list circumstances where their system will not generate sufficiently compliant documents, and how they propose to repair these shortcomings.

The PAS also recognizes that it takes two to tango—if you do your bit to author accessibly and design to meet the standards, the user must come equipped with a browser and any necessary assistive technologies that are smart enough to understand your pages, specifically noting that this is beyond the control of the developer (6.4.4.4).

The Impact of PAS 78

It is possible that the cost alone may prevent momentum towards PAS 78's adoption by opinion formers. The cost inhibits the number of people who can debate and discuss its content, particularly as the BSI vigorously enforces its copyright.

Also, compliance with the PAS is voluntary (it is simply *guidance*, after all). It doesn't have the force of a full-fledged British Standard, although the names of the BSI and DRC should give it some prestige.

Nevertheless, I believe PAS 78 offers some good advice, including practical checklists on how to choose prepackaged software and how to choose a developer. It contains many sensible, practical suggestions to nontechnical commissioners, and the material describes best practice that is applicable far beyond the borders of the UK.

The Legal Impact of PAS 78

Some in the UK have complained that it costs £30 for a document upon which "legal cases may be brought," but this is a false argument. The legal criteria that a UK website must meet are defined by the Disability Discrimination Act. It is perfectly possible to make accessible websites without reading the PAS.

However, PAS 78 is sponsored and supported by the DRC, and it would therefore seem likely that a business in the process of implementing the PAS could claim that it was attempting to do its duty under the Disability Discrimination Act, if it came to court.

Struan Robertson, of the legal firm Pinsent Masons, and editor of the useful OUT-LAW.com, commented (www.out-law.com/page-6713):

> The DRC's endorsement of PAS 78 is significant and it could be used in court to illustrate whether a business has complied with the Disability Discrimination Act. A failure to follow it could be damaging to an organisation's case; but compliance would be evidence of steps being taken to fulfill the legal duty.

It will be interesting indeed to see whether the PAS is cited in any court cases in the next few years, or whether the DRC and its successors will remain in the role of toothless watchdog.

INDEX

Symbols

! important operator 258
* selector 258
@import rule
  <style> element 257
@media rule
  <link> element 287

A

<a> element
  See also anchors 136
  combining active images with text 147
  href attribute 136
  title attribute 610
absolute positioning 273–275
ACB (American Council of the Blind)
  skip navigation links 187–188
Access Board
  See also Section 508
  frames title requirements 196
  recommendations for server-side maps 203
Access Instruction pages
  San José Access Standards require 58
access keys standard 493
Access Now v. Southwest Airlines 520–521, 540
accessibility
  See also Web accessibility
  addressing accessibility early in web design 61
  design principles of WCAG 2.0 462–464
  fostering positive approach to 47–49
  guidelines for web development 54
  incorporating at design phase of planning 79
accessibility awareness 74–75
accessibility checker
  Adobe Acrobat 404
accessibility checking software
  Bobby 420–424
  InFocus 424–429
  introduction 419–420
  LIFT Machine 429–433
  Ramp Ascend 434–437
  test suite 446–456
  WebKing 437–441
  WebXM 441–445

accessibility features
  Adobe Reader 368–379
  Green Methods homepage 185
Accessibility for Ontarians with Disabilities Act. *See* AODA
Accessibility in the User-Centered Design Process 28
Accessibility Internet Rally (AIR) 234–235
accessibility laws and policies 548
  Australia 548–550
  Austria 550–551
  Belgium 551–553
  Brazil 553
  Canada 554
  Denmark 555
  European Union 556–558
  Finland 558
  France 559
  Germany 559–560
  Hong Kong 561
  Ireland 561–562
  Italy 562–565
  Japan 565–568
  Korea 569
  Luxembourg 569
  Netherlands 570
  New Zealand 571–573
  Norway 573–574
  Portugal 574–575
  Singapore 576
  Spain 577
  Sweden 577
  Thailand 577
  United Kingdom 578–579
Accessibility object
  isActive() method 357
accessibility organization
  accessibility awareness 74–75
  authority required 72–73
  feedback process 75–76
  implementation
    handover to AO 82
    initiall assessment 81–82
    phased approach 80
    plan 82
  makeup of 71
  need for 70
  problems with ad hoc approach 70–71
  public representation 80
  quality assurance 76–77
  scope, goals and functions 73–74
  staff for legal matters 78

  standards, external and internal 78–79
  support infrastructure 77–78
Accessibility panel
  assigning reading order 354
  assigning text equivalents 346
  Description field 350
  Make Child Objects Accessible option 357
  Make Object Accessible option 348
  Shortcut field 358
  turning off auto-labeling 350
Accessibility section
  Preferences dialog box 368
accessibility settings
  Preferences pane of RealPlayer 95
Accessibility Task Force (ATF) 582
accessible content, creating 128–176
accessible technologies
  CSS (Cascading Style Sheets) 88–89
  Flash 91–92
  HTML and XHTML 87–88
  introduction 86
  Java 99
  JavaScript 89
  PDF 93
  QuickTime, Windows Media, and RealPlayer 96–97
  Section 508 requirement 524, 526, 536
  SMIL (Synchronized Multimedia Integration Language) 93–94, 96
  SVG (Scalable Vector Graphics) 97–98
  XML and XSL 99–100
AccessiWeb label
  BrailleNet Association 559
achromatopsia 154
Act on equal treatment on the grounds of handicap or chronic illness 570
ActionScript
  accessibility properties 348
  forceSimple property 357
  shortcut property 358
  tabIndex property 355
ADA (Americans with Disabilities Act, 1990) 512, 523–528, 582
  accessibility of state and local government websites 517–518
  and the Internet 513

CPSIA information can be obtained
at www.ICGtesting.com
Printed in the USA
LVOW03s1916111215
466369LV00005B/9/P